JUSTICE
Alternative Political Perspectives

Fourth Edition

James P. Sterba
University of Notre Dame

THOMSON

WADSWORTH ™

Australia • Canada • Mexico • Singapore • Spain • United Kingdom • United States

Publisher: Holly J. Allen
Philosophy Editor: Steve Wainwright
Assistant Editor: Lee McCracken
Editorial Assistant: Anna Lustig
Technology Project Manager: Susan DeVanna
Marketing Manager: Worth Hawes
Marketing Assistant: Justine Ferguson
Advertising Project Manager: Bryan Vann

Print/Media Buyer: Judy Inouye
Composition Buyer: Ben Schroeter
Permissions Editor: Joohee Lee
Production Service: Matrix Productions
Copy Editor: Cheryl Smith
Cover Designer: Ross Carron
Compositor: G&S Typesetters
Text and Cover Printer: Webcom Ltd.

For more information about our
products, contact us at: Thomson
Learning Academic Resource Center
1-800-423-0563
For permission to use material from this
text, contact us by:
Phone: 1-800-730-2214
Fax: 1-800-730-2215
Web: http://www.thomsonrights.com.

Library of Congress Cataloging-in-Publication Data
   Justice : alternative political perspectives / [edited by]
James P. Sterba. — 4th ed.
      p. cm.
   Includes bibliographical references.
   ISBN 0-534-60219-3
   1. Justice.   I. Sterba, James P.

JC578.J87 2003
320'.01'1—dc21   2002066172

Wadsworth/Thomson Learning
10 Davis Drive
Belmont, CA 94002-3098
USA

Asia
Thomson Learning
60 Albert Street, #15-01
Albert Complex
Singapore 189969

Australia
Nelson Thomson Learning
102 Dodds Street
South Melbourne, Victoria 3205
Australia

Canada
Nelson Thomson Learning
1120 Birchmont Road
Toronto, Ontario M1K 5G4
Canada

Europe/Middle East/Africa
Thomson Learning
Berkshire House
168-173 High Holborn
London WC1V 7AA
United Kingdom

Latin America
Thomson Learning
Seneca, 53
Colonia Polanco
11560 Mexico D.F.
Mexico

Spain
Paraninfo Thomson Learning
Calle/Magallanes, 25
28015 Madrid, Spain

To Janet
As always
A philosopher's philosopher

Contents

Preface

The fourth edition of *Justice: Alternative Political Perspectives* has been revised and expanded to keep abreast of current discussions of conceptions of justice. This edition contains selections from the most recent work of John Rawls (2001) and Alasdair MacIntyre (1999) as well as a critique of Rawls's new work. There is also a new section of Environmental Justice. In all, there are eight new readings. *Justice: Alternative Political Perspectives* still remains the only anthology of its kind. It contains classic and contemporary defenses and critiques of seven major conceptions of justice, and the Introduction provides background and critique for each of the selections. All of the selections have been class tested and edited for accessibility.

For helping in putting together this fourth edition, I would like to thank Erin Kelly of Tufts University, Anthony Laden at the University of Illinois at Chicago, Peter Wenz at the University of Illinois at Springfield, and my colleague and partner Janet A. Kourany. I would also like to thank the following reviewers: John D. Arras, University of Virginia; Robert Carroll, Sacramento City College; Ann P. Conrad, The Catholic University of America; Donald Hatcher, Baker University; Ted Stolze, California State University, Hayward; Harry vanderLinden, Butler University, as well as Steve Wainwright, Philosophy Editor, at Wadsworth Publishing Co. and Merrill Peterson of Matrix Productions Inc. who both assisted me in countless ways. Financial and other support from the National Humanities Center in Research Triangle Park, North Carolina, the University of California at Irvine, and the University of Notre Dame is also greatly appreciated.

Part I

Introduction

Introduction

JAMES P. STERBA

Virtually all of us become involved at one time or another in disputes about justice. Sometimes our involvement in such disputes is rooted in the fact that we believe ourselves to be victims of some form of injustice; sometimes our involvement is rooted in the fact that others believe us to be the perpetrators or at least the beneficiaries of some form of injustice affecting them. Sometimes the injustice at issue seems to require eliminating a drastic reform, or even a revolutionary change in the political system—such as has taken place in Eastern Europe. Sometimes elimination only seems to require some electoral pressure or administrative decision—what might be required, say, in ending a war. But whatever the origin and whatever the practical effect, such disputes about justice are difficult to avoid, especially when dealing with issues (such as the distribution of income, the control and use of natural resources, and the distribution of educational and employment opportunities) that have widespread social effects.

How can we resolve such disputes in a reasonable way? Reasonable resolution of such disputes requires careful consideration of whatever reasons have been, or might be, advanced in favor of the alternative conceptions of justice that are available to us. Hopefully, through such a process of critical evaluation, one of these conceptions will begin to emerge as the most defensible—maybe it will even be the conception we initially endorsed.

This anthology has been designed to help you carry out this process of critical evaluation. The readings in it defend and critique seven contemporary conceptions of justice. All of these conceptions of justice regard their requirements as belonging to the domain of obligation rather than to the domain of charity; they simply disagree about where to draw the line between these two domains. Each is concerned with giving people what they deserve or should rightfully possess; they simply tend to disagree about what it is that people deserve or rightfully possess.

Turning from common ground to disputed territory, each of these conceptions of justice appeals to a different political ideal. First is a Libertarian Conception of Justice. In recent years, libertarian party candidates have not done very well. But Ronald Reagan, George Bush Sr., and Margaret Thatcher, whose views on economic issues are close to a Libertarian Conception of Justice, were successful politically and succeeded in refashioning the economies of their respective nations. According to this conception of justice, liberty is the ultimate political ideal. Thus all assignments of rights and duties are ultimately to be justified in terms of an ideal of liberty.

Second is a Socialist Conception of Justice. In the United States there has never been a viable socialist presidential candidate, but elsewhere there have been many successful socialist candidates. For example, the late Olof Palme led the Social Democrats back to power in Sweden and the late François Mitterand, a socialist, was the longest serving president in France, holding office for 14 years until May of 1995. According to a Socialist Conception of Justice, equality is the ultimate political ideal. Thus all assignments of rights and duties are ultimately to be justified in terms of an ideal of equality.

Third is a Liberal Democratic Conception of Justice. This is the conception of justice endorsed, for example, by the left wing of the Democratic Party in the United States, whose leaders have been George McGovern, Ted Kennedy, and Jesse Jackson. According to this conception of justice, the ultimate political ideal is a blend of liberty and equality, and this blend can be characterized as contractual fairness, maximal utility, or discourse ethics. Thus all assignments of rights and duties are ultimately to be justified in terms of these ideals.

Fourth is a Communitarian Conception of Justice. This conception is somewhat difficult to associate with any particular political group, but it does seem to be reflected in a wide range of Supreme Court decisions in the United States today, and has its roots in the republicanism of Madison and Jefferson. According to this Communitarian Conception of Justice, the common good is proclaimed to be the ultimate political ideal, and this ideal is said to support a virtue-based conception of human flourishing.

Fifth is a Feminist Conception of Justice. This is the conception endorsed by the National Organization for Women (NOW) and by numerous other women's organizations in the United States and elsewhere. According to a Feminist Conception of Justice, the ultimate political ideal can be seen to be androgyny. Thus all assignments of rights and duties can ultimately be justified in terms of an ideal of androgyny.

Sixth is a Postmodern Conception of Justice. This conception is also somewhat difficult to associate with any particular political group, but it has many adherents in literary and academic circles. According to a Postmodern Conception of Justice, we should reject all metanarratives or grand theories, which would seem to include our other six conceptions of justice. According to this conception, the justification for rights and duties is local and limited. It applies only with respect to individuals in a given setting and is not universalizable.

Seventh is an Environmental Conception of Justice. This conception has only recently been widely recognized as a conception of justice, that is, with requirements that belong to the domain of obligation and legal enforcement rather than simply to the domain of charity or aspiration. This conception is associated with many moderate and radical environmental groups today, such as Greenpeace and Earth First! According to this conception of justice, species equality or nondomination is the ultimate political ideal. Moreover, as Peter Singer argues, acceptance of this ideal would lead to radical changes in our diet, in farming methods, experimental procedures in many fields of science, our approach to wildlife and to hunting and trapping, and to our use of animals in circuses, rodeos, and zoos.

What we need to do, therefore, is examine each of these conceptions of justice, along with their historical roots where appropriate, in order to determine which is most defensible. Happily the readings in this anthology have been designed to help you do just that by providing classical and contemporary defenses and critiques of each of the seven conceptions of justice. Working through the readings in this anthology will not always be an easy task. Some articles will be clear on the first reading, whereas others will require closer scrutiny. You should also make sure you give each selection a fair hearing, for while some will accord with your current views, others will not. It is important that you evaluate the latter with an open mind, allowing for the possibility that after sufficient reflection you may come to view them as the most defensible. Indeed, to approach the selections of this anthology in any other way would surely undermine your ability to reasonably resolve those disputes about justice in which you are inescapably involved.

Libertarian Justice

In 1972, John Hospers was nominated as the first U.S. presidential candidate of the Libertarian Party. In the first selection, Hospers takes liberty to be the ultimate moral and political ideal, and he defines *liberty* as "the state of being unconstrained by other persons from doing what one wants." This definition limits the scope of liberty in two ways. First, not all constraints, whatever the source, count as a restriction on liberty; the constraints must come from other persons. For example, people who are constrained by natural forces from getting to the top of Mount Everest do not lack liberty in this regard. Second, the constraints must run counter to people's wants. Thus, people who do not want to hear Beethoven's Fifth Symphony do not feel their liberty is restricted when other people forbid its performance, even though the proscription does in fact constrain what they are able to do.

Of course, libertarians may argue that these constraints do restrict a person's liberty because people normally want to be unconstrained by others. But other philosophers have claimed that such constraints point to a serious defect in the libertarian's definition of liberty, which can only be remedied by defining *liberty* more broadly as "the state of being unconstrained by other persons from doing what one is able to do." If we apply this revised definition to the previous example, we find that people's liberty to hear Beethoven's Fifth Symphony would be restricted even if they did not want to hear it (and even if, perchance, they did not want to be unconstrained by others) because other people would still be constraining them from doing what they are able to do.

Confident that problems of defining liberty can be overcome in some satisfactory manner, libertarians go on to characterize their moral and political ideal as requiring that each person should have the greatest amount of liberty commensurate with the same liberty for all. From this ideal, libertarians claim that a number of more specific requirements—in particular a right to life, a right to freedom of speech, press, and assembly, and a right to property—can be derived.

It is important to note that the libertarian's right to life is not a right to receive from others the goods and resources necessary for preserving one's life; it is simply a right not to be killed. So understood, the right to life is not a right to receive welfare. In fact, libertarians are concerned to show that there are no welfare rights in their view. Accordingly, the libertarian's understanding of the right to property is not a right to receive from others the goods and resources necessary for one's welfare, but rather a right to acquire goods and resources either by initial acquisition or by voluntary agreement.

Obviously, by defending rights such as these, libertarians can only support a limited role for government. That role is simply to prevent and punish initial acts of coercion—the only wrongful actions for libertarians.

Libertarians do not deny that it is a good thing for people to have sufficient goods and resources to meet at least their basic nutritional needs, but libertarians do deny that government has a duty to provide for such needs. Some good things, such as the provision of welfare to the needy, are requirements of charity rather than justice, libertarians claim. Accordingly, failure to make such provisions is neither blameworthy nor punishable.

In selection 2, I argue that a libertarian ideal of liberty, which appears to reject the rights of a welfare state, can be seen to support such rights through an application of the "ought" implies "can" principle to conflicts between the rich and the poor. In one interpretation, the principle supports such rights by favoring the liberty of the poor over the liberty of the rich. In another interpretation, the principle supports such rights by favoring a conditional right to property over an unconditional right to property. In either interpretation, what is crucial in the derivation of these rights is the claim that it would be unreasonable to ask the poor to deny their basic needs and accept anything less than these rights as the condition for their willing cooperation.

In selection 3, Tibor Machan attacks my view that a libertarian ideal of liberty leads to what I call "action welfare rights." An action welfare right is the right of the poor, under certain conditions, not to be interfered with when taking from the rich what is required to satisfy their basic needs. An action welfare right differs from what are usually called "welfare rights" because it is a negative right rather than a positive right. However, I further argue that when libertarians are brought to see the legitimacy of action welfare rights they will want to institutionalize positive welfare rights in order to avoid the possibly arbitrary exercise by the poor of their action welfare rights. In this way, I claim, a liberal democratic state would come to have a grounding in a libertarian ideal of (negative) liberty.

In criticizing my argument that a libertarian ideal of liberty leads to action welfare rights and thence to positive welfare rights, Machan accepts the theoretical thrust of my argument, but rejects its practical significance. In the revised version of the argument, which is reprinted as selection 2, I have responded to this criticism. In selection 3, however, Machan, seeking to further undercut the practical force of my argument, has contended that when we compare economic systems to determine which produce more poverty

> No one can seriously dispute that the near-libertarian systems have fared much better than those going in the opposite direction, including the welfare state.[1]

Here one would think that Machan has the United States in mind as a "near-libertarian system" because earlier in the same paragraph he claims

> America is still the freest of societies, with many of its legal principles giving expression to classical liberal, near-libertarian ideas.[2]

Yet apparently this is not what Machan thinks because in a footnote to the same text he says,

> It is notable that the statistics that Sterba cites [in my above response to Machan's critique] are drawn from societies, including the United States of America, which are far from libertarian in their legal construction and are far closer to the welfare state, if not to outright socialism.[3]

Obviously, then, Machan is surprisingly unclear as to whether he wants to call the United States a near-libertarian state, a welfare state, or a socialist state. Yet, whichever of these designations is most appropriate, what is clear is that the poor do less well in the United States than they do in the liberal democratic or socialist states of Western Europe such as Germany, Sweden, and Switzerland.[4] For example, 22.4 percent of children live below the poverty line in the United States as compared to 4.9 percent in Germany, 5 percent in Sweden, and 7.8 percent in Switzerland, and the United States shares with Italy the highest infant mortality rate of the major industrialized nations. The United States also ranks 67 among all nations in the percentage of national income received by the poorest 20 percent of its population, ranking the absolute lowest among industrialized nations.[5] Accordingly, the success that liberal democratic and socialist states have had, especially in Western Europe, in coming close to truly meeting the basic needs of their deserving poor should give us good reason to doubt what Machan proclaims is the superior practical effectiveness of "near-libertarian states" in dealing with poverty.

In selection 4, Jan Narveson argues for libertarianism by trying to give it a contractarian foundation in what people want. Narveson argues that if we consider the choice between

1. knowing that I will be forced to help others whom I wouldn't choose to help if I had my choice, with all others, in turn, being similarly forced to help me; and
2. knowing that our right to use our resources as we judge best, without interference by others, will always be respected, even though we also know that we won't *necessarily* be helped by others when the chips are down, (i.e., nobody will *force* them to help)

not everyone will favor (1) over (2). But since Narveson also acknowledges that most people want a social minimum (see p. 61), which is equivalent to favoring (1), he should presumably abandon his contractarian defense and claim instead that, despite what most people want, the best reasons really do favor libertarianism. But do the best reasons favor libertarianism? Narveson argues that if there are enough votes to legislate the welfare state, then there must be enough charitable people out there to easily meet welfare needs without requiring anyone to help. Yet is this really the case? Historically, haven't tax-supported welfare systems come into existence because voluntary giving turned out to be insufficient?[6] If so, then tax-supported welfare institutions are needed to take care of the poor who are not provided for by the available private charity just as tax-supported educational institutions are needed to take care of the educational needs of those who are not provided for by existing private educational institutions.

Narveson in his response to my article argues that the constraints that a welfare system would impose on the rich would be unreasonable for them to accept. Yet in my article I argued that the constraints of a property system without welfare would be even more unreasonable for the poor to accept. Moreover, even if Narveson were right that the (European) poor in the United States did not starve in the early days when the United States was nearly a libertarian society, that would not show that the poor today, as I argued above, are not better off in the liberal democratic or socialist countries of Western Europe. Nor should we neglect to note that the well-being of early European settlers was frequently secured by decimating and exterminating American Indian nations, precisely those who should, on libertarian principles, have been regarded as the rightful owners of the land.

Socialist Justice

In contrast with libertarians, socialists take equality to be the ultimate political ideal. In the first part of selection 5, which is taken from the *Communist Manifesto,* Karl Marx and Friedrich Engels maintain that the abolition of bourgeois property and bourgeois family structure is a necessary first requirement for building a society that accords with the political ideal of equality. In the second part of selection 5 Marx provides a much more positive account of what is required to build a society based upon the political ideal of equality. In such a society, Marx claims that the distribution of social goods must conform, at least initially, to the principle "from each according to his ability, to each according to his contribution." But when the highest stage of communist society has been reached, Marx adds, distribution will conform to the principle "from each according to his ability, to each according to his need."

This final principle of socialist justice is discussed and defended by Edward Nell and Onora O'Neill in selection 6. They argue that any incentive problems associated with the principle will be resolved when, quoting Marx, "labor is no longer a means of life but has become life's principal need." They further contend that when it is at last appropriate to apply this principle of socialist justice there will exist a system for distributing the burdens of nonfulfilling but socially necessary tasks as well as a system for equitably distributing the benefits of goods not required for anyone's needs. What this means is that because some jobs, such as collecting garbage or changing bedpans, probably can't be made intrinsically rewarding, socialists propose to divide them up in some equitable manner. Some people might, for example, collect garbage one day a week and then work at intrinsically rewarding jobs for the rest of the week. Others would change bedpans or do some other slop job one day a week and then work at an intrinsically rewarding job the other days of the week. By making jobs as intrinsically rewarding as possible, in part through democratic control of the workplace and an equitable assignment of unrewarding tasks, socialists believe people will contribute according to their ability even when distribution proceeds according to need.

Finally, it is important to note that the socialist ideal of equality does not accord with what existed in countries such as the Soviet Union or Albania. Judging the acceptability of the socialist ideal of equality by what took place in those countries would be as unfair as judging the acceptability of the libertarian ideal of liberty by what took place in countries such as Chile or South Korea, where citizens are arrested and imprisoned without cause. By analogy, it would be like judging the merits of college football by the way Vanderbilt or Rutgers plays rather than by the way Michigan or Florida State plays. Actually, a fairer comparison would be to judge the socialist ideal of equality by what takes place in countries such as Norway or Sweden and to judge the libertarian ideal of liberty by what takes place in the United States. Even these comparisons, however, are not wholly appropriate because none of these countries fully conforms to those ideals.

To justify the ideal of equality, Kai Nielson (selection 7) argues that it is required by *liberty* or at least by a fair distribution of liberty. By *liberty* Nielson means both "positive liberty to receive certain goods" and "negative liberty not to be interfered with," so his argument from liberty will not have much weight with libertarians, who only value negative liberty. Rather, his argument is directed primarily at liberal democrats, who value both positive and negative liberty as well as a fair distribution of liberty.

Another basic difficulty with Nielson's socialist conception of justice concerns the proclaimed necessity of abolishing private property and socializing the means of production. It seems perfectly possible to give workers more control over their workplace while at the same time the means of production remain privately owned. Of course, private ownership would have a somewhat different character in a society with democratic control of the workplace, but it need not cease to be private ownership. After all, private ownership would also have a somewhat different character in a society where private holdings, and hence bargaining power, were distributed more equally than is found in most capitalist societies, yet it would not cease to be private ownership. Accordingly, we could imagine a society where the means of production are privately owned but where—because ownership is so widely dispersed throughout the society (e.g., nearly everyone owns 10 shares of major industrial stock and no one more than 20 shares) and because of the degree of democratic control of the workplace—many of the valid criticisms socialists make of existing capitalist societies would no longer apply.

In selection 8, Robert Nozick illustrates another argument often used against a socialist conception of justice—that it is opposed to liberty. Nozick asks us to imagine that we are in a society that has just distributed income according to some ideal pattern, possibly a pattern of equality. We are to further imagine that in such a society Wilt Chamberlain (or Michael Jordan, if we wish to update the example) offers to play basketball for us provided that he receives a quarter for every home game ticket that is sold. Suppose we agree to these terms and a million people attend the home games to see Wilt Chamberlain (or Michael Jordan) play, thereby securing him an income of $250,000. Because such an income would surely upset the initial pattern of income distribution, whatever that happened to be, Nozick contends that this illustrates how an ideal of liberty upsets the patterns required by other political ideals and hence calls for their rejection.

Nozick's critique, however, seems to apply only to political ideals that require an absolute equality of income. Yet for many political ideals, the inequalities of income generated in Nozick's example would be objectionable only if they deprived people of something to which they had a right, such as equal opportunity. And whether people were so deprived would depend on to what uses the Wilt Chamberlains or Michael Jordans of the world put their greater income. However, there is no necessity for those who have legitimately acquired greater income to use it in ways that violate the rights of others.

Liberal Democratic Justice: The Contractarian Perspective

Finding merit in both the libertarian's ideal of liberty and the socialist's ideal of equality, liberal democrats attempt to combine both liberty and equality into one political ideal that can be characterized as contractual fairness, maximal utility, or discourse ethics.

A classical example of the contractual approach to liberal democratic justice is found in the work of Immanuel Kant, from which selection 9 is taken. In this selection, Kant claims that a civil state ought to be founded on an original contract satisfying the requirements of freedom (the freedom to seek happiness in whatever way one sees fit as long as one does not infringe upon the freedom of others to pursue a similar end), equality (the equal right of each person to coerce others to use their freedom in a way that harmonizes with one's own freedom), and independence (that independence of each person that is necessarily presupposed by the free agreement of the original contract).

According to Kant, the original contract, which ought to be the foundation of every civil state, does not have to "actually exist as a fact." It suffices that the laws of a civil state are such that people would agree to them under conditions in which requirements of freedom, equality, and independence obtain. Laws that accord with this original contract would then, Kant claims, give all members of society the right to reach any degree of rank that they could earn through their labor, industry, and good fortune. Thus, the equality demanded by the original contract would not, in Kant's view, exclude a considerable amount of economic liberty.

The Kantian ideal of a hypothetical contract as the moral foundation for a welfare liberal conception of justice has been further developed in the work of John Rawls. In selection 10, taken from Rawls's most recent work, *Justice as Fairness: A Restatement*, Rawls, like Kant before him, argues that principles of justice are those principles that free and rational persons who are concerned with advancing their own interests would accept in an initial position of equality. Yet Rawls goes beyond Kant by interpreting the conditions of his "original position" to explicitly require a "veil of ignorance." This veil of ignorance, Rawls claims, requires that we discount certain knowledge about ourselves in order to reach fair agreements.

In *Justice as Fairness: A Restatement*, Rawls now reformulates the principles of justice that he claims would be chosen in the original position somewhat differently, as follows:

1. Each person has the same indefeasible claim to a fully adequate scheme of equal basic liberties, which scheme is compatible with the same scheme of liberties for all; and
2. Social and economic inequalities are to satisfy two conditions: First they are to be attached to offices and positions open to all under conditions of fair equality of opportunity; second, they are to be to the greatest benefit of the least advantaged members of society (the difference principle).

What is significantly different in Rawls's current theory of justice is how he now argues for these two principles from the perspective of the original position. In his earlier work, *A Theory of Justice*, Rawls had defended his principles of justice primarily by appealing to the maximin strategy. By contrast, in *Justice as Fairness: A Restatement*, Rawls defends his principles of justice by making two comparisons, one of which does not appeal to the maximin strategy at all. In the first comparison, the two principles taken as a unit are compared with the principle of average utility. In the second comparison, the two principles taken as a unit are compared with an alternative formed by substituting for the difference principle the principle of average utility combined with a stipulated social minimum. In the first comparison, Rawls holds that his two principles of justice would be chosen over the principle of average utility because persons in the original position would find it reasonable to follow the conservative dictates of the maximin strategy and <u>max</u>imize the <u>min</u>imum payoff primarily because they fear that the principle of average utility could require that the basic rights and liberties of some be restricted to secure greater benefits for others. In the second comparison, however, Rawls holds that the difference principle would be favored over the principle of average utility combined with a stipulated social minimum primarily because the difference principle expresses an ideal of reciprocity absent from the principle of average utility, even with a stipulated social minimum.

In selection 11, I sketch out the earlier defense that Rawls provided for his welfare liberal conception of justice in *A Theory of Justice,* and contrast that defense with Rawls's current defense in *Justice as Fairness: A Restatement.* I then assess the moral defensibility of Rawls's conception of justice.

Liberal Democratic Justice: The Utilitarian Perspective

It is clear that John Rawls takes utilitarianism to be the main rival to his contractarian defense of liberal democratic justice. Utilitarianism claims that the requirements of a liberal democratic conception of justice can be derived from considerations of utility in such a way that following these requirements will result in the maximization of total happiness or satisfaction in society. The best-known classical defense of this utilitarian approach is certainly that presented by John Stuart Mill in Chapter 5 of *Utilitarianism,* from which selection 12 is drawn.

In this selection, Mill surveys various types of actions and situations that are ordinarily described as just or unjust and concludes that justice (by which he understands a liberal democratic conception of justice) simply denotes a certain class of fundamental rules, the adherence to which is essential for maximizing social utility. Thus Mill rejects the ideal that justice and social utility are ultimately distinct ideals, maintaining instead that (liberal democratic) justice is in fact derivable from the moral ideal of social utility.

Nevertheless, various problems remain for the utilitarian defense of liberal democratic justice. Consider, for example, a society in which the members are equally divided between the Privileged Rich and the Alienated Poor, and suppose that the incomes for two alternative social arrangements for this society are the following:

	Social Arrangement A	*Social Arrangement B*
Privileged Rich	$100,000	$60,000
Alienated Poor	$5,000	$15,000

Given these alternatives, considerations of maximizing utility would appear to favor Social Arrangement A over Social Arrangement B. But suppose that liberal justice required a high minimum for each person in society. Then it would seem that liberal democratic justice would favor Social Arrangement B over Social Arrangement A, in apparent conflict with the requirements of utility. Obviously, the possibility of such a conflict places the utilitarian defense of liberal democratic justice in some doubt. In selection 13, R. M. Hare attempts to remove the grounds for that doubt.

Hare argues that in fashioning a theory of justice we must proceed in accordance with the formal constraints of the concept of justice; that is, our judgments must be universalizable and impartial. But in addition, Hare argues, we must take relevant empirical considerations into account, such as the fact that people experience a declining marginal utility for money and other social goods. For example, considerations of declining marginal utility of money and other social goods, Hare believes, would render a utilitarian approach to a theory of justice moderately egalitarian in its requirements. Applied to our example, considerations of declining marginal utility of money and other social goods would seem to render Social Arrangement B preferable to Social Arrangement A from a utilitarian point of view, thus removing the grounds for thinking that liberal justice and social utility conflict in this case.

Of course, when considerations of declining marginal utility of money and other social goods are taken into account, the utility values for the two alternatives given above might end up to be something like:

Social Arrangement A	*Social Arrangement B*
Privileged Rich 55	40
Alienated Poor 10	20

And if they did, then there would still remain a conflict between liberal democratic justice and utility, with liberal democratic justice favoring Social Arrangement B, and utility favoring Social Arrangement A . . . unless, of course, additional empirical considerations could be advanced to show that this is not the case.

Still another objection to a utilitarian defense of liberal justice is developed by John Rawls in selection 14. In this selection Rawls criticizes utilitarianism, particularly classical utilitarianism, for applying to society as a whole the principle of rational choice for one person, and thereby treating the desires and satisfactions of separate persons as if they were the desires and satisfactions of just one person. In this way, Rawls claims, utilitarianism fails to preserve the distinction between persons.

What Rawls must be claiming is that even after considerations of declining marginal utility of money and other social goods are taken into account, utilitarianism will still fail to adequately preserve the distinction between persons. But is Rawls right? It may well be that a proper assessment of the relative merits of the contractual and utilitarian approaches to liberal democratic justice will turn on this very issue.

Liberal Democratic Justice:
The Discourse Ethics Perspective

The Kantian ideal of a hypothetical contract as the moral foundation for a liberal democratic conception of justice has been developed in a somewhat different direction by Jürgen Habermas. A significant part of Habermas's work has been to show that the basic requirements of a political conception of justice can be derived from the common presuppositions of argumentation to which we all are committed. In selection 15, however,

Habermas tries to show how the most defensible political conception of justice also strikes a balance between popular sovereignty and human rights or between "the freedom of the ancients" and "the freedom of the moderns." What Habermas wants to avoid is conceiving of humans rights either as simply external constraints imposed on legislators or as simply means to legislative goals. Accordingly, he maintains that human rights are what makes the exercise of popular sovereignty possible. For him, they are not constraints but rather enabling conditions for the proper exercise of popular sovereignty. Habermas then goes on to draw out the implications of his analysis for the case of women, arguing that the individual rights necessary to guarantee women the autonomy to pursue their lives in the private sphere cannot be formulated adequately unless women and their male supporters first articulate and justify in public debate those aspects of women's lives that are relevant to equal or unequal treatment in typical cases.

In selection 16, Charles Larmore challenges two aspects of Habermas's defense of a liberal democratic conception of justice. First, Larmore challenges Habermas's tendency to reject metaphysics and religion as obsolete. While allowing that a political conception of justice cannot be based on metaphysical or religious views that reasonable people can reject, Larmore holds that reasonable people can and still do disagree about the validity of particular metaphysical or religious views, so that reason does not require that we all reject such views. Nevertheless, Habermas's view here may be closer to Larmore's than Larmore allows. Thus, Habermas may not be rejecting metaphysics and religion as a private doctrine but only as a public foundation for a political conception of justice, and that is exactly what Larmore does as well.

Second, Larmore questions whether Habermas succeeds in striking a proper balance between popular sovereignty and human rights. As Larmore sees it, Habermas favors the former over the latter since he maintains that human rights are what makes democratic self-rule possible; for example, a right to freedom of speech recommends itself simply as a means to the formation of a common political will. Larmore thinks that a further sign that Habermas is privileging popular sovereignty is the way he conceives of both popular sovereignty and human rights in terms of autonomy, public autonomy in the one case and private autonomy in the other. According to Larmore, however, there is a better way to interpret Habermas's view. Given that Habermas thinks that a political conception of justice ought to be rationally acceptable to all those who are bound by it, Larmore thinks that this implies an underlying requirement that each person be treated as an end and thus be shown respect. So interpreted, Larmore contends, popular sovereignty would itself rest on a fundamental individual right to equal respect.

In selection 17, Seyla Benhabib provides an even more expansive discussion of the discourse ethics perspective. She begins by discussing the presuppositions of argumentation on which a discourse ethics is grounded and then goes on to consider two criticisms of a strong model of deliberative democracy. The first is that this model leads to the corrosion of individual liberties. The second is by feminist theorists who are skeptical about the model because they see it as privileging a certain mode of discourse at the cost of silencing others that are more utilized by women and minorities.

Benhabib responds to the first criticism by noting that in her version of discourse ethics, which she shares with Habermas, all the participants in a deliberative democracy are entitled to mutual respect and egalitarian reciprocity. Since these fundamental rights both require and guide deliberative democracy, she contends that there is no sense in which the model can lead to the corrosion of individual rights.

In response to the second criticism, Benhabib argues that her model of deliberative democracy will not silence women and minorities, but, in fact, will take into account their different perspectives. She also criticizes Iris Young for requiring the participants in deliberative democracy to transcend and transform their initial situated knowledge at the same time that she denies them the standards of fairness and impartiality to do so properly.

Communitarian Justice

Another prominent political ideal defended by contemporary philosophers is the communitarian ideal of the common good. As one might expect, many contemporary defenders of a communitarian conception of justice regard their conception as rooted in Aristotelian moral theory. In selection 18, Aristotle distinguishes between different varieties of justice. He first distinguishes between justice as the whole of virtue and justice as a particular part of virtue. In the former sense, justice is understood as what is lawful and the just person is equivalent to the moral person. In the latter sense, justice is understood as what is fair or equal and the just person is the person who takes only a proper share. Aristotle focuses his discussion on justice in the latter sense, which further divides into distributive justice, corrective justice, and justice in exchange. Each of these varieties of justice can be understood to be concerned with achieving equality. For distributive justice it is equality between equals; for corrective justice it is equality between punishment and the crime; and for justice in exchange it is equality between whatever goods are exchanged. Aristotle also claims that justice has both its natural and conventional aspects: This twofold character of justice seems to be behind Aristotle's discussion of equity, in which equality is described as a corrective to legal or conventional justice.

Note that few of the distinctions Aristotle makes here seem tied to the acceptance of any particular conception of justice. One could, for example, accept the view that justice requires formal equality but then specify the equality that is required in different ways. Even the ideal of justice as giving people what they deserve, which has its roots in Aristotle's account of distributive justice, is also subject to various interpretations. For a correct analysis of the concept of desert would show that there is no conceptual difficulty with claiming, for example, that everyone deserves to have his or her needs satisfied or that everyone deserves an equal share of the goods distributed by his or her society.[7] Consequently, Aristotle's account is primarily helpful for getting clear about the distinctions belonging to the concept of justice that can be made without committing oneself to any particular conceptions of justice.

Yet rather than draw out the particular requirements of their own conception of justice, contemporary communitarians have frequently chosen to defend their conception by attacking other conceptions of justice, and, by and large, they have focused their attacks on the liberal democratic conception of justice.

One of the best-known attacks of this sort has been put forth by Michael J. Sandel (selection 19). According to Sandel, our current political philosophy is that of a procedural republic. We hold to the priority of fair procedures over particular ends. We emphasize toleration and respect for individual rights. We respect people's freedom to choose. This political philosophy, Sandel claims, comes in both utilitarian and Kantian varieties. While allowing that Rawls rightly criticizes utilitarianism for failing to take into account the separateness of persons, Sandel claims that Rawls's conception of the self as prior to the ends or purposes that are affirmed by it has a problem of its own. This is because it leads to the view that the obligations we have are either universally owed or voluntarily incurred. The problem with this, Sandel argues, is that we have obligations of membership and solidarity that are neither universally owed nor voluntarily incurred. Sandel cites here the example of Robert E. Lee's obligations to his relations and to Virginia at the outbreak of the Civil War.

Sandel also questions the view held by Rawls and other liberals that we should set aside moral and religious views about which there is reasonable disagreement when fashioning a political conception of justice. Here Sandel discusses two examples, the current abortion debate and the Lincoln–Douglas debate of 1858. Sandel claims that in both cases whether we should set aside our moral and religious views to achieve agreement depends upon whether or not we think those moral and religious views are true. According to Sandel, if we think that the Catholic Church's official doctrine on abortion is true, then it isn't clear why we should set aside this belief when fashioning a political conception of justice. But surely, we could believe something to be true while granting that other people in our society who lack our particular background or experience will not come to see it as true. Knowing this, we can see how they can reasonably disagree with us, and, for that reason, we might not think it right to coercively require them to live in accord with our (true) belief. Generally, it would seem that beliefs that are true but not accessible should not be the basis for coercive policies by the state.

In addition, the fact that there is disagreement as there was at the time of the Lincoln–Douglas debate does not show that those who disagreed were all reasonable. One could even argue that by 1858 there were sufficient reasons generally accessible to everyone to show that slavery was morally wrong, and that those who failed to believe this at the time were simply being unreasonable and could, therefore, be coercively required to oppose slavery.

In selection 20, Alasdair MacIntyre argues that the requirements for a common good cannot be secured by either the nation-state or the nuclear family. The nation-state is too large and the interests operating in it are too conflicted for it to provide for a common good, and families generally lack the self-sufficiency to provide for it. Only through the intermediate institutions of the local community, MacIntyre argues, can this common good characterized by a just generosity and other virtues of acknowledged dependence be achieved. To understand how best to achieve this common good of local community, MacIntyre suggests that we would do well to study the different types of local community that currently exist, or have existed in the past, such as fishing communities in New England, Welsh mining communities, farming cooperatives in Donegal, Mayan towns in Guatemala and Mexico, and city-states from a more distant past.

In selection 21, Jean Hampton defends liberalism against the communitarian perspective. She argues that both liberals and communitarians acknowledge the sociality of human nature while differing in their views of state power. Communitarians want the state to use its power to protect and encourage the development of communities and community values while liberals want the state to stay out of community life. She argues that liberalism has implicit within it a kind of critical facility for judging cultures that communitarianism appears to lack. At the same time, she allows that liberalism has trouble appreciating the moral wisdom implicit in community practices.

Feminist Justice

Defenders of a feminist conception of justice present a distinctively challenging critique to defenders of other conceptions of justice. John Stuart Mill, one of the earliest male defenders of women's liberation argues in selection 22 that the subjection of women was never justified but was imposed upon them because they were physically weaker than men and that later this subjection was confirmed by law. Mill argues that society must remove the legal restrictions that deny women the same opportunities that are enjoyed by men in society. However, Mill does not consider whether because of past discrimination against women it may be necessary to do more than simply remove legal restrictions to provide women with the same opportunities that men now enjoy. He doesn't consider whether positive assistance may also be required.

But usually it is not enough simply to remove unequal restrictions to make a competition fair among those who have been participating. Positive assistance to those who have been disadvantaged in the past may also be required, as would be the case if one were running a race in which one was unfairly impeded by having to carry a 10-pound weight. Similarly, positive assistance, such as affirmative action programs, may be necessary if women who have been disadvantaged in the past are now for the first time to enjoy equal opportunity with men.

In selection 23, Susan Okin points out that in the face of the radical inequality that exists between women and men in our society there is still a widespread failure of political philosophers to address gender issues in their political theories. Ironically this is true even among those philosophers who have seen the need to adopt gender neutral language. Okin argues that no theory of justice can be adequate until it addresses these issues.

In selection 24, I set out and defend an ideal of androgyny that I identify with feminist justice. This ideal requires that traits that are truly desirable in society be equally available to both women and men, or in the case of virtues, equally inculcated in both women and men. I consider attempts to derive the ideal of androgyny either from a right to equal opportunity that is a central requirement of a liberal democratic conception of justice or from an equal right of self-development that is a central requirement of a socialist conception of justice. I argue that although the ideal of androgyny is compatible with the requirements of these two conceptions of justice, it also transcends them by requiring that all virtue be equally inculcated in both women and men.

I further argue that the ideal of androgyny would require 1) that all children irrespective of their sex must be given the same type of upbringing consistent with their native capabilities and 2) that mothers and fathers must also have the same opportunities for education and employment consistent with their native capabilities. I go on to consider how achieving equal opportunity for women and men requires vastly improved day care facilities and flexible (usually part-time) work schedules for both women and men.

In Selection 25, Christina Sommers criticizes the attack by feminist philosophers, such as Okin and myself, on the traditional family structures. She distinguishes liberal feminists from radical feminists. She contends that liberal feminists, like herself, want equal opportunity in the workplace and politics, but would leave marriage and motherhood "untouched and unimpugned." By contrast, Sommers contends that radical feminists are committed to an assimilationist or androgynous ideal that would destroy the (traditional) family and deny most women what they want. Sommers, however, never explains how it is possible to secure for women equal opportunity in the workplace and politics while rejecting androgyny in favor of traditional gender roles. For example, how could women be passive, submissive, dependent, indecisive, and weak and still enjoy the same opportunities in the workplace and politics that are enjoyed by men who are aggressive, dominant, independent, decisive, and strong?

Marilyn Friedman (selection 26) does not challenge Sommers's contention that radical feminists are committed to an assimilationist or androgynous ideal. There is, however, an important distinction between these two ideals. According to an assimilationist ideal, "one's sex should be no more noticeable than one's eye color," but according to an androgynous ideal, this need not be the case, as long as all desirable traits are equally open to both women and men, and all virtues equally expected of both women and men.

Friedman does, however, question whether what Sommers supports is really what most women want. She quotes a 1983 survey which indicated that 63 percent of women preferred nontraditional family relationships, and points out that in 1977 only 16 percent of American households were traditional families in the sense of families consisting of a legally married heterosexual couple and their children, in which the man is the sole breadwinner and "head" of the household, and the woman does the domestic work and childcare. In responding to Friedman, Sommers explains that what she means by a traditional family is one that consists of two heterosexual parents and one or more children in which the mother plays a distinctive gender role in caring for the children.[8] This definition obviously broadens the class of families to which Sommers is referring. But in her response, Sommers goes on to renounce any attempt at promoting even the traditional family as she defines it. What she claims to be promoting is simply "the right and liberty to live under the arrangement of one's choice." According to Sommers, if people want to live in nontraditional families, they should be free to do so.

Friedman further disagrees with Sommers, contending that no woman should "swoon at the sight of Rhett Butler carrying Scarlett O'Hara up the stairs to a fate undreamt of in feminist philosophy." According to Friedman, what Rhett Butler is doing in *Gone With the Wind* is raping Scarlett O'Hara. In a subsequent response to Sommers, Friedman, noting that Scarlett O'Hara, although initially unwilling, later appears to be a willing sexual partner, defines "rape" as "any very intimate sexual contact which is *initiated* forcefully or against the will of the recipient."[9] Friedman allows that others might want to define such activity as sexual domination rather than rape, but under either definition, Friedman condemns it, whereas Sommers does not. In her response, Sommers cites approvingly the following passage from *Scarlett's Women: Gone With the Wind and Its Female Fans.*

[T]he majority of my correspondents (and I agree) recognize the ambiguous nature of the encounter and interpret it as a scene of mutually pleasurable rough sex . . . By far the majority of women who responded to me saw the episode as erotically exciting, emotionally stirring and profoundly memorable. Few of them referred to it as "rape."[10]

Postmodern Justice

Jean-Francois Lyotard is usually given credit for first introducing the term "postmodern" into the current discussions of philosophy, politics, and social theory with his book *The Postmodern Condition* from which selection 27 is taken. Lyotard defines postmodernism as incredulity toward metanarratives or grand theories. By metanarratives, Lyotard is primarily referring to Marxism and Hegelianism, but the term also refers to any univeralistic theory including our other six conceptions of justice. In its place, Lyotard wants justification to proceed by way of a multitude of localized mini-narratives, because he takes this to be the only form of justification possible.

According to Jeffrey Reiman in selection 28, modernism is the Enlightenment belief in a single unified rational perspective. By contrast, postmodernism, Reiman claims, rejects the idea of a given and claims that any interpretation can be shown to have been purchased only by the exclusion of other possible ones. Accordingly, postmodernists regard libertarians who interpret liberty to be our ultimate political ideal to be arbitrarily excluding other possible interpretations, but the same could be said of liberal democrats, socialists, communitarians, or feminists as well. Reiman's response to the postmodern challenge is to maintain that all arguments must proceed from beliefs that people already hold, which is to say they must be ad hominem. While Reiman thinks that an argument for liberalism can be derived from beliefs that everybody shares, that may not be necessary. For instance, if we could show that the libertarian ideal of liberty requires a right to welfare and further that implementing this right around the world and into the future would lead to the equality that socialists favor, that should serve to bring libertarians, liberal democrats and socialists together at a practical level despite their differing starting points.[11]

In selection 29, Nancy Fraser and Linda Nicholson try to combine the best elements of both postmodernism and feminism into a postmodern feminism. According to Fraser and Nicholson, feminists should learn from postmodernists to attend to the cultural specificity of different societies and historical periods and beware of oversimplistic explanations or false generalizations as they seek to uncover the cause or causes of the domination of women. Nevertheless, Fraser and Nicholson claim that this can be done without abandoning the large-scale historical narratives and analyses that is needed for a wide-ranging critical theory or theory of justice. All postmodern feminism has to do is be concerned with the subordination of women in both its "endless variety and monotonous similarity." In addition, if people could be led to see that feminist justice is compatible with or required by the ideals of libertarian justice, liberal democratic justice, socialist justice, and communitarian justice that they hold dear, then the case for feminist justice would be strengthened immeasurably. It could make the practical requirements of feminist justice virtually inescapable.

Environmental Justice

Like defenders of a feminist conception of justice, defenders of environmental justice present a distinctive challenge to defenders of other conceptions of justice. Environmental justice raises the question of who is to count morally. The usual assumption (which is almost never argued for) is that only humans are to count morally. One of the reasons given for thinking that only humans count morally is the belief that only humans are capable of morality. In selection 30, however, Frans De Waal challenges this belief by showing how chimpanzees practice social reciprocity. This raises the question of whether social reciprocity as practiced by chimpanzees is all that different from the reciprocity that John Rawls thinks grounds his conception of justice.

In Selection 31, Peter Singer further argues for the liberation of animals by comparing the bias against animals, which he calls "speciesism," with biases against blacks and women. According to Singer, the grounds we have for opposing racism and sexism are also grounds for opposing speciesism because all forms of discrimination run counter to the principle of equal consideration. Racists violate this principle by giving greater weight to the interests of members of their own race in cases of conflict; sexists violate this principle by giving greater weight to the interests of members of their own sex in cases of conflict; and speciesists violate this principle by giving greater weight to the interests of members of their own species in cases of conflict.

Animals have interests, Singer maintains, because they have a capacity for suffering and enjoyment. According to the principle of equal consideration, there is no justification for regarding the pain animals feel as less important than the same amount of pain (or pleasure) humans feel. As for the practical requirements of this view, Singer contends that we cannot go astray if we give the same respect to the lives of animals that we give to the lives of humans at a similar mental level. In the end, Singer thinks, this will require us to make radical changes in our diet, the farming methods we use, experimental procedures in many fields of science, our approach to wildlife and to hunting, trapping, and the wearing of furs, and areas of entertainment such as circuses, rodeos, and zoos.

A serious problem with Singer's view, however, is that it still appears to be biased against certain forms of life. Singer does not make it clear why only sentient beings count and not all living beings. He maintains that only sentient beings have interests in the sense that what we do matters to them. But why should this be grounds for excluding nonsentient living beings from moral consideration, given that although they are nonsentient, they still have a good of their own? This particular challenge to Singer's view is taken up by Paul Taylor in selection 32.

Taylor presents the following argument:

1. Humans are members of the earth's community of life.
2. All living things are related to one another in an order of interdependence.
3. Each organism is a teleological center of life.
4. The assertion of human superiority is groundless.
5. Therefore, we should recognize the equal inherent worth of every living being.

Given the general acceptability of the premises (1–3), Taylor devotes most of his time to arguing for (4) on the grounds that we have no non-question-begging reason for maintaining human superiority in the sense that it would justify our domination of other living beings.

The main difficulty with Taylor's argument concerns how we are to weigh human welfare against the welfare of other living beings once we grant that human beings are not superior to other species. In a later book that develops the argument of this essay, Taylor distinguishes between basic and nonbasic interests of living beings, but because he doesn't hold that the basic interests always have priority over nonbasic interests, it is difficult to know how decisions are to be made when there is conflict between human and nonhuman interests.

In Selection 33, I try to show that environmental ethics is grounded in rationality. This requires not simply showing that an environmental ethics is rationally permissible, because that would imply that a rejection of an environmental ethics is rationally permissible as well. Rather, what needs to be shown is that an environmental ethics is rationally required, thus excluding its rejection as rationally permissible. In the selection, I defend an environmental ethics which I call "Morality as Compromise" as more rationally defensible than either anthropocentrism or nonanthropocentrism, and I further provide a set of conflict resolution principles which determine how that compromise is to be specified. Obviously, the crucial questions for evaluating my view are whether these principles represent common ground between the opposing perspectives, and whether they can be effectively applied.

In Selection 34, Karen Warren argues that the domination of nature is connected to the domination of women and that at least within Western culture, the following argument is sanctioned:

1. Women are identified with nature and the realm of the physical; men are identified with the "human" and the realm of the mental. (For example, naturist language describes women as cows, foxes, chicks, serpents, bitches, beavers, old bats, pussycats, cats, bird-brains, hare-brains. Sexist language feminizes and sexualizes Nature: Nature is raped, mastered, conquered, controlled, mined. Her "secrets" are "penetrated" and her "womb" is put into the services of the "man of science." "Virgin timber" is felled, cut down. "Fertile soil" is tilled and land that lies "fallow" is "barren," useless.)
2. Whatever is identified with nature and the realm of the physical is inferior to whatever is identified with the "human" and the realm of the mental; or, conversely, the latter is superior to the former.
3. Thus, women are inferior to men; or, conversely, men are superior to women.
4. For any X and Y, if X is superior to Y, then X is justified in subordinating Y.
5. Thus, men are justified in subordinating women.

Warren points out that there is a "logic of domination" to this argument. It begins with a *claim of difference*. It then moves from a claim of difference to a *claim of superiority* and then from a claim of superiority to a *claim of subordination or domination*. Warren contends that this same logic of domination is common to all forms of domination and so is used to support, for example, racism, classism, and ageism, as well as sexism and naturism (Warren's term for the domination of nature). If Warren is correct, it follows that if one is against any one of these forms of domination, one should be against them all.

What this suggests is that our overall task of critically evaluating alternative conceptions of justice in order to reasonably resolve disputes about justice may not be as difficult as it initially appeared. If libertarian justice, liberal democratic justice, socialist justice, communitarian justice, feminist justice, postmodern justice, and environmental justice, when correctly interpreted, are interconnected and can all be seen to have virtually the same practical requirements, then there is really no need to choose between them. To reasonably resolve our disputes about justice, all we would have to do is get clear about what are the shared practical requirements of these conceptions of justice and then simply act upon them.[12]

NOTES

1. Selection 3.

2. *Ibid.*

3. *Ibid.*

4. Richard Rose and Rei Shiratori, eds. *The Welfare State East and West* (Oxford: Oxford University Press, 1986). In fact, the living standards of poor children in Switzerland, Sweden, Finland, Denmark, Belgium, Norway, Luxembourg, Germany, the Netherlands, Austria, Canada, France, Italy, the United Kingdom, and Australia are all better than they are in the United States. See James Carville, *We're Right They're Wrong* (New York: Random House, 1996), pp. 31–32.

5. Michael Wolff, *Where We Stand* (New York: Bantam Books, 1992) pp. 23 and 115; George Kurian, *The New Book of Work Rankings,* 3rd ed. (New York: Facts on File, 1990), p. 73; *New York Times,* April 17, 1995.

6. Joel Handler, *Poverty of Welfare Reform* (New Haven: Yale University Press, 1995); Herbert Gans, *The War Against the Poor* (New York: Basic Books, 1995).

7. For further argument, see my article "Justice and the Concept of Desert," *The Personalist* (1976), pp. 118–197.

8. Christina Sommers, "Do These Feminists Like Women?" *The Journal of Social Philosophy* (1991), pp. 66–74.

9. Marilyn Friedman, "Does Sommers Like Women?" *The Journal of Social Philosophy* (1991), pp. 75–90.

10. *Ibid.,* p. 72.

11. For further argument for this practical reconciliation thesis, see my book *How To Make People Just* (Rowman and Littlefield, 1988) and *Justice for Here and Now* (Cambridge University Press, 1998).

12. For further argument for this practical reconciliation thesis, see *How To Make People Just* and *Justice for Here and Now.*

Part II

Libertarian Justice

1 The Libertarian Manifesto

JOHN HOSPERS

THE POLITICAL PHILOSOPHY that is called libertarianism (from the Latin *libertas,* liberty) is the doctrine that every person is the owner of his own life, and that no one is the owner of anyone else's life: and that consequently every human being has the right to act in accordance with his own choices, unless those actions infringe on the equal liberty of other human beings to act in accordance with their choices.

There are several other ways of stating the same libertarian thesis:

1. *No one is anyone else's master, and no one is anyone else's slave.* Since I am the one to decide how my life is to be conducted just as you decide about yours, I have no right (even if I had the power) to make you my slave and be your master, nor have you the right to become the master by enslaving me. Slavery is *forced* servitude, and since no one owns the life of anyone else, no one has the right to enslave another. Political theories past and present have traditionally been concerned with who should be the master (usually the king, the dictator, or government bureaucracy) and who should be the slaves, and what the extent of the slavery should be. Libertarianism holds that no one has the right to use force to enslave the life of another, or any portion or aspect of that life.

2. *Other men's lives are not yours to dispose of.* I enjoy seeing operas; but operas are expensive to produce. Opera-lovers often say, "The state (or the city, etc.) should subsidize opera, so that we can all see it. Also it would be for people's betterment, cultural benefit, etc." But what they are advocating is nothing more or less than legalized plunder. They can't pay for the productions themselves, and yet they want to see opera, which involves a large number of people and their labor; so what they are saying in effect is, "Get the money through legalized force. Take a little bit more out of every worker's paycheck every week to pay for the operas we want to see." But I have no right to take by force from the workers' pockets to pay for what I want.

Perhaps it would be better if he *did* go to see opera—then I should try to convince him to go voluntarily. But to take the money from him forcibly, because in my opinion it would be good for *him,* is still seizure of his earnings, which is plunder.

Besides, if I have the right to force him to help pay for my pet projects, hasn't he equally the right to force me to help pay for his? Perhaps he in turn wants the government to subsidize rock-and-roll, or his new car, or a house in the country? If I have the right to milk him, why hasn't he the right to milk me? If I can be a moral cannibal, why can't he too?

We should beware of the inventors of utopias. They would remake the world ac-

From "What Libertarianism Is," in The Libertarian Alternative, *edited by Tibor Machan (1974). Reprinted by permission of Nelson-Hall, Inc.*

cording to their vision—with the lives and fruits of the labor of *other* human beings. Is it someone's utopian vision that others should build pyramids to beautify the landscape? Very well, then other men should provide the labor; and if he is in a position of political power, and he can't get men to do it voluntarily, then he must *compel* them to "cooperate"—i.e. he must enslave them.

A hundred men might gain great pleasure from beating up or killing just one insignificant human being; but other men's lives are not theirs to dispose of. "In order to achieve the worthy goals of the next five-year-plan, we must forcibly collectivize the peasants . . ."; but other men's lives are not theirs to dispose of. Do you want to occupy, rent-free, the mansion that another man has worked for twenty years to buy? But other men's lives are not yours to dispose of. Do you want operas so badly that everyone is forced to work harder to pay for their subsidization through taxes? But other men's lives are not yours to dispose of. Do you want to have free medical care at the expense of other people, whether they wish to provide it or not? But this would require them to work longer for you whether they want to or not, and other men's lives are not yours to dispose of. . . .

3. *No human being should be a nonvoluntary mortgage on the life of another.* I cannot claim your life, your work, or the products of your effort as mine. The fruit of one man's labor should not be fair game for every freeloader who comes along and demands it as his own. The orchard that has been carefully grown, nurtured, and harvested by its owner should not be ripe for the plucking for any bypasser who has a yen for the ripe fruit. The wealth that some men have produced should not be fair game for looting by government, to be used for whatever purposes its representatives determine, no matter what their motives in so doing may be. The theft of your

money by a robber is not justified by the fact that he used it to help his injured mother.

It will already be evident that libertarian doctrine is embedded in a view of the rights of man. Each human being has the right to live his life as he chooses, compatibly with the equal right of all other human beings to live their lives as they choose.

All man's rights are implicit in the above statement. Each man has the right to life: any attempt by others to take it away from him, or even to injure him, violates this right, through the use of coercion against him. Each man has the right to liberty: to conduct his life in accordance with the alternatives open to him without coercive action by others. And every man has the right to property: to work to sustain his life (and the lives of whichever others he chooses to sustain, such as his family) and to retain the fruits of his labor.

People often defend the rights of life and liberty but denigrate property rights, and yet the right to property is as basic as the other two: indeed, without property rights no other rights are possible. Depriving you of property is depriving you of the means by which you live. . . .

I have no right to decide how *you* should spend your time or your money. I can make that decision for myself, but not for you, my neighbor. I may deplore your choice of life-style, and I may talk with you about it provided you are willing to listen to me. But I have no right to use force to change it. Nor have I the right to decide how you should spend the money you have earned. I may appeal to you to give it to the Red Cross, and you may prefer to go to prize-fights. But that is your decision, and however much I may chafe about it I do not have the right to interfere forcibly with it, for example by robbing you in order to use the money in accordance with *my* choices. (If I have the right to rob you, have you also the right to rob me?)

When I claim a right, I carve out a niche, as it were, in my life, saying in effect, "This activity I must be able to perform without interference from others. For you and everyone else, this is off limits." And so I put up a "no trespassing" sign, which marks off the area of my right. Each individual's right is his "no trespassing" sign in relation to me and others. I may not encroach upon his domain any more than he upon mine, without my consent. Every right entails a duty, true—but the duty is only that of *forbearance*—that is, of *refraining* from violating the other person's right. If you have a right to life, I have no right to take your life; if you have a right to the products of your labor (property), I have no right to take it from you without your consent. The nonviolation of these rights will not guarantee you protection against natural catastrophes such as floods and earthquakes, but it will protect you against the aggressive activities *of other men*. And rights, after all, have to do with one's relations to other human beings, not with one's relations to physical nature.

Nor were these rights created by government; governments—some governments, obviously not all—*recognize* and *protect* the rights that individuals already have. Governments regularly forbid homicide and theft; and, at a more advanced stage, protect individuals against such things as libel and breach of contract. . . .

The *right to property* is the most misunderstood and unappreciated of human rights, and it is one most constantly violated by governments. "Property" of course does not mean only real estate; it includes anything you can call your own—your clothing, your car, your jewelry, your books and papers.

The right of property is not the right to just *take* it from others, for this would interfere with *their* property rights. It is rather the right to work for it, to obtain non-coercively, the money or services which you can present in voluntary exchange.

The right to property is consistently underplayed by intellectuals today, sometimes even frowned upon, as if we should feel guilty for upholding such a right in view of all the poverty in the world. But the right to property is absolutely basic. It is your hedge against the future. It is your assurance that what you have worked to earn will still be there and be yours, when you wish or need

to use it, especially when you are too old to work any longer.

Government has always been the chief enemy of the right to property. The officials of government, wishing to increase their power, and finding an increase of wealth an effective way to bring this about, seize some or all of what a person has earned—and since government has a monopoly of physical force within the geographical area of the nation, it has the power (but not the right) to do this. When this happens, of course, every citizen of that country is insecure: he knows that no matter how hard he works the government can swoop down on him at any time and confiscate his earnings and possessions. A person sees his life savings wiped out in a moment when the tax-collectors descend to deprive him of the fruits of his work; or, an industry which has been fifty years in the making and cost millions of dollars and millions of hours of time and planning, is nationalized overnight. Or the government, via inflation, cheapens the currency, so that hard-won dollars aren't worth anything any more. The effect of such actions, of course, is that people lose hope and incentive: if no matter how hard they work the government agents can take it all away, why bother to work at all, for more than today's needs? Depriving people of property is *depriving them of the means by which they live*—the freedom of the individual citizen to do what he wishes with his own life and to plan for the future. Indeed only if property rights are respected is there any point to planning for the future and working to achieve one's goals. *Property rights are what makes long-range planning possible*—the kind of planning which is a distinctively human endeavor, as opposed to the day-to-day activity of the lion who hunts, who depends on the supply of game tomorrow but has no real insurance against starvation in a day or a week. Without the right to property, the right to life itself amounts to little: how can you sustain your life if you cannot plan ahead? and how can you plan ahead if the fruits of your labor can at any moment by confiscated by government? . . .

Indeed, the right to property may well be considered second only to the right to life. Even the freedom of speech is limited by considerations of property. If a person visiting in your home behaves in a way undesired by you, you have every right to evict him; he can scream or agitate elsewhere if he wishes, but not in your home without your consent. Does a person have a right to shout obscenities in a cathedral? No, for the owners of the cathedral (presumably the Church) have not allowed others on their property for that purpose; one may go there to worship or to visit, but not just for any purpose one wishes. Their property right is prior to your or my wish to scream or expectorate or write graffiti on their building. Or, to take the stock example, does a person have a right to shout "Fire!" falsely in a crowded theater? No, for the theater owner has permitted others to enter and use his property only for a specific purpose, that of seeing a film or watching a stage show. If a person heckles or otherwise disturbs other members of the audience, he can be thrown out. (In fact, he can be removed for any reason the owner chooses, provided his admission money is returned.) And if he shouts "Fire!" when there is no fire, he may be endangering other lives by causing a panic or a stampede. The right to free speech doesn't give one the right to say anything anywhere; it is circumscribed by property rights.

Again, some people seem to assume that the right of free speech (including written speech) means that they can go to a newspaper publisher and demand that he print in his newspaper some propaganda or policy statement for their political party (or other group). But of course they have no right to the use of his newspaper. Ownership of the newspaper is the product of his labor, and he has a right to put into his newspaper whatever he wants, for whatever reason. If he excludes material which many readers would like to have in, perhaps they can find it in another newspaper or persuade him to print it himself (if there are enough of them, they will usually do just that). Perhaps they can even cause his newspaper to fail. But as long as he owns it, he has the right to put in it what he wishes; what would a property right be if he could not do this? They have no right to place their material in his newspaper without his consent—not

for free, nor even for a fee. Perhaps other newspapers will include it, or perhaps they can start their own newspaper (in which case they have a right to put in it what they like). If not, an option open to them would be to mimeograph and distribute some handbills.

In exactly the same way, no one has a right to "free television time" unless the owner of the television station consents to give it; it is his station, he has the property rights over it, and it is for him to decide how to dispose of his time. He may not decide wisely, but it is his right to decide as he wishes. If he makes enough unwise decisions, and courts enough unpopularity with the viewing public or the sponsors, he may have to go out of business; but as he is free to make his own decisions, so is he free to face their consequences. (If the government owns the television station, then government officials will make the decisions, and there is no guarantee of *their* superior wisdom. The difference is that when "the government" owns the station, you are forced to help pay for its upkeep through your taxes, whether the bureaucrat in charge decides to give you television time or not.)

"But why have *individual* property rights? Why not have lands and houses owned by everybody together?" Yes, this involves no violation of individual rights, as long as everybody consents to this arrangement and no one is forced to join it. The parties to it may enjoy the communal living enough (at least for a time) to overcome certain inevitable problems: that some will work and some not, that some will achieve more in an hour than others can do in a day, and still they will all get the same income. The few who do the most will in the end consider themselves "workhorses" who do the work of two or three or twelve, while the others will be "freeloaders" on the efforts of these few. But as long as they can get out of the arrangement if they no longer like it, no violation of rights is involved. They got in voluntarily, and they can get out voluntarily; no one had used force.

"But why not say that everybody owns everything? That we *all* own everything there is?"

To some this may have a pleasant ring—but let us try to analyze what it means. If everybody owns everything, then everyone has an equal right to go everywhere, do what he pleases, take what he likes, destroy if he wishes, grow crops or burn them, trample them under, and so on. Consider what it would be like in practice. Suppose you have saved money to buy a house for yourself and your family. Now suppose that the principle, "everybody owns everything," becomes adopted. Well then, why shouldn't every itinerant hippie just come in and take over, sleeping in your beds and eating in your kitchen and not bothering to replace the food supply or clean up the mess? After all, it belongs to all of us, doesn't it? So we have just as much right to it as you, the buyer, have. What happens if we *all* want to sleep in the bedroom and there's not room for all of us? Is it the strongest who wins?

What would be the result? Since no one would be responsible for anything, the property would soon be destroyed, the food used up, the facilities nonfunctional. Beginning as a house that *one* family could use, it would end up as a house that *no one* could use. And if the principle continued to be adopted, no one would build houses any more—or anything else. What for? They would only be occupied and used by others, without remuneration.

Suppose two men are cast ashore on an island, and they agree that each will cultivate half of it. The first man is industrious and grows crops and builds a shelter, making the most of the situation with which he is confronted. The second man, perhaps thinking that the warm days will last forever, lies in the sun, picks coconuts while they last, and does a minimum of work to sustain himself. At the time of harvest, the second man has nothing to harvest, nor does he assist the first man in his labors. But later when there is a dearth of food on the island, the second man comes to the first man and demands half of the harvest as his right. But of course he has no right to the product of the first man's labors. The first man may freely choose to give part of his harvest to the second out of charity rather than see him starve; but that is just what it is—charity, not the second man's right.

How can any of man's rights be violated? Ultimately, only by the use of force. I can make suggestions to you, I can reason with you, entreat you (if you are willing to listen), but I cannot *force* you without violating your rights; only by forcing you do I cut the cord between your free decisions and your actions. Voluntary relations between individuals involve no deprivation of rights, but murder, assault, and rape do, because in doing these things I make you the unwilling victim of my actions. A man's beating his wife involves no violation of rights if she *wanted* to be beaten. *Force is behavior that requires the unwilling involvement of other persons.*

Thus the use of force need not involve the use of physical violence. If I trespass on your property or dump garbage on it, I am violating your property rights, as indeed I am when I steal your watch; although this is not force in the sense of violence, it *is* a case of your being an unwilling victim of my action. Similarly, if you shout at me so that I cannot be heard when I try to speak, or blow a siren in my ear, or start a factory next door which pollutes my land, you are again violating my rights (to free speech, to property); I am, again, an unwilling victim of your actions. Similarly, if you steal a manuscript of mine and publish it as your own, you are confiscating a piece of my property and thus violating my right to keep what is the product of my labor. Of course, if I give you the manuscript with permission to sign your name to it and keep the proceeds, no violation of rights is involved—any more than if I give you permission to dump garbage on my yard.

According to libertarianism, the role of government should be limited to the retaliatory use of force against those who have initiated its use. It should not enter into any other areas such as religion, social organization, and economics.

Government

Government is the most dangerous institution known to man. Throughout history it has violated the rights of men more than any individual or groups of individuals could do: it has killed people, enslaved them, sent them to forced labor and concentration camps, and regularly robbed and pillaged them of the fruits of their expended labor. Unlike individual criminals, government has the power to arrest and try; unlike individual criminals, it can surround and encompass a person totally, dominating every aspect of one's life, so that one has no recourse from it but to leave the country (and in totalitarian nations even that is prohibited). Government throughout history has a much sorrier record than any individual, even that of a ruthless mass murderer. The signs we see on bumper stickers are chillingly accurate: "Beware: the Government Is Armed and Dangerous."

The only proper role of government, according to libertarians, is that of the protector of the citizen against aggression by other individuals. The government, of course, should never initiate aggression; its proper role is as the embodiment of the *retaliatory* use of force against anyone who initiates its use.

If each individual had constantly to defend himself against possible aggressors, he would have to spend a considerable portion of his life in target practice, karate exercises, and other means of self-defense, and even so he would probably be helpless against groups of individuals who might try to kill, maim, or rob him. He would have little time for cultivating those qualities which are essential to civilized life, nor would improvements in science, medicine, and the arts be likely to occur. The function of government is to take this responsibility off his shoulders: the government undertakes to defend him against aggressors and to punish them if they attack him. When the government is effective in doing this, it enables the citizen to go about his business unmolested and without constant fear for his life. To do this, of course, government must have physical power—the police, to protect the citizen from aggression within its borders, and the armed forces, to protect him from aggressors outside. Beyond that, the government should not intrude upon his life, either to run his business, or adjust his daily activities, or prescribe his personal moral code.

Government, then, undertakes to be the individual's protector; but historically governments have gone far beyond this function. Since they already have the physical power, they have not hesitated to use it for purposes far beyond that which was entrusted to them in the first place. Undertaking initially to protect its citizens against aggression, it has often itself become an aggressor— a far greater aggressor, indeed, than the criminals against whom it was supposed to protect its citizens. Governments have done what no private citizen can do: arrest and imprison individuals without a trial and send them to slave labor camps. Government must have power in order to be effective—and yet the very means by which alone it can be effective make it vulnerable to the abuse of power, leading to managing the lives of individuals and even inflicting terror upon them.

What then should be the function of government? In a word, the *protection of human rights*.

1. *The right to life:* libertarians support all such legislation as will protect human beings against the use of force by others, for example, laws against killing, attempting killing, maiming, beating, and all kinds of physical violence.
2. *The right to liberty:* there should be no laws compromising in any way freedom of speech, of the press, and peaceable assembly. There should be no censorship of ideas, books, films, or of anything else by government.
3. *The right to property:* libertarians support legislation that protects the property rights of individuals against confiscation, nationalization, eminent domain, robbery, trespass, fraud and misrepresentation, patent and copyright, libel and slander.

Someone has violently assaulted you. Should he be legally liable? Of course. He has violated one of your rights. He has knowingly injured you and since he has initiated aggression against you he should be made to expiate.

Someone has negligently left his bicycle on the sidewalk where you trip over it in the dark and injure yourself. He didn't do it intentionally; he didn't mean you any harm. Should he be legally liable? Of course; he has, however unwittingly, injured you, and since the injury is caused by him and you are the victim, he should pay.

Someone across the street is unemployed. Should you be taxed extra to pay for his expenses? Not at all. You have not injured him, you are not responsible for the fact that he is unemployed (unless you are a senator or bureaucrat who agitated for further curtailing of business, which legislation passed, with the result that your neighbor was laid off by the curtailed business). You may voluntarily wish to help him out, or better still, try to get him a job to put him on his feet again; but since you have initiated no aggressive act against him, and neither purposely nor accidentally injured him in any way, you should not be legally penalized for the fact of his unemployment. (Actually, it is just such penalties that increase unemployment.)

One man, A, works hard for years and finally earns a high salary as a professional man. A second man, B, prefers not to work at all, and to spend wastefully what money he has (through inheritance), so that after a year or two he has nothing left. At the end of this time he has a long siege of illness and lots of medical bills to pay. He demands that the bills be paid by the government—that is, by the taxpayers of the land, including Mr. A.

But of course B has no such right. He chose to lead his life in a certain way—that was his voluntary decision. One consequence of that choice is that he must depend on charity in case of later need. Mr. A chose not to live that way. (And if everyone lived like Mr. B, on whom would he depend in case of later need?) Each has a right to live in the way he pleases, but each must live with the consequences of his own decision (which, as always, fall primarily on himself). He cannot, in time of need, claim A's beneficence as his right.

If a house-guest of yours starts to carve his initials in your walls and break up your furniture, you have a right to evict him, and call the police if he makes trouble. If someone starts to destroy the machinery in a factory, the factory-owner is also entitled to evict him and call the police. In both cases, persons other than the owner are permitted on the property only under certain conditions, at the pleasure of the owner. If those conditions are

violated, the owner is entitled to use force to set things straight. The case is exactly the same on a college or university campus: if a campus demonstrator starts breaking windows, occupying the president's office, and setting fire to a dean, the college authorities are certainly within their rights to evict him forcibly; one is permitted on the college grounds only under specific conditions, set by the administration: study, peaceful student activity, even political activity if those in charge choose to permit it. If they do not choose to permit peaceful political activity on campus, they may be unwise, since a campus is after all a place where all sides of every issue should get discussed, and the college that doesn't permit this may soon lose its reputation and its students. All the same, the college official who does not permit it is quite within his rights; the students do not own the campus, nor do the hired troublemakers imported from elsewhere. In the case of a privately owned college, the owners, or whoever they have delegated to administer it, have the right to make the decisions as to who shall be permitted on the campus and under what conditions. In the case of a state university or college, the ownership problem is more complex: one could say that the "government" owns the campus or that "the people" do since they are the taxpayers who support it; but in either case, the university administration has the delegated task of keeping order, and until they are removed by the state administration or the taxpayers, it is theirs to decide who shall be permitted on campus, and what nonacademic activities will be permitted to their students on the premises.

Property rights can be violated by physical trespass, of course, or by anyone entering on your property for any reason without your consent. (If you *do* consent to having your neighbor dump garbage on your yard, there is no violation of your rights.) But the physical trespass of a person is only a special case of violation of property rights. Property rights can be violated by sound-waves, in the form of a loud noise, or the sounds of your neighbor's hi-fi set while you are trying to sleep. Such violations of property rights are of course the subject of action in the courts.

But there is another violation of property rights that has not thus far been honored by the courts; this has to do with the effects of *pollution* of the atmosphere.

> From the beginnings of modern air pollution, the courts made a conscious decision not to protect, for example, the orchards of farmers from the smoke of nearby factories or locomotives. They said, in effect, to the farmers: yes, your private property is being invaded by this smoke, but we hold that "public policy" is more important than private property, and public policy holds factories and locomotives to be good things. These goods were allowed to override the defense of property rights—with our consequent headlong rush into pollution disaster. The remedy is both "radical" and crystal clear, and it has nothing to do with multibillion dollar palliative programs at the expense of the taxpayers which do not even meet the real issue. The remedy is simply to enjoin anyone from injecting pollutants into the air, and thereby invading the rights of persons and property. Period. The argument that such an injunction prohibition would add to the costs of industrial production is as reprehensible as the pre-Civil War argument that the abolition of slavery would add to the costs of growing cotton, and therefore should not take place. For this means that the polluters are able to impose the high costs of pollution upon those whose property rights they are allowed to invade with impunity.[1]

What about automobiles, the chief polluters of the air? One can hardly sue every automobile owner. But one can sue the manufacturers of automobiles who do not install anti-smog devices on the cars which they distribute—and later (though this is more difficult), owners of individual automobiles if they discard the equipment or do not keep it functional.

The violation of rights does not apply only to air-pollution. If someone with a factory upstream on a river pollutes the river, anyone living downstream from him, finding his water polluted, should be able to sue the owner of the factory. In this way the price of adding the anti-pollutant devices will be the owner's responsibility, and will probably be added to the cost of the products which the factory produces and thus spread around among all consumers, rather than the entire cost being borne by the users of the river in the form of polluted water, with the consequent impossibility of fishing, swimming, and so on. In each case, pollution would be stopped at the source rather than having its ill effects spread around to numerous members of the population.

What about property which you do not work to earn, but which you *inherit* from someone else? Do you have a right to that? You have no right to it until someone decides to give it to you. Consider the man who willed it to you; it was his, he had the right to use and dispose of it as *he* saw fit; and if he decided to give it to you, this is a windfall for you, but it was only the exercise of *his* right. Had the property been seized by the government at the man's death, or distributed among numerous other people designated by the government, it *would* have been a violation of his rights: for he, who worked to earn and sustain it, would not have been able to dispose of it according to his own judgment. If he doesn't have the right to determine who shall have it, who does?

What about the property status of your intellectual activity, such as inventions you may devise and books you write? These, of course, are your property also; they are the products of your mind; you worked at them, you created them. Prior to that, they did not exist. If you worked five years to write a book, and someone stole it and published it as his own, receiving royalties from its sales, he would have stolen your property just as surely as if he had robbed your home. The same is true if someone used and sold without your permission an invention which was the product of your labor and ingenuity.

The role of government with respect to this issue, at least most governments of the Western world, is a proper one: government protects the products of your labor from the moment they materialize. Copyright law protects your writings from piracy. In the United States, one's writings are protected for a period of twenty-seven years, and another twenty-seven if one applies for renewal of the copyright. In most other countries, they are protected for a period of fifty years after the author's death, permitting both himself and his surviving heirs to reap the fruits of his labor. After that they enter the "public domain"—that is, anyone may reprint them without your or your heir's permission. Patent law protects your inventions for a limited period, which varies according to the type of invention. In no case are you forced to avail yourself of this protection; you need not apply for patent or copyright coverage if you do not wish to do so. But the protection of your intellectual property is there, in case you wish to use it.

What about the property status of the airwaves? Here the government's position is far more questionable. The government now claims ownership of the airwaves, leasing them to individuals and corporations. The government renews leases or refuses them depending on whether the programs satisfy authorities in the Federal Communications Commission. The official position is that "we all own the airwaves"; but since only one party can broadcast on a certain frequency at a certain time without causing chaos, it is simply a fact of reality that "everyone" cannot use it. In fact the government decides who shall use the airwaves and one courts its displeasure only at the price of a revoked license. One can write without government approval, but one cannot use the airwaves without the approval of government.

What policy should have been observed with regard to the airwaves? Much the same as the policy that was followed in the case of the Homestead Act, when the lands of the American West were opening up for settlement. There was a policy of "first come, first served," with the government parcelling out a certain acreage for each individual who wanted to claim the land as his own. There was no charge for the land, but if a man had not used it and built a dwelling during the first two-year period, it was assumed that he was not homesteading and the land was given to the next man in line. The airwaves too could have been given out on a "first come, first served" basis. The first man who used a given frequency would be its owner, and the government would protect him in the use of it against trespassers. If others wanted to use the same frequency, they would have to buy it from the first man, if he was willing to sell, or try to buy another, just as one now does with the land.

Laws may be classified into three types: (1) laws protecting individuals against themselves, such as laws against fornication and other sexual behavior, alcohol, and drugs; (2) laws protecting individuals against aggressions by other individuals, such as laws against murder, robbery, and fraud; (3) laws requiring people to help one another; for example, all laws which rob Peter to pay Paul, such as welfare.

Libertarians reject the first class of laws totally. Behavior which harms no one else is strictly the individual's own affair. Thus, there should be no laws against becoming intoxicated, since whether or not to become intoxicated is the individual's own decision: but there should be laws against driving while intoxicated, since the drunken driver is a threat to every other motorist on the highway (drunken driving falls into type 2). Similarly, there should be no laws against drugs (except the prohibition of sale of drugs to minors) as long as the taking of these drugs poses no threat to anyone else. Drug addiction is a psychological problem to which no present solution exists. Most of the social harm caused by addicts, other than to themselves, is the result of thefts which they perform in order to continue their habit—and then the *legal* crime is the theft, not the addiction. The actual cost of heroin is about ten cents a shot; if it were legalized, the enormous traffic in illegal sale and purchase of it would stop, as well as the accompanying proselytization to get new addicts (to make more money for the pusher) and the thefts performed by addicts who often require eighty dollars a day just to keep up the habit. Addiction would not stop, but the crimes would: it is estimated that 75 percent of the burglaries in New York City today are performed by addicts, and all these crimes could be wiped out at one stroke though the legalization of drugs. (Only when the taking of drugs could be shown to constitute a threat to *others,* should it be prohibited by law. It is only laws protecting people against *themselves* that libertarians oppose.)

Laws should be limited to the second class only: aggression by individuals against other individuals. These are laws whose function is to protect human beings against encroachment by others; and this, as we have seen, is (according to libertarianism) the sole function of government.

Libertarians also reject the third class of laws totally: no one should be forced by law to help others, not even to tell them the time of day if requested, and certainly not to give them a portion of one's weekly paycheck. Governments, in the guise of humanitarianism, have given to some by taking from others (charging a "handling fee" in the process, which, because of the government's waste and inefficiency, sometimes is several hundred percent). And in so doing they have decreased incentive, violated the rights of individuals and lowered the standard of living of almost everyone.

All such laws constitute what libertarians call *moral cannibalism*. A cannibal in the physical sense is a person who lives off the flesh of other human beings. A *moral* cannibal is one who believes he has a right to live off the "spirit" of other human beings—who believes that he has a moral claim on the productive capacity, time, and effort expended by others.

It has become fashionable to claim virtually everything that one needs or desires as one's *right*. Thus, many people claim that they have a right to a job, the right to free medical care, to free food and clothing, to a decent home, and so on. Now if one asks, apart from any specific context, whether it would be desirable if everyone had these things, one might well say yes. But there is a gimmick attached to each of them: *At whose expense*? Jobs, medical care, education, and so on, don't grow on trees. These are goods and services *produced only by men*. Who then is to provide them, and under what conditions?

If you have a right to a job, who is to supply it? Must an employer supply it even if he doesn't want to hire you? What if you are unemployable, or incurably lazy? (If you say "the government must

supply it," does that mean that a job must be created for you which no employer needs done, and that you must be kept in it regardless of how much or little you work?) If the employer is forced to supply it at his expense even if he doesn't need you, then isn't *he* being enslaved to that extent? What ever happened to *his* right to conduct his life and his affairs in accordance with his choices?

If you have a right to free medical care, then, since medical care doesn't exist in nature as wild apples do, some people will have to supply it to you for free: that is, they will have to spend their time and money and energy taking care of you whether they want to or not. What ever happened to *their* right to conduct their lives as they see fit? Or do you have a right to violate theirs? Can there be a right to violate rights?

All those who demand this or that as a "free service" are consciously or unconsciously evading the fact that there is in reality no such thing as free services. All man-made goods and services are the result of human expenditure of time and effort. There is no such thing as "something for nothing" in this world. If you demand something free, you are demanding that other men give their time and effort to you without compensation. If they voluntarily choose to do this, there is no problem; but if you demand that they be *forced* to do it, you are interfering with their right not to do it if they so choose. "Swimming in this pool ought to be free!" says the indignant passerby. What he means is that others should build a pool, others should provide the material and still others should run it and keep it in functioning order, so that *he* can use it without fee. But what right has he to the expenditure of *their* time and effort? To expect something "for free" is to expect it *to be paid for by others* whether they choose to or not.

Many questions, particularly about economic matters, will be generated by the libertarian account of human rights and the role of government. Should government have a role in assisting the needy, in providing social security, in legislating minimum wages, in fixing prices and putting a ceiling on rents, in curbing monopolies, in erecting tariffs, in guaranteeing jobs, in managing the money supply? To these and all similar questions the libertarian answers with an equivocal no.

"But then you'd let people go hungry!" comes the rejoinder. This, the libertarian insists, is precisely what would not happen; with the restrictions removed, the economy would flourish as never before. With the controls taken off business, existing enterprises would expand and new ones would spring into existence satisfying more and more consumer needs; millions more people would be gainfully employed instead of subsisting on welfare, and all kinds of research and production, released from the stranglehold of government, would proliferate, fulfilling man's needs and desires as never before. It has always been so whenever government has permitted men to be free traders on a free market. But *why* this is so, and how the free market is the best solution to all problems relating to the material aspect of man's life, is another and far longer story.

NOTE

1. Murray Rothbard, "The Great Ecology Issue," *The Individualist, 2,* no. 2 (Feb. 1970), p. 5.

2　From Liberty to Welfare

JAMES P. STERBA

LIBERTARIANS TODAY are deeply divided over whether a night watchman state can be morally justified. Some, like Robert Nozick, hold that a night watchman state would tend to arise by an invisible-hand process if people generally respected each other's Lockean rights.[1] Others, like Murray Rothbard, hold that even the free and informed consent of all the members of a society would not justify such a state.[2] Despite this disagreement, libertarians are strongly united in opposition to welfare rights and the welfare state. According to Nozick, "the state may not use its coercive apparatus for the purpose of getting some citizens to aid others."[3] For Rothbard, "the libertarian position calls for the complete abolition of governmental welfare and reliance on private charitable aid."[4] Here I argue that this libertarian opposition to welfare rights and a welfare state is ill-founded. Welfare rights can be given a libertarian justification, and once this is recognized, a libertarian argument for a welfare state, unlike libertarian arguments for the night watchman state, is both straightforward and compelling. . . .

Libertarians have defended their view in basically two different ways. Some libertarians, following Herbert Spencer, have 1) defined liberty as the absence of constraints, 2) taken a right to liberty to be the ultimate political ideal, and 3) derived all other rights from this right to liberty. Other libertarians, following John Locke, have 1) taken a set of rights, including, typically, a right to life or self-ownership and a right to property, to be the ultimate political ideal, 2) defined liberty as the ab-

sence of constraints in the exercise of these fundamental rights, and 3) derived all other rights including a right to liberty, from these fundamental rights.

Each of these approaches has its difficulties. The principal difficulty with the first approach is that unless one arbitrarily restricts what is to count as an interference, conflicting liberties will abound, particularly in all areas of social life.[5] The principal difficulty with the second approach is that as long as a person's rights have not been violated, her liberty would not have been restricted either, even if she were kept in prison for the rest of her days.[6] I don't propose to try to decide between these two approaches. What I do want to show, however, is that on either approach welfare rights and a welfare state are morally required.

Spencerian Libertarianism

Thus suppose we were to adopt the view of those libertarians who take a right to liberty to be the ultimate political ideal. According to this view, liberty is usually defined as follows:

The Want Conception of Liberty: Liberty is being unconstrained by other persons from doing what one wants.

This conception limits the scope of liberty in two ways. First, not all constraints whatever their source count as a restriction of liberty; the constraints must come from other persons. For example, people who are constrained by natural

From Social Theory and Practice, *vol. 11, no. 3 (fall 1985), pp. 285–305, with revisions.*

forces from getting to the top of Mount Everest do not lack liberty in this regard. Second, constraints that have their source in other persons, but that do not run counter to an individual's wants, constrain without restricting that individual's liberty. Thus, for people who do not want to hear Beethoven's Fifth Symphony, the fact that others have effectively proscribed its performance does not restrict their liberty, even though it does constrain what they are able to do.

Of course, libertarians may wish to argue that even such constraints can be seen to restrict a person's liberty once we take into account the fact that people normally want, or have a general desire, to be unconstrained by others. But other philosophers have thought that the possibility of such constraints points to a serious defect in this conception of liberty,[7] which can only be remedied by adopting the following broader conception of liberty:

> *The Ability Conception of Liberty:* Liberty is being unconstrained by other persons from doing what one is able to do.

Applying this conception to the above example, we find that people's liberty to hear Beethoven's Fifth Symphony would be restricted even if they did not want to hear it (and even if, perchance, they did not want to be unconstrained by others) since other people would still be constraining them from doing what they are able to do. . . .

Of course, there will be numerous liberties determined by the Ability Conception that are not liberties according to the Want Conception. For example, there will be highly talented students who do not want to pursue careers in philosophy, even though no one constrains them from doing so. Accordingly, the Ability Conception but not the Want Conception would view them as possessing a liberty. And even though such liberties are generally not as valuable as those liberties that are common to both conceptions, they still are of some value, even when the manipulation of people's wants is not at issue.

Yet even if we accept all the liberties specified by the Ability Conception, problems of interpretation still remain. The major problem in this re-gard concerns what is to count as a constraint. On the one hand, libertarians would like to limit constraints to positive acts (that is, acts of commission) that prevent people from doing what they are otherwise able to do. On the other hand, . . . liberal [democrats] and socialists interpret constraints to include, in addition, negative acts (that is, of omission) that prevent people from doing what they are otherwise able to do. In fact, this is one way to understand the debate between defenders of "negative liberty" and defenders of "positive liberty." For defenders of negative liberty would seem to interpret constraints to include only positive acts of others that prevent people from doing what they otherwise are able to do, while defenders of positive liberty would seem to interpret constraints to include both positive and negative acts of others that prevent people from doing what they are otherwise able to do.[8]

Suppose we interpret constraints in the manner favored by libertarians to include only positive acts by others that prevent people from doing what they are otherwise able to do, and let us consider a typical conflict situation between the rich and the poor.

In this conflict situation, the rich, of course, have more than enough resources to satisfy their basic needs. By contrast, the poor lack the resources to meet their most basic nutritional needs even though they have tried all the means available to them that libertarians regard as legitimate for acquiring such resources. Under circumstances like these, libertarians usually maintain that the rich should have the liberty to use their resources to satisfy their luxury needs if they so wish. Libertarians recognize that this liberty might well be enjoyed at the expense of the satisfaction of the most basic nutritional needs of the poor. Libertarians just think that a right to liberty always has priority over other political ideals, and since they assume that the liberty of the poor is not at stake in such conflict situations, it is easy for them to conclude that the rich should not be required to sacrifice their liberty so that the basic nutritional needs of the poor may be met.

From a consideration of the liberties involved, libertarians claim to derive a number of more specific requirements, in particular, a right to life, a right to freedom of speech, press and assembly, and a right to property.

Here it is important to observe that the libertarian's right to life is not a right to receive from others the goods and resources necessary for preserving one's life; it is simply a right not to be killed unjustly. Correspondingly, the libertarian's right to property is not a right to receive from others the goods and resources necessary for one's welfare, but rather a right to acquire goods and resources either by initial acquisition or by voluntary agreement.

Rights such as these, libertarians claim, can at best support only a limited role for government. That role is simply to prevent and punish initial acts of coercion—the only wrongful actions for libertarians. And, as we noted before, libertarians are deeply divided over whether a government with even such a limited role, that is, a night watchman state, can be morally justified.

Of course, libertarians would allow that it would be nice of the rich to share their surplus resources with the poor. Nevertheless, according to libertarians, such acts of charity should not be coercively required, because the liberty of the poor is not thought to be at stake in such conflict situations.

In fact, however, the liberty of the poor is at stake in such conflict situations. What is at stake is the liberty of the poor to take from the surplus possessions of the rich what is necessary to satisfy their basic nutritional needs. When libertarians are brought to see that this is the case, they are often genuinely surprised, for they had not previously seen the conflict between the rich and the poor as a conflict of liberties.[9]

When the conflict between the rich and the poor is viewed as a conflict of liberties, we can either say that the rich should have the liberty to use their surplus resources for luxury purposes, or we can say that the poor should have the liberty to take from the rich what they require to meet their basic nutritional needs. If we choose one liberty, we must reject the other. What needs to be determined, therefore, is which liberty is morally preferable: the liberty of the rich or the liberty of the poor.

I submit that the liberty of the poor, which is the liberty to take from the surplus resources of others what is required to meet one's basic nutritional needs, is morally preferable to the liberty of the rich, which is the liberty to use one's surplus resources for luxury purposes. To see that this is the case we need only appeal to one of the most fundamental principles of morality, one that is common to all political perspectives, namely, the "ought" implies "can" principle. According to this principle, people are not morally required to do what they lack the power to do or what would involve so great a sacrifice that it would be unreasonable to ask them to perform such an action.[10] For example, suppose I promised to attend a meeting on Friday, but on Thursday I am involved in a serious car accident which puts me into a coma. Surely it is no longer the case that I ought to attend the meeting now that I lack the power to do so. Or suppose instead that on Thursday I develop a severe case of pneumonia for which I am hospitalized. Surely I could legitimately claim that I no longer ought to attend the meeting on the grounds that the risk to my health involved in attending is a sacrifice that it would be unreasonable to ask me to bear.

Now applying the "ought" implies "can" principle to the case at hand, it seems clear that the poor have it within their power to willingly relinquish such an important liberty as the liberty to take from the rich what they require to meet their basic nutritional needs. Nevertheless, it would be unreasonable to require them to make so great a sacrifice. In the extreme case, it would involve requiring the poor to sit back and starve to death. Of course, the poor may have no real alternative to relinquishing this liberty. To do anything else may involve worse consequences for themselves and their loved ones and may invite a painful death. Accordingly, we may expect that the poor would acquiesce, albeit unwillingly, to a political system that denied them the welfare rights supported by such a liberty, at the same time that we recognize that such a system imposed an unreasonable sacrifice upon the poor—a sacrifice that we could not morally blame the poor for trying to evade.[11] Analogously, we might expect that a woman whose life was threatened would submit to a rapist's demands, at the same time that we recognize the utter unreasonableness of those demands.

By contrast, it would not be unreasonable to require the rich to sacrifice the liberty to meet some of their luxury needs so that the poor can have the liberty to meet their basic nutritional needs. Naturally, we might expect that the rich for reasons of self-interest and past contribution might be disinclined to make such a sacrifice. We might even suppose that the past contribution of the rich provides a good reason for not sacrificing their liberty to use their surplus for luxury purposes. Yet, unlike the poor, the rich could not claim that relinquishing such a liberty involved so great a sacrifice that it would be unreasonable to require them to make it; unlike the poor, the rich could be morally blameworthy for failing to make such a sacrifice.

Consequently, if we assume that however else we specify the requirements of morality, they cannot violate the "ought" implies "can" principle, it follows that, despite what libertarians claim, the right to liberty endorsed by libertarians actually favors the liberty of the poor over the liberty of the rich.

Yet couldn't libertarians object to this conclusion, claiming that it would be unreasonable to require the rich to sacrifice the liberty to meet some of their luxury needs so that the poor could have the liberty to meet their basic nutritional needs? As I have pointed out, libertarians don't usually see the situation as a conflict of liberties, but suppose they did. How plausible would such an objection be? Not very plausible at all, I think.

Consider this: what are libertarians going to say about the poor? Isn't it clearly unreasonable to require the poor to sacrifice the liberty to meet their basic nutritional needs so that the rich can have the liberty to meet their luxury needs? Isn't it clearly unreasonable to require the poor to sit back and starve to death? If it is, then there is no resolution of this conflict that would be reasonable to require both the rich and the poor to accept. But that would mean that the libertarian ideal of liberty cannot be a moral ideal that re-

solves conflicts of interest in ways that it would be reasonable to require everyone affected to accept. Therefore, as long as libertarians think of themselves as putting forth such a moral ideal, they cannot allow that it would be unreasonable both to require the rich to sacrifice the liberty to meet some of their luxury needs in order to benefit the poor and to require the poor to sacrifice the liberty to meet their basic nutritional needs in order to benefit the rich. But I submit that if one of these requests is to be judged reasonable, then, by any neutral assessment, it must be the requirement that the rich sacrifice the liberty to meet some of their luxury needs so that the poor can have the liberty to meet their basic nutritional needs; there is no other plausible resolution, if libertarians intend to be putting forth a moral ideal that reasonably resolves conflicts of interest.

But might not libertarians hold that putting forth a moral ideal means no more than being willing to universalize one's fundamental commitments? Surely we have no difficulty imagining the rich willing to universalize their commitments to relatively strong property rights. Yet, at the same time, we have no difficulty imagining the poor and their advocates willing to universalize their commitments to relatively weak property rights. Consequently, if the libertarian's moral ideal is interpreted in this fashion, it would not be able to provide a basis for reasonably resolving conflicts of interest between the rich and the poor. But without such a basis for conflict resolution, how could societies flourish, as libertarians claim they would, under a minimal state or with no state at all?[12] Surely, in order for societies to flourish in this fashion, the libertarian ideal must resolve conflicts of interest in ways that it would be reasonable to require everyone affected to accept. But, as we have seen, that requirement can only be satisfied if the rich sacrifice the liberty to meet some of their luxury needs so that the poor can have the liberty to meet their basic nutritional needs.

It should also be noted that this case for restricting the liberty of the rich depends upon the willingness of the poor to take advantage of whatever opportunities are available to them for satisfying their basic needs by engaging in mutually beneficial work, so that failure of the poor to take advantage of such opportunities would normally either cancel or at least significantly reduce the obligation of the rich to restrict their own liberty for the benefit of the poor.[13] In addition, the poor would be required to return the equivalent of any surplus possessions they have taken from the rich once they are able to do so and still satisfy their basic needs. Nor would the poor be required to keep the liberty to which they are entitled. They could give up part of it, or all of it, or risk losing it on the chance of gaining a greater share of liberties or other social goods.[14] Consequently, the case for restricting the liberty of the rich for the benefit of the poor is neither unconditional nor inalienable.

Even so, libertarians would have to be disconcerted about what turns out to be the practical upshot of taking a right to liberty to be the ultimate political ideal. For libertarians contend that their political ideal would support welfare rights only when constraints are "illegitimately" interpreted to induce both positive and negative acts by others that prevent people from doing what they are otherwise able to do. By contrast, when constraints are interpreted to include only positive acts, libertarians contend, no such welfare rights can be justified.

Nevertheless, what the foregoing argument demonstrates is that this view is mistaken. For even when the interpretation of constraints favored by libertarians is employed, a moral assessment of the competing liberties still requires an allocation of liberties to the poor that will be generally sufficient to provide them with the goods and resources necessary for satisfying their basic nutritional needs.

One might think that once the rich realize that the poor should have the liberty not to be interfered with when taking from the surplus possessions of the rich what they require to satisfy their basic needs, it would be in the interest of the rich to stop producing any surplus whatsoever. Yet that would only be the case if first, the recognition of the rightful claims of the poor would exhaust the surplus of the rich and second, the poor would

never be in a position to be obligated to repay what they appropriated from the rich. Fortunately for the poor both of these conditions are unlikely to obtain.

Of course, there will be cases where the poor fail to satisfy their basic nutritional needs, not because of any direct restriction of liberty on the part of the rich, but because the poor are in such dire need that they are unable even to attempt to take from the rich what they require to meet their basic nutritional needs. Accordingly, in such cases, the rich would not be performing any act of commission that prevents the poor from taking what they require. Yet, even in such cases, the rich would normally be performing acts of commission that prevent other persons from aiding the poor by taking from the surplus possessions of the rich. And when assessed from a moral point of view, restricting the liberty of these other persons would not be morally justified for the very same reason that restricting the liberty of the poor to meet their own basic nutritional needs would not be morally justified: it would not be reasonable to ask all of those affected to accept such a restriction of liberty. . . .

In brief, what this shows is that if a right to liberty is taken to be the ultimate political ideal, then, contrary to what libertarians claim, not only would a system of welfare rights be morally required, but also such a system would clearly benefit the poor.

Lockean Libertarianism

Yet suppose we were to adopt the view of those libertarians who do not take a right to liberty to be the ultimate political ideal. According to this view, liberty is defined as follows:

> *The Rights Conception of Liberty.* Liberty is being unconstrained by other persons from doing what one has a right to do.

The most important ultimate rights in terms of which liberty is specified are, according to this view, a right to life understood as a right not to be killed unjustly and a right to property understood as a right to acquire goods and resources either by initial acquisition or voluntary agreement. In order to evaluate this view, we must determine what are the practical implications of these rights.

Presumably, a right to life understood as a right not to be killed unjustly would not be violated by defensive measures designed to protect one's person from life-threatening attacks. Yet would this right be violated when the rich prevent the poor from taking what they require to satisfy their basic nutritional needs? Obviously, as a consequence of such preventive actions poor people sometimes do starve to death. Have the rich, then, in contributing to this result, killed the poor, or simply let them die; and, if they have killed the poor, have they done so unjustly?

Sometimes the rich, in preventing the poor from taking what they require to meet their basic nutritional needs, would not in fact be killing the poor, but only causing them to be physically or mentally debilitated. Yet since such preventive acts involve resisting the life-preserving activities of the poor, when the poor do die as a consequence of such acts, it seems clear that the rich would be killing the poor, whether intentionally or unintentionally.

Of course, libertarians would want to argue that such killing is simply a consequence of the legitimate exercise of property rights, and hence, not unjust. But to understand why libertarians are mistaken in this regard, let us appeal again to that fundamental principle of morality, the "ought" implies "can" principle. In this context, the principle can be used to assess two opposing accounts of property rights. According to the first account, a right to property is not conditional upon whether other persons have sufficient opportunities and resources to satisfy their basic needs. This view holds that the initial acquisition and voluntary agreement of some can leave others, through no fault of their own, dependent upon charity for the satisfaction of their most basic needs. By contrast, according to the second account, initial acquisition and voluntary agreement can confer title of property on all goods and resources except those surplus goods and resources of the rich that are required to satisfy the basic needs of those poor who through no fault of their own lack opportunities and resources to satisfy their own basic needs.

Clearly, only the first of these two accounts of property rights would generally justify the killing of the poor as a legitimate exercise of the property rights of the rich. Yet it would be unreasonable to require the poor to accept anything other than some version of the second account of property rights. Moreover, according to the second account, it does not matter whether the poor would actually die or are only physically or mentally debilitated as a result of such acts of prevention. Either result would preclude property rights from arising. Of course, the poor may have no real alternative to acquiescing to a political system modeled after the first account of property rights, even though such a system imposes an unreasonable sacrifice upon them—a sacrifice that we could not blame them for trying to evade. At the same time, although the rich would be disinclined to do so, it would not be unreasonable to require them to accept a political system modeled after the second account of property rights—the account favored by the poor.

Consequently, if we assume that however else we specify the requirements of morality, they cannot violate the "ought" implies "can" principle, it follows that, despite what libertarians claim, the right to life and the right to property endorsed by libertarians actually support a system of welfare rights. . . .

Nevertheless, it might be objected that the welfare rights that have been established against the libertarian are not the same as the welfare rights endorsed by . . . liberal [democrats]. We could mark this difference by referring to the welfare rights that have been established against the libertarian as "action welfare rights" and referring to the welfare rights endorsed by liberal [democrats] as both "action and recipient welfare rights." The significance of this difference is that a person's action welfare right can be violated only when other people through acts of commission interfere with a person's exercise of that right, whereas a person's action and recipient welfare right can be violated by such acts of commission and by acts of omission as well. However, this difference will have little practical import. For once libertarians come to recognize the legitimacy of action welfare rights, then in order not to be subject to the poor person's discretion in choosing when and how to exercise her action welfare right, libertarians will tend to favor two morally legitimate ways of preventing the exercise of such rights. First, libertarians can provide the poor with mutually beneficial job opportunities. Second, libertarians can institute adequate recipient welfare rights that would take precedence over the poor's action welfare rights. Accordingly, if libertarians adopt either or both of these ways of legitimately preventing the poor from exercising their action welfare rights, libertarians will end up endorsing the same sort of welfare institutions favored by . . . liberal [democrats].

Finally, once a system of welfare rights is seen to follow irrespective of whether one takes a right to liberty or rights to life and property as the ultimate political ideal, the justification for a welfare state becomes straightforward and compelling. For while it is at least conceivable that rights other than welfare rights could be adequately secured in a society without the enforcement agencies of a state, it is inconceivable that welfare rights themselves could be adequately secured without such enforcement agencies. Only a welfare state would be able to effectively solve the large-scale coordination problem necessitated by the provision of welfare. Consequently, once a system of welfare rights can be seen to have a libertarian justification, the argument for a welfare state hardly seems to need stating.[15]

Libertarian Objections

In his book, *Individuals and their Rights,* Tibor Machan criticizes the preceding argument that a libertarian ideal of liberty leads to a right to welfare, accepting its theoretical thrust but denying its practical significance.[16] He appreciates the force of the argument enough to grant that if the

type of conflict cases that we have described between the rich and the poor actually obtained, the poor would have a right to welfare. But he denies that such cases—in which the poor have done all that they legitimately can to satisfy their basic needs in a libertarian society—actually obtain. "Normally," he writes, "persons do not lack the opportunities and resources to satisfy their basic needs."[17]

But this response virtually concedes everything that the preceding argument intended to establish, for the poor's right to welfare is not claimed to be unconditional. Rather, it is said to be conditional principally upon the poor doing all that they legitimately can to meet their own basic needs. So it follows that only when the poor lack sufficient opportunity to satisfy their own basic needs would their right to welfare have any practical moral force. Accordingly, on libertarian grounds, Machan has conceded the legitimacy of just the kind of right to welfare that the preceding argument hoped to establish.

The only difference that remains is a practical one. Machan thinks that virtually all of the poor have sufficient opportunities and resources to satisfy their basic needs and that, therefore, a right to welfare has no practical moral force. In contrast, I think that many of the poor do not have sufficient opportunities and resources to satisfy their basic needs and that, therefore, a right to welfare has considerable practical moral force.

But isn't this practical disagreement resolvable? Who could deny that most of the 1.2 billion people who are currently living in conditions of absolute poverty "lack the opportunities and resources to satisfy their basic needs?"[18] And even within our own country, it is estimated that some 32 million Americans live below the official poverty index, and that one-fifth of American children are growing up in poverty.[19] Surely, it is impossible to deny that many of these Americans also "lack the opportunities and resources to satisfy their basic needs." Given the impossibility of reasonably denying these factual claims, Machan would have to concede that the right to welfare, which he grants can be theoretically established on libertarian premises, also has practical moral force.[20]

Douglas Rasmussen has developed another libertarian challenge to the previous argument that begins by conceding what Machan denied—that the poor lack the opportunity to satisfy their basic needs.[21] Rasmussen distinguishes two ways that this can occur. In one case, only a few of the poor lack the opportunity to satisfy their basic needs. Here, Rasmussen contends that libertarian property rights still apply even though the poor who are in need morally ought to take from the surplus property of the rich what they need for survival. Because libertarian property rights still apply, Rasmussen contends that the poor who do take from the legal property of the rich can be arrested and tried for their actions, but what their punishment should be, Rasmussen contends, should simply be left up to judges to decide.[22] Rasmussen also rejects the suggestion that the law should make an exception for the poor in such cases on the grounds that one can never have perfect symmetry between what is moral and what the law requires.[23]

But why should the question of punishment be simply left up to judges to decide? If the judicial proceedings determine what is assumed in this case—that the poor morally ought to take from the legal property of the rich what they need for survival—then it is difficult to see on what grounds a judge could inflict punishment. Surely, if it would be unreasonable to require the poor to do anything contrary to meeting their basic needs at minimal cost to the rich, it would be equally unreasonable to punish the poor for actually doing just that—meeting their basic needs at minimal cost to the rich.

Nor will it do to claim that we cannot expect symmetry between what morality requires and what the law requires in this case. Of course, there is no denying that sometimes the law can justifiably require us to do what is morally wrong. In such cases opposing the law, even when what it requires is immoral, would do more harm than good. This can occur when there is a bona fide disagreement over whether what the law requires is

morally wrong (for example, the *Roe* v. *Wade* decision), with those in favor of the law justifiably thinking that it is morally right and those against the law justifiably thinking that it is morally wrong. When this occurs, failing to obey the law, even when what it requires is immoral, could, by undermining the legal system, do more harm than good. However, in our case of severe conflict of interest between the rich and the poor, nothing of the sort obtains. In our case, it is judged that the poor morally ought to take from the legal property of the rich and that no other moral imperative favoring the rich overrides this moral imperative favoring the poor. So it is clear in this case that there are no grounds for upholding any asymmetry between what morality and the law require. Accordingly, the law in this case should be changed to favor the poor.

However, Rasmussen distinguishes another case in which many of the poor lack the opportunity to satisfy their basic needs.[24] In this case, so many of the poor lack the opportunity to satisfy their basic needs that Rasmussen claims that libertarian property rights no longer apply. Here Rasmussen contends that morality requires that the poor should take what they need for survival from the legal property of the rich and that the rich should not refuse assistance. Still Rasmussen contends that the poor have no right to assistance in this case, nor the rich presumably any corresponding obligation to help the poor because "the situation cannot be judged in social and political terms."[25]

But why cannot the situation be judged in social and political terms? If we know what the moral directives of the rich and the poor are in the case, as Rasmussen admits that we do, why would we not be justified in setting up a legal system or altering an existing legal system so that the poor would have a guaranteed right to welfare? Now it may be that Rasmussen is imagining a situation where it is not possible for the basic needs of everyone to be met. Such situations are truly lifeboat cases. But while such cases are difficult to resolve (maybe only a chance mechanism would offer a reasonable resolution) they surely do not represent the typical conflict situation between the rich and the poor. For in such situations, it is recognized that it is possible to meet everyone's basic needs, and what is at issue is whether (some of) the nonbasic or luxury needs of the rich should be sacrificed so that everyone's basic needs can be met. So when dealing with typical conflict situations between the rich and the poor, there is no justification for not securing a legal system that reflects the moral directives in these cases.

In sum, both Machan's and Rasmussen's objections to grounding a right to welfare on libertarian premises have been answered. Machan's attempt to grant the theoretical validity of a libertarian right to welfare, but then deny its practical validity, fails once we recognize that there are many poor who lack the opportunity to satisfy their basic needs. Rasmussen's attempt to grant that there are poor who lack the opportunity to meet their basic needs, but then deny that the poor have any right to welfare, fails once we recognize that the moral directives that Rasmussen grants apply to the rich and the poor in severe conflict of interest cases provide ample justification for a right to welfare.

NOTES

1. Robert Nozick, *Anarchy, State and Utopia* (New York: Basic Books, 1974), Part I.
2. Murray Rothbard, *The Ethics of Liberty* (Atlantic Highlands: Humanities Press, 1982), p. 230.
3. Nozick, *Anarchy, State and Utopia*, p. ix.
4. Murray Rothbard, *For a New Liberty* (New York: Collier Books, 1978), p. 148.
5. See, for example, James P. Sterba, "Neo-Libertarianism," *American Philosophical Quarterly* 15 (1978): 17–19; Ernest Loevinsohn, "Liberty and the Redistribution of Property," *Philosophy and Public Affairs* 6 (1977): 226–39; David Zimmerman, "Coercive Wage Offers," *Philosophy and Public Affairs* 10 (1981): 121–45. To limit what is to count as coercive, Zimmerman claims that in order for P's offer to be coercive (I)t must be the case that P does more than merely prevent Q *from taking from* P resources necessary for securing Q's strongly preferred preproposal situation; P must prevent Q *from acting on his own* (or with the help of others) *to produce or procure* the strongly preferred proposal situation.

But this restriction seems arbitrary, and Zimmerman provides little justification for it. See David Zimmerman, "More on Coercive Wage Offers," *Philosophy and Public Affairs* 12 (1983): 67–68.
6. It might seem that this second approach could avoid this difficulty if a restriction of liberty is understood as the curtailment of one's prima facie rights. But in order to avoid the problem of a multitude of conflicting liberties, which plagues the first approach, the specification of prima facie rights must be such that they only can be overridden when one or more of them is violated. And this may involve too much precision for our notion of prima facie rights.
7. Isaiah Berlin, *Four Essays on Liberty* (New York: Oxford University Press, 1969), pp. XXXVIII–XL.
8. On this point, see Maurice Cranston, *Freedom* (New York: Basic Books, 1953), pp. 52–53; C. B. Macpherson, *Democratic Theory* (Oxford: Oxford University Press, 1973), p. 95; Joel Feinberg, *Rights, Justice and the Bounds of Liberty* (Princeton, N.J.: Princeton University Press, 1980). Chapter 1.
9. See John Hospers, *Libertarianism* (Los Angeles: Nash Publishing Co., 1971), Chapter 7.
10. Alvin Goldman, *A Theory of Human Action* (Englewood Cliffs, N.J.: Prentice-Hall, 1970), pp. 208–15; William Frankena, "Obligation and Ability," in *Philosophical Analysis,* edited by Max Black (Ithaca, N.Y.: Cornell University Press, 1950), pp. 157–75.

Judging from some recent discussions of moral dilemmas by Bernard Williams and Ruth Marcus, one might think that the "ought" implies "can" principle would only be useful for illustrating moral conflicts rather than resolving them. (See Bernard Williams, *Problems of the Self* (Cambridge: Cambridge University Press, 1977), Chapters 11 and 12; Ruth Marcus, "Moral Dilemmas and Consistency," *The Journal of Philosophy* 80 (1980): 121–36. See also Terrance C. McConnell, "Moral Dilemmas and Consistency in Ethics," *Canadian Journal of Philosophy* 18 (1978): 269–87. But this is only true if one interprets that "can" in the principle to exclude only "what a person lacks the power to do." If one interprets the "can" to exclude in addition "what would involve so great a sacrifice that it would be unreasonable to ask the person to do it" then the principle can be used to resolve moral conflicts as well as state them. Nor would libertarians object to this broader interpretation of the "ought" implies "can" principle since they do not ground their claim to liberty on the existence of irresolvable moral conflicts.
11. See James P. Sterba, "Is there a Rationale for Punishment?", *The American Journal of Jurisprudence* 29 (1984): 29–44.
12. As further evidence, notice that those libertarians who justify a minimal state do so on the grounds that such a state would arise from reasonable disagreements

concerning the application of libertarian rights. They do not justify the minimal state on the grounds that it would be needed to keep in submission large numbers of people who could not come to see the reasonableness of libertarian rights.

13. Obviously, the employment opportunities offered to the poor must be honorable and supportive of self-respect. To do otherwise would be to offer the poor the opportunity to meet some of their basic needs at the cost of denying some of their other basic needs.

14. The poor cannot, however, give up the liberty to which their children are entitled.

15. Of course, someone might still want to object to welfare states on the grounds that they "force workers to sell their labor" (see G. A. Cohen, "The Structure of Proletarian Unfreedom," *Philosophy and Public Affairs* 12 (1982): 3–33) and subject workers to "coercive wage offers." (See Zimmerman, "Coercive Wage Offers.") But for a defense of at least one form of welfare state against such an objection, see James P. Sterba, "A Marxist Dilemma for Social Contract Theory," *American Philosophical Quarterly* 21 (1981): 51–59.

16. Tibor Machan, *Individuals and their Rights* (La Salle: Open Court, 1989), pp. 100–111.

17. *Ibid.*, p. 107.

18. Alan Durning, "Life on the Brink," *World Watch,* Vol. 3 (1990), p. 24.

19. *Ibid.*, p. 29.

20. Machan also sketches another line of argument which unfortunately proceeds from premises that contradict his line of argument that I have discussed here. The line of argument that I have discussed here turns on Machan's claim that "normally, persons do not lack the opportunities and resources to satisfy their basic needs." Machan's second line of argument, by contrast, concedes that many of the poor lack the opportunities and resources to satisfy their basic needs but then contends that this lack is the result of political oppression in the absence of libertarian institutions. See Machan, *Individuals and their Rights,* p. 109. See also Machan's contribution to James P. Sterba, Tibor Machan, et. al., *Morality and Social Justice: Point and Counterpoint* (Lanham: Rowman and Littlefield, 1994), pp. 59–106, where Machan develops this second line of argument in more detail. For my response to this line of argument, see "Comments by James P. Sterba," in *Morality and Social Justice: Point and Counterpoint,* pp. 110–113.

21. Douglas Rasmussen, "Individual Rights and Human Flourishing," *Public Affairs Quarterly,* Vol. 3 (1989), pp. 89–103. See also Douglas Rasmussen and Douglas Den Uyl, *Liberty and Nature* (La Salle: Open Court, 1991), Chapters 2–4.

22. Rasmussen, "Individual Rights and Human Flourishing," p. 98.

23. *Ibid.*, p. 99.

24. *Ibid.*, p. 100.

25. *Ibid.*, p. 101.

3   The Nonexistence of Basic Welfare Rights

TIBOR R. MACHAN

JAMES STERBA AND OTHERS maintain that we all have the right to "receive the goods and resources necessary for preserving" ourselves. This is not what I have argued human beings have a right to. They have the right, rather, not to be killed, attacked, and deprived of their property—by persons in or outside of government. As Abraham Lincoln put it, "no man is good enough to govern another man, without that other's consent."[1]

Sterba claims that various political outlooks would have to endorse these "rights." He sets out to show, in particular, that welfare rights follow from libertarian theory itself.[2] Sterba wishes to show that *if* Lockean libertarianism is correct, then we all have rights to welfare and equal (economic) opportunity. What I wish to show is that since Lockean libertarianism—as developed in this work—is true, and since the rights to welfare and equal opportunity require their violation, no one has these latter rights. The reason some people, including Sterba, believe otherwise is that they have found some very rare instances in which some citizens could find themselves in circumstances that would require disregarding rights altogether. This would be in situations that cannot be characterized to be "where peace is possible."[3] And every major libertarian thinker from Locke to the present has treated these kinds of cases.[4]

Let us be clear about what Sterba sets out to show. It is that libertarians are philosophically unable to escape the welfare-statist implications of their commitment to negative liberty. This means that despite their belief that they are only sup-

porting the enforceable right of every person not to be coerced by other persons, libertarians must accept, by the logic of their own position, that individuals also possess basic enforceable rights to being provided with various services from others. He holds, then, that basic negative rights imply basic positive rights.

To Lockean libertarians the ideal of liberty means that we all, individually, have the right not to be constrained against our consent within our realm of authority—ourselves and our belongings. Sterba states that for such libertarians "Liberty is being unconstrained by persons from doing what one has a right to do."[5] Sterba adds, somewhat misleadingly, that for Lockean libertarians "a right to life [is] a right not to be killed unjustly and a right to property [is] a right to acquire goods and resources either by initial acquisition or voluntary agreement."[6] Sterba does realize that these rights do not entitle one to receive from others the goods and resources necessary for preserving one's life.

A problem with this foundation of the Lockean libertarian view is that political justice—not the justice of Plato, which is best designated in our time as "perfect virtue"—for natural-rights theorists presupposes individual rights. One cannot then explain rights in terms of justice but must explain justice in terms of rights.

For a Lockean libertarian, to possess any basic right to receive the goods and resources necessary for preserving one's life conflicts with possessing the right not to be killed, assaulted, or stolen

Reprinted from Individuals and Their Rights *by Tibor Machan by permission of The Open Court Publishing Company, a division of Carus Publishing Company, Peru, IL.*

from. The latter are rights Lockean libertarians consider to be held by all individual human beings. Regularly to protect and maintain—that is, enforce—the former right would often require the violation of the latter. A's right to the food she has is incompatible with B's right to take this same food. Both the rights could not be fundamental in an integrated legal system. The situation of one's having rights to welfare, and so forth, and another's having rights to life, liberty, and property is thus theoretically intolerable and practically unfeasible. The point of a system of rights is the securing of mutually peaceful and consistent moral conduct on the part of human beings. As Rand observes,

> "Rights" are . . . the link between the moral code of a man and the legal code of a society, between ethics and politics. *Individual rights are the means of subordinating society to moral law.*[7]

Sterba asks us—in another discussion of his views—to consider what he calls "a *typical* conflict situation between the rich and the poor." He says that in his situation "the rich, of course, have more than enough resources to satisfy their basic needs. By contrast, the poor lack the resources to meet their most basic needs even though *they have tried all the means available to them that libertarians regard as legitimate for acquiring such resources*"[8] (my emphasis).

The goal of a theory of rights would be defeated if rights were typically in conflict. Some bureaucratic group would have to keep applying its moral intuitions on numerous occasions when rights claims would *typically* conflict. A constitution is workable if it helps remove at least the largest proportion of such decisions from the realm of arbitrary (intuitive) choice and avail a society of men and women of objective guidelines that are reasonably integrated, not in relentless discord.

Most critics of libertarianism assume some doctrine of basic needs that they invoke to show that whatever basic needs are not satisfied for some people, while others have "resources" that are not basic needs for them, the former have just claims against the latter. (The language of resources of course loads the argument in the critic's favor since it suggests that these goods simply come into being and happen to be in the possession of some people, quite without rhyme or reason, arbitrarily [as John Rawls claims].)[9]

This doctrine is full of difficulties. It lacks any foundation for why the needs of some persons must be claims upon the lives of others. And why are there such needs anyway—to what end are they needs, and whose ends are these and why are not the persons whose needs they are held responsible for supplying the needs? (Needs, as I have already observed, lack any force in moral argument without the prior justification of the purposes they serve, or the goals they help to fulfill. A thief has a basic need of skills and powers that are clearly not justified if theft is morally unjustified. If, however, the justification of basic needs, such as food and other resources, presupposes the value of human life, and if the value of human life justifies, as I have argued earlier, the principle of the natural rights to life, liberty and property, then the attainment or fulfillment of the basic need for food may not involve the violation of these rights.)

Sterba claims that without guaranteeing welfare and equal-opportunity rights, Lockean libertarianism violates the most basic tenets of any morality, namely, that "ought" implies "can." The thrust of " 'ought' implies 'can' " is that one ought to do that which one is free to do, that one is morally responsible only for those acts that one had the power either to choose to engage in or not to engage in. (There is debate on just how this point must be phrased—in terms of the will being free or the person being free to will something. For our purposes, however, all that counts is that the person must have [had] a genuine option to do X or not to do X before it can be true that he or she ought to do X or ought to have done X.) If an innocent person is forced by the actions of another to forgo significant moral choices, then that innocent person is not free to act morally and thus his or her human dignity is violated.

This is not so different from the common-sense legal precept that if one is not sound of mind one cannot be criminally culpable. Only free agents, capable of choosing between right and wrong, are open to moral evaluation. This indeed is the reason that many so-called moral theories fail to be anything more than value theories. They omit from consideration the issue of self-determination. If either hard or soft determinism is true, morality is impossible, although values need not disappear.[10]

If Sterba were correct about Lockean libertarianism typically contradicting "'ought' implies 'can,'" his argument would be decisive. (There are few arguments against this principle that I know of and they have not convinced me. They trade on rare circumstances when persons feel guilt for taking actions that had bad consequences even though they could not have avoided them.)[11] It is because Karl Marx's and Herbert Spencer's systems typically, normally, indeed in every case, violate this principle that they are not bona fide moral systems. And quite a few others may be open to a similar charge.[12]

Sterba offers his strongest argument when he observes that "'ought' implies 'can'" is violated "when the rich prevent the poor from taking what they require to satisfy their basic needs even though they have tried all the means available to them that libertarians regard as legitimate for acquiring such resources."[13]

Is Sterba right that such are—indeed, must be—typical conflict cases in a libertarian society? Are the rich and poor, even admitting that there is some simple division of people into such economic groups, in such hopeless conflict all the time? Even in the case of homeless people, many find help without having to resort to theft. The political factors contributing to the presence of helpless people in the United States and other Western liberal democracies are a hotly debated issue, even among utilitarians and welfare-state supporters. Sterba cannot make his argument for the typicality of such cases by reference to history alone. (Arguably, there are fewer helpless poor in near-libertarian, capitalist systems than anywhere else—why else would virtually everyone wish to live in these societies rather than those where welfare is guaranteed, indeed enforced? Not, at least originally, for their welfare-statist features. Arguably, too, the disturbing numbers of such people in these societies could be due, in part, to the lack of consistent protection of all the libertarian natural rights.)

Nonetheless, in a system that legally protects and preserves property rights there will be cases where a rich person prevents a poor person from taking what belongs to her (the rich person)—for example, a chicken that the poor person might use to feed herself. Since after such prevention the poor person might starve, Sterba asks the rhetorical question, "Have the rich, then, in contributing to this result, killed the poor, or simply let them die; and if they have killed the poor, have they done so unjustly?"[14] His answer is that they have. Sterba holds that a system that accords with the Lockean libertarian's idea that the rich person's preventive action is just "imposes an unreasonable sacrifice upon" the poor, one "that we could not blame them for trying to evade." Not permitting the poor to act to satisfy their basic needs is to undermine the precept that "'ought' implies 'can,'" since, as Sterba claims, that precept means, for the poor, that they ought to satisfy their basic needs. This they must have the option to do if they ought to do it.

When people defend their property, what are they doing? They are protecting themselves against the intrusive acts of some other person, acts that would normally deprive them of something to which they have a right, and the other has no right. As such, these acts of protectiveness make it possible for men and women in society to retain their own sphere of jurisdiction intact, protect their own "moral space."[15] They refuse to have their human dignity violated. They want to be sovereigns and govern their own lives, including their own productive decisions and actions. Those who mount the attack, in turn, fail or refuse to refrain from encroaching upon the moral space of their victims. They are treating the victim's life and its productive results as though these were unowned resources for them to do with as they choose.

Now the argument that cuts against the above account is that on some occasions there can be people who, with no responsibility for their situation, are highly unlikely to survive without disregarding the rights of others and taking from them what they need. This is indeed possible. It is no less possible that there be cases in which someone is highly unlikely to survive without obtaining the services of a doctor who is at that moment spending time healing someone else, or in which there is a person who is highly unlikely to survive without obtaining one of the lungs of another person, who wants to keep both lungs so as to be able to run the New York City marathon effectively. And such cases could be multiplied indefinitely.

But are such cases typical? The argument that starts with this assumption about a society is already not comparable to the libertarianism that has emerged in the footsteps of Lockean natural-rights doctrine, including the version advanced in this book. That system is developed for a human community in which "peace is possible." Libertarian individual rights, which guide men and women in such an adequately hospitable environment to act without thwarting the flourishing of others, are thus suitable bases for the legal foundations of a human society. It is possible for people in the world to pursue their proper goals without thwarting a similar pursuit by others.

The underlying notion of society in such a theory rejects the description of human communities implicit in Sterba's picture. Sterba sees conflict as typically arising from some people producing and owning goods, while others having no alternative but to take these goods from the former in order to survive. But these are not the typical conflict situations even in what we today consider reasonably free human communities—most thieves and robbers are not destitute, nor are they incapable of doing something aside from taking other people's property in order to obtain their livelihood.

The typical conflict situation in society involves people who wish to take shortcuts to earning their living (and a lot more) by attacking others, not those who lack any other alternative to attacking others so as to reach that same goal. This may not

be evident from all societies that teem with human conflict—in the Middle East, or Central and South America, for example. But it must be remembered that these societies are far from being even near-libertarian. Even if the typical conflicts there involved the kind Sterba describes, that would not suffice to make his point. Only if it were true that in comparatively free countries the typical conflict involved the utterly destitute and helpless arrayed against the well-to-do, could his argument carry any conviction.

The Lockean libertarian has confidence in the willingness and capacity of *virtually all persons* to make headway in life in a free society. The very small minority of exceptional cases must be taken care of by voluntary social institutions, not by the government, which guards self-consistent individual rights.

The integrity of law would be seriously endangered if the government entered areas that required it to make very particular judgments and depart from serving the interest of the public as such. We have already noted that the idea of "satisfying basic needs" can involve the difficulty of distinguishing those whose actions are properly to be so characterized. Rich persons are indeed satisfying their basic needs as they protect and preserve their property rights. . . . Private property rights are necessary for a morally decent society.

The Lockean libertarian argues that private property rights are morally justified in part because they are concrete requirements for delineating the sphere of jurisdiction of each person's moral authority, where her own judgment is decisive.[16] This is a crucial basis for the right to property. And so is the contention that we live in a metaphysically hospitable universe wherein people normally need not suffer innocent misery and deprivation—so that such a condition is usually the result of negligence or the violation of Lockean rights, a violation that has made self-development and commerce impossible. If exceptional emergencies set the agenda for the law, the law itself will disintegrate. (A just legal system makes provision for coping with emergencies that are brought to the attention of the authorities, for example, by way of judicial discretion, without allowing such cases to determine the direction of the system. If legislators and judges don't uphold the integrity of the system, disintegration ensues. This can itself encourage the emergence of strong leaders, demagogues, who promise to do what the law has not been permitted to do, namely, satisfy people's sense of justice. Experience with them bodes ill for such a prospect.)

Normally persons do not "lack the opportunities and resources to satisfy their own basic needs." Even if we grant that some helpless, crippled, retarded, or destitute persons could offer nothing to anyone that would merit wages enabling them to carry on their lives and perhaps even flourish, there is still the other possibility for most actual, known hard cases, namely seeking help. I am not speaking here of the cases we know: people who drop out of school, get an unskilled job, marry and have kids, only to find that their personal choice of inadequate preparation for life leaves them relatively poorly off. "'Ought' implies 'can'" must not be treated ahistorically—some people's lack of current options results from their failure to exercise previous options prudently. I refer here to the "truly needy," to use a shop-worn but still useful phrase—those who have never been able to help themselves and are not now helpless from their own neglect. Are such people being treated *unjustly,* rather than at most uncharitably, ungenerously, indecently, pitilessly, or in some other respect immorally—by those who, knowing of the plight of such persons, resist forcibly efforts to take from them enough to provide the ill-fated with what they truly need? Actually, if we tried to pry the needed goods or money from the well-to-do, we would not even learn if they would act generously. Charity, generosity, kindness, and acts of compassion presuppose that those well enough off are not coerced to provide help. These virtues cannot flourish, nor can the corresponding vices, of course, without a clearly identified and well-protected right to private property for all.

If we consider the situation as we are more likely to find it, namely, that desperate cases not caused by previous injustices (in the libertarian sense) are rare, then, contrary to what Sterba suggests, there is much that unfortunate persons can and should do in those plausible, non-emergency situations that can be considered typical. They need not resort to violating the private-property rights of those who are better off. The destitute can appeal for assistance both from the rich and from the many voluntary social service agencies that emerge from the widespread compassion of people who know about the mishaps that can at times strike perfectly decent people.

Consider, as a prototype of this situation on which we might model what concerns Sterba, that if one's car breaks down on a remote road, it would be unreasonable to expect one not to seek a phone or some other way of escaping one's unfortunate situation. So one ought to at least try to obtain the use of a phone.

But should one break into the home of a perfect stranger living nearby? Or ought one instead to request the use of the phone as a favor? "'Ought' implies 'can'" is surely fully satisfied here. Actual practice makes this quite evident. When someone is suffering from misfortune and there are plenty of others who are not, and the unfortunate person has no other avenue for obtaining help than to obtain it from others, it would not be unreasonable to expect, morally, that the poor seek such help as surely might be forthcoming. We have no justification for assuming that the rich are all callous, though this caricature is regularly painted by communists and in folklore. Supporting and gaining advantage from the institution of private property by no means implies that one lacks the virtue of generosity. The rich are no more immune to virtue than the poor are to vice. The contrary view is probably a legacy of the idea that only those concerned with spiritual or intellectual matters can be trusted to know virtue—those concerned with seeking material prosperity are too base.

The destitute typically have options other than to violate the rights of the well-off. "'Ought' implies 'can'" is satisfiable by the moral imperative that the poor ought to seek help, not loot. There is then no injustice in the rich preventing the poor from seeking such loot by violating the right to private property. "'Ought' implies 'can'" is fully satisfied if the poor can take the kind of action that could gain them the satisfaction of their basic needs, and this action could well be asking for help.

All along here I have been considering only the helplessly poor, who through no fault of their own, nor again through any rights violation by others, are destitute. I am taking the hard cases seriously, where violation of "'ought' implies 'can'" would appear to be most probable. But such cases are by no means typical. They are extremely rare. And even rarer are those cases in which all avenues regarded as legitimate from the libertarian point of view have been exhausted, including appealing for help.

The bulk of poverty in the world is not the result of natural disaster or disease. Rather it is political oppression, whereby people throughout many of the world's countries are not legally permitted to look out for themselves in production and trade. The famines in Africa and India, the poverty in the same countries and in Central and Latin America, as well as in China, the Soviet Union, Poland, Rumania, and so forth, are not the result of lack of charity but of oppression. It is the kind that those who have the protection of even a seriously compromised document and system protecting individual negative human rights, such as the U.S. Constitution, do not experience. The first requirement for men and women to ameliorate their hardship is to be free of other people's oppression, not to be free to take others people's belongings.

Of course, it would be immoral if people failed to help out when this was clearly no sacrifice for them. But charity or generosity is not a categorical imperative, even for the rich. There are more basic moral principles that might require the rich to refuse to be charitable—for example, if they are using most of their wealth for the protection of freedom or a just society. Courage can be more important than charity or benevolence or compassion. But a discussion of the ranking of moral virtues would take us far afield. One reason that many critics of libertarians find their own cases persuasive is that they think the libertarian can only subscribe to *political* principles or values. But this is mistaken.[17]

There can be emergency cases in which there is no alternative available to disregarding the rights of others. But these are extremely rare, and not at all the sort invoked by critics such as Sterba. I have in mind the desert-island case found in ethics books where instantaneous action, with only one violent alternative, faces persons—the sort we know from the law books in which the issue is one of immediate life and death. These are not cases, to repeat the phrase quoted from Locke by H. L. A. Hart, "where peace is possible." They are discussed in the libertarian literature and considerable progress has been made in integrating them with the concerns of law and politics. Since we are here discussing law and politics, which are general systematic approaches to how we normally ought to live with one another in human communities, these emergency situations do not help us except as limiting cases. And not surprisingly many famous court cases illustrate just this point as they now and then confront these kinds of instances after they have come to light within the framework of civilized society.

Since the time of the original publication of the above discussion—as part of my book *Individuals and Their Rights*—James Sterba has made several attempts to counter the arguments advanced here. The central claim on which he attempts to rest the argument that within a libertarian system many people would have no chance for self-directed flourishing goes as follows:

> [W]ho could deny that most of 1.2 billion people who are currently living in conditions of absolute poverty "lack the opportunities and necessities to satisfy their basic needs"? And even within our country [USA], it is estimated that some 32 million Americans live below the official poverty index [$14,000 per annum for a family, $7,000 per annum for an individual], and that one fifth of American children are growing up in poverty. Surely, it is impossible to deny that many of these

Americans also "lack the opportunities and resources to satisfy their basic needs."[18]

There is little discussion in Sterba's work of why people are poor or otherwise experience circumstances that afford them little or no opportunity for flourishing. Among libertarians, however, there is considerable agreement on the position that many who face such circumstances make significant contribution to their own plight. Many others suffer such circumstances because their negative rights to liberty (to produce and to keep what they produce) are violated.

Certainly, libertarians draw a sharp distinction between those who are in dire straits because they are unfortunate, through no fault of their own, and those who fail to act in ways that would probably extricate them from their adverse living conditions. In the philosophical literature that draws on the legacy of Marx, Engels, and their followers, this distinction is not easy to make, since in this tradition human behavior is taken to be determined by a person's economic circumstances, so one is bound by one's situation and cannot make choices that would overcome them. More generally, in modern political philosophy there has been a strong tendency to view human beings as passive, unable to initiate their own conduct and moved by innate drives or environmental stimuli. Thus, those who are well-off could not have achieved this through their own initiative, nor could those who are badly off have failed in significant ways. Accordingly, all the poor or badly off, be they victims of others' oppression, casualties of misfortune, or products of their own misconduct are regarded alike. It is not clear how much Sterba's reasoning may be influenced by these considerations. In the absence of significant discussion of the matter, it is understandable why Sterba appears to view life as largely a zero sum game.[19]

Sterba claims, then, that poverty is typical, including, we must assume, of libertarian societies. Without that assumption, the story about poverty would have no bearing on libertarian politics. Sterba, therefore, needs to argue, as he does, that in a fully libertarian system, which respects and protects only negative individual rights (to life, liberty, and property), massive poverty would ensue—it would be the typical situation for there to be great masses of poor people.

Libertarians, as suggested above, seriously dispute this point. Indeed, they are not pure deontologists regarding negative individual liberty or the right to it, for they believe that respect for and protection of it would produce a better life for most people, in all relevant respects (moral, economic, intellectual, psychological, and cultural), provided they make an effort to improve themselves. They argue, in the main, that the most prosperous and otherwise beneficial societies are also those that give greatest respect and protection to negative individual rights. In turn, they hold, that where poverty is widespread, negative individual liberty is, in the main, left unrespected and unprotected.

This part of their argument is, for most libertarians, a fairly reasonable analytical and historical stance. They would argue, analytically, that it is the protection of negative individual liberty—the right to free association, freedom of trade, freedom of wealth accumulation, freedom of contract, freedom of entrepreneurship, freedom of speech, freedom of thought—that provides the most hospitable social climate for the creation of wealth. While no libertarian claims that this guarantees that no one will be destitute, those who are poor would either have failed of their own accord or would have been the few unfortunate people who are innocently incapacitated and do not enjoy the benefit of others' generosity, charity, compassion, and similar support. According to libertarians, there is no reason to think that there would be many such persons, at least compared to the numbers one can expect in societies lacking respect and protection for negative individual rights. Thus, even the most well known opponent of capitalism (the economic system of libertarianism), Karl Marx, was aware that unless human nature itself changes and the "new man" develops, socialism can do no more than to socialize poverty, i.e., make everyone poor.

As to the historical evidence, it is hard to argue that other than substantially capitalist economic systems, which tend in the direction of libertarianism (at least as far as the legal respect for and protection of private property or the right to it are concerned) have fared much better in reducing poverty than have others, without also causing massive political and other social failures (such as abolition of civil liberties, institution for forced labor and involuntary servitude, regimentation of the bulk of social relations, arresting scientific and technological progress, or censorship of the arts and other intellectual endeavors). Thus, America is still the freest of societies, with many of its legal principles giving expression to classical liberal, near-libertarian ideas, and it is, at the same time, the most generally productive (creative and culturally rich) of all societies, with its wealth aiding in the support of hundreds of other societies across the globe. Barring the impossible-to-conduct controlled sociopolitical-economic experiment, such historical evidence is all we can adduce to examine which political economic system produces more poverty. No one can seriously dispute that the near-libertarian systems have fared much better than those going in the opposite direction, including the welfare state. Even though some people wish for more in the way of empirical backing, it is difficult to know what they could wish for apart from the relatively plain fact of history that societies in which negative liberty flourishes produce far more (tangible) wealth than do ones in which such freedom is systematically denied. It is no secret that the Western liberal nations in general and the United States of America in particular contribute the most to the rescue of casualties of famines and other natural disasters across the globe. The US supports the United Nations' treasury far more than do other nations. While factors other than the political-economic conditions of a country contribute to these circumstances, barring some kind of controlled experiment in which those factors can be isolated, this will have to do for present purposes.

There is another point to be stressed, though, that Sterba has not taken into consideration. This is that there can be people in a libertarian society—indeed, in any society—for whom a lack of wealth, even extreme poverty relative to the mean, may not be a great liability. Not everyone wants to, or even ought to, live prosperously. For some individuals a life of ostensible poverty could be of substantial benefit. Contenders would be monks, hobos, starving artists, and the like who, despite the protection of their negative liberty or the right to it, do not elect to seek economic prosperity, at least in preference to other important objectives. Among the citizens of a libertarian society, then, we could find some who are poor but who are not, therefore, worse off than the rich, provided we do not confine ourselves to counting economic prosperity as the prime source of well-being.

At one point, Sterba suggests that libertarians, because they do not see the need to affirm as a principle of justice the right to welfare, may not care sufficiently for the poor. As he puts it:

> Machan seems reluctant to take the steps required to secure the basic needs of the poor. Why then does he balk at taking any further steps? Could it be that he does not see the oppression of the poor as truly oppressive after all?[20]

There is perhaps something to this, although not in the way Sterba's rhetorical question suggests, namely, that libertarians are callous or uncaring where the cultivation of care is warranted. But it is true enough that just being poor does not necessarily warrant being cared for, just as simply being sick does not place upon another the obligation to help, if the sickness is the result of self-abuse or gross negligence, or affects a thoroughly evil person.

Furthermore, some artists who are poor are happier than some merchants who are rich. There is no justification for feeling compassion for such artists, despite their poverty. In short, being poor in and of itself does not justify special consideration.[21] Being in need of what it takes to attain one's well-being warrants, if the need is a matter of natural misfortune or injury from others, feelings and conduct amounting to care, generosity, and charity. Poverty does not always constitute such neediness.

Nevertheless, Sterba may also underestimate what Marxists might call the objective generosity or charity of libertarians. One must consider just how much greater the long range prospects for economic well-being are for everyone within a libertarian political economy, and how benevolent it is for people not to be cuddled and treated as if they were inept in attaining prosperity; this system fosters institutional conditions within which they will probably be much better off than they would be in any welfare state (which seems clearly to encourage long-range economic ineptitude and dependence) the libertarian could well be regarded as the political theory with the greatest concern for the poor.[22]

It seems, therefore, that Sterba hasn't supported his main contention: that libertarianism implies the welfare state. The reason is that he has failed to appreciate the analytical and historical context within which libertarianism is argued. But there is more.

Sterba has also failed to appreciate that, although in some cases a person might not be required to respect the negative individual rights all citizens have—e.g., in some rare case of helpless destitution—nothing follows from this regarding the rights that everyone in society has by virtue of being a human individual living in a community of other human individuals. As Rasmussen and Den Uyl so carefully argue, the system of negative individual rights is a metanormative system or, in other words, a political framework within which human beings normally would and should pursue their highly varied flourishing. Focusing on exceptional, rare cases, wherein "peace is not possible," and, thus, it is justified to disregard consideration of basic (political) rights, does not justify the abrogation of the system of justice based on such rights that does, in fact, best befit human beings in their communities. On rare occasions, for particular persons, exceptions might be made, just as courts in extraordinary circumstances make such exceptions in the criminal law by pardoning someone who has violated a law but could not be expected to abide by it; these pardons do not abolish the law in question.

The point is, one ought not to abandon political principles to accommodate what can only be deemed extraordinary circumstances, Sterba's advice to the contrary notwithstanding.

NOTES

1. Quoted in Harry V. Jaffa, *How to Think About the American Revolution* (Durham, NC: Carolina Academic Press, 1978), p. 41 (from *The Collected Works of Abraham Lincoln* [R. Basler (ed.), 1953], 108–15).

2. See, in particular, James Sterba, "A Libertarian Justification for a Welfare State," *Social Theory and Practice*, 11 (Fall 1985), 285–306. I will be referring to this essay as well as a more developed version, titled "The U.S. Constitution: A Fundamentally Flawed Document" in *Philosophy Reflections on the United States Constitution*, edited by Christopher Gray (1989).

3. H. L. A. Hart, "Are There Any Natural Rights?" *Philosophical Review* 64 (1955), 175.

4. See, for my own discussions, Tibor R. Machan, *Human Rights and Human Liberties* (Chicago: Nelson-Hall, 1975), 213–22; "Prima Facie versus Natural (Human) Rights," *Journal of Value Inquiry* 10 (1976), 119–31; "Human Rights: Some Points of Clarification," *Journal of Critical Analysis* 5 (1973), 30–39.

5. Sterba, op. cit, "A Libertarian Justification," 295.

6. Ibid.

7. Ayn Rand, "Value and Rights," in J. Hospers, (ed.), *Readings in Introductory Philosophical Analysis* (Englewood Cliffs, NJ: Prentice-Hall, 1968), 382.

8. Sterba, "The U.S. Constitution: A Fundamentally Flawed Document."

9. John Rawls, *A Theory of Justice* (Cambridge, MA: Harvard University Press, 1971), 101–02. For a discussion of the complexities in the differential attainments of members of various ethnic groups—often invoked as evidence for the injustice of a capitalist system, see Thomas Sowell, *Ethnic America: A History* (New York: Basic Books, 1981). There is pervasive prejudice in welfare-state proponents' writings against crediting people with the ability to extricate themselves from poverty without special political assistance. The idea behind the right to negative liberty is to set people free from others so as to pursue their progressive goals. This is the ultimate teleological justification of Lockean libertarian natural rights. See Tibor R. Machan, *Human Rights and Human Liberties: A Radical Reconsideration of the American Political Tradition* (Chicago: Nelson-Hall, 1975). Consider also this thought from Herbert Spencer:

The feeling which vents itself in "poor fellow!" on seeing one in agony, excludes the thought of "bad fellow," which might at another time arise.

Naturally, then, if the wretched are unknown or but vaguely known, all the demerits they may have are ignored: and thus it happens that when the miseries of the poor are dilated upon, they are thought of as the miseries of the deserving poor, instead of being thought of as the miseries of undeserving poor, which in large measure they should be. Those whose hardships are set forth in pamphlets and proclaimed in sermons and speeches which echo throughout society, are assumed to be all worthy souls, grievously wronged; and none of them are thought of as bearing the penalties of their own misdeeds.

(*Man versus the State* [Caldwell, ID: Caxton Printers, 1940], 22)

10. Tibor R. Machan, "Ethics vs. Coercion: Morality of Just Values?" in L. H. Rockwell, Jr. et al., (ed.), *Man, Economy and Liberty: Essays in Honor of Murray N. Rothbard* (Auburn, AL: Ludwig von Mises Institute, 1988), 236–46.

11. John Kekes, "'Ought Implies Can' and Two Kinds of Morality," *The Philosophical Quarterly* 34 (1984), 459–67.

12. Tibor R. Machan, "Ethics vs. Coercion." In a vegetable garden or even in a forest, there can be good things and bad, but no morally good things and morally evil things (apart from people who might be there).

13. Sterba, "The U.S. Constitution: A Fundamentally Flawed Document."

14. Sterba, "A Libertarian Justification," 295–96.

15. Robert Nozick, *Anarchy, State, and Utopia* (New York: Basic Books, 1974), 57. See, also, Tibor R. Machan, "Conditions for Rights, Sphere of Authority," *Journal of Human Relations* 19 (1971), 184–87, where I argue that "within the context of a legal system where the *sphere of authority* of individuals and groups of individuals cannot be delineated independently of the sphere of authority of the public as a whole, there is an inescapable conflict of rights specified by the same legal system." (186). See, also, Tibor R. Machan, "The Virtue of Freedom in Capitalism," *Journal of Applied Philosophy* 3 (1986), 49–58, and Douglas J. Den Uyl, "Freedom and Virtue," in Tibor R. Machan (ed.), *The Main Debate: Communism versus Capitalism* (New York: Random House, 1987), 200–16. This last essay is especially pertinent to the understanding of the ethical or moral merits of coercion and coerced conduct. Thus it is argued here that "coercive charity" amounts to an oxymoron.

16. See, Machan, op. cit., "The Virtue of Freedom in Capitalism" and "Private Property and the Decent Society" in J. K. Roth and R. C. Whittemore (eds.), *Ideology and American Experience* (Washington, DC: Washington Institute Press, 1986).

17. E.g., James Fishkin, *Tyranny and Legitimacy* (Baltimore, MD: Johns Hopkins University Press, 1979). Cf., Tibor R. Machan, "Fishkin on Nozick's Absolute Rights," *Journal of Libertarian Studies* 6 (1982), 317–20.

Sterba has gone on to raise further objections, for example, in his "From Liberty to Welfare," *Ethics* 105 (October 1994), 64–98. All these rest on Sterba's refusal to examine the ethical foundations of natural rights. Thus Sterba can claim that "Machan seems reluctant to take the steps required to secure the basic needs of the poor." This, simply because I will not sanction theft as a means to "secure" those needs. What about generosity, charity, philanthropy, kindness, compassion, help, assistance, etc.? All these appear not to interest Sterba, since they do not involve the force of law or coercion, whereby Machan and others can be compelled, one may assume by Sterba & Co., "to secure the basic needs of the poor." But there is more to coping with life's problems than foisting political "solutions" on people.

If history is any indication, what the oppressed poor need is not giving them permission to steal but a polity of liberty where they can put their own initiative to productive use, where what they create or obtain by trade may be kept by them, invested and built into nest eggs or substantial wealth. The poor, as the saying goes, need to become rich, not be placed into a polity wherein no one is allowed to get too rich and all those who have unsatisfied basic needs can legally raid the wealth of others.

18. James P. Sterba, *Morality and Social Justice* (Lanham, MD: Rowman & Littlefield, 1995), 15.

19. In so far as Sterba is a reasonably close follower of John Rawls' thinking in politics, and since Rawls denies the efficacy of individual initiative in the formation of personal assets such as one's character, it is quite possible that Sterba follows suit. (See John Rawls, *A Theory of Justice* [Cambridge: Harvard University Press, 1971], 104.) Since, however, Sterba also endorses the Kantian notion of "ought implies can" and advances numerous claims as to what people ought to do, there is evidence that he is also committed to a theory of free will. Which view dominates is unclear since there is no explicit discussion of this matter in Sterba's work with which I am familiar.

In contrast, most libertarians would invoke views drawn from philosophers of human nature, action theory, or motivational psychology, and embrace the position that when human beings are not kept in subjugation, they will tend or have good reasons to work toward their improvement, regardless of where they are on the continuum between destitution and abundance. Libertarians differ on the details, of course, with some subscribing to a neo-Hobbesian idea about what leads people to act and others to an agency view drawing from Ayn Rand and others. Some embrace the

Hayekian notion of natural evolution. None accept what seems to underlie many statist positions, namely, that most people are congenitally passive, even when they are not actively kept in subjugation. On this view, of course, neither the poor (and some among them who are lazy) nor the rich (and some among them who are greedy) are personally responsible for their economic position in life. Nor, of course, can those who resist Sterba's analysis be blamed for possible moral blindness (a charge implicit in some of what Sterba has said about libertarians), since they, too, presumably are the way they are because of circumstances beyond their control.

It is notable that the statistics Sterba cites are drawn from societies, including the United States of America, which are far from libertarian in their legal construction and are far closer to the welfare state, if not to outright socialism. It is surprising why Sterba does not consider that perhaps what accounts for those statistics is the absence of libertarianism, given that there is ample historical evidence for the impact of socialism on the economic conditions of the members of various societies around the globe. Seeing, then, that socialism does not improve the general welfare and the welfare state leaves a great many people badly off, a not unreasonable alternative would be that greater stress on the protection of negative individual liberty would promise the results Sterba desires. In contrast to Sterba's empirical assertions about poverty *vis-a-vis* capitalism (the economic system of libertarianism), see Nathan Rosenberg, *How the West Grew Rich: The economic transformation of the industrial world* (New York: Basic Books, 1986), and Nathan Rosenberg, Ralph Landau, and David C. Mowery, *Technology and the Wealth of Nations* (Stanford, CA: Stanford University Press, 1992). Both works go a long way toward demonstrating the superior wealth-creating record of economies that rest, more so than alternative systems, on the principles of the right to private property, free competition and the pursuit of private profit.

20. James P. Sterba, "Liberty and Welfare," note 34. In this paper Sterba repeats the claims about the alleged connection between libertarianism and significantly widespread poverty, with no attempt to establish them except by reference to unanalyzed statistics. (An attempt by the present author to challenge his analysis was rejected by the editors on grounds that the challenge was based on no more than "confident empirical speculations." See note 19, above, however, for references to works containing historical evidence supportive of the claim against Sterba's unanalyzed statistics.)

21. This may account, in part, for the indignation felt by some poor when they are offered help. Their dignity has been offended, for they know that their poverty follows from their conscious or implicit choices, ones they find and which may indeed be fully justified. For a general argument against the enforceable duty to serve others, see Lester H. Hunt, "An Argument Against a Legal Duty to Rescue," *Journal of Social Philosophy* 36 (1994), 22.

22. Let me spend a few paragraphs on the difference between meaning and doing good, for Sterba's implied charge gains its moral force from what seems to me a misunderstanding of morality along certain Kantian lines. (See, for a comment along lines similar to what follows, Shelby Steele, "How Liberals Lost Their Virtue Over Race," *Newsweek,* January 1995, 41–42.)

There is, among many moral theorists as well as politicians and pundits, much concern with who is mean spirited, who lacks compassion, who is kinder and gentler among those vying to be political leaders. For too many people what appears to count most for having moral character is the quality of the feelings that motivate one's conduct. If you *mean or intend* well, if what you feel in your heart is good, decent, caring and such, what follows is supposed to be morally upstanding, commendable. It doesn't even matter much what actually results from the conduct motivated by such good feelings. "It's the thought that counts," as the saying goes.

Yet there is clearly something wrong with this idea. People may feel good for having done one thing or another from certain generous, charitable, kind or compassionate sensibilities or motives but it doesn't follow at all that this assures that the consequences are actually going to produce much benefit. Indeed, it is often quite likely that by focusing on how one feels about what one does, one loses sight of whether the action actually achieves any good at all. Furthermore, by focusing on these evaluating feelings, one can run the very real risk of trying to please others instead of actually helping them.

Very often, indeed, helpful conduct does not square with conduct that pleases. One knows this well enough in personal relations: some friends or relatives want us to do for them things that are definitely not very helpful. Such conduct more often simply satisfies some desire, never mind whether it is actually worthy of being satisfied. Consider young friends who want to have, say, cigarettes or alcohol purchased for them, never mind what these actually produce. Consider the deadbeat who would so much like another loan, or the lazy person who would like to escape all hardship and just sit around. Or consider the moments when you, too, are tempted to plead merely to be satisfied, hoping that no one will critically examine the merits of your desires. Those who comply with such calls for unwise generosity may often fool themselves and feel moral righteousness about what they do. And they are certainly often liked for this by the people whom they have "helped."

In contrast, bona fide help is much more risky. And it is demanding. One needs to learn what actually is good for the person who seeks it. One needs to do some research. And one often upsets those whom one helps, just as doctors often displease patients with treatments or prescriptions that are unpleasant, as coaches do with the training they demand from athletes.

The more remote one is from those in need of help, the less likely it is going to be that such research is going to be undertaken. Instead some standard formulas will be invoked and the gauge to success will be how much gratitude is forthcoming, never mind whether such gratitude means serious thanks for useful help or mere pleasure in response to compliance.

In the current political climate there is a lot of talk about how some people are mean-spirited, who lack compassion, versus others who care and feel for those in need. It will pay handsomely, especially for those who are to be benefited from various public policies, to take a very close look at what actually is at issue. Are those derided for callousness perhaps thinking harder than their critics about what will be most helpful to the targeted beneficiaries? Are their proposals perhaps more fruitful in the long run, than those motivated by kinder and gentler feelings, regarding the actual task of securing for people a better life? And are these so called mean spirited policy architects perhaps the ones who ought to obtain real moral credit for generosity and compassion, rather than those who are flooded with feelings of compassion and kindness and thus are filled with moral pride and righteousness?

If one considers, also, that the generosity and compassion of those full of good feelings for others tend to come at other people's expense, the answer might be quite easy to discover.

4   Contracting for Liberty

JAN NARVESON

Politics and Reason

MANY HAVE FOUND THE POLITICAL outlook now generally known as "libertarianism" attractive, but most of them have held it in much the same way as most who adhere strongly to any other political outlook: they regard it as *obviously* true—scarcely in need of argument. They might even hold that no argument at this level is possible—just what people often say about religious beliefs. And in both cases, there is the same result: they are virtually barred from convincing anyone who doesn't already incline toward their outlook. Only nonrational methods are possible—not rational discourse, but maneuvering for power, if not by naked force of arms, then by conspiring to wield the arm of the law against all rivals.

It would be nice if we could do better than that. It may even be of genuine practical importance that the basic tenets of a political society should be amenable to reasoned discussion instead of war, soap-box rhetoric, or back-room machinations. The present essay is a brief defense of the proposal that there are actually good reasons for adopting the libertarian program above any other, and that these reasons can be explicated in a plausible way. I am proposing, then, that there actually are reasonable "foundations" for this political theory. . . .

The Other Views

Political and moral theories have been argued for on such bases as ideals of virtue, the will of God, self-evidence, and, in one way or another, nature. Why reject all these? Actually, as we will see, we needn't reject them all, quite: the contractarian view may be aligned with one kind of "natural law."

Meanwhile, we can say something about the inadequacy of such theories. *Virtue theories* fail because their ideas of virtue are never shared by *all*, and are unprovable to those who disagree. Appeals to *authority* are useless because they are circular. What the Authority says is right, we are told. And why? Well, because he knows what is right. His commands are a fifth wheel. And if we appeal to "self-evidence," what do we do about those who, alas, do not "see" the self-evident? The usual answer—kick'em!—lacks cogency.

Morals are for people: if a theory is to work, it must be shown that it appeals to people. Those who propose that politics are based on "natural law" or "nature" may be obscurely appreciating this point. But the claim that some view is "based on the nature of things" or on "human nature" is unclear. Talk of "conforming to nature" makes no literal sense; nature simply *is*. It sets limits to what is possible, but can prescribe nothing.

Can the idea of natural law be given a useful interpretation? I suggest this: a natural law theory should say, in the end, that in view of the way

From Liberty for the Twenty-First Century: Contemporary Libertarian Thought, *edited by Tibor R. Machan and Douglas B. Rasmussen, pp. 19–39, 217–221. Reprinted by permission of Rowman & Littlefield Publishers, Inc.*

things and people are, subscribing to *this* set of rules or virtues is our *best* means of accommodating them.

So, what *makes* it best, then? People make choices. To say that nature *determines* which choice to make is pointless: *we* must choose. But given that I *want* this or that, then with good information I can see that *this* is the thing to do. And so we might adapt the terminology of natural law for this purpose and suggest that a rule or a value is "natural" when it is one's rationally best response to one's circumstances. In just that spirit, Hobbes proposed his Laws of Nature. And he got them right: modern decision-theoretic arguments confirm Hobbes' basic moral ideas, even as they fail to support his argument for the State.

The Contractarian Idea

John Stuart Mill declared that "society is not founded on a contract, and . . . no good purpose is answered by inventing a contract in order to deduce social obligations from it"—yet he adds the remarkably contract-like suggestion that "everyone who receives the protection of society owes a return for the benefit, and the fact of living in society renders it indispensable that each should be bound to observe a certain line of conduct toward the rest."[1] To any who envisage a need to justify the ways of their fellows to themselves or vice versa, that line of argument is inevitable. There is no alternative. . . .

Contract

Why "contract"? And especially, why the "social" contract? Does the idea of a "contract" at the universal level we contemplate here make any sense? We need a characterization sufficiently general to capture what is in common both to the many explicit arrangements normally so-called in ordinary life, and to that pattern or principle of interactions, *not* the result of explicit negotiations, that the social-contract theorist proposes as the basis of morals and politics.

The answer has been identified plausibly by Hobbes and Hume, and latterly, in a more precise and general form, by David Gauthier.[2] In contracts, people make their behavior *conditional on each other's performance*. In so doing, at least one of them typically makes himself vulnerable to the other's decision not to carry through on it.[3] An inward impetus of the will is required to make it work. That is morality. Now and again, one of the parties concerned may lack the necessary inner commitment. We may then have to resort to external imposition, sometimes to force.

A contract in the relevant sense is *social* when it is a conditional arrangement of *each with all*. The building block of such a contract is an arrangement between oneself and whomever comes to treat them thus-and-so *provided* they do likewise. "Social contract" does not refer to anything not analyzable into the plans of action of particular individuals. And if, as is likely, we fall short of unanimity, near-unanimity contract will somehow have to serve. That problem will be carefully considered below. Meanwhile, though, the prospect of mutual benefit is what underwrites social reinforcement of contracts generally, and in particular the commitment to refrain from force in the pursuit of one's goals. We rationally expect all to adhere to that rule: it is a rational commitment.

Commitment is rational only where one can expect reciprocity—which in turn can only be expected if the other party can expect it from you. Can either really expect it, though? Here we must make an obvious and familiar distinction, between two senses of "expect": (1) to *predict,* and (2) to *insist,* that is, to feel entitled to performance. As to (1), whether we can expect others to perform depends on their characters, and we sometimes know enough of that to form reliable predictions, and sometimes not. But (2) we can always *insist* on others' keeping the terms of any particular promise, provided that we do our share and provided that it was made in a suitably well-informed and uncoerced fashion. In so insisting, we invoke the support of anyone and everyone in the social environment—not just that of our interactee.

This social element is a substantial reinforcer, if applied consistently and carefully. Being the general object of disapprobation, with accompanying withdrawal of assorted amenities of civilized exchange, is a heavy price to pay for displaying a tendency to renege, and those who are motivated to avoid getting caught at their reneging pay a price in having to devote effort to covering their tracks and avoiding detection. They can and sometimes do succeed, more or less, and just what that shows is debatable—certainly that morality is imperfect, but not that it is irrational nor even that it is less than fully rational. Any doctrine that made immorality incomprehensible would be convicted of unreality on that account. My claim is only that rational people will give weight to morality as here explained, in the form of a disposition to abide by agreements and to refrain from trying to get one's way by sheer force.

The "social contract" has in common with all contracts that (1) it is the reciprocal conditionalizing of behavior and (2) it involves commitment from those concerned. But it is, of course, an unspoken understanding, a *non*-negotiated agreement—an agreement in action, not in words nor preceded by words. Each party adopts a disposition to respond in ways that make the resulting interaction mutually preferable to its alternatives. Such dispositions are moral virtues: dispositions we do well to have. But the contractarian view differs from theories claiming to found morals on a prior discernment of what is virtuous, independently of interaction. On the view defended here, we can *show* that this disposition is a virtue. It isn't a matter of what's "in the eye of the beholder."

The Libertarian Idea[4]

It cannot be too strongly emphasized that libertarianism is not a view about the same thing as contractarianism. The latter is a *metatheory* of morals and politics. It holds that the principles of morals, whatever they may turn out to be, are those we all do have reason to agree on provided all others accept them as well. The reason for agreeing is simple: we do better in the condition where all comply with the proposed principles. But only if others agree too; absent agreement, we revert to the unsatisfactory condition in which no one can trust anyone else. Libertarianism is a view about the substance of that agreement.

That substance is the principle that force—the stick, as I call it—ought to be restricted, in human affairs, to countering those who would or do employ force without that restriction: namely, to the initiators of violence, those who propose to make their way by removing the human obstacles to it by brute force or threat of same. The libertarian strategy, then, is *to resort to force only to counter the aggression of others.* And the libertarian theory is contractually *grounded* only if (1) libertarianism is the best rule for everybody in the way of general restrictions on behavior, and (2) no other way of arriving at the virtue in question is plausible. Our argument is that the Universal Social Contract, the agreement of all with all, calls for nothing more nor less than to refrain from the use of force to attain one's goals. In Hobbes' words, it is to "seek peace, and follow it," which, together with its famous corollary, that when peace is unattainable, one may then use "all the helps and advantages of war"[5] constitute his First Law of Nature, and really the only one, if he is right in holding that all the others flow from it. The job is to show that it is indeed the only reasonable candidate for the role of fundamental principle of morality, and showing that is not a purely a priori matter. The argument may not only be difficult, but varyingly plausible under different conditions.

Why is this "libertarian"? To be at liberty, in general, is to have no obstacles impeding one's efforts. To be at *social* liberty, liberty in relation to one's fellows, is for them to refrain from impeding one's efforts. For people in general to have social liberty is for all to refrain from impeding each other's efforts—that each person, A, has no obstacles to A's efforts imposed by the voluntary actions of A's fellow persons. Of course the expectation of liberty at the hands of others is unreasonable if it is not reciprocal: A won't impede B, but only on condition that B in turn will not impede A. The social contract is necessary for liberty. But is it sufficient? That is the big question.

Liberty cannot sensibly be regarded as an *intrinsic* value. One values liberty because there are things that one values, and liberty is necessary for getting them by one's own efforts. But what if we can get it by somebody else's efforts? Terrific—if we can. But how can we? Perhaps by happenstance appeal to the goodness of their hearts—which, no doubt, will sometimes work and sometimes not. But if not, then what? The answer, as we have already seen, is by force or fraud—means that the person against whom they are used has the strongest reason for objecting to. Universal agreement precludes use of those methods.

Others will talk of "positive" liberty, perhaps. Of what use to a paraplegic is the liberty to walk, it will be asked? The answer to that is easy: none, until he becomes equipped with devices to move him around; and then it's plenty of use, just as it is for the rest of us. But those who propose to equip him at our expense, involuntarily incurred, need to tell *us* why *we* should accept that imposition. To look myopically at the paraplegic alone is absurd, and it is dishonest. "We" do *not* prefer supposed positive liberty, which must always be at the expense of others, to negative liberty, which can be had by all. Only *some* prefer that.

Liberty and Property

Liberty is the absence of impediments, and thus of impositions. What constitutes an "impediment" must, then, be one of the first questions on our conceptual agenda. The libertarian has a specific view about this. He proposes that in general nonimpediment entails respecting *property*, broadly speaking. Explicating this idea carefully and plausibly is our first conceptual task. If we don't know what constitutes impediment, then we don't know what constitutes liberty, and if we don't know that, we don't know what we are advocating under the banner of libertarianism. If we do know what it is, however, then we can also understand how to formulate a workable notion of property.

The libertarian holds, in effect, that *liberty = property*. To own something is to have the right to do with it as one pleases: the disposition of that thing is up to you, not someone else. Take the special case in which the "something" is the person himself, and it follows immediately that liberty consists in self-ownership. Locke's confidence that a man owns himself was, therefore, correct. To act is to make use of one's own capacities, one's own equipment and abilities—limbs, memory, pianistic talents, the works. Too many talk as though property were not only entirely distinct from but perhaps antithetical to liberty. That is nonsense. If one's tongue is not one's own, what means freedom of speech? If one's mind isn't, what sense is there in freedom of thought?

The large question about this must concern external property: land, amplifiers, hotels, metalworking machines. Many writers seem to think that there is a terrible problem about extending a right of personal freedom to the use of items in the external world. While too large an issue for this essay to deal with completely,[6] the basic idea is simple: just as we can do what we wish with the natural parts of our own person, bodily and psychological, so we may do what we wish with bits of external nature, so long only as we do not thereby damage or impede the uses by others of such objects. In particular, it is not an impediment that if A acquires x, B is thereby unable to do so. The implication of an argument along those lines is that nobody may use anything—a strange doctrine of *liberty*! The correct view is that you can use *whatever* you find if nobody else already has it. Once you begin to use it, then anyone else who comes along will interfere with your already-commenced train of action if he renders it impossible for you to continue. To own x is to have control over the further disposition of x. Once we acquire hitherto unowned nature, all further acquisition of property must be via agreement: that is, by voluntary exchange, of things for things, things for services, or services for services. Liberty = property. If we have no property rights, we have no rights. Period. . . .

The "State of Nature"

The classic political philosophers of the modern era thought to derive the principles of politics from hypotheses about how things would be for people in a "state of nature," this being the situation where people interact in the absence of *any* authoritatively exercised general controls. They then hoped to justify proposals by demonstrating the superiority of the situations envisaged by them over the original condition. This raises two questions. First, can this be a useful conception, seeing that such states do not seem to occur in human affairs? Second, does the utility of contractarianism depend on the real possibility of such states? We briefly consider these central issues here.

First, let us note three distinctions. One is the familiar distinction between hypothetical and actual states of nature. Even if they are never actual, the idea may be useful. If (1) such a condition is at least possible, and if (2) from the point of view of any individual it would be terrible if it did occur, and if (3) certain behavior patterns in humans do head us toward such a condition unless certain social arrangements are made, then there need not ever actually be any such to show that we have reason to avoid those patterns.

The second distinction is between *political* and *moral* versions of the idea. A political state of nature is a social condition without political institutions. A moral state of nature is a social condition without morals: no one has any moral inhibitions about doing *anything*. The moral version is the more general and profound.

A third distinction is between *partial* and *complete* states of nature. A social condition is a partial state of nature if it has aspects of apoliticality or amorality, even though in other respects there are laws or moral inhibitions. A more abstract and useful characterization of the "state of nature" is that it displays certain game-theoretic structures, in particular what is called a prisoner's dilemma.

State of nature is then identified with the default option. This again is relevant to our two questions: there are plenty of such dilemmas at hand; we needn't go to the ultimate one envisaged by Hobbes in order to make the argument for morality. (Or maybe the state? Note that I do *not* assume that the argument can work to justify a state, but do not pursue the question here.)

We can now make progress on the question before us. A state of nature that couldn't even approximately obtain under *any* circumstances is indeed pointless. But if the condition in question is clearly possible, and it can be established that we really would tend toward that condition unless we do x, while x produces a condition clearly superior to it, then we have an argument for doing x. So, for example, it is *logically* impossible that we should actually be behind Rawls' "veil of ignorance." But it is not obviously impossible at all to be in a situation where no body of people has effective political power—where there is a "breakdown of law and order." And we know cases of immoral behavior; generalizing from them doesn't seem impossible either. And so there is no problem about the reality of states of nature. At any given time, there are many matters that are not subject to specific controls of either the legal or the moral type, and where arguably all concerned would be better off if they were. That's all we need.

Starting Where We Are

The fundamental question in life is: what do I do *now*? Speculation on what we should have done yesterday might help answer that question, or it might not; the past is, after all, past. Speculation on what we should do if some or another condition should obtain is useful if the condition is probable. But deliberation about what to do right now isn't speculation—it's life. In my daily doings, I will encounter various people and innumerable features of my environment that are substantially different from what they would have been had previous human activity been different, and that are decidedly subject to change at the hands of further human activity in the foreseeable future. Having helpful dispositions at hand for dealing with various of these is likely to be useful. The contractarian proposal is that among these handy dispositions are recognizably moral ones, whose utility has a lot to do with the network of expectations we can or do generate by encountering and reflecting on the behavior of others with whom we interact. It is a useful idea if, and only if, features of our social situations answer to the contractarian descriptions and call for their sort of solutions.

The status quo itself may be taken as our point of departure for many purposes of theory, as it must for all purposes of practice. If my proposed action and your proposed response would produce alterations for the better from both our points of view, as compared with any obvious alternatives, and by reference to the status quo, then agreement between us about that particular interaction is, *prima facie,* rational. If a proposed rule would make for improvement over the current situation for all concerned, then we have a plausible argument for adopting such a rule. These are options that obviously can and often do obtain—thus showing that the contractarian idea is at least partially practical and cannot be rejected out of hand.

That the status quo itself may be affected by injustice, stupidity, or other defects is clearly possible. But we show this by looking at aspects of *preceding* states of affairs and showing how certain departures from those states were contrary to the contractual criterion. If we learn, for example, that the reason why A has $100 to offer and B has nothing is that A got it from B by threatening to beat him to a pulp if he didn't hand it over, that makes quite a difference. No *general* agreement could have led to that development. Of course the status quo is not sacred. But we detect defects by looking back as far as necessary to see where the alleged defects came from and whether those involved agreed or could have agreed to what produced them. . . .

Nonunanimity?

Any contract view must address the question of what to do about those who will agree to nothing. My answer is Hobbes's: everyone else's behavior is, obviously, utterly unrestricted in relation to them. If in the process they end up on the gallows or in the tar-pit, that's tough for them—but it is not unjust. And the same for us, of course: if he does us in, that's too bad for us. All we can say is that in an all-out war, victory goes to the strong. However, our bet is that there are a great many more of us than of them—especially after they have finished doing each other in! . . .

Sorting Interests

For purposes of morals, what matters about an interest in others is whether that interest is positive or negative: would its satisfaction be a pro or a con to those others? If positive, then we have, prima facie, a situation of harmony, and there should be no problem, nuances apart; but if satisfying A's interest in B requires dissatisfying B, we have problems. What would we do about public controls on the pursuit of interests of these types? No one will allow others routinely to block his pursuit of his own interest. Where interests conflict, agreement requires a rationale for allowing one to be subject to overturning at the hands of some other. This agreement is not going to be forthcoming from the one who loses out. It must be shown that there's something in it *for him*—that he stands to gain from the rule even if it is imposed on him by force. Inherently, conflictual interests cannot be accommodated by a public charter. There simply is no basis for agreement to actions on interests that from their very nature can only be satisfied at the expense of someone else. These necessarily set people against each other.

We may now define a class of what we may call *liberal* interests. These are interests that do not take as their object the dissatisfaction of anyone else. There are no inherent obstacles to acceptance of interests that have no bearing on others' interests. They may be pursued unrestrictedly. On the other hand, interests that do affect the interest of others must be cleared with those others before we proceed.

To take an extremely important example, the pursuit of private wealth—contrary to the doctrines of socialists—is, if pursued by consensual means, inherently nonconflictual. One person's having more than he had before does not entail that any other persons have less than they had before. And if we make our way by exchange, then both of us must, barring accident or mistake, do better in each instance. This furthers the case for private property; such relations are inherently nonconflictual.

Of course, A's having more than B implies that B has less than A. But the interest in having more, or less, or the same as B has no status in the public charter. For example, egalitarianism, the passion for equality, has exactly the same inherently conflict structure as any other relational motive. Society may not adopt as a goal that persons in class X have more, or less, *or the same,* as persons in class Y. By contrast, endeavoring to increase one's own wealth has no logical relation to other persons' levels of wealth. Each may do the best he or she can do; in principle, we can *all* win, improving our wealth with no adverse affects on any others. But we should also note that when we improve it by commerce—free exchange with others—then we benefit others even as we benefit ourselves. For this reason, it is plausible to propose that free exchange benefits the community maximally. Thus, the familiar policy of "soaking the rich" is absurd in all cases where the rich get rich by buying and selling. To have gotten rich by that means is to have improved the lot of many others. Reducing the incentive to acquire by such means reduces the real incomes of those other people, as well as of the immediate victim. Theft is counterproductive from the public point of view. It improves the lot of the thief (if it does) only by worsening the lot of someone else.

Charity, on the other hand, has a place of honor. The charitable person enjoys helping others; when they are helped, so is he. It should be noted, though, that charity has to be the exception, not the rule. If we *all* tried to live by charity, that would be the end of all wealth. Someone must actually produce in order for there to be anything to give away. . . .

Welfare

Would contractarianism confirm the libertarian's refusal to allow coercively extracted support of the so-called safety net for the poor, public schooling, socialized medicine, and so on? I shall argue that it would indeed.

Nobody can deny that people enjoying a higher rather than a lower level of welfare is, generally speaking, a good thing. Even those who profess not to care about the well-being of their fellows will, in the first place, sign up for a general duty of nonaggression: they too will "seek peace and follow it," using violence only when necessary to counter the violence of aggressors.

It has to be pointed out that if this duty is perfectly general, it extends also to the case where the supposedly caring A steals from B in order to feed needy C. But it's not enough to point that out, as if it were a proof. What must be shown is that rational people will not modify or qualify the general duty of nonimposition, and opt instead for the idea that we do all owe each other something: for instance, a social minimum, funds for which we may extract from everyone, by force if need be. Unfortunately, most people we know do think that a social minimum is owed. They think there is a difference between my putting a gun in your ribs and extracting a transfer of cash from you to me, on the one hand, and representatives of "the public" doing the same thing, with the difference that the transfer is only partly from you to them—some of the extracted cash really does end up in the pockets of the supposed poor or provides schooling "free" to all who can benefit from it; or pays for the appendectomies of those who might not otherwise be able to afford them. Are they right to make such a distinction? No—or so I will argue.

First, let's attend to what most defenders of the welfare state overlook. The world we live in has around five billion inhabitants at present, of whom perhaps one billion enjoy "first world" status. But if the alleged duty to provide a safety net for the poor had the status of a general duty to poor humans, no state welfare program would make any sense. All such programs would have to become universal-scope foreign aid programs. Yet virtually no supporter of the Welfare State accepts this obligation. Why not?

The short answer is that politics and the self-interest of some few play the major role in the equation, high principle having little to do with it. In fact, the supposed "high" principle is considered by most people to be *too* high. They do not believe that all well-off people have an enforceable duty to provide for all badly off ones. Yet they don't actually have a *reason* for confining welfare programs to their own nations or their own communities.

The libertarian principle says that force is to be confined to dealing with aggression, and may not be used for any other end, however noble it may seem. That includes the welfare of others such as the poor. Why, it may be asked, should we insist on sticking only with the Scrooge-like principle advocated by us libertarians at the most fundamental level? There is a ready answer. If person A does not in fact care about person B, why would he accept an enforceable duty to help care for B? Perhaps A anticipates the possibility that one day he might be in bad shape and would like B to help him. This is solid reasoning. We should all be disposed to help those in need. But should we be so disposed to the point where we agree that if we don't help those people, we'll go to jail? Or the point where we allow others to garnish our wages forever after? Surely not! The scope of the familiar idea of aid is much more restricted than that. If we can be very helpful without much cost to us, we should do so—yet we will not consent to being *forced* to do so.

On the other hand, there is good reason to consider arrangements whereby many people agree each to pay for the operations of the others, should need arise, for example, by paying a certain set sum each month. That is precisely what insurance systems do, and they make perfect sense. But they in no way involve the involuntary duties considered in the foregoing. The fact of their availability in principle, however, makes a huge difference to arguments about welfare. It is not rational to sign up for an "insurance" pact from which you are certain to lose. Agreement to pay for operations by fellow "members" who didn't pay, didn't even have to join, and will never be any use to the ones who do pay makes no sense. Hardly fit material for a rational agreement!

Now consider the choice between (1) knowing that I will be forced to help others whom I wouldn't choose to help if I had my choice, with all others, in turn, being similarly forced to help me; and (2) knowing that our right to use our resources as we judge best, without interference by others, will always be respected, even though we also know that we won't *necessarily* be helped by others when the chips are down (i.e., nobody will *force* them to help). Is it obvious that everyone would take (1) rather than (2)? Certainly not. But that is not all. For to (2) let us add the knowledge that people are generally well-disposed toward their fellows and inclined to help when they can, and, of course, that no one may prevent them from helping when they are so inclined; add the fact that one has the right to refuse unwanted help, and you have a package that dominates the alternatives. Any supposed advantage that anyone might derive from being a beneficiary is utterly negated by his also being a forced contributor, whatever he might have preferred to do with his life.

How do we know, though, that this argument really holds? There are two points. First, it has to be noted that if most people were not at least disposed to be charitable, they also would not choose the welfare state in a social contract. But if there are enough votes to legislate the welfare state, then there must be so many charitable people out there that they can easily fulfill welfare needs without forcing their neighbors to help: most will help in any case.

Most have conceived the social contract as being concerned only with enforceable duties, that is, with strict justice. But that is a mistake. There are such things as public attitudes as well. In opting for the carrot rather than the stick in matters relating to welfare, what we are opting for is a public resolution that all will prefer that others be well-off to their being badly off, apart from any personal relation they may have to those others. That is to say, the way we should regard each other *qua* fellow persons, rather than in more local capacities such as fellow inhabitant of this part of town or fellow believer in the same religion, is not as indifferent pieces of furniture but as fellow humans trying to live good lives, and we are more likely to do so if people are well-disposed than if they are ill-disposed. This kind of disposition costs us little, after all. We do not take on a great burden when we agree that, all else being at least roughly equal, it is a better thing that Jones or Smith do well than badly, and to be disposed—but not conscripted—to lend an occasional hand or an occasional dollar if need be.

If by contrast we take the welfare-state option, it would mean that others over whom you have no control would be authorized to decide that a sizable fraction of your money will be spent on "the poor," whatever you may have wanted to do with it if you had your own way. Empirical considerations add to the case. Welfare expenditures tend to be counterproductive, discouraging or even effectively preventing the recipient from working, and thus from acquiring useful skills. And those who do not work when they might leave us as well as themselves with a lesser array of goods and services than we would otherwise enjoy. . . .

According to James Sterba, libertarians, far from being committed to the free market and the absence of welfare legislation as I have suggested, "must endorse a welfare system." He arrives at this conclusion in the following way. Consider, he says, "a typical conflict situation between the rich and the poor. In this situation, the rich have more than enough goods and resources to satisfy their basic needs."

In such a situation, he thinks, "What is at stake is the liberty of the poor not to be interfered with in taking from the surplus possessions of the rich what is necessary to satisfy their basic needs." The rich, he says, have "more than enough," while the poor do not. So if we stop the latter from taking from the former, we deny them liberty. There is, he thinks, a "conflict of liberties" here, those of the rich vs. those of the poor.

Whether you are at liberty is a question of whether people restrict you from doing as you would like to do. But some restrictions may be made in the interests of liberty, and others not—that is the whole point of talking of a right to liberty, since rights, as such, restrict. Now, the "rich" in his argument, we are assuming, got where they are by fair means: they always acquired only by finding what was previously unowned, or by making things out of what they found, or by trading things got by one of those ways, or by other liberty-respecting trades, with others on mutually agreed terms. Whenever anyone has done so, he has satisfied the condition that his activities do not, as such, interfere with the activities of anyone else. They are harmonious. Now along come the poor with their proposal to take from the rich, and to do so without an agreement by the latter to have them do so. What the rich have is acquired in the ways noted; thus the poor do not have a right to take anything from them, so far as the right to liberty only is concerned. Whether they have such a right has nothing to do with how much they need the things in question. But it has everything to do with the fundamental moral agreement among us all: do we let each other live in peace, or don't we? The rich whom we are considering in this argument do not make war on anyone, poor or otherwise, in the process of getting rich. How, then, can Sterba imagine that what we have here is a "conflict of liberties" which cannot be decided on libertarian grounds? If his specifications are strictly observed, then the rich in question have the right to refuse to allow the poor to take what they need, and the poor, presumably, will starve.

Sterba thinks, of course, that it would be "unreasonable" to ask the poor to accept a principle such as I have been advocating. It is not clear whether he thinks this to be a distinct issue from the issue of what a liberty principle, of the type I have been supporting, as such implies. If we stick to the latter question, it is plain that the liberty principle does not imply that the poor have a right, *qua* right of liberty, to do what he describes. They do, of course, have a right to ask, and the rich a right to give as well as refuse.

Now, Aquinas supposed that the poor taking from the rich in such cases wouldn't even be theft; perhaps Sterba is following in his footsteps here. But that is surely just special pleading on Aquinas' part; it seems clearly to be a question of whether the theft in question is somehow excusable, and not whether it is theft at all.

That it is "unreasonable" to ask people to accept that principle is plainly a discussable claim. Is it unreasonable? I think not. On the contrary, welfarism, which makes everyone in principle a slave to anyone in need, is unreasonable. Welfarism taken to the extreme of socialism is an invitation to the productive to cease producing, since they are not allowed to enjoy the fruits of their labor, except in the special case where they are Mother Theresa. But the principles of morals are not made for Mother Theresa: They are made for us all.

On the very different, but certainly important, question of whether the poor would do better in a libertarian society where people have rights to their property, or in a welfare liberal society where, in effect, they do not, it is not clear what our terms of reference are. But insofar as we can point to real-world cases, certainly the evidence is overwhelmingly on the side of the libertarians. In Mao's China, as we now know, tens of millions of people starved to death; in America, cases of actual starvation, even during the days when it was pretty nearly a "libertarian" country, were extremely rare. If we are permitted to equip the information base of the poor with facts like that, the appearance of unreason will surely diminish drastically. Giving people the right to get rich if they can assures us that the social world will be well equipped with people who can feed the hungry should they need feeding; and people being what they are, it is extremely unlikely that persons in need will go long without, with all those wealthy persons' doors to knock on.

The welfare liberal "guarantee" is a delusion. All you can guarantee is that the people who are done down will indeed be done down. But as to a guarantee that people who would otherwise starve will not starve—which is what the socialist claims to be offering us—it is hollow. Absence of starvation is a function of ample supply and some generous hearts. Only libertarianism actually gets us the former, and the latter is the only real refuge for those genuinely in need. The efficacy of both depends on security of property and freedom of exchange. Systems biased toward the incapable are systems that perpetuate poverty, with no compensating advantages.

Concluding Note

The position here advocated takes on, I suppose, the heaviest burden of proof in the field. On the one hand, it disavows any appeal to transcendental considerations in its defense of liberty—including a priori impositions on what the people who are party to the social contract may believe. On the other hand, it refuses to assume that we *must* sign some social contract or other. Everything needs to be supported, nothing simply assumed. Yet this is a burden of proof that can be borne. The appeal of social life for everyone is so enormous that our motivation to accept the terms proposed here greatly exceeds any interest in remaining outside. What we would sign for, I have argued, is, purely and simply, liberty—not, for instance, a package of handouts from our hapless fellows. Your private club or religion, and certainly your marriage or your job, may indeed involve much more. The advantage of liberty in that respect is precisely that it leaves the widest possible array of such further involvements open to all who, together with willing others, are ready to take them on. Precisely what makes that possible is the exclusion of arrangements that press unwilling participants into the act.

My argument, then, does not *presuppose* the libertarian scheme of rights. Instead it argues for those rights, by showing that that scheme of rights can be expected to work out better for every reasonable person, if applied uniformly to all, than any alternative scheme. That is why we should support strong rights of individual liberty rather than schemes imposing involuntary duties for the alleged benefit of the public, on shaky or confused grounds. The best politics, in short, is no politics.

NOTES

1. Mill, *On Liberty,* Ch. IV, 3rd paragraph.
2. The central source is David Gauthier, *Morals by Agreement* (New York: Oxford University Press, 1986).

3. Anthony De Jasay, *Social Contract, Free Ride* (New York: Oxford University Press, 1989) distinguishes three sorts of contract: the "spot" contract, where performance is essentially immediate for both parties, the "half-forward" contract where one acts significantly before the other, and the "fully forward" contract where both act in the medium to far future. Of these, only the second poses a major problem; it is my standard model, though he is right to point out that the others are at least as frequent. See 22–25 for starters.

4. See Jan Narveson, *The Libertarian Idea* (Philadelphia: Temple University Press, 1988).

5. Hobbes, *Leviathan,* Ch. XIV.

6. The author's unpublished study, "Property Rights, Original Acquisition, and Lockean Provisos," read at the meetings of the Canadian Philosophical Association. Calgary, Alberta, June 1994, goes into this at length. See also the exposition in *The Libertarian Idea,* Chs. 6–8.

Part III

Socialist Justice

5 The Socialist Ideal

KARL MARX AND FRIEDRICH ENGELS

A SPECTRE IS HAUNTING EUROPE—the spectre of Communism. All the Powers of old Europe have entered into a holy alliance to exorcise this spectre: Pope and Czar, Metternich and Guizot, French Radicals and German police-spies.

Where is the party in opposition that has not been decried as Communistic by its opponents in power? Where the Opposition that has not hurled back the branding reproach of Communism, against the more advanced opposition parties, as well as against its reactionary adversaries?

Two things result from this fact.

I. Communism is already acknowledged by all European Powers to be itself a Power.

II. It is high time that Communists should openly, in the face of the whole world, publish their views, their aims, their tendencies, and meet this nursery tale of the Spectre of Communism with a Manifesto of the party itself. . . .

The Communist Program

The Communists do not form a separate party opposed to other working-class parties.

They have no interests separate and apart from those of the proletariat as a whole.

They do not set up any sectarian principles of their own, by which to shape and mould the proletarian movement.

The Communists are distinguished from the other working-class parties by this only: (1) In the national struggles of the proletarians of the different countries, they point out and bring to the front the common interests of the entire proletariat, independently of all nationality. (2) In the various stages of development which the struggle of the working class against the bourgeoisie has to pass through they always and everywhere represent the interests of the movement as a whole.

The Communists, therefore, are on the one hand, practically, the most advanced and resolute section of the working-class parties of every country, that section which pushes forward all others; on the other hand, theoretically, they have over the great mass of the proletariat the advantage of clearly understanding the line of march, the conditions and the ultimate general results of the proletarian movement.

The immediate aim of the Communists is the same as that of all the other proletarian parties: formation of the proletariat into a class, overthrow of the bourgeois supremacy, conquest of political power by the proletariat.

The theoretical conclusions of the Communists are in no way based on ideas or principles that have been invented, or discovered, by this or that would-be universal reformer.

They merely express, in general terms, actual relations springing from an existing class struggle, from a historical movement going on under our very eyes. The abolition of existing property relations is not at all a distinctive feature of Communism.

From the Communist Manifesto, *first published in English by Friedrich Engels in 1888, and the* Critique of the Gotha Program, *edited by C. P. Dutt (1966), pp. 5–11. Reprinted by permission of International Publishers.*

All property relations in the past have continually been subject to historical change consequent upon the change in historical conditions.

The French Revolution, for example, abolished feudal property in favour of bourgeois property.

The distinguishing feature of Communism is not the abolition of property generally, but the abolition of bourgeois property. But modern bourgeois private property is the final and most complete expression of the system of producing and appropriating products, that is based on class antagonisms, on the exploitation of the many by the few.

In this sense, the theory of the Communists may be summed up in the single sentence: Abolition of private property.

We Communists have been reproached with the desire of abolishing the right of personally acquiring property as the fruit of man's own labour, which property is alleged to be the groundwork of all personal freedom, activity and independence.

Hard-won, self-acquired, self-earned property! Do you mean the property of the petty artisan and of the small peasant, a form of property that preceded the bourgeois form? There is no need to abolish that; the development of industry has to a great extent already destroyed it, and is still destroying it daily.

Or do you mean modern bourgeois private property?

But does wage-labour create any property for the labourer? Not a bit. It creates capital, *i.e.,* that kind of property which exploits wage-labour, and which cannot increase except upon condition of begetting a new supply of wage-labour for fresh exploitation. Property, in its present form, is based on the antagonism of capital and wage-labour. Let us examine both sides of this antagonism.

To be capitalist, is to have not only a purely personal, but a social *status* in production. Capital is a collective product, and only by the united action of many members, nay, in the last resort, only by the united action of all members of society, can it be set in motion.

Capital is, therefore, not a personal, it is a social power.

When, therefore, capital is converted into common property, into the property of all members of society, personal property is not thereby transformed into social property. It is only the social character of the property that is changed. It loses its class-character.

Let us now take wage-labour.

The average price of wage-labour is the minimum wage, *i.e.,* that quantum of the means of subsistence, which is absolutely requisite to keep the labourer in bare existence as a labourer. What, therefore, the wage-labourer appropriates by means of his labour, merely suffices to prolong and reproduce a bare existence. We by no means intend to abolish this personal appropriation of the products of labour, an appropriation that is made for the maintenance and reproduction of human life, and that leaves no surplus wherewith to command the labour of others. All that we want to do away with, is the miserable character of this appropriation, under which the labourer lives merely to increase capital, and is allowed to live only in so far as the interest of the ruling class requires it.

In bourgeois society, living labour is but a means to increase accumulated labour. In Communist society, accumulated labour is but a means to widen, to enrich, to promote the existence of the labourer.

In bourgeois society, therefore, the past dominates the present; in Communist society, the present dominates the past. In bourgeois society capital is independent and has individuality, while the living person is dependent and has no individuality.

And the abolition of this state of things is called by the bourgeois, abolition of individuality and freedom! And rightly so. The abolition of bourgeois individuality, bourgeois independence, and bourgeois freedom is undoubtedly aimed at.

By freedom is meant, under the present bourgeois conditions of production, free trade, free selling and buying.

But if selling and buying disappears, free selling and buying disappears also. This talk about free selling and buying, and all the other "brave words" of our bourgeoisie about freedom in general, have a meaning, if any, only in contrast with restricted selling and buying, with the fettered traders of the Middle Ages, but have no meaning when opposed to the Communistic abolition of buying and selling, of the bourgeois conditions of production, and of the bourgeoisie itself.

You are horrified at our intending to do away with private property. But in your existing society, private property is already done away with for nine-tenths of the population; its existence for the few is solely due to its non-existence in the hands of those nine-tenths. You reproach us, therefore, with intending to do away with a form of property, the necessary condition for whose existence is the non-existence of any property for the immense majority of society.

In one word, you reproach us with intending to do away with your property. Precisely so; that is just what we intend.

From the moment when labour can no longer be converted into capital, money, or rent, into a social power capable of being monopolised, *i.e.*, from the moment when individual property can no longer be transformed into bourgeois property, into capital, from that moment, you say, individuality vanishes.

You must, therefore, confess that by "individual" you mean no other person than the bourgeois, than the middle-class owner of property. This person must, indeed, be swept out of the way, and made impossible.

Communism deprives no man of the power to appropriate the products of society; all that it does is to deprive him of the power to subjugate the labour of others by means of such appropriation.

It has been objected that upon the abolition of private property all work will cease, and universal laziness will overtake us.

According to this, bourgeois society ought long ago to have gone to the dogs through sheer idleness; for those of its members who work, acquire nothing, and those who acquire anything, do not work. The whole of this objection is but another expression of the tautology: that there can no longer be any wage-labour when there is no longer any capital.

All objections urged against the Communistic mode of producing and appropriating material products, have, in the same way, been urged against the Communistic modes of producing and appropriating intellectual products. Just as, to the bourgeois, the disappearance of class property is the disappearance of production itself, so the disappearance of class culture is to him identical with the disappearance of all culture.

That culture, the loss of which he laments, is, for the enormous majority, a mere training to act as a machine.

But don't wrangle with us so long as you apply, to our intended abolition of bourgeois property, the standard of your bourgeois notions of freedom, culture, law, [and so on]. Your very ideas are but the outgrowth of the conditions of your bourgeois production and bourgeois property, just as your jurisprudence is but the will of your class made into a law for all, a will, whose essential character and direction are determined by the economical conditions of existence of your class.

The selfish misconception that induces you to transform into eternal laws of nature and reason, the social forms springing from your present mode of production and form of property—historical relations that rise and disappear in the progress of production—this misconception you share with every ruling class that has preceded you. What you see clearly in the case of ancient property, what you admit in the case of feudal property, you are of course forbidden to admit in the case of your own bourgeois form of property.

Abolition of the family! Even the most radical flare up at this infamous proposal of the Communists.

On what foundation is the present family, the bourgeois family, based? On capital, on private gain. In its completely developed form this family exists only among the bourgeoisie. But this state of things finds its complement in the practical absence of the family among the proletarians, and in public prostitution.

The bourgeois family will vanish as a matter of course when its complement vanishes, and both will vanish with the vanishing of capital.

Do you charge us with wanting to stop the exploitation of children by their parents? To this crime we plead guilty.

But, you will say, we destroy the most hallowed of relations, when we replace home education by social.

And your education! Is not that also social, and determined by the social conditions under which you educate, by the intervention, direct or indirect, of society, by means of schools, [and so on]? The Communists have not invented the intervention of society in education; they do but seek to alter the character of that intervention, and to rescue education from the influence of the ruling class.

The bourgeois clap-trap about the family and education, about the hallowed co-relation of parent and child, becomes all the more disgusting, the more, by the action of Modern Industry, all family ties among the proletarians are torn asunder, and their children transformed into simple articles of commerce and instruments of labour.

But you Communists would introduce community of women, screams the whole bourgeoisie in chorus.

The bourgeois sees in his wife a mere instrument of production. He hears that the instruments of production are to be exploited in common, and, naturally, can come to no other conclusion than that the lot of being common to all will likewise fall to the women.

He has not even a suspicion that the real point aimed at is to do away with the status of women as mere instruments of production.

For the rest, nothing is more ridiculous than the virtuous indignation of our bourgeois at the community of women which, they pretend, is to be openly and officially established by the Communists. The Communists have no need to introduce community of women; it has existed almost from time immemorial.

Our bourgeois, not content with having the wives and daughters of their proletarians at their disposal, not to speak of common prostitutes, take the greatest pleasure in seducing each other's wives.

Bourgeois marriage is in reality a system of wives in common and thus, at the most, what the Communists might possibly be reproached with, is that they desire to introduce, in substitution for a hypocritically concealed, an openly legalised community of women. For the rest, it is self-evident that the abolition of the present system of production must bring with it the abolition of the community of women springing from that system, *i.e.*, of prostitution both public and private.

The Communists are further reproached with desiring to abolish countries and nationality.

The working men have no country. We cannot take from them what they have not got. Since the proletariat must first of all acquire political supremacy, must rise to be the leading class of the nation, must constitute itself *the* nation, it is, so far, itself national, though not in the bourgeois sense of the word.

National differences and antagonisms between peoples are daily more and more vanishing, owing to the development of the bourgeoisie, to freedom of commerce, to the world-market, to uniformity in the mode of production and in the conditions of life corresponding thereto.

The supremacy of the proletariat will cause them to vanish still faster. United action, of the leading civilised countries at least, is one of the first conditions for the emancipation of the proletariat.

In proportion as the exploitation of one individual by another is put an end to, the exploitation of one nation by another will also be put an end to. In proportion as the antagonism between classes within the nation vanished, the hostility of one nation to another will come to an end.

The charges against Communism made from a religious, a philosophical, and, generally, from an ideological standpoint, are not deserving of serious examination.

Does it require deep intuition to comprehend that man's ideas, views and conceptions, in one word, man's consciousness, changes with every change in the conditions of his material existence, in his social relations and in his social life?

What else does the history of ideas prove, than that intellectual production changes its character in proportion as material production is changed? The ruling ideas of each age have ever been the ideas of its ruling class.

When people speak of ideas that revolutionise society, they do but express the fact, that within the old society, the elements of a new one have been created, and that the dissolution of the old ideas keeps even pace with the dissolution of the old conditions of existence.

When the ancient world was in its last throes, the ancient religions were overcome by Christianity. When Christian ideas succumbed in the 18th century to rationalist ideas, feudal society fought its death battle with the then revolutionary bourgeoisie. The ideas of religious liberty and freedom of conscience merely gave expression to the sway of free competition within the domain of knowledge.

"Undoubtedly," it will be said, "religious, moral, philosophical and juridical ideas have been modified in the course of historical development. But religion, morality, philosophy, political science, and law, constantly survived this change."

"There are, besides, eternal truths, such as Freedom, Justice, etc., that are common to all states of society. But Communism abolishes eternal truths, it abolishes all religion, and all morality, instead of constituting them on a new basis; it therefore acts in contradiction to all past historical experience."

What does this accusation reduce itself to? The history of all past society has consisted in the development of class antagonisms, antagonisms that assumed different forms at different epochs.

But whatever form they may have taken, one fact is common to all past ages, *viz.*, the exploitation of one part of society by the other. No wonder, then, that the social consciousness of past ages, despite all the multiplicity and variety it displays, moves within certain common forms, or general ideas, which cannot completely vanish except with the total disappearance of class antagonisms.

The Communist revolution is the most radical rupture with traditional property relations; no wonder that its development involves the most radical rupture with traditional ideas.

But let us have done with the bourgeois objections to Communism.

We have seen above, that the first step in the revolution by the working class, is to raise the proletariat to the position of ruling class, to win the battle of democracy.

The proletariat will use its political supremacy to wrest, by degrees, all capital from the bourgeoisie, to centralise all instruments of production in the hands of the State, *i.e.*, of the proletariat organised as the ruling class; and to increase the total of productive forces as rapidly as possible.

Of course, in the beginning, this cannot be effected except by means of despotic inroads on the rights of property, and on the conditions of bourgeois production; by means of measures, therefore, which appear economically insufficient and untenable, but which, in the course of the movement, outstrip themselves, necessitate further inroads upon the old social order, and are unavoidable as a means of entirely revolutionising the mode of production.

These measures will of course be different in different countries.

Nevertheless in the most advanced countries, the following will be pretty generally applicable.

1. Abolition of property in land and application of all rents of land to public purposes.
2. A heavy progressive or graduated income tax.
3. Abolition of all right of inheritance.
4. Confiscation of the property of all emigrants and rebels.
5. Centralisation of credit in the hands of the State, by means of a national bank with State capital and an exclusive monopoly.

6. Centralisation of the means of communication and transport in the hands of the State.

7. Extension of factories and instruments of production owned by the State; the bringing into cultivation of waste-lands, and the improvement of the soil generally in accordance with a common plan.

8. Equal liability of all to labour. Establishment of industrial armies, especially for agriculture.

9. Combination of agriculture with manufacturing industries; gradual abolition of the distinction between town and country, by a more equable distribution of the population over the country.

10. Free education for all children in public schools. Abolition of children's factory labour in its present form. Combination of education with industrial production [and so on].

When, in the course of development, class distinctions have disappeared, and all production has been concentrated in the hands of a vast association of the whole nation, the public power will lose its political character. Political power, properly so called, is merely the organized power of one class for oppressing another. If the proletariat during its contest with the bourgeoisie is compelled, by the force of circumstances, to organise itself as a class, if, by means of a revolution, it makes itself the ruling class, and, as such, sweeps away by force the old conditions of production, then it will, along with these conditions, have swept away the conditions for the existence of class antagonisms and of class generally, and will thereby have abolished its own supremacy as a class.

In place of the old bourgeois society, with its classes and class antagonisms, we shall have an association, in which the free development of each is the condition for the free development of all. . . .

Critique of Social Democracy

In present-day society, the instruments of labour are the monopoly of the capitalist class; the resulting dependence of the working class is the cause of misery and servitude in all its forms.

This sentence, borrowed from the Statutes of the International, is incorrect in this "improved" edition.

In present-day society the instruments of labour are the monopoly of the landowners (the monopoly of property in land is even the basis of the monopoly of capital) *and* the capitalists. In the passage in question, the Statutes of the International do not mention by name either the one or the other class of monopolists. They speak of the *"monopoly of the means of labour, that is the sources of life."* The addition, *"sources of life,"* makes it sufficiently clear that land is included in the instruments of labour.

The correction was introduced because Lassalle, for reasons now generally known, attacked *only* the capitalist class and not the landowners. In England, the capitalist is usually not even the owner of the land on which his factory stands.

> The emancipation of labour demands the promotion of the instruments of labour to the common property of society, and the co-operative regulation of the total labour with equitable distribution of the proceeds of labour.

"Promotion of the instruments of labour to the common property" ought obviously to read, their "conversion into the common property," but this only in passing.

What are the "proceeds of labour"? The product of labour or its value? And in the latter case, is it the total value of the product or only that part of the value which labour has newly added to the value of the means of production consumed?

The "proceeds of labour" is a loose notion which Lassalle has put in the place of definite economic conceptions.

What is "equitable distribution"?

Do not the bourgeois assert that the present-day distribution is "equitable"? And is it not, in fact, the only "equitable" distribution on the basis of the present-day mode of production? Are economic relations regulated by legal conceptions or do not, on the contrary, legal relations arise from economic ones? Have not also the socialist sectarians the most varied notions about "equitable" distribution?

To understand what idea is meant in this connection by the phrase "equitable distribution," we must take the first paragraph and this one together. The latter implies a society wherein "the instruments of labour are common property, and the total labour is co-operatively regulated," and from the first paragraph we learn that "the proceeds of labour belong undiminished with equal right to all members of society."

"To all members of society"? To those who do not work as well? What remains then of the "undiminished proceeds of labour"? Only to those members of society who work? What remains then of the "equal right" of all members of society?

But "all members of society" and "equal right" are obviously mere phrases. The kernel consists in this, that in this communist society every worker must receive the "undiminished" Lassallean "proceeds of labour."

Let us take first of all the words "proceeds of labour" in the sense of the product of labour, then the co-operative proceeds of labour are the *total social product*.

From this is then to be deducted:

First, cover for replacement of the means of production used up.

Secondly, additional portion for expansion of production.

Thirdly, reserve or insurance fund to provide against mis-adventures, disturbances through natural events, etc.

These deductions from the "undiminished proceeds of labour" are an economic necessity and their magnitude is to be determined by available means and forces, and partly by calculation of probabilities, but they are in no way calculable by equity.

There remains the other part of the total product, destined to serve as means of consumption.

Before this is divided among the individuals, there has to be deducted from it:

First, the general costs of administration not belonging to production.

This part will, from the outset, be very considerably restricted in comparison with present-day society and it diminishes in proportion as the new society develops.

Secondly, that which is destined for the communal satisfaction of needs, such as schools, health services, etc.

From the outset this part is considerably increased in comparison with present-day society and it increases in proportion as the new society develops.

Thirdly, funds for those unable to work, etc., in short, what is included under so-called official poor relief today.

Only now do we come to the "distribution" which the programme, under Lassallean influence, alone has in view in its narrow fashion, namely that part of the means of consumption which is divided among the individual producers of the co-operative society.

The "undiminished proceeds of labour" have already quietly become converted into the "diminished" proceeds, although what the producer is deprived of in his capacity as a private individual benefits him directly or indirectly in his capacity as a member of society.

Just as the phrase "undiminished proceeds of labour" has disappeared, so now does the phrase "proceeds of labour" disappear altogether.

Within the co-operative society based on common ownership of the means of production, the producers do not exchange their products; just as little does the labour employed on the products appear here *as the value* of these products, as a material quality possessed by them, since now, in contrast to capitalist society, individual labour no longer exists in an indirect fashion but directly as a component part of the total labour. The phrase "proceeds of labour," objectionable even today on account of its ambiguity, thus loses all meaning.

What we have to deal with here is a communist society, not as it has *developed* on its own foundations, but, on the contrary, as it *emerges* from capitalist society; which is thus in every respect, economically, morally and intellectually, still stamped with the birthmarks of the old society from whose womb it emerges. Accordingly the individual producer receives back from society—after the deductions have been made—exactly what he gives to it. What he has given to it is his individual amount of labour. For example, the social working day consists of the sum of the individual labour hours; the individual labour time of the individual producer is the part of the social labour day contributed by him, his share in it. He receives a certificate from society that he has furnished such and such an amount of labour (after deducting his labour for the common fund), and with this certificate he draws from the social stock of means of consumption as much as the same amount of labour costs. The same amount of labour which he has given to society in one form, he receives back in another.

Here obviously the same principle prevails as that which regulates the exchange of commodities, as far as this is exchange of equal values. Content and form are changed, because under the altered circumstances no one can give anything except his labour, and because, on the other hand, nothing can pass into the ownership of individuals except individual means of consumption. But, as far as the distribution of the latter among the individual producers is concerned, the same principle prevails as in the exchange of commodity-equivalents, so much labour in one form is exchanged for an equal amount of labour in another form.

Hence, *equal right* here is still in principle—*bourgeois right*, although principle and practice are no longer in conflict, while the exchange of equivalents in commodity exchange only exists on the *average* and not in the individual case.

In spite of this advance, this *equal right* is still stigmatised by a bourgeois limitation. The right of the producers is *proportional* to the labour they supply; the equality consists in the fact that measurement is made with an *equal standard*, labour.

But one man is superior to another physically or mentally and so supplies more labour in the same time, or can labour for a longer time; and labour, to serve as a measure, must be defined by its duration or intensity, otherwise it ceases to be a standard of measurement. This *equal* right is an unequal right for unequal labour. It recognises no class differences, because everyone is only a worker like everyone else; but it tacitly recognises unequal individual endowment and thus productive capacity as natural privileges. *It is therefore a right of inequality in its content, like every right.* Right by its very nature can only consist in the application of an equal standard; but unequal individuals (and they would not be different individuals if they were not unequal) are only measurable by an equal standard in so far as they are brought under an equal point of view, are taken from one *definite* side only, *e.g.,* in the present case are regarded *only as workers,* and nothing more seen in them, everything else being ignored. Further, one worker is married, another not; one has more children than another and so on and so forth. Thus with an equal output, and hence an equal share in the social consumption fund, one will in fact receive more than another, one will be richer than another, and so on. To avoid all these defects, right, instead of being equal, would have to be unequal.

But these defects are inevitable in the first phase of communist society as it is when it has just emerged after prolonged birth pangs from capitalist society. Right can never be higher than the economic structure of society and the cultural development thereby determined.

In a higher phase of communist society, after the enslaving subordination of individuals under division of labour, and therewith also the antithesis between mental and physical labour, has vanished; after labour, from a mere means of life, has itself become the prime necessity of life; after the productive forces have also increased with the all-round development of the individual, and all the springs of co-operative wealth flow more abundantly—only then can the narrow horizon of bourgeois right be fully left behind and society inscribe on its banners: from each according to his ability, to each according to his needs!

I have dealt more at length with the "undiminished proceeds of labour" on the one hand, and with "equal right" and "equitable distribution" on the other, in order to show what a crime it is to attempt, on the one hand, to force on our party again, as dogmas, ideas which in a certain period had some meaning but have now become obsolete rubbishy phrases, while on the other, perverting the realistic outlook, which has cost so much effort to instill into the party, but which has now taken root in it, by means of ideological nonsense about "right" and other trash common among the democrats and French Socialists.

Quite apart from the analysis so far given, it was in general incorrect to make a fuss about so-called "*distribution*" and put the principal stress on it.

The distribution of the means of consumption at any time is only a consequence of the distribution of the conditions of production themselves. The latter distribution, however, is a feature of the mode of production itself. The capitalist mode of production, for example, rests on the fact that the material conditions of production are in the hands of non-workers in the form of property in capital and land, while the masses are only owners of the personal condition of production, *viz.*, labour power. Once the elements of production are so distributed, then the present-day distribution of the means of consumption results automatically. If the material conditions of production are the co-operative property of the workers themselves, then this likewise results in a different distribution of the means of consumption from the present one. Vulgar socialism (and from it in turn a section of democracy) has taken over from the bourgeois economists the consideration and treatment of distribution as independent of the mode of production and hence the presentation of socialism as turning principally on distribution. After the real position has long been made clear, why go back again?

6 Justice Under Socialism

EDWARD NELL AND ONORA O'NEILL

"From each according to his ability, to each according to his need."

THE STIRRING SLOGAN THAT ENDS *The Critique of the Gotha Program* is generally taken as a capsule summary of the socialist approach to distributing the burdens and benefits of life. It can be seen as the statement of a noble ideal and yet be found wanting on three separate scores. First, there is no guarantee that, even if all contribute according to their abilities, all needs can be met: the principle gives us no guidance for distributing goods when some needs must go unmet. Second, if all contribute according to their abilities, there may be a material surplus after all needs are met: again, the principle gives us no guidance for distributing such a surplus. Third, the principle incorporates no suggestion as to why each man would contribute according to his ability: no incentive structure is evident.

These apparent shortcomings can be compared with those of other principles a society might follow in distributing burdens and benefits. Let us call

1. "From each according to his ability, to each according to his need," the *Socialist Principle of Justice.*

Its Capitalist counterpart would be

2. From each according to his choice, given his assets, to each according to his contribution. We shall call this the *Laissez-Faire Principle.*

These two principles will require a good deal of interpretation, but at the outset we can say that in the Socialist Principle of Justice "abilities" and "needs" refer to persons, whereas the "choices" and "contributions" in the Laissez-Faire Principle refer also to the management of impersonal property, the given assets. It goes without saying that some of the "choices," particularly those of the propertyless, are normally made under considerable duress. As "choice" is the ideologically favored term, we shall retain it.

In a society where the Socialist Principle of Justice regulates distribution, the requirement is that everyone use such talents as have been developed in him (though this need not entail any allocation of workers to jobs), and the payment of workers is contingent not upon their contributions but upon their needs. In a laissez-faire society, where individuals may be endowed with more or less capital or with bare labor power, they choose in the light of these assets how and how much to work (they may be dropouts or moonlighters), and/or how to invest their capital, and they are paid in proportion.

None of the three objections raised against the Socialist Principle of Justice holds for the Laissez-Faire Principle. Whatever the level of contribution individuals choose, their aggregate product can be distributed in proportion to the contribution—whether of capital or of labor—each individual

From "Justice Under Socialism," Dissent, *Vol. 18 (1972), pp. 483–491. Reprinted by permission of the authors and Dissent Publishing Corporation.*

chooses to make. The Laissez-Faire Principle is applicable under situations both of scarcity and of abundance, and it incorporates a theory of incentives: people choose their level of contribution in order to get a given level of material reward.

Principles 1 and 2 can be crossfertilized, yielding two further principles:

3. From each according to his ability, to each according to his contribution.
4. From each according to his choice, to each according to his need.

Principle 3 could be called an *Incentive Socialist Principle* of distribution. Like the Socialist Principle of Justice, it pictures a society in which all are required to work in proportion to the talents that have been developed in them. Since unearned income is not available and rewards are hinged to contribution rather than need, all work is easily enforced in an economy based on the Incentive Socialist Principle. This principle, however, covers a considerable range of systems. It holds for a Stalinist economy with an authoritarian job allocation. It also holds for a more liberal, market socialist economy in which there is a more or less free labor market, though without an option to drop out or live on unearned income, or the freedom to choose the level and type of qualification one is prepared to acquire. The Incentive Socialist Principle rewards workers according to their contribution: it is a principle of distribution in which an incentive system—reliance on material rewards—is explicit. Marx believed this principle would have to be followed in the early stages of socialism, in a society "still stamped with the birthmarks of the old society."

Under the Incentive Socialist Principle, each worker receives back the value of the amount of work he contributes to society in one form or another. According to Marx, this is a form of bourgeois right that "tacitly recognizes unequal individual endowments, and thus natural privileges in respect of productive capacity." So this principle holds for a still deficient society where the needs of particular workers, which depend on many things other than their productive capacity, may

not be met. Although it may be less desirable than the Socialist Principle of Justice, the Incentive Socialist Principle clearly meets certain criteria the Socialist Principle of Justice cannot meet. It provides a principle of allocation that can be applied equally well to the various situations of scarcity, sufficiency, and abundance. Its material incentive structure explains how under market socialism, given a capital structure and a skill structure, workers will choose jobs and work hard at them—and also why under a Stalinist economy workers will work hard at jobs to which they have been allocated.

Under the Incentive Socialist Principle, workers—whether assigned to menial work or to specific jobs—respond to incentives of the same sort as do workers under the Laissez-Faire Principle. The difference is that, while the Laissez-Faire Principle leaves the measurement of the contribution of a worker to be determined by the level of wage he is offered, the Incentive Socialist Principle relies on a bureaucratically determined weighting that takes into account such factors as the difficulty, duration, qualification level, and risk involved in a given job.

There is another difference between societies living under the Laissez-Faire Principle and those following the Incentive Socialist Principle. Under the Laissez-Faire Principle, there is no central coordination of decisions, for assets are managed according to the choices of their owners. This gives rise to the well-known problems of instability and unemployment. Under the Incentive Socialist Principle, assets are managed by the central government; hence one would expect instability to be eliminated and full employment guaranteed. However, we do not regard this difference as a matter of principle on the same level with others we are discussing. Moreover, in practice some recognizable capitalist societies have managed to control fluctuations without undermining the Laissez-Faire Principle as the principle of distribution.

Let us call Principle 4 the *Utopian Principle of Justice*. It postulates a society without any requirement of contribution or material incentives, but with guaranteed minimal consumption. This principle suffers from the same defect as the Socialist Principle of Justice: it does not determine distributions of benefits under conditions either of scarcity or of abundance, and it suggests no incentive structure to explain why enough should be contributed to its economy to make it possible to satisfy needs. Whether labor is contributed according to choice or according to ability, it is conceivable that the aggregate social product should be such that either some needs cannot be met or that, when all needs are met, a surplus remains that cannot be divided on the basis of needs.

On the surface, this Utopian Principle of Justice exudes the aroma of laissez-faire: though needs will not go unmet in utopia, contributions will be made for no more basic reason than individual whim. They are tied neither to the reliable effects of the incentive of material reward for oneself, nor to those of the noble ideal of filling the needs of others, nor to a conception of duty or self-sacrifice. Instead, contributions will come forth, if they do, according to the free and unconstrained choices of individual economic agents, on the basis of their given preferences. Preferences, however, are not "given"; they develop and change, are learned and unlearned, and follow fashions and fads. Whim, fancy, pleasure, desire, wish are all words suggesting this aspect of consumer choice. By tying the demand for products to needs and the supply of work to choice, the Utopian Principle of Justice ensures stability in the former but does not legislate against fluctuations and unpredictable variability in the latter.

So the Socialist Principle of Justice and the Utopian Principle of Justice suffer from a common defect. There is no reason to suppose these systems will operate at precisely the level at which aggregate output is sufficient to meet all the needs without surplus. And since people do not need an income in money terms but rather an actual and quite precisely defined list of food, clothing, housing, etc. (bearing in mind the various alternatives that might be substituted), the *aggregate* measured in value terms could be right, yet the *composition* might still be unable to meet all the people's

needs. People might choose or have the ability to do the right amount of work, but on the wrong projects. One could even imagine the economy growing from a situation of scarcity to one of abundance without ever passing through any point at which its aggregate output could be distributed to meet precisely the needs of its population.

So far, we have been considering not the justification or desirability of alternative principles of distribution, but their practicality. It appears that, in this respect, principles hinging reward on contribution rather than on need have a great advantage. They can both provide a general principle of distribution and indicate the pattern of incentives to which workers will respond.

It might be held that these advantages are restricted to the Incentive Socialist Principle in its various versions, since under the Laissez-Faire Principle there is some income—property income—which is not being paid in virtue of any contribution. This problem can be dealt with either, as we indicated above, by interpreting the notion of contribution to cover the contribution of one's assets to the capital market, or by restricting the scope of the Laissez-Faire Principle to cover workers only, or by interpreting the notion of property income so as to regard wages as a return to property, i.e., property in one's labor power. One can say that under capitalism part of the aggregate product is set aside for the owners of capital (and another part, as under market socialism, for government expenditure) and the remainder is distributed according to the Laissez-Faire Principle. Or one may say that property income is paid in virtue of past contributions, whose reward was not consumed at the time it was earned but was stored. Apologists tend to favor interpretations that make the worker a sort of capitalist or the capitalist a sort of slow-consuming worker. Whichever line is taken, it is clear that the Laissez-Faire Principle—however undesirable we may find it—is a principle of distribution that can be of general use in two senses. Appropriately interpreted, it covers the distribution of earned and of unearned income, and it applies in situations both of scarcity and of abundance.

So we seem to have reached the paradoxical conclusion that the principle of distribution requiring that workers' needs be met is of no use in situations of need, since it does not assign priorities among needs, and that the principle demanding that each contribute according to his ability is unable to explain what incentives will lead him to do so. In this view, the Socialist Principle of Justice would have to be regarded as possibly noble but certainly unworkable.

The Socialist Principle Defended

But this view should not be accepted. Marx formulated the Socialist Principle of Justice on the basis of a conception of human abilities and needs that will yield some guidance to its interpretation. We shall now try to see whether the difficulties discussed above can be alleviated when we consider this principle in the light of Marxian theory.

Marx clearly thought that the Socialist Principle of Justice was peculiarly relevant to situations of abundance. In the last section we argued that, on the contrary, it was an adequate principle of distribution only when aggregate output exactly covered total needs. The source of this discrepancy lies in differing analyses of human needs.

By fulfillment of needs we understand at least a subsistence income. Needs are not met when a person lacks sufficient food, clothing, shelter, medical care, or socially necessary training/education. But beyond this biological and social minimum we can point to another set of needs, which men do not have qua men but acquire qua producers. Workers need not merely a biological and social minimum, but whatever other goods—be they holidays or contacts with others whose work bears on theirs or guaranteed leisure, which they need to perform their jobs as well as possible. So a principle of distribution according to needs will not be of use only to a subsistence-level economy. Very considerable goods over and above those necessary for biological subsistence can be distributed according to a principle of need.

But despite this extension of the concept of need the Socialist Principle of Justice still seems to face the three problems listed [earlier]:

1. What guarantees are there that even under abundance the *composition* of the output with all contributing according to their abilities, will suffice to fill all needs? (There may still be scarcities of goods needed to fill either biological or job-related needs.)
2. What principle can serve to distribute goods that are surplus both to biological and to job-related needs?
3. What system of incentives explains why each will contribute to the full measure of his abilities, though he is not materially rewarded for increments of effort? Whether or not there is authoritative job allocation, job performance cannot be guaranteed.

Marx's solution to these problems does not seem too explicit. But much is suggested by the passage at the end of the *Critique of the Gotha Program* where he describes the higher phase of communist society as one in which "labor is no longer merely a means of life but has become life's principal need."

To most people it sounds almost comic to claim that labor could become life's principal need: it suggests a society of compulsive workers. Labor in the common view is intrinsically undesirable, but undertaken as a means to some further, typically material, end. For Marx this popular view would have been confirmation of his own view of the degree to which most labor under capitalism is alienating. He thought that under capitalism laborers experienced a threefold alienation: alienation from the *product* of their labor, which is for them merely a means to material reward; alienation from the *process* of labor, which is experienced as forced labor rather than as desirable activity; and alienation from *others*, since activities undertaken with others are undertaken as a means to achieving further ends, which are normally scarce and allocated competitively. Laborers cooperate in production but, under capitalism, compete for job and income, and the competition overrides the cooperation. Hence Marx claims (in the *Economic and Philosophical Manuscripts*) that "life itself appears only as a means to life." Though the horror of that situation is apparent in the very words, many people accept that labor should be only a means to life—whose real ends lie elsewhere; whether in religion, consumption, personal relations, or leisure.

Marx, on the other hand, held that labor could be more than a means; it could also be an end of life, for labor in itself—*the activity*—can, like other activities, be something for whose sake one does other things. We would be loath to think that activity itself should appear only as a means to life—on the contrary, life's worth for most people lies in the activities undertaken. Those we call labor do not differ intrinsically from the rest, only in relation to the system of production. In Marx's view a system was possible in which all activities undertaken would be nonalienating. Nobody would have to compete to engage in an activity he found unpleasant for the sake of a material reward. Instead, workers would cooperate in creative and fulfilling activities that provide occasions for the experience of talents, for taking responsibilities, and that result in useful or beautiful products. In such a situation one can see why labor would be regarded as life's greatest need, rather than as its scourge. Nonalienated labor is humanly fulfilling activity.

In the course of switching from the conception of alienating labor to that of nonalienating labor, it might seem that we have moved into a realm for which principles of distribution may be irrelevant. What can the Socialist Principle of Justice tell us about the distribution of burdens and benefits in "the higher phase of Communist society?"

In such a society each is to contribute according to his abilities. In the light of the discussion of nonalienated labor, it is clear that there is no problem of incentives. Each man works at what he wants to work at. He works because that is his need. (This is not a situation in which "moral incentives" have replaced material ones, for both moral and material incentives are based on alienating labor. The situation Marx envisages is one for which incentives of *all* sorts are irrelevant.)

Though this disposes of the problem of incentives under the Socialist Principle of Justice, it is much less clear whether this principle can work for a reasonable range of situations. Can it cope with both the situation of abundance and that of scarcity?

In the case of abundance, a surplus of goods over and above those needed is provided. But if all activities are need-fulfilling, then no work is done that does not fulfill some need. In a sense there is no surplus to be distributed, for nothing needless is being done. Nevertheless, there may be a surplus of material goods that are the by-product of need-fulfilling activity. In a society where everybody fulfills himself by painting pictures, there may be a vast surplus of pictures. If so, the Socialist Principle of Justice gives no indication of the right method for their distribution; they are not the goal for which the task was undertaken. Since they do not fulfill an objective need, the method for their distribution is not important. In this the higher phase of communist society is, as one might expect, the very antithesis of consumerism; rather than fabricate reasons for desiring and so acquiring what is not needed, it disregards anything that is not needed in decisions of distribution.

There, nevertheless, is a problem of distribution the Socialist Principle of Justice does not attempt to solve. Some of the products of need-fulfilling activity may be things other people either desire or detest. When need-fulfilling activity yields works of art or noisy block parties, its distribution cannot be disregarded. Not all planning problems can be solved by the Socialist Principle of Justice. We shall not discuss the merits of various principles that could serve to handle these cases, but shall only try to delimit the scope of the Socialist Principle of Justice.

This brings us to the problem of scarcity. Can the Socialist Principle of Justice explain why, when all contribute to the extent of their abilities, all needs can be met? Isn't it conceivable that everyone should find fulfillment in painting, but nobody find fulfillment in producing either biological necessities or the canvases, brushes, and paints everybody wants to use? Might not incentive payments be needed, even in this higher phase of communist society, to guarantee the production of subsistence goods and job-related necessities? In short, will not any viable system involve some alienating labor?

Marx at any rate guarantees that communism need not involve much alienating labor. He insists that the Socialist Principle of Justice is applicable only in a context of abundance. For only when man's needs can be met is it relevant to insist that they ought to be met. The Socialist Principle of Justice comes into its own only with the development of the forces of production. But, of course, higher productivity does not by itself guarantee the right composition of output. Subsistence goods and job-related services and products might not be provided as the population fulfills itself in painting, poetry, and sculpture. Man cannot live by works of art alone.

This socialist version of the story of Midas should not alarm us too much. The possibility of starvation amidst abundant art works seemed plausible only because we abstracted it from other features of an abundant socialist society. Such a society is a planned society, and part of its planning concerns the ability structure of the population. Such a society would include people able to perform all tasks necessary to maintain a high level of material well-being.

Nevertheless, there may be certain essential tasks in such a society whose performance is not need-fulfilling for anybody. Their allocation presents another planning problem for which the Socialist Principle of Justice, by hypothesis, is not a solution. But the degree of coercion need not be very great. In a highly productive society the amount of labor expended on nonfulfilling tasks is a diminishing proportion of total labor time. Hence, given equitable allocation of this burden (and it is here that the planning decisions are really made), nobody would be prevented from en-

gaging principally in need-fulfilling activities. In the limiting case of abundance, where automation of the production of material needs is complete, nobody would have to do any task he did not find intrinsically worthwhile. To the extent that this abundance is not reached, the Socialist Principle of Justice cannot be fully implemented.

However, the degree of coercion experienced by those who are allocated to necessary but nonfulfilling chores may be reducible if the planning procedure is of a certain sort. To the extent that people participate in planning and that they realize the necessity of the nonfulfilling chores in order for everyone to be able to do also what he finds need-fulfilling, they may find the performance of these chores less burdensome. As they want to achieve the ends, so — once they are informed — they cannot rationally resent the means, provided they perceive the distribution of chores as just.

The point can be taken a step further. Under the Socialist Principle of Justice, households do not put forth productive effort to be rewarded with an aliquot portion of time and means for self-fulfillment. It is precisely this market mentality from which we wish to escape. The miserable toil of society should be

> performed gratis for the benefit of society . . . performed not as a definite duty, not for the purpose of obtaining a right to certain products, not according to previously established and legally fixed quotas, but voluntary labor . . . performed because it has become a habit to work for the common good, and because of a conscious realization (that has become a habit) of the necessity of working for the common good.[1]

Creative work should be done for its own sake, not for any reward. Drudgery should be done for the common good, not to be rewarded with opportunity and means for creative work. Of course, the better and more efficient the performance of drudgery, the more will be the opportunities for creative work. To realize this, however, is to understand the necessity of working for the common good, not to be animated by private material incentives. For the possibilities of creative work are opened by the simultaneous and parallel development of large numbers of people. To take the arts, poets need a public, authors readers, performers audiences, and all need (though few want) critics. One cannot sensibly wish, under the Socialist Principle of Justice, to be rewarded *privately* with opportunities and means for nonalienated work.

There is a question regarding the distribution of educational opportunities. Before men can contribute according to their abilities, their abilities must be developed. But in whom should society develop which abilities? If we regard education as consumption, then according to the Socialist Principle of Justice, each should receive it according to his need.

It is clear that all men require some early training to make them viable social beings; further, all men require certain general skills necessary for performing work. But we could hardly claim that some men need to be doctors or economists or lawyers, or need to receive any other specialized or expensive training. If, on the other hand, we regard education as production of those skills necessary for maintaining society and providing the possibility of fulfillment, then the Socialist Principle of Justice can determine a lower bound to the production of certain skills: so-and-so many farmers/doctors/mechanics must be produced to satisfy future subsistence and job-related needs. But the Socialist Principle of Justice cannot determine who shall get which of these educational opportunities. One traditional answer might be that each person should specialize at whatever he is relatively best suited to do. Yet this only makes sense in terms of tasks done as onerous means to desirable ends. Specialization on the basis of comparative advantage minimizes the effort in achieving given ends; but if work is itself fulfilling, it is not an "effort" that must be minimized.

In conditions of abundance, it is unlikely that anyone will be denied training they want and can absorb, though they may have to acquire skills they do not particularly want, since some onerous tasks may still have to be done. For even in conditions of abundance, it may be necessary to compel some or all to undertake certain unwanted training in the interests of the whole. But it is not necessary to supplement the Socialist Principle of Justice with an incentive scheme, whether material or moral. The principle already contains the Kantian maxim: develop your talents to the utmost, for only in this way can a person contribute to the limits of his ability. And if a society wills the end of self-fulfillment, it must will sufficient means. If the members of society take part in planning to maintain and expand the opportunities for everyone's nonalienated activity, they must understand the necessity of allocating the onerous tasks, and so the training for them.

Perhaps we can make our point clearer by looking briefly at Marx's schematic conception of the stages of modern history—feudalism, capitalism, socialism, communism—where each stage is characterized by a higher productivity of labor than the preceding stage. In feudalism, the principle of distribution would be:

5. From each according to his status, to each according to his status—the *Feudal Principles of Justice.*

There is no connection between work and reward. There are no market incentives in the "ideal" feudal system. Peasants grow the stuff for their own subsistence and perform traditional labor services for their lord on domain land. He in turn provides protection and government in traditional fashion. Yet, though labor is not performed as a means to a distant or abstract end, as when it is done for money, it still is done for survival, not for its own sake, and those who do it are powerless to control their conditions of work or their own destinies. Man lives on the edge of famine and is subject to the vagaries of the weather and the dominion of tradition. Only a massive increase in productive powers frees him. But to engender this increase men must come to connect work directly with reward. This provides the incentive to labor, both to take those jobs most needed (moving from the farm to the factory) and to work sufficiently hard once on the job.

But more than work is needed; the surplus of output over that needed to maintain the work force (including materials) and replace and repair the means of production (machines, raw materials) must be put to productive use; it must be reinvested, not consumed. In capitalism, station at birth determines whether one works or owns capital; workers are rewarded for their contribution of work, capitalists for theirs of reinvestment. There is a stick as well as a carrot. Those workers who do not work, starve; those capitalists who fail to reinvest, fail to grow and will eventually be crushed by their larger rivals. Socialism rationalizes this by eliminating the two-class dichotomy and by making reinvestment a function of the institutions of the state, so that the capital structure of the society is the collective property of the citizenry, all of whom must work for reward. In this system the connection between work and reward reaches its fullest development, and labor in one sense is most fully alienated. The transition to communism then breaks this link altogether.

The link between work and rewards serves a historical purpose; namely, to encourage the development of the productive forces. But as the productive forces continue to develop, the demand for additional rewards will tend to decline, while the difficulty of stimulating still further growth in productivity may increase. This at least, seems to be implied by the principles of conventional economics—diminishing marginal utility and diminishing marginal productivity. Even if one rejects most of the conventional wisdom of economics, a good case can be made for the diminishing efficacy of material incentives as prosperity increases. For as labor productivity rises, private consumption needs will be met, and the most urgent needs remaining will be those requiring *collective* consumption—and, indeed, some of these needs will be generated by the process of growth and technical progress. These last needs, if left unmet, may hinder further attempts to raise the productive power of labor. So the system of material incentives could in principle come to a point where the weakened encouragements to extra productivity offered as private reward for con-

tribution might be offset by the accumulated hindrances generated by the failures to meet collective needs and by the wastes involved in competition. At this point, it becomes appropriate to break the link between work and reward. Breaking the link, however, is not enough. Both the Socialist Principle of Justice and the Utopian Principle of Justice break the link between work and reward. But the Utopian Principle of Justice leaves the distinction between them. Work is a means, the products of work are the ends. Given a high productivity of labor, workers would in principle choose their occupations and work-leisure patterns, yet still producing enough to satisfy everyone's needs. This would be a society devoted to minimizing effort, a sort of high-technology Polynesia. Since it neither makes consumption dependent upon work nor regards work as other than a regrettable means to consumption, it fails to explain why sufficient work to supply basic needs should ever be done. The alienation of labor cannot be overcome by eliminating labor rather than alienation.

Breaking the link, between work and reward, while leaving the distinction itself intact, may also lead to the loss of the productive powers of labor. For without reward, and when the object is to work as little as possible, why expend the effort to acquire highly complex skills? What is the motive to education, self-improvement, self-development? A high-technology Polynesia contains an inner contradiction.

By contrast, the Socialist Principle of Justice not only does not make reward depend upon work but denies that there is a distinction between the two. Because man needs fulfilling activity—work that he chooses and wants—men who get it contribute according to their ability.

Yet there still may remain routine and menial, unfulfilling jobs. But who wills the end wills the means. The society must plan to have such jobs done. No doubt many will be mechanized or automated, but the remaining ones will form a burden that must be allocated.

The Socialist Principle of Justice cannot solve this problem of allocation. But everyone has some interest in getting uncoveted but essential work done. Hence it should not be difficult to find an acceptable supplementary principle of distribution for allocating these chores. For instance, the Principle of Comparative Advantage might be introduced to assign each the drudgery at which he is relatively best. There can be no quarrel with this so long as such alienating work is only a small fraction of a man's total activity, conferring no special status. It is only when alienating work takes up the bulk of one's waking hours, and determines status, that specialization inevitably entails some form of class structure.

The Socialist Principle of Justice cannot solve all allocation problems. But once one understands that it is based on a denial of a distinction between work, need, and reward, it is clear that it can solve an enormous range of such problems. In a highly productive society the only allocation problems the Socialist Principle of Justice cannot solve are the distribution of unmechanized and uncoveted chores and of the material by-products of creative endeavor.

NOTE

1. V. I. Lenin, "From the Destruction of the Old Social System to the Creation of the New," April 11, 1920. From *Collected Works,* English trans., 40 vols. (London: Lawrence & Wishart, 1965), vol. 30, p. 517.

7 Radical Egalitarianism

KAI NIELSON

I

I HAVE TALKED OF EQUALITY as a right and of equality as a goal. And I have taken, as the principal thing, to be able to state what goal we are seeking when we say equality is a goal. When we are in a position actually to achieve that goal, then that same equality becomes a right. The goal we are seeking is an equality of basic condition for everyone. Let me say a bit what this is: everyone, as far as possible, should have equal life prospects, short of genetic engineering and the like and the rooting out of any form of the family and the undermining of our basic freedoms. There should, where this is possible, be an equality of access to equal resources over each person's life as a whole, though this should be qualified by people's varying needs. Where psychiatrists are in short supply only people who are in need of psychiatric help should have equal access to such help. This equal access to resources should be such that it stands as a barrier to there being the sort of differences between people that allow some to be in a position to control and to exploit others; such equal access to resources should also stand as a barrier to one person having power over other adult persons that does not rest on the revokable consent on the part of the persons over whom he comes to have power. Where, because of some remaining scarcity in a society of considerable productive abundance, we cannot reasonably distribute resources equally, we should first, where considerations of desert are not at issue, distribute according to stringency of need, second according to the strength of unmanipulated preferences and third, and finally, by lottery. We should, in trying to attain equality of condition, aim at a condition of autonomy (the fuller and the more rational the better) for everyone and at a condition where everyone alike, to the fullest extent possible, has his or her needs and wants satisfied. The limitations on the satisfaction of people's wants should be only where the satisfaction is incompatible with everyone getting the same treatment. Where we have conflicting wants, such as where two persons want to marry the same person, the fair thing to do will vary with the circumstances. In the marriage case, freedom of choice is obviously the fair thing. But generally, what should be aimed at is having everyone have their wants satisfied as far as possible. To achieve equality of condition would be, as well, to achieve a condition where the necessary burdens of the society are equally shared, where to do so is reasonable, and where each person has an equal voice in deciding what these burdens shall be. Moreover, everyone, as much as possible, should be in a position—and should be equally in that position—to control his own life. The goals of egalitarianism are to achieve such equalities.

Minimally, classlessness is something we should all aim at if we are egalitarians. It is necessary for the stable achievement of equalities of the type discussed in the previous paragraph. Beyond that, we should also aim at a statusless society, though

Abridged from Equality and Liberty *(1985), pp. 283–292, 302–306, 309. Reprinted by permission of Rowman & Littlefield, Publishers. Notes renumbered.*

not at an undifferentiated society or a society which does not recognize merit. . . . It is only in such a classless, statusless society that the ideals of equality (the conception of equality as a very general goal to be achieved) can be realized. In aiming for a statusless society, we are aiming for a society which, while remaining a society of material abundance, is a society in which there are to be no extensive differences in life prospects between people because some have far greater income, power, authority or prestige than others. This is the *via negativa* of the egalitarian way. The *via positiva* is to produce social conditions, where there is generally material abundance, where well-being and satisfaction are not only maximized (the utilitarian thing) but, as well, a society where this condition, as far as it is achievable, is sought equally for all (the egalitarian thing). This is the underlying conception of the egalitarian commitment to equality of condition.

II

Robert Nozick asks, "How do we decide how much equality is enough?"[1] In the preceding section we gestured in the direction of an answer. I should now like to be somewhat more explicit. Too much equality, as we have been at pains to point out, would be to treat everyone identically, completely ignoring their differing needs. Various forms of "barracks equality" approximating that would also be too much. Too little equality would be to limit equality of condition, as did the old egalitarianism, to achieving equal legal and political rights, equal civil liberties, to equality of opportunity and to a redistribution of gross disparities in wealth sufficient to keep social peace, the rationale for the latter being that such gross inequalities if allowed to stand would threaten social stability. This Hobbesist stance indicates that the old egalitarianism proceeds in a very pragmatic manner. Against the old egalitarianism I would argue that we must at least aim at an equality of whole life prospects, where that is not ready simply as the right to compete for scarce positions of

advantage, but where there is to be brought into being the kind of equality of condition that would provide everyone equally, as far as possible, with the resources and the social conditions to satisfy their needs as fully as possible compatible with everyone else doing likewise. (Note that between people these needs will be partly the same but will still often be importantly different as well.) Ideally, as a kind of ideal limit for a society of wondrous abundance, a radical egalitarianism would go beyond that to a similar thing for wants. We should, that is, provide all people equally, as far as possible, with the resources and social conditions to satisfy their wants, as fully as possible compatible with everyone else doing likewise. (I recognize that there is a slide between wants and needs. As the wealth of a society increases and its structure changes, things that started out as wants tend to become needs, e.g. someone in the Falkland Islands might merely reasonably want an auto while someone in Los Angeles might not only want it but need it as well. But this does not collapse the distinction between wants and needs. There are things in any society people need, if they are to survive at all in anything like a commodious condition, whether they want them or not, e.g., they need food, shelter, security, companionship and the like. An egalitarian starts with basic needs, or at least with what are taken in the cultural environment in which a given person lives to be basic needs, and moves out to other needs and finally to wants as the productive power of the society increases.)

I qualified my above formulations with "as far as possible" and with "as fully as possible compatible with everyone else doing likewise." These are essential qualifications. Where, as in societies that we know, there are scarcities, even rather minimal scarcities, not everyone can have the resources or at least all the resources necessary to have their needs satisfied. Here we must first ensure that, again as far as possible, their basic needs are all satisfied and then we move on to other needs and finally to wants. But sometimes, to understate it, even in very affluent societies, everyone's needs cannot be met, or at least they cannot be equally met. In such circumstances we have to make some hard choices. I am thinking of a situation where there are not enough dialysis machines to go around so that everyone who needs one can have one. What then should we do? The thing to aim at, to try as far as possible to approximate, if only as a heuristic ideal, is the full and equal meeting of needs and wants of everyone. It is when we have that much equality that we have enough equality. But, of course, "ought implies can," and where we can't achieve it we can't achieve it. But where we reasonably can, we ought to do it. It is something that fairness requires.

The "reasonably can" is also an essential modification: we need situations of sufficient abundance so that we do not, in going for such an equality of condition, simply spread the misery around or spread very Spartan conditions around. Before we can rightly aim for the equality of condition I mentioned, we must first have the productive capacity and resource conditions to support the institutional means that would make possible the equal satisfaction of basic needs and the equal satisfaction of other needs and wants as well.

Such achievements will often not be possible; perhaps they will never be fully possible, for, no doubt, the physically handicapped will always be with us. Consider, for example, situations where our scarcities are such that we cannot, without causing considerable misery, create the institutions and mechanisms that would work to satisfy all needs, even all basic needs. Suppose we have the technology in place to develop all sorts of complicated life-sustaining machines all of which would predictably provide people with a quality of life that they, viewing the matter clearly, would rationally choose if they were simply choosing for themselves. But suppose, if we put such technologies in place, we will then not have the wherewithal to provide basic health care in outlying regions in the country or adequate educational services in such places. We should not, under those circumstances, put those technologies in place. But we should also recognize that where it becomes possible to put these technologies in place without sacrificing other more pressing needs, we should do so. The underlying egalitarian rationale is evident enough: produce the conditions for the most extensive satisfaction of needs for everyone. Where A's need and B's need are equally important (equally stringent) but cannot both be satisfied, satisfy A's need rather than B's if the satisfaction of A's need would be more fecund for the satisfaction of the needs of others than B's, or less undermining of the satisfaction of the needs of others than B's. (I do not mean to say that this is our only criterion of choice but it is the criterion most relevant for us here.) We should seek the satisfaction of the greatest compossible set of needs where the conditions for compossibility are (a) that everyone's needs be considered, (b) that everyone's needs be *equally* considered and where two sets of needs cannot both be satisfied, the more stringent set of needs shall first be satisfied. (Do not say we have no working criteria for what they are. If you need food to keep you from starvation or debilitating malnutrition and I need a vacation to relax after a spate of hard work, your need is plainly more stringent than mine. There would, of course, be all sorts of disputable cases, but there are also a host of perfectly determinate cases indicating that we have working criteria.) The underlying rationale is to seek compossible sets of needs so that we approach as far as possible as great a satisfaction of needs as possible for everyone.

This might, it could be said, produce a situation in which very few people got those things that they needed the most, or at least wanted the most. Remember Nozick with his need for the resources of Widener Library in an annex to his house. People, some might argue, with expensive tastes and extravagant needs, say a need for really good wine, would never, with a stress on such compossibilia, get things they are really keen about.[2] Is that the kind of world we would reflectively want? Well, *if* their not getting them is the price we have to pay for everyone having their basic needs met, then it is a price we ought to pay. I am very fond of very good wines as well as fresh ripe mangoes, but if the price of my having them is that people starve or suffer malnutrition in the Sahel, or indeed anywhere else, then plainly fairness, if not just plain human decency, requires that I forgo them.

In talking about how much equality is enough, I have so far talked of the benefits that equality is meant to provide. But egalitarians also speak of an equal sharing of the necessary burdens of the society as well. Fairness requires a sharing of the burdens, and for a radical egalitarian this comes to an equal sharing of the burdens where people are equally capable of sharing them. Translated into the concrete this does *not* mean that a child or an old man or a pregnant woman are to be required to work in the mines or that they be required to collect garbage, but it would involve something like requiring every able bodied person, say from nineteen to twenty, to take his or her turn at a fair portion of the necessary unpleasant jobs in the world. In that way all, where we are able to do it, would share equally in these burdens—in doing the things that none of us want to do but that we, if we are at all reasonable, recognize the necessity of having done. (There are all kinds of variations and complications concerning this—what do we do with the youthful wonder at the violin? But, that notwithstanding, the general idea is clear enough.) And, where we think this is reasonably feasible, it squares with our considered judgments about fairness.

I have given you, in effect appealing to my considered judgments but considered judgments I do not think are at all eccentric, a picture of what I would take to be enough equality, too little equality and not enough equality. But how can we know that my proportions are right? I do not think we can avoid or should indeed try to avoid an appeal to considered judgments here. But working with them there are some arguments we can appeal to get them in wide reflective equilibrium. Suppose we go back to the formal principle of justice, namely that we must treat like cases alike. Because it does not tell us *what* are like cases, we cannot derive substantive criteria from it. But it may, indirectly, be of some help here. We all, if we are not utterly zany, want a life in which

our needs are satisfied and in which we can live as we wish and do what we want to do. Though we differ in many ways, in our abilities, capacities for pleasure, determination to keep on with a job, we do not differ about wanting our needs satisfied or being able to live as we wish. Thus, *ceterus paribus,* where questions of desert, entitlement and the like do not enter, it is only fair that all of us should have our needs equally considered and that we should, again *ceterus paribus,* all be able to do as we wish in a way that is compatible with others doing likewise. From the formal principle of justice and a few key facts about us, we can get to the claim that *ceterus paribus* we should go for this much equality. But this is the core content of a radical egalitarianism.

However, how do we know that *ceterus* is *paribus* here? What about our entitlements and deserts? Suppose I have built my house with my own hands, from materials I have purchased and on land that I have purchased and that I have lived in it for years and have carefully cared for it. The house is mine and I am entitled to keep it even if by dividing the house into two apartments greater and more equal satisfaction of need would obtain for everyone. Justice requires that such an entitlement be respected here. (Again, there is an implicit *ceterus paribus* clause. In extreme situations, say after a war with housing in extremely short supply, that entitlement could be rightly overridden.)

There is a response on the egalitarian's part similar to a response utilitarianism made to criticisms of a similar logical type made of utilitarians by pluralistic deontologists. One of the things that people in fact need, or at least reflectively firmly want, is to have such entitlements respected. Where they are routinely overridden to satisfy other needs or wants, we would *not* in fact have a society in which the needs of everyone are being maximally met. To the reply, but what if more needs for everyone were met by ignoring or overriding such entitlements, the radical egalitarian should respond that that is, given the way we are, a thoroughly hypothetical situation and that theories of morality cannot be expected to give guidance for all logically possible worlds but only for worlds which are reasonably like what our actual world is or plausibly could come to be. Setting this argument aside for the moment, even if it did turn out that the need satisfaction linked with having other things—things that involved the overriding of those entitlements—was sufficient to make it the case that more need satisfaction all around for *everyone* would be achieved by overriding those entitlements, then, for reasonable people who clearly saw that, these entitlements would not have the weight presently given to them. They either would not have the importance presently attached to them or the need for the additional living space would be so great that their being overridden would seem, everything considered, the lesser of two evils (as in the example of the postwar housing situation).

There are without doubt genuine entitlements and a theory of justice must take them seriously, but they are not absolute. If the need is great enough we can see the merit in overriding them, just as in law as well as morality the right of eminent domain is recognized. Finally, while I have talked of entitlements here, parallel arguments will go through for desert.

III

I want now to relate this articulation of what equality comes to to my radically egalitarian principles of justice. My articulation of justice is a certain spelling out of the slogan proclaimed by Marx "From each according to his ability, to each according to his needs." The egalitarian conception of society argues for the desirability of bringing into existence a world, once the springs of social wealth flow freely, in which everyone's needs are as fully satisfied as possible and in which everyone gives according to his ability. Which means, among other things, that everyone, according to his ability, shares the burdens of society. There is an equal giving and equal responsibility here according to ability. It is here, with respect to giving according to ability and with respect to receiving according to need, that a complex equality of re-

sult, i.e., equality of condition, is being advocated by the radical egalitarian. What it comes to is this: each of us, where each is to count for one and none to count for more than one, is to give according to ability and receive according to need.

My radical egalitarian principles of justice read as follows:

1. Each person is to have an equal right to the most extensive total system of equal basic liberties and opportunities (including equal opportunities for meaningful work, for self-determination and political and economic participation) compatible with a similar treatment of all. (This principle gives expression to a commitment to attain and/or sustain equal moral autonomy and equal self-respect.)

2. After provisions are made for common social (community) values, for capital overhead to preserve the society's productive capacity, allowances made for differing unmanipulated needs and preferences, and due weight is given to the just entitlements of individuals, the income and wealth (the common stock of means) is to be so divided that each person will have a right to an equal share. The necessary burdens requisite to enhance human well-being are also to be equally shared, subject, of course, to limitations by differing abilities and differing situations. (Here I refer to different natural environments and the like and not to class position and the like.)

Here we are talking about equality as a right rather than about equality as a goal as has previously been the subject matter of equality in this chapter. These principles of egalitarianism spell out rights people have and duties they have under *conditions of very considerable productive abundance*. We have a right to certain basic liberties and opportunities and we have, subject to certain limitations spelled out in the second principle, a right to an equal share of the income and wealth in the world. We also have a duty, again subject to the qualifications mentioned in the principle, to do our equal share in shouldering the burdens necessary to protect us from ills and to enhance our well-being.

What is the relation between these rights and the ideal of equality of condition discussed earlier? That is a goal for which we can struggle now to bring about conditions which will some day make its achievement possible, while these rights only become rights when the goal is actually achievable. We have no such rights in slave, feudal or capitalist societies or such duties in those societies. In that important way they are not natural rights for they depend on certain social conditions and certain social structures (socialist ones) to be realizable. What we can say is that it is always desirable that socio-economic conditions come into being which would make it possible to achieve the goal of equality of condition so that these rights and duties I speak of could obtain. But that is a far cry from saying we have such rights and duties now.

It is a corollary of this, if these radical egalitarian principles of justice are correct, that capitalist societies (even capitalist welfare state societies such as Sweden) and statist societies such as the Soviet Union or the People's Republic of China cannot be just societies or at least they must be societies, structured as they are, which are defective in justice. (This is not to say that some of these societies are not juster than others. Sweden is juster than South Africa, Canada than the United States and Cuba and Nicaragua than Honduras and Guatemala.) But none of these statist or capitalist societies can satisfy these radical egalitarian principles of justice, for equal liberty, equal opportunity, equal wealth or equal sharing of burdens are not at all possible in societies having their social structure. So we do not have such rights now but we can take it as a goal that we bring such a society into being with a commitment to an equality of condition in which we would have these rights and duties. Here we require first the massive development of productive power.

The connection between equality as a goal and equality as a right spelled out in these principles of justice is this. This equality of condition appealed to in equality as a goal would, if it were actually to obtain, have to contain the rights and duties enunciated in those principles. There could be no equal life prospects between all people or anything approximating an equal satisfaction of needs if there were not in place something like the system of equal basic liberties referred to in the first principle. Furthermore, without the rough equality of wealth referred to in the second principle, there would be disparities in power and self-direction in society which would render impossible an equality of life prospects or the social conditions required for an equal satisfaction of needs. And plainly, without a roughly equal sharing of burdens, there cannot be a situation where everyone has equal life prospects or has the chance equally to satisfy his needs. The principles of radical egalitarian justice are implicated in its conception of an ideally adequate equality of condition.

IV

The principles of radical egalitarian justice I have articulated are meant to apply globally and not just to particular societies. But it is certainly fair to say that not a few would worry that such principles of radical egalitarian justice, if applied globally, would force the people in wealthier sections of the world to a kind of financial hari-kari. There are millions of desperately impoverished people. Indeed millions are starving or malnourished and things are not getting any better. People in the affluent societies cannot but worry about whether they face a bottomless pit. Many believe that meeting, even in the most minimal way, the needs of the impoverished is going to put an incredible burden on people—people of all classes—in the affluent societies. Indeed it will, if acted on non-evasively, bring about their impoverishment, and this is just too much to ask. Radical egalitarianism is forgetting Rawls' admonitions about "the strains of commitment"—the recognition that in any rational account of what is required of us, we must at least give a minimal healthy self-interest its due. We must construct our moral philosophy for human beings and not for saints. Human nature is less fixed than conservatives are wont to assume, but it is not so elastic that we can reasonably expect people to impoverish themselves to make the massive transfers between North and South—the industrialized world and the Third World—required to begin to approach a situation where even Rawls' principles would be in place on a global level, to say nothing of my radical egalitarian principles of justice.[3]

The first thing to say in response to this is that my radical egalitarian principles are meant actually to guide practice, to directly determine what we are to do, only in a world of extensive abundance where, as Marx put it, the springs of social wealth flow freely. If such a world cannot be attained with the underminings of capitalism and the full putting into place, stabilizing, and developing of socialist relations of production, then such radical egalitarian principles can only remain as heuristic ideals against which to measure the distance of our travel in the direction of what would be a perfectly just society.

Aside from a small capitalist class, along with those elites most directly and profitably beholden to it (together a group constituting not more than 5 percent of the world's population), there would, in taking my radical egalitarian principles as heuristic guides, be no impoverishment of people in the affluent societies, if we moved in a radically more egalitarian way to start to achieve a global fairness. There would be massive transfers of wealth between North and South, but this could be done in stages so that, for the people in the affluent societies (capitalist elites apart), there need be no undermining of the quality of their lives. Even what were once capitalist elites would not be impoverished or reduced to some kind of bleak life though they would, the incidental Spartan types aside, find their life styles altered. But their health and general well being, including their opportunities to do significant and innovative work, would, if anything, be enhanced. And while some of the sources of their enjoyment would be a thing of the past, there would still be a considerable range of enjoyments available to them sufficient to afford anyone a rich life that could be lived with verve and zest.

A fraction of what the United States spends on defense spending would take care of immediate problems of starvation and malnutrition for most of the world. For longer range problems such as bringing conditions of life in the Third World more in line with conditions of life in Sweden and Switzerland, what is necessary is the dismantling of the capitalist system and the creation of a socio-economic system with an underlying rationale directing it toward producing for needs—everyone's needs. With this altered productive mode, the irrationalities and waste of capitalist production would be cut. There would be no more built-in obsolescence, no more merely cosmetic changes in consumer durables, no more fashion roulette, no more useless products and the like. Moreover, the enormous expenditures that go into the war industry would be a thing of the past. There would be great transfers from North to South, but it would be from the North's capitalist fat and not from things people in the North really need. (There would, in other words, be no self-pauperization of people in the capitalist world.) . . .

V

It has been repeatedly argued that equality undermines liberty. Some would say that a society in which principles like my radical egalitarian principles were adopted, or even the liberal egalitarian principles of Rawls or Dworkin were adopted, would not be a free society. My arguments have been just the reverse. I have argued that it is only in an egalitarian society that full and extensive liberty is possible.

Perhaps the egalitarian and the anti-egalitarian are arguing at cross purposes? What we need to recognize, it has been argued, is that we have two kinds of rights both of which are important to freedom but to rather different freedoms and which are freedoms which not infrequently conflict.[4] We have rights to *fair terms of cooperation* but we also have rights to non-interference. If a right of either kind is overridden our freedom is diminished. The reason why it might be thought that the egalitarian and the anti-egalitarian may be arguing at cross purposes is that the egalitarian is pointing to the fact that rights to fair terms of cooperation and their associated liberties require equality while the anti-egalitarian is pointing to the fact that rights to noninterference and their associated liberties conflict with equality. They focus on different liberties.

What I have said above may not be crystal clear, so let me explain. People have a right to fair terms of cooperation. In political terms this comes to the equal right of all to effective participation in government and, in more broadly social terms, and for a society of economic wealth, it means people having a right to a roughly equal distribution of the benefits and burdens of the basic social arrangements that affect their lives and for them to stand in such relations to each other such that no one has the power to dominate the life of another. By contrast, rights to non-interference come to the equal right of all to be left alone by the government and more broadly to live in a society in which people have a right peacefully to pursue their interests without interference.

The conflict between equality and liberty comes down to, very essentially, the conflicts we get in modern societies between rights to fair terms of cooperation and rights to noninterference. As Joseph Schumpeter saw and J. S. Mill before him, one could have a thoroughly democratic society (at least in conventional terms) in which rights to noninterference might still be extensively violated. A central anti-egalitarian claim is that we cannot have an egalitarian society in which the very precious liberties that go with the rights to non-interference would not be violated.

Socialism and egalitarianism plainly protect rights to fair terms of cooperation. Without the social (collective) ownership and control of the means of production, involving with this, in the initial stages of socialism at least, a workers' state, economic power will be concentrated in the hands of a few who will in turn, as a result, dominate effective participation in government. Some right-wing libertarians blind themselves to that reality, but it is about as evident as can be. Only an utter

turning away from the facts of social life could lead to any doubts about this at all. But then this means that in a workers' state, if some people have capitalistic impulses, that they would have their rights peacefully to pursue their own interests interfered with. They might wish to invest, retain and bequeath in economic domains. In a workers' state these capitalist acts in many circumstances would have to be forbidden, but that would be a violation of an individual's right to non-interference and the fact, if it was a fact, that we by democratic vote, even with vast majorities, had made such capitalist acts illegal would still not make any difference because individuals' rights to noninterference would still be violated.

We are indeed driven, by egalitarian impulses, of a perfectly understandable sort, to accept interference with laissez-faire capitalism to protect non-subordination and non-domination of people by protecting the egalitarian right to fair terms of cooperation and the enhanced liberty that that brings. Still, as things stand, this leads inevitably to violations of the right to non-interference and this brings with it a diminution of liberty. There will be people with capitalist impulses and they will be interfered with. It is no good denying, it will be said, that egalitarianism and particularly socialism will not lead to interference with very precious individual liberties, namely with our right peacefully to pursue our interests without interference.[5]

The proper response to this, as should be apparent from what I have argued throughout, is that to live in any society at all, capitalist, socialist or whatever, is to live in a world in which there will be some restriction or other on our rights peacefully to pursue our interests without interference. I can't lecture in Albanian or even in French in a standard philosophy class at the University of Calgary, I can't jog naked on most beaches, borrow a book from your library without your permission, fish in your trout pond without your permission, take your dog for a walk without your say so and the like. At least some of these things have been thought to be things which I might peacefully pursue in my own interests. Stopping me from doing them is plainly interfering with my peaceful pursuit of my own interests. And indeed it is an infringement on liberty, an interference with my doing what I may want to do.

However, for at least many of these activities, and particularly the ones having to do with property, even right-wing libertarians think that such interference is perfectly justified. But, justified or not, they still plainly constitute a restriction on our individual freedom. However, what we must also recognize is that there will always be some such restrictions on freedom in any society whatsoever, just in virtue of the fact that a normless society, without the restrictions that having norms implies, is a contradiction in terms.[6] Many restrictions are hardly felt as restrictions, as in the attitudes of many people toward seat-belt legislation, but they are, all the same, plainly restriction on our liberty. It is just that they are thought to be unproblematically justified.

To the question would a socialism with a radical egalitarianism restrict some liberties, including some liberties rooted in rights to noninterference, the answer is that it indeed would; but so would laissez-faire capitalism, aristocratic conceptions of justice, liberal conceptions or any social formations at all, with their associated conceptions of justice. The relevant question is which of these restrictions are justified.

The restrictions on liberty preferred by radical egalitarianism and socialism, I have argued, are justified for they, of the various alternatives, give us both the most extensive and the most abundant system of liberty possible in modern conditions with their thorough protection of the right to fair terms of cooperation. Radical egalitarianism will also, and this is central for us, protect our civil liberties and these liberties are, of course, our most basic liberties. These are the liberties which are the most vital for us to protect. What it will not do is to protect our unrestricted liberties to invest, retain and bequeath in the economic realm and it will not protect our unrestricted freedom to buy and sell. There is, however, no good reason to think that these restrictions are restrictions of anything like a basic liberty. Moreover, we are jus-

tified in restricting our freedom to buy and sell if such restrictions strengthen, rather than weaken, our total system of liberty. This is in this way justified, for only by such market restrictions can the rights of the vast majority of people to effective participation in government and an equal role in the control of their social lives be protected. I say this because if we let the market run free in this way, power will pass into the hands of a few who will control the lives of the many and determine the fundamental design of the society. The actual liberties that are curtailed in a radically egalitarian social order are inessential liberties whose restriction in contemporary circumstances enhances human well-being and indeed makes for a firmer entrenchment of basic liberties and for their greater extension globally. That is to say, we here restrict some liberty in order to attain more liberty and a more equally distributed pattern of liberty. More people will be able to do what they want and have a greater control over their own lives than in a capitalist world order with its at least implicit inegalitarian commitments.

However, some might say I still have not faced the most central objection to radical egalitarianism, namely its statism. (I would prefer to say its putative statism.) The picture is this. The egalitarian state must be in the redistribution business. It has to make, or make sure there is made, an equal relative contribution to the welfare of every citizen. But this in effect means that the socialist state or, for that matter, the welfare state, will be deeply interventionist in our personal lives. It will be in the business, as one right-winger emotively put it, of cutting one person down to size in order to bring about that person's equality with another person who was in a previously disadvantageous position.[7] That is said to be morally objectionable and it would indeed be deeply morally objectionable in many circumstances. But it isn't in the circumstances in which the radical egalitarian presses for redistribution. (I am not speaking of what might be mere equalizing upwards.) The circumstances are these: Capitalist A gets his productive property confiscated so that he could no longer dominate and control the lives of proletarians B,

C, D, E, F, and G. But what is wrong with it where this "cutting down to size"—in reality the confiscation of productive property or the taxation of the capitalist—involves no violation of A's civil liberties or the harming of his actual well-being (health, ability to work, to cultivate the arts, to have fruitful personal relation, to live in comfort and the like) and where B, C, D, E, F, and G will have their freedom and their well-being thoroughly enhanced if such confiscation or taxation occurs? Far from being morally objectionable, it is precisely the sort of state of affairs that people ought to favor. It certainly protects more liberties and more significant liberties that it undermines.

There is another familiar anti-egalitarian argument designed to establish the liberty-undermining qualities of egalitarianism. It is an argument we have touched upon in discussing meritocracy. It turns on the fact that in any society there will be both talents and handicaps. Where they exist, what do we want to do about maintaining equal distribution? Egalitarians, radical or otherwise, certainly do not want to penalize people for talent. That being so, then surely people should be allowed to retain the benefits of superior talent. But this in some circumstances will lead to significant inequalities in resources and in the meeting of needs. To sustain equality there will have to be an ongoing redistribution in the direction of the less talented and less fortunate. But this redistribution from the more to the less talented does plainly penalize the talented for their talent. That, it will be said, is something which is both unfair and an undermining of liberty.

The following, it has been argued, makes the above evident enough.[8] If people have talents they will tend to want to use them. And if they use them they are very likely to come out ahead. Must not egalitarians say they ought not to be able to come out ahead no matter how well they use their talents and no matter how considerable these talents are? But that is intolerably restrictive and unfair.

The answer to the above anti-egalitarian argument is implicit in a number of things I have already said. But here let me confront this familiar argument directly. Part of the answer comes out in probing some of the ambiguities of "coming out ahead." Note, incidentally, that (1) not all reflective, morally sensitive people will be so concerned with that, and (2) that being very concerned with that is a mentality that capitalism inculcates. Be that as it may, to turn to the ambiguities, note that some take "coming out ahead" principally to mean "being paid well for the use of those talents" where "being paid well" is being paid sufficiently well so that it creates inequalities sufficient to disturb the preferred egalitarian patterns. (Without that, being paid well would give one no relative advantage.) But, as we have seen, "coming out ahead" need not take that form at all. Talents can be recognized and acknowledged in many ways. First, in just the respect and admiration of a fine employment of talents that would naturally come from people seeing them so displayed where these people were not twisted by envy; second, by having, because of these talents, interesting and secure work that their talents fit them for and they merit in virtue of those talents. Moreover, having more money is not going to matter much—for familiar marginal utility reasons—where what in capitalist societies would be called the welfare floors are already very high, this being made feasible by the great productive wealth of the society. Recall that in such a society of abundance everyone will be well off and secure. In such a society people are not going to be very concerned about being a little better off than someone else. The talented are in no way, in such a situation, robbed to help the untalented and handicapped or penalized for their talents. They are only prevented from amassing wealth (most particularly productive wealth), which would enable them to dominate the untalented and the handicapped and to control the social life of the world of which they are both a part. . . .

I think that the moral authority for abstract egalitarianism, for the belief that the interests of everyone matter and matter equally, comes from its being the case that it is *required by the moral point of view*.[9] What I am predicting is that a person who has a good understanding of what morality is, has a good knowledge of the facts, is not ideologically mystified, takes an impartial point of view, and has an attitude of impartial caring, would, if not conceptually confused, come to accept the abstract egalitarian thesis. I see no way of arguing someone into such an egalitarianism who does not in this general way have a love of humankind.[10] A hard-hearted Hobbesist is not reachable here. But given that a person has that love of humankind—that impartial and impersonal caring—together with the other qualities mentioned above, then, I predict, that that person would be an egalitarian at least to the extent of accepting the abstract egalitarian thesis. What I am claiming is that if these conditions were to obtain (if they ceased to be just counterfactuals), then there would be a consensus among moral agents about accepting the abstract egalitarian thesis. . . .

NOTES

1. See the debate between Robert Nozick, Daniel Bell and James Tobin, "If Inequality Is Inevitable, What Can Be Done About It?", *The New York Times,* January 3, 1982, p. E5. The exchange between Bell and Nozick reveals the differences between the old egalitarianism and right-wing libertarianism. It is not only that the right and left clash but sometimes right clashes with right.

2. Amartya Sen, "Equality of What?", *The Tanner Lectures on Human Values,* vol. 1 (1980), ed. Sterling M. McMurrin (Cambridge, England: Cambridge University Press, 1980), pp. 198–220.

3. Henry Shue, "The Burdens of Justice," *The Journal of Philosophy* 80, no. 10 (October 1983): 600–601; 606–8.

4. Richard W. Miller, "Marx and Morality," in *Marxism,* eds. J. R. Pennock and J. W. Chapman, Nomos 26 (New York: New York University Press, 1983), pp. 9–11.

5. Ibid., p. 10.

6. This has been argued from both the liberal center and the left. Ralf Dahrendorf, *Essays in the Theory of Society* (Stanford, Calif.: Stanford University Press, 1968), pp. 151–78; and G. A. Cohen, "Capitalism, Freedom and the Proletariat," in *The Idea of Freedom: Essays in Honour of Isaiah Berlin,* ed. Alan Ryan (Oxford: Oxford University Press, 1979).

7. The graphic language should be duly noted. Jan Narveson, "On Dworkinian Equality," *Social Philosophy and Policy* 1, no. 1 (autumn 1983): 4.

8. Ibid., pp. 1–24.

9. Some will argue that there is no such thing as a moral point of view. My differences with him about the question of whether the amoralist can be argued into morality not withstanding, I think Kurt Baier, in a series of articles written subsequent to his *The Moral Point of View,* has clearly shown that there is something reasonably determinate that can, without ethnocentrism, be called "the moral point of view."

10. Richard Norman has impressively argued that this is an essential background assumption of the moral point of view. Richard Norman, "Critical Notice of Rodger Beehler's *Moral Life,*" *Canadian Journal of Philosophy* 11, no. 1 (March 1981): 157–83.

8   How Liberty Upsets Patterns

ROBERT NOZICK

IT IS NOT CLEAR HOW those holding alternative conceptions of distributive justice can reject the entitlement conception of justice in holdings. For suppose a distribution favored by one of the nonentitlement conceptions is realized. Let us suppose it is your favorite one and let us call this distribution D_1; perhaps everyone has an equal share, perhaps shares vary in accordance with some dimension you treasure. Now suppose that Wilt Chamberlain is greatly in demand by basketball teams, being a great gate attraction. (Also suppose contracts run only for a year, with players being free agents.) He signs the following sort of contract with a team: In each home game, twenty-five cents from the price of each ticket of admission goes to him. (We ignore the question of whether he is "gouging" the owners, letting them look out for themselves.) The season starts, and people cheerfully attend his team's games; they buy their tickets, each time dropping a separate twenty-five cents of their admission price into a special box with Chamberlain's name on it. They are excited about seeing him play; it is worth the total admission price to them. Let us suppose that in one season one million persons attend his home games, and Wilt Chamberlain winds up with $250,000, a much larger sum than the average income and larger even than anyone else has. Is he entitled to this income? Is this new distribution D_2, unjust? If so, why? There is *no* question about whether each of the people was entitled to the control over the resources they held in D_1, because that was the distribution (your favorite) that (for the purposes of argument) we assumed was acceptable. Each of these persons *chose* to give twenty-five cents of their money to Chamberlain. They could have spent it on going to the movies, or on candy bars, or on copies of *Dissent* magazine, or of *Monthly Review*. But they all, at least one million of them, converged on giving it to Wilt Chamberlain in exchange for watching him play basketball. If D_1 was a just distribution, and people voluntarily moved from it to D_2 transferring parts of their shares they were given under D_1 (what was it for if not to do something with?), isn't D_2 also just? If people were entitled to dispose of the resources to which they were entitled (under D_1), didn't this include their being entitled to give it to, or exchange it with, Wilt Chamberlain? Can anyone else complain on grounds of justice? Each other person already has his legitimate share under D_1. Under D_1, there is nothing that anyone has that anyone else has a claim of justice against. After someone transfers something to Wilt Chamberlain, third parties *still* have their legitimate shares; *their* shares are not changed. By what process could such a transfer among two persons give rise to a legitimate claim of distributive justice on a portion of what was transferred, by a third party who had no claim of justice on any holding of the others *before* the transfer?[1] To cut off objections irrelevant here, we might imagine the exchanges occurring in a socialist society, after hours: After playing whatever basketball he does in his daily work, or doing whatever other daily work he does, Wilt Chamberlain decides to put in *overtime* to earn additional money. (First his work quota is set; he works time over that.) Or imagine it is a skilled juggler people like to see, who puts on shows after hours.

Why might someone work overtime in a society in which it is assumed their needs are satisfied? Perhaps because they care about things other than needs. I like to write in books that I read, and to have easy access to books for browsing at odd hours. It would be very pleasant and convenient to have the resources of Widener Library in my backyard. No society, I assume, will provide such resources close to each person who would like them as part of his regular allotment (under D_1). Thus, persons either must do without some extra things that they want, or be allowed to do something extra to get some of these things. On what basis could the inequalities that would eventuate be forbidden? Notice also that small factories would spring up in a socialist society, unless forbidden. I melt down some of my personal possessions (under D_1) and build a machine out of the material. I offer you, and others, a philosophy lecture once a week in exchange for your cranking the handle on my machine, whose products I exchange for yet other things, and so on. (The raw materials used by the machine are given to me by others who possess them under D_1, in exchange for hearing lectures.) Each person might participate to gain things over and above their allotment under D_1. Some persons even might want to leave their job in socialist industry and work full time in this private sector. [In any case] I wish merely to note how private property even in means of production would occur in a socialist society that did not forbid people to use as they wished some of the resources they are given under the socialist distribution D_1.[2] The socialist society would have to forbid capitalist acts between consenting adults.

The general point illustrated by the Wilt Chamberlain example and the example of the entrepreneur in a socialist society is that no end-state principle or distributional patterned principle of justice can be continuously realized without continuous interference with people's lives. Any favored pattern would be transformed into one unfavored by the principle, by people choosing to act in various ways; for example, by people exchanging goods and services with other people, or giving things to other people, things the transferrers are entitled to under the favored distribution pattern. To maintain a pattern one must either continually interfere to stop people from transferring resources as they wish to, or continually (or periodically) interfere to take from some persons resources that others for some reason chose to transfer to them. (But if some time limit is to be set on how long people may keep resources others voluntarily transfer to them, why let them keep these resources for *any* period of time? Why not have immediate confiscation?) It might be objected that all persons voluntarily will choose to refrain from actions which would upset the pattern. This presupposes unrealistically (1) that all will most want to maintain the pattern (are those who don't, to be "reeducated" or forced to undergo "self-criticism"?), (2) that each can gather enough information about his own actions and the ongoing activities of others to discover which of his actions will upset the pattern, and (3) that diverse and far-flung persons can coordinate their actions to dovetail into the pattern. Compare the manner in which the market is neutral among persons' desires, as it reflects and transmits widely scattered information via prices, and coordinates persons' activities.

It puts things perhaps a bit too strongly to say that every patterned (or end-state) principle is liable to be thwarted by the voluntary actions of the individual parties transferring some of their shares they receive under the principle. For perhaps some *very* weak patterns are not so thwarted.[3] Any distributional pattern with any egalitarian component is overturnable by the voluntary actions of individual persons over time, as is every patterned condition with sufficient content so as actually to have been proposed as presenting the central core of distributive justice. Still, given the possibility that some weak conditions or patterns may not be unstable in this way, it would be better to formulate an explicit description of the kind of interesting and contentful patterns under discussion, and to prove a theorem about their instability. Since the weaker the patterning, the more likely it is that the entitlement system itself satisfies it, a plausible conjecture is that any patterning either is unstable or is satisfied by the entitlement system. . . .

NOTES

1. Might not a transfer have instrumental effects on a third party, changing his feasible options? (But what if the two parties to the transfer independently had used their holdings in this fashion?) I discuss this question below, but note here that this question concedes the point for distributions of ultimate intrinsic noninstrumental goods (pure utility experiences, so to speak) that are transferable. It also might be objected that the transfer might make a third party more envious because it worsens his position relative to someone else. I find it incomprehensible how this can be thought to involve a claim of justice. . . .

Here and elsewhere in this chapter, a theory which incorporates elements of pure procedural justice might find what I say acceptable, *if* kept in its proper place; that is, if background institutions exist to ensure the satisfaction of certain conditions on distributive shares. But if these institutions are not themselves the sum or invisible-hand result of people's voluntary (nonaggressive) actions, the constraints they impose require justification. At no point does *our* argument assume any background institutions more extensive than those of the minimal nightwatchman state, a state limited to protecting persons against murder, assault, theft, fraud, and so forth.

2. See the selection from John Henry MacKay's novel, *The Anarchists*, reprinted in Leonard Krimmerman and Lewis Perry, eds., *Patterns of Anarchy* (New York: Doubleday Anchor Books, 1966), in which an individualist anarchist presses upon a communist anarchist the following question: "Would you, in the system of society which you call 'free Communism' prevent individuals from exchanging their labor among themselves by means of their own medium of exchange? And further: Would you prevent them from occupying land for the purpose of personal use?" The novel continues: "[the] question was not to be escaped. If he answered 'Yes!' he admitted that society had the right of control over the individual and threw overboard the autonomy of the individual which he had always zealously defended; if, on the other hand, he answered 'No!' he admitted the right of private property which he had just denied so emphatically. . . . Then he answered, 'In Anarchy any number of men must have the right of forming a voluntary association, and so realizing their ideas in practice. Nor can I understand how anyone could justly be driven from the land and house which he uses and occupies . . . every serious man must declare himself: for Socialism, and thereby for force and against liberty, or for Anarchism, and thereby for liberty and against force.'" In contrast, we find Noam Chomsky writing, "Any consistent anarchist must oppose private ownership of the means of production," "the consistent anarchist then . . . will be a socialist . . . of a particular sort." Introduction to Daniel Guerin, *Anarchism: From Theory to Practice* (New York: Monthly Review Press, 1970), pages xiii, xv.

3. Is the patterned principle stable that requires merely that a distribution be Pareto-optimal? One person might give another a gift or bequest that the second could exchange with a third to their mutual benefit. Before the second makes this exchange there is not Pareto-optimality. Is a stable pattern presented by a principle choosing that among the Pareto-optimal positions that satisfies some further condition C? It may seem that there cannot be a counter-example, for won't any voluntary exchange made away from a situation show that the first situation wasn't Pareto-optimal. (Ignore the implausibility of this last claim for the case of bequests.) But principles are to be satisfied over time, during which new possibilities arise. A distribution that at one time satisfies the criterion of Pareto-optimality might not do so when some new possibilities arise (Wilt Chamberlain grows up and starts playing basketball); and though people's activities will tend to move then to a new Pareto-optimal position, *this* new one need not satisfy the contentful condition C. Continual interference will be needed to insure the continual satisfaction of C. (The theoretical possibility of a pattern's being maintained by some invisible-hand process that brings it back to an equilibrium that fits the pattern when deviations occur should be investigated.)

Part IV

Liberal Democratic Justice

9   The Contractual Basis for a Just Society

IMMANUEL KANT

AMONG ALL THE CONTRACTS by which a large group of men unites to form a society, . . . the contract establishing a *civil constitution* . . . is of an exceptional nature. For while, so far as its execution is concerned, it has much in common with all others that are likewise directed toward a chosen end to be pursued by joint effort, it is essentially different from all others in the principle of its constitution. . . . In all social contracts, we find a union of many individuals for some common end which they all *share*. But a union as an end in itself which they all *ought to share* and which is thus an absolute and primary duty in all external relationships whatsoever among human beings (who cannot avoid mutually influencing one another), is only found in a society insofar as it constitutes a civil state, i.e. a commonwealth. . . .

The civil state, regarded purely as a lawful state, is based on the following *a priori* principles:

1. the *freedom* of every member of society as a *human being*
2. the *equality* of each with all the others as a *subject*
3. the *independence* of each member of a commonwealth as a *citizen*

These principles are not so much laws given by an already established state, as laws by which a state can alone be established in accordance with pure rational principles of external human right. Thus:

1. Man's *freedom* as a human being, as a principle for the constitution of a commonwealth, can be expressed in the following formula. No one can compel me to be happy in accordance with his conception of the welfare of others, for each may seek his happiness in whatever way he sees fit, so long as he does not infringe upon the freedom of others to pursue a similar end which can be reconciled with the freedom of everyone else within a workable general law—i.e., he must accord to others the same right as he enjoys himself. A government might be established on the principle of benevolence toward the people, like that of a father toward his children. Under such a *paternal government* . . . the subjects, as immature children who cannot distinguish what is truly useful or harmful to themselves, would be obliged to behave purely passively and to rely upon the judgement of the head of state as to how they *ought* to be happy, and upon his kindness in willing their happiness at all. Such a government is the greatest conceivable *despotism,* i.e., a constitution which suspends the entire freedom of its subjects, who thenceforth have no rights whatsoever. The only conceivable government for men who are capable of possessing rights, even if the ruler is benevolent, is not a *paternal* but a *patriotic* government. . . . A *patriotic* attitude is one where everyone in the state, not excepting its head, regards the commonwealth as a maternal womb, or the land as the paternal ground from which he himself sprang and which he must leave to his descendants as a treasured pledge. Each regards himself as authorized to protect the rights of the common-

From Kant's Political Writings, *edited by Hans Reiss and translated by H. B. Nisbet (1970), pp. 73–81. Reprinted by permission of Cambridge University Press.*

wealth by laws of the general will, but not to submit it to his personal use at his own absolute pleasure. This right of freedom belongs to each member of the commonwealth as a human being, insofar as each is a being capable of possessing rights.

2. Man's equality as a subject might be formulated as follows. Each member of the commonwealth has rights of coercion in relation to all the others, except in relation to the head of state. For he alone is not a member of the commonwealth, but its creator or preserver, and he alone is authorized to coerce others without being subject to any coercive law himself. But all who are subject to laws are the subjects of a state, and are thus subject to the right of coercion along with all other members of the commonwealth; the only exception is a single person (in either the physical or the moral sense of the word), the head of state, through whom alone the rightful coercion of all others can be exercised. For if he too could be coerced, he would not be the head of state, and the hierarchy of subordination would ascend infinitely. But if there were two persons exempt from coercion, neither would be subject to coercive laws, and neither could do to the other anything contrary to right, which is impossible.

This uniform equality of human beings as subjects of a state is, however, perfectly consistent with the utmost inequality of the mass in the degree of its possessions, whether these take the form of physical or mental superiority over others, or of fortuitous external property and of particular rights (of which there may be many) with respect to others. Thus the welfare of the one depends very much on the will of the other (the poor depending on the rich), the one must obey the other (as the child its parents or the wife her husband), the one serves (the laborer) while the other pays, etc. Nevertheless, they are all equal as subjects *before the law,* which, as the pronouncement of the general will, can only be single in form, and which concerns the form of right and not the material or object in relation to which I possess rights. For no one can coerce anyone else other

than through the public law and its executor, the head of state, while everyone else can resist the others in the same way and to the same degree. No one, however, can lose this authority to coerce others and to have rights toward them except through committing a crime. And no one can voluntarily renounce his rights by a contract or legal transaction to the effect that he has no rights but only duties, for such a contract would deprive him of the right to make a contract, and would thus invalidate the one he had already made.

From this idea of the equality of men as subjects in a commonwealth, there emerges this further formula: every member of the commonwealth must be entitled to reach any degree of rank which a subject can earn through his talent, his industry and his good fortune, And his fellow-subjects may not stand in his way by *hereditary* prerogatives or privileges of rank and thereby hold him and his descendants back indefinitely.

All right consists solely in the restriction of the freedom of others, with the qualification that their freedom can co-exist with my freedom within the terms of a general law; and public right in a commonwealth is simply a state of affairs regulated by a real legislation which conforms to this principle and is backed up by power, and under which a whole people live as subjects in a lawful state. . . . This is what we call a civil state, and it is characterized by equality in the effects and countereffects of freely willed actions which limit one another in accordance with the general law of freedom. Thus the *birthright* of each individual in such a state (i.e., before he has performed any acts which can be judged in relation to right) is absolutely *equal* as regards his authority to coerce others to use their freedom in a way which harmonizes with his freedom. Since birth is not an act on the part of the one who is born, it cannot create any inequality in his legal position and cannot make him submit to any coercive laws except insofar as he is subject, along with all the others, of the one supreme legislative power. Thus no member of the commonwealth can have a hereditary privilege as against his fellow-subjects; and no one can hand down to his descendants the privileges attached to the rank he occupies in the commonwealth, nor act as if he were qualified as a ruler by birth and forcibly prevent others from reaching the higher levels of the hierarchy (which are *superior* and *inferior,* but never *imperans* and *subiectus*) through their own merit. He may hand down everything else, so long as it is material and not pertaining to his person, for it may be acquired and disposed of as property and may over a series of generations create considerable inequalities in wealth among the members of the commonwealth (the employee and the employer, the landowner and the agricultural servants, etc.). But he may not prevent his subordinates from raising themselves to his own level if they are able and entitled to do so by their talent, industry and good fortune. If this were not so, he would be allowed to practise coercion without himself being subject to coercive countermeasures from others, and would thus be more than their fellow-subject. No one who lives within the lawful state of a commonwealth can forfeit this equality other than through some crime of his own, but never by contract or through military force. . . . For no legal transaction on his part or on that of anyone else can make him cease to be his own master. He cannot become like a domestic animal to be employed in any chosen capacity and retained therein without consent for any desired period, even with the reservation (which is at times sanctioned by religion, as among the Indians) that he may not be maimed or killed. He can be considered happy in any condition so long as he is aware that, if he does not reach the same level as others, the fault lies either with himself (i.e., lack of ability or serious endeavour) or with circumstances for which he cannot blame others, and not with the irresistible will of any outside party. For as far as right is concerned, his fellow-subjects have no advantage over him.

3. The *independence* . . . of a member of the commonwealth as a *citizen,* i.e., as a co-legislator, may be defined as follows. In the question of actual legislation, all who are free and equal under existing public laws may be considered equal, but not as regards the right to make these laws. Those who are not entitled to this right are nonetheless obliged, as members of the commonwealth, to comply with these laws, and they thus likewise enjoy their protection (not as *citizens* but as co-beneficiaries of this protection). For all right depends on laws. But a public law which defines for everyone that which is permitted and prohibited by right, is the act of a public will, from which all right proceeds and which must not therefore itself be able to do an injustice to any one. And this requires no less than the will of the entire people (since all men decide for all men and each decides for himself). For only toward oneself can one never act unjustly. But on the other hand, the will of another person cannot decide anything for someone without injustice, so that the law made by this other person would require a further law to limit his legislation. Thus an individual will cannot legislate for a commonwealth. For this requires freedom, equality and *unity* of the will of *all* the members. And the prerequisite for unity, since it necessitates a general vote (if freedom and equality are both present), is independence. The basic law, which can come only from the general, united will of the people, is called the *original contract.*

Anyone who has the right to vote on this legislation is a *citizen* . . . (i.e., citizen of a state). . . . The only qualification required by a citizen (apart, of course, from being an adult male) is that he must be his *own master,* . . . and must have some *property* (which can include any skill, trade, fine art or science) to support himself. In cases where he must earn his living from others, he must earn it only by *selling* that which is his,[1] and not by allowing others to make use of him; for he must in the true sense of the word *serve* no one but the commonwealth. In this respect, artisans and large or small landowners are all equal, and each is entitled to one vote only. As for landowners, we leave aside the questions of how anyone can have rightfully acquired more land than he can cultivate with his own hands (for acquisition by military seizure is not primary acquisition), and how it came about that numerous people who might otherwise have acquired permanent property were thereby reduced to serving someone else in order to live at all. It would certainly conflict with the above principle of equality if a law were to grant them a privileged status so that their descendants would always remain feudal landowners, without their land being sold or divided by inheritance and thus made useful to more people; it would also be unjust if only those belonging to an arbitrarily selected class were allowed to acquire land, should the estates in fact be divided. The owner of a large estate keeps out as many smaller property owners (and their votes) as could otherwise occupy his territories. He does not vote on their behalf, and himself has only *one* vote. It should be left exclusively to the ability, industry and good fortune of each member of the commonwealth to enable each to acquire a part and all to acquire the whole, although this distinction cannot be observed within the general legislation itself. The number of those entitled to vote on matters of legislation must be calculated purely from the number of property owners, not from the size of their properties.

Those who possess this right to vote must agree *unanimously* to the law of public justice, or else a legal contention would arise between those who agree and those who disagree, and it would require yet another higher legal principle to resolve it. An entire people cannot, however, be expected to reach unanimity, but only to show a majority of votes (and not even of direct votes, but simply of the votes of those delegated in a large nation to represent the people). Thus the actual principle of being content with majority decisions must be accepted unanimously and embodied in a contract; and this itself must be the ultimate basis on which a civil constitution is established.

Conclusion

This, then is an *original contract* by means of which a civil and thus completely lawful constitution and commonwealth can alone be established. But we need by no means assume that this contract . . . , based on a coalition of the wills of all private individuals in a nation to form a common, public will for the purposes of rightful legislation,

actually exists as a *fact,* for it cannot possibly be so. Such an assumption would mean that we would first have to prove from history that some nation, whose rights and obligations have been passed down to us, did in fact perform such an act, and handed down some authentic record or legal instrument, orally or in writing, before we could regard ourselves as bound by a preexisting civil constitution. It is in fact merely an *idea* of reason, which nonetheless has undoubted practical reality; for it can oblige every legislator to frame his laws in such a way that they could have been produced by the united will of a whole nation, and to regard each subject, insofar as he can claim citizenship, as if he had consented within the general will. This is the test of the rightfulness of every public law. For if the law is such that a whole people could not *possibly* agree to it (for example, if it stated that a certain class of *subjects* must be privileged as a hereditary *ruling class*), it is unjust; but if it is at least *possible* that a people could agree to it, it is our duty to consider the law as just, even if the people is at present in such a position or attitude of mind that it would probably refuse its consent if it were consulted.[2] But this restriction obviously applies only to the judgment of the legislator, not to that of the subject. Thus if a people, under some existing legislation, were asked to make a judgment which in all probability would prejudice its happiness, what should it do? Should the people not oppose the measure? The only possible answer is that they can do nothing but obey. For we are not concerned here with any happiness which the subject might expect to derive from the institutions or administration of the commonwealth, but primarily with the rights which would thereby be secured for everyone. And this is the highest principle from which all maxims relating to the commonwealth must begin, and which cannot be qualified by any other principles. No generally valid principle of legislation can be based on happiness. For both the current circumstances and the highly conflicting and variable illusions as to what happiness is (and no one can prescribe to others how they should attain it) make all fixed principles impossible, so that happiness alone can never be a suitable principle of legislation. The doctrine that *salus publica suprema civitatis lex est*[3] retains its value and authority undiminished; but the public welfare which demands *first* consideration lies precisely in that legal constitution which guarantees everyone his freedom within the law, so that each remains free to seek his happiness in whatever way he thinks best, so long as he does not violate the lawful freedom and rights of his fellow subjects at large. If the supreme power makes laws which are primarily directed toward happiness (the affluence of the citizens, increased population, etc.), this cannot be regarded as the end for which a civil constitution was established, but only as a means of *securing the rightful state,* especially against external enemies of the people. The head of state must be authorized to judge for himself whether such measures are necessary for the commonwealth's prosperity, which is required to maintain its strength and stability both internally and against external enemies. The aim is not, as it were, to make the people happy against its will, but only to ensure its continued existence as a commonwealth.[4] The legislator may indeed err in judging whether or not the measures he adopts are *prudent*, but not in deciding whether or not the law harmonizes with the principle of right. For he has ready to hand as an infallible *a priori* standard, the idea of an original contract, and he need not wait for experience to show whether the means are suitable, as would be necessary if they were based on the principle of happiness. For so long as it is not self-contradictory to say that an entire people could agree to such a law, however painful it might seem, then the law is in harmony with right. But if a public law is beyond reproach (i.e., *irreprehensible*) with respect to right, it carries with it the authority to coerce those to whom it applies, and conversely, it forbids them to resist the will of the legislator by violent means. In other words, the power of the state to put the law into effect is also *irresistible,* and no rightfully established commonwealth can exist without a force of this kind to suppress all internal resistance. For such resistance would be dictated by a maxim which, if it became general, would destroy the whole civil constitution and put an end to the only state in which men can possess rights.

NOTES

1. He who does a piece of work (*opus*) can sell it to someone else, just as if it were his own property. But guaranteeing one's labor (*praestatio operae*) is not the same as selling a commodity. The domestic servant, the shop assistant, the laborer, or even the barber, are merely laborers (*operarii*), not *artists* (*artifices*, in the wider sense) or members of the state, and are thus unqualified to be citizens. And although the man to whom I give my firewood to chop and the tailor to whom I give material to make into clothes both appear to have a similar relationship toward me, the former differs from the latter in the same way as the barber from the wigmaker (to whom I may in fact have given the requisite hair) or the laborer from the artist or tradesman, who does a piece of work which belongs to him until he is paid for it. For the latter, in pursuing his trade, exchanges his property with someone else (*opus*), while the former allows someone else to make use of him. But I do admit that it is somewhat difficult to define the qualifications which entitle anyone to claim the status of being his own master.

2. If, for example, a war tax were proportionately imposed on all subjects, they could not claim, simply because it is oppressive, that it is unjust because the war is in their opinion unnecessary. For they are not entitled to judge this issue, since it is at least *possible* that the war is inevitable and the tax indispensable, so that the tax must be deemed rightful in the judgment of the subjects. But if certain estate owners were oppressed with levies for such a war, while others of the same class were exempted, it is easily seen that a whole people could never agree to a law of this kind, and it is entitled at least to make representations against it, since an unequal distribution of burdens can never be considered just.

3. "The public welfare is the supreme law of the state."

4. Measures of this kind might include certain restrictions on imports, so that the means of livelihood may be developed for the benefit of the subjects themselves and not as an advantage to foreigners or an encouragement for their industry. For without the prosperity of the people, the state would not have enough strength to resist external enemies or to preserve itself as a commonwealth.

10 Justice as Fairness: A Restatement

JOHN RAWLS

The Original Position: the Setup

[This section] considers two main topics in this order: the setup of the original position, and the argument from the original position for the two principles of justice. This argument is divided into two fundamental comparisons: the first fundamental comparison; and the second fundamental comparison. Since we have already discussed the original position as a device of representation, I focus here on a few details about how it is set up.[1]

Keep in mind throughout that, as a device of representation, the original position models two things.

First, it models what we regard—here and now—as fair conditions under which the representatives of citizens, viewed solely as free and equal persons, are to agree to the fair terms of social cooperation (as expressed by principles of justice) whereby the basic structure is to be regulated.

Second, it models what we regard—here and now—as acceptable restrictions on the reasons on the basis of which the parties (as citizens' representatives), situated in those fair conditions, may properly put forward certain principles of justice and reject others.

Keep in mind also that the original position serves other purposes as well. As we have said, it provides a way to keep track of our assumptions. We can see what we have assumed by looking at the way the parties and their situation have been described. The original position also brings out the combined force of our assumptions by uniting them into one surveyable idea that enables us to see their implications more easily.

I now turn to matters of detail. Note first the similarity between the argument from the original position and arguments in economics and social theory. The elementary theory of the consumer (the household) contains many examples of the latter. In each case we have rational persons (or agents) making decisions, or arriving at agreements, subject to certain conditions. From these persons' knowledge and beliefs, their desires and interests, and the alternatives they face, as well as the likely consequences they expect from adopting each alternative, we can figure out what they will decide, or agree to, unless they make a mistake in reasoning or otherwise fail to act sensibly. If the main elements at work can be modeled by mathematical assumptions, it may be possible to prove what they will do, ceteris paribus.

Despite the similarity between familiar arguments in economics and social theory and the argument from the original position, there are fundamental differences. One difference is that our aim is not to describe and explain how people actually behave in certain situations, or how institutions actually work. Our aim is to uncover a public basis for a political conception of justice, and doing this belongs to political philosophy and not social theory. In describing the parties we are not describing persons as we find them. Rather, the parties are described according to how we want to model rational representatives of free and equal citizens. In addition, we impose on the parties certain reasonable conditions as seen in the symmetry of their situation with respect to one another and the limits of their knowledge (the veil of ignorance).

Formal Constraints and the Veil of Ignorance

Although the argument from the original position could be presented formally, I use the idea of the original position as a natural and vivid way to convey the kind of the reasoning the parties may engage in. Many questions about the original position answer themselves if we remember this and see it is a device of representation modeling reasonable constraints that limit the reasons that the parties as rational representatives may appeal to. Is that position a general assembly which includes at one moment everyone who lives at some time? No. Is it a gathering of all actual or possible persons? Plainly not. Can we enter it, so to speak, and if so when? We can enter it at any time. How? Simply by reasoning in accordance with the modeled constraints, citing only reasons those constraints allow.

It is essential that the parties as rational representatives be led to the same judgment as to which principles to adopt. This allows that a unanimous agreement can be reached. The veil of ignorance achieves this result by limiting the parties to the same body of general facts (the presently accepted facts of social theory) and to the same information about the general circumstances of society: that it exists under the circumstances of justice, both objective and subjective, and that reasonably favorable conditions making a constitutional democracy possible obtain.

Along with other conditions on the original position, the veil of ignorance removes differences in bargaining advantages, so that in this and other respects the parties are symmetrically situated. Citizens are represented solely as free and equal persons: as those who have to the minimum

sufficient degree the two moral powers and other capacities enabling them to be normal cooperating members of society over a complete life. By situating the parties symmetrically, the original position respects the basic precept of formal equality, or Sidgwick's principle of equity: those similar in all relevant respects are to be treated similarly. With this precept satisfied, the original position is fair.

We suppose that the parties are rational, where rationality (as distinguished from reasonableness) is understood in the way familiar from economics. Thus the parties are rational in that they can rank their final ends consistently; they deliberate guided by such principles as: to adopt the most effective means to one's ends; to select the alternative most likely to advance those ends; to schedule activities so that, ceteris paribus, more rather than less of those ends can be fulfilled.

There is, be it noted, one important modification in this idea of rationality in regard to certain special psychologies.[2] These include a liability to envy and spite, a peculiarly high aversion to risk and uncertainty, and a strong will to dominate and exercise power over others. The parties (in contrast to persons in society) are not moved by such desires and inclinations. Remember it is up to us, you and me, who are setting up justice as fairness, to describe the parties (as artificial persons in our device of representation) as best suits our aims in developing a political conception of justice. Since envy, for instance, is generally regarded as something to be avoided and feared, at least when it becomes intense, it seems desirable that, if possible, the choice of principles should not be influenced by this trait.[3] So we stipulate that the parties are not influenced by these psychologies as they try to secure the good of those they represent.

Since the veil of ignorance prevents the parties from knowing the (comprehensive) doctrines and conceptions of the good of the persons they represent, they must have some other grounds for deciding which principles to select in the original position. Here we face a serious problem: unless we can set up the original position so that the parties can agree on principles of justice moved by appropriate grounds, justice as fairness cannot be carried through.

To solve this problem is one reason we introduced the idea of primary goods and enumerated a list of items falling under this heading. As we saw, these goods are identified by asking which things are generally necessary as social conditions and all-purpose means to enable citizens, regarded as free and equal, adequately to develop and fully exercise their two moral powers, and to pursue their determinate conceptions of the good. Primary goods, we said, are things persons need as citizens, rather than as human beings apart from any normative conception. Here the political conception, and not a comprehensive moral doctrine, helps to specify these needs and requirements. . . .

Two Principles of Justice

[V]iewing society as a fair system of cooperation between citizens regarded as free and equal, what principles of justice are most appropriate to specify basic rights and liberties, and to regulate social and economic inequalities in citizens' prospects over a complete life? These inequalities are our primary concern.

To find a principle to regulate these inequalities, we look to our firmest considered convictions about equal basic rights and liberties, the fair value of the political liberties as well as fair equality of opportunity. We look outside the sphere of distributive justice more narrowly construed to see whether an appropriate distributive principle is singled out by those firmest convictions once their essential elements are represented in the original position as a device of representation. This device is to assist us in working out which principle, or principles, the representatives of free and equal citizens would select to regulate social and economic inequalities in these prospects over a complete life when they assume that the equal basic liberties and fair opportunities are already secured.

The idea here is to use our firmest considered convictions about the nature of a democratic society as a fair system of cooperation between free and equal citizens—as modeled in the original

position—to see whether the combined assertion of those convictions so expressed will help us to identify an appropriate distributive principle for the basic structure with its economic and social inequalities in citizens' life-prospects. Our convictions about principles regulating those inequalities are much less firm and assured; so we look to our firmest convictions for guidance where assurance is lacking and guidance is needed (*Theory*, 4, 20). . . .

To try to answer our question, let us turn to a revised statement of the two principles of justice discussed in *Theory* §§11–14. They should now read: [4]

(a) Each person has the same indefeasible claim to a fully adequate scheme of equal basic liberties, which scheme is compatible with the same scheme of liberties for all; and

(b) Social and economic inequalities are to satisfy two conditions: first, they are to be attached to offices and positions open to all under conditions of fair equality of opportunity; and second, they are to be to the greatest benefit of the least-advantaged members of society (the difference principle). . . . [5]

First Fundamental Comparison

The preceding survey completes a brief account of the setup of the original position. . . . We now start on the second topic of this part, the reasoning of the parties for the two principles of justice. This reasoning is organized as two fundamental comparisons. [6] Doing this enables us to separate the reasons that lead the parties to select the difference principle from the reasons that lead them to select the principle of the basic equal liberties. Despite the formal resemblance between the difference principle as a principle of distributive justice and the maximin rule as a rule of thumb for decisions under uncertainty, . . . the reasoning for the difference principle does not rely on this rule. The formal resemblance is misleading. [7]

To proceed: we assume that the parties reason by comparing alternatives two at a time. They begin with the two principles of justice and compare those principles with the other available alternatives on the list. If the two principles are supported by a stronger balance of reasons in each such comparison, the argument is complete and those principles are adopted. In any comparison there may be reasons, possibly strong ones, for and against each of the two alternatives. Still, it may be clear that the balance of reasons favors one alternative over the other. Plainly an argument for the two principles depends on judgment—on judging the balance of reasons—and is also relative to a given list. We do not claim that the two principles would be agreed to from a complete, or any possible, list.[8] To claim that would be excessive and I attempt no general argument.

The two comparisons we will discuss are, then, but a small part of the argument that would be required to provide a reasonably conclusive argument for the two principles of justice. This is because the two principles are compared, each time in a different way, with the principle of average utility, and the comparison shows at best their superiority over that principle. The first comparison, which gives the reasoning for the first principle, is, I think, quite conclusive; the second comparison, which gives the reasoning for the difference principle, is less conclusive. It turns on a more delicate balance of less decisive considerations. Nevertheless, despite the limited scope of this two-part argument, it is instructive in suggesting how we can proceed in other comparisons to bring out the merits of the two principles.

The two comparisons arise as follows. In the history of democratic thought two contrasting ideas of society have a prominent place: one is the idea of society as a fair system of social cooperation between citizens regarded as free and equal; the other is the idea of society as a social system organized so as to produce the most good summed over all its members, where this good is a complete good specified by a comprehensive doctrine. The tradition of the social contract elaborates the first idea, the utilitarian tradition is a special case of the second.

Between these two traditions there is a basic contrast: the idea of society as a fair system of social cooperation is quite naturally specified so as to include the ideas of equality (the equality of basic rights, liberties, and fair opportunities) and of reciprocity (of which the difference principle is an example). By contrast, the idea of society organized to produce the most good expresses a maximizing and aggregative principle of political justice. In utilitarianism, the ideas of equality and of reciprocity are accounted for only indirectly, as what is thought to be normally necessary to maximize the sum of social welfare. The two comparisons turn on this contrast: the first brings out the advantage of the two principles with respect to equality, the second their advantage with respect to reciprocity, or mutuality.

As I said above, presenting the case for the two principles by way of these two comparisons separates the reasons that particularly favor the equal basic liberties from the reasons that particularly favor the difference principle. Given this separation, the situation is not as one might have thought. The first comparison, which uses the guidelines of the maximin rule for decisions under uncertainty, is quite decisive in supporting the equal basic rights and liberties; but those guidelines lend little support to the difference principle. In fact, when we formulate the second comparison they are not used at all.

In the first comparison the two principles of justice, taken as a unit, are compared with the principle of average utility as the sole principle of justice. The principle of average utility says that the institutions of the basic structure are to be arranged so as to maximize the average welfare of the members of society, beginning now and extending into the foreseeable future.

The second fundamental comparison is that in which the two principles, again taken as a unit, are compared with an alternative formed by substituting for the difference principle the principle of average utility (combined with a stipulated social minimum). In all other respects the two principles of justice are unchanged. In the second comparison, then, the principles prior to the difference principle are already accepted and the parties are selecting a principle for regulating economic and social inequalities (differences in citizens' prospects over a complete life) for a society in which those prior principles are assumed to be effective in regulating the basic structure. This means that people already view themselves as free and equal citizens of a democratic society, and the parties must take that into account.

The first comparison is the more fundamental because the aim of justice as fairness is to work out an alternative conception of political justice to those found in utilitarianism, perfectionism, and intuitionism (the first has been particularly dominant in our political tradition), while at the same time finding a more appropriate moral basis for the institutions of a modern democratic society. Should the two principles win in the first comparison, this aim is already in good part achieved; but should they lose, all is lost. The first comparison is also essential in replying to recent libertarian views, as we may call them, of Buchanan, Gauthier, and Nozick, . . . the first two being explicitly contractarian.

The first comparison with the principle of average utility is important for another reason: it illustrates how arguments from the original position proceed, and it provides a fairly simple case which displays the nature of those arguments. Surveying them prepares us for the second comparison, which turns on a less decisive balance of reasons.

The Structure of the Argument and the Maximin Rule

First, a statement of the maximin rule: it tells us to identify the worst outcome of each available alternative and then to adopt the alternative whose worst outcome is better than the worst outcomes of all the other alternatives. To follow this rule in selecting principles of justice for the basic structure we focus on the worst social positions that would be allowed when that structure is effectively regulated by those principles under various cir-

cumstances. What this means will become clearer by looking at the argument from the original position in the first comparison.[9]

The argument can be described as follows:

(i) If there are certain conditions in which it is rational to be guided by the maximin rule when agreeing to principles of justice for the basic structure, then under those conditions the two principles of justice would be agreed to rather than the principle of average utility.

(ii) There are certain conditions, three in particular, such that, when they obtain, it is rational to be guided by the maximin rule when agreeing to principles of justice for the basic structure.

(iii) These three conditions obtain in the original position.

(iv) Therefore, the two principles would be agreed to by the parties rather than the principle of average utility.

While each of the premises (i)–(iii) might be disputed, for the time being let's assume that (i) is acceptable. It is (iii) that calls for the most explanation; but (ii) also requires comment, so let's start with (ii).

Let us review the three conditions referred to in (ii) above.[10]

(a) Since the maximin rule takes no account of probabilities, that is, of how likely it is that the circumstances obtain for their respective worst outcomes to be realized, the first condition is that the parties have no reliable basis for estimating the probabilities of the possible social circumstances that affect the fundamental interests of the persons they represent. This condition fully obtains when the concept of probability does not even apply.

(b) Since the maximin rule directs the parties to evaluate the alternatives only by their worst possible outcomes, it must be rational for the parties as trustees not to be much concerned for what might be gained above what can be guaranteed (for those they represent) by adopting the alternative whose worst outcome is better than the worst outcomes of all the other alternatives. Let's call this best worst outcome the "guaranteeable level." The second condition obtains, then, when the guaranteeable level is itself quite satisfactory. It fully obtains when this level is completely satisfactory.

(c) Since the maximin rule directs the parties to avoid alternatives whose worst outcomes are below the guaranteeable level, the third condition is that the worst outcomes of all the other alternatives are significantly below the guaranteeable level. When those outcomes are far below that level and altogether intolerable, and must, if possible, be avoided, the third condition fully obtains.

Three comments about these conditions: First, being guided by the maximin rule in these conditions is compatible with the familiar principle of maximizing the fulfillment of one's interests, or (rational) good. The parties' use of the rule to organize their deliberations in no way violates this familiar principle of rationality. Rather, they use the rule to guide them in deciding in accordance with that principle in the highly unusual, if not unique, circumstances of the original position when the matter at hand is of such fundamental significance.

Note, however, this caveat: the argument guided by the rule fits with the idea that rational agents maximize their expected utility, but only if that expected utility is understood to have no substantive content. That is, it does not mean expected pleasure, or agreeable consciousness (Sidgwick), or satisfaction. Expected utility is a purely formal idea specified by a rule or a mathematical function. As such, the rule or function simply represents the order, or ranking, in which the alternatives are judged better and worse in meeting the agent's fundamental interests, which are in this case the interests of citizens as free and equal.

A second point is that it is not necessary that all, or any, of the three conditions fully obtain for the maximin rule to be a sensible way to organize deliberation. For should the third condition fully obtain, this suffices to bring the maximin rule into play, provided that the guaranteeable level is rea-

sonably satisfactory, so long as the first condition at least partially obtains. However, in the first comparison the first condition has a relatively minor role. As we shall see, what is crucial is that the second and third conditions should obtain to a high degree.

Finally, it is not essential for the parties to use the maximin rule in the original position. It is simply a useful heuristic device. Focusing on the worst outcomes has the advantage of forcing us to consider what our fundamental interests really are when it comes to the design of the basic structure. This is not a question that we would often, if ever, ask ourselves in ordinary life. Part of the point of the original position is that it forces us to ask that question and moreover to do so in a highly special situation which gives it a definite sense.

Let us now review why the second and third conditions obtain to a high degree for the parties given their situation in the original position.

The second condition obtains because the guaranteeable level is quite satisfactory. What is this level? It is the situation of the least-advantaged members of the well-ordered society that results from the full realization of the two principles of justice (given reasonably favorable conditions). Justice as fairness claims that a well-ordered society paired with the two principles of justice is a highly satisfactory political and social world . . . . This basic point about the guaranteeable level is crucial for the argument.[11]

The third condition obtains given the assumption we make that there are realistic social circumstances, even with reasonably favorable conditions, under which the principle of utility would require, or allow, that the basic rights and liberties of some be in various ways restricted, or even denied altogether, for the sake of greater benefits for others or for society as a whole. These circumstances are among the possibilities that the parties must guard against on behalf of those they represent.

Utilitarians may question this assumption. But to support it we need not invoke such drastic infringements of liberty as slavery and serfdom, or oppressive religious persecution. Consider instead a possible balance of social advantages to a sizable majority from limiting the political liberties and religious freedoms of small and weak minorities.[12] The principle of average utility seems to allow possible outcomes that the parties, as trustees, must regard as altogether unacceptable and intolerable. So the third condition obtains to a high degree. . . .

In this comparison, we do not stress the first condition: we assume it to hold, not fully, but only to some significant degree. This we do because the first condition raises difficult points in the theory of probability that so far as possible we want to avoid. Hence we stipulate that knowledge and well-founded beliefs about probabilities must be based on at least some established facts or well-supported beliefs about the world. This fits any interpretation of probability except a general subjectivist (or Bayesian) one. We then say the parties lack the requisite information, and so cannot have well-founded probabilities in selecting among alternatives.

The point is this: the parties know the general commonsense facts of human psychology and political sociology. They also know that the society in question exists in the circumstances of justice under reasonably favorable conditions. These are conditions that, provided the political will exists, make a constitutional regime possible. Yet whether the political will exists depends on a society's political culture and traditions, its religious and ethnic composition, and much else. Favorable conditions may exist when the political will does not.[13] Thus the knowledge that reasonably favorable conditions exist is far too little for the parties to specify a well-grounded probability distribution over the forms of political culture and tradition that might exist. History tells of more aristocracies and theocracies, dictatorships and class-states, than democracies. Of course, the parties don't have this particular knowledge. In any case, does that make those outcomes more likely than democracy? Surely such speculation is far beyond the reach of common sense, or uncommon sense, for that matter. About the first condition of the maximin rule, we claim, then, only that it holds sufficiently so that the argument of the first comparison emphasizing the second and third conditions is not put in doubt.

The argument emphasizing the second and third conditions is essentially as follows: if it is indeed the case that a well-ordered society regulated by the two principles of justice is a highly satisfactory form of political society that secures the basic rights and liberties equally for all (and thus represents a highly satisfactory guaranteeable level), and if the principle of utility may sometimes permit or else require the restriction or suppression of the rights and liberties of some for the sake of a greater aggregate of social well-being, then the parties must agree to the two principles of justice. Only in this way (in the first comparison) can they act responsibly as trustees: that is, effectively protect the fundamental interests of the person each represents, and at the same time make sure to avoid possibilities the realization of which would be altogether intolerable.

This argument rests on the parties' assuming that, given the capacity of those they represent to be free and equal persons and fully cooperating members of society over a complete life, those persons would never put their basic rights and liberties in jeopardy so long as there was a readily available and satisfactory alternative. What aim could the parties suppose those persons might have for doing that? Do they wish to take a chance on having ever more adequate material means to fulfill their ends? But the parties as representatives of citizens regarded as free and equal cannot for that purpose jeopardize citizens' basic rights and liberties. Their responsibility as trustees for citizens so regarded does not allow them to gamble with the basic rights and liberties of those citizens. . . .

Second Fundamental Comparison . . .

We have now completed our survey of the first fundamental comparison: the reasoning favoring the two principles of justice (as a unit) over the principle of average utility (as the sole principle of justice). While the outcome of that comparison achieves the most fundamental aim of justice as fairness, it does not give much support to the difference principle. The most it shows is that this principle adequately secures the general all-purpose means we need to take advantage of our basic freedoms. But other principles may be superior to it on that count.

To explore this question let us now discuss a second fundamental comparison in which the two principles of justice taken as a unit are compared to an alternative exactly the same as those principles except in one respect. The principle of average utility, combined with a suitable social minimum, is substituted for the difference principle. A minimum must be included, for the parties will always insist on some insurance of that kind: the question is how much is appropriate. The basic structure is, then, to be arranged so as to maximize average utility consistent, first, with guaranteeing the equal basic liberties (including their fair value) and fair equality of opportunity, and second, with maintaining a suitable social minimum. We refer to this mixed conception as the principle of restricted utility.[14]

The second comparison is fundamental for this reason: among the conceptions of justice in which the principle of utility has a prominent role, the principle of restricted utility would seem to be the strongest rival to the two principles of justice. Should these principles still be favored in this comparison, then it would appear that other forms of the restricted utility principle would also be rejected. Their role would be that of subordinate norms regulating social policies within the limits allowed by more fundamental principles.

Note that the third condition of the maximin rule no longer obtains since both alternatives ensure against the worst possibilities, not only against the denial or restriction of the basic liberties and of fair equality of opportunity, but also, given the social minimum in the utility principle, against the more serious losses of well-being. Since we do not want to put any weight on the first condition of that rule, we exclude probability arguments entirely. We assume that there are two groups in society, the more and the less advantaged; and then we try to show that both would favor the difference principle over that of re-

stricted utility. In effect, we argue that the second condition of the maximin rule is fully satisfied, or nearly enough so to provide an independent argument for the two principles. . . .

Grounds Falling under Reciprocity

. . . [T]he fact that the difference principle includes an idea of reciprocity distinguishes it from the restricted utility principle. The latter is a maximizing aggregative principle with no inherent tendency toward either equality or reciprocity; any such tendency depends on the consequences of applying it in given circumstances, which vary from case to case. The two fundamental comparisons exploit this fact: as we have said, the first brings out the advantage of the two principles with respect to equality (the equal basic liberties), the second with respect to reciprocity.

To simplify matters, let us assume that there are only two groups in society, the more and the less advantaged, and focus on inequalities of income and wealth alone. In its simplest form, the difference principle regulates these inequalities. Since the parties in the original position are symmetrically situated and know (from the common content of the two alternatives) that the principle adopted will apply to citizens viewed as free and equal, they take equal division of income and wealth (equal life-prospects as indexed by those primary goods) as the starting point. They then ask: are there good reasons for departing from equal division, and if so, which inequalities arising in what ways are acceptable?

A political conception of justice must take into account the requirements of social organization and economic efficiency. The parties would accept inequalities in income and wealth when these work effectively to improve everyone's situation starting from equal division. This suggests the difference principle: taking equal division as the benchmark, those who gain more are to do so on terms acceptable to those who gain less, and in particular to those who gain the least.

We get that principle, then, by taking equal division as the starting point, together with an idea

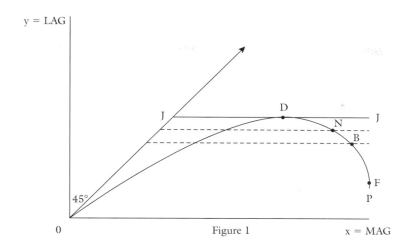

Figure 1

of reciprocity. The principle selects the highest point on the (most efficient) OP curve; and we saw that this point is the efficient point closest to the 45° line, which line represents equality and preserves equal division (see Figure 1). The idea of reciprocity implicit in the difference principle selects a natural focal point between the claims of efficiency and equality.[15]

To see one way the parties might arrive at the difference principle, consider Figure 1. Imagine they have agreed to move from O to D, as everyone gains in the segment OD and D is the first (Pareto) efficient point.

At D the parties ask whether they should proceed from D to B, which is on the southeast-sloping part of the OP curve to the right of D. B is the Bentham point at which average utility (so far as it depends on income and wealth) is maximized (subject to the constraints). The points in the segment D to B and on to the point F (the feudal point), where the utility of the most advantaged is maximized, are also efficient points: movements along that segment can raise the index of one group only by lowering the index of the other. The segment DF is the conflict segment in contrast to the segment OD along which everyone benefits by moving northeast.

The difference principle represents an agreement to stop at D and not to enter the conflict segment. D is the only point on the (highest) OP curve that meets the following reciprocity condition: those who are better off at any point are not better off to the detriment of those who are worse off at that point. Since the parties represent citizens as free and equal, and thus take equal division as the appropriate starting point, we say this is an (not the only) appropriate reciprocity condition. We haven't shown there is no other such condition. But it is hard to imagine what it might be.

To sum up: the difference principle expresses the idea that, starting from equal division, the more advantaged are not to be better off at any point to the detriment of the less well off. But since the difference principle applies to the basic structure, a deeper idea of reciprocity implicit in it is that social institutions are not to take advantage of contingencies of native endowment, or of initial social position, or of good or bad luck over the course of life, except in ways that benefit everyone, including the least favored. This represents a fair undertaking between the citizens seen as free and equal with respect to those inevitable contingencies.

Recall what we said [earlier] the better endowed (who have a place in the distribution of native endowments they do not morally deserve) are encouraged to seek still further benefits—they are already favored by their fortunate place in the distribution—provided they train their endowments and use them in ways that contribute to the good of all, and in particular to the good of the least endowed (who have a less fortunate place in the distribution, a place they also do not morally deserve). This idea of reciprocity is implicit in the idea of regarding the distribution of native endowments as a common asset. Parallel but not identical considerations hold for the contingencies of social position and of good and bad luck.

NOTES

1. See *Theory,* §§20–25. John Rawls, *Theory of Justice* (Cambridge: Harvard University Press, 1971) pp. 20–25.

2. See *Theory,* §25: 123ff.

3. [See *Theory,* §80: 465.]

4. This section summarizes some points from "The Basic Liberties and Their Priority, *Tanner Lectures on Human Values,* vol. 3, ed. Sterling McMurrin (Salt Lake City: University of Utah Press, 1982), §1, reprinted in *Political Liberalism.* In that essay I try to reply to what I believe are two of the more serious objections to my account of liberty in *Theory* raised by H. L. A. Hart in his splendid critical review essay, "Rawls on Liberty and Its Priority," *University of Chicago Law Review* 40 (Spring 1973): 551–555, reprinted in his *Essays in Jurisprudence and Philosophy* (Oxford: Oxford University Press, 1983). No changes made in justice as fairness in this restatement are more significant than those forced by Hart's review.

5. Instead of the "the difference principle," many writers prefer the term "the maximin principle," or simply "maximin justice," or some such locution. See, for example, Joshua Cohen's very full and accurate account of the difference principle in "Democratic Equality," *Ethics* 99 (July 1989): 727–751. But I still use the term "difference principle" to emphasize first, that this principle and the maximin rule for decision under uncertainty are two very distinct things; and second, that in arguing for the difference principle over other distributive principles (say a restricted principle of (average) utility, which includes a social minimum), there is no appeal at all to the maximin rule for decision under uncertainty. The widespread idea that the argument for the difference principle depends on extreme aversion to uncertainty is a mistake, although a mistake unhappily encouraged by the faults of exposition in *Theory,* faults to be corrected in Part III of this restatement.

6. This way of organizing the reasoning for the two principles was first sketched in "Reply to Alexander and Musgrave," *Quarterly Journal of Economics* 88 (November 1974) §§III–VI, pp. 639–653, reprinted in *Collected Papers.*

7. The failure to explain this was a serious fault in *Theory.*

8. See *Theory,* §87: 509.

9. *Theory,* §26: 132–135. As the account of this and later sections shows, the maximin rule was never proposed as the general principle of rational decision in all cases of risk and uncertainty, as some seem to have thought. For example, see J. C. Harsanyi, in his review essay, "Can the Maximin Principle Serve as a Basis for Morality?" *American Political Science Review* 69 (1975): 594–606, and reprinted in his *Essays on Ethics, Social Behavior, and Scientific Explanation* (Dordrecht: D. Reidel Pub. Co., 1976). Such a proposal would be simply irrational, as Harsanyi argues, pp. 39f. On this point there was, and is, no disagreement. The only question is whether, given the highly special, indeed unique, conditions of the original position, the maximin rule is a useful heuristic rule of thumb for the parties to use to organize their deliberations.

10. Here we follow William Fellner, *Probability and Profit* (Homewood, Ill.: R. D. Irwin, 1965), pp. 140–142.

11. This important point about the guaranteeable level, while perhaps obvious, is never expressly stated in *Theory.* The failure to do so led some to think of the guaranteeable level as a natural, nonsocial, level below which individual utility drops precipitously to minus infinity, as it were. Thus they hoped to explain why *Theory* used the maximin rule even though they rejected the idea of such a natural, nonsocial level. But, as the text shows, this was not the intention. See the discussion by Joshua Cohen in "Democratic Equality," pp. 733f.

12. To block this kind of argument some utilitarians have imposed restrictions on the kind of advantages to individuals relevant to their utility function. For example, Harsanyi in his essay "Morality and the Theory of Rational Behavior," in *Utilitarianism and Beyond,* ed. Sen and Williams, p. 56, excludes what he calls antisocial preferences, for example, malice, envy, resentment, and the pleasures of cruelty. Now this is a fundamental departure from the classical (and traditional) utilitarian view in which all pleasures, or the satisfaction of actual preferences, regardless of their source, are intrinsically good. When Harsanyi abandons that view (a view he held in 1955 in his "Cardinal Welfare, Individualistic Ethics, and Interpersonal Comparisons," *Journal of Political Economy* 63 (1955): 309–321, reprinted in *Essays on Ethics, Social Behavior, and Scientific Expla-*

nation, pp. 18ff.), he owes us an explanation of the grounds for counting certain pleasures, or satisfactions, for naught. Calling them antisocial is not enough. We need to know where his restrictions on entries in utility functions come from and how they are justified. Until these questions are answered within a suitably specified framework that is recognizably utilitarian, we cannot decide whether Harsanyi is entitled to impose them. One might ask whether a theory of basic rights and liberties, or a nonutilitarian ideal, lies in the background, tacit and unexpressed.

13. Germany between 1870 and 1945 is an example of a country where reasonably favorable conditions existed—economic, technological and no lack of resources, an educated citizenry and more—but where the political will for a democratic regime was altogether lacking. One might say the same of the United States today, if one decides our constitutional regime is largely democratic in form only.

14. For mixed conceptions, see *Theory,* §21: 107.

15. See E. S. Phelps, "Taxation of Wage Income for Economic Justice," *Quarterly Journal of Economics* 87 (1973), §1. The idea of a focal point is due to Thomas Schelling, *Strategy of Conflict* (Cambridge, Mass.: Harvard University Press, 1960), e.g., pp. 57f.

11 Rawls and a Morally Defensible Conception of Justice

JAMES P. STERBA

In *Justice as Fairness: A Restatement,* John Rawls attempts to improve upon the conception of justice that he defended in his much acclaimed *A Theory of Justice* written over thirty years ago. In what follows, I will first sketch out the earlier defense that Rawls provided in *A Theory of Justice,* and then contrast that defense with Rawls's current defense in *Justice as Fairness: A Restatement.* My ultimate goal is to determine the moral defensibility of Rawls's conception of justice.

I

In *A Theory of Justice,* John Rawls, like Immanuel Kant before him, argues that principles of justice are those principles that free and rational persons who are concerned with advancing their own interests would accept in an initial position of equality. Yet Rawls goes beyond Kant by interpreting the conditions of his "original position" to explicitly require a "veil of ignorance." This veil of ignorance, Rawls claims, requires that we discount certain knowledge about ourselves in order to reach fair agreements. A good example of what is at issue here is the practice of withholding information from juries. As we know, judges sometimes refuse to allow juries to hear certain testimony. The rationale behind this practice is that certain information is highly prejudicial or irrelevant to the case at hand. The hope is that without this information, juries will be more likely to reach fair verdicts. Similarly, when prejudicial or irrelevant information is blurted out in the courtroom, intentionally or unintentionally, judges will usually instruct juries to discount that information to

increase the likelihood that juries will reach fair verdicts. Of course, whether judges and juries in fact carry out their responsibilities in this regard is beside the point. What is crucial is that it is recognized in these contexts that justice demands that we discount certain information in order to achieve just results.

Rawls's ideal of justice can be seen as simply a generalization of this practice. It maintains that if we are to achieve a fair system of rights and duties in general, then we must discount certain information about ourselves when choosing our system of rights and duties. In particular, we must discount our knowledge of whether we are rich or poor, talented or untalented, male or female. In general, this ideal of justice requires that we should choose as though we were standing behind an imaginary "veil of ignorance" with respect to most particular facts about ourselves, anything that would bias our choice or stand in the way of unanimous agreement. Rawls calls this choice situation "the original position" because it is the position we should start from when determining what fundamental rights and duties people should have.

But what rights and duties would be chosen in the original position? *In A Theory of Justice,* Rawls argues that a system of rights and duties that maximizes benefit to the least advantaged position would be chosen. This would be the result of using the maximin strategy which requires that we <u>maxi</u>mize benefit to those who have the <u>mini</u>mum. Rawls argues that persons in the original position would use the maximin strategy because

1. Persons so situated would have no reliable basis for estimating the probabilities of

outcomes that would affect them because they are choosing in ignorance of the probabilities of their occupying any particular place in society, for example, the probability of their being rich or poor, talented or untalented.

2. Persons so situated would care very little, if anything, for what might be gained above what is guaranteed by maximizing the minimum.

3. All other alternatives have outcomes that persons so situated could hardly accept.

Given that these three conditions are meet, Rawls claims, it is rational to follow the maximin strategy.

To better understand what this maximin strategy requires, consider a society with just three individuals, A, B and C, each facing the following alternatives:

Alternatives	Individuals			
	A	B	C	Average
I	4	7	12	7⅔
II	3	8	14	8⅓
III	5	6	8	6⅓

Imagine that the numbers represent comparable social goods or utilities to the three members of this society. Now the maximin strategy would favor alternative III, because only that alternative maximizes the benefit to the least advantaged member of this society, despite the fact that the other two alternatives offer a higher average expected index of social good or utility to each member of the society. According to the maximin strategy when making important choices in (imagined) ignorance of how those choices will affect one personally, it is most rational to maximize the benefit to the least advantaged individual in order to guard against the possibility that this individual will turn out to be oneself.

Others, however, most notably John Harsanyi, have argued that persons in the original position would reject the maximin strategy in favor of a system of rights and duties that maximizes average expected benefit or utility.[1] This is called the utilitarian strategy because it requires that we maximize average expected benefit or utility over the relevant group. In our example, the utilitarian strategy would favor alternative II because that alternative provides the highest average expected benefit or utility. According to the utilitarian strategy, when making important choices in (imagined) ignorance of how those choices will affect one personally, it is most rational to first assign an equal probability to one's occupying each particular position and then select the alternative with the highest average expected benefit or utility.

According to Rawls, the principles of justice that would be derived in the original position are the following:

I. Special conception of justice

1. Each person is to have an equal right to the most extensive basic liberty compatible with a similar system of liberty for others

2. Social and economic inequalities are to be arranged so that they are (a) to the greatest benefit of the least advantaged, consistent with the just savings principle and (b) attached to offices and position open to all under conditions of fair equality of opportunity.

II. General conception of justice

1. All social goods—liberty and opportunity, income and wealth, and the bases of self-respect—are to be distributed equally unless an unequal distribution of any or all of these goods is to the advantage of the least favored.

The general conception of justice differs from the special conception of justice by allowing trade-offs between liberty and other social goods. According to Rawls, persons in the original position would want the special conception of justice to be applied in place of the general conception of justice whenever social conditions allowed all representative persons to exercise their basic liberties.

In *Justice as Fairness: A Restatement,* Rawls now reformulates his principles of justice somewhat differently as follows:

1. Each person has the same indefeasible claim to a fully adequate scheme of equal basic liberties, which scheme is compatible with the same scheme of liberties for all; and
2. Social and economic inequalities are to satisfy two conditions: first they are to be attached to offices and positions open to all under conditions of fair equality of opportunity; second, they are to be to the greatest benefit of the least advantaged members of society (the difference principle).

In this formulation, there is no longer a general conception of justice and except for dropping a reference to liberty in general in his first principle, the only remaining changes are stylistic.

What is significantly different in Rawls's current theory of justice is how he now argues for these two principles from the perspective of the original position. In *A Theory of Justice,* Rawls had defended his principles of justice primarily by appealing to the maximin strategy. By contrast, in *Justice as Fairness: A Restatement,* Rawls defends his principles of justice by making two comparisons, one of which does not appeal to the maximin strategy at all. In the first comparison, the two principles taken as a unit are compared with the principle of average utility. In the second comparison, the two principles taken as a unit are compared with an alternative formed by substituting for the difference principle the principle of average utility combined with a stipulated social minimum. In the first comparison, Rawls holds that his two principles of justice would be chosen over the principle of average utility because persons in the original position would find it reasonable to follow the conservative dictates of the maximin strategy and <u>maximize</u> the <u>minimum</u> payoff primarily because they fear that the principle of average utility could require that the basic rights and liberties of some be restricted to secure greater benefits for others. In the second comparison, however, Rawls holds that the difference

principle would be favored over the principle of average utility combined with a stipulated social minimum primarily because the difference principle expresses an ideal of reciprocity absent from the principle of average utility, even with a stipulated social minimum. In this second comparison, Rawls is comparing his principles of justice to a modified form of utilitarianism. Because this modified form of utilitarianism differs from Rawls's principles of justice only to the extent that it substitutes the principle of average utility combined with a stipulated social minimum for the difference principle, this form of utilitarianism is clearly able to guarantee a presumptively acceptable minimum. As a result, the maximin strategy would be neutral between Rawls's principles of justice and this modified form of utilitarianism. This is why, in the second comparison, Rawls now relies not on the maximin strategy, but primarily on an argument from reciprocity to support his two principles of justice. According to Rawls, the difference principle provides for a reciprocity not matched by the principle of average utility, even with a stipulated social minimum. This is because, starting from a point of equal division, the difference principle requires that those who gain more are to do so on terms acceptable to those who gain less, and thereby secures a reciprocity not matched by the principle of average utility, even with a stipulated social minimum.

II

What needs to be determined is how successful Rawls's defense of his two principles of justice is? Rawls's two principles of justice do appear to look good against traditional forms of utilitarianism, which tell us to simply maximize either total or average utility. The problem with these views, according to Rawls, is that they cannot guarantee even a presumptively acceptable minimum, because at least in theory these traditional forms of utilitarianism must be willing to sacrifice an acceptable minimum for some in order to secure some greater good overall. The general problem with these forms of utilitarianism, as Rawls sees it, is that they justify imposing harms on a few (innocent individuals) to secure a greater benefit for others.

Yet actually this cannot be what makes these forms of utilitarianism objectionable because any defensible moral theory will justify imposing harms on a few (innocent individuals) for the sake of greater benefit for others, at least in certain circumstances. For example, suppose that the only way a doctor can get out of a crowded subway in an emergency situation is by stepping on a few people's toes. Surely, the harm that the doctor inflicts on these innocent individuals would be justified by any defensible moral theory by the greater benefit the doctor is able to do in an emergency situation. In this case, the harm inflicted for the sake of the greater benefit is trivial. In other cases, however, the harm inflicted is not trivial, but it is still reparable, as when one might lie to a temporarily depressed friend to keep her from committing suicide. Here too any defensible moral theory would hold that the harm inflicted on an innocent person in this case is justified by the greater benefit that results.

Clearly, the most difficult cases of this sort are where the harm inflicted is not trivial, nor reparable, but is still arguably justified by the good consequences that result. A widely discussed case of this sort is provided by Bernard Williams. In Williams's case, an explorer, let us call her Sonya, arrives in a South American village just as Pedro, an army officer, is about to kill a random group of twenty Indians in retaliation for protests against the local government. In honor of Sonya's arrival, Pedro offers to spare nineteen of the twenty Indians provided that Sonya will shoot one of them. For this case, even Williams, who is a critic of utilitarianism, admits that the explorer should shoot one of the Indians in order to save the other nineteen. One way to see why this course of action is justified in this case is to imagine that all twenty of the Indians are behind Rawls's veil of ignorance, not knowing which of them would be killed by the explorer but knowing that if the explorer does not kill one of them, they all will be killed by Pedro and his troops. In this situation, all twenty Indians

would agree to have the explorer arbitrarily shoot one of them in order to save the other nineteen. If you need to be further convinced that this type of irreversible harm to innocents can be justified for the sake of achieving greater benefit for others, then just imagine that larger and larger numbers of innocents (e.g., one hundred, one thousand, one million, whatever number you want) would be lost unless one particular (innocent) individual is killed. Surely, at some point, any defensible moral theory will justify such sacrifices.[2]

So what is wrong with at least certain forms of utilitarianism cannot be that they justify doing harm to innocents in order to secure a greater benefit for others. As I just argued, any defensible moral theory will have to do that. Rather what must be wrong with at least certain forms of utilitarianism is that they permit or require harms of this sort in cases when the trade-offs cannot be justified.

But when are such trade-offs not justified? I maintain that such trade-off are not justified when they violate one of the most fundamental principles of morality, one that is common to all moral and political perspectives, namely, the "ought" implies "can" principle. According to this principle, people are not morally required to do what they lack the power to do or what would involve so great a sacrifice that it would be unreasonable to ask, and/or in cases of severe conflict of interest, unreasonable to require them to abide by.

For example, suppose I promised to attend a departmental meeting on Friday, but on Thursday I am involved in a serious car accident that puts me into a coma. Surely it is no longer the case that I ought to attend the meeting now that I lack the power to do so. Or suppose instead that on Thursday I develop a severe case of pneumonia for which I am hospitalized. Surely I could legitimately claim that I cannot attend the meeting on the grounds that the risk to my health involved in attending is a sacrifice that it would be unreasonable to ask me to bear. Or suppose the risk to my health from having pneumonia is not so serious that it would be unreasonable to ask me to attend the meeting (a supererogatory request), it might still be serious enough to be unreasonable to require my attendance at the meeting (a demand that is backed up by blame or coercion).

This "ought" implies "can" principle claims that reason and morality must be linked in an appropriate way, especially if we are going to be able to justifiably use blame or coercion to get people to abide by the requirements of morality. It should be noted, however, that while major figures in the history of philosophy, and most philosophers today accept this linkage between reason and morality, this linkage is not usually conceived to be part of the "ought" implies "can" principle. Nevertheless, I claim that there are good reasons for associating this linkage between reason and morality with the "ought" implies "can" principle, namely, our use of the word "can" as in the example just given, and the natural progression from logical, physical and psychological possibility found in the traditional "ought" implies "can" principle to the notion of moral possibility found in this formulation of the "ought" implies "can" principle. In any case, the acceptability of this formulation of the "ought" implies "can" principle is determined by the virtual universal acceptance of its components and not by the manner in which I have proposed to join those components together.

Now applying the "ought" implies "can" principle to the cases at hand, where the sacrifices for the sake of greater benefit to others are either trivial, reparable, or nonreparable but greatly outweighed by their consequences, the principle would not be violated. In all of these cases, the sacrifices involved are not unreasonable to ask those affected to bear. Nevertheless, the "ought" implies "can" principle would be violated by cases of the sort Rawls has in mind where the least advantaged would be asked to sacrifice an acceptable minimum so that greater benefits would be enjoyed by the more advantaged. For example, Rawls envisions a case where limiting the political liberties and religious freedoms of small and weak minorities would be outweighed by the social advantages to a sizable majority. This is not a

sacrifice that it is reasonable to ask and/or require these minorities to bear. Accordingly, when utilitarianism is appropriately interpreted to be constrained by the "ought" implies "can" principle, it would then appear not to have the practical implications to which Rawls objects.

But what then becomes of utilitarianism's requirement to maximize utility overall? Because people are not morally required to do what would involve so great a sacrifice that it would be unreasonable to ask, and/or in cases of severe conflict of interest, unreasonable to require them to abide by, then at least in some cases, the requirement to maximize utility can only be a supererogatory requirement, not something we can reasonably require of people, but something that people may choose to do in any case for the sake of the greater good that would result. Moreover, if, due to the declining marginal utility of goods, it will only rarely be the case that we can maximize utility overall by transferring benefits from the least advantaged to the more advantaged in society (as utilitarians argue), then, as I just argued, we have the option of understanding the requirement of maximizing utility in such cases to be morally supererogatory. Alternatively, we can interpret the constraints of the "ought" implies "can" principle, which generally favor the poor and disadvantaged over the rich and advantaged, as producing greater utility overall in the sense of producing morally greater or morally better utility overall.[3]

It is interesting to note here how the "ought" implies "can" principle similarly constrains other moral and political theories as well. Take, for example, libertarianism.[4] According to John Hospers, libertarianism requires that each person should have the greatest amount of liberty commensurate with the same liberty for all. But how is this principle to apply to cases of conflict between the rich and the poor? Imagine that the rich have more than enough resources to satisfy their basic needs, and that the poor, by contrast, lack the resources to meet their most basic needs even though they have tried all the means available to them that libertarians regard as legitimate for acquiring such resources. Under circumstances such as these, the rich could have the liberty not to be interfered with in using their resources to satisfy their luxury needs if they so wish. Alternatively, the poor could have the liberty not to be interfered with in taking from the surplus possessions of the rich what is necessary to satisfy their basic needs. Because these liberties are in direct conflict, what needs to be determined, therefore, is which liberty is morally preferable: the liberty of the rich or the liberty of the poor.

It is here that the "ought" implies "can" principle is extremely relevant. Applying the principle to the conflict between the rich and the poor, it seems clear that the poor have it within their power willingly to relinquish such an important liberty as the liberty to take from the rich what they require to meet their basic needs. Nevertheless, it would be unreasonable to ask or require them to make so great a sacrifice. By contrast, it would not be unreasonable to ask and require the rich to sacrifice the liberty to meet some of their luxury needs so that the poor can have the liberty to meet their basic needs. Consequently, when libertarianism, is appropriately constrained by the "ought" implies "can" principle, it favors the liberty of the poor over the liberty of the rich.[5]

This means that within the bundle of liberties alloted to each person by the basic principle of libertarianism, there must be the liberty not to be interfered with (when one is poor) in taking from the surplus possessions of the rich what is necessary to satisfy one's basic needs. This must be part of the bundle that constitutes the greatest liberty for each person because this liberty is morally superior to the liberty with which it directly conflicts, that is, the liberty not to be interfered with (when one is rich) in using one's resources to satisfy one's luxury needs if one so wishes. In this context, the "ought" implies "can" principle establishes the moral superiority of the liberty of the poor over the liberty of the rich. Here, too, the application of the "ought" implies "can" principle can be said to support greater liberty overall in the sense of supporting the morally greater or morally better liberty overall.

III

Of course, Rawls does not think that utilitarianism, as traditionally understood, could generate an acceptable minimum, left to its own resources. Unfortunately, in arriving at this conclusion, Rawls does not consider whether applying the "ought" implies "can" principle to utilitarianism could secure that minimum. In a way, this is surprising because Rawls is sympathetic to Thomas Scanlon's characterization of moral requirements as those to which no one could reasonably reject, and this constraint is quite similar to that described by the "ought" implies "can" principle.[6] Unfortunately, neither Rawls nor Scanlon sees this similarity, which presumably explains why neither of them recognizes the possibility of internally reforming utilitarianism.

It also explains why Rawls, in his second comparison, simply considers whether his two principles of justice can be shown to be superior to an *externally* constrained utilitarian view. Actually, this view is so externally constrained that it is hard to recognize it as a form of utilitarianism. What it is is Rawls's two principles of justice with the principle of average utility combined with a stipulated social minimum substituted for the difference principle. The utilitarian element of this view—the principle of average utility—is really buried and heavily constrained by the other requirements of the view. Nevertheless, Rawls thinks that his two principles of justice would still be judged superior in the original position to this heavily constrained form of utilitarianism. This is because, Rawls argues, his difference principle expresses an ideal of reciprocity absent from this constrained form of utilitarianism.

But how does this argument go? According to Rawls, starting from a point of equal division, the difference principle requires that those who gain more are to do so on terms acceptable to those who gain less, thereby securing a reciprocity not matched by the principle of average utility, even with a stipulated social minimum. Unfortunately, the equal division starting point of this argument is a little difficult to concretely imagine. It would appear to involve a society that is bound together by the rule that whatever primary social goods (e.g., basic liberties and opportunities, income and wealth) are produced or available in the society are to be divided equally among all the members of the society. Under these circumstances, it would seem that those who have the greater talents and abilities to be productive are going to use their talents and abilities to at least ensure that the equal share that is guaranteed to everyone is an acceptable minimum because otherwise they would not receive an acceptable minimum themselves.

It is less clear, however, what we can reasonably expect from the perspective of those who have lesser talents and abilities. Would they be willing to make a corresponding contribution? If those who with lesser talents and abilities know that they will get an equal share whatever they do, maybe they would just decide to free-ride, more or less, requiring those with greater talents and abilities to work harder than they would otherwise have to do in order to secure an acceptable minimum for themselves and everyone else. Of course, this could be avoided if everyone at the equal sharing starting point were required to do what he or she can to provide an acceptable minimum for themselves and those in need. But in his *Restatement,* Rawls explicitly rejects the required contribution part of Karl Marx's principle: From each according to his or her abilities to each according to his or her needs. Rawls thinks that this requirement would lead people to conceal their talents and abilities or to choose for themselves more productive but less desirable jobs or occupations.[7] But how else are we going to prevent free-riding on the part of the would-be least advantaged from the perspective of the original position?

Even leaving aside the problem of how an equal sharing starting point would be generated in the first place, consider what would motivate people in the original position to move beyond it. Sup-posedly, we are to imagine that those with greater talents and abilities would offer to be even more productive than they presently are, provided that they would receive a larger share of the increased social goods that thereby would be produced. Let's say, for example, that under the new arrangement those with greater talents and abilities would get five more units of income and wealth while those who would be the least advantaged in the society would get only one more unit. The question is why should those who would be the least advantaged under the proposed new arrangement agree to this differential improvement? If they reject it, then presumably they, and everyone else, would stay at the equal division point; everyone would have just an acceptable minimum. So why wouldn't they reject this proposed differential sharing arrangement and propose instead an equal sharing of everything that is produced above what is necessary to provide everyone with an acceptable minimum? Surely, those with greater talents and abilities would want to receive more than the acceptable minimum that they are currently getting. But if they were to reject this counter proposal, they, along with everyone else, would surely lose out. Of course, the same would hold for those who would have been the least advantaged under the proposed differential sharing arrangement. If they reject that arrangement, and their own equal sharing arrangement is similarly rejected, then they too lose out. So what should persons in the original position do? Should they just flip a coin between the two proposals?

Suppose we try to use the idea of reciprocity to achieve a resolution here. According to Rawls, reciprocity requires "that those who gain more are to do so on terms acceptable to those who gain less." This would imply that resolution that would be most favored in the original position starting from a point of equal sharing would be an arrangement of continuing equal sharing. This is the arrangement that benefits those who would otherwise be the most disadvantaged. But clearly this is not the sort of arrangement that Rawls envisioned that his difference principle would endorse.

IV

Clearly, the underlying problem here is that Rawls's equal sharing starting point seems to overly favor those with less talent and ability in society. It goes so far as to guarantee them an acceptable minimum even if they are unwilling to productively contribute to their society. We could, however, imagine an alternative that overly favors those with more talent and ability in society. Thus, suppose that persons in the original position assumed that those with more talent and ability could do well for themselves if they simply cooperated with each other, although they could do even better if they also cooperated with those with less talent and ability. Framing the original position choice situation this way would have the effect of putting those with more talent and ability in a very strong bargaining position. Conceivably, their terms of cooperation with those with less talent and ability might not even include an acceptable minimum. Surely, this alternative construal of the original position choice situation would overly favor those with more talent and ability.[8] So we have one alternative, Rawls's equal sharing starting point, that overly favors those with less talent and ability in society, and another alternative that overly favors those with more talent and ability in society. Ideally, we would like to go in between.

Trying to go in between these two unacceptable construals, we might envision persons in the original position assuming that those with more talent and ability would tend to survive, but not all that well, without cooperative arrangement with those with less talent and ability, and that those with less talent and ability would do far worse in the absence of a cooperative arrangement with those with more talent and ability. Under such conditions, it would seem reasonable to guarantee an acceptable minimum to those with less talent and ability, provided that they do what they can to productively contribute to their

society. It would also seem reasonable to permit those with talent and ability to achieve more than the acceptable minimum provided that everyone in need is guaranteed an acceptable minimum. This outcome would be preferable to what would emerge either from Rawls's equal sharing starting point that overly favors those with less talent and ability or from the other alternative we considered that overly favors those with more talent and ability.

V.

It is important, however, to understand what are the practical implications of this conditional acceptable minimum for Rawls's theory of justice. First, let us specify the conditional acceptable minimum in terms of the satisfaction of a person's basic needs. A person's basic needs are those that must be satisfied in order not to seriously endanger a person's mental or physical well-being. Needs in general, if not satisfied, lead to lacks and deficiencies with respect to various standards. Basic needs, if not satisfied, lead to significant lacks and deficiencies with respect to a standard of mental and physical well-being. A person's needs for food, shelter, medical care, protection, companionship, and self-development are, at least in part, needs of this sort. Obviously, societies vary in their ability to satisfy the basic needs of their members, but the needs themselves would vary only to the degree that there is a corresponding variation in what constitutes health and sanity in different societies. Consequently, requiring the satisfaction of a person's basic needs is a fairly determinate way of specifying the minimum of goods and resources that each person has a right to receive.

Second, we need to appropriately extend the veil of ignorance in the original position to include distant peoples and future generations as well as the members of our own society. Once the veil of ignorance is extended in this fashion, persons in the original position would choose to have this basic needs minimum guaranteed to everyone. Now at present, there is a sufficient worldwide supply of goods and resources to meet the normal costs of satisfying the basic nutritional needs of all existing persons. According to former U.S. Secretary of Agriculture, Bob Bergland

> For the past 20 years, if the available world food supply had been evenly divided and distributed, each person would have received more than the minimum number of calories.[9]

Other authorities have made similar assessments of the available world food supply.[10]

Needless to say, the adoption of a policy of providing an acceptable minimum for all existing persons would necessitate significant changes, especially in developed countries. For example, the large percentage of the U.S. population whose food consumption clearly exceeds even an adequately adjusted poverty index would have to substantially alter their eating habits. In particular, they would have to reduce their consumption of beef and pork in order to make more grain available for direct human consumption. (Currently, 37 percent of worldwide production of grain and 70 percent of U.S. production is fed to animals.[11]) Thus, the satisfaction of at least some of the nonbasic needs of the more advantaged in developed societies would have to be forgone, leading to greater equality, so that the basic nutritional needs of all existing persons in developing and underdeveloped societies could be met. Of course, meeting the long-term basic nutritional needs of all existing persons in developing and underdeveloped societies will require other kinds of aid, including appropriate technology and training, and the removal of trade barriers favoring developed societies.[12] Furthermore, to raise the standard of living in developing and underdeveloped countries will require substantial increases in the consumption of energy and other resources. But such an increase would have to be matched by a substantial decrease in the consumption of these goods in developed countries, otherwise global ecological disaster would result from increased global warming, ozone depletion and acid rain, lowering virtually everyone's standard of living.[13]

Nevertheless, once the basic nutritional needs of future generations are also taken into account, the satisfaction of the nonbasic needs of the more advantaged in developed countries would have to be further restricted in order to preserve the fertility of cropland and other food-related natural resources for the use of future generations. Obviously, the only assured way to guarantee the energy and resources necessary for the satisfaction of the basic needs of future generations is by setting aside resources that would otherwise be used to satisfy the nonbasic needs of existing generations. And once basic needs other than nutritional needs are taken into account as well, still further restrictions would be required. For example, it has been estimated that presently a North American uses 50 times more resources than an Indian. This means that in terms of resource consumption the North American continent's population is the equivalent of 12.5 billion Indians.[14] So unless we assume that basic resources such as arable land, iron, coal, oil, etc. are in unlimited supply, this unequal consumption would have to be radically altered if the basic needs of distant peoples and future generations are to be met.[15] As a consequence, securing an acceptable minimum for both the distant peoples and future generations would lead to a state of affairs in which few resources would be available for directly meeting nonbasic needs. Thus, the basic needs minimum that would be guaranteed to those with less talent and ability, provided that they did what they can to productively contribute to society, would turn out to be the most that anyone in society, even those with more talent and ability, could justifiably possess. Moreover, those with more talent and ability would have to be making their best contributions to society in order that an acceptable minimum could be secured for all. This would lead, despite Rawls's protests, to an instantiation of Marx's principle from each according to his or her ability to each according to his or her (basic) needs, but it would also lead to an instantiation of Rawls's own difference principle because those who are "least advantaged" in this egalitarian society would be clearly as well off as they could reasonably expect to be. Of course, this is not the sort of conception of justice that Rawls thought his original position decision-procedure would favor, nor does it follow from Rawls's equal sharing starting point construal of choice in the original position. Nevertheless, given the problems I have raised for Rawls's equal sharing starting point, it would seem that this is the conception of justice that would be most favored by Rawls's own original position decision procedure.

So it turns out that while the conception of justice that emerges from Rawls's original position is morally acceptable, it is not the conception of justice that Rawls's thought emerged, nor is it as incompatible with a defensible utilitarian perspective as Rawls thought.

NOTES

1. John C. Harsanyi, *Essays on Ethics, Social Behavior, and Scientific Explanation* (Dordrecht, 1976).

2. There are moral theories, like John Finnis's, that would seem to reject what I have just said any defensible moral theory must support. Thus, Finnis's moral theory contains the principle that one should never do evil that good may come. But Finnis would probably want to interpret my first two cases (stepping on people's toes to respond to an emergency and even lying (not telling the truth to one's friend to keep her from committing suicide) as not really cases of doing evil that good may come of it. In my third case, (shooting one Indian to save nineteen others) Finnis would surely see this as a case of doing evil that good may come of it and so impermissible. But what about the consequences of not doing evil in this case? Finnis contends that we need not worry about consequences because God will take care of things. Obviously this is not a stance that a nonbeliever can take. And even for the believer, how does Finnis know that God does want us to take consequences into account in these difficult cases?

3. For a fuller argument for this conclusion, see my *Justice for Here and Now* (Cambridge, 1998) Chapter 3.

4. Check the articles in Section II of this anthology.

5. I first appealed to this interpretation of the "ought" implies "can" principle to internally constrain libertarianism in an expanded version of an article entitled "Neo-Libertarianism," which appeared in the fall of 1979 in my edited volume, *Justice: Alternative Political Perspectives,* 1st ed. (Belmont: Wadsworth Publishing Co), pp. 172–186. In my judgment, the "ought" implies "can" principle can be more effectively used as a constraint on libertarianism than as a constraint on utilitarianism because the sacrifices that libertarians standardly seek to impose on the less advantaged are more outrageous and, hence, more easily shown to be contrary to reason than those sacrifices utilitarians are seemingly led to defend.

6. See T. M. Scanlon in "Contractualism and Utilitarianism" *Utilitarianism and Beyond,* edited by Amartya Sen and Bernard Williams (Cambridge: Cambridge University Press, 1982), pp. 103–128. See also his *What We Owe Each Other* (Harvard, 1998), Chapter 2.

7. John Rawls, *Justice as Fairness: A Restatement* (Harvard, 2001), pp. 157–8.

8. Rawls assumes that other political views start with some such construal of their favored "state of nature" choice situation. Joshua Cohen makes a similar point and argues that John Locke's is one such theory. See his "Structure and Choice, and Legitimacy: Locke's Theory of the State," *Philosophy and Public Affairs* (1986), pp. 301–324.

9. Bob Bergland, "Attacking the Problem of World Hunger," *The National Forum* (1979) Vol. 69, No. 2, p. 4.

10. *Hunger 1995: Fifth Annual Report on the State of World Hunger* (Silver Springs, Md.: Bread for the World Institute, 1994) p. 10; Ruth Sivard, *World Military and Social Expenditures,* (Washington, DC.: World Priorities, 1993) p. 28; Frances Moore Lappe, *World Hunger* (New York: Grove Press, 1986) p. 9.

11. Lester Brown, Christopher Flavin, and Hal Kane, *Vital Signs 1996* (New York: W.W. Norton & Co., 1996) pp. 34–5; Jeremy Rifkin, *Beyond Beef* (New York: Penguin, 1992), p. 1.

12. See Henry Shue, *Basic Rights* (Princeton: Princeton University Press, 1980), Chapter 7.

13. For a discussion of these causal connections, see Cheryl Silver, *One Earth One Future* (Washington, DC, 1990); Bill McKibben, *The End of Nature* (New York: Anchor Books, 1989); Jeremy Leggett, ed., *Global Warming* (New York: Oxford University Press, 1990); Lester Brown, ed., *The World Watch Reader,* (New York: Nelson, 1991).

14. Janet Besecker and Phil Elder, "Lifeboat Ethics: A Reply to Hardin," in *Readings in Ecology, Energy and Human Society: Contemporary Perspectives,* edited by William R. Burdi, Jr. (New York: Harper and Row, 1977), p. 229.

15. Currently, the U.S. which constitutes 6% of the world's population consumes 30% of the world's

natural resources. There is no way that the resource consumption of the United States can be matched by developing and underdeveloped countries, and even if it could be matched, doing so would clearly lead to ecological disaster. See *Planet under Stress,* edited by Constance Mungall and Digby McLaren (Oxford: Oxford University Press, 1990) and *World Hunger: Twelve Myths* by Frances Lappe and Joseph Collins (New York: Grove Press, 1986).

The Utilitarian Perspective

12   On the Connection Between Justice and Utility

JOHN STUART MILL

IN ALL AGES OF SPECULATION one of the strongest obstacles to the reception of the doctrine that utility or happiness is the criterion of right and wrong has been drawn from the idea of justice. The powerful sentiment and apparently clear perception which that word recalls with a rapidity and certainty resembling an instinct have seemed to the majority of thinkers to point to an inherent quality in things; to show that the just must have an existence in nature as something absolute, generically distinct from every variety of the expedient and, in idea, opposed to it, though (as is commonly acknowledged) never, in the long run, disjoined from it in fact.

In the case of this, as of our other moral sentiments, there is no necessary connection between the question of its origin and that of its binding force. That a feeling is bestowed on us by nature does not necessarily legitimate all its promptings. The feeling of justice might be a peculiar instinct, and might yet require, like our other instincts, to be controlled and enlightened by a higher reason. If we have intellectual instincts leading us to judge in a particular way, as well as animal instincts that prompt us to act in a particular way, there is no necessity that the former should be more infallible in their sphere than the latter in theirs; it may as well happen that wrong judgments are occasionally suggested by those, as wrong actions by these. But though it is one thing to believe that we have natural feelings of justice, and another to acknowledge them as an ultimate criterion of conduct,

these two opinions are very closely connected in point of fact. Mankind is always predisposed to believe that any subjective feeling not otherwise accounted for, is a revelation of some objective reality. Our present object is to determine whether the reality to which the feeling of justice corresponds is one which needs any such special revelation, whether the justice or injustice of an action is a thing intrinsically peculiar and distinct from all its other qualities or only a combination of certain of those qualities presented under a peculiar aspect. For the purpose of this inquiry it is practically important to consider whether the feeling itself, of justice and injustice, is *sui generis* like our sensations of color and taste or a derivative feeling formed by a combination of others. And this it is the more essential to examine, as people are in general willing enough to allow that objectively the dictates of justice coincide with a part of the field of general expediency; but inasmuch as the subjective mental feeling of justice is different from that which commonly attaches to simple expediency, and, except in the extreme cases of the latter, is far more imperative in its demands, people find it difficult to see in justice only a particular kind or branch of general utility, and think that its superior binding force requires a totally different origin.

To throw light upon this question, it is necessary to attempt to ascertain what is the distinguishing character of justice, or of injustice; what is the quality, or whether there is any quality,

From Utilitarianism, *Chapter V. First published 1863.*

attributed in common to all modes of conduct designated as unjust (for justice, like many other moral attributes, is best defined by its opposite), and distinguishing them from such modes of conduct as are disapproved, but without having that particular epithet of disapprobation applied to them. If in everything which men are accustomed to characterize as just or unjust some one common attribute or collection of attributes is always present, we may judge whether this particular attribute or combination of attributes would be capable of gathering round it a sentiment of that peculiar character and intensity by virtue of the general laws of our emotional constitution, or whether the sentiment is inexplicable and requires to be regarded as a special provision of nature. If we find the former to be the case, we shall, in resolving this question, have resolved also the main problem; if the latter, we shall have to seek for some other mode of investigating it.

To find the common attributes of a variety of objects, it is necessary to begin by surveying the objects themselves in the concrete. Let us therefore advert successively to the various models of action and arrangements of human affairs which are classed by universal or widely spread opinion, as just or as unjust. The things well known to excite the sentiments associated with those names are of a very multifarious character. I shall pass them rapidly in review, without studying any particular arrangement.

In the first place, it is mostly considered unjust to deprive anyone of his personal liberty, his property, or any other thing which belongs to him by law. Here, therefore, is one instance of the application of the terms "just" and "unjust" in a perfectly definite sense, namely, that it is just to respect, unjust to violate, the *legal rights* of anyone. But this judgment admits of several exceptions, arising from the other forms in which the notions of justice and injustice present themselves. For example, the person who suffers the deprivation may (as the phrase is) have *forfeited* the rights which he is so deprived of—a case to which we shall return presently But also—

Secondly, the legal rights of which he is deprived may be rights which *ought* not to have belonged to him; in other words, the law which confers on him these rights may be a bad law. When it is or when (which is the same thing for our purpose) it is supposed to be so, opinions will differ as to the justice or injustice of infringing it. Some maintain that no law, however, bad, ought to be disobeyed by an individual citizen; that his opposition to it, if shown at all, should only be shown in endeavoring to get it altered by competent authority. This opinion (which condemns many of the most illustrious benefactors of mankind, and would often protect pernicious institutions against the only weapons which, in the state of things existing at the time, have any chance of succeeding against them) is defended by those who hold it on grounds of expediency, principally on that of the importance to the common interest of mankind, of maintaining inviolate the sentiment of submission to law. Other persons, again, hold the directly contrary opinion that any law, judged to be bad, may blamelessly be disobeyed, even though it be not judged to be unjust but only inexpedient, while others would confine the license of disobedience to the case of unjust laws; but, again, some say that all laws which are inexpedient are unjust, since every law imposes some restriction on the natural liberty of mankind, which restriction is an injustice unless legitimated by tending to their good. Among these diversities of opinion it seems to be universally admitted that there may be unjust laws, and that law, consequently, is not the ultimate criterion of justice, but may give to one person a benefit, or impose on another an evil, which justice condemns. When, however, a law is thought to be unjust, it seems always to be regarded as being so in the same way in which a breach of law is unjust; namely, by infringing somebody's right, which, as it cannot in this case be a legal right, receives a different appellation and is called a moral right. We may say, therefore, that a second case of injustice consists in taking or withholding from any person that to which he has a *moral right*.

Thirdly, it is universally considered just that each person should obtain that (whether good or evil) which he *deserves,* and unjust that he should obtain a good or be made to undergo an evil which he does not deserve. This is, perhaps, the clearest and most emphatic form in which the idea of justice is conceived by the general mind. As it involves the notion of desert, the question arises, what constitutes desert? Speaking in a general way, a person is understood to deserve good if he does right, evil if he does wrong; and in a more particular sense, to deserve good from those to whom he does or has done good, and evil from those to whom he does or has done evil. The precept of returning good for evil has never been regarded as a case of the fulfillment of justice, but as one in which the claims of justice are waived, in obedience to other considerations.

Fourthly, it is confessedly unjust to *break faith* with anyone: to violate an engagement, either express or implied, or disappoint expectations raised by our own conduct, at least if we have raised those expectations knowingly and voluntarily. Like the other obligations of justice already spoken of, this one is not regarded as absolute, but as capable of being overruled by a stronger obligation of justice on the other side, or by such conduct on the part of the person concerned as is deemed to absolve us from our obligation to him and to constitute a *forfeiture* of the benefit which he has been led to expect.

Fifthly, it is, by universal admission, inconsistent with justice to be *partial*—to show favor or preference to one person over another in matters to which favor and preference do not properly apply. Impartiality, however, does not seem to be regarded as a duty in itself, but rather as instrumental to some other duty; for it is admitted that favor and preference are not always censurable, and, indeed, the cases in which they are condemned are rather the exception than the rule. A person would be more likely to be blamed than applauded for giving his family or friends no superiority in good offices over strangers when he could do so without violating any other duty; and no one thinks it unjust to seek one person in preference to another as a friend, connection, or companion. Impartiality where rights are concerned is of course obligatory, but this is involved in the more general obligations of giving to everyone his right. A tribunal, for example, must be impartial because it is bound to award, without regard to any other consideration, a disputed object to the one of two parties who has the right to it. There are other cases in which impartiality means being solely influenced by desert, as with those who, in the capacity of judges, preceptors, or parents, administer reward and punishment as such. There are cases, again, in which it means being solely influenced by considerations for the public interest, as in making a selection among candidates for a government employment. Impartiality, in short, as an obligation of justice, may be said to mean being exclusively influenced by the considerations which it is supposed ought to influence the particular case in hand, and resisting solicitation of any motives which prompt to conduct different from what those considerations would dictate.

Nearly allied to the idea of impartiality is that of *equality,* which often enters as a component part of both into the conception of justice and into the practice of it, and, in the eyes of many persons, constitutes its essence. But in this, still more than in any other case, the notion of justice varies in different persons, and always conforms in its variations to their notion of utility. Each person maintains that equality is the dictate of justice, except where he thinks that expediency requires inequality. The justice of giving equal protection to the rights of all is maintained by those who support the most outrageous inequality in the rights themselves. Even in slave countries it is theoretically admitted that the rights of the slave, such as they are, ought to be as sacred as those of the master, and that a tribunal which fails to enforce them with equal strictness is wanting injustice; while, at the same time, institutions which leave to the slave scarcely any rights to enforce are not deemed unjust because they are not deemed inexpedient. Those who think that utility requires distinctions of rank do not consider it unjust that riches and social privileges should be unequally dispensed; but those who think this inequality inexpedient think it unjust also. Whoever thinks that government is necessary sees no injustice in as much inequality as is constituted by giving to the magistrate powers not granted to other people. Even among those who hold leveling doctrines, there are differences of opinion about expediency. Some communists consider it unjust that the produce of the labor of the community should be shared on any other principle than that of exact equality; others think it just that those should receive most whose wants are greatest; while others hold that those who work harder, or who produce more, or whose services are more valuable to the community, may justly claim a larger quota in the division of the produce. And the sense of natural justice may be plausibly appealed to in behalf of every one of these opinions.

Among so many diverse applications of the term "justice," which yet is not regarded as ambiguous, it is a matter of some difficulty to seize the mental link which holds them together, and on which the moral sentiment adhering to the term essentially depends. Perhaps, in this embarrassment, some help may be derived from the history of the word, as indicated by its etymology.

In most if not all languages, the etymology of the word which corresponds to "just" points distinctly to an origin connected with the ordinances of law. *Justum* is a form of *jussum,* that which has been ordered. *Dikaion* comes directly from *dike,* a suit at law. *Recht,* from which came *right* and *righteous,* is synonymous with law. The courts of justice, the administration of justice, are the courts and the administration of law. *La justice,* in French, is the established term for judicature. I am not committing the fallacy, imputed with some show of truth to Horne Tooke, of assuming that a word must still continue to mean what it originally meant. Etymology is slight evidence of what the idea now signified is, but the very best evidence of how it sprang up. There can, I think, be no doubt that the *idée mère,* the primitive element, in the formation of the notion of justice was conformity to law. It constituted the entire idea among the Hebrews, up to the birth of Christianity; as might be expected in the case of a people whose laws attempted to embrace all subjects on which precepts were required, and who believed those laws to be a direct emanation from the Supreme Being. But other nations, and in particular the Greeks and Romans, who knew that their laws had been made originally, and still continued to be made, by men, were not afraid to admit that those men might make bad laws; might do, by law, the same things, and from the same motives, which if done by individuals without the sanction of law would be called unjust. And hence the sentiment of injustice came to be attached, not to all violations of law, but only to violations of such laws as *ought* to exist, including such as ought to exist but do not, and to laws themselves if supposed to be contrary to what ought to be law. In this manner the idea of law and of its injunctions was still predominant in the notion of justice, even when the laws actually in force ceased to be accepted as the standard of it.

It is true that mankind consider the idea of justice and its obligations as applicable to many things which neither are, nor is it desired that they should be, regulated by law. Nobody desires that laws should interfere with the whole detail of private life; yet everyone allows that in all daily conduct a person may and does show himself to be either just or unjust. But even here, the idea of the breach of what ought to be law still lingers in a modified shape. It would always give us pleasure, and chime in with our feelings of fitness, that acts which we deem unjust should be punished, though we do not always think it expedient that this should be done by the tribunals. We forego that gratification on account of incidental inconveniences. We should be glad to see just conduct enforced and injustice repressed, even in the minutest details, if we were not, with reason, afraid of trusting the magistrate with so unlimited an amount of power over individuals. When we think that a person is bound in justice to do a thing, it is an ordinary form of language to say that he ought to be compelled to do it. We should be gratified to see the obligation enforced by anybody who had the power. If we see that its enforcement by law would be inexpedient, we lament the impossibility, we consider the impunity given to injustice as an evil and strive to make amends for it by bringing a strong expression of our own and the public disapprobation to bear upon the offender. Thus the idea of legal constraint is still the generating idea of the notion of justice, though undergoing several transformations before that notion as it exists in an advanced state of society becomes complete.

The above is, I think, a true account, as far as it goes, of the origin and progressive growth of the idea of justice. But we must observe that it contains as yet nothing to distinguish that obligation from moral obligation in general. For the truth is that the idea of penal sanction, which is the essence of law, enters not only into the conception of injustice, but into that of any kind of wrong. We do not call anything wrong unless we mean to imply that a person ought to be punished in some way or other for doing it—if not by law, by the opinion of his fellow creatures; if not by opinion, by the reproaches of his own conscience. This seems the real turning point of the distinction between morality and simple expediency. It is a part of the notion of duty in every one of its forms that a person may rightfully be compelled to fulfill it. Duty is a thing which may be *exacted* from a person, as one exacts a debt. Unless we think that it may be exacted from him, we do not call it his duty. Reasons of prudence, or the interest of other people, may militate against actually exacting it, but the person himself, it is clearly understood, would not be entitled to complain. There are other things, on the contrary, which we wish that people should do, which we like or admire them for doing, perhaps dislike or despise them for not doing, but yet admit they are not bound to do; it is not a case of moral obligation; we do not blame them; that is, we do not think that they are proper objects of punishment. How we come by these ideas of deserving and not deserving punishment will appear, perhaps, in the sequel; but I think there is no doubt that this distinction lies at the

bottom of the notions of right and wrong; that we call any conduct wrong, or employ, instead, some other term of dislike or disparagement, according as we think that the person ought, or ought not, to be punished for it; and we say it would be right to do so and so, or merely that it would be desirable or laudable, according as we would wish to see the person whom it concerns compelled, or only persuaded and exhorted, to act in that manner.

Justice Correlated with Certain Rights

This, therefore, being the characteristic difference which marks off, not justice, but morality in general from the remaining provinces of expediency and worthiness, the character is still to be sought which distinguishes justice from other branches of morality. Now it is known that ethical writers divide moral duties into two classes, denoted by the ill-chosen expressions, duties of perfect and of imperfect obligation; the latter being those in which, though the act is obligatory, the particular occasions of performing it are left to our choice, as in the case of charity or beneficence, which we are indeed bound to practice but not toward any definite person, nor at any prescribed time. In the more precise language of philosophic jurists, duties of perfect obligation are those duties in virtue of which a correlative *right* resides in some person or persons; duties of imperfect obligation are those moral obligations which do not give birth to any right. I think it will be found that this distinction exactly coincides with that which exists between justice and the other obligations of morality. In our survey of the various popular acceptations of justice, the term appeared generally to involve the idea of a personal right—a claim on the part of one or more individuals, like that which the law gives when it confers a proprietary or other legal right. Whether the injustice consists in depriving a person of a possession, or in breaking faith with him, or in treating him worse than he deserves, or worse than other people who have no greater claims—in each case the supposition implies two things: a wrong done, and some assignable person who is wronged. Injustice may also be done by treating a person better than others; but the wrong in this case is to his competitors, who are also assignable persons. It seems to me that this feature in the case—a right in some person, correlative to the moral obligation—constitutes a specific difference between justice and generosity or beneficence. Justice implies something which it is not only right to do, and wrong not to do, but which some individual person can claim from us as his moral right. No one has a moral right to our generosity or beneficence because we are not morally bound to practice those virtues toward any given individual. And it will be found with respect to this as to every correct definition that the instances which seem to conflict with it are those which most confirm it. For if a moralist attempts, as some have done, to make out that mankind generally, though not any given individual, have a right to all the good we can do them, he at once, by that thesis, includes generosity and beneficence within the category of justice. He is obliged to say that our utmost exertions are *due* to our fellow creatures, thus assimilating them to a debt; or that nothing less can be a sufficient *return* for what society does for us, thus classing the case as one of gratitude; both of which are acknowledged cases of justice, and not of the virtue of beneficence; and whoever does not place the distinction between justice and morality in general, where we have now placed it, will be found to make no distinction between them at all, but to merge all morality in justice. . . . When we call anything a person's right, we mean that he has a valid claim on society to protect him in the possession of it, either by the force of law or by that of education and opinion. If he has what we consider a sufficient claim, on whatever account, to have something guaranteed to him by society, we say that he has a right to it. If we desire to prove that anything does not belong to him by right, we think this done as soon as it is admitted that society ought not to take measures for securing it to him, but should leave him to chance or to his own exertions. Thus a person is said to have a right to what he can earn in fair professional competition,

because society ought not to allow any other person to hinder him from endeavoring to earn in that manner as much as he can. But he has not a right to three hundred a year, though he may happen to be earning it; because society is not called on to provide that he shall earn that sum. On the contrary, if he owns ten thousand pounds three-percent stock, he *has* a right to three hundred a year because society has come under an obligation to provide him with an income of that amount.

To have a right, then, is I conceive, to have something which society ought to defend me in the possession of. If the objector goes on to ask why it ought, I can give him no other reason than general utility. If that expression does not seem to convey a sufficient feeling of the strength of the obligation, nor to account for the peculiar energy of the feeling, it is because there goes to the composition of the sentiment, not a rational only but also an animal element—the thirst for retaliation; and this thirst derives its intensity, as well as its moral justification, from the extraordinarily important and impressive kind of utility which is concerned. The interest involved is that of security, to everyone's feelings the most vital of all interests. All other earthly benefits are needed by one person, not needed by another; and many of them can, if necessary be cheerfully foregone or replaced by something else; but security no human being can possibly do without; on it we depend for all our immunity from evil and for the whole value of all and every good, beyond the passing moment, since nothing but the gratification of the instant could be of any worth to us if we could be deprived of everything the next instant by whoever was momentarily stronger than ourselves. Now this most indispensable of all necessaries, after physical nutriment, cannot be had unless the machinery for providing it is kept unintermittedly in active play. Our notion, therefore, of the claim we have on our fellow creatures to join in making safe for us the very groundwork of our existence gathers feelings around it so much more intense than those concerned in any of the more common cases of utility that the difference in degree (as is often the case in psychology) becomes a real difference in kind. The claim assumes that character of absoluteness, that apparent infinity and incommensurability with all other considerations which constitute the distinction between the feeling of right and wrong and that of ordinary expediency and inexpediency. The feelings concerned are so powerful, and we count so positively on finding a responsive feeling in others (all being alike interested) that *ought* and *should* grow into *must,* and recognized indispensability becomes a moral necessity, analogous to physical, and often not inferior to it in binding force.

Justice and Utility

If the preceding analysis, or something resembling it, be not the correct account of the notion of justice—if justice be totally independent of utility, and be a standard *per se,* which the mind can recognize by simple retrospection of itself—it is hard to understand why that internal oracle is so ambiguous, and why so many things appear either just or unjust, according to the light in which they are regarded.

We are continually informed that utility is an uncertain standard, which every different person interprets differently, and that there is no safety but in the immutable, ineffaceable, and unmistakable dictates of justice, which carry their evidence in themselves and are independent of the fluctuations of opinion. One would suppose from this that on questions of justice there could be no controversy; that, if we take that for our rule, its application to any given case could leave us in as little doubt as a mathematical demonstration. So far is this from being the fact that there is as much difference of opinion, and as much discussion, about what is just as about what is useful to society. Not only have different nations and individuals different notions of justice, but in the mind of one and the same individual, justice is not some one rule, principle, or maxim, but many which do not always coincide in their dictates, and, in choosing between which, he is guided either by some extraneous standard or by his own personal predilec-

tions. . . . [to take an] example from a subject already once referred to. In cooperative industrial association, is it just or not that talent or skill should give a title to superior remuneration? On the negative side of the question it is argued that whoever does the best he can deserves equally well, and ought not in justice to be put in a position of inferiority for no fault of his own; that superior abilities have already advantages more than enough, in the admiration they excite, the personal influence they command, and the internal sources of satisfaction attending them, without adding to these a superior share of the world's goods; and that society is bound in justice rather to make compensation to the less favored for this unmerited inequality of advantages than to aggravate it. On the contrary side it is contended that society receives more from the more efficient laborer; that, his services being more useful, society owes him a larger return for them; that a greater share of the joint result is actually his work, and not to allow his claim to it is a kind of robbery; that, if he is only to receive as much as others, he can only be justly required to produce as much, and to give a smaller amount of time and exertion, proportioned to his superior efficiency. Who shall decide between these appeals to conflicting principles of justice? Justice has in this case two sides to it, which it is impossible to bring into harmony, and the two disputants have chosen opposite sides; the one looks to what it is just that the individual should receive, the other to what it is just that the community should give. Each, from his own point of view, is unanswerable; and any choice between them, on the grounds of justice, must be perfectly arbitrary. Social utility alone can decide the preference.

How many, again, and how irreconcilable are the standards of justice to which reference is made in discussing the repartition of taxation. One opinion is that the payment to the state should be in numerical proportion to pecuniary means. Others think that justice dictates what they term graduated taxation—taking a higher percentage from those who have more to spare. In point of natural justice a strong case might be made for disregarding means altogether, and taking the same absolute sum (whenever it could be got) from everyone; as the subscribers to a mess or to a club all pay the same sum for the same privileges, whether they can all equally afford it or not. Since the protection (it might be said) of law and government is afforded to and is equally required by all, there is no injustice in making all buy it at the same price. It is reckoned justice, not injustice, that a dealer should charge to all customers the same price for the same article, not a price varying according to their means of payment. This doctrine, as applied to taxation, finds no advocates because it conflicts so strongly with man's feelings of humanity and of social expediency; but the principle of justice which it invokes is as true and as binding as those which can be appealed to against it. Accordingly it exerts a tacit influence on the line of defense employed for other modes of assessing taxation. People feel obliged to argue that the state does more for the rich man than for the poor, as a justification for its taking more from them, though this is in reality not true, for the rich would be far better able to protect themselves, in the absence of law or government, than the poor, and indeed would probably be successful in converting the poor into their slaves. Others, again, so far defer to the same conception of justice as to maintain that all should pay an equal capitation tax for the protection of their persons (these being of equal value to all), and an unequal tax for the protection of their property, which is unequal. To this others reply that the all of one man is as valuable to him as the all of another. From these confusions there is no other mode of extrication than the utilitarian.

Is, then, the difference between the just and the expedient a merely imaginary distinction? Have mankind been under a delusion in thinking that justice is a more sacred thing than policy, and that the latter ought only to be listened to after the former has been satisfied? By no means. The exposition we have given of the nature and origin of the sentiment recognizes a real distinction; and no one of those who profess the most sublime contempt for the consequences of actions as an element in their morality attaches more importance to the distinction than I do. While I dispute the pretensions of any theory which sets up an imaginary standard of justice not grounded on utility, I account the justice which is grounded on utility to be the chief part and incomparably the most sacred and binding part, of all morality. Justice is a name for certain classes of moral rules which concern the essentials of human well-being more nearly, and are therefore of more absolute obligation, than any other rules of the guidance of life; and the notion which we have found to be of the essence of the idea of justice—that of a right residing in an individual—implies and testifies to this more binding obligation.

The moral rules which forbid mankind to hurt one another (in which we must never forget to include wrongful interference with each other's freedom) are more vital to human well-being than any maxims, however important, which only point out the best mode of managing some department of human affairs. They have also the peculiarity that they are the main element in determining the whole of the social feelings of mankind. It is their observance which alone preserves peace among human beings; if obedience to them were not the rule, and disobedience the exception, everyone would see in everyone else an enemy against whom he must be perpetually guarding himself. What is hardly less important, these are the precepts which mankind have the strongest and the most direct inducements for impressing upon one another. By merely giving to each other prudential instruction or exhortation, they may gain, or think they gain, nothing; in inculcating on each other the duty of positive beneficence, they have an unmistakable interest, but far less in degree; a person may possibly not need the benefits of others, but he always needs that they should not do him hurt. Thus the moralities which protect every individual from being harmed by others, either directly or by being hindered in his freedom of pursuing his own good, are at once those which he himself has most at heart and those which he has the strongest interest in publishing and enforcing by word and deed. It is by a person's observance of these that his fitness to exist as one of the fellowship of human beings is tested and decided; for on that depends his being a nuisance or not to those with whom he is in contact. Now it is these moralities primarily which compose the obligations of justice. The most marked cases of injustice, and those which give the tone to the feeling of repugnance which characterizes the sentiment, are acts of wrongful aggression or wrongful exercise of power over someone; the next are those which consist in wrongfully withholding from him something which is his due—in both cases inflicting on him a positive hurt, either in the form of direct suffering or of the privation of some good which he had reasonable ground, either of a physical or of a social kind, for counting upon.

The same powerful motives which command the observance of these primary moralities enjoin the punishment of those who violate them; and as the impulses of self-defense, of defense of others, and of vengeance are all called forth against such persons, retribution, or evil for evil, becomes closely connected with the sentiment of justice, and is universally included in the idea. Good for good is also one of the dictates of justice; and this, though its social utility is evident, and though it carries with it a natural human feeling, has not at first sight that obvious connection with hurt or injury which, existing in the most elementary cases of just and unjust, is the source of the characteristic intensity of the sentiment. But the connection, though less obvious, is not less real. He who accepts benefits and denies a return of them when needed inflicts a real hurt by disappointing one of the most natural and reasonable of expectations, and one which he must at least tacitly have encouraged, otherwise the benefits would seldom have been conferred. The important rank, among human evils and wrongs, of the disappointment of expectation is shown in the fact that it constitutes the principal criminality of two such highly immoral acts as a breach of friendship and a breach of promise. Few hurts which human beings can sustain are greater, and none wound more, than when that on which they habitually and with full assurance relied fails them in the hour of need; and

few wrongs are greater than this mere withholding of good; none excite more resentment, either in the person suffering or in a sympathizing spectator. The principle, therefore, of giving to each what they deserve, that is, good for good as well as evil for evil, is not only included within the idea of justice as we have defined it, but is a proper object of that intensity of sentiment which places the just in human estimation above the simply expedient.

Most of the maxims of justice current in the world, and commonly appealed to in its transactions, are simply instrumental to carrying into effect the principles of justice which we have now spoken of. That a person is only responsible for what he has done voluntarily, or could voluntarily have avoided; that it is unjust to condemn any person unheard; that the punishment ought to be proportioned to the offense; and the like, are maxims intended to prevent the just principle of evil for evil from being perverted to the infliction of evil without that justification. The greater part of these common maxims have come into use from the practice of courts of justice, which have been naturally led to a more complete recognition and elaboration than was likely to suggest itself to others, of the rules necessary to enable them to fulfill their double function—of inflicting punishment when due, and of awarding to each person his right.

That first of judicial virtues, impartiality, is an obligation of justice, partly for the reason last mentioned, as being a necessary condition of the fulfillment of other obligations of justice. But this is not the only source of the exalted rank, among human obligations, of those maxims of equality and impartiality which, both in popular estimation and in that of the most enlightened, are included among the precepts of justice. In one point of view, they may be considered as corollaries from the principles already laid down. If it is a duty to do to each according to his deserts, returning good for good, as well as repressing evil by evil, it necessarily follows that we should treat all equally well (when no higher duty forbids) who have deserved equally well of *us,* and that society should treat all equally well who have deserved equally well of *it,* that is, who have deserved equally well absolutely. This is the highest abstract standard of social and distributive justice, toward which all institutions and the efforts of all virtuous citizens should be made in the utmost possible degree to converge. But this great moral duty rests upon a still deeper foundation, being a direct emanation from the first principle of morals, and not a mere logical corollary from secondary or derivative doctrines. It is involved in the very meaning of utility, or the greatest happiness principle. That principle is a mere form of words without rational signification unless one person's happiness, supposed equal in degree (with the proper allowance made for kind), is counted for exactly as much as another's. Those conditions being supplied, Bentham's dictum, "everybody to count for one, nobody for more than one," might be written under the principle of utility as an explanatory commentary.[1] The equal claim of everybody to happiness, in the estimation of the moralist and of the legislator, involves an equal claim to all the means of happiness except insofar as the inevitable conditions of human life and the general interest in which that of every individual is included set limits to the maxim; and those limits ought to be strictly construed. As every other maxim of justice, so this is by no means applied or held applicable universally; on the contrary, as I have already remarked, it bends to every person's ideas of social expediency. But in whatever case it is deemed applicable at all, it is held to be the dictate of justice. All persons are deemed to have a *right* to equality of treatment, except when some recognized social expediency requires the reverse. And hence all social inequalities which have ceased to be considered expedient assume the character, not of simple inexpediency, but of injustice, and appear so tyrannical that people are apt to wonder how they ever could have been tolerated—forgetful that they themselves, perhaps, tolerate other inequalities under an equally mistaken notion of expediency, the correction of which would make that which they approve seem quite as monstrous as what they have at last learned to condemn. The

entire history of social improvement has been a series of transitions by which one custom or institution after another, from being a supposed primary necessity of social existence, has passed into the rank of a universally stigmatized injustice and tyranny. So it has been with the distinction of slaves and freemen, nobles and serfs, patricians and plebeians; and so it will be, and in part already is, with the aristocracies of color, race, and sex.

It appears from what has been said that justice is a name for certain moral requirements which, regarded collectively, stand higher in the scale of social utility, and are therefore of more paramount obligation, than any others, though particular cases may occur in which some other social duty is so important as to overrule any one of the general maxims of justice. Thus, to save a life, it may not only be allowable, but a duty, to steal or take by force the necessary food or medicine, or to kidnap and compel to officiate the only qualified medical practitioner. In such cases, as we do not call anything justice which is not a virtue, we usually say, not that justice must give way to some other moral principle, but that what is just in ordinary cases is, by reason of that other principle, not just in the particular case. By this useful accommodation of language, the character of indefeasibility attributed to justice is kept up, and we are saved from the necessity of maintaining that there can be laudable injustice.

The considerations which have now been adduced resolve, I conceive, the only real difficulty in the utilitarian theory of morals. It has always been evident that all cases of justice are also cases of expediency; the difference is in the peculiar sentiment which attaches to the former, as contradistinguished from the latter. If this characteristic sentiment has been sufficiently accounted for; if there is no necessity to assume for it any peculiarity of origin; if it is simply the natural feeling of resentment, moralized by being made co-extensive with the demands of social good; and if this feeling not only does but ought to exist in all the classes of cases to which the idea of justice corresponds—that idea no longer presents itself as a stumbling block to the utilitarian ethics. Justice remains the appropriate name for certain social utilities which are vastly more important, and therefore more absolute and imperative, than any others are as a class (though not more so than others may be in particular cases); and which, therefore, ought to be, as well as naturally are, guarded by a sentiment, not only different in degree, but also in kind; distinguished from the milder feeling which attaches to the mere idea of promoting human pleasure or convenience at once by the more definite nature of its commands and by the sterner character of its sanctions.

NOTE

1. This implication, in the first principle of the utilitarian scheme, of perfect impartiality between persons is regarded by Mr. Herbert Spencer (in his *Social Statics*) as a disproof of the pretensions of utility to be a sufficient guide to right; since (he says) the principle of utility presupposes the anterior principle that everybody has an equal right to happiness. It may be more correctly described as supposing that equal amounts of happiness are equally desirable, whether felt by the same or different persons. This, however, is not a *pre*supposition, not a premise needful to support the principle of utility, but the very principle itself; for what is the principle of utility if it be not that "happiness" and "desirable" are synonymous terms? If there is any anterior principle implied, it can be no other than this, that the truths of arithmetic are applicable to the valuation of happiness, as of all other measurable quantities.

(Mr. Herbert Spencer, in a private communication on the subject of the preceding note, objects to being considered an opponent of utilitarianism and states that he regards happiness as the ultimate end of morality; but deems that end only partially attainable by empirical generalizations from the observed results of conduct, and completely attainable only by deducing, from the laws of life and the conditions of existence, what kinds of action necessarily tend to produce happiness, and what kinds to produce unhappiness. With the exception of the word "necessarily," I have no dissent to express from this doctrine; and (omitting that word) I am not aware that any modern advocate of utilitarianism is of a different opinion. Bentham, certainly, to whom in the *Social Statics* Mr. Spencer particularly referred, is, least of all writers, chargeable with unwillingness to deduce the effect of actions on happiness from the laws of human nature and the universal conditions of human life. The common charge against him is of relying too exclusively upon such deductions and declining altogether to be bound by the generalizations from specific experience which Mr. Spencer thinks that utilitarians generally confine themselves to. My own opinion (and, as I collect, Mr. Spencer's) is that in ethics, as in all other branches of scientific study, the concilience of the results of both these processes, each corroborating and verifying the other, is requisite to give to any general proposition the kind and degree of evidence which constitutes scientific proof.)

13   Justice and Equality

R. M. HARE

THERE ARE SEVERAL REASONS why a philosopher of my persuasion should wish to write about justice. The first is the general one that ethical theory ought to be applied to practical issues, both for the sake of improving the theory and for any light it may shed on the practical issues, of which many of the most important involve questions of justice. This is shown by the frequency with which appeals are made to justice and fairness and related ideals when people are arguing about political or economic questions (about wages for example, or about schools policy or about relations between races or sexes). If we do not know what "just" and "fair" mean (and it looks as if we do not) and therefore do not know what would settle questions involving these concepts, then we are unlikely to be able to sort out these very difficult moral problems. I have also a particular interest in the topic: I hold a view about moral reasoning which has at least strong affinities with utilitarianism;[1] and there is commonly thought to be some kind of antagonism between justice and utility or, as it is sometimes called, expediency. I have therefore a special need to sort these questions out.

We must start by distinguishing between different kinds of justice, or between different senses or uses of the word "just" (the distinction between these different ways of putting the matter need not now concern us). In distinguishing between different kinds of justice we shall have to make crucial use of a distinction between different levels of moral thinking which I have explained at length in other places.[2] It is perhaps simplest to distinguish three levels of thought, one ethical or meta-ethical and two moral or normative-ethical. At the meta-ethical level we try to establish the meanings of the moral words, and thus the formal properties of the moral concepts, including their logical properties. Without knowing these a theory of normative moral reasoning cannot begin. Then there are two levels of (normative) moral thinking which have often been in various ways distinguished. I have myself in the past called them "level 2" and "level 1"; but for ease of remembering I now think it best to give them names, and propose to call level 2 the *critical* level and level 1 the *intuitive* level. At the intuitive level we make use of *prima facie* moral principles of a fairly simple general sort, and do not question them but merely apply them to cases which we encounter. This level of thinking cannot be (as intuitionists commonly suppose) self-sustaining; there is a need for a critical level of thinking by which we select the *prima facie* principles for use at the intuitive level, settle conflict between them, and give to the whole system of them a justification which intuition by itself can never provide. It will be one of the objects of this paper to distinguish those kinds of justice whose place is at the intuitive level and which are embodied in *prima facie* principles from those kinds which have a role in critical and indeed in meta-ethical thinking.

The principal result of meta-ethical enquiry in this field is to isolate a sense or kind of justice

From *"Justice and Equality,"* Justice and Economic Distribution, *edited by John Arthur and William Shaw (1978), pp. 116–131. Reprinted by permission of the author.*

which has come to be known as "formal justice." Formal justice is a property of all moral principles (which is why Professor Rawls heads his chapter on this subject not "Formal constraints of the concept of *just*" but "Formal constraints of the concept of *right*,"[3] and why his disciple David Richards is able to make a good attempt to found the whole of morality, and not merely a theory of justice, on a similar hypothetical-contrast basis).[4] Formal justice is simply another name for the formal requirement of universality in moral principles on which, as I have explained in detail elsewhere,[5] golden-rule arguments are based. From the formal, logical properties of the moral words, and in particular from the logical prohibition of individual references in moral principles, it is possible to derive formal canons of moral argument, such as the rule that we are not allowed to discriminate morally between individuals unless there is some qualitative difference between them which is the ground for the discrimination; and the rule that the equal interests of different individuals have equal moral weight. Formal justice consists simply in the observance of these canons in our moral arguments; it is widely thought that this observance by itself is not enough to secure justice in some more substantial sense. As we shall see, one is not offending against the first rule if one says that extra privileges should be given to people just because they have white skins; and one is not offending against either rule if one says that one should take a cent from everybody and give it to the man with the biggest nose, provided that he benefits as much in total as they lose. The question is, How do we get from formal to substantial justice?

This question arises because there are various kinds of material or substantial justice whose content cannot be established directly by appeal to the uses of moral words or the formal properties of moral concepts (we shall see later how much can be done indirectly by appeal to these formal properties *in conjunction with* other premises or postulates or presuppositions). There is a number of different kinds of substantial justice, and we

can hardly do better than begin with Aristotle's classification of them,[6] since it is largely responsible for the different senses which the word "just" still has in common use. This is a case where it is impossible to appeal to common use, at any rate of the word "just" (the word "fair" is better) in order to settle philosophical disputes, because the common use is itself the product of past philosophical theories. The expressions "distributive" and "retributive" justice go back to Aristotle,[7] and the word "just" itself occupies the place (or places) that it does in our language largely because of its place in earlier philosophical discussions.

Aristotle first separated off a generic sense of the Greek word commonly translated "just," a sense which had been used a lot by Plato: the sense in which justice is the whole of virtue in so far as it concerns our relations with other people.[8] The last qualification reminds us that this is not the most generic sense possible. Theognis had already used it to include the whole of virtue, full stop.[9] These very generic senses of the word, as applied to men and acts, have survived into modern English to confuse philosophers. One of the sources of confusion is that, in the less generic sense of "just" to be discussed in most of this paper, the judgment that an act would be unjust is sometimes fairly easily overridden by other moral considerations ("unjust," we may say, "but right as an act of mercy"; or "unjust, but right because necessary in order to avert an appalling calamity"). It is much more difficult for judgments that an act is required by justice in the generic sense, in which "unjust" is almost equivalent to "not right," to be overridden this way.

Adherents of the "*fiat justitia ruat caelum*"[10] school seldom make clear whether, when they say "Let justice be done though the heavens fall," they are using a more or less generic sense of "justice"; and they thus take advantage of its non-overridability in the more generic sense in order to claim unchallengeable sanctity for judgments made using one of the less generic senses. It must be right to do the just thing (whatever that may be) in the sense (if there still is one in English) in which "just" *means* "right." In this sense, if it were right to cause the heavens to fall, and therefore just in the most generic sense, it would of course be right. But we might have to take into account, in deciding whether it would be right, the fact that the heavens would fall (that causing the heavens to fall would be one of the things we were doing if we did the action in question). On the other hand, if it were merely the just act in one of the less generic senses, we might hold that, though just, it was not right, because it would not be right to cause the heavens to fall merely in order to secure justice in this more limited sense; perhaps some concession to mercy, or even to common sense, would be in order.

This is an application of the "split-level" structure of moral thinking sketched above. One of the theses I wish to maintain is that principles of justice in these less generic senses are all *prima facie* principles and therefore overridable. I shall later be giving a utilitarian account of justice which finds a place, at the intuitive level, for these *prima facie* principles of justice. At this level they have great importance and utility, but it is in accordance with utilitarianism, as indeed with common sense, to claim that they can on unusual occasions be overridden. Having said this, however, it is most important to stress that this does *not* involve conceding the overridability of either the generic kind of justice, which has its place at the critical level, or of formal justice, which operates at the meta-ethical level. These are preserved intact, and therefore defenders of the sanctity of justice ought to be content, since these are the core of justice as of morality. We may call to mind here Aristotle's[11] remarks about the "better justice" or "equity" which is required in order to rectify the crudities, giving rise to unacceptable results in particular cases, of a justice whose principles are, as they have to be, couched in general (i.e. simple) terms. The lawgiver who, according to Aristotle, "would have" given a special prescription if he had been present at this particular case, and to whose prescription we must try to conform if we can, corresponds to the critical moral thinker, who operates under the constraints of formal justice and whose

principles are not limited to simple general rules but can be specific enough to cover the peculiarities of unusual cases.

Retributive and Distributive Justice

After speaking briefly of generic justice, Aristotle goes on[12] to distinguish two main kinds of justice in the narrow or more particular sense in which it means "fairness." He calls these retributive and distributive justice. They have their place, respectively, in the fixing of penalties and rewards for bad and good actions, and in the distribution of goods and the opposite between the possible recipients. One of the most important questions is whether these two sorts of justice are reducible to a single sort. Rawls, for example, thinks that they are, and so do I. By using the expression "justice as fairness," he implies that all justice can be reduced to kinds of distributive justice, which itself is founded on procedural justice (i.e. on the adoption of fair procedures) in distribution.[13]

We may (without attempting complete accuracy in exposition) explain how Rawls might effect this reduction as follows. The parties in his 'original position' are prevented by his "veil of ignorance" from knowing what their own positions are in the world in which they are to live; so they are unable when adopting principles of justice to tailor them to suit their own individual interests. Impartiality (a very important constituent, at least, of justice) is thus secured. Therefore the principles which govern *both* the distribution of wealth and power and other good things *and* the assignment of rewards and penalties (and indeed all other matters which have to be regulated by principles of justice) will be impartial as between individuals, and in this sense just. In this way Rawls in effect reduces the justice of acts of retribution to justice in distributing between the affected parties the good and bad effects of a system of retributions, and reduces this distributive justice in turn to the adoption of a just procedure for selecting the system of retributions to be used.

This can be illustrated by considering the case of a criminal facing a judge (a case which has been thought to give trouble to me too, though I dealt with it adequately, on the lines which I am about to repeat here, in my book *Freedom and Reason*).[14] A Rawlsian judge, when sentencing the criminal, could defend himself against the charge of injustice or unfairness by saying that he was faithfully observing the principles of justice which would be adopted in the original position, whose conditions are procedurally fair. What these principles would be requires, no doubt, a great deal of discussion, in the course of which I might find myself in disagreement with Rawls. But my own view on how the judge should justify his action is, in its formal properties, very like his. On my view likewise, the judge can say that, when he asks himself what universal principles he is prepared to adopt for situations exactly like the one he is in, and considers examples of such logically possible situations in which *he* occupies, successively, the positions of judge, and of criminal, and of all those who are affected by the administration and enforcement of the law under which he is sentencing the criminal, including, of course, potential victims of possible future crimes—he can say that when he asks himself this, he has no hesitation in accepting the principle which bids him impose such and such a sentence in accordance with the law.

I am assuming that the judge is justifying himself at the critical level. If he were content with justifying himself at the intuitive level, his task would be easier, because, we hope, he, like most of us, has intuitions about the proper administration of justice in the courts, embodying *prima facie* principles of a sort whose inculcation in judges and in the rest of us has a high social utility. I say this while recognizing that *some* judges have intuitions about these matters which have a high social *disu*tility. The question of what intuitions judges ought to have about retributive justice is a matter for *critical* moral thinking.

On both Rawls' view and mine retributive justice has thus been reduced to distributive; on Rawls' view the principles of justice adopted are those which *distribute* fairly between those affected the good and the evil consequences of hav-

ing or not having certain enforced criminal laws; on my own view likewise it is the impartiality secured by the requirement to universalize one's prescription which makes the judge say what he says, and here too it is an impartiality in distributing good and evil consequences between the affected parties. For the judge to let off the rapist would not be *fair* to all those who would be raped if the law were not enforced. I conclude that retributive justice can be reduced to distributive, and that therefore we shall have done what is required of us if we can give an adequate account of the latter.

What is common to Rawls' method and my own is the recognition that to get solutions to particular questions about what is just or unjust, we have to have a way of selecting principles of justice to answer such questions, and that to ask them in default of such principles is senseless. And we both recognize that the method for selecting the principles has to be founded on what he calls "the formal constraints of the concept of right." This measure of agreement can extend to the method of selecting principles of distributive justice as well as retributive. Neither Rawls nor I need be put off our stride by an objector who says that we have not addressed ourselves to the question of what acts are just, but have divagated on to the quite different question of how to select principles of justice. The point is that the first question cannot be answered without answering the second. Most of the apparently intractable conflicts about justice and rights that plague the world have been generated by taking certain answers to the first question as obvious and requiring no argument. We shall resolve these conflicts only by asking what arguments are available for the principles by which questions about the justice of individual acts are to be answered. In short, we need to ascend from intuitive to critical thinking; as I have argued in my review of his book, Rawls is to be reproached with not *completing* the ascent.[15]

Nozick, however, seems hardly to have begun it.[16] Neither Rawls nor I have anything to fear from him, so long as we stick to the formal part of our systems which we in effect share. When it comes to the application of this formal method to produce substantial principles of justice, I might find myself in disagreement with Rawls, because he relies much too much on his own intuitions which are open to question. Nozick's intuitions differ from Rawls', and sometimes differ from, sometimes agree with mine. This sort of question is simply not to be settled by appeal to intuitions, and it is time that the whole controversy ascended to a more serious, critical level. At this level, the answer which both Rawls and I should give to Nozick is that whatever sort of principles of justice we are after, whether structural principles, as Rawls thinks, or historical principles, as Nozick maintains, they have to be supported by critical thinking, of which Nozick seems hardly to see the necessity. This point is quite independent of the structural-historical disagreement.

For example, if Nozick thinks that it is just for people to retain whatever property they have acquired by voluntary exchange which benefited all parties, starting from a position of equality but perhaps ending up with a position of gross inequality, and if Rawls, by contrast, thinks that such inequality should be rectified in order to make the position of the least advantaged in society as good as possible, how are we to decide between them? Not by intuition, because there seems to be a deadlock between their intuitions. Rawls has a procedure, which *need* not appeal to intuition, for justifying distributions; this would give him the game, if he were to base the procedure on firm logical grounds, and if he followed it correctly. Actually he does not so base it, and mixes up so many intuitions in the argument that the conclusions he reaches are not such as the procedure really justifies. But Nozick has no procedure at all: only a variety of considerations of different sorts, all in the end based on intuition. Sometimes he seems to be telling us what arrangements in society would be arrived at if bargaining took place in accordance with games-theory between mutually disinterested parties; sometimes what arrangements would maximize the welfare of members of society; and sometimes what arrangements would strike them as fair. He does not often warn us

when he is switching from one of these grounds to another; and he does little to convince us by argument that the arrangements so selected would be in accordance with justice. He hopes that we will think what he thinks; but Rawls at least thinks otherwise.

Formal Justice and Substantial Equality

How then do we get from formal to substantial justice? We have had an example of how this is done in the sphere of retributive justice; but how is this method to be extended to cover distributive justice as a whole, and its relation, if any, to equality in distribution? The difficulty of using formal justice in order to establish principles of substantial justice can indeed be illustrated very well by asking whether, and in what sense, justice demands equality in distribution. The complaint is often made that a certain distribution is unfair or unjust because unequal; so it looks, at least, as if the substantial principle that goods ought to be distributed equally in default of reasons to the contrary forms part of some people's conception of justice. Yet, it is argued, this substantial principle cannot be established simply on the basis of the formal notions we have mentioned. The following kind of schematic example is often adduced: consider two possible distributions of a given finite stock of goods, in one of which the goods are distributed equally, and in the other of which a few of the recipients have nearly all the goods, and the rest have what little remains. It is claimed with some plausibility that the second distribution is unfair, and the first fair. But it might also be claimed that impartiality and formal justice alone will not establish that we ought to distribute the goods equally.

There are two reasons which might be given for this second claim, the first of them a bad one, the other more cogent. The bad reason rests on an underestimate of the powers of golden-rule arguments. It is objected, for example, that people with white skins, if they claimed privileges in distributing purely on the ground of skin-colour, would not be offending against the formal principle of impartiality or universalizability, because no individual reference need enter into the principle to which they are appealing. Thus the principle that blacks ought to be subservient to whites is impartial as between *individuals;* any individual whatever who has the bad luck to find himself with a black skin or the good luck to find himself with a white skin is impartially placed by the principle in the appropriate social rank. This move receives a brief answer in my *Freedom and Reason,*[17] and a much fuller one in a forthcoming paper.[18] If the whites are faced with the decision, not merely of whether to frame this principle, but of whether to prescribe its adoption universally in all cases, including hypothetical ones in which their own skins turn black, they will at once reject it.

The other, more cogent-sounding argument is often used as an argument against utilitarians by those who think that justice has a lot to do with equality. It could also, at first sight, be used as an argument against the adequacy of formal justice or impartiality as a basis for distributive justice. That the argument could be leveled against both these methods is no accident; as I have tried to show elsewhere,[19] utilitarianism of a certain sort is the embodiment of—the method of moral reasoning which fulfills in practice—the requirement of universalizability or formal justice. Having shown that neither of these methods can produce a direct justification for equal distribution, I shall then show that both can produce indirect justifications, which depend, not on a priori reasoning alone, but on likely assumptions about what the world and the people in it are like.

The argument is this. Formal impartiality only requires us to treat everybody's interest as of equal weight. Imagine, then, a situation in which utilities are equally distributed. (There is a complication here which we can for the moment avoid by choosing a suitable example. Shortly I shall be mentioning the so-called principle of diminishing marginal utility, and shall indeed be making important use of it. But for now let us take a case in which it does not operate, so that we can, for ease of illustration, treat money as a linear measure of utility.) Suppose that we can vary the equal distri-

bution that we started with by taking a dollar each away from everybody in the town, and that the loss of purchasing power is so small that they hardly notice it, and therefore the utility enjoyed by each is not much diminished. However, when we give the resulting large sum to one man, he is able to buy himself a holiday in Acapulco, which gives him so much pleasure that his access of utility is equal to the sum of the small losses suffered by all the others. Many would say that this redistribution was unfair. But we were, in the required sense, being impartial between the equal interests of all the parties; we were treating an equal access or loss of utility to any part as of equal value or disvalue. For, on our suppositions, the taking away of a dollar from one of the unfortunate parties deprived him of just as much utility as the addition of that dollar gave to the fortunate one. But if we are completely impartial, we have to regard *who has* that dollar or that access of utility as irrelevant. So there will be nothing to choose, from an impartial point of view, between our original equal distribution and our later highly unequal one, in which everybody else is deprived of a dollar in order to give one person a holiday in Acapulco. And that is why people say that formal impartiality alone is not enough to secure social justice, nor even to secure impartiality itself in some more substantial sense.

What is needed, in the opinion of these people, is some principle which says that it is unjust to give a person more when he already has more than the others—some sort of egalitarian principle. Egalitarian principles are only one possible kind of principles of distributive justice; and it is so far an open question whether they are to be preferred to alternative inegalitarian principles. It is fairly clear as a matter of history that different principles of justice have been accepted in different societies. As Aristotle says, "everybody agrees that the just distribution is one in accordance with desert of some kind; but they do not call desert the same thing, but the democrats say it is being a free citizen, the oligarchs being rich, others good lineage, and the aristocrats virtue."[20] It is not difficult to think of some societies in which it would be thought unjust for one man to have privileges not possessed by all men, and of others in which it would be thought unjust for a slave to have privileges which a free man would take for granted, or for a commoner to have sort of house which a nobleman could aspire to. Even Aristotle's democrats did not think that slaves, but only citizens, had equal rights; and Plato complains of democracy that it "bestows equality of a sort on equals and unequals alike."[21] We have to ask, therefore, whether there are any reasons for preferring one of these attitudes to another.

At this point some philosophers will be ready to step in with their intuitions, and tell us that some distributions or ways of achieving distributions are *obviously* more just than others, or that *everyone will agree on reflection* that they are. These philosophers appeal to our intuitions or prejudices in support of the most widely divergent methods or patterns of distribution. But this is a way of arguing which should be abjured by anybody who wishes to have rational grounds for his moral judgments. Intuitions prove nothing; general consensus proves nothing; both have been used to support conclusions which *our* intuitions and our consensus may well find outrageous. We want arguments, and in this field seldom get them.

However, it is too early to despair of finding some. The utilitarian, and the formalist like me, still have some moves to make. I am supposing that we have already made the major move suggested above, and have ruled out discrimination on grounds of skin colour and the like, in so far as such discrimination could not be accepted by all for cases where they were the ones discriminated against. I am supposing that our society has absorbed this move, and contains no racists, sexists or in general discriminators, but does still contain economic men who do not think it wrong, in pursuit of Nozickian economic liberty, to get what they can, even if the resulting distribution is grotesquely unequal. Has the egalitarian any moves to make against them, and are they moves which can be supported by appeal to formal justice, in conjunction with the empirical facts?

Two Arguments for Equal Distribution

He has two. The first is based on that good old prop of egalitarian policies, the diminishing marginal utility, within the ranges that matter, of money and of nearly all goods. Almost always, if money or goods are taken away from someone who has a lot of them already, and given to someone who has little, total utility is increased, other things being equal. As we shall see, they hardly ever are equal; but the principle is all right. Its ground is that the poor man will get more utility out of what he is given than the rich man from whom it is taken would have got. A millionaire minds less about the gain or loss of a dollar than I do, and I than a pauper.

It must be noted that this is not an *a priori* principle. It is an empirical fact (if it is) that people are so disposed. The most important thing I have to say in this paper is that when we are, as we now are, trying to establish *prima facie* principles of distributive justice, it is enough if they can be justified in the world as it actually is, among people as they actually are. It is a wholly illegitimate argument against formalists or utilitarians that states of society or of the people in it could be *conceived of* in which gross inequalities could be justified by formal or utilitarian arguments. We are seeking principles for practical use in the world as it is. The same applies when we ask what qualifications are required to the principles.

Diminishing marginal utility is the firmest support for policies of progressive taxation of the rich and other egalitarian measures. However, as I said above, other things are seldom equal, and there are severe empirical, practical restraints on the equality that can sensibly be imposed by governments. To mention just a few of these hackneyed other things: the removal of incentives to effort may diminish the total stock of goods to be divided up; abrupt confiscation or even very steep progressive taxation may antagonize the victims so much that a whole class turns from a useful element in society to a hostile and dangerous one; or, even if that does not happen, it may merely become demoralized and either lose all enterprise and readiness to take business risks, or else just emigrate if it can. Perhaps one main cause of what is called the English sickness is the alienation of the middle class. It is an empirical question, just when egalitarian measures get to the stage of having these effects; and serious political argument on this subject should concentrate on such empirical questions, instead of indulging in the rhetoric of equal (or for that matter of unequal) rights. Rights are the offspring of *prima facie,* intuitive principles, and I have nothing against them; but the question is, What *prima facie* principles ought we to adopt? What intuitions ought we to have? On these questions the rhetoric of rights sheds no light whatever, any more than do appeals to intuition (i.e. to prejudice, i.e. to the *prima facie* principles, good or bad, which our upbringings happen to have implanted in us). The worth of intuitions is to be known by their fruits; as in the case of the principles to be followed by judges in administering the law, the best principles are those with the highest acceptance-utility, i.e. those whose general acceptance maximizes the furtherance of the interests, in sum, of all the affected parties, treating all those interests as of equal weight, i.e. impartially, i.e. with formal justice.

We have seen that, given the empirical assumption of diminishing marginal utility, such a method provides a justification for moderately egalitarian policies. The justification is strengthened by a second move that the egalitarian can make. This is to point out that inequality itself has a tendency to produce envy, which is a disagreeable state of mind and leads people to do disagreeable things. It makes no difference to the argument whether the envy is a good or a bad quality, nor whether it is justified or unjustified— any more than it makes a difference whether the alienation of the middle class which I mentioned above is to be condemned or excused. These states of minds are facts, and moral judgments have to be made in the light of the facts as they are. We have to take account of the actual state of the world and of the people in it. We can very easily

think of societies which are highly unequal, but in which the more fortunate members have contrived to find some real or metaphorical opium of some Platonic noble lie[22] to keep the people quiet, so that the people feel no envy of privileges which we should consider outrageous. Imagine, for example, a society consisting of happy slave-owners and of happy slaves, all of whom know their places and do not have ideas above their station. Since there is *ex hypothesi* no envy, this source of disutility does not exist, and the whole argument from envy collapses.

It is salutary to remember this. It may make us stop looking for purely formal, *a priori* reasons for demanding equality, and look instead at the actual conditions which obtain in particular societies. To make the investigation more concrete, albeit oversimplified, let us ask what would have to be the case before we ought to be ready to push this happy slaveowning society into a revolution— peaceful or violent—which would turn the slaves into free and moderately equal wage-earners. I shall be able only to sketch my answer to this question, without doing nearly enough to justify it.

Arguments For and Against Egalitarian Revolutions

First of all, as with all moral questions, we should have to ask what would be the actual consequences of what we were doing—which is the same as to ask what we should be *doing,* so that accusations of "consequentialism"[23] need not be taken very seriously. Suppose, to simplify matters outrageously, that we can actually predict the consequences of the revolution and what will happen during its course. We can then consider two societies (one actual and one possible) and a possible process of transition from one to the other. And we have to ask whether the transition from one to the other will, all in all, promote the interest of all those affected more than to stay as they are, or rather, to develop as they would develop if the revolution did not occur. The question can be divided into questions about the process of transition and questions about the relative merits of the actual society (including its probably subsequent "natural" development) and the possible society which would be produced by the revolution.

We have supposed that the slaves in the existing society feel no envy, and that therefore the disutility of envy cannot be used as an argument for change. If there *were* envy, as in actual cases is probable, this argument *could* be employed; but let us see what can be done without it. We have the fact that there is gross inequality in the actual society and much greater equality in the possible one. The principle of diminishing marginal utility will therefore support the change, provided that its effects are not outweighed by a reduction in total utility resulting from the change and the way it comes about. But we have to be sure that this condition is fulfilled. Suppose, for example, that the actual society is a happy bucolic one and is likely to remain so, but that the transition to the possible society initiates the growth of an industrial economy in which everybody has to engage in a rat-race and is far less happy. We might in that case pronounce the actual society better. In general it is not self-evident that the access of what is called wealth makes people happier, although they nearly always think that it will.

Let us suppose, however, that we are satisfied that the people in the possible society will be better off all round than in the actual. There is also the point that there will be more generations to enjoy the new regime than suffer in the transition from the old. At least, this is what revolutionaries often say; and we have set them at liberty to say it by assuming contrary to what is likely to be the case, that the future state of society is predictable. In actual fact, revolutions usually produce states of society very different from, and in most cases worse than, what their authors expected—which does not always stop them being better than what went before, once things have settled down. However, let us waive these difficulties and suppose that the future state of society can be predicted, and that it is markedly better than the existing state, because a greater equality of distri-

bution has, owing to diminishing marginal utility, resulted in greater total utility.

Let us also suppose that the more enterprising economic structure which results leads to increased production without causing a rat-race. There will then be more wealth to go round and the revolution will have additional justification. Other benefits of the same general kind may also be adduced; and what is perhaps the greatest benefit of all, namely liberty itself. That people like having this is an empirical fact; it may not be a fact universally, but it is at least *likely* that by freeing slaves we shall *pro tanto* promote their interests. Philosophers who ask for *a priori* arguments for liberty or equality often talk as if empirical facts like this were totally irrelevant to the question. Genuine egalitarians and liberals ought to abjure the aid of these philosophers, because they have taken away the main ground for such views, namely the fact that people are as they are.

The arguments so far adduced support the call for a revolution. They will have to be balanced against the disutilities which will probably be caused by the process of transition. If heads roll, that is contrary to the interests of their owners; and no doubt the economy will be disrupted at least temporarily, and the new rulers, whoever they are, may infringe liberty just as much as the old, and possibly in an even more arbitrary manner. Few revolutions are pleasant while they are going on. But if the revolution can be more or less smooth or even peaceful, it may well be that (given the arguments already adduced about the desirability of the future society thereby achieved) revolution can have a utilitarian justification, and therefore a justification on grounds of formal impartiality between people's interests. But it is likely to be better for all if the same changes can be achieved less abruptly by an evolutionary process, and those who try to persuade us that this is not so are often merely giving way to impatience and showing a curious indifference to the interests of those for whom they purport to be concerned.

The argument in favour of change from a slave-owning society to a wage-earning one has been extremely superficial, and has served only to illustrate the lines on which a utilitarian or a formalist might argue. If we considered instead the transition from a capitalist society to a socialist one, the same forms of argument would have to be employed, but might not yield the same result. Even if the introduction of a fully socialist economy would promote greater equality, or more equal liberties (and I can see no reason for supposing this, but rather the reverse; for socialism tends to produce very great inequalities of *power*), it needs to be argued what the consequences would be, and then an assessment has to be made of the relative benefits and harms accruing from leaving matters alone and from having various sorts of bloody or bloodless change. Here again the rhetoric of rights will provide nothing but inflammatory material for agitators on both sides. It is designed to lead to, not to resolve, conflicts.

Remarks about Methods

But we must now leave this argument and attend to a methodological point which has become pressing. We have not, in the last few pages, been arguing about what state of society would be just, but about what state of society would best promote the interests of its members. All the arguments have been utilitarian. Where then does justice come in? It is likely to come into the propaganda of revolutionaries, as I have already hinted. But so far as I can see it has no direct bearing on the question of what would be the better society. It has, however, an important indirect bearing which I shall now try to explain. Our *prima facie* moral principles and intuitions are, as I have already said, the products of our upbringings; and it is a very important question *what* principles and intuitions it is best to bring up people to have. I have been arguing on the assumption that this question is to be decided by looking at the consequences for society, and the effects on the interests of people in society, of inculcating different principles. We are looking for the set of principles with the highest acceptance-utility.

Will these include principles of justice? The answer is obviously "Yes," if we think that society

and the people in it are better off with *some* principles of justice than without any. A "land without justice" (to use the title of Milovan Djilas' book)[24] is almost bound to be an unhappy one. But what are the principles to be? Are we, for example, to inculcate the principle that it is just for people to perform the duties of their station and not envy those of higher social rank? Or the principle that all inequalities of any sort are unjust and ought to be removed? For my part, I would think that neither of these principles has a very high acceptance-utility. It may be that the principle with the highest acceptance-utility is one which makes just reward vary (but not immoderately) with desert, and assesses desert according to service to the interests of one's fellow-men. It would have to be supplemented by a principle securing equality of opportunity. But it is a partly empirical question what principles would have the highest acceptance-utility, and in any case beyond the scope of this paper. If some such principle is adopted and inculcated, people will *call* breaches of it unjust. Will they *be* unjust? Only in the sense that they will be contrary to a *prima facie* principle of distributive justice which we ought to adopt (not because it is itself a just principle, but because it is the best principle). The only sense that can be given to the question of whether it is a just principle (apart from the purely circular or tautological question of whether the principle obeys itself), is by asking whether the procedure by which we have selected the principle satisfies the logical requirements of critical moral thinking, i.e. is *formally* just. We might add that the adoption of such a formally just procedure and of the principles it selects is just in the *generic* sense mentioned at the beginning of this paper: it is the right thing to do; we morally ought to do it. The reason is that critical thinking, because it follows the requirements of formal justice based on the logical properties of the moral concepts, especially "ought" and "right," can therefore not fail, if pursued correctly in the light of the empirical facts, to lead to principles of justice which are in accord with morality. But because the requirements are all formal, they do not by themselves determine the content of the principles of justice. We have to do the thinking.

What principles of justice are best to try to inculcate will depend on the circumstances of particular societies, and especially on psychological facts about their members. One of these facts is their readiness to accept the principles themselves. There might be a principle of justice which it would be highly desirable to inculcate, but which we have no chance of successfully inculcating. The best principles for a society to *have* are, as I said, those with the highest acceptance-utility. But the best principles to *try to inculcate* will not necessarily be these, if these are impossible to inculcate. Imagine that in our happy slave-society both slaves and slave-owners are obstinately conservative and know their places, and that the attempt to get the slaves to have revolutionary or egalitarian thoughts will result only in a very few of them becoming discontented, and probably going to the gallows as a result, and the vast majority merely becoming unsettled and therefore more unhappy. Then we ought not to try to inculcate such an egalitarian principle. On the other hand, if, as is much more likely, the principle stood a good chance of catching on, and the revolution was likely to be as advantageous as we have supposed, then we ought. The difference lies in the dispositions of the inhabitants. I am not saying that the probability of being accepted is the same thing as acceptance-utility; only that the rationality of trying to inculcate a principle (like the rationality of trying to do anything else) varies with the likelihood of success. In this sense the advisability of trying to inculcate principles of justice (though not their merit) is relative to these states of mind of those who, it is hoped, will hold them.

It is important to be clear about the extent to which what I am advocating is a kind of relativism. It is certainly not relativistic in any strong sense. Relativism is the doctrine that the truth of some moral statement depends on whether people accept it. A typical example would be the thesis that if in a certain society people think that they ought to get their male children circumcised, then they ought to get them circumcised, full stop. Needless

to say, I am not supporting any such doctrine, which is usually the result of confusion, and against which there are well-known arguments. It is, however, nearly always the case that among the facts relevant to a moral decision are facts about people's thoughts or dispositions. For example, if I am wondering whether I ought to take my wife for a holiday in Acapulco, it is relevant to ask whether she would like it. What I have been saying is to be assimilated to this last example. If we take as given certain dispositions in the members of society (namely dispositions not to accept a certain principle of justice however hard we work at propagating it) then we have to decide whether, in the light of these facts, we ought to propagate it. What principles of justice we ought to propagate will vary with the probable effects of propagating them. The answer to this "ought"-question is not relative to what we, who are asking it, think about the matter; it is to be arrived at by moral thought on the basis of the facts of the situation. But among these facts are facts about the dispositions of people in the society in question.

The moral I wish to draw from the whole argument is that ethical reasoning *can* provide us with a way of conducting political arguments about justice and rights rationally and with hope of agreement; that such rational arguments have to rest on an understanding of the concepts being used, *and* of the facts of our actual situation. They key question is "What principles of justice, what attitudes towards the distribution of goods, what ascriptions of rights, are such that their acceptance is in the general interest?" I advocate the asking of this question as a substitute for one which is much more commonly asked, namely "What rights do I have?" For people who ask this latter question will, being human, nearly always answer that they have just those rights, whatever they are, which will promote a distribution of goods which is in the interest of their own social group. The rhetoric of rights, which is engendered by this question, is a recipe for class war, and civil war. In pursuit of these rights, people will, because they have convinced themselves that justice demands it, inflict almost any harms on the rest of society and on themselves. To live at peace, we need principles such as critical thinking can provide, based on formal justice and on the facts of the actual world in which we have to live. It is possible for all to practise this critical thinking in cooperation, if only they would learn how; for all share the same moral concepts with the same logic, if they could understand them and follow it.

NOTES

1. See my "Ethical Theory and Utilitarianism" (*ETU*), in *Contemporary British Philosophy* 4, ed. H. D. Lewis (London, 1976).
2. See, e.g., my "Principles," *Ar. Soc.* 72 (1972/3), "Rules of War and Moral Reasoning," *Ph. and Pub. Aff.* 1 (1972) and *ETU*.
3. Rawls, J., *A Theory of Justice* (Cambridge, Mass., 1971), p. 130.
4. Richards, D. A. J., *A Theory of Reasons for Action* (Oxford, 1971).
5. See my *Freedom and Reason,* pt. II (Oxford, 1963) and *ETU*.
6. *Nicomachean Ethics,* bk. V.
7. ib. 1130 b 31, 1131 b 25.
8. ib. 1130 a 8.
9. Theognis 147; also attr. to Phocylides by Aristotle, ib. 1129 b 27.
10. The earliest version of this tag is attr. by the *Oxford Dictionary of Quotations* to the Emperor Ferdinand I (1503–64).
11. ib. 1137 b 8.
12. ib. 1130 a 14 ff.
13. *A Theory of Justice,* p. 136.
14. Pp. 115–7, 124.
15. *Ph Q.* 23 (1973), repr. in *Reading Rawls,* ed. N. Daniels (Oxford, 1975).
16. Nozick, R. D., *Anarchy, State and Utopia* (New York, 1974).
17. Pp. 106f.
18. "Relevance," in a volume in *Values and Morals,* eds. A Goldman and J. Kim (Reidel, 1978).
19. See note 2 above.
20. ib. 1131 a 25.
21. *Republic* 558 c.
22. ib. 414 b.
23. See, e.g., Anscombe, G. E. M., "Modern Moral Philosophy," *Philosophy* 33 (1958), and Williams, B. A. O., in Smart, J. J. C., and Williams, B. A. O., *Utilitarianism: For and Against* (Cambridge, Eng., 1973), p. 82.
24. Djilas, M., *Land without Justice* (London, 1958).

14 Utilitarianism and the Distinction Between Persons

JOHN RAWLS

THERE ARE MANY FORMS of utilitarianism, and the development of the theory has continued in recent years. I shall not survey these forms here, nor take account of the numerous refinements found in contemporary discussions. My aim is to work out a theory of justice that represents an alternative to utilitarian thought generally and so to all of these different versions of it. I believe that the contrast between the contract view and utilitarianism remains essentially the same in all these cases. Therefore I shall compare justice as fairness with familiar variants of intuitionism, perfectionism, and utilitarianism in order to bring out the underlying differences in the simplest way. With this end in mind, the kind of utilitarianism I shall describe here is the strict classical doctrine which receives perhaps its clearest and most accessible formulation in Sidgwick. The main idea is that society is rightly ordered, and therefore just, when its major institutions are arranged so as to achieve the greatest net balance of satisfaction summed over all the individuals belonging to it.[1]

We may note first that there is, indeed, a way of thinking of society which makes it easy to suppose that the most rational conception of justice is utilitarian. For consider: each man in realizing his own interests is certainly free to balance his own losses against his own gains. We may impose a sacrifice on ourselves now for the sake of a greater advantage later. A person quite properly acts, at least when others are not affected, to achieve his own greatest good, to advance his rational ends as far as possible. Now why should not a society act on precisely the same principle applied to the group and therefore regard that which is rational for one man as right for an association of men? Just as the well-being of a person is constructed from the series of satisfactions that are experienced at different moments in the course of his life, so in very much the same way the well-being of society is to be constructed from the fulfillment of the systems of desires of the many individuals who belong to it. Since the principle for an individual is to advance as far as possible his own welfare, his own system of desires, the principle for society is to advance as far as possible the welfare of the group, to realize to the greatest extent the comprehensive system of desire arrived at from the desires of its members. Just as an individual balances present and future gains against present and future losses, so a society may balance satisfactions and dissatisfactions among different individuals. And so by these reflections one reaches the principle of utility in a natural way: a society is properly arranged when its institutions maximize the net balance of satisfaction. The principle of choice for an association of men is interpreted as an extension of the principle of choice for one man. Social justice is the principle of rational prudence applied to an aggregative conception of the welfare of the group. . . .[2]

This idea is made all the more attractive by a further consideration. The two main concepts of ethics are those of the right and the good; the concept of a morally worthy person is, I believe, derived from them. The structure of an ethical theory is, then, largely determined by how it defines and connects these two basic notions. Now it seems that the simplest way of relating them is taken by teleological theories: the good is defined independently from the right, and then the right is defined as that which maximizes the good.[3] More precisely, those institutions and acts are right which, of the available alternatives, produce the most good, or at least as much good as any of the other institutions and acts open as real possibilities (a rider needed when the maximal class is not a singleton). Teleological theories have a deep intuitive appeal since they seem to embody the idea of rationality. It is natural to think that rationality is maximizing something and that in morals it must be maximizing the good. Indeed, it is tempting to suppose that it is self-evident that things should be arranged so as to lead to the most good.

It is essential to keep in mind that in a teleological theory the good is defined independently from the right. This means two things. First, the theory accounts for our considered judgments as to which things are good (our judgments of value) as a separate class of judgments intuitively distinguishable by common sense, and then proposes the hypothesis that the right is maximizing the good as already specified. Second, the theory enables one to judge the goodness of things without referring to what is right. For example, if pleasure is said to be the sole good, then presumably pleasures can be recognized and ranked in value by criteria that do not presuppose any standards of right, or what we would normally think of as such. Whereas if the distributions of goods is also counted as a good, perhaps a higher order one, and the theory directs us to produce the most good (including the good of distribution among others), we no longer have a teleological view in the classical sense. The problem of distribution

falls under the concept of right as one intuitively understands it, and so the theory lacks an independent definition of the good. The clarity and simplicity of classical teleological theories derive largely from the fact that they factor our moral judgments into two classes, the one being characterized separately while the other is then connected with it by a maximizing principle.

Teleological doctrines differ, pretty clearly, according to how the conception of the good is specified. If it is taken as the realization of human excellence in the various forms of culture, we have what may be called perfectionism. This notion is found in Aristotle and Nietzsche, among others. If the good is defined as pleasure, we have hedonism; if as happiness, eudaimonism, and so on. I shall understand the principle of utility in its classical form as defining the good as the satisfaction of desire, or perhaps better, as the satisfaction of rational desire. This accords with the view in all essentials and provides, I believe, a fair interpretation of it. The appropriate terms of social cooperation are settled by whatever in the circumstances will achieve the greatest sum of satisfaction of the rational desires of individuals. It is impossible to deny the initial plausibility and attractiveness of this conception.

The striking feature of the utilitarian view of justice is that it does not matter, except indirectly, how this sum of satisfactions is distributed among individuals any more than it matters, except indirectly, how one man distributes his satisfactions over time. The correct distribution in either case is that which yields the maximum fulfillment. Society must allocate its means of satisfaction whatever these are, rights and duties, opportunities and privileges, and various forms of wealth, so as to achieve this maximum if it can. But in itself no distribution of satisfaction is better than another except that the more equal distribution is to be preferred to break ties.[4] It is true that certain common sense precepts of justice, particularly those which concern the protection of liberties and rights, or which express the claims of desert, seem to contradict this contention. But from a utilitarian standpoint the explanation of these precepts and of their seemingly stringent character is that they are those precepts which experience shows should be strictly respected and departed from only under exceptional circumstances if the sum of advantages is to be maximized.[5] Yet, as with all other precepts, those of justice are derivative from the one end of attaining the greatest balance of satisfaction. Thus there is no reason in principle why the greater gains of some should not compensate for the lesser losses of others; or more importantly, why the violation of the liberty of a few might not be made right by the greater good shared by many. It simply happens that under most conditions, at least in a reasonably advanced stage of civilization, the greatest sum of advantages is not attained in this way. No doubt the strictness of common sense precepts of justice has a certain usefulness in limiting men's propensities to injustice and to socially injurious actions, but the utilitarian believes that to affirm this strictness as a first principle of morals is a mistake. For just as it is rational for one man to maximize the fulfillment of his system of desires, it is right for a society to maximize the net balance of satisfaction taken over all of its members.

The most natural way, then, of arriving at utilitarianism (although not, of course, the only way of doing so) is to adopt for society as a whole the principle of rational choice for one man. Once this is recognized, the place of the impartial spectator and the emphasis on sympathy in the history of utilitarian thought is readily understood. For it is by the conception of the impartial spectator and the use of sympathetic identification in guiding our imagination that the principle for one man is applied to society. It is this spectator who is conceived as carrying out the required organization of the desires of all persons into one coherent system of desire; it is by this construction that many persons are fused into one. Endowed with ideal powers of sympathy and imagination, the impartial spectator is the perfectly rational individual who identifies with and experiences the desires of others as if these desires were his own. In this way, he ascertains the intensity of these desires and assigns

them their appropriate weight in the one system of desire the satisfaction of which the ideal legislator then tries to maximize by adjusting the rules of the social system. On this conception of society separate individuals are thought of as so many different lines along which rights and duties are to be assigned and scarce means of satisfaction allocated in accordance with rules so as to give the greatest fulfillment of wants. The nature of the decision made by the ideal legislator is not, therefore, materially different from that of an entrepreneur deciding how to maximize his profit by producing this or that commodity, or that of a consumer deciding how to maximize his satisfaction by the purchase of this or that collection of goods. In each case there is a single person whose system of desires determines the best allocation of limited means. The correct decision is essentially a question of efficient administration. This view of social cooperation is the consequence of extending to society the principle of choice for one man, and then, to make this extension work, conflating all persons into one through the imaginative acts of the impartial sympathetic spectator. Utilitarianism does not take seriously the distinction between persons.

NOTES

1. I shall take Henry Sidgwick's *The Methods of Ethics*, 7th ed. (London, 1907), as summarizing the development of utilitarian moral theory. Book III of his *Principles of Political Economy* (London, 1883) applies this doctrine to questions of economic and social justice, and is a precursor of A. C. Pigou, *The Economics of Welfare* (London, Macmillan, 1920). Sidgwick's *Outlines of the History of Ethics*, 5th ed. (London, 1902), contains a brief history of the utilitarian tradition. We may follow him in assuming, somewhat arbitrarily, that it begins with Shaftesbury's *An Inquiry Concerning Virtue and Merit* (1911) and Hutcheson's *An Inquiry Concerning Moral Good and Evil* (1725). Hutcheson seems to have been the first to state clearly the principle of utility. He says in *Inquiry*, sec. III, §8, that "that action is best, which procures the greatest happiness for the greatest numbers; and that, worst, which, in like manner, occasions misery." Other major eighteenth-century works are Hume's *A Treatise of Human Nature* (1739), and *An Enquiry Concerning the Principles of*

Morals (1751); Adam Smith's *A Theory of the Moral Sentiments* (1759); and Bentham's *The Principles of Morals and Legislation* (1789). To these we must add the writings of J. S. Mill represented by *Utilitarianism* (1863) and F. Y. Edgeworth's *Mathematical Psychics* (London, 1888).

The discussion of utilitarianism has taken a different turn in recent years by focusing on what we may call the coordination problem and related questions of publicity. This development stems from the essays of R. F. Harrod, "Utilitarianism Revised," *Mind*, vol. 45 (1936); J. D. Mabbott, "Punishment," *Mind*, vol. 48 (1939); Jonathan Harrison, "Utilitarianism, Univerali-sation, and Our Duty to be Just," *Proceedings of the Aristotelian Society*, vol. 53 (1952–53); and J. O. Urmson, "The Interpretation of the Philosophy of J. S. Mill," *Philosophical Quarterly*, vol. 3 (1953). See also J. J. C. Smart, "Extreme and Restricted Utilitarianism," *Philosophical Quarterly*, vol. 6 (1956), and his *An Outline of a System of Utilitarian Ethics* (Cambridge, The University Press, 1961). For an account of these matters, see David Lyons, *Forms and Limits of Utilitarianism* (Oxford, The Clarendon Press, 1965); and Allan Gibbard, "Utilitarianisms and Coordination" (dissertation, Harvard University, 1971). The problems raised by these works, as important as they are, I shall leave aside as not bearing directly on the more elementary question of distribution which I wish to discuss.

Finally, we should note here the essay of J. C. Harsanyi, in particular, "Cardinal Utility in Welfare Economics and in the Theory of Risk-Taking," *Journal of Political Economy*, 1953, and "Cardinal Welfare, Individualistic Ethics, and Interpersonal Comparisons of Utility," *Journal of Political Economy*, 1955; and R. B. Brandt, "Some Merits of One Form of Rule—Utilitarianism," *University of Colorado Studies* (Boulder, Colorado, 1967). . . .

2. On this point see also D. P. Gauthier, *Practical Reasoning* (Oxford, Clarendon Press, 1963), pp. 126f. The text elaborates the suggestion found in "Constitutional Liberty and the Concept of Justice," *Nomos VI: Justice*, ed. C. J. Friedrich and J. W. Chapman (New York, Atherton Press, 1963), pp. 124f, which in turn is related to the idea of justice as a higher-order administrative decision. See "Justice as Fairness," *Philosophical Review*, 1958, pp. 185–187. . . . That the principle of social integration is distinct from the principle of personal integration is stated by R. B. Perry, *General Theory of Value* (New York, Longmans, Green, and Company, 1926), pp. 674–677. He attributes the error of overlooking this fact to Emile Durkheim and others with similar views. Perry's conception of social integration is that brought about by a shared and dominant benevolent purpose. . . .

3. Here I adopt W. K. Frankena's definition of teleological theories in *Ethics* (Englewood Cliffs, N.J., Prentice Hall, Inc., 1963), p. 13.

4. On this point see Sidgwick, *The Methods of Ethics*, pp. 416f.

5. See J. S. Mill, *Utilitarianism*, ch. V, last two parts.

The Discourse Ethics Perspective

15 The Rule of Law and Democracy

JÜRGEN HABERMAS

IN ACADEMIA WE OFTEN MENTION law and politics in the same breath, yet at the same time we are accustomed to consider law, including the rule of law, and democracy as subjects of different disciplines: jurisprudence deals with law, political science with democracy, and each deals with the constitutional state in its own way, one side in normative terms, the other from an empirical perspective. Even when legal scholars and social scientists refer from their different standpoints to the same objects, they treat law and the rule of law and, on the other hand, democracy as different matters. There are good reasons for this. Because political authority is, in whatever kind of regime, always exercised in forms of law, there exist legal orders where political force has not yet been domesticated by the rule of law. And there may again exist a rule of law, where the government has not yet been democratized. In short, there are legal systems without a rule of law, and a rule of law may exist without democratic forms of political will-formation. Both come together only within the frame of constitutional states. However, these *empirical* grounds for a division of labour in the analysis of the two subjects by no means implies that, from the *normative* standpoint of legal philosophy, the rule of law could be implemented without democracy. In this paper I want to treat several aspects of this internal relationship between the rule of law and democracy, which is essential for any constitutional state.

This relation results from the concept of modern law itself (section 1) as well as from the fact that positive law can no longer draw its legitimacy from a higher law (section 2). Modern law is legitimated by the autonomy guaranteed equally to each citizen, and legitimated in such a way that private and public autonomy reciprocally presuppose each other (section 3). This conceptual interrelation also makes itself felt in the dialectic of legal and factual equality. It was this dialectic that first elicited the social welfare paradigm of law as a response to the liberal understanding of law, and today this same dialectic necessitates a proceduralist self-understanding of constitutional democracy (section 4). In closing I will elucidate this proceduralist legal paradigm with the example provided by the feminist politics of equality (section 5).

1. Formal Properties of Modern Law

Since Locke, Rousseau, and Kant, a certain concept of law has gradually prevailed not only in philosophical thought but in the constitutional reality of Western societies. This concept is supposed to account simultaneously for both the positivity and the freedom-guaranteeing character of coercive law. The positivity of law, the fact that norms backed by the threat of state sanction stem from the changeable decisions of a political legislator, is bound up with the demand for legitimation. According to this demand, positively enacted

From European Journal of Philosophy 3:1, pp. 12–20. Copyright © 1995 Basil Blackwell Ltd. Reprinted by permission.

law should equally guarantee the autonomy of all legal persons; and the democratic procedure of legislation should in turn satisfy this demand. In this way, an internal relation is established between, on the one hand, the coercibility and changeability of positive law and, on the other, a mode of law-making that engenders legitimacy. Hence, from a normative perspective there is a conceptual relation—and not simply an historically accidental relation—between law and democracy, between legal and democratic theory.

At first glance, this has the look of a philosophical trick. Yet, as a matter of fact, this internal relation is deeply rooted in the presuppositions of our everyday practice of law. For in the mode of validity that attaches to law, the facticity of the state's legal enforcement is intermeshed with the legitimating force of a legislative procedure that claims to be rational because it guarantees freedom. This is shown in the peculiar ambivalence with which the law presents itself to its addressees and expects their obedience: that is, it leaves its addressees free to approach the law in either of two ways. They can either consider norms merely as factual constraints on their freedom and take a strategic approach to the calculable consequences of possible rule-violations, or they can comply with legal statutes in a performative attitude, indeed comply out of respect for results of a common will-formation that claim legitimacy. Kant already expressed this point with his specific concept of 'legality', which highlighted the connection between these two moments without which legal obedience cannot reasonably be expected: legal norms must be so fashioned that they can be viewed simultaneously in two different ways, as coercive laws and as laws of freedom. These two aspects belong to our understanding of modern law; we consider the validity of a legal norm as equivalent to the explanation that the state can simultaneously guarantee factual enforcement and legitimate enactment—and thus it can guarantee, on the one hand, the legality of behaviour in the sense of average compliance, which can if necessary be compelled by sanctions; and, on the other hand, the legitimacy of the rule itself, which should always make it possible to comply with the norm out of reasonable respect for the law.

Of course, this immediately raises the question of how the legitimacy of rules should be grounded when the rules in questions can be changed at any time by the political legislator. Constitutional norms too are changeable; and even the basic norms that the Constitution itself has declared non-amendable share, along with all positive law, the fate that they can be abrogated, say, after a change of regime. As long as one was able to fall back on a religiously or metaphysically grounded natural law, the whirlpool of temporality enveloping positive law could be held in check by morality. Situated in a hierarchy of law, temporalized positive law was supposed to remain *subordinate* to an eternally valid moral law and therefrom receive its lasting orientations. But even aside from the fact that in pluralistic societies such integrating worldviews and collectively binding comprehensive doctrines have disintegrated, modern law, simply by virtue of its formal properties, resists the direct control of a post-traditional morality of conscience, which is so to speak, all we have left.

2. The Complementary Relation between Positive Law and Autonomous Morality

Modern legal systems are built out of individual rights. Such rights have the character of releasing legal persons from moral obligations in a carefully circumscribed manner. By introducing rights that concede to agents the latitude to act according to personal preferences, modern law as a whole implements the principle that whatever is not explicitly prohibited is permitted. Whereas in morality an inherent symmetry exists between rights and duties, legal duties are a consequence of entitlements, that is, they result only from statutory constraints of individual liberties. This basic conceptual privileging of rights over duties is explained by the modern concepts of the 'legal person' and the 'legal community'. The moral universe, which is *unlimited* in social space and historical time, includes *all natural* persons in their life-historical complexity; morality itself extends protection to the integrity of fully individuated persons (*Einzelner*). By contrast, the legal community, which is always localized in space and time, protects the integrity of its members precisely insofar as they acquire the artificial status of *rights-bearers*. For this reason, the relation between law and morality is more one of complementarity than of subordination.

The same is true if one compares their relative scope. The matters that require legal regulation are at once narrower and broader in scope than morally relevant concerns: they are narrower in scope inasmuch as legal regulation has access only to external, that is, coercible, behavior; they are broader in scope inasmuch as law, as an organizational form of politics, pertains not only to the regulation of interpersonal conflicts but also to the pursuit of political goals and the implementation of policies. Hence, legal regulations touch not only on moral questions in the narrow sense, but also on pragmatic and ethical questions, and on compromise formation among conflicting interests. Moreover, unlike the clearly delimited normative validity claimed by moral norms, the *legitimacy* claimed by legal norms is based on various sorts of reasons. The legislative practice of justification depends on a complex network of discourses and bargaining, and not just on moral discourse.

The natural law idea of a hierarchy of laws (*Rechten*) at different levels of dignity is misleading. Law is better understood as a functional complement to morality. As positively valid, legitimately enacted and adjudicated, that is actionable, law can relieve the morally judging and acting person of the considerable cognitive, motivational, and organization demands of morality based entirely on individual conscience. Law can compensate for the weaknesses of a highly demanding morality that—if we judge from its empirical results—provides only cognitively indeterminate and motivationally unreliable results. Naturally, this does not absolve legislators and judges from a concern that the law be in harmony with morality. But legal regulations are too concrete to be legitimated *solely* through their compatibility with moral principles. From what, then, can positive law borrow its legitimacy, if not from a superior moral law?

Like morality, law too is supposed to protect the autonomy of all persons equally. Law too must prove its legitimacy under this aspect of securing freedom. Interestingly enough, though, the positive character of law forces autonomy to split up in a peculiar way, which has no parallel in morality. Moral self-determination in Kant's sense is a unified concept insofar as it demands of each person, *in propria persona,* that she obey just those norms that she herself posits according to her own impartial judgment, or according to judgment reached in common with all other persons. However, the binding quality of legal norms does not stem solely from processes or opinion- and will-formation, but arises also from the collectively binding decisions of authorities who make and apply law. This circumstance makes it conceptually necessary to distinguish the role of authors who make (and adjudicate) law from that of addressees who are subject to established law. The autonomy that in the moral domain is all of a piece, so to speak, appears in the legal domain only in the dual form of private and public autonomy.

However, these two moments must then be mediated in such a way that the one form of autonomy does not detract from the other. Each form of autonomy, the individual liberties of the subject of private law and the public autonomy of the citizen, makes the other form possible. This reciprocal relation is expressed by the idea that legal persons can be autonomous only insofar as they can understand themselves, in the exercise of their civil rights, as authors of just those rights which they are supposed to obey as addressees.

3. The Mediation of Popular Sovereignty and Human Rights

It is therefore not surprising that modern natural law theories have answered the legitimation question by referring, on the one hand, to the principle of *popular sovereignty* and, on the other, to the *rule of law* as guaranteed by human rights. The principle of popular sovereignty is expressed in rights of communications and participation that secure the public autonomy of citizens; the rule of law is expressed in those classical basic rights that guarantee the private autonomy of members of society. Thus the law is legitimated as an instrument for the equal protection of private and public autonomy. To be sure, political philosophy has never really been able to strike a balance between popular sovereignty and human rights, or between the 'freedom of the ancients' and the 'freedom of the moderns'. The political autonomy of citizens is supposed to be embodied in the self-organization of a community that gives itself its laws through the sovereign will of the people. The private autonomy of citizens, on the other hand, is supposed to take the form of basic rights that guarantee the anonymous rule of law. Once the issue is set up in this way, the one idea can be upheld only at the expense of the other. The intuitively plausible co-originality of both ideas falls by the wayside.

Republicanism, which goes back to Aristotle and the political humanism of the Renaissance, has always given the public autonomy of citizens priority over the pre-political liberties of private persons. *Liberalism,* which goes back to John Locke, has invoked the danger of tyrannical majorities and postulated the priority of human rights. According to republicanism, human rights owed their legitimacy to the ethical self-understanding and self-determination achieved by a political community; in liberalism, such rights were supposed to provide, from the very start, legitimate barriers that prevented the sovereign will of the people from encroaching on inviolable spheres of individual freedom. In their concepts of the legal person's autonomy, Rousseau and Kant certainly aimed to conceive of sovereign will and practical reason as unified in such a way that popular sovereignty and human rights would reciprocally interpret one another. But even they failed to do justice to the co-originality of the two ideas; Rousseau suggests more of a republican reading,

Kant more of a liberal one. They missed the intuition they wanted to articulate: the idea of human rights, which is expressed in the right to equal individual liberties, must neither be merely imposed on the sovereign legislator as an external barrier, nor be instrumentalist as a functional requisite for legislative goals.

To express this intuition properly it helps to view the democratic procedure—which alone provides legitimating force to the law-making process in the context of social and ideological pluralism—from a discourse-theoretical standpoint. Here I assume a principle that I cannot discuss in detail, namely, that a regulation may claim legitimacy only if all those possibly affected by it could consent to it after participating in rational discourses. Now, if discourses—and bargaining processes as well, whose fairness is based on discursively grounded procedures—represent the place where a reasonable political will can develop, then the presumption of reasonability, which the democratic procedure is supposed to ground, ultimately rests on an elaborate communicative arrangement: the presumption depends on the conditions under which one can legally institutionalize the forms of communication necessary for legitimate lawmaking. In that case, the desired internal relation between human rights and popular sovereignty consists in this: human rights themselves are what satisfy the requirement that a civic practice of the public use of communicative freedom be legally institutionalized. Human rights, which make the exercise of popular sovereignty legally *possible,* cannot be imposed on this practice as an external constraint. Enabling conditions must not be confused with such constraints.

Naturally, this analysis is at first plausible only for those civil rights, specifically the rights of communication and participation, that safeguard the exercise of political autonomy. It is less plausible for the classical human rights that guarantee the citizen's private autonomy. Here we think of the fundamental right to the greatest possible degree of equal individual liberties, though we also think of basic rights that constitute membership status in a state and provide the individual with comprehensive legal protection. These rights, which are meant to guarantee to everyone an equal opportunity to pursue his or her private conceptions of the good, have an intrinsic value, or at least they are not reducible to their instrumental value for democratic will-formation. We will do justice to the intuition that the classical liberties are co-original with political rights only if we state more precisely the thesis that human rights legally enable the citizens' practice of self-determination. I turn now to this more precise statement.

4. The Relation between Private and Public Autonomy

However well-grounded human rights are, they may not be paternalistically foisted, as it were, on a sovereign. Indeed, the idea of citizens' legal autonomy demands that the addressees of law be able to understand themselves at the same time as its authors. It would contradict this idea if the democratic legislator were to discover human rights as though they were (pre-existing) moral facts that one merely needs to enact as positive law. At the same time, one must also not forget that when citizens occupy the role of co-legislators they are no longer free to choose the medium in which alone they can realize their autonomy. They participate in legislation only as legal subjects; it is no longer in their power to decide which language they will make use of. The democratic idea of self-legislation *must* acquire its validity in the medium of law itself.

However, when citizens judge in the light of the discourse principle whether the law they make is legitimate, they do so under communicative presuppositions that must themselves be legally institutionalized in the form of civil rights, and for such institutionalization to occur, the legal code as such must be available. But to establish this legal code it is necessary to create the status of legal persons who as bearers of individual rights belong to a voluntary association of citizens and when necessary effectively claim their rights. There is no law without the private autonomy of legal persons

in general. As a result, without basic rights that secure the private autonomy of citizens there also would not be any medium in which to legally institutionalize the conditions under which these citizens, as citizens of a state, could make use of their public autonomy. Thus private and public autonomy mutually presuppose each other in such a way that neither human rights nor popular sovereignty can claim primacy over its counterpart.

This expresses the intuition that, on the one hand, citizens can make adequate use of their public autonomy only if, on the basis of their equally protected private autonomy, they are sufficiently independent; but that, on the other hand, they can arrive at a consensual regulation of their private autonomy only if they make adequate use of their political autonomy as enfranchised citizens.

This internal relation between the rule of law and democracy has been concealed long enough by the competition between the legal paradigms that have been dominant up to the present. The liberal legal paradigm reckons with an economic society that is institutionalized through private law—above all through property rights and contractual freedom—and left to the spontaneous workings of the market. This 'private law society' is tailored for the autonomy of legal subjects who as market participants more or less rationally pursue their personal life-plans. This model of society is associated with the normative expectation that social justice can be realized by guaranteeing such a negative legal status, and thus solely by delimiting spheres of individual freedom. The critique of this supposition gave rise to the social welfare model. The objection is obvious: if the free 'capacity to have and acquire' is supposed to guarantee social justice, then an equality in 'legal capacity' must exist. As a matter of fact, however, the growing inequalities in economic power, assets, and living conditions have increasingly destroyed the factual preconditions for an equal opportunity to make effective use of equally distributed legal powers. If the normative content of legal equality is not to be inverted into its opposite, then two correctives are necessary. On the one hand, existing norms of private law must be substantively specified and on the other hand, basic social rights must be introduced, rights that ground claims to a more just distribution of socially produced wealth and to more effective protection against socially produced dangers.

In the meantime, of course, this *materialization* of law has in turn created the unintended side effects of *welfare paternalism*. Clearly, efforts to compensate for actual living conditions and power positions must not lead to 'normalizing' interventions of a sort that once again restrict the presumptive beneficiaries' pursuit of an autonomous life-project. The further development of the dialectic of legal and factual equality has shown that both legal paradigms are equally committed to the productivist image of an economic society based on industrial capitalism. This society is supposed to function in such a way that the expectation of social justice can be satisfied by securing each individual's private pursuit of his or her conception of the good life. The only dispute between the two paradigms concerns whether private autonomy can be guaranteed straightaway by negative liberties (*Freiheitsrechte*), or whether (on the contrary) the conditions for private autonomy must be secured through the provisions of welfare entitlements. In both cases, however, the internal relation between private and public autonomy drops out of the picture.

5. *The Example of the Feminist Politics of Equality*

In closing, I want to examine the feminist politics of equality to show that policies and legal strategies oscillate helplessly between the conventional paradigms as long as they remain limited to securing private autonomy and disregard how the individual rights of private persons are related to the public autonomy of citizens engaged in lawmaking. For, in the final analysis, private legal subjects cannot enjoy even equal individual liberties if they themselves do not exercise their civic autonomy in common in order to specify clearly which interests and standards are justified, and to agree on the relevant respects that determine when like

cases should be treated alike and different cases differently.

Initially, the goal of liberal policies was to uncouple the acquisition of status from gender identity and to guarantee to women equal opportunities in the competition for jobs, social recognition, education, political power, etc., regardless of the outcome. However, the formal equality that was partially achieved merely made it more obvious how women were *in fact* treated unequally. Social welfare politics responded to this, especially in the areas of social labour, and family law, by passing special regulations relating, for example, to pregnancy and child care, or to social hardship in the case of divorce. In the meantime feminist critique has targeted not only the unredeemed demands, but also the ambivalent consequences of successfully implemented welfare programmes—for example, the higher risk of women losing their jobs as a result of compensatory regulations, the over-representation of women in lower wage brackets, the problematic issue of 'what is in the child's best interests', and in general the progressive feminization of poverty. From a legal standpoint, one reason for this reflexively generated discrimination is found in the over-generalized classifications used to label disadvantaged situations and disadvantaged groups of persons, because these 'false' classifications lead to 'normalizing' interventions into how people conduct their lives, interventions that transform what was intended as compensation for damages into new forms of discrimination. Thus instead of guaranteeing liberty, such over-protection takes it away. In areas of law that are of concern to feminism, welfare paternalism takes on literal meaning to the extent that legislation and adjudication are oriented by traditional patterns of interpretation and thus serve to buttress existing stereotypes of sexual identity.

The classification of gender-specific roles and differences touches on fundamental levels of a society's cultural self-understanding. Radical feminism has only now made us aware of the fallible character of this self-understanding, an understanding that is essentially contested and in need of revision. It rightly insists that the appropriate interpretation of needs and criteria be a matter of public debate *in the political public sphere*. It is here that citizens must clarify the aspects that determine which differences between the experiences and living situations of (specific groups of) men and women are relevant for an equal opportunity to exercise individual liberties. Thus, this struggle for the equal status of women is a particularly good example of the need for a change of the legal paradigm.

The dispute between the two received paradigms—whether the autonomy of legal persons is better secured through individual liberties for private competition or through publicly guaranteed entitlements for clients of welfare bureaucracies—this dispute is superseded by a *proceduralist conception of law*. According to this conception, the democratic process must secure private and public autonomy at the same time: the individual rights that are meant to guarantee to women the autonomy to pursue their lives in the private sphere cannot even be adequately formulated unless the affected persons themselves first articulate and justify in public debate those aspects which are relevant to equal or unequal treatment in typical cases. The private autonomy of equally entitled citizens can be secured only insofar as citizens actively exercise their civic autonomy.

16 The Foundations of Modern Democracy[1]

CHARLES LARMORE

JÜRGEN HABERMAS IS ONE of the very few indisputably great moral and social thinkers of our time. We must situate our own thought with respect to his, in order to know what it is we truly think, even when we then find that we must disagree. Over a number of years, Habermas has been working out a new conception of moral philosophy which he calls 'discourse ethics' (*Diskursethik*). To some extent, this line of thought has developed at a very abstract level. Its most prominent feature perhaps has been the attempt to find the source of morality in a general principle of universalization which any agent must assume just by virtue of being a competent speaker with an understanding of the concept of reasons for action. It cannot be said that this attempt has met with evident success. Like all efforts to draw some fundamental set of moral obligations from the notion of practical rationality as such, Habermas' reflections at this level seem caught in a well-known, but inescapable dilemma: either the idea Habermas proposes of practical rationality (or 'communicative reason', as he terms it) proves too weak to deliver any moral principles, or it is made to yield the desired conclusions only by virtue of moral content having been built into it from the outset.

These exercises in 'first philosophy' have been however, only one part, and doubtlessly not the most deeply felt, of Habermas' project of a discourse ethics. Far more important has been the vision of a truly democratic politics which has driven this project. That is why one of Habermas' most recent books, *Faktizität und Geltung,* represents so significant an event.[2] In it Habermas' political philosophy and his guiding conception of radical democracy have finally achieved the detailed articulation they deserve. This book allows us to take a more just measure of the contribution which Habermas' discourse ethics can make to an understanding of the nature and promise of political association.

1. Argument and Context

In the book, Habermas sets out to reply to the frequent objection that his discourse ethics promotes a sort of excessive moralizing which betrays a lack of contact with the reality of the modern liberal-democratic state. The general form of Habermas' response is to argue that reality (*Faktizität*) and validity (*Geltung*) form a relation of tension, which his political philosophy pursues in two opposing directions. On the one hand, he aims to show that social reality, even in the most elementary aspects of language use, rests on a normative dimension. Whenever we act or think reasonably, or believe we do, we make a 'validity claim' (*Geltungsanspruch*): we suppose that the reasons we have possess a certain objectivity and would command the rational assent of others in an appropriately conducted discussion (*Diskurs*). No satisfactory theory of the political life of modern societies, however complex they may be, can

From European Journal of Philosophy 3:1, pp. 55–68. Copyright © 1995 Basil Blackwell Ltd. *Reprinted by permission.*

therefore ignore or dismiss the normative claims of the modern liberal-democratic state. This conclusion is familiar from many of his earlier works, particularly from his *Theory of Communicative Action*.

But on the other hand, Habermas also acknowledges that the cultural and social realities of modern society impose certain tasks and constraints on our attempt to make sense of the proper nature of political association today. Modern societies are highly complex, he observes, in that they can no longer be understood as politically constituted. In functionally differentiated, or 'decentered' societies such as our own, where different social domains (or 'subsystems') such as law, the economy, political life, and religion take on specialized tasks in accord with their own criteria, the state may no longer serve, he claims, as the expression and guarantee of the goals and ideals of society as a whole (pp. 65, 365f.). For my part, I think one might better say that modern societies are so complex that such holistic conceptions are likely to have considerably less appeal, and not that they have only now become untrue. For probably they were never really adequate to their object. Be that as it may, Habermas is surely right to maintain (here principally in opposition to Niklas Luhmann's systems theory) that we need not think society to be politically constituted in order to suppose that the collectively binding decisions of the legal system and the underlying principles of our political life have a normative basis and can become an appropriate object of reflection for moral philosophy (pp. 70ff.). Sensitivity to the complexities of social reality cannot replace our need to reflect on the validity of the principles by which we live together. . . .

2. Politics and Modernity

In Habermas' view, the moral self-understanding of modern political association must today satisfy the requirements of 'post-metaphysical thought' (pp. 24, 127, 135, 492). One might well wonder just how 'post-metaphysically' Habermas himself is disposed to think, when he resorts so freely to his ideal of the Unconditioned. But let us begin by looking more closely at what he means by 'post-metaphysical'.

According to his earlier book, *Post-Metaphysical Thought* (*Nachmetaphysisches Denken*), our epoch requires that, in place of metaphysical modes of thought, we regard reason as finite, fallible, oriented toward achieving intersubjective agreement, and tied to procedural rationality.[3] Habermas' most recent book defends basically the same conception. Concepts of justice, and the legal systems corresponding to them, are constructed in a post-metaphysical fashion, he claims, when they aim to remain neutral with respect to religious and metaphysically conceived forms of life which have themselves become problematic and disputed. The normative foundations of the modern liberal-democratic state must consist in procedural principles of justice that do not presuppose the validity of controversial ideas of the good life (pp. 375f.). Here the right, as he says, must be prior to the good. Societies such as our own, which are functionally differentiated and culturally heterogeneous, have no common good other than a legal system that treats free citizens equally and deals with their conflicts according to standards of procedural justice. If patriotism is the virtue of loyalty to the common values constituting political life, then Habermas' position, succinctly put, is that only a 'constitutional patriotism' (*Verfassungspatriotismus*) is truly coherent today (p. 642).[4]

Consequently, Habermas turns a cold eye on some of the recent revivals of the 'civic republican' tradition. To the extent that these revivals have taken a 'communitarian' form (Habermas cites the work of Frank Michelman and Charles Taylor), and long for citizenship to express the substantial ethic (or *Sittlichkeit*) of a common vision of the meaning of life, they do not fit with the exigencies of modern political life (pp. 338f., 642). I agree. But I should point out that in reality the republican tradition is not essentially communitarian. The strand of republican thought represented paradigmatically by Machiavelli's *Discorsi* and recovered today in particular by Quentin Skinner appeals, not to the fusion of politics around a common ideal of the good life, and in particular not to the idea that political participation is itself the highest form of activity, but rather to the importance, limited but real, of the active virtues of citizenship and to the need to nurture the rule of law which is necessary for individual liberty.[5] As such, republicanism ought to be a central ingredient in the self-understanding of the modern liberal-democratic state and of Habermas' own political philosophy.

A principle of neutrality similar to that of Habermas, expressed as the demand that liberalism take the form of a 'political', not a 'comprehensive' doctrine, lies at the heart of the theory of justice John Rawls has made so famous. It is also a principle that I have defended, in some earlier writings of mine. Despite this common ground, which Habermas is kind enough to point out (pp. 376ff.), there are several respects in which I find myself in disagreement.

The first objection concerns an important matter, though it is one which does not affect, I believe, the basic contours of Habermas' position. It seems to me that, though he rightly rejects the communitarian longing to have politics express a common vision of the good life, Habermas rather underestimates the depth of the common life necessary, even today, for the fundamental principles of political association to command allegiance. This common life must run deeper than just constitutional patriotism. If the political identity of a people did not extend beyond that level, if it consisted therefore only in the affirmation of procedural principles of equal freedom and respect, which clearly purport to govern political life everywhere, then such a people would have to espouse as its ultimate goal the construction of a world political order. Its fundamental political aspiration would have to be cosmopolitan. Whether or not this goal is really desirable, it seems to me wrong to regard it as inscribed in the very logic of the modern liberal-democratic state. Political allegiance today, even when its object is liberal democracy, remains essentially shaped by the conviction that a people can rightly enjoy a form of political association that sets it off from other peoples, even from those sharing the same fundamental political values.

How then should we understand this further, necessary dimension of the common life underlying political association? The mistake of communitarians, but apparently of Habermas as well, is to suppose that it can consist only in a shared allegiance to additional values. That is not so. It can instead be a matter of being shaped by common circumstances. For example, a people can think of itself as a distinct people in terms of a shared language and geographical situation. Neither of these is either necessary or sufficient for the sense of belonging to a people, though each can certainly play a significant role. The most important factor, however, is that a people can be bound together by a common historical experience, including the memory of past conflicts, even bloody ones, which were ignited by political programmes attempting to impose contrary ideals of the good life (different religious confessions, for instance), but which have been superseded by a practice of equal respect. The political identity of a people may be forged by a shared memory of the violent struggles they have been through and the quarrels they have left behind, in addition to the principles of a 'constitutional patriotism' they have put in their place.

This was the idea Ernest Renan sought to express when he observed (in his *Qu'est-ce qu'une nation?* of 1882) that 'every French citizen must have forgotten the St Bartholomew's Day massacre.'[6] This famous statement is paradoxical, not just because many Frenchmen had not forgotten that fateful day when Catholics slaughtered Protestants by the thousands, but also because Renan addressed the statement to his French readers. In fact, what Renan meant to highlight is not a shared amnesia, but rather a shared memory. A common sense of French citizenship has been forged precisely by people forsaking together, though not forgetting, the passions that once drove their ancestors to make political authority an instrument of religious confession. Similarly formative memories play a role in the self-understanding of other Western liberal democracies.

Only by keeping in mind this aspect of its underlying common life, can we make sense of an important fact about liberal democracy. Not just as a matter of historical record, but in its very character, it presents itself as a *latecomer* amongst the forms of political life. Liberal democracy builds upon the memory of past conflict and the hard-won knowledge that many of the ideals that used to shape political life now form the object of reasonable disagreement. For this reason, individuals may rightly see themselves as sharing a political destiny that goes beyond the values they can affirm in patriotic declarations. They may feel united in what they have learned together from the things that came to divide them. This shared memory is itself sustained, of course, by a common allegiance to the constitutional principles of equal freedom and respect. It is indeed, the historical colouring these principles have for a specific people, the expression of how they came to accept them. That is why a recognition of this further dimension of common life is compatible with the principle of neutrality mentioned above. And why it can be fitted into the basic structure of Habermas's thought as well.

There are, however, two fundamental and consequential points where it seems to me Habermas goes wrong in his reconstruction of the normative basis of modern liberal democracy. The first of them concerns the very designation of 'post-metaphysical'. In Habermas' view, reason should proceed 'post-metaphysically' in the political realm, not simply in order to solve the problem of the principles of political association, but rather in order to apply to this realm the general philosophical perspective which alone, he believes, fits our contemporary intellectual situation. Again and again he insists that certain political principles (the primacy of procedural justice or the priority of the right over the good, the idea of popular sovereignty as the source of individual rights) recommend themselves because the age of metaphysical and religious worldviews is over and practical reason must thus abandon the frameworks of natural law and of the individual subject in favour of his own model of communicative interaction (pp. 17, 24, 51f., 127).

This argumentative strategy seems to me a mistake. It is not that I want to assert that the ambitions of metaphysics retain their plausibility or that some particular religious worldview has not really lost its authority. My own considered views on these matters are, in fact, somewhat more complex than those of Habermas. But the present question properly involves not all that we might reasonably believe to be true of the world, but rather what we ought to consider as relevant to the establishment of principles of political association. These two perspectives are not, I continue to believe, the same.[7] So the important point here is that in modern culture such assertions about the vitality or obsolescence of metaphysics and religion are something about which reasonable people — aiming, that is, to think and converse in good faith and apply, as best they can, the general capacities of reason — can disagree. Even today, reasonable people can come to believe that the naturalistic worldview should be replaced by a broader, metaphysical or 'platonistic', vision that recognizes the existence of ideal entitles, neither physical nor psychological in character. Thus, I myself think that we must believe there to exist such things as reasons, which we discover by reflection, if we are to suppose that there can be normative knowledge, that is, knowledge of how we ought to think and act.[8] Similarly, reasonable people can also find a basis for believing that the world is guided by divine providence; just as other people equally reasonable — and this includes Habermas himself — can conclude, to the contrary, that mind and knowledge must be understood without platonistic assumptions and that religion can belong (at best) to the realm of subjective conviction. Indeed, people can also find themselves in reasonable disagreement, as we have seen, about what should count as metaphysical and what should not.

As a political principle, the priority of the right over the good should therefore not be thought dependent on the supposed obsolescence of metaphysical and religious worldviews. This principle is not 'post-metaphysical', if that means that it gives expression to a new, general vision of thought and world. Instead, the priority of the right should be seen as stemming from the recognition that such worldviews, like the philosophical attempts to overcome them, are and will remain the object of controversy among reasonable people. Again, it may well be the case, on general philosophical grounds, that our best understanding of reason today would be along the lines of the 'post-metaphysical' characterization Habermas gives: finite, fallible, oriented toward achieving agreement, and tied to procedural rationality. Such a conception of reason is indeed one I am inclined to share, though I think Habermas wrongly supposes that it escapes the need to assume the existence of ideal entities. But the point here is that such a conception, however ultimately correct, remains the object of reasonable disagreement. To that extent, it shows itself to be unfit to play a foundational role in what ought to be the moral self-understanding of the modern liberal-democratic state. For the priority of the right, as a political principle, expresses the conviction that in the wake of ongoing ethical, religious, and philosophical controversy political association today must rest on a core morality, which reasonable people despite their deep differences can all accept. At the heart of this core morality lies, as I shall explain in the next section, a principle of equal respect. This political doctrine of liberalism is 'post-metaphysical' only in a trivial sense: metaphysical and religious assumptions are too controversial to have a place at its basis. But the same is equally true for general philosophical conceptions of so-called 'post-metaphysical thought'.

Habermas' aim is to bring out the fundamental dimension of modern experience that finds expression in the liberal-democratic state. This project is a very sensible one. But to me it seems that Habermas has missed the feature of modern experience which is relevant. It does not lie in the demise of metaphysical and religious worldviews, though the widespread abandonment of such views is certainly a significant aspect of modernity. It consists instead in the growing recognition that reasonable disagreement about the nature of the good life and even about the philosophical foundations of morality is not a passing phenomenon, but rather is the situation we should expect. The more we discuss with one another, and in a thoughtful and informed way, the meaning of life, the more likely it is that we will find that we differ and disagree. The expectation of reasonable disagreement is the phenomenon that ought to guide our political thought today.

Though I have discussed in detail elsewhere this fundamental experience of modern life,[9] let me point out here again that it is very far from recommending a general moral scepticism. First, there is the fact that the expectation of irresolvable controversy has been aroused most of all by questions of the speculative sort. However much such controversies may engage our deepest aspirations, they still leave generally untouched the moral commitments of everyday life. Controversy about ultimate and fundamental matters can go hand in hand with the conviction that we can nonetheless agree upon a core morality that is adequate for the purposes of political association. Indeed, it is only such a core morality that can tell us that we ought to give reasonable disagreement about the meaning of life a decisive role in the establishment of political principles.

Secondly, the fact that our vision of the good life is the object of reasonable disagreement does not entail that we should withdraw our allegiance to it or regard it as henceforth a mere article of faith. On the contrary, we may still have good reasons to affirm it, based on our experience and reflection. We should remember only that such reasons are not likely to be acceptable to other people, who are equally reasonable, but have a different history of experience and reflection. Just as the basis they have for their different conceptions of life will not be such as to win our assent. The good reasons which move reasonable people, disposed as they are to think and converse in good faith and to exercise, to the best of their abilities, the general capacities of reason, need not be reasons they all must share. Their grounds for belief and action draw upon their different background convictions. As their starting points differ, so do the positions at which they may legitimately arrive. Reasonable people may thus have good reason to believe in the visions which divide them. But they would be foolish not to expect that a careful and informed discussion would lead them into disagreement.

I could sum up this criticism of Habermas, therefore, by saying that he has presented a concept of modernity which is not sufficiently broad. Modern experience is characterized, not just by a new, 'post-metaphysical' understanding of the true and the right, but also by the expectation that metaphysics and post-metaphysics will remain an enduring object of reasonable disagreement.

3. Liberalism and Democracy

My second major criticism is directed toward the way in which Habermas proposes to conceive the relation between basic individual rights (the right to freedom of conscience, freedom of speech, assembly and private property) and the democratic ideal of popular sovereignty. As I have noted, he does not share the communitarian assumption that individual rights need to be nurtured and shaped by an antecedent, substantial vision of the good life (*Sittlichkeit*). But equally significantly, he rejects the contrary standpoint of liberalism. As Habermas rightly observes, liberalism has usually assigned to individual rights—at least those of a fundamental kind—the function of delimiting the proper scope of popular sovereignty (pp. 130, 329, 610). That is, liberal thinkers have generally seen fundamental individual rights as a distinct value from democratic self-rule and as taking precedence over it. This outlook finds expression indeed in the very term 'liberal democracy', but it is nonetheless one Habermas refuses. His explicit aim is to cut a middle way between the opposing camps of liberalism and communitarianism, which divide between them

so much of contemporary Anglo-American political philosophy.

This *via media* is announced in the thesis that fundamental individual rights and democratic self-rule are 'co-original' (*gleichursprünglich*) values. At one level this co-originality is for Habermas a relation of mutual presupposition. Just as self-government can serve to protect individual rights, so rights are best understood as providing the necessary conditions for the exercise of popular sovereignty (pp. 133f., 161, 610). But at bottom Habermas unmistakably privileges the second of these values. Individual rights in his view draw their rationale from their supposed ability to make democratic self-rule possible. Their basic purpose cannot be, as liberals generally believe, to limit the authority of popular sovereignty.

A clear sign of the priority Habermas assigns to democracy is the basic value he sees as underlying the co-originality of rights and self-government. It is what he calls 'autonomy' (pp. 52f.). In a post-metaphysical age, he argues, where the appeal of metaphysical and religious world-pictures is on the wane, we can have reason to consider ourselves subject to practical norms only if we are able at the same time to see ourselves as the source of these norms. Democratic self-rule is but the application of this idea of autonomy to the political realm (pp. 52, 153f., 160). Citizens can regard themselves as legitimately bound by the rules of political association, only to the extent that these rules spring from no higher source than the citizens themselves. Again, because of widespread and deeply rooted controversies about the nature of the good life, however, citizens must locate their role as the source of law, not in a given substantial form of life they might already share, but instead in their own common will, which they mobilize for this political purpose alone. This is why communitarianism is unacceptable. Citizens can form and express this collective will only in public discussion (*Diskurs*) with one another about the principles of the common life which they are to affirm.

This line of Habermas' thought contains an important element which other liberal-democratic thinkers have embraced before him: legitimate principles of political association must be rationally acceptable to all citizens whom they are meant to bind. This is why in the face of reasonable disagreement about the good life, political association must rely on the priority of the right. But the distinctive feature of Habermas' position is the further claim which he believes to underlie this and which breaks with the usual conception of liberal democracy. It is his claim that fundamental individual rights have their proper basis only in the ideal of popular sovereignty, so that citizens will understand their collective will as the source of all the norms which bind them. In Habermas' eyes, the essentially protective function of such rights does not lie primarily in restricting the power of the state, but instead at the deeper level of empowering individuals to participate in this democratic self-rule. The right to freedom of speech, for example, is held to recommend itself as a means to the formation of a common political will. Individual rights serve, not to protect us against the collective will, but rather to protect the means necessary for creating a collective will.

In essence, Habermas thus wants to see democratic self-rule as the sole normative foundation of the modern liberal-democratic state. Liberal democracy ought best to be understood, he believes, not as that term itself suggests (the subordination of democracy to liberal principles), but rather as *radical democracy*. Political association must be understood as truly and thoroughly self-governing. It cannot subordinate itself to any pre-given norms. It can acknowledge only those moral norms to which it has itself given rise (pp. 123, 154). This ideal of popular sovereignty forms the heart of Habermas' political philosophy. It is why he thinks, for example, that instead of regarding fundamental legal, i.e. constitutional, principles as the application of moral principles already held to be valid, we should understand law and morality as equally basic, though often overlapping, specifications of an even more general normative principle D, which gives expression to the fundamental value of autonomy (pp. 135–138): 'Only those action norms are valid to which all those who

might be affected by their establishment could assent as the result of a rational discussion.'

At first glance, Habermas' vision of radical democracy seems to lack the defining features of the liberal point of view. Liberal thinkers have always argued that political association must rest ultimately on moral principles that serve to protect certain basic individual freedoms. Typically, such principles have consisted in the affirmation of fundamental rights, with the result that democratic self-rule is subordinated to the protection of individual freedoms. Habermas' unqualified fondness for the ideal of popular sovereignty seems to make him something very different from a liberal.

But the appearance is misleading. In reality, Habermas' description of his theory as involving the primacy of popular sovereignty fails to capture its actual structure. Democratic self-rule, at least as Habermas understands it, depends on an unacknowledged premise, a premise expressing an antecedent moral commitment and affirming the existence of a fundamental individual right. Other conceptions of popular sovereignty would have, no doubt, a different character. But Habermas' conception is so constituted as to imply that political principles ought to be rationally acceptable to all those whom they are to bind. And that is the feature which brings his idea of democracy back within the liberal fold, as generally understood.

For let us ask why indeed we should believe that political principles ought to be rationally acceptable to all. It will not do to reply, as Habermas suggests, that the authority of traditional views of the world, in which being subject to law and being the source of the law do not coincide, has simply vanished. For that is first of all false. As I have pointed out, the authority of such worldviews remains for many the object of a living conviction. Indeed, we cannot in particular understand how there can be such a thing as moral knowledge, I have suggested, unless we suppose 'metaphysically' that there exist such things as reasons that we do not create, but rather discover by reflection. It is too narrow a conception of modernity, or at least of that aspect of it which is relevant to the problem of political association, that fails to recognize the existence of reasonable disagreement on this point. Secondly, the waning of these worldviews, where it has occurred, cannot suffice to justify the idea that the principles of political association must be rationally acceptable to all. It would, for example, be just as possible under these circumstances for political principles to be geared instead to the maximization of the general welfare.

The crucial fact about the idea that the rules of political association must be rationally acceptable to all those whom they are to bind is that it takes into account the respect in which political principles differ from other moral principles. In general, political principles are precisely those principles which we believe may be enforced by coercion, if need be. The idea that such principles must be rationally acceptable to those who are to be subject to them rests on a moral view about the conditions under which norms may be backed up by force. This underlying moral commitment is that no one should be made by force to comply with a norm of action when it is not possible for him to recognize through reason the validity of that norm. Moral principles with which we do not intend to bring about compliance by force if necessary need not meet this condition: we may judge others in their light, without having to suppose they would agree to their validity. There is nothing *per se* wrong with doing so: we do it all the time when we judge others in terms of our religious convictions or ideals of the good life, which they do not and cannot share given their own settled convictions. (Consequently, I cannot accept Habermas' view that his Principle D concerns all moral norms, and not just politically instituted ones.) But the matter is different with moral principles we mean to back up with coercive force. Such principles, which are precisely political in nature, are ones we should accept only if they could command the rational assent of those whom they are to bind. It is, as I have said, a fundamental moral commitment that makes this so.

This moral conviction amounts, in fact, to the Kantian formula that every person is always to be treated as an end in himself. No one should be made to do, for the sake of some ulterior end, what cannot also win his rational assent. This is, at root, a norm of equal respect, according to which individuals are to be treated as beings whose exercise of their capacity of rational agency cannot be sacrificed for the sake of achieving some social goal. It lies at the heart of the core morality which can be affirmed by people who otherwise differ about the merits of metaphysical and post-metaphysical views of the world, and which sustains the political principle of the priority of the right. Most importantly of all in the present context, this moral principle gives expression to an individual right, though certainly one more fundamental than the political rights which tend to be the object of explicit constitutional guarantees. Habermas is probably right that the familiar individual rights serve to make possible democratic self-rule. But that cannot be their entire rationale. They also give concrete expression to the deepest individual right which is that of equal respect and which itself underlies the ideal of democratic self-rule. Popular sovereignty cannot form therefore the ultimate layer of our political self-understanding. It draws instead on a fundamentally liberal conception of the political world.

This result also means that, contrary to Habermas, the concept of discussion (*Diskurs*)—be it the actual public discussion in which democratic self-rule is exercised or even the hypothetical discussion we might imagine to be carried out under ideal conditions—cannot play the fundamental role in our moral and political self-understanding. At a deeper level still must lie the moral principle of respect for persons. The 'ideal conditions of justification' which political argument in a liberal democracy must aim to heed have to embody at their heart this moral principle. For equal respect is precisely what makes democratic self-rule the proper form of political association. Citizens can therefore understand themselves as the source of law only insofar as they have already accepted this principle and judge the validity of their collective decisions from this standpoint. The moral principle of equal respect belongs to the innermost core of our moral consciousness. It forms the historically situated point of departure for our moral reflection, the framework within which we can conceive of moral argument.

Charles Larmore
Columbia University

NOTES

1. This article draws on material originally published as a review of Jürgen Habermas' book, *Faktizität und Geltung,* in the *Deutsche Zeitschrift für Philosophie,* 41 (1993), pp. 321–327.
2. J. Habermas (1992). All page references in the text are to this book.
3. J. Habermas (1988), pp. 41 ff.
4. This formulation appears in a celebrated essay, 'Staatsbürgerschaft und nationale Identität' (1990), reprinted at the end of Habermas (1992).
5. See Skinner (1991).
6. See Renan (1992), p. 42.
7. See Larmore (1987), chapter 4.
8. See the chapter 'De la connaissance morale' in Larmore (1993a) and the chapter 'Moral Knowledge' in Larmore (forthcoming).
9. See Larmore (1994).

REFERENCES

Habermas, J. (1988), *Nachmetaphysisches, Denken.* Frankfurt: Suhrkamp.
Habermas, J. (1992), *Faktizität und Geltung.* Frankfurt: Suhrkamp.
Larmore, C. (1987), *Patterns of Moral Complexity.* Cambridge: Cambridge University Press.
Larmore, C. (1993a), *Modernité et morale.* Paris: Presses Universitaires de France.
Larmore, C. (1993b), 'Beyond Religion and Enlightenment', in *San Diego Law Review,* vol. 30, no. 4, pp. 799–815.
Larmore, C. (1994), 'Pluralism and Reasonable Disagreement', in E. F. Paul *et al.* (eds.), *Cultural Pluralism and Moral Knowledge.* Cambridge: Cambridge University Press.
Larmore, C. (1996), *The Morals of Modernity.* Cambridge: Cambridge University Press.
Renan, E. (1992), *Qu'est-ce qu'une nation? et autres essais politiques,* ed. by J. Roman. Paris: Presses Pocket.
Skinner, Q. (1991), 'Two Views on the Maintenance of Liberty', in P. Pettit (ed.), *Contemporary Political Theory.* New York: Macmillan.

17 Toward a Deliberative Model of Democratic Legitimacy

SEYLA BENHABIB

Democratic Legitimacy and Public Goods

COMPLEX MODERN DEMOCRATIC societies since the Second World War face the task of securing three public goods. These are legitimacy, economic welfare, and a viable sense of collective identity. These are "goods" in the sense that their attainment is considered worthy and desirable by most members of such societies; furthermore, not attaining one or a combination thereof would cause problems in the functioning of these societies such as to throw them into crises.

These goods stand in a complex relation to one another: excessive realization of one such good may be in conflict with and may jeopardize the realization of others. For example, economic welfare may be attained at the cost of sacrificing legitimacy by curtailing union rights, by limiting a more rigorous examination of business accounting practices, or by encouraging the unfair use of protectionist state measures. Too great an emphasis on collective identity may come at the cost of minorities and dissidents whose civil and political rights may be impinged upon by a revival of a sense of collective identity. Thus legitimacy claims and collective identity demands, particularly if they take a nationalist tone, may come into conflict. There can also be conflicts between the claims of economic welfare and the demands of collective identity, as when excessive forms of protectionism and nationalism isolate countries in the world economic context, possibly leading to declining standards of living. Conversely, too great an emphasis on economic welfare may undermine a sense of collective identity by increasing competition among social groups and by weakening the claims of political sovereignty vis-à-vis other states. In a well-functioning democratic society the demands of legitimacy, economic welfare, and collective identity ideally exist in some form of equilibrium.

The present essay is concerned with one good among others which democratic societies must at-

This essay is a much-revised version of an article that originally appeared in Constellations 1, no. 1 (April 1994), under the title "Deliberative Rationality and Models of Democratic Legitimacy." It is part of a manuscript in progress tentatively entitled In Search of the Civic Polity: Democracy, Legitimacy, and Citizenship at Century's End.

I would like to acknowledge my thanks to members of the New York University "Law and Social Theory" symposium and the Yale University "Legal Theory Workshop" for comments and criticisms on earlier drafts. In particular, I am thankful to Professors Ronald Dworkin and Thomas Nagel for their rigorous criticisms on the question of the status of basic rights and liberties within the framework of a theory of deliberative democracy. I would also like to thank Stephen Macedo, whose comments on an earlier version of this paper delivered at the Political Theory Colloquium of the Harvard University Department of Government in the spring of 1994 have greatly contributed to my thoughts.

172

tain: the good of legitimacy. I am concerned to examine the philosophical foundations of democratic legitimacy. I will argue that legitimacy in complex democratic societies must be thought to result from the free and unconstrained public deliberation of all about matters of common concern. Thus a public sphere of deliberation about matters of mutual concern is essential to the legitimacy of democratic institutions.

Democracy, in my view, is best understood as a model for organizing the collective and public exercise of power in the major institutions of a society on the basis of the principle that decisions affecting the well-being of a collectivity can be viewed as the outcome of a procedure of free and reasoned deliberation among individuals considered as moral and political equals. Certainly any definition of essentially contested concepts like democracy, freedom, and justice is never a mere definition; the definition itself already articulates the normative theory that justifies the term. Such is the case with the preceding definition. My understanding of democracy privileges a deliberative model over other kinds of normative considerations. This is not to imply that economic welfare, institutional efficiency, and cultural stability would not be relevant in judging the adequacy of a normative definition of democracy. Economic welfare claims and collective identity needs must also be satisfied for democracies to function over time. However, the normative basis of democracy as a form of organizing our collective life is neither the fulfillment of economic welfare nor the realization of a stable sense of collective identity. For just as the attainment of certain levels of economic welfare may be compatible with authoritarian political rule, so too antidemocratic regimes may be more successful in assuring a sense of collective identity than democratic ones.

My goal in the first half of this article will be to examine the relationship between the normative presuppositions of democratic deliberation and the idealized content of practical rationality. The approach I follow is consonant with what John Rawls has called "Kantian constructivism," and

what Jürgen Habermas refers to as "reconstruction."[1] In this context, the differences in their methodologies are less significant than their shared assumption that the institutions of liberal democracies embody the idealized content of a form of practical reason. This idealized content can be elucidated and philosophically articulated; in fact, the task of a philosophical theory of democracy would consist in the clarification and articulation of the form of practical rationality represented by democratic rule.[2]

The methodology of "philosophical reconstruction" differs from "ethnocentric liberalism" (Richard Rorty) as well as from more a prioristic forms of Kantianism.[3] As distinguished from certain kinds of Kantianism, I would like to acknowledge the historical and sociological specificity of the project of democracy while, against ethnocentric liberalism, I would like to insist that the practical rationality embodied in democratic institutions has a culture-transcending validity claim. This form of practical reason has become the collective and anonymous property of cultures, institutions, and traditions as a result of the experiments and experiences, both ancient and modern, with democratic rule over the course of human history.[4] The insights and perhaps illusions resulting from these experiments and experiences are sedimented in diverse constitutions, institutional arrangements, and procedural specifics. When one thinks through the form of practical rationality at the core of democratic rule, Hegel's concept of "objective Spirit" (*objektiver Geist*) appears to me particularly appropriate. [5] To make this concept useful today we have to think of it without recourse to the metaphorical presence of a supersubject; we have to desubstantialize the model of a thinking and acting supersubject that still governs Hegelian philosophy. Without this metaphor of the subject implicitly governing it, the term "objective spirit" would refer to those *anonymous yet intelligible* collective rules, procedures, and practices that form a way of life. It is the rationality intrinsic to these anonymous yet intelligible rules, procedures and practices that any attempt aiming at the reconstruction of the logic of democracies must focus upon.

A Deliberative Model of Democracy

According to the deliberative model of democracy, it is a necessary condition for attaining legitimacy and rationality with regard to collective decision-making processes in a polity, that the institutions of this polity are so arranged that what is considered in the common interest of all results from processes of collective deliberation conducted rationally and fairly among free and equal individuals.[6] The more collective decision-making processes approximate this model the more increases the presumption of their legitimacy and rationality. Why?

The basis of legitimacy in democratic institutions is to be traced back to the presumption that the instances which claim obligatory power for themselves do so because their decisions represent an impartial standpoint said to be equally in the interests of all. This presumption can be fulfilled only if such decisions are in principle open to appropriate public processes of deliberation by free and equal citizens.

The discourse model of ethics formulates the most *general principles* and *moral intuitions* behind the validity claims of a deliberative model of democracy.[7] The basic idea behind this model is that only those norms (i.e., general rules of action and institutional arrangements) can be said to be valid (i.e., morally binding), which would be agreed to by all those affected by their consequences, if such agreement were reached as a consequence of a process of deliberation that had the following features: 1) participation in such deliberation is governed by the norms of equality and symmetry; all have the same chances to initiate speech acts, to question, to interrogate, and to open debate; 2) all have the right to question the assigned topics of conversation; and 3) all have the right to initiate reflexive arguments about the very rules of the discourse procedure and the way in which they are applied or carried out. There are no prima facie rules limiting the agenda of the conversation, or the identity of the participants, as long as each excluded person or group can justifiably show that they are relevantly affected by the proposed norm under question. In certain circumstances this would mean that citizens of a democratic community would have to enter into a practical discourse with noncitizens who may be residing in their countries, at their borders, or in neighboring communities if there are matters that affect them all. Ecology and environmental issues in general are a perfect example of such instances when the boundaries of discourses keep expanding because the consequences of our actions expand and affect increasingly more people.

The procedural specifics of those special argumentation situations called "practical discourses" are not automatically transferable to a macroinstitutional level, nor is it necessary that they should be so transferable. A theory of democracy, as opposed to a general moral theory, would have to be concerned with the question of institutional specifications and practical feasibility. Nonetheless, the procedural constraints of the discourse model can act as test cases for critically evaluating the criteria of membership and the rules for agenda setting, and for the structuring of public discussions within and among institutions. . . .

According to the deliberative model, procedures of deliberation generate legitimacy as well as assure some degree of practical rationality.[8] But what are the claims to practical rationality of such deliberative democratic processes? Deliberative processes are essential to the rationality of collective decision-making processes for three reasons. First, as Bernard Manin has observed in an excellent article "On Legitimacy and Deliberation," deliberative processes are also processes that impart information.[9] New information is imparted because 1) no single individual can anticipate and foresee all the variety of perspectives through which matters of ethics and politics would be perceived by different individuals; and 2) no single individual can possess all the information deemed relevant to a certain decision affecting all.[10] Deliberation is a procedure for being informed.

Furthermore, much political theory under the influence of economic models of reasoning in particular proceeds from a methodological fiction: this is the methodological fiction of an individual with an ordered set of coherent preferences. This fiction does not have much relevance in the political world. On complex social and political issues, more often than not, individuals may have views and wishes but no ordered set of preferences, since the latter would imply that they would be enlightened not only about the preferences but about the consequences and relative merits of each of their preferred choices in advance. It is actually the deliberative process itself that is likely to produce such an outcome by leading the individual to further critical reflection on his already held views and opinions; it is incoherent to assume that individuals can start a process of public deliberation with a level of conceptual clarity about their choices and preferences that can actually result only from a successful process of deliberation. Likewise, the formation of coherent preferences cannot precede deliberation; it can only succeed it. Very often individuals' wishes as well as views and opinions conflict with one another. In the course of deliberation and the exchange of views with others, individuals become more aware of such conflicts and feel compelled to undertake a coherent ordering.

More significantly, the very procedure of articulating a view in public imposes a certain reflexivity on individual preferences and opinions. When presenting their point of view and position to others, individuals must support them by articulating good reasons in a public context to their co-deliberators. This process of *articulating good reasons in public* forces the individual to think of what would count as a good reason for all others involved. One is thus forced to think from the standpoint of all involved for whose agreement one is "wooing." Nobody can convince others in public of her point of view without being able to state why what appears good, plausible, just, and expedient to her can also be considered so from the standpoint of all involved. Reasoning from the standpoint of all involved not only forces

a certain coherence upon one's own views but also forces one to adopt a standpoint that Hannah Arendt, following Kant, had called the "enlarged mentality."[11]

A deliberative model of democracy suggests a necessary but not sufficient condition of practical rationality, because, as with any procedure, it can be misinterpreted, misapplied, and abused. Procedures can neither dictate outcomes nor define the quality of the reasons advanced in argumentation nor control the quality of the reasoning and rules of logic and inference used by participants. Procedural models of rationality are underdetermined. Nonetheless, the discourse model makes some provisions against its own misuses and abuses in that the reflexivity condition built into the model allows abuses and misapplications at the first level to be challenged at a second, metalevel of discourse. Likewise, the equal chance of all affected to initiate such discourse of deliberation suggests that no outcome is prima facie fixed but can be revised and subjected to reexamination. Such would be the normative justification of majority rule as a decision procedure following from this model: in many instances the majority rule is a fair and rational decision procedure, not because legitimacy resides in numbers but because if a majority of people are convinced at one point on the basis of reasons formulated as closely as possible as a result of a process of discursive deliberation that conclusion A is the right thing to do, then this conclusion can remain valid until challenged by good reasons by some other group. It is not the sheer numbers that support the rationality of the conclusion, but the presumption that if a large number of people see certain matters a certain way as a result of following certain kinds of rational procedures of deliberation and decision-making, then such a conclusion has a presumptive claim to being rational until shown to be otherwise. The simple practice of having a ruling and an opposition party in democracies in fact incorporates this principle: we accept the will of the majority at the end of an electoral process that has been fairly and correctly carried out, but even when we accept the legitimacy of the process we may have grave doubts about the rationality of the outcome. The practice of there being parliamentary opposition says that the grounds on which the majority party claims to govern can be examined, challenged, tested, criticized, and rearticulated. Parliamentary procedures of opposition, debate, questioning, and even impeachment proceedings, and investigatory commissions incorporate this rule of deliberative rationality that majoritarian decisions are temporarily agreed-upon conclusions, the claim to rationality and validity of which can be publicly reexamined.

This deliberative model of democracy is proceduralist in that it emphasizes first and foremost certain institutional procedures and practices for attaining decisions on matters that would be binding on all. Three additional points are worthy of note with respect to such a conception of democracy: first, I proceed from the assumption of value pluralism. Disagreement about the highest goods of human existence and the proper conduct of a morally righteous life are a fundamental feature of our modern value-universe since the end of natural law cosmologies in the sixteenth and seventeenth centuries, and the eventual separation of church and state.[12] The challenge to democratic rationality is to arrive at acceptable formulations of the common good despite this inevitable value-pluralism. We cannot resolve conflicts among value systems and visions of the good by reestablishing a strong unified moral and religious code without forsaking fundamental liberties. Agreements in societies living with value-pluralism are to be sought for not at the level of substantive beliefs but at that of procedures, processes, and practices for attaining and revising beliefs. Proceduralism is a rational answer to persisting value conflicts at the substantive level.[13]

Second, the deliberative model of democracy proceeds not only from a conflict of values but also from a conflict of interests in social life. Social life necessitates both conflict of interests and cooperation. Democratic procedures have to convince, even under conditions when one's interests as an individual or as a group are negatively affected, that the conditions of mutual cooperation are still legitimate. Procedures can be regarded as methods for articulating, sifting through, and weighing conflicting interests. The more conflicts of interests there are the more it is important to have procedural solutions of conflict adjudication through which parties whose interests are negatively affected can find recourse to other methods of the articulation and representation of their grievances. Proceduralist models of democracy allow the articulation of conflicts of interests under conditions of social cooperation mutually acceptable to all.[14]

Finally, any proceduralist and deliberative model of democracy is prima facie open to the argument that no modern society can organize its affairs along the fiction of a mass assembly carrying out its deliberations in public and collectively. Here more than an issue of size is at stake. The argument that there may be an invisible limit to the size of a deliberative body that, when crossed, affects the nature of the reasoning process is undoubtedly true. Nonetheless the reason why a deliberative and proceduralist model of democracy does not need to operate with the fiction of a general deliberative assembly is that the procedural specifications of this model privilege a *plurality of modes of association* in which all affected can have the right to articulate their point of view. These can range from political parties, to citizens' initiatives, to social movements, to voluntary associations, to consciousness-raising groups, and the like. *It is through the interlocking net of these multiple forms of associations, networks, and organizations that an anonymous "public conversation" results. It is central to the model of deliberative democracy that it privileges such a public sphere of mutually interlocking and overlapping networks and associations of deliberation, contestation, and argumentation.* The fiction of a general deliberative assembly in which the united people expressed their will belongs to the early history of democratic theory; today our guiding model has to be that of a medium of loosely associated, multiple foci of opinion formation and dissemination which affect one another in free and spontaneous processes of communication.[15]

Such a strong model of deliberative democracy is subject to three different kinds of criticism: first, liberal theorists will express concern that such a strong model would lead to the corrosion of individual liberties and may in fact destabilize the rule of law. In his earlier work, Bruce Ackerman had formulated a theory of "conversational neutrality" to voice some of these concerns.[16] Stephen Holmes has defended the plausibility of certain "gag rules" on public conversation.[17] Second, feminist theorists are skeptical about this model, because they see it as privileging a certain mode of discourse at the cost of silencing others: this is the rationalist, male, univocal, hegemonic discourse of a transparent polity that disregards the emotions, polyvocity, multiplicity, and differences in the articulation of the voice of the public. . . .

Basic Rights and Deliberative Democracy

Deliberative democracy models often seem subject to the argument that they do not protect individuals' basic rights and liberties sufficiently.[18] This objection is rooted in two assumptions: first, insofar as deliberative models appear to make a high degree of consensus or unanimity of public issues a value, it is fair to suspect that such unanimity could only be attained at the cost of silencing dissent and curtailing minority viewpoints. Second, what protection does a deliberative model allow against the tyranny of democratic majorities from imposing its choices and norms upon the minority?

I believe that these objections are fair when raised against most versions of radical participatory democratic theories that also prioritize political deliberation. I think it is fair to ask whether the radical democratic theories of Hannah Arendt, Benjamin Barber, or Mouffe and Laclau allow for a coherent theory of rights such as would protect both basic rights and liberties for all, and defend minority rights against the tyranny of the majority. But such objections are not applicable to the model of deliberative democracy developed here.

Precisely because I share with the Kantian liberal tradition the assumption that moral respect for the autonomous personality is a fundamental norm of morality and democracy, the deliberative model of democracy presupposes a discourse theory of ethics to supply it with the most general moral principles upon which rights claims would be based.[19] Insofar as a discourse theory of ethics considers participants to be equal and free beings, equally entitled to take part in those discourses which determine the norms that are to affect their lives, it proceeds from a view of persons as beings entitled to certain "moral rights." I have named this moral right the entitlement to *universal moral respect,* and have attempted in *Situating the Self* to give a nonfoundationalist but principled justification for the recognition of this norm.[20] I further maintain that within a discourse theory each individual has the same symmetrical rights to various speech acts, to initiate new topics, to ask for reflection about the presuppositions of the conversations, and so on. I call this the principle of *egalitarian reciprocity.* In my view the norms of universal moral respect and egalitarian reciprocity are moral rights in that they are entitlements that accrue to individuals insofar as we view them as moral persons.

The step that would lead from a recognition of these two moral rights to the formulation of a principle of basic rights and liberties is certainly not very wide.[21] Basically it would involve a hypothetical answer to the question, If it is plausible for individuals to view one another as beings entitled to universal moral respect and egalitarian reciprocity, which most general principles of basic rights and liberties would such individuals also be likely to accept as determining the conditions of their collective existence?[22]

Although the discourse theory shares this kind of hypothetical and counter-factual moral reasoning procedure with Kant and Rawls, it would be different from a Kantian deduction of the concept of right and from a Rawlsian construction of the "original position," in that it would privilege a discourse model of practical debate as being the appropriate forum for determining rights claims. But are we not thereby landing in a vicious circle, that is, discourses, even to get started, presuppose the recognition of one another's moral rights among discourse participants; on the other hand, such rights are said to be specified as a result of the discursive situation.

I have indicated elsewhere that this is not a vicious circle but rather the hermeneutic circle that characterizes all reasoning about morals and politics.[23] We never begin our deliberations concerning these matters at a "moral ground zero." Rather, in moral theory as in everyday morality, in political theory as in everyday political discourse, we are always situated within a horizon of presuppositions, assumptions, and power relations, the totality of which can never become wholly transparent to us. This much we must have learned from all the criticisms of rationalism in the last three centuries. Discourse ethics in this sense presupposes the reciprocal moral recognition of one another's claims to be participants in the moral-political dialogue. I am still enough of a Hegelian to maintain, however, that such reciprocal recognition of one another's rights to moral personality is a result of a world-historical process that involves struggle, battle and resistance, as well as defeat, carried out by social classes, genders, groups, and nations.

What is distinctive about the discourse model is that although it presupposes that participants must recognize one another's entitlement to moral respect and reciprocity in some sense, the determination of the precise content and extent of these principles would be a consequence of discourses themselves.[24] Insofar as the precise meaning and entailment of the norms of universal moral respect and egalitarian reciprocity would be subject to discursive validation, we can speak here of a procedure of "recursive validation."[25] The methodological procedure of recursive validation rules out the two consequences most feared by liberals vis-à-vis the model of deliberative democracy—namely, too strong a formulation of the conditions of consent, and the tyranny of the majority. The norms of universal moral respect and egalitarian reciprocity allow minorities and dissenters both the right to withhold their assent and the right to challenge the rules as well as the

agenda of public debate. For what distinguishes discourses from compromises and other agreements reached under conditions of coercion is that only the *freely given assent of all concerned* can count as a condition of having reached agreement in the discourse situation.[26]

Deliberative Democracy and Constitutionalism

Upon reflection, we can see that institutionally as well, complex constitutional democracies, and particularly those in which a *public sphere* of opinion formation and deliberation has been developed, engage in such recursive validation continually. Basic human civil and political rights, as guaranteed by the Bill of Rights to the U.S. Constitution and as embodied in the constitution of most democratic governments, are never really "off the agenda" of public discussion and debate. They are simply constitutive and regulative institutional norms of debate in democratic societies that cannot be transformed and abrogated by simple majority decisions. The language of keeping these rights off the agenda mischaracterizes the nature of democratic debate in our kinds of societies: although we cannot change these rights without extremely elaborate political and juridical procedures, we are always disputing their meaning, their extent, and their jurisdiction. Democratic debate is like a ball game where there is no umpire to interpret the rules of the game and their application definitively. Rather, in the game of democracy the rules of the game no less than their interpretation and even the position of the umpire are essentially contestable. Contestation means neither the complete abrogation of these rules nor silence about them. When basic rights and liberties are violated the game of democracy is suspended and becomes either martial rule, civil war, or dictatorship; when democratic politics is in full session, the debate about the meaning of these rights, what they do or do not entitle us to, their scope and enforcement, is what politics is all about. One cannot challenge the specific interpretation of basic rights and liberties in a democracy without taking these absolutely seriously.

The deliberative theory of democracy transcends the traditional opposition of majoritarian politics vs. liberal guarantees of basic rights and liberties to the extent that the normative conditions of discourses, like basic rights and liberties, are to be viewed as rules of the game that can be contested within the game but only insofar as one first accepts to abide by them and play the game at all. This formulation seems to me to correspond to the reality of democratic debate and public speech in real democracies much more accurately than the liberal model of deliberation upon constitutional essentials or the reasoning of the Supreme Court. Crucial to the deliberative model of democracy is the idea of a "public sphere" of opinion-formation, debate, deliberation, and contestation among citizens, groups, movements, and organizations in a polity. When this concept of a public sphere is introduced as the concrete embodiment of discursive democracy in practice, it also becomes possible to think of the issue of conversational constraints in a more nuanced way. While the deliberative model of democracy shares with liberalism a concern for the protection of the rights to autonomy of equal citizens, the conceptual method of discursive validation and the institutional reality of a differentiated public sphere of deliberation and contestation provide plausible beginning points for a mediation of the stark opposition between liberalism and deliberative democracy.

Bruce Ackerman's conception of dualist democracy is based upon a similar strategy of overcoming the opposition between the standpoint of foundationalist rights-liberals on the one hand and monist majoritarian democrats on the other: "The basic mediating device is the dualist's two-track system of democratic lawmaking. It allows an important place for the foundationalist's view of 'rights as trumps' without violating the monist's deeper commitment to the primacy of democracy."[27] In a constitutional democracy the question as to which aspects of the higher law are entrenched against revision by the people as opposed to which aspects may be repealed is itself always open and contestable. Conceptually as well as sociologically, models of deliberative and dualistic democracy focus on this process of "recursive" and "hermeneutic" interdependence between constitution-making and democratic politics.[28]

Feminist Suspicions toward Deliberative Democracy

While liberals criticize the model of deliberative democracy for possibly overextending itself and corroding the sphere of individual privacy, feminist theorists criticize this model for not extending itself broadly enough to be truly inclusive. In an illuminating article entitled "Impartiality and the Civic Public," Iris Young, for example, has argued:

> The distinction between public and private as it appears in modern political theory expresses a will for homogeneity that necessitates the exclusion of many persons and groups, particularly women and radicalized groups culturally identified with the body, wildness and rationality. In conformity with the modern idea of normative reason, the idea of the public in modern political theory and practice designates a sphere of human existence in which citizens express their rationality and universality, abstracted from their particular situations and need, and opposed to feeling. . . . Examination of the exclusionary and homogeneous ideal in modern political theory, however, shows that we cannot envision such renewal of public life as a recovery of Enlightenment ideals. Instead, we need to transform the distinction between public and private that does not correlate with an opposition between reason and affectivity and desire, or universal and particular.[29]

Iris Young's cogent and penetrating feminist critique of the ideal of the impartial public applies to the model of deliberative democracy suggested in the preceding only in certain respects. Certainly, the model of a general deliberative assembly that governed our conceptions of the public sphere well into the twentieth century was historically, socially, and culturally a space for male bodies. I mean this not only in the sense that only men were active citizens entitled to hold office and appear in public, but also in the sense that the institutional iconography of early democratic theory privileged the male mode of self-representation.[30]

Yet here we must distinguish between the *institutional* and the *conceptual* critiques. There is a certain ambivalence in the feminist critique of such models of the public sphere and deliberative democracy. On the one hand, the critique appears to take democratic institutions at their principled best and to criticize their biased and restrictive implementations in practice; on the other hand, the feminist critique appears to aim at a rejection of the ideals of free public reason and impartiality altogether. As Joan Landes puts it, the democratic public sphere appears to be essentially and not just accidentally "masculinist."[31] A normative theory of deliberative democracy requires a strong concept of the public sphere as its institutional correlate. The public sphere replaces the model of the general deliberative assembly found in early democratic theory. In this context, it is important for feminist theorists to specify the level of their conceptual objection, and to differentiate among institutional and normative presuppositions.[32]

Iris Young does not reject the ideal of a public sphere, only its Enlightenment variety. She proposes to replace the ideal of the "civil public" with that of a heterogeneous public. In her recent work she has advocated a number of institutional measures that would guarantee and solidify group representation in such a public sphere.[33] Yet wanting to retain the public sphere and according it a place in democratic theory is not compatible with the more radical critique of the ideal of impartial reason that Young also develops in some of her essays.

In her essay "Communication and the Other: Beyond Deliberative Democracy" Iris Young distinguishes between "deliberative" and "communicative" democracy on the grounds that most theories of deliberative democracy offer too narrow a conception of the democratic process because they continue to privilege an ideal of "a common good in which [the discussion participants] are all supposed to leave behind their particular experience and interests"(126).

By contrast, Young advocates a theory of communicative democracy according to which individuals would attend to one another's differences in class, gender, race, religion, and so on. Each social position has a partial perspective on the public that it does not abandon; but through the communicative process participants transcend and transform their initial situated knowledges (127). Instead of critical argumentation, such processes of communicative confrontation privilege modalities of communication like "greeting, rhetoric, and storytelling"(120).

I think this distinction between deliberative and communicative democracy is more apparent than real. To sustain her critique of the ideals of impartiality and objectivity, which she associates with the deliberative model, Young must be able to distinguish the kind of *transformation* and *transcendence* of partial perspectives that occurs in communicative democracy from the *mutual agreement* to be reached in processes of deliberative democracy. Yet how can we distinguish between the emergence of common opinion among members of one group, if we do not apply to such processes of communication or deliberation some standards of fairness and impartiality in order to judge the manner in which opinions were allowed to be brought forth, groups were given chances to express their points of view, and the like? The model of communicative democracy, far from dispensing with the need for standards of impartiality and fairness, requires them to make sense of its own formulations. Without some such standards, Young could not differentiate the genuine transformation of partial and situated perspectives from mere agreements of convenience or apparent unanimity reached under conditions of duress.

With respect to modes of communication like "greeting, rhetoric, and storytelling," I would say that each of these modes may have their place within the *informally structured process of everyday communication among individuals who share a cultural and historical life world*. However, it is neither necessary for the democratic theorist to try to formalize and institutionalize these aspects of communicative everyday competence, nor is it plausible—and this is the more important objection—to build an opposition between them and critical argumentation. Greeting, storytelling, and rhetoric, although they may be aspects of informal communication in our everyday life, cannot become the public language of institutions and legislatures in a democracy for the following reason: to attain legitimacy, democratic institutions require the articulation of the bases of their actions and policies in discursive language that appeals to commonly shared and accepted public reasons. In constitutional democracies such public reasons take the form of general statements consonant with the rule of law. The rule of law has a certain rhetorical structure of its own: it is general, applies to all members of a specified reference group on the basis of legitimate reasons. Young's attempt to transform the language of the rule of law into a more partial, affective, and situated mode of communication would have the consequence of inducing arbitrariness, for who can tell how far the power of a greeting can reach? It would further create capriciousness—what about those who simply cannot understand my story? It would limit rather than enhance social justice because rhetoric moves people and achieves results without having to render an account of the bases upon which it induces people to engage in certain courses of action rather than others. In short, some moral ideal of impartiality is a regulative principle that should govern not only our *deliberations* in public but also the *articulation* of reasons by public institutions. What is considered impartial has to be "in the best interests of all equally." Without such a normative principle, neither the ideal of the rule of law can be sustained nor deliberative reasoning toward a common good occur. Some Enlightenment ideals are part of any conception of democratic legitimacy and the public sphere. The point therefore is not a rejection of the Enlightenment in toto but a critical renegotiation of its legacy.

Expanding on the model of a heterogeneous, dispersed network of many publics, Nancy Fraser has suggested how, in fact, once the unitary model of the public sphere is abandoned, women's concerns, as well as those of other excluded groups, can be accommodated. Such a nonunitary and dispersed network of publics can accommodate women's desires for their own spaces, in their own terms. In such "subaltern counterpublics," to use Fraser's term,[34] the lines between the public and the private, for example, can be renegotiated, rethought, challenged, and reformulated. It is nonetheless a long step from the cultural and social rethinking and reformulation of such distinctions as between the public and the private to their implementation in legislation and governmental regulation. While sharing the concern of liberal theorists that the precipitous reformulation of such a divide may corrode individual liberties, Fraser rightly points out that there is a distinction between "opinion-making" and "policy-making" public bodies, and that the same kinds of constraints may not apply to each alike.[35] Opinion-making publics, as found in social movements, for example, can lead us to reconsider and rethink very controversial issues about privacy, sexuality, and intimacy; but this does not imply that the only or even most desirable consequence of such processes of public deliberation should be general legislation. Thus when conceived as an anonymous, plural, and multiple medium of communication and deliberation, the public sphere need not homogenize and repress difference. Heterogeneity, otherness, and difference can find expression in the multiple associations, networks, and citizens' forums, all of which constitute public life under late capitalism.[36]

Institutionalist Distrust of Deliberative Democracy

. . . My goal in this essay has been to outline a deliberative model of democracy that incorporates features of practical rationality. Central to practical rationality is the possibility of free public deliberation about matters of mutual concern to all. The discourse model of ethics and politics suggests a procedure for such free public deliberation among all concerned. Such processes of public deliberation have a claim to rationality because they increase and make available necessary information, because they allow the expression of arguments in the light of which opinions and beliefs need to be revised, and because they lead to the formation of conclusions that can be challenged publicly for good reasons. Furthermore, such procedures allow self-referential critique of their own uses and abuses. The chief institutional correlate of such a model of deliberative democracy is a multiple, anonymous, heterogeneous network of many publics and public conversations. In other domains of social life as well, the model of deliberative democracy based on the centrality of public deliberation can inspire the proliferation of many institutional designs.

NOTES

1. See John Rawls, "Kantian Constructivism in Moral Theory," *Journal of Philosophy* 77, no 9 (1980): 515–72, a revised and enlarged version of which is included in *Political Liberalism* (New York: Columbia University Press, 1993), 89–131; Jürgen Habermas, *Moral Consciousness and Communicative Action,* trans. Christian Lenhardt and Shierry Weber Nicholsen (Cambridge, Mass.: MIT Press, 1990), and in particular the essay "Discourse Ethics: Notes on a Program of Philosophical Justification," 76ff.

2. In a helpful survey article entitled "Freedom, Consensus, and Equality in Collective Decision Making," *Ethics* 101, no. 1 (October 1990): 151ff., Thomas Christiano examines different approaches to the philosophical foundations of democracy.

3. It is well known that nearly a decade ago now, John Rawls retracted the Kantian strategy of normative justification followed in his *Theory of Justice* in favor of a more historicist, and social and politically situated concept of an "overlapping consensus." The two principles of justice were valid, he claimed, not sub specie aeternitatis but because they articulated some deeply shared convictions in liberal democracies of the West about the foundations of their forms of government. These deeply held convictions would constitute, when properly sifted through, clarified, and articulated, the bases of an "overlapping consensus" in such societies. See John Rawls, "Justice as Fairness: Political Not Metaphysical," *Philosophy and Public Affairs* 14 (1985): 223–51; and "The Idea of an Overlapping Consensus," *Oxford Journal of Legal Studies* 7 (1987): 1–25. This

shift from a Kantian strategy of justification to a more historicist mode has been celebrated by some. Richard Rorty has seen in these recent developments of Rawls's work a confirmation for his own brand of "ethnocentric liberalism." See Richard Rorty, "The Priority of Democracy to Philosophy," in *Objectivism, Relativism, and Truth* (New York: Cambridge University Press, 1991), 175–96. For a lucid account of these developments in Rawls's position and a critical examination of the idea of an "overlapping consensus," see Kenneth Baynes, "Constructivism and Practical Reason in Rawls," in *Analyse und Kritik. Zeitschrift für Sozialwissenschaften* 14 (June 1992): 18–32.

4. See M. I. Finley's still-classic essays in *Democracy: Ancient and Modern* (New Brunswick, N. J.: Rutgers University Press, 1985).

5. The most brilliant example of Hegels methodology remains the 1821 *Philosophy of Right,* trans. T. M. Knox (New York: Oxford University Press, 1973). The kind of anonymous collective rationality I have in mind has been developed by Karl Popper in the domain of epistemology. See Karl R. Popper, *Objective Knowledge: An Evolutionary Approach* (Oxford: Clarendon, 1972).

6. My formulation is wholly akin to that proposed by Joshua Cohen, "Deliberation and Democratic Legitimacy," in *The Good Polity: Normative Analysis of the State,* ed. Alan Hamlin and Philip Pettit (London: Blackwell, 1989), 17–34; see also Joshua Cohen, "Procedure and Substance in Deliberative Democracy."

7. I have outlined my understanding of this project as well as indicating the manner in which my interpretation of the general program of discourse ethics differs from that of Habermas and Apel in *Situating the Self* (New York: Routledge, 1992). This article presupposes the general argument set forth in that book in chapters 1, 2, and 3 in particular, and documents my effort to apply the principles of discourse ethics to political-institutional life. Independently of the project of discourse ethics but in fascinating affinity to it, in recent years there has also been a revival of deliberative models of democracy among political theorists and legal philosophers. See in particular Frank I. Michelman, "Law's Republic," *Yale Law Journal* 93 (1984): 1013ff.; and Cass R. Sunstein, "Beyond the Republican Revival," *Yale Law Journal* 97 (1988): 1539.

8. In some contemporary models of deliberative democracy, a distinction between "constitutional" (high) politics and "ordinary" (low) politics dominates. The claim is that deliberative politics more properly characterizes constitution-making processes, whereas mundane, day-to-day politics may be governed by nondeliberative and narrowly instrumental, self-regarding pursuits. See David Gauthier, "Constituting Democracy," in *The Idea of Democracy,* ed. David Copp et al. (Cambridge: Cambridge University Press, 1993), 314–

15; and David M. Estlund's very instructive discussion, "Who's Afraid of Deliberative Democracy? On the Strategic/Deliberative Dichotomy in Recent Constitutional Jurisprudence." *Texas Law Review* 71, no. 7 (June 1993): 1437–77. Although I believe that a distinction between "constitution-making" and "ordinary" politics is extremely useful and unavoidable for democratic theory, I think that it can be and has been overdrawn. The main motivation for overdrawing this distinction seems to be traditional liberal fears about unbridled majoritarian decisions and distrust in the rationality of political judgment as exercised by ordinary people. The deliberative model of democracy that I am advocating seeks to bridge the gap between high and low politics by raising the quality of ordinary people's everyday deliberations. This does not mean that constitutional issues are always and at all times open for reconsideration. Not at all; but it does suggests that ordinary politics cannot but be informed by such constitutional issues and principles—as examples take debates ranging from prayer in public schools to violence in the media to pornography and abortion. My assumption is that the more such ordinary political deliberation approximates the model suggested above, the more the likelihood increases that it will be informed by constitutional principles in the "right way." For further discussion see also the "Deliberative Democracy and Constitutionalism" section that follows.

9. Bernard Manin, "On Legitimacy and Political Deliberation." *Political Theory* 15, no. 3 (August 1987): 338–68.

10. In a recent article, "The Voice of the People," Sidney Verba discusses citizens' communications to their representatives and other governmental offices via letters, calls, and increasingly faxes and e-mail. (677ff.) Reflecting upon the phenomenal increase of such direct communication (about a fifth to a quarter of the public in the U.S.A. report contacting an official—"depending on the way the question is framed" [679]), Verba expresses the hope that "perhaps citizen-initiated messages, especially when enhanced by new technology, can become part of a public discourse" (685). See Sidney Verba, "The Voice of the People," 1993 James Madison Award Lecture, *PS: Political Science and Politics* 26, no 4 (December 1993): 677–86.

11. Hannah Arendt, "The Crisis in Culture," in *Between Past and Future: Six Exercises in Political Thought* (New York: Meridian, 1961), 220–21.

12. Charles Larmore has provided an eloquent statement of this view in recent years. See *Patterns of Moral Complexity* (Cambridge: Cambridge University Press, 1987), 119ff.; and "Political Liberalism," *Political Theory* 18, no. 3 (August 1990): 342ff.

13. I would like to attempt to answer here a very important objection raised by Donald Moon. How plausible is it to distinguish value disagreements concerning *substantive* moral, religious, or philosophical doctrines from *procedural* agreement about processes for adjudicating and revising beliefs in a public context? Very often, such substantive beliefs will not permit one to distinguish so sharply between content and form, substance and procedure. As examples of cases when value systems do not permit a sharp distinction between substance and procedure we can think of religious sects living within the boundaries of the liberal-democratic constitutional state such as certain Orthodox Jewish sects in Israel who refuse to recognize the secular authority of the State of Israel; Orthodox Moslems living in some European states, like Germany and France for example, who experience conflict between their views of the proper education and place of women and the views of the liberal-democratic state; or Christian Scientists in the United States who want to provide medical treatment to their children consonant with their own beliefs and who come into conflict with local and federal authorities. In each of these cases clashes can and do arise that prima facie cannot be solved by resorting to a simple substance/form distinction. To deal properly with the issues raised by such examples and in particular to explore the ways in which a deliberative model of democracy based upon discourse ethics may or may not presuppose too strong a model of agreement clearly goes beyond the scope of this article. However, I do think that in the face of all these cases as well a form of deliberative proceduralism is the most viable normative answer.

Insofar as these groups live within the jurisdiction of the liberal-constitutional and democratic state they have accepted certain "constitutional minimums." Debates usually arise not around these constitutional minimal rights, which are guaranteed to all citizens and residents (in varying degrees) under the rule of law, but around whether certain cultural and religious practices do or do not contradict these constitutional minimums or whether they can be considered matters of the religious and cultural autonomy of a group. Is the duty to serve in the Israeli army a constitutional obligation to which there can be no exceptions on religious grounds? Can Orthodox Muslim families choose not to send their daughters to public schools? And when they do send them to public schools, should these children be allowed to wear head scarves or should they be obliged to wear school uniforms? Can a Christian Scientist family refuse medical treatment to a child suffering from an infectious disease that requires standard medication? Should the state protect the rights of the child against the judgment of the family in this case? I am inclined to think that vis-à-vis such issues there is no single answer applicable to each case but more or less a gradation of moral and political principles and intuitions. The possibility not to serve in the army on the basis of religious beliefs is a right of conscientious objection recognized by many modern states, which can be made consonant with the principle of the separation of church and state. On the other hand, to deny a child the fundamentals of a secular education in our world or the best treatment that medical science can offer violate the respect and equality we owe that child as a future citizen of our polity. Yet whether Muslim girls can wear their head scarves (the chador) to French schools or whether Sikh soldiers can wear their turbans in the Canadian Royal Police strikes me as being a qualitatively different matter from the provision of either education or health care. A more pluralistic conception of the public sphere and of civic identity than that displayed by the French public and authorities in the debate around the chador is perfectly compatible with, and in fact required by, the model of deliberative democracy and public dialogue developed in this essay.

14. See Jane Mansbridge's article "Using Power/Fighting Power: The Polity" for an exploration of the dilemmas of deliberative democracy models in the face of persistent and ineliminable conflicts of interests and wills in public life, and the problems involved in the use of coercion.

15. For a recent statement of the transformation of the concept of the public sphere from a centralized to a decentered model, see Jürgen Habermas, "Ist der Herzschlag der Revolution zum Stillstand gekommen? Volkssouveränität als Verfahren. Ein normativer Begriff der Öffentlichkeit?" in *Die Iden von* 1789, ed. Forum für Philosophie Bad Homburg (Frankfurt: Suhrkamp, 1989), 7ff.

16. Bruce Ackerman, *Social Justice in the Liberal State* (New Haven: Yale University Press, 1980) and "Why Dialogue?" *Journal of Philosophy* 86 (January 1989). I have dealt with Bruce Ackerman's model of liberal conversation in several articles. See Benhabib, "Liberal Dialogue vs. a Critical Model of Discursive Legitimacy" and "Models of Public Space: Hannah Arendt, the Liberal Tradition and Jürgen Habermas," in *Situating the Self.*

17. Cf. Stephen Holmes, "Gag Rules or the Politics of Omission," in *Constitutionalism and Democracy,* ed. Jon Elster and R. Slagstad (Cambridge: Cambridge University Press, 1988), 19–58; and John Rawls, "The Idea of an Overlapping Consensus."

18. For a further exploration of these themes see the article by Josh Cohen, "Procedure and Substance in Deliberative Democracy," in this volume.

19. This issue has been recently well formulated by Kenneth Baynes in "The Liberal/Communitarian Controversy and Communicative Ethics," *Philosophy and Social Criticism* 14, nos. 3–4 (1988): 305 (my emphasis).

20. See *Situating the Self,* 29ff.

21. Jürgen Habermas has embarked on this task in his new book, *Faktizität und Geltung* (Frankfurt: Suhrkamp, 1992), chap. 3.

22. In her contribution to this volume, "Diversity and Democracy: Representing Differences," Carol Gould objects that discourse-ethical theory cannot justify fundamental human rights. I would counter her criticisms by further exploring the implications of the counterfactual suggested above for a theory of rights.

23. In *Situating the Self,* 30ff.

24. Perhaps an example may clarify this procedure further: let us take the cases of Great Britain, the United States of America, and Israel as three models of liberal-democratic societies whose political and legal order is based upon some form of recognition of the norm of moral respect for persons. Certainly all three societies enjoy a system of parliamentary democracy in which, through legislatively or constitutionally determined periodic elections, public officials are brought to and removed from office. In all three societies individuals enjoy certain rights and liberties that are upheld by the political system and protected by the courts. However, these societies have radically divergent and at times incompatible views of what constitutes the legitimate exercise of the right of free speech. Whereas in the United States considerations of public propriety, fair trial, or national security would hardly serve as routine grounds on the basis of which to curtail First Amendment rights, in Great Britain and Israel they are commonly invoked. In Great Britain the media's access to court hearings and trials is restricted, while in Israel even the publication of certain scholarly articles can be subjected to the prohibition of the military censor if they are deemed to contain "security-sensitive information."

The relevance of this example to the theoretical principle of discursive validation is the following: just as differences in the extent and application of the fundamental right of free speech would not lead us to deny that Great Britain and Israel are democratic societies just as the United States is, so too a number of more specific interpretations of the norms of universal moral respect and egalitarian reciprocity are compatible with democratic political dialogue. What results from a deliberative theory of democracy based upon the discourse model is not a catalog of unabridgeable basic rights and liberties but two most general moral norms that are compatible, within certain well-defined limits, with a variety of legal and political arrangements.

25. See Kenneth Baynes, *The Normative Grounds of Political Criticism: Kant, Rawls, Habermas* (Albany: SUNY Press, 1992). 1ff.

26. In his interesting criticism of some of my earlier formulations concerning discourse ethics in *Critique, Norm, and Utopia* (New York: Columbia University

Press, 1986), Donald Moon charges that practical discourse could be potentially "coercive, leading to institutional forms that involve domination or imposition. It is hard to see how any form of 'discourse' could achieve a consensus that is genuinely free and uncoerced unless participants enjoy some rights of privacy and personal integrity, unless they can resist the demand for self-disclosure." Donald Moon, *Constructing Community: Moral Pluralism and Tragic Conflicts* (Princeton: Princeton University Press, 1993), 95. Given the norms of universal moral respect and egalitarian reciprocity presupposed by discourses, and given the strong emphasis on voluntarily given assent, based upon one's evaluation of certain kinds of validity claims, I fail to see how discourses could violate individual privacy or force self-disclosure. I maintain, however, that discourses can challenge the line between the public and the private spheres, in the sense that citizens in a polity may make into a public issue some areas of concern that were hitherto considered private matters, such as domestic violence, or, conversely, may plead for the privacy of certain kinds of information, such as buying and consumption patterns or other kinds of personal facts contained in data banks, for example. What moral and political theory should not do is freeze the historical and essentially contestable outcomes of democratic discourses into some immutable catalog of rights; rather moral and political theory should provide us with general principles to guide our moral intuitions and concrete deliberations when we are confronted with such controversial cases as domestic violence, child abuse, and marital rape, or using the sex of an unborn baby as a basis for aborting that fetus.

27. Bruce Ackerman, *We the People,* vol. 1: *Foundations* (Cambridge, Mass.: Harvard University Press, 1991), 12.

28. Some questions of democratic legitimacy and antifoundationalism as they apply to the Supreme Court's dilemma in a democracy have been most fruitfully explored by Morton J. Horwitz in "The Constitution of Change: Legal Fundamentality without Fundamentalism," *Harvard Law Review* 107 (1993): 32–117.

29. Iris Young, "Impartiality and the Civic Public," in *Feminism as Critique,* ed. Seyla Benhabib and Drucilla Cornell (London: Polity Press), 73.

30. For historical analyses, see Joan B. Landes, *Women and the Public Sphere in the Age of the French Revolution* (Ithaca: Cornell University Press, 1988); and Linda Kerber, *Women of the Republic: Intellect and Ideology in Revolutionary America* (New York: Norton, 1986).

31. Landes's illuminating early work *Women and the Public Sphere in the Age of the French Revolution* was marred by one conceptual issue. Particularly in her critique of Habermas's work on the public sphere, Landes conflated the Habermasian model of the public sphere that was part of civil society with the Rousseauian-republican model based upon an opposition to civil society. Much of criticism of the "masculinism" of the public sphere applies only to this republican, civic-virtue version that has little to do with the Enlightenment conception of the public sphere, which Habermas defines as "private individuals using their reason about public matters." Clearly the concept of the public sphere developed in this essay emerges out of this second tradition. See Keith Baker's illuminating discussion of this issue in "Defining the Public Sphere in Eighteenth-Century France: Variations on a Theme by Habermas," in *Habermas and the Public Sphere,* ed. Craig Calhoun (Cambridge, Mass.: MIT Press, 1992), 181–212.

32. A provocative but inadequate critique of the public sphere concept has been given by Dana Villa who minimizes the role and significance of this concept in securing legitimation in democratic theory while focusing on its agonistic and performative dimensions. See "Postmodernism and the Public Sphere," *American Political Science Review* 86, no. 3 (September 1992): 712–25.

33. Iris Marion Young, *Justice and the Politics of Difference* (Princeton: Princeton University Press, 1990).

34. Nancy Fraser, "Rethinking the Public Sphere: A Contribution to the Critique of Actually Existing Democracy," in Calhoun, ed. *Habermas and the Public Sphere,* 123.

35. Ibid., 132ff.

36. Ibid., 108ff.

Part V

Communitarian Justice

18   The Nature of Justice

ARISTOTLE

WITH REGARD TO JUSTICE[1] and injustice, the points we have to consider are—with what class of actions are they connected, in what sense is justice a middle state, and between what extremes is that which is just intermediate? Our enquiry shall follow the same procedure as our previous investigations.

We observe that by the term justice everybody means that state of character which renders men disposed to act justly, and which causes them to do and to wish what is just; and similarly by injustice they mean the disposition that makes men do and wish what is unjust. Let us then accept these definitions to go upon as broadly correct.

The fact is that it is not the same with a state of character as with the sciences and faculties. It appears that the same science or faculty deals with opposite objects,[2] but a state that produces one result does not also produce the opposite result—for instance, health does not cause us to do actions that are the reverse of healthy, but only those that are healthy: A sound gait in walking means walking like a man in good health, not walking lame.

Hence it is often possible to infer one of two opposite states from the other, and often states can be identified from the subjects that exhibit them. Thus if we find out what constitutes good bodily condition we learn what bad condition is as well; but we can also learn what good bodily condition is from actual persons that are in good condition, while from knowing what good condition is we can recognize things that produce good con-

dition. If good condition is firmness of flesh, bad condition must necessarily be flabbiness of flesh, and also 'wholesome' must mean productive of firmness of flesh. Also if one of two opposite terms has more than one meaning, it follows as a rule that the other also has more than one meaning—for instance, the terms "just" and "unjust." And "justice" and "injustice" appear to have more than one meaning, but owing to their two meanings not being widely separate, the ambiguity escapes notice and is not rather obvious, as it is in the case of two meanings that are widely separate. Let us then take the different senses in which the word "unjust" is used. A man who breaks the law is unjust, and so also is a man who is grasping and unfair; so that obviously a law-abiding man and a man who is fair in business are both of them just. "Just" therefore denotes both what is lawful and what is fair, and "unjust" denotes both what is unlawful and what is unfair.

As the unjust man is grasping, his injustice will be exercised in regard to things that are good—not all of them but those with which good and bad fortune are concerned, which though always good in the absolute sense are not always good for a particular person. These are the goods that men pray for and seek after, although they ought not to do so; they ought to pray that the things which are good in the absolute sense may also be good for themselves, though choosing the things that are good for themselves. The unjust man does not always choose the larger share—in the case of

From Chapter V of Aristotle's Ethics for English Readers, *rendered from the Greek of the* Nicomachean Ethics *by H. Rackham (1943). Reprinted by permission of Basil Blackwell, Publisher.*

things that are bad absolutely he chooses the smaller share; but because the smaller quantity of a bad thing seems to be good in a sense, and a grasping nature means that one grasps something good, this makes him appear to be grasping. Let us call him "unfair," as that term includes taking too much of good things and taking too little of bad ones, and covers both.

We saw that the man who breaks the law is unjust and the law-abiding man just. This shows that all that is lawful is just in a sense, since it is the business of legislature to define what is lawful, and the various decisions of the legislature are what we term the principles of justice. Now all the edicts of the laws are aimed either at the common advantage of everybody or at the interest of a ruling class selected by merit or in some other similar way. Consequently in one sense we apply the word "just" to things which produce and preserve happiness, and the things that form part of happiness for the community. And the law prescribes certain conduct: the conduct of a brave man (for instance, not to desert one's post, not to run away in battle, not to throw down one's arms); that of a self-controlled man (for instance, not to commit adultery or violent assault); that of a good-tempered man (for instance, not to strike a person or to use abusive language), and similarly as to all the other forms of virtue—some acts the law enjoins and others it forbids, rightly if the law has been rightly framed and not so well if it has been drafted carelessly.

Justice in this sense then is perfect virtue, though with the qualification that it is virtue in relation to our neighbors. Because of this the view is often held that in the list of virtues justice occupies the top place, and that

Neither the evening nor the morning star[3] is so sublime; and we have the proverb:

The whole of virtue is comprised in justice.[4]

Justice is perfect because it is our mode of practicing perfect virtue; and it is supremely perfect because its possessor can use it in his relations with others and not only by himself. There are plenty of people who can practice virtue in their personal affairs but who are incapable of displaying it in their relations with others. This shows the truth of the saying of Bias,[5] "Office will show a real man"; when somebody obtains a position of authority he is brought into contact with other people, and is a member of a partnership. For this same reason, justice alone among the virtues is thought to be "another person's good,"[6] because it is exercised in relation to one's neighbors; it does what is in the interest of somebody else, a superior or a partner. The wickedest man therefore is he who exercises his wickedness in his relations with his friends and not merely in his personal affairs; and the best man is the one who practices his virtue not in regard to himself but in relation to someone else, as that is a difficult thing to do.

Justice thus understood therefore is not a part of virtue, but the whole of it; and its opposite, injustice, is not a part of vice, but the whole. The distinction between justice in this sense and virtue is clear from what has been said; they are the same quality of character but differently viewed: what as exercised in relation to others is justice, considered simply as a disposition of a certain sort is virtue.

Justice as a Part of Virtue

But it is justice as a particular part of virtue that we are investigating, that being as we say one sort of justice; and similarly we are considering injustice as a particular vice, not in the sense of wickedness in general.

That there is such a vice is indicated by the following considerations: When a man practices one of the other vices (for instance, when owing to cowardice he throws away his shield,[7] or owing to ill-temper uses abusive language, or owing to meanness refuses to help a friend out of a difficulty with money), he is committing an injustice but he is not taking an unfair share of something. But when he takes an unfair share, he is not displaying one of the vices of the kind specified, and certainly not all of them, but clearly he does display a vice of some sort, as we blame his conduct—in fact he displays injustice. Therefore there is another sort of injustice which is a part of injustice as a whole, and there is a form of unjust action which is a subdivision of unjust and illegal conduct in general. Again, suppose that A commits adultery for gain and gets something by it, whereas B does it out of inclination and loses by his indulgence. B would appear to be self-indulgent rather than avaricious, whereas A would seem unjust but not self-indulgent at all. It is clear then that A's motive would be profit. And yet another reason—whereas all other offenses are always attributed to some particular vice; for instance, adultery is ascribed to self-indulgence, desertion of a comrade in battle to cowardice, assault to anger—an offense out of which a man has made a profit is not put down to any other vice but injustice.

Hence it is clear that beside injustice in the wide sense there is another kind of injustice which is a particular form of vice. It bears the same name because it comes under the same general definition—both forms of injustice being exercised in our relations with other people; but injustice in the special sense is concerned with honor or money or security, or perhaps all of these things included under some general term, and its motive is the pleasure derived from gain, whereas injustice in the wide sense is concerned with the whole of things in relation to which virtue is displayed.

The next step is to ascertain the nature and the attributes of justice in this special sense of the term, as distinct from justice denoting the whole of virtue.

Now we have distinguished two meanings of the term "unjust"—namely, unlawful and unequal or unfair; and we have shown that "just" means both lawful and equal or fair. Injustice of the kind mentioned above corresponds with "unlawful." But the unfair is not the same thing as the unlawful, but is related to it as part to whole—everything unfair is unlawful, but not everything unlawful is unfair. Consequently the unjust and injustice in the special sense are not the same as the unjust and injustice in the wide sense; although they also are related to each other as part to whole—injustice in this sense is a part of injustice in the wide sense, and likewise justice in this sense is a part of justice in the wide sense. We must consequently discuss justice and injustice, and what is just and unjust, in the special sense also. We may therefore leave on one side that form of justice which is coextensive with virtue as a whole, and the corresponding form of injustice—namely, the exercise of the whole of virtue and of vice in our relations with another person.

It is also clear how we should define what is just and what unjust in the corresponding senses; for almost a majority of the actions ordained by law are those which are prescribed on the basis of virtue taken as a whole, since the law specifies the particular virtues which we are to practice and the particular vices which we are to avoid; and the means for producing virtue as a whole are the regulations laid down by law for education in the duties of a citizen. But in regard to our education as individuals, which renders us simply good *men*, the question whether this is the concern of politics or of another art will have to be decided later,[8] for perhaps to be a good man is not the same thing as to be a good citizen of some particular state.

Special justice, on the other hand, and that which is just in the sense corresponding to it, is of two kinds. One kind is the principle that regulates distributions of honor or money or the other divisible assets of the community, which may be divided among its members in equal or unequal shares. The other kind is that which regulates private transactions. The latter form of justice has two divisions, inasmuch as some transactions are voluntary and others nonvoluntary.[9] Instances of voluntary transactions are selling, buying, lending at interest, lending free of interest, pledging, depositing, letting for hire: these are called voluntary because they are voluntarily entered upon. Of nonvoluntary transactions some are clandestine, such as theft, adultery, poisoning, procuring, enticing slaves to leave their owners, assassination, giving false witness; and some are violent, such as assault, imprisonment, murder, rape, mutilation, abusive language, contumelious treatment.

Distributive and Corrective Justice

Now as an unjust man is unfair and an unjust thing unequal, it is clear that corresponding to the unequal there is a middle point or mean; namely, that which is equal; for any kind of action admitting of more or less also admits what is equal. If then what is unjust is unequal, what is just is equal, as everyone will agree without argument; and since the equal is a mean, the just will be a sort of mean too. Now equality involves at least two terms; it follows therefore not only that the just is a mean and equal, but also that (1) as a mean it implies two extremes, the more and the less, (2) as equal it implies two equal shares, and (3) as just it implies certain persons for whom it is just. Consequently justice involves at least four terms, two persons for whom it is just and two shares which are just. And there will be the same equality between the shares as between the persons, that is, the ratio between the shares will be the same as the ratio between the persons. If the persons are not equal, they will not have equal shares; it is when equals possess or are assigned unequal shares, or persons who are not equal equal shares, that quarrels and complaints arise.

Moreover the same point also clearly follows from the principle of assignment by merit. Everybody agrees that just distribution must be in accordance with merit of some sort, though everybody does not mean the same sort of merit. Democrats take merit to mean free status, adherents of oligarchy take it to mean wealth or noble birth, supporters of aristocracy excellence.

The just then is that which is proportionate and the unjust is that which runs counter to proportion; the man who acts unjustly has too much, and the man who is unjustly treated too little, of the good. In the case of evil, it is the other way about, as the lesser evil is accounted as good in comparison with the greater evil, because the lesser

evil is more desirable than the greater, and what is desirable is a good, and what is more desirable a greater good.

This then is one species of justice.

The species of justice that remains is the justice of redress, which operates in the case of voluntary and involuntary transactions. This form of justice has a different specific character from the preceding one. The justice that distributes common property always follows the kind of proportion mentioned above (because in the case of distribution from the common funds of a partnership it will follow the same ratio as that existing between the sums put into the business by the partners); and the unjust that is opposed to this form of the just is that which violates that proportion. But justice in transactions between individuals, although it is equality of a sort and injustice inequality, does not go by the kind of proportion mentioned, but by arithmetical proportion.[10] It makes no difference[11] whether a good man has defrauded a bad one or a bad man a good one, nor whether a good man or a bad man has committed adultery; the law only looks at the nature of the injury, and treats the parties as equal if one has done and the other suffered a wrong or if one has inflicted and the other sustained damage. Consequently, in such cases the judge tries to equalize this injustice, which consists in inequality—for even in a case where one person has received and the other has inflicted a blow, or where one has killed and the other been killed, the suffering and the action have been distributed in unequal shares, while the judge's endeavor is to make them equal by means of the penalty he inflicts, taking something away from the gain of the assailant. The term "gain" is applied to such cases in a general sense, even though to some, for instance a person who has inflicted a wound, it is not specially appropriate, and the term "loss" is applied to the sufferer; at all events the terms "gain" and "loss" are employed when the amount of the suffering inflicted has been assessed. Consequently, while equal is intermediate between more and less, gain and loss are at once both more and less in contrary ways—

more of what is good and less of what is bad are gain, and more of what is bad and less of what is good are loss, intermediate between them being, as we said, the equal, which we pronounce to be just. Consequently the justice of redress will be what is intermediate between loss and gain. This is why when a dispute arises the parties have recourse to a judge; to go to a judge is to appeal to the just, inasmuch as a judge is virtually justice personified;[12] and they have recourse to a judge as intermediary—indeed, in some countries judges are called "mediators"—on the ground that if the litigants get the medium amount they will get what is just. Thus justice is a sort of medium, as the judge is a medium between the litigants. What he does is to restore equality: it is as if there were a line divided into two unequal parts, and he took away the amount by which the larger segment exceeded half the line and added it to the smaller segment. When the whole has been divided into two equal parts, people say that they "have got their own," having got an equal share. This is the arithmetic mean between the greater amount and the less.

Therefore the just is intermediate between gain and loss due to breach of contract; it consists in having an equal amount both before and after the transaction.

Justice in Exchange

Some people hold the view that mere reciprocity is justice. But reciprocity does not coincide with either distributive justice or with corrective justice; it often conflicts with them—for example, if an officer strikes a man it is wrong for the man to hit back, but if a man strikes an officer, not only should the officer hit him but he must be punished as well. Further, there is a wide distinction between an act done with the consent of the other party and one done without consent. But in association for exchange this sort of justice, reciprocity, is the bond uniting the parties; but it must be reciprocity on a basis of proportion and not of equality. It is proportionate requital that keeps the state together. Men seek to return either evil for

evil, failing which they feel themselves mere slaves, or good for good, in default of which no exchange of goods and services takes place; but it is exchange which holds society together. This is why men build a shrine of the Graces in their cities, as a reminder that favors should be returned, since to return favors received is a characteristic of grace. When somebody has done one a service, it behoves one not only to do him a service in return but also on the next occasion to take the initiative in doing him a service oneself.

Proportional requital is achieved by diagonal conjunction. Let A be a builder, B a shoemaker, C a house, and D a pair of shoes. Then the builder has to take from the shoemaker a part of the produce of his labor and give him in return a part of his own product. If proportionate equality between the products be first established, and then reciprocation takes place, the condition indicated will have been satisfied. But if this is not done, the bargain is not equal, and does not hold, since it may happen that the work of one party is worth more than that of the other, so that they have to be equalized. For two doctors do not combine to exchange their services, but a doctor and a farmer, and in general persons who are different and who may be unequal, but in that case they need to be equated. Consequently exchange of commodities requires that the commodities must be in some way commensurable; and it was to achieve this that money was invented. Money serves as a sort of middle term, as it measures all things, and so indicates their superior or inferior value—just how many shoes are the equivalent of a house or a certain quantity of food. The number of shoes exchanged for a house must correspond to the ratio between a builder and a shoemaker. Failing this, there will be no exchange, and no business will be done. And this cannot be secured unless the goods are equated in some way.

It is therefore necessary to have some one standard of measurement for all commodities, as was said before. And this standard is in reality demand; it is demand which keeps commerce together, since if people were to cease to have wants or if their wants were to alter, exchange will not go on, or it will be on different lines. But it has been agreed to accept money as representing demand. Money is a convention, and we can alter the currency if we choose, rendering the old coinage useless. Thus reciprocity will be achieved when the factors have been equated, bringing it about that as farmer is to shoemaker so the amount of shoemaker's work is to the amount of farmer's work exchanged for it.

That demand serves as a single factor holding commerce together is shown by the fact that when there is no demand for mutual service in the case of both parties or at least of one of the two, exchange of services does not take place. And money serves us as a security for future exchange, if we do not need a thing now; money guarantees that we shall have it if we do need it, as we shall be able to get it by producing the money. Now money fluctuates in value, just like goods; but it tends to be steadier. Consequently all goods must have a price given to them, as then exchange of goods will always be possible, and consequently association between men. Currency therefore is a sort of measure, which equates goods by making them commensurable. In fact there would be no association between man and man if there were no exchange, and no exchange if there were no equalization of values, and no equalization of values if there were no commensurability. No doubt it is not really possible for articles that are so different to be made exactly commensurable in value, but they can be made sufficiently commensurable for the practical purpose of exchange. That is why there has to be a single standard fixed by agreement, making all commodities commensurable; for everything can be measured by money. Let A be a house, B 20 minae and C a bedstead. Then $A = B/2$ (supposing a house to be worth—that is, equal to—5 minae) and C (the bedstead) = $B/10$. We can now say how many bedsteads are equal to one house; namely, five. Obviously before money existed this is how the rate of exchange was quoted—five beds for a house; there is no real difference between bartering five bedsteads for a house and buying the house for the price of five bedsteads.

We have now defined "just" and "unjust"; and our definitions show that just action is intermediate between doing injustice and suffering injustice, since the former is to get too much and the latter is to get too little. Justice is a sort of middle state, but not in the same manner as the other virtues are middle states; it is middle because it attaches to a middle amount, injustice being the quality of extremes. Also justice is the virtue which disposes the just man to resolve to act justly, and which leads him, when distributing things between himself and another, not to give himself a larger portion and his neighbor a smaller one of what is desirable, and the other way about in regard to what is detrimental, but to allot shares that are proportionately equal; and similarly when making a distribution between two other persons. Injustice on the contrary stands in the same relation to what is unjust, this being disproportionate excess or deficiency of something useful or harmful. Thus injustice is excess and deficiency in the sense of being productive of excess and deficiency, in one's own case excess of what is simply useful and deficiency of what is harmful, and in the case of others taken as a whole it is the same as in one's own case, but the disproportion may be in either direction.[13] In an unjust distribution to get too little is to suffer injustice and to get too much is to do injustice.

Political Justice and Analogous Kinds of Justice

But it must be borne in mind that what we are investigating is not only justice in the abstract but also political justice. This exists between men living in a community for the purpose of satisfying their needs, men who are free and who enjoy either absolute or proportional equality. Between men who do not fulfill these conditions no political justice exists, but only justice in a special sense and so called by analogy. Justice exists between those whose mutual relations are regulated by law; and law exists for those between whom there is a possibility of injustice, the administration of the law being the discrimination of what is just and what is unjust. Persons therefore between whom may be injustice may act unjustly toward each other (although unjust action does not necessarily imply injustice); and unjust action means appropriating too large a share of things essentially good and taking too small a share of things essentially bad. On this account we do not allow a man to govern, but only the law, because a human ruler governs in his own interest and becomes a tyrant; whereas the true function of a ruler is to be the guardian of justice, and therefore of equality. A just ruler, we think, gets no profit out of his office, as he does not assign to himself the larger share of what is essentially good unless such a share is proportionate to his merits. So he labors for the sake of others: this explains the saying "Justice is other men's good." Consequently it is necessary to give him some recompense in the form of honor and privilege. Rulers not content with such rewards become tyrants.

The justice of a master or a father is not the same thing as absolute justice or political justice, but only analogous to them; for there is no such thing as injustice in the absolute sense toward things that belong to one. Slaves, who are a man's chattels, and also children till they reach a certain age and start an independent life, are in a manner part of oneself, and nobody deliberately does harm to himself, so that there is no such thing as being unjust to oneself. Therefore justice and injustice in the political sense are not exercised in these relations, because they are regulated by law, as we saw, and exist between persons naturally governed by law, who, as we saw, are people who have an equal share in governing and being governed. Consequently justice exists in a fuller degree between a man and his wife than between a man and his children and chattels; it is in fact domestic justice. But this also is different from political justice.

Natural and Conventional Justice

Civil justice is partly natural and partly conventional.[14] A natural rule of justice is one which has the same validity everywhere, independently of

whether people accept it or not. A conventional rule is a practice that at the outset may equally well be settled one way or the other, but which when once enacted becomes a regulation—for instance, the rule that the ransom for a prisoner of war shall be a mina, or that a certain sacrifice shall consist of one goat or two sheep; as well as enactments dealing with particular cases; for instance, the sacrifice celebrated in honor of Brasidas;[15] and special regulations promulgated by decree. Some people hold that all justice is a matter of fixed regulations, because a law of nature never alters and has the same validity everywhere—for instance, fire burns both here and in Persia—but they see men's conceptions of justice changing. This is not absolutely true, but only with qualifications—among the gods indeed it is perhaps not true at all. But among us, although there is such a thing as natural justice, nevertheless all rules can be altered. For instance, the right hand is naturally stronger than the left, but anybody can train himself to be ambidextrous. And in all other matters the same distinction will apply. But among things which admit of variation, it is not clear what kind is natural and what is not natural but due to convention and based on agreements, as both kinds alike are equally susceptible of change. But nevertheless it is the case that one thing is natural and another not natural. Rules of justice fixed by agreement and for the sake of expediency are like weights and measures. Wine and corn measures are not the same everywhere, but are larger in wholesale and smaller in retail markets. Similarly those rules of justice which are not due to nature but are enacted by man are not the same everywhere, since the constitution of the state is not the same everywhere; yet there is only one form of constitution which is everywhere in accordance with nature, namely the best form. . . .

Justice and Equity

The next subject to discuss is equity and its relation to justice. They appear on examination to be neither absolutely identical nor yet different in kind. Sometimes, it is true, we praise equity and the equitable man, and virtually employ the word as a term of general approval, using "more equitable" to mean merely "better."[16] But sometimes, when we think the matter out, it seems curious that the equitable should be praiseworthy if it is something different from what is just. If they are different, either the just or the equitable is not good, or if both are good, they are the same thing.

These then more or less are the considerations that make the meaning of "equity" a difficult problem. In one way, however, all the different uses of the term are correct, and there is no real inconsistency between them. Although equity is superior to one kind of justice, it is not better than justice as being generically different from it. Justice and equity are the same thing, and both are good, although equity is the better of the two.

The problem arises from the fact that equity, although just, is not justice as enacted by law, but a rectification of legal justice. The reason of this is that all law is universal, but there are some things about which it is not possible to make a universal statement which will be correct. In matters therefore in which a universal statement is necessary but it is not possible for it to be absolutely correct, the law follows the line that is valid as a general rule—though with full recognition of the error involved. Nevertheless this does not make it bad law, for the error does not lie in the law nor in the lawgiver, but in the nature of the case: the material of practical affairs is essentially irregular. When therefore the law lays down a general rule and afterwards a case arises that is not covered by the rule, the proper course is to rectify the omission in the law where it is defective and where it errs by oversimplification, and to insert the provision which the author of the law would himself suggest if he were present, and would have inserted if he had been cognizant of the case in question. Therefore while equity is just, and is better than one kind of justice, it is not superior to absolute justice, but only to the error that is caused by the absolute statement of what is just. This is the essential nature of equity—it is a rectification of the law where it is defective owing to its universality. Indeed this is the reason why law does not cover everything:

there are some things for which it is impossible to provide by legislation, and consequently they require a special decree. When a thing is indefinite the rule dealing with it is also indefinite, like the mason's rule made of lead that is used by builders in Lesbos. This is not rigid but can be bent to fit the shape of the stone; and similarly a special decree can be adapted to suit the circumstances of the case.

The nature of equity has now been explained, and it has been shown to be just, and to be superior to one kind of justice. And from this it is clear what the equitable man is: he is a man who is of set purpose and habitually does what is equitable, and does not stand on his rights unduly but is ready to accept less than his share although he has the law on his side. This quality of character is equity; it is a special kind of justice, not an entirely distinct quality.

Can a Man Treat Himself Unjustly?

The foregoing remarks supply an answer to the question, is it possible for a man to do an injustice to himself? One class of just acts consists of those acts, in conformity with one of the virtues, which are ordained by law. For instance, the law does not sanction suicide, and any form of homicide which it does not expressly permit it must be understood to forbid. Further, when a man in violation of the law voluntarily injures another man (not in retaliation), he acts unjustly ("voluntarily" meaning with a knowledge of the person affected and the instrument employed). Now a man who in a fit of anger stabs himself commits voluntarily an injury that is not a legitimate act of retaliation, and this the law does not permit. He is therefore committing an unjust offense. But against whom? Presumably against the state, not himself, for he suffers the act voluntarily, and no one is voluntarily treated unjustly. Moreover it is for this that the state inflicts a penalty: suicide is punished by certain marks of dishonor, as an offense against the state.[17]

Secondly, in one sense a man who "acts unjustly" is merely unjust, and not wicked in every way; and in this sense it is not possible to act un-justly toward oneself (this is a different sense of the term from the one above; in one sense injustice is a particular evil quality, and does not imply complete wickedness, so that the unjust act specified does not display general wickedness). For, (1) that would imply that a quality was both present and absent in the same person at the same time, which is impossible. Justice and injustice must always belong to different people. Moreover, (2) to be unjust an act must be voluntary and deliberate, and also unprovoked: a man who retaliates and does to another what that other has done to him is not thought to commit an injustice. But one who does harm to himself is both doing and suffering the same thing at the same time. Again, (3) if it were possible for a man to inflict an injustice on himself, it would be possible voluntarily to suffer injustice. And in addition, (4) acting unjustly means committing a particular act of injustice; for instance, adultery, burglary, theft; but a man cannot commit adultery with his own wife or steal his own property. And broadly speaking, the question "Can a man act unjustly toward himself?" is solved by our answer to the question about suffering injustice voluntarily.

(It is also clear that although both doing and receiving injustice are bad things, the former meaning to have more and the latter to have less than the medium amount, which corresponds to health in the art of medicine and to good bodily condition in the art of athletic training, yet to act unjustly is the worse of the two. For it involves wickedness and deserves reprehension, and its wickedness is complete or nearly complete; but to suffer injustice does not involve wickedness, viz., injustice, in the victim. In itself therefore to suffer injustice is the lesser evil, although it may well be the greater evil incidentally. But with this science is not concerned: it pronounces pleurisy to be a more serious malady than a sprain, in spite of the fact that a sprain might on occasion be a more serious mishap, if owing to it you stumbled in a battle and were taken prisoner and killed by the enemy.)

But in a metaphorical and analogical sense there is such a thing as justice not toward oneself but between the different parts of one's nature, not indeed justice in the full sense of the term but such as exists between master and servant or the head of a household and the members of his family. For in the discourses on these questions[18] distinction is made between the rational and irrational parts of the soul; and this has suggested the view that there is such a thing as injustice toward oneself, because these parts of the self may thwart each other in their respective desires, and consequently there is a sort of mutual justice between them as there is between ruler and subject.

NOTES

1. The Greek term normally thus rendered is stated in what follows to have two senses, the wider sense of righteousness in general, any right conduct in relation to others, and the narrower sense of right conduct in matters involving gain or loss to the agent or to others. It is justice in the latter sense that this chapter deals with; in some places we should rather term it honesty.

2. For instance, medicine studies both health and disease.

3. A quotation from a play of Euripides that has not come down to us.

4. From the poet Theognis.

5. One of the Seven Sages.

6. Plato, *Republic* 343 c.—the definition given by the sophist Thrasymachus.

7. I.e., so as to be able to run away quickly.

8. It is discussed in Aristotle's *Politics,* Book III.

9. Viz., lacking the consent of one of the parties.

10. I.e., two pairs of terms (e.g., 1, 3, 7, 9) the second of which exceeds the first by the same amount as the fourth exceeds the third. We do not call this proportion, but if the third term also exceeds the second by the same amount (e.g., 1, 3, 5, 7), an arithmetical progression.

11. For corrective justice the merits of the parties are immaterial.

12. Cf. our expressions "Mr. Justice So-and-so," "Justice of the Peace."

13. When A makes an unjust distribution not between himself and B but between B and C, the result for either B or C may be either too large or too small a share of something beneficial and either too small or too large a share of something detrimental.

14. The word thus rendered also means "legal."

15. This Spartan general won the city of Amphipolis from the Athenian Empire, 424 B.C., and fell in defending it two years later. He was consecrated as a local hero, and an annual celebration was held in his honor, with sacrifices and races (for the Greeks races had religious associations).

16. In English "reasonable" is similarly used as a term of general approval.

17. At Athens a suicide's hand, as the guilty instrument, was cut off and buried separately from the body.

18. Plato's *Republic* and the writings of Plato's pupils in the Academy.

19 The Public Philosophy of Contemporary Liberalism

MICHAEL SANDEL

Liberal and Republican Freedom

THE POLITICAL PHILOSOPHY by which we live is a certain version of liberal political theory. Its central idea is that government should be neutral toward the moral and religious views its citizens espouse. Since people disagree about the best way to live, government should not affirm in law any particular vision of the good life. Instead, it should provide a framework of rights that respects persons as free and independent selves, capable of choosing their own values and ends.[1] Since this liberalism asserts the priority of fair procedures over particular ends, the public life it informs might be called the procedural republic.[2]

In describing the prevailing political philosophy as a version of liberal political theory, it is important to distinguish two different meanings of liberalism. In the common parlance of American politics, liberalism is the opposite of conservatism; it is the outlook of those who favor a more generous welfare state and a greater measure of social and economic equality.[3] In the history of political theory, however, liberalism has a different, broader meaning. In this historical sense, liberalism describes a tradition of thought that emphasizes toleration and respect for individual rights and that runs from John Locke, Immanuel Kant, and John Stuart Mill to John Rawls. The public philosophy

of contemporary American politics is a version of this liberal tradition of thought, and most of our debates proceed within its terms.

The idea that freedom consists in our capacity to choose our ends finds prominent expression in our politics and law. Its province is not limited to those known as liberals rather than conservatives in American politics; it can be found across the political spectrum. Republicans sometimes argue, for example, that taxing the rich to pay for welfare programs is a form of coerced charity that violates people's freedom to choose what to do with their own money. Democrats sometimes argue that government should assure all citizens a decent level of income, housing, and health, on the grounds that those who are crushed by economic necessity are not truly free to exercise choice in other domains. Although the two sides disagree about how government should act to respect individual choice, both assume that freedom consists in the capacity of persons to choose their values and ends.

So familiar is this vision of freedom that it seems a permanent feature of the American political and constitutional tradition. But Americans have not always understood freedom in this way. As a reigning public philosophy, the version of liberalism that informs our present debates is a recent arrival, a development of the last forty or fifty years. Its distinctive character can best be seen by contrast with a rival public philosophy that it gradually displaced. This rival public philosophy is a version of republican political theory.

Central to republican theory is the idea that liberty depends on sharing in self-government. This idea is not by itself inconsistent with liberal freedom. Participating in politics can be one among the ways in which people choose to pursue their ends. According to republican political theory, however, sharing in self-rule involves something more. It means deliberating with fellow citizens about the common good and helping to shape the destiny of the political community. But to deliberate well about the common good requires more than the capacity to choose one's ends and to respect others' rights to do the same. It requires a knowledge of public affairs and also a sense of belonging, a concern for the whole, a moral bond with the community whose fate is at stake. To share in self-rule therefore requires that citizens possess, or come to acquire, certain qualities of character, or civic virtues. But this means that republican politics cannot be neutral toward the values and ends its citizens espouse. The republican conception of freedom, unlike the liberal conception, requires a formative politics, a politics that cultivates in citizens the qualities of character self-government requires.

Both the liberal and republican conceptions of freedom have been present throughout our political experience, but in shifting measure and relative importance. Broadly speaking, republicanism predominated earlier in American history, liberalism later. In recent decades, the civic or formative aspect of our politics has largely given way to the liberalism that conceives persons as free and independent selves, unencumbered by moral or civic ties they have not chosen.

This shift sheds light on our present political predicament. For despite its appeal, the liberal vision of freedom lacks the civic resources to sustain self-government. This defect ill-equips it to address the sense of disempowerment that afflicts our public life. The public philosophy by which we live cannot secure the liberty it promises, because it cannot inspire the sense of community and civic engagement that liberty requires.

How the liberal conception of citizenship and freedom gradually crowded out the republican conception involves two intersecting tales. One traces the advent of the procedural republic from the first stirrings of American constitutionalism to recent debates about religious liberty, free speech, and privacy rights. Another traces the decline of the civic strand of American political discourse from Thomas Jefferson's day to the present.[4]

These stories, taken together, bring to clarity the self-image that animates—and sometimes debilitates—our public life. They do not reveal a golden age when all was right with American democracy. The republican tradition coexisted with slavery, with the exclusion of women from the public realm, with property qualifications for voting, with nativist hostility to immigrants; indeed it sometimes provided the terms within which these practices were defended.

And yet, for all its episodes of darkness, the republican tradition with its emphasis on community and self-government, may offer a corrective to our impoverished civic life. Recalling the republican conception of freedom as self-rule may prompt us to pose questions we have forgotten how to ask: What economic arrangements are hospitable to self-government? How might our political discourse engage rather than avoid the moral and religious convictions people bring to the public realm? And how might the public life of a pluralist society cultivate in citizens the expansive self-understandings that civic engagement requires? If the public philosophy of our day leaves little room for civic considerations, it may help to recall how earlier generations of Americans debated such questions, before the procedural republic took hold. But in order to identify the relevant strands of the story, we need to specify more fully the version of liberalism that informs our present politics.

The Aspiration to Neutrality

The idea that government should be neutral on the question of the good life is distinctive to modern political thought. Ancient political theory held that the purpose of politics was to cultivate the virtue, or moral excellence, of citizens. All associations aim at some good, Aristotle wrote, and the polis, or political association, aims at the highest, most comprehensive good: "any polis which is truly so called, and is not merely one in name, must devote itself to the end of encouraging goodness. Otherwise, a political association sinks into a mere alliance, which only differs in space from other forms of alliance where the members live at a distance from one another. Otherwise, too, law becomes a mere covenant—or (in the phrase of the Sophist Lycophron) 'a guarantor of men's rights against one another'—instead of being, as it should be, a rule of life such as will make the members of a polis good and just."[5]

According to Aristotle, political community is more than "an association for residence on a common site, or for the sake of preventing mutual injustice and easing exchange." Although these are necessary conditions for political community, they are not its purpose of ultimate justification. "The end and purpose of a polis is the good life, and the institutions of social life are means to that end." It is only as participants in political association that we can realize our nature and fulfill our highest ends.[6]

Unlike the ancient conception, liberal political theory does not see political life as concerned with the highest human ends or with the moral excellence of its citizens. Rather than promote a particular conception of the good life, liberal political theory insists on toleration, fair procedures, and respect for individual rights—values that respect people's freedom to choose their own values. But this raises a difficult question. If liberal ideals cannot be defended in the name of the highest human good, then in what does their moral basis consist?

It is sometimes thought that liberal principles can be justified by a simple version of moral relativism. Government should not "legislate morality," because all morality is merely subjective, a matter of personal preference not open to argument or rational debate. "Who is to say what is literature and what is filth? That is a value judgment, and whose values should decide?" Relativism usually appears less as a claim than as a question: "Who is to judge?" But the same question can be asked of the values that liberals defend. Toleration and freedom and fairness are values too, and they can hardly be defended by the claim that no values can be defended. So it is a mistake to affirm liberal values by arguing that all values are merely subjective. The relativist defense of liberalism is no defense at all.

Utilitarianism versus Kantian Liberalism

What, then, is the case for the neutrality the liberal invokes? Recent political philosophy has offered two main alternatives—one utilitarian, the other Kantian.[7] The utilitarian view, following John Stuart Mill, defends liberal principles in the name of maximizing the general welfare. The state should not impose on its citizens a preferred way of life, even for their own good, because doing so will reduce the sum of human happiness, at least in the long run. It is better that people choose for themselves, even if, on occasion, they get it wrong.

"The only freedom which deserves the name," writes Mill in *On Liberty*, "is that of pursuing our own good in our own way, so long as we do not attempt to deprive others of theirs, or impede their efforts to obtain it." He adds that his argument does not depend on any notion of abstract right, only on the principle of the greatest good for the greatest number. "I regard utility as the ultimate appeal on all ethical questions; but it must be utility in the largest sense, grounded on the permanent interests of man as a progressive being."[8]

Many objections have been raised against utilitarianism as a general doctrine of moral philosophy. Some have questioned the concept of utility and the assumption that all human goods are in principle commensurable. Others have objected that by reducing all values to preferences and desires, utilitarians are unable to admit qualitative distinctions of worth, unable to distinguish noble desires from base ones. But most recent debate has focused on whether utilitarianism offers a convincing basis for liberal principles, including respect for individual rights.[9]

At first glance, utilitarianism seems well suited to liberal purposes. Seeking to maximize overall happiness does not require judging people's values, only aggregating them. And the willingness to aggregate preferences without judging them suggests a tolerant spirit, even a democratic one. When people go to the polls we count their votes, whatever they are.

But the utilitarian calculus is not always as liberal as it first appears. If enough cheering Romans pack the Coliseum to watch the lion devour the Christian, the collective pleasure of the Romans will surely outweigh the pain of the Christian, intense though it be. Or if a big majority abhors a small religion and wants it banned, the balances of preferences will favor suppression, not toleration. Utilitarians sometimes defend individual rights on the grounds that respecting them now will serve utility in the long run. But this calculation is precarious and contingent. It hardly secures the liberal promise not to impose on some the values of others.

The case against utilitarianism was made most powerfully by Immanuel Kant. He argued that empirical principles such as utility were unfit to serve as a basis for morality. A wholly instrumental defense of freedom and rights not only leaves rights vulnerable but fails to respect the inherent dignity of persons. The utilitarian calculus treats people as means to the happiness of others, not as ends in themselves, worthy of respect.[10]

Contemporary liberals extend Kant's argument with the claim that utilitarianism fails to take seriously the distinction between persons. In seeking above all to maximize the general welfare, the utilitarian treats society as a whole as if it were a single person; it conflates our many, diverse desires into a single system of desires. It is indifferent to the

distribution of satisfactions among persons, except insofar as this may affect the overall sum. But this fails to respect our plurality and distinctness. It uses some as means to the happiness of all, and so fails to respect each as an end in himself or herself.

In the view of modern-day Kantians, certain rights are so fundamental that even the general welfare cannot override them. As John Rawls writes in *A Theory of Justice*, "Each person possesses an inviolability founded on justice that even the welfare of society as a whole cannot override. . . . The rights secured by justice are not subject to political bargaining or to the calculus of social interests."[11]

So Kantian liberals need an account of rights that does not depend on utilitarian considerations. More than this, they need an account that does not depend on any particular conception of the good, that does not presuppose the superiority of one way of life over others. Only a justification neutral among ends could preserve the liberal resolve not to favor any particular ends or to impose on its citizens a preferred way of life. But what sort of justification could this be? How is it possible to affirm certain liberties and rights as fundamental without embracing some vision of the good life, without endorsing some ends over others?

The solution proposed by Kantian liberals is to draw a distinction between the "right" and the "good"—between a framework of basic rights and liberties, and the conceptions of the good that people may choose to pursue within the framework. It is one thing for the state to support a fair framework, they argue, something else to affirm some particular ends. For example, it is one thing to defend the right to free speech so that people may be free to form their own opinions and choose their own ends, but something else to support it on grounds that a life of political discussion is inherently worthier than a life unconcerned with public affairs, or on the grounds that free speech will increase the general welfare. Only the first defense is available on the Kantian view, resting as it does on the ideal of a neutral framework.

Now the commitment to a framework neutral with respect to ends can be seen as a kind of value—in this sense the Kantian liberal is no relativist—but its value consists precisely in its refusal to affirm a preferred way of life or conception of the good. For Kantian liberals, then, the right is prior to the good, and in two senses. First, individual rights cannot be sacrificed for the sake of the general good; and second, the principles of justice that specify these rights cannot be premised on any particular vision of the good life. What justifies the rights is not that they maximize the general welfare or otherwise promote the good, but rather that they constitute a fair framework within which individuals and groups can choose their own values and ends, consistent with a similar liberty for others.

The claim for the priority of the right over the good connects the ideal of neutrality with the primacy of individual rights. For Kantian liberals, rights "function as trump cards held by individuals." They protect individuals from policies, even democratically enacted ones, that would impose a preferred conception of the good and so fail to respect people's freedom to choose their own conceptions.[12]

Of course, proponents of the liberal ethic notoriously disagree about what rights are fundamental and what political arrangements the ideal of the neutral framework requires. Egalitarian liberals support the welfare state and favor a scheme of civil liberties together with certain social and economic rights—rights to welfare, education, health care, and so on. They argue that respecting the capacity of persons to pursue their own ends requires government to assure the minimal prerequisites of a dignified life. Libertarian liberals (usually called conservatives in contemporary politics) defend the market economy and claim that redistributive policies violate people's rights. They argue that respect for persons requires assuring to each the fruits of his or her own labor, and so favor a scheme of civil liberties combined with a strict regime of private property rights. Whether egalitarian or libertarian, Kantian liberalism begins with the claim that we are separate, individual persons, each with our own aims, interests, and conceptions of the good life. It seeks a framework of rights that will enable us to realize our capacity as free moral agents, consistent with a similar liberty for others.

The Liberal Self

The Kantian case against utilitarianism derives much of its force from its contrasting conception of the person, its view of what it means to be a moral agent. Where utilitarians conflate our many desires into a single system of desire, Kantian liberals insist on the separateness of persons. Where the utilitarian self is simply defined as the sum of its desires, the Kantian self is a choosing self, independent of the desires and ends it may have at any moment. Kant expressed this idea by attributing to human beings the capacity to act with an autonomous will. Contemporary liberals rely on the similar notion of a self given prior to and independent of its purposes and ends.

The claim for the priority of the right over the good, and the conception of the person that attends it, oppose Kantian liberalism not only to utilitarianism but also to any view that regards us as obligated to fulfill ends we have not chosen—ends given by nature or God, for example, or by our identities as members of families, peoples, cultures, or traditions. Encumbered identities such as these are at odds with the liberal conception of the person as free and independent selves, unbound by prior moral ties, capable of choosing our ends for ourselves. This is the conception that finds expression in the ideal of the state as a neutral framework. For Kantian liberals, it is precisely because we are freely choosing, independent selves that we need a neutral framework, a framework of rights that refuses to choose among competing values and ends. For the liberal self, what matters above all, what is most essential to our personhood, is not the ends we choose but our capacity to choose them. "It is not our aims that primarily reveal our nature," but rather the framework of rights we would agree to if we could abstract from our aims. "For the self is prior to the ends which are affirmed by it; even a dominant end must be chosen from among numerous possibilities."[13]

The liberal ethic derives much of its moral force from the appeal of the self-image that animates it. This appeal has at least two sources. First, the image of the self as free and independent, unencumbered by aims and attachments it does not choose for itself, offers a powerful liberating vision. Freed from the sanctions of custom and tradition and inherited status, unbound by moral ties antecedent to choice, the liberal self is installed as sovereign, cast as the author of the only obligations that constrain. More than the simple sum of circumstance, we become capable of the dignity that consists in being persons of our "own creating, making, choosing."[14] We are agents and not just instruments of the purposes we pursue. We are "self-originating sources of valid claims."[15]

A second appeal of the liberal self-image consists in the case it implies for equal respect. The idea that there is more to a person than the roles he plays or the customs she keeps or the faith he affirms suggests a basis for respect independent of life's contingencies. Liberal justice is blind to such differences between persons as race, religion, ethnicity, and gender, for in the liberal self-image, these features do not really define our identity in the first place. They are not constituents but merely attributes of the self, the sort of things the state should look beyond. "Our social position and class, our sex and race should not influence deliberations made from a moral point of view."[16] Once these contingencies are seen as products of our situation rather than as aspects of our person, they cease to supply the familiar grounds for prejudice and discrimination.

Nor does it matter, from the standpoint of liberal justice, what virtues we display or what values we espouse. "That we have one conception of the good rather than another is not relevant from a moral standpoint. In acquiring it we are influenced by the same sort of contingencies that lead us to rule out a knowledge of our sex and class."[17] Despite their many differences, libertarian and egalitarian liberals agree that people's entitlements should not be based on their merit or virtue or moral desert, for the qualities that make people virtuous or morally deserving depend on factors "arbitrary from a moral point of view."[18] The liberal state therefore does not discriminate; none of its policies or laws may presuppose that any person or way of life is intrinsically more virtuous than any other. It respects persons as persons, and secures their equal right to live the lives they choose.

Critique of Kantian Liberalism

Kantian liberals thus avoid affirming a conception of the good by affirming instead the priority of the right, which depends in turn on a picture of the self given prior to its ends. But how plausible is this self-conception? Despite its powerful appeal, the image of the unencumbered self is flawed. It cannot make sense of our moral experience, because it cannot account for certain moral and political obligations that we commonly recognize, even prize. These include obligations of solidarity, religious duties, and other moral ties that may claim us for reasons unrelated to a choice. Such obligations are difficult to account for if we understand ourselves as free and independent selves, unbound by moral ties we have not chosen. Unless we think of ourselves as encumbered selves, already claimed by certain projects and commitments, we cannot make sense of these indispensable aspects of our moral and political experience.

Consider the limited scope of obligation on the liberal view. According to Rawls, obligations can arise in only one of two ways, as "natural duties" we owe to human beings as such or as voluntary obligations we incur by consent. The natural duties are those we owe persons *qua* persons—to do justice, to avoid cruelty, and so on. All other obligations, the ones we owe to particular others, are founded in consent and arise only in virtue of agreements we make, be they tacit or explicit.[19]

Conceived as unencumbered selves, we must respect the dignity of all persons, but beyond this, we owe only what we agree to owe. Liberal justice requires that we respect people's rights (as defined by the neutral framework), not that we advance their good. Whether we must concern ourselves with other people's good depends on whether, and with whom, and on what terms, we have agreed to do so.

One striking consequence of this view is that "there is no political obligation, strictly speaking, for citizens generally." Although those who run for office voluntarily incur a political obligation (that is, to serve their country if elected), the ordinary citizen does not. "It is not clear what is the requisite binding action or who has performed it."[20] The average citizen is therefore without any special obligations to his or her fellow citizens, apart from the universal, natural duty not to commit injustice.

The liberal attempt to construe all obligation in terms of duties universally owed or obligations voluntarily incurred makes it difficult to account for civic obligations and other moral and political ties that we commonly recognize. It fails to capture those loyalties and responsibilities whose moral force consists partly in the fact that living by them is inseparable from understanding ourselves as the particular persons we are—as members of this family or city or nation or people, as bearers of that history, as citizens of this republic. Loyalties such as these can be more than values I happen to have, and to hold, at a certain distance. The moral responsibilities they entail may go beyond the obligations I voluntarily incur and the "natural duties" I owe to human beings as such.[21]

Some of the special responsibilities that flow from the particular communities I inhabit I may owe to fellow members, such as obligations of solidarity. Others I may owe to members of those communities with which my own community has some morally relevant history, such as the morally burdened relations of Germans to Jews, of American whites to American blacks, or of England and France to their former colonies.[22] Whether they look inward or outward, obligations of membership presuppose that we are capable of moral ties antecedent to choice. To the extent that we are, the meaning of our membership resists redescription in contractarian terms.

It is sometimes argued, in defense of the liberal view, that loyalties and allegiances not grounded in consent, however psychologically compelling, are matters of sentiment, not of morality, and so do not suggest an obligation unavailable to unencumbered selves. But it is difficult to make sense of certain familiar moral and political dilemmas without acknowledging obligations of solidarity and the thickly constituted, encumbered selves that they imply.

Consider the case of Robert E. Lee on the eve of the Civil War. Lee, then an officer in the Union army, opposed secession, in fact regarded it as treason. And yet when war loomed, Lee concluded that his obligation to Virginia outweighed his obligation to the Union and also his reported opposition to slavery. "With all my devotion to the Union," he wrote, "I have not been able to make up my mind to raise my hand against my relatives, my children, my home. . . . If the Union is dissolved, and the Government disrupted, I shall return to my native State and share the miseries of my people. Save in her defense, I will draw my sword no more."[23]

One can appreciate the poignance of Lee's predicament without necessarily approving of the choice he made. But one cannot make sense of his dilemma as a *moral* dilemma without acknowledging that the call to stand with his people, even to lead them in a cause he opposed, was a claim of moral and not merely sentimental import, capable at least of weighing in the balance against other duties and obligations. Otherwise, Lee's predicament was not really a moral dilemma at all, but simply a conflict between morality on the one hand and mere sentiment or prejudice on the other.

A merely psychological reading of Lee's predicament misses the fact that we not only sympathize with people such as Lee but often admire them, not necessarily for the choices they make but for the quality of character their deliberation reflects. The quality at stake is the disposition to see and bear one's life circumstances as a reflectively situated being—claimed by the history that implicates me in a particular life, but self-conscious of its particularity, and so alive to other ways, wider horizons. But this is precisely the quality that is lacking in those who would think of themselves as unencumbered selves, bound only by the obligations they choose to incur.

As the Lee example illustrates, the liberal conception of the person is too thin to account for the full range of moral and political obligations we commonly recognize, such as obligations of solidarity. This counts against its plausibility generally. But it may even be too weak to support the less strenuous communal obligations expected of citizens in the modern welfare state. Some stronger conception of community may be required, not only to make sense of tragic-heroic dilemmas such as Lee's, but even to sustain the rights that many liberals defend.

While libertarian liberals ask little of citizens, more generous expressions of the liberal ethic support various policies of public provision and redistribution. Egalitarian liberals defend social and economic rights as well as civil and political rights, and so demand of their fellow citizens a high measure of mutual engagement. They insist on the "plurality and distinctness" of individuals but also require that we "share one another's fate" and regard the distribution of natural talents as "a common asset."[24]

Liberalism as an ethic of sharing emphasizes the arbitrariness of fortune and the importance of certain material prerequisites for the meaningful exercise of equal liberties. Since "necessitous men are not free men," and since in any case the distribution of assets and endowments that make for success is "arbitrary from a moral point of view," egalitarian liberals would tax the rich to help the poor secure the prerequisites of a dignified life. Thus the liberal case for the welfare state depends not on a theory of the common good or on some strong notion of communal obligation, but instead on the rights we would agree to respect if we could abstract from our interests and ends.

The liberal case for public provision seems well suited to conditions in which strong communal ties cannot be relied on, and this is one source of its appeal. But it lies vulnerable nonetheless to the libertarian objection that redistributive policies use some people as means to others's ends, and so offend the "plurality and distinctness" of individuals that liberalism seeks above all to secure.[25] In the contractual vision of community alone, it is unclear how the libertarian objection can be met. If those whose fate I am required to share really are, morally speaking, *others*, rather than fellow participants in a way of life with which my identity is bound, then liberalism as an ethic of sharing seems open to the same objections as utilitarianism. Its claim on me is not the claim of a community with which I identify, but rather the claim of an arbitrarily defined collectivity whose aims I may or may not share.

If the egalitarian replies that social and economic rights are required as a matter of equal respect for persons, the question remains why *these* persons, the ones who happen to live in my country, have a claim on my concern that others do not. Tying the mutual responsibilities of citizenship to the idea of respect for persons *qua* persons puts the moral case for welfare on a par with the case for foreign aid—a duty we owe strangers with whom we share a common humanity but possibly little else. Given its conception of the person, it is unclear how liberalism can defend the particular boundaries of concern its own ethic of sharing must presuppose.

What egalitarian liberalism requires, but cannot within its own terms provide, is some way of defining the relevant community of sharing, some way of seeing the participants as mutually indebted and morally engaged to begin with. It needs a way of answering Emerson's challenge to the man who solicited his contribution to the poor—"Are they *my* poor?"[26] Since liberal social and economic rights cannot be justified as expressing or advancing a common life of shared pursuits, the basis and bounds of communal concern become difficult to defend. For as we have seen, the strong notion of community or membership that would save and situate the sharing is precisely the one denied to the liberal self. The moral encumbrances and antecedent obligations it implies would undercut the priority of right.

Minimalist Liberalism

If we are not the freely choosing, unencumbered selves that Kantian liberals imagine us to be, does it follow that government need not be neutral, that politics should cultivate the virtue of its citizens after all? Some political philosophers argue that the case for neutrality can be detached from the Kantian conception of the person. The case for liberalism, they argue, is political, not philosophical or metaphysical, and so does not depend on controversial claims about the nature of the self. The priority of the right over the good is not the application to politics of Kantian moral philosophy, but a practical response to the familiar fact that people in modern democratic societies typically disagree about the good. Since this defense of neutrality does not depend on a Kantian conception of the person but instead "stays on the surface, philosophically speaking," it might be described as minimalist liberalism.[27]

Minimalist liberals acknowledge that we may sometimes be claimed by moral or religious obligations unrelated to a choice. But they insist that we set these obligations aside when we enter the public realm, that we bracket our moral and religious convictions when deliberating about politics and law. In our personal lives, we may regard it as unthinkable to view ourselves "apart from certain religious, philosophical, and moral convictions, or from certain enduring attachments and loyalties." But we should draw a distinction between our personal and our political identities. However encumbered we may be in private, however claimed by moral or religious convictions, we should bracket our encumbrances in public and regard ourselves, *qua* public selves, as independent of any particular loyalties or conceptions of the good.[28]

The insistence that we separate our identity as citizens from our identity as persons gives rise to an obvious challenge. Why should our political identities not express the moral and religious convictions we affirm in our personal lives? Why, in deliberating about justice and rights, must we set aside the moral judgments that inform the rest of our lives? Minimalist liberals reply that separating our identity as citizens from our identity as persons honors an important fact about modern democratic life. In traditional societies, people sought to shape political life in the image of their own moral and religious ideals. But modern democratic societies are marked by a plurality of moral and religious ideals. Moreover, this pluralism is reasonable; it reflects the fact that, even after reasoned reflection, decent, intelligent people will come to different conceptions about the nature of the good life. Given the fact of reasonable pluralism, we should try to decide questions of justice and rights without affirming one conception of the good over others. Only in this way can we affirm the political value of social cooperation based on mutual respect.[29]

Minimalist liberalism seeks to detach liberal principles from political controversy, including debates about the nature of the self. It presents itself "not as a conception of justice that is true," but as one that can serve as a basis for political agreement in a democratic society. It asserts "the priority of democracy over philosophy." It offers a political conception of justice, not a metaphysical or philosophical one.[30]

The minimalist case for liberalism depends on the plausibility of separating politics from philosophy, of bracketing moral and religious questions where politics is concerned. But this raises the question why the practical interest in securing social cooperation and mutual respect is always so compelling as to defeat any competing moral interest that could arise from within a substantive moral or religious view. One way of assuring the priority of the practical is to deny that any of the moral or religious conceptions it brackets could be true. But this is precisely the sort of controversial metaphysical claim the minimalist liberal wants to avoid. If the liberal must therefore allow that some such conceptions might be true, then the question remains: What guarantees that no moral or religious doctrine can generate interests sufficiently compelling to burst the brackets, so to speak, and morally outweigh the practical interest in social cooperation?

Critique of Minimalist Liberalism

Minimalist liberalism lacks a convincing answer to this question. For notwithstanding the importance of political values such as toleration, social cooperation, and mutual respect, it is not always reasonable to set aside competing values that may arise from substantive moral and religious doctrines. At least where grave moral questions are concerned, whether it is reasonable to bracket moral and religious controversies for the sake of political agreement partly depends on which of the contending moral or religious doctrines is true. Minimalist liberalism wants to separate the case for toleration from any judgment about the moral worth of the practices being tolerated. But this separation is not always defensible. We cannot determine whether toleration is justified in any given case without passing moral judgment on the practice in question.

This difficulty is illustrated by two political controversies that bear on grave moral and religious questions. One is the contemporary debate about abortion rights. The other is the famous debate in 1858 between Abraham Lincoln and Stephen Douglas over popular sovereignty and slavery.[31]

THE ABORTION DEBATE

Given the intense disagreement over the moral permissibility of abortion, the case for seeking a political solution that brackets the moral and religious issues—that is neutral with respect to them—would seem especially strong. But whether it is reasonable to bracket, for political purposes, the moral and religious doctrines at stake depends largely on which of those doctrines is true. If the doctrine of the Catholic church is true, if human life in the relevant moral sense really does begin at conception, then bracketing the moral-theological question of when human life begins is far less reasonable than it would be on rival moral and religious assumptions. The more confident we are that fetuses are, in the relevant moral sense, *different* from babies, the more confident we can be in affirming a political conception of justice that

sets aside the controversy about the moral status of fetuses.

As the contemporary debate over abortion reflects, even a political conception of justice presupposes a certain view of the controversies it would bracket. For the debate about abortion is not only a debate about when human life begins, but also a debate about how reasonable it is to abstract from that question for political purposes. Opponents of abortion resist the translation from moral to political terms because they know that more of their view will be lost in the translation; the neutral territory offered by minimalist liberalism is likely to be less hospitable to their religious convictions than to those of their opponents. For defenders of abortion, little comparable is at stake; there is little difference between believing that abortion is morally permissible and agreeing that, as a political matter, women should be free to decide the moral question for themselves. The moral price of political agreement is far higher if abortion is wrong than if it is permissible. How reasonable it is to bracket the contending moral and religious views depends partly on which of those views is more plausible.

The minimalist liberal might reply that the political values of toleration and equal citizenship for women are sufficient grounds for concluding that women should be free to choose for themselves whether to have an abortion; government should not take sides on the moral and religious controversy over when human life begins. But if the Catholic church is right about the moral status of the fetus, if abortion is morally tantamount to murder, then it is not clear why the political values of toleration and women's equality, important though they are, should prevail. If the Catholic doctrine is true, then the minimalist liberal's case for the priority of political values must become an instance of just-war theory; he or she would have to show why these values should prevail even at the cost of some 1.5 million civilian deaths each year.

Of course, to suggest the impossibility of bracketing the moral-theological question of when human life begins is not to argue against a right to abortion. It is simply to show that the case for abortion rights cannot be neutral with respect to the underlying moral and religious controversy. It must engage rather than avoid the substantive moral and religious doctrines at stake. Liberals often resist this engagement because it violates the priority of the right over the good. But the abortion debate shows that this priority cannot be sustained. The case for respecting a woman's right to decide for herself whether to have an abortion depends on showing that there is a relevant moral difference between aborting a fetus at a relatively early stage of development and killing a child.

THE LINCOLN–DOUGLAS DEBATES

Perhaps the most famous case for bracketing a controversial moral question for the sake of political agreement was made by Stephen Douglas in his debates with Abraham Lincoln. Since people were bound to disagree about the morality of slavery, Douglas argued, national policy should be neutral on that question. The doctrine of popular sovereignty he defended did not judge slavery right or wrong but left the people of the territories free to make their own judgments. "To throw the weight of federal power into the scale, either in favor of the free or the slave states," would violate the fundamental principles of the constitution and run the risk of civil war. The only hope of holding the country together, he argued, was to agree to disagree, to bracket the moral controversy over slavery and respect "the right of each state and each territory to decide these questions for themselves."[32]

Lincoln argued against Douglas' case for a political conception of justice. Policy should express rather than avoid a substantive moral judgment about slavery, he maintained. Although Lincoln was not an abolitionist, he believed that government should treat slavery as the moral wrong it was and prohibit its extension to the territories. "The real issue in this controversy—pressing upon every mind—is the sentiment on the part of one class that looks upon the institution of slavery as a wrong, and of another class that does not look upon it as a wrong." Lincoln and the Republican party viewed slavery as a wrong and insisted that it "be treated as a wrong, and one of the methods of treating it as a wrong is to make provision that it shall grow no larger."[33]

Whatever his personal moral views, Douglas claimed that, for political purposes at least, he was agnostic on the question of slavery; he did not care whether slavery was "voted up or voted down." Lincoln replied that it was reasonable to bracket the question of the morality of slavery only on the assumption that it was not the moral evil he regarded it to be. Any man can advocate political neutrality "who does not see anything wrong in slavery, but no man can logically say it who does see a wrong in it; because no man can logically say he don't care whether a wrong is voted up or voted down."[34]

The debate between Lincoln and Douglas was not primarily about the morality of slavery, but about whether to bracket a moral controversy for the sake of political agreement. In this respect, their debate over popular sovereignty is analogous to the contemporary debate over abortion rights. As some contemporary liberals argue that government should not take a stand one way or another on the morality of abortion, but let each woman decide the question for herself, so Douglas argued that national policy should not take a stand one way or the other on the morality of slavery, but let each territory decide the question for itself. There is of course the difference that in the case of abortion rights, those who would bracket the substantive moral question typically leave the choice to the individual, while in the case of slavery, Douglas' way of bracketing was to leave the choice to the territories.

But Lincoln's argument against Douglas was an argument about bracketing as such, at least where grave moral questions are at stake. Lincoln's point was that the political conception of justice defended by Douglas depended for its plausibility on a particular answer to the substantive moral question it sought to bracket. Even in the face of so dire a threat to social cooperation as the prospect of civil war, it made neither moral nor political sense to aspire to political neutrality. As Lincoln concluded in his final debate with Douglas, "Is it not a false statesmanship that undertakes to build up a system of policy upon the basis of caring nothing about the very thing that every body does care the most about?"[35]

Present-day liberals will surely resist the company of Douglas and want national policy to oppose slavery, presumably on the grounds that slavery violates people's rights. But it is doubtful that liberalism conceived as a political conception of justice can make this claim without violating its own strictures against appeals to comprehensive moral ideals. For example, a Kantian liberal can oppose slavery as a failure to treat persons as ends in themselves, worthy of respect. But this argument, resting as it does on a Kantian conception of the person, is unavailable to minimalist liberalism. So too are the antislavery arguments of many American abolitionists in the 1830s and 1840s, who emphasized the sin of slavery and made their case in religious terms.

The debates over abortion and slavery show that a political conception of justice must sometimes presuppose an answer to the moral and religious questions it purports to bracket. At least where grave moral questions are at stake, it is not possible to detach politics and law from substantive moral judgment. But even in cases where it is possible to conduct political debate without reference to our moral and religious convictions, it may not always be desirable. The effort to banish moral and religious argument from the public realm for the sake of political agreement may end up impoverishing political discourse and eroding the moral and civic resources necessary to self-government.

This tendency can be seen in our present public life. With a few notable exceptions, such as the civil rights movement of the 1950s and 1960s, our political discourse in recent decades has come to reflect the liberal resolve that government be neutral on moral and religious questions, that matters of policy and law be debated and decided without reference to any particular conception of the good life. But we are beginning to find that a politics that brackets morality and religion too completely soon generates its own disenchantment. A procedural republic cannot contain the moral energies of a vital democratic life. It creates a moral void that opens the way for narrow, intolerant moralisms. And it fails to cultivate the qualities of character that equip citizens to share in self-rule.

In the chapters that follow, I try to show that the liberalism of the procedural republic provides the public philosophy by which we live. Despite its philosophical failings, it is the theory most thoroughly embodied in our practices and institutions. Now it might be thought that the very existence of the procedural republic as a sustained practice puts to rest the philosophical objections raised against it. If the neutral state succeeds in securing a scheme of rights without appealing to a sense of community beyond the social contract, if its members can exercise their agency as free citizens without seeing themselves as claimed by civic obligations beyond consent, then abstract worries about community and self-government, toleration and moral judgment, would seem at best beside the point. Either those objections are mistaken, or liberal politics is sufficiently autonomous of theory to proceed unimpaired by philosophical infirmity.

But its prevalence as practice is no proof against its poverty as theory. To the contrary, what goes wrong with the philosophy shows up in the practice. The predicament of liberal democracy in contemporary America recapitulates the tensions that inhabit its ideals. Far from proving the autonomy of liberal politics, its practice confirms what its philosophy foretells: The procedural republic cannot secure the liberty it promises, because it cannot sustain the kind of political community and civic engagement that liberty requires.

NOTES

1. See John Rawls, *A Theory of Justice* (Cambridge, Mass.: Harvard University Press, 1971); Ronald Dworkin, "Liberalism," in Stuart Hampshire, ed., *Public and Private Morality* (Cambridge: Cambridge University Press, 1978), pp. 114–143; idem, *Taking Rights Seriously* (Cambridge, Mass.: Harvard University Press,

1977); Robert Nozick, *Anarchy, State, and Utopia* (New York: Basic Books, 1977); Bruce Ackerman, *Social Justice in the Liberal State* (New Haven: Yale University Press, 1980).

2. The term "procedural republic" was suggested to me by Judith N. Shklar.

3. On the meaning of "liberal" as used in contemporary American politics, see Ronald D. Rotunda, *The Politics of Language* (Iowa City: Iowa University Press, 1986).

4. Chapters 2–4 tell the first story; Chapters 5–9 tell the second.

5. Aristotle, *The Politics*, trans. Ernest Barker, book 3, chap. 9 (London: Oxford University Press, 1946), p. 119.

6. Ibid., pp. 119–120.

7. In this section I draw on my introduction to Michael Sandel, ed., *Liberalism and Its Critics* (Oxford: Basil Blackwell, 1984), pp. 1–11.

8. John Stuart Mill, *On Liberty* (1859), chap. 1.

9. For a sampling of arguments for and against utilitarianism, see Amartya Sen and Bernard Williams, eds., *Utilitarianism and Beyond* (Cambridge: Cambridge University Press, 1982).

10. See Immanuel Kant, *Groundwork of the Metaphysics of Morals* (1785), trans. H. J. Paton (New York: Harper and Row, 1956); idem, *Critique of Practical Reason* (1788), trans. L. W. Beck (Indianapolis: Bobbs-Merrill, 1956); idem, "On the Common Saying: 'This May Be True in Theory, But It Does Not Apply in Practice,'" in *Kant's Political Writings*, ed. Hans Reiss (Cambridge: Cambridge University Press, 1970), pp. 61–92.

11. Rawls, *A Theory of Justice*, pp. 3–4.

12. Dworkin, "Liberalism," p. 136.

13. Rawls, *A Theory of Justice*, p. 560.

14. George Kateb, "Democratic Individuality and the Claims of Politics," *Political Theory*, 12 (August 1984), 343.

15. John Rawls, "Kantian Constructivism in Moral Theory," *Journal of Philosophy*, 77 (Summer 1980), 543.

16. John Rawls, "Fairness to Goodness," *Philosophical Review*, 84 (October 1985), 537.

17. Ibid.

18. Rawls, *A Theory of Justice*, p. 312, and, generally, pp. 310–315. See also Friedrich A. Hayek, *The Constitution of Liberty* (Chicago: University of Chicago Press,

1960), chap. 7; and Nozick, *Anarchy, State, and Utopia*, pp. 155–160.

19. Rawls, *A Theory of Justice*, pp. 108–117.

20. Ibid., p. 114.

21. See Michael J. Sandel, *Liberalism and the Limits of Justice* (Cambridge: Cambridge University Press, 1982), pp. 179–183.

22. Alasdair MacIntyre, *After Virtue* (Notre Dame: University of Notre Dame Press, 1981), pp. 204–206.

23. Lee quoted in Douglas Southall Freeman, *R. E. Lee* (New York: Charles Scribner's Sons, 1934), pp. 443, 421. See also the discussions of Lee in Morton Grodzins, *The Loyal and the Disloyal* (Chicago: University of Chicago Press, 1965), pp. 142–143; and Judith Shklar, *Ordinary Vices* (Cambridge, Mass.: Harvard University Press, 1984), p. 160.

24. Rawls, *A Theory of Justice*, pp. 101–102.

25. See Nozick, *Anarchy, State, and Utopia*, p. 228.

26. Ralph Waldo Emerson, "Self Reliance," in Emerson, *Essays and Lectures* (New York: Library of America, 1983), p. 262.

27. The view I describe here as minimalist liberalism is represented by John Rawls's recent book, *Political Liberalism* (New York: Columbia University Press, 1993), and his article "Justice as Fairness: Political Not Metaphysical," *Philosophy & Public Affairs*, 14 (1985), 223–251. It is also presented in a somewhat different version, in Richard Rorty, "The Priority of Democracy to Philosophy," in *The Virginia Statute for Religious Freedom*, ed. Merrill D. Peterson and Robert C. Vaughan (Cambridge: Cambridge University Press, 1988). The quotation is from Rawls, "Justice as Fairness," p. 230.

28. Rawls, *Political Liberalism*, p. 31; see generally pp. 29–35.

29. Ibid., pp. xvi–xviii.

30. Rawls, "Justice as Fairness," p. 230; Rorty, "Priority of Democracy," p. 257.

31. I draw in this discussion from Michael J. Sandel, "Political Liberalism," *Harvard Law Review*, 107 (1994), 1765–94.

32. Paul M. Angle, ed., *Created Equal? The Complete Lincoln-Douglas Debates of 1858* (Chicago: University of Chicago Press, 1958), pp. 369, 374.

33. Ibid., p. 390.

34. Ibid., p. 392.

35. Ibid., p. 389.

20   The Political and Social Structures of the Common Good

ALASDAIR MACINTYRE

WHAT ARE THE TYPES of political and social society that can embody those relationships of giving and receiving through which our individual and common goods can be achieved? They will have to satisfy three conditions. First they must afford expression to the political decision-making of independent reasoners on all those matters on which it is important that the members of a particular community be able to come through shared rational deliberation to a common mind. So there will have to be institutionalized forms of deliberation to which all those members of the community who have proposals, objections and arguments to contribute have access. And the procedures of decision-making will have to be generally acceptable, so that both deliberation and decisions are recognizable as the work of the whole.

Secondly, in a community in which just generosity is counted among the central virtues the established norms of justice will have to be consistent with the exercise of this virtue. No single simple formulation will be capable of capturing the different kinds of norm that will be necessary for different kinds of just relationship. Between independent practical reasoners the norms will have to satisfy Marx's formula for justice in a socialist society, according to which what each receives is proportionate to what each contributes. Between those capable of giving and those who are most dependent and in most need of receiving—children, the old, the disabled—the norms will have to satisfy a revised version of Marx's formula for justice in a communist society, "From each according to her or his ability, to each, so far as is possible, according to her or his needs" (*Critique of the Gotha Program,* I). Marx of course understood his second formula as having application only in an as yet unrealizable future. And we must recognize that limited economic resources allow only for its application in imperfect ways. But without its application, even if imperfectly, even if *very* imperfectly, we will be unable to sustain a way of life characterized both by effective appeals to desert and by effective appeals to need, and so by justice to and for both the independent and the dependent.

Thirdly, the political structures must make it possible both for those capable of independent practical reason and for those whose exercise of reasoning is limited or nonexistent to have a voice in communal deliberation about what these norms of justice require. And the only way in which the latter can have a voice is if there are others who are able and prepared to stand proxy for them and if the role of proxy is given a formal place in the political structures.

What I am trying to envisage then is a form of political society in which it is taken for granted that disability and dependence on others are something that all of us experience at certain times in our lives and this to unpredictable degrees, and

From Dependent Rational Animals *by Alasdair MacIntyre (University of Notre Dame Press, 1999) by permission.*

that consequently our interest in how the needs of the disabled are adequately voiced and met is not a special interest, the interest of one particular group rather than of others, but rather the interest of the whole political society, an interest that is integral to their conception of their common good. What kind of society might possess the structures necessary to achieve a common good thus conceived?

If at this point we turn for assistance to recent social and political philosophy, we will be for the most part disappointed, since with rare exceptions work in that area ignores questions about the common goods of associations and relationships that are intermediate between on the one hand the nation-state and on the other the individual and the nuclear family. Yet it is with just this intermediate area that we shall need to be concerned, since those whose relationships embody both a recognition of the independence of practical reasoners and an acknowledgment of the facts of human dependence, and for whom therefore the virtue of just generosity is a key virtue, presuppose in their activities, explicitly, or more usually implicitly, the sharing of a common good that is constitutive of a type of association that can be realized neither in the forms of the modern state nor in those of the contemporary family.

Why not? What is it about the modern state and the contemporary family that renders them incapable of providing the kind of communal association within which this type of common good can be achieved? Let me consider each in turn. Modern nation-states are governed through a series of compromises between a range of more or less conflicting economic and social interests. What weight is given to different interests varies with the political and economic bargaining power of each and with its ability to ensure that the voices of its protagonists are heard at the relevant bargaining tables. What determines both bargaining power and such ability is in key part money, money used to provide the resources to sustain political power: electoral resources, media resources, relationships to corporations. This use of money procures very different degrees and kinds

of political influence for different interests. And the outcome is that although most citizens share, although to greatly varying extents, in such public goods as those of a minimally secure order, the distribution of goods by government in no way reflects a common mind arrived at through widespread shared deliberation governed by norms of rational enquiry. Indeed the size of modern states would itself preclude this. It does not follow that relationships to the nation-state, or rather to the various agencies of government that collectively compose it, are unimportant to those who practice the politics of the virtues of acknowledged dependence. No one can avoid having some significant interest in her or his relationships to the nation-state just because of its massive resources, its coercive legal powers, and the threats that its blundering and distorted benevolence presents. But any rational relationship of the governed to the government of modern states requires individuals and groups to weigh any benefits to be derived from it against the costs of entanglement with it, at least so far as that aspect of states is concerned in which they are and present themselves as giant utility companies.

There is of course another aspect of the modern state in which it presents itself as the guardian of our values and from time to time invites us to die for it. This invitation is one issued by every ruling power that asserts its legitimate and justifiable political and legal sovereignty over its subjects. For no state can justify that assertion unless it is able to provide at least minimal security for its subjects from external aggression and from internal criminality. And the provision of such security generally requires that there be police officers, firefighters, and soldiers prepared, if need arise — and it does arise remarkably often — to give up their lives in the course of their duties. But the importance of the good of public security, although it is a good served by this admirable devotion, and although it is a good without which none of us in our various local communities could achieve our common goods, must not be allowed to obscure the fact that the shared public goods of the modern nation-state are not the common goods of a genuine nationwide community and, when the nation-state masquerades as the guardian of such a common good, the outcome is bound to be either ludicrous or disastrous or both. For the counterpart to the nation-state thus misconceived as itself a community is a misconception of its citizens as constituting a *Volk*, a type of collectivity whose bonds are simultaneously to extend to the entire body of citizens and yet to be as binding as the ties of kinship and locality. In a modern, large scale nation-state no such collectivity is possible and the pretense that it is is always an ideological disguise for sinister realities. I conclude then that insofar as the nation-state provides necessary and important public goods, these must not be confused with the type of common good for which communal recognition is required by the virtues of acknowledged dependence, and that insofar as the rhetoric of the nation-state presents it as the provider of something that is indeed, in this stronger sense, a common good, that rhetoric is a purveyor of dangerous fictions.

The virtues of acknowledged dependence and the virtues of independence require for their practice a very different kind of shared pursuit of a common good. Where the virtues of acknowledged dependence are practiced, there will have to be a common mind as to how responsibilities for and to dependent others are allocated and what standards of success or failure in discharging these responsibilities are appropriate. And, where the virtues of independent practical reasoning are practiced, such a common mind will have to emerge from shared deliberation, so that social agreement on responsibilities will not only be, but be seen to be rationally justified. Hence those who practice both sets of virtues will have a double attitude to the nation-state. They will recognize that it is an ineliminable feature of the contemporary landscape and they will not despise the resources that it affords. It may and on occasion does provide the only means for removing obstacles to humane goals and we all have reason, for example, to be very grateful indeed to those who secured the passage of the Americans with Disabilities Act and to those who have used its provi-

sions constructively and creatively. But they will also recognize that the modern state cannot provide a political framework informed by the just generosity necessary to achieve the common goods of networks of giving and receiving.

If then the nation-state cannot provide a form of association directed towards the relevant type of common good, what of the family? Families at their best are forms of association in which children are first nurtured, and then educated for and initiated into the activities of an adult world in which their parents' participatory activities provide them both with resources and models. It follows that the quality of life of a family is in key part a function of the quality of the relationships of the individual members of the family to and in a variety of other institutions and associations: workplaces, schools, parishes, sports clubs, trade union branches, adult education classes, and the like. And it is insofar as children learn to recognize and to pursue as their own, and parents and other adult members of the family continue to recognize and to pursue, the goods internal to the practices of which such associations and institutions are the milieu that the goods of family life are realized. The family flourishes only if its social environment also flourishes. And since the social environments of families vary a great deal, so do the modes of flourishing of families. All happy families are not alike and only a very great novelist could have got away with telling us otherwise. And as it is with the strengths and achievements of family life, so it is also with its weaknesses and failures. They too are inseparable from features of the social environment of the family. (I do not want to suggest by this that families cannot sometimes flourish in highly unfavorable conditions. They can and do. But, when they can and do, it is always because the family members and more especially the parents have been able to construct for that family a range of activities and opportunities that substitute for those of a more favorable social environment. So, for example, for a family living successfully in conditions of extreme isolation, perhaps a hundred miles from their nearest neighbors, the activity of workplace, of school, of parish, and of play may all become activities of the household. That household will have become a microcosm of community and not only a family. Yet this must clearly be an exceptional type of case.)

Generally and characteristically then the goods of family life are achieved in and with the goods of various types of local community. And generally and characteristically the common good of a family can only be achieved in the course of achieving the common goods of the local community of which it is a part. It is because of the family's lack of self-sufficiency that the type of common good recognition of which is required by the virtues of acknowledged dependence cannot be achieved within the family, at least insofar as the family is conceived of as a distinct and separate social unit. Yet families are of course key and indispensable constituents of local community and there are many areas of family life in which the exercise of the virtues of acknowledged dependence is called for. Indeed, as I suggested earlier, the relationships of parents to young children and of adults to their elderly parents are both paradigm cases of relationships that can be sustained only by those virtues. And so is the relationship of the able and independent members of a family to other members who are temporarily or permanently disabled and largely or wholly dependent.

Neither the state nor the family then is the form of association whose common good is to be both served and sustained by the virtues of acknowledged dependence. It must instead be some form of local community within which the activities of families, workplaces, schools, clinics, clubs dedicated to debate and clubs dedicated to games and sports, and religious congregations may all find a place. What kind of place then are those who are temporarily or permanently disabled able to have in such a community? What kind of recognition is the recognition required to sustain respect both for them and for those not disabled, as well as their self-respect? It will build upon that regard for each individual, however badly disabled, that I characterized earlier. But it will add to that regard

a recognition that each member of the community is someone from whom we may learn and may have to learn about our common good and our own good, and who always may have lessons to teach us about those goods that we will not be able to learn elsewhere. It is not primarily because others find what we achieve worthwhile that we are owed this respect. For even at those times when we are disabled so that we cannot engage in worthwhile projects we are still owed by others and we still owe to others that attentive care without which neither we nor they can learn what we have to teach each other. . . .

Political reasoning at the level of practice is not a special kind of reasoning, one distinct from ordinary practical reasoning. One cannot generally become an effective practical reasoner without becoming in some measure a political reasoner, and this for two reasons. First, because participants in networks of giving and receiving are only able to identify their individual goods in the course of identifying their common goods, and because their identification of those common goods can only be achieved by contributing to and learning from shared deliberation with those others whose common goods they are, an ability to reason practically about the common good is indispensable. But to reason together about the common good is to reason politically.

Secondly, so many of our goods, individual as well as common, are shared goods that generally my decisions about what part certain goods are to play in my life will not be and cannot be independent of our decisions about what part those goods are to play in the life of our community. I will not be able to find a place, whether a larger or smaller place, for dramatic art in my own life—as amateur or professional actor, as director or stagehand, as a member of the orchestra or the audience—in a community in which the goods of theater are not given a certain priority in the allocation of communal resources. It is in and through political decisions about these priorities that we determine the range of possibilities open for the shaping of our individual lives and, if we exclude ourselves or are excluded by others from contributing to such political decision-making, we diminish the scope and effectiveness of our decision-making.

This suggests that the account advanced so far of the prerequisites for a political community whose common good would be that of social networks of giving and receiving badly needs to be supplemented, if it is not to be misleading. For I have asked what attitudes of regard we should take to each other, whether able or disabled, if we are to satisfy the requirements of such virtues as that of just generosity, as though we could first answer that question and only then as a secondary matter enquire what kinds of political structures might give expression to such attitudes. But it now becomes clear that these attitudes of regard must be understood from the outset as political attitudes. To treat someone else as someone for whom we have a regard because of what, one way or another, they contribute to our shared education in becoming rational givers and receivers is to accord them political recognition. It is to treat them as someone whom it would be wrong to ignore or to exclude from political deliberation.

This conception of political reasoning as one aspect of everyday practical reasoning has as its counterpart a conception of political activity as one aspect of the everyday activity of every adult capable of engaging in it. The contrast is with the conception of political activity embodied in the modern state, according to which there is a small minority of the population who are to make politics their active occupation and preoccupation, professional and semiprofessional politicians, and a huge largely passive majority who are to be mobilized only at periodic intervals, for elections or national crises. Between the political elites on the one hand and the larger population on the other there are important differences, as in, for example, how much or how little information is required and provided for each. A modern electorate can only function as it does, so long as it has only a highly simplified and impoverished account of the issues that are presented to it. And the modes of presentation through which elites address electorates are designed to conceal as much as to reveal.

These are not accidental features of the politics of modern states any more than is the part that money plays in affording influence upon the decision-making process. The sometimes revolutionary struggles of the past that broke down the barriers to achieving modern citizenship—to abolish slavery, to extend the suffrage, especially to women, to secure for the labor movement defenses against capitalist exploitation and victimization—involved degrees and kinds of effective political participation that are quite as alien to the democratic forms of the politics of the contemporary state as they are to nondemocratic forms. It is not at all, as I have already stressed, that the politics of the state have become unimportant. There are numerous crucial needs of local communities that can only be met by making use of state resources and invoking the interventions of state agencies. But it is the quality of the politics of local communities that will be crucial in defining those needs adequately and in seeing to it that they are met.

It is therefore a mistake, the communitarian mistake, to attempt to infuse the politics of the state with the values and modes of participation in local community. It is a further mistake to suppose that there is anything good about local community as such. The relatively small-scale character and the face-to-face encounters and conversations of local community are necessary for the shared achievement of the common goods of those who participate in the rational deliberation needed to sustain networks of giving and receiving, but, absent the virtues of just generosity and of shared deliberation, local communities are always open to corruption by narrowness, by complacency, by prejudice against outsiders and by a whole range of other deformities, including those that arise from a cult of local community.

This is one point at which the discussion of moral and political philosophers benefit from becoming historical and sociological. We need to set side by side for comparative study examples of different types of local community, examples of such communities at their best and at their worst, and most of all examples of communities that have been or are open to alternative possibilities and that sometimes move towards the better and sometimes towards the worse. So it would be instructive to look at the history of some fishing communities in New England over the past hundred and fifty years and to examine the different ways in which at different times their virtues have enabled them to cope with the stress of adversity and with the stress of prosperity. And it would be similarly instructive to examine the history of Welsh mining communities and of a way of life informed by the ethics of work at the coal face, by a passion for the goods of choral singing and of rugby football and by the virtues of trade union struggle against first coal-owners and then the state. Such examples can be multiplied: farming cooperatives in Donegal, Mayan towns in Guatemala and Mexico, some city-states from a more distant past.

What such comparative studies will bring home to us is both the variety of social forms within which networks of giving and receiving can be institutionalized and the variety of ways in which such networks can be sustained and strengthened or weakened and destroyed. Different conditions pose different threats that in turn require different responses. Yet the tasks that have to be undertaken to meet those threats share a great deal in common. So it is, for example, with the tasks of providing for the security of a local community from internal crime or external aggression, tasks that can never safely be handed over completely to the agencies of the state. (On occasion it is the danger presented by just those agencies that has to be guarded against.) Those who perform such tasks on behalf of the community are asked by the community to be prepared, if necessary, to risk their lives, but to ask this can only be justified, if those who accept this risk can be confident that they, if disabled, or their dependents, if they die, will receive adequate care. The defense of a community whose structures are governed by norms of relatively uncalculated giving and receiving, if it is in

good order, will itself be similarly structured. Yet the forms taken by those structures will vary with the culture and the history of the community.

What extended comparative study of the varying characteristics of communities that embody networks of giving and receiving may teach us is how better to identify what relationships of the relevant kinds of giving and receiving already exist in our own local community and how perhaps to greater extent than we have realized there is already a degree of shared recognition of the common good. About such communities we will need to bear in mind three things. First, even when they are at their best, the exercise of shared deliberative rationality is always imperfect and what should impress us is not so much the mistakes made and the limitations upon its exercise at any particular stage as the ability through time and conflict to correct those mistakes and to move beyond those limitations. The exercise of practical relationships in communities always has a history and it is the direction of that history that is important.

Secondly, the politics of such communities, when they are at their best or are at least moving in the right direction, is not a politics of competing interests in the way in which the politics of the modern state is. For the basic political question is what resources each individual and group needs, if it is to make its particular contribution to the common good, and, insofar as the community is in good order, it is to the interest of all that each should be able to make its contribution. Of course because local communities are always to some degree imperfect, competing interests are always apt to emerge. And it is therefore important that, so far as is possible, communities are structured so as to limit such emergence. Economically what matters is that there should be relatively small inequalities of income or wealth. For gross inequality of income or wealth is by itself always liable to generate conflicts of interest and to obscure the possibility of understanding one's social relationships in terms of a common good.

This is of course only one example of how economic considerations will have to be subordinated to social and moral considerations, if a local community that is a network of giving and receiving is to survive, let alone thrive. There may have to be self-imposed limits to labor mobility for the sake of the continuities and the stabilities of families and other institutions. There will have to be what from an economic point of view is disproportionate investment in types of education of children that are not economically productive. Everyone, so far as is possible, will have to take their turn in performing the tedious and the dangerous jobs, in order to avoid another disruptive form of social inequality. These are of course Utopian standards, not too often realized outside Utopia, and only then, as I have already suggested, in flawed ways. But trying to live by Utopian standards is not Utopian, although it does involve a rejection of the economic goals of advanced capitalism. For the institutional forms through which such a way of life is realized, although economically various, have this in common: they do not promote economic growth and they require some significant degree of insulation from and protection from the forces generated by outside markets. Most importantly, such a society will be inimical to and in conflict with the goals of a consumer society. But to take note of this directs our attention to the extent to which these norms are to some extent already accepted in a variety of those settings—households, workplaces, schools, parishes—in which resistance to the goals and norms of a consumer society is recurrently generated. And, where such resistance is found, it is characteristically within groups whose social relationships are those of giving and receiving.

Thirdly, among the distinguishing marks of communities thus structured is the importance that they attach to the needs of children and the needs of the disabled. Partly this is a matter of the allocation of attention and other resources. Children are never able to constitute an interest group in the modern sense of that word. And what children need can rarely be adequately supplied only by their own families. They are therefore cared for adequately only when the care that they receive, although inevitably constrained by the limits of the community's resources, is not constrained by predictions about how much those children will one day give in return. And as it is with the care needed by children, so it is too with the care needed by the old and the mentally and physically infirm. What matters is not only that in this kind of community children and the disabled are objects of care and attention. It matters also and correspondingly that those who are no longer children recognize in children what they once were, that those who are not yet disabled by age recognize in the old what they are moving towards becoming, and that those who are not ill or injured recognize in the ill and injured what they often have been and will be and always may be. It matters also that these recognitions are not a source of fear. For such recognitions are a condition of adequate awareness of both the common needs and the common goods that are served by networks of giving and receiving and by the virtues, both of independence and of acknowledged dependence. Yet that awareness cannot itself be achieved without those same virtues.

21   The Liberals Strike Back

JEAN HAMPTON

Communitarianism

SINCE THE 1980s some political theorists have criticized not just particular liberal views but the entire liberal family of theories, claiming they are too focused on the individual, too focused on the importance of individual liberty, and insufficiently appreciative of the way in which human beings require a place in a well-functioning community in order to flourish. One might say that whereas liberals encourage each person to define and seek her own "good" within a political structure that defines and enforces what is "right," communitarians believe that a political structure has an important role to play in defining both the right and the good and in helping those people in that political structure to seek the good. This is because like Plato, communitarians believe human beings can achieve a good life only if they live within a well-functioning society that government must help to create (although, as I noted, communitarians, are unlike Plato, generally committed to democratic forms of government).

As their name suggests, communitarians are first and foremost concerned with *community*: They insist that each of us, as an individual, develops an identity, talents, and pursuits in life only in the context of a community. Political life, then, must start with a concern for the community (not the individual), since the community is what determines and shapes individuals' natures. One communitarian, Alasdair MacIntyre, ridicules the liberals' "autonomous moral agent" operating disconnected from any social context and argues that individuals flourish only within the context of what he calls "practices," through which individuals develop and perfect virtues. For MacIntyre, a practice is

> any coherent and complex form of socially established cooperative human activity through which goods internal to that form of activity are realized in the course of trying to achieve those standards of excellence which are appropriate to, and partially definitive of, that form of activity, with the result that human powers to achieve excellence, and human conceptions of the ends and goods involved, are systematically extended.[1]

So on this view the state's role is to help develop and protect practices that encourage the development of human excellence. Were the state to let individuals loose to realize their "autonomy" (as liberals seem to wish), treating them as if they were socially disconnected beings who are concerned with their "rights," MacIntyre and other communitarians believe that the result would be social disintegration and moral disaster. Indeed, they argue that such disintegration and degeneration have already started to occur in modern liberal states, given the prevalence of crime and violence, the breakdown of the family and drug abuse in these societies.[2]

MacIntyre's criticisms have been echoed by Charles Taylor, who attacks the plausibility of the

From Political Philosophy *by Jean Hampton. Copyright © 1996 by Westview Press. Reprinted by permission of Westview Press.*

liberals' "atomistic" conception of human beings as autonomous choosers, arguing that it treats the human being as primarily a "will" and does not acknowledge the complexities of the human personality and the fact that it is (and must be) situated in a society in order to develop.[3] These same themes have been echoed by some feminists: As Jean Bethke Elshtain has put it, "There is no way to create real communities out of an aggregate of 'freely choosing' adults."[4] Such sentiments are usually attended by dissatisfaction with the morality of rights upon which many (albeit not all) liberal theories are based.[5] Finally, certain religious thinkers have argued that liberals' reliance on individualism and reason are in reality hostile to religious belief and religious community life.[6]

Another communitarian critic of liberalism is Michael Sandel, whose work focuses on the form of liberalism exemplified by Rawls in *A Theory of Justice*. Sandel is struck by the disconnected, disembodied nature of the people in Rawls's original position. That Rawls could even conceive of people in this way shows, according to Sandel, the extent to which he and many other liberals in the past few hundred years try to understand human beings independently of all activities, desires, ideas, roles, and pursuits that characterize human lives in an actual society. But why should we think there is anything left of the person when we subtract all of this? Isn't the Rawlsian (and for that matter any liberal) view of the person woefully impoverished? Writes Sandel:

> We cannot regard ourselves as independent in this way without great cost to those loyalties and convictions whose moral force consists partly in the fact that living by them is inseparable from understanding ourselves as the particular persons we are—as members of this family or community or nation or people, as bearers of this history, as sons and daughters of that revolution, as citizens of this republic. Allegiances such as these are more than values I happen to have or aims I "espouse at any given time." They go beyond the obligations I voluntarily incur and the "natural duties" I owe to human beings as such. They allow that

to some I owe more than justice requires or even permits, not by reason of agreements I have made but instead in virtue of those more or less enduring attachments and commitments which taken together partly define the person that I am.[7]

So Sandel is saying that liberal theories fail to come to grips with the nature of our "embeddedness" in a particular time, place, and culture. Not only is this embeddedness a fact, it is also a fact that a political theory must recognize if it is going to generate laws, institutions, and practices that are genuinely good for us and constitutive of an ideal and fully just society. He calls for us to pursue justice not by working out ways that independent and separately conceived selves might profitably relate to one another (e.g., in markets or in political institutions) but by thinking about how people with attachments that partially constitute their identities can come to know and relate to one another as friends.[8] Only in this way, says Sandel, can we create a "deeper commonality" than benevolence allows, one of "shared self-understanding" as well as affection.[9]

Communitarians have also taken issue with the liberal penchant for freedom and autonomy. Communitarians insist that many adult human beings (because of illness, personality, mental impairment, or immaturity) are simply not capable of the kind of autonomous choice of life plan that liberals believe a state must respect, and they point out that even highly mature and intelligent people frequently use their freedom to make bad (sometimes dreadfully bad) choices. Does a state respect its citizen if it tries to pretend that the residual "childishness" in all of our natures simply isn't there? Does it respect people when it permits them to make choices that will clearly preclude their own future happiness (and indirectly affect the happiness of those who are connected to them)? And finally, why think that autonomy is one of the most important political values that a society must respect? (Wouldn't Plato be profoundly puzzled by the liberal penchant for liberty as a primary political value?) Aren't there other values a government must implement that are at least as important as—and maybe more important than—autonomy, such as stability, the preservation of social bonds, the preservation of culture, and the safety of its citizens? . . .[10]

Whereas liberals believe that the most important political values are freedom and equality, . . . communitarians regard other values to be as important, and perhaps more important—in particular, what might be called the "values of community life," as I have just articulated them above. Moreover, whereas liberals are committed to the idea that the state's role must be defined such that it enhances the freedom and equality of the people, meaning that it should be democratically organized, pursue policies that implement toleration and freedom of conscience for all citizens, and stay out of the individual's construction of his own life plans and "conception of the good", . . . communitarians believe the state's primary role is to ensure the health and well-being of the community life that makes possible all human flourishing and all human good. They are particularly adamant in rejecting the idea that in order to ensure human liberty the state must refrain from articulating a conception of the good to which all people must conform. Communitarians regard as a ridiculous illusion the liberal idea that we can autonomously pursue the good as individuals independent of cultural traditions and social roles; instead, they believe, in order to ensure that its citizens flourish, the ideal state must use its power and authority to encourage the continuation and health of the cultural traditions and roles through which each person must find her good life. . . .

Finally, communitarians dismiss the liberal acceptance of . . . reason as the tool by which the liberal state governs. The problem with the liberals' reliance on reason, say the communitarians, is that their conception of reason is disconnected from social traditions, operating in a vacuum (think of the reasoning in Rawls's original position) and hence unconnected to the real concerns, assumptions, goals, aspirations, and belief systems that real, socially embedded people actually have. In contrast, communitarians insist that the way to social harmony and health is through discourse that is informed by the culture of the community. We can achieve the ideal state only by engaging in discourse that is tied to the social practices that constitute and define the goals of the culture of the community.

The communitarian challenge has generated considerable response by liberals, the outlines of which I review and evaluate here. The first response liberals have made to the communitarians is: We care about communities, too! Whereas Hobbes (as we saw) was inclined to think that people were radically asocial, other liberals, including Locke, Rousseau, Kant, and, in modern times, Rawls, Gauthier, and Feinberg, have insisted on the social nature of human beings.[11] To quote Feinberg:

> Whatever else a human being is "by nature", he is essentially a social product. He is born into a family, itself part of a tribe or clan and a larger political community, each with its ongoing record or history, his first concepts shaped by a language provided for him by the larger group of which he is a member, his roles and status assigned by social custom and practice, his membership and sense of belonging imprinted from the start. He finds himself, as Alasdair MacIntyre puts it, "embedded" in a human culture not of his own original design or "contractual agreement," but one that is simply given.[12]

Such remarks endorse all sorts of communitarian ideas, yet they are made by a liberal who obviously feels that an enthusiastic endorsement of human sociality in no way threatens liberal political theory. Indeed, much of the liberal interest in allowing individuals to pursue their own conception of the good comes from their view that individuals should be able (and need to be able) to develop or pursue social connections—especially of a religious nature—that they take to be vital to their well-being and identity without being in any way impeded by government.

So both groups care about communities and acknowledge the sociality of human nature. What really differentiates them is their different views of state power: Whereas communitarians want the state to use its power to protect and encourage the development of communities and community values, liberals want the state to stay out of community life, so as not to harm, threaten, or limit those who are participating in it. This way of putting their disagreement shows that liberals and communitarians have very different views of the dangers, advantages, and consequences of state power. Whereas communitarians "seem to assume that whatever is properly social must become the province of the political,"[13] liberals want to limit the state's role in this province since they distrust it, fear its effects, and have faith in the ability of social groups to flourish without its help.

There are at least two reasons for the liberals' concern to limit the state's responsiveness to and interference in community life. The first reason has to do with the liberal commitment to the value of human autonomy. It is really this value that is driving the liberals' concern for the individual, and not some sort of implausible theory of the person as a socially naked atom. Again, to quote Feinberg: "The liberal can give up the excesses of individualism, acknowledge the social nature of man, and still hold on to what is essential in his normative theory, the doctrine of the human right of autonomous self-government within the private sphere."[14] The liberal is convinced that the best way to ensure that an individual can flourish within the community is to give her the freedom she needs to live (what will surely be) a highly social life in the way that she chooses.

The second reason arises from the liberals' deep distrust of state power and authority. Judith Shklar has argued that this distrust was born in the early modern period, in the midst of Calvinist proclamations of the innate sinfulness of the human soul, misanthropic writings of men of letters such as Michel de Montaigne, and grim experiences with the abusiveness and cruelty of state power and authority.[15] The lesson learned by the early moderns, whose thinking provides . . . the foundation for modern liberals, is that no human being can be counted upon to be "good enough" not to abuse extensive state power and authority. (As the saying goes, power corrupts and absolute power corrupts absolutely. . . . Hence in order to ensure that individuals will not be harmed in their pursuits—pursuits that (particularly when they concern religion) are generally highly social—liberals have insisted on constraining state power and authority in order to protect those subject to it from being abused by it.

Communitarians, in contrast, have been influenced by different thinkers and different historical experiences in ways that have given them a far more benign view of state power. They tend to agree, for example, with the nineteenth-century German philosopher G. W. F. Hegel, who considered the state "the actuality of the ethical idea"[16]—that is, that aspect of society which articulates and maintains the conditions for moral life in a society, drawing from the social traditions that compose it. They are also influenced by the way in which many modern states appear to have successfully taken on all sorts of moral roles, including the provision of education, health care, and art (supporting dramatic arts, fine arts, literature, music); the responsibility for caring for the poor; even the moral improvement of the citizenry (through programs designed to improve their mental health and social functioning). Those liberals who reject these Hegelian sentiments are either hostile to many of the moral roles Hegelians would have the state play or are concerned to limit them, lest the state's power and authority get out of control and compromise the liberty of the people.

Liberals and communitarians, however, disagree not only about the benignity of state authority and power but also about the benignity of culture. Consider that the communitarian sees the state as playing a moral role that is responsive to and at least partly defined by the traditions and moral views of the cultural traditions of the society it governs. But in many ways liberals have been just as suspicious of cultures as they have been of governments—and with good reason. For example, the American cultural experience has been sexist, racist, and antihomosexual. It has also been strongly influenced by a variety of philosophical traditions, ethnic groups, and religions. Were a U.S. government to rule in a way that was responsive to any one of these elements in American cultural life, many other groups would be subject to state power that enforced ideas they would regard as discordant with or antithetical to their beliefs and interests. So if communitarians would have the state respond to "social roles" and "community values," how can they ensure that when it does so, it will not, say, compromise religious liberty or enact laws that reflect the prejudices of a majority against a minority? Why couldn't either use of state power and authority endanger not only the liberty and equality of certain people but also their very well-being? As one liberal critic of communitarianism puts it:

> The communitarian critics [of liberalism] want us to live in Salem, but not to believe in witches. Or human rights. Perhaps the Moral Majority would cease to be a threat were the United States a communitarian society; benevolence and fraternity might take the place of justice. Almost anything is possible, but it does not make moral sense to leave liberal politics behind on the strength of such speculation.[17]

Such worries show that to persuade the liberal opposition, communitarians can't simply hope for the best. They need to develop their theory so that it can show us how we can take a morally critical attitude toward community, even while recognizing the importance of community. Otherwise, their theory gives them no critical moral distance from existing social practices, which means that it could be used to license any abuse, injustice, and cruelty implicit in the community's culture.

Liberals influenced by those early modern thinkers who were impressed by the human capacity for cruelty have been very willing to recognize the way in which human beings and human social institutions can be morally corrupted and abusive. It is, I believe, for this reason that in their argumentation liberals start from the individual. By insisting that the individual is the focus of moral concern, the liberal gets the critical moral distance from community and the government that the communitarian lacks. In particular, by requiring that social arrangements are to work to the benefit of each person, the liberal has a way of recommending political policies that are not indebted to potentially cruel or unjust cultural practices of that community. This means liberal arguments start from the individual, not because they deny the sociality of human beings, but because they require that *all* social arrangements, to be morally acceptable, must be morally acceptable from the individual standpoint.

Hence liberalism has implicit within it a kind of critical facility for judging cultures that communitarianism appears to be lacking. Perhaps the best example of this is Rawls's original position procedure: That procedure, contra some communitarians, doesn't deny human sociality. Instead, quite the opposite is true—it affirms the extent to which our lives are influenced by a variety of social structures. The point of the original position procedure is to give us a way of *morally evaluating those social structures* or, in other words, a moral vantage point from which to reliably assess and evaluate social structures (what Rawls calls an "Archimedian point").[18] The original position is a moral standpoint from which we attempt to assess the effects of a social practice on *every* member of society by freeing ourselves of beliefs, biases, and traditions that can prejudice that assessment. A social practice is easy to affirm if one uses the ideas generated by that practice to do so; the trick is to figure out a way of freeing oneself of the effects of a practice (which might be racist or sexist or in some other way unjust) so that one can come up with an effective moral assessment of it.

Indeed, this sort of "freeing" is what Rawls's original position procedure aims to do. Communitarians have attacked that procedure, . . . contending that it implicitly denies our thoroughly social natures. But is each of us *entirely* a product of the confluence of social forces on her biological nature? Can none of us critically assess the social forces to which we have been subject, because each of us is so completely a product of those forces that anything we would use to assess those forces would itself be generated by them? To say yes to this question is to raise an interesting (and chilling) possibility: If such complete social definition of human beings were possible, could not a government learn to control these social forces so effectively that it could design a society in which some individuals were socially constructed so as to be contented subordinates (happy "socialized" slaves), while other individuals were socially constructed to be fully comfortable in their role as superiors (happy "socialized" masters)?

If one answers no to this last question, one is postulating that there is something in individuals that will inevitably object to and fight social "definition" that attempts to oppress and subordinate them. It is this "something" that Rawls attempts to isolate in his original position procedure: The veil of ignorance, he says, tries to isolate each individual's "moral conception"—that is, that aspect of our personhood that is the source of our moral evaluations not only of individuals (including ourselves) but also of societies, cultures, and governments. Whether or not Rawls succeeds in defining this moral component of individuals is arguable, but it would seem that communitarians must recognize such a component if they are to construct a way of morally assessing cultures. And doing so would seem to require them to take individuals, rather than social groups, as the foundational moral concern of all well-ordered societies, because social groups can be as much the source of the abuse of individuals as they are the source of roles that contribute to their happiness.

Still, communitarians can insist that even if they have trouble formulating a critical stance toward the community, liberalism has trouble formulating a way to respect and use (what might be called) the "moral wisdom" implicit in that community. If one's political theorizing is too individualistic and fails to focus on the community, it can fail to acknowledge that all sorts of social structures in our society, including our legal institutions, family structures, and systems of educating the young, have been worked out by generations of people responding to a variety of problems in ways that are complicated, nuanced, and often highly successful. One argument in favor of communitariansim . . . is that it encourages us to respect the moral wisdom implicit in these social structures and not to adopt the hubristic attitude

that any one of us could do better by reasoning about these social structures by ourselves. This argument for communitarianism therefore links it with philosophical conservatism, a position associated with the writings of Edmund Burke (1729–1797).[19] An important political figure and member of the British Parliament, Burke argued that a society is ill advised to try to govern itself by relying on abstract reasoning, because such reasoning cannot compete with the accumulated wisdom of generations of people struggling with highly complicated issues in various areas. How can a single individual, for example, generate an adequate code of criminal conduct simply by using her reason? Moreover, Burke argued that custom, human sentiments, and the lessons we learn from experience are as important as reason in giving us the tools to construct a well-functioning political society. (These themes are also present in the novels of George Eliot, who criticized certain zealous attempts at reform in the nineteenth century by people who had no respect for the moral life of the community.[20])

As we have seen, liberals such as Feinberg have also been persuaded of the importance of respect for custom and community life and have sought to incorporate such respect in their theories. Still, these liberals are committed to assessing these commitments by reference to a reason-based theory of what is good for, or owed to, individuals. Such liberals will surely want to know how communitarians can assess and criticize the status quo in their society unless they rely upon some such reason-based individualistic theory. Thus far, communitarians have not yet developed a way of supplementing their respect for custom and culture with a fully worked out theory of how we are to critically assess custom and culture.

Liberals have other arguments against the communitarian position. For example, they can object to the way such a position seems to license a paternalistic attitude toward the citizenry. That is, rather than respecting individual pursuits of the good, the communitarian state seems to be licensed to dismiss them as "wrong" in the way that a parent may dismiss a child's pursuits as wrong.

They can also contend that communitarianism rests on the wildly implausible idea that governmental officials know better than those whom they rule what counts as the good in life. Unless a group of Platonic guardians turns up among us, liberals would insist that state officials as a group are no wiser about what ought to be pursued in life than any other group of human beings and thus should not be allowed to use the state's power to insist that *their* view of the good be accepted. Such sentiments may also be related to the liberals' commitment to the Jeffersonian idea that truth is something each individual must seek for herself if she is to be rightly related to it and effectively incorporate it into her own life, so that it cannot be foisted upon her by culture or society.[21]

These liberal responses to communitarianism, while compelling, do not refute the communitarian view completely, but they do show that communitarians have more work to do in order to develop their theory effectively: In particular, they must defend their trust of government power to pursue the good, and they must develop a way of achieving critical moral distance from the communities they would have the government respect so that this "respect" does not end up encouraging any oppression, subordination, and abuse that has been part of that culture's traditions.

NOTES

1. See Alasdair MacIntyre, *After Virtue* (Notre Dame: University of Notre Dame Press, 1981), p. 187; see also chaps. 5 and 6, where MacIntyre argues for the failure of moral theories of the sort that undergird liberalism.

2. For an argument that uses communitarian ideas to attack the effect of current liberal ideas on university education, see Allan Bloom, *The Closing of the American Mind* (New York: Simon and Schuster, 1987).

3. These views are put forward in a series of essays assembled in Taylor's *Philosophical Papers* (Cambridge; Cambridge University Press, 1985). Note that communitarians such as Taylor and Michael Sandel also object to liberalism because of what they take to be its advocacy of the neutral state; for example, see Sandel's "Morality and the Liberal Ideal," *New Republic,* May 7, 1984, and Taylor's "Alternative Futures: Legitimacy, Identity and Alienation in Late Twentieth Century

Canada," in Alan Cairns and Cynthia Williams, eds., *Constitutionalism, Citizenship and Society in Canada* (Toronto Press, 1986). However, that is to object to only one *form* of liberalism. As my discussion in the previous section shows, there are nonneutral forms of liberalism that advocate a moral role for the liberal state, such as rights-based liberalism and perfectionist liberalism, and neither Sandel's nor Taylor's attack on neutrality refutes these forms of liberal theory.

4. Jean Bethke Elshtain, "Family, Feminism and Community," *Dissent* 29 (Fall 1982): 442. See also Elshtain's *Public Man, Private Woman* (Princeton University Press, 1981.)

5. See MacIntyre, *After Virtue,* p. 67.

6. For a discussion of whether or not religious life and liberalism are in conflict, see William Galston, *Liberal Purposes: Goods, Virtues and Diversity in the Liberal State* (Cambridge: Cambridge University Press, 1991), chap. 12.

7. Michael J. Sandel, *Liberalism and the Limits of Justice* (Cambridge: Cambridge University Press, 1982), p. 179.

8. Ibid., p. 181.

9. Ibid., p. 182.

10. For a discussion of some of these objections, see Will Kymlicka, *Contemporary Political Philosophy: An Introduction* (Oxford: Clarendon Press, 1990), pp. 199–207. Kymlicka also discusses some communitarians' objections to some liberals' view of the autonomous self as "empty"; see ibid., pp. 208–209.

11. I have already discussed Rawls's insistence on the social construction of human beings as a motivation for constructing the original position procedure, which tries to give us a vantage point from which we can assess that social construction. See the section on Rawls in Chapter 4. Gauthier's commitment to our sociality comes out not only in his book *Morals by Agreement* (Oxford: Oxford University Press, 1986) but also in a very interesting essay, "The Social Contract as ideology," *Philosophy and Public Affairs* 6, 2 (1977): 130–164. For a discussion of the way in which liberals are able to accommodate the sociality of persons, see Kymlicka, *Contemporary Political Philosophy,* pp. 216–230.

12. Feinberg, *Harmless Wrongdoing,* p. 83.

13. Kymlicka, *Contemporary Political Philosophy,* p. 222.

14. Feinberg, *Harmless Wrongdoing,* p. 84.

15. See Judith Shklar, *Ordinary Vices* (Cambridge: Harvard University Press, 1984).

16. G. W. F. Hegel, *The Philosophy of Right,* trans. T. M. Knox (London: Oxford University Press, 1976), sec. 257, p. 155.

17. Amy Gutmann, "Communitarian Critics of Liberalism," *Philosophy and Public Affairs* 14, 3 (Summer 1985): 319.

18. Rawls, *A Theory of Justice*, pp. 260–263.

19. Burke's most famous political works include *Reflections on the Revolution in France* (1790) and *A Philosophical Enquiry into the Origin of Our Ideas of the Sublime and the Beautiful*. These and other political works are available in Edmund Burke, *Reflections on the Revolution in France* (Harmondsworth: Penguin, 1969).

20. But Eliot did believe that her society needed reform, and she had respect for those reformers who were not contemptuous of custom. Both respect for and Burkian concern about reformist zeal are present in her masterpiece, *Middlemarch*.

21. Jefferson maintains that one reason there must be freedom of religion in an ideal political society is that coercion is useless in bringing a person to religious truth "Constraint may make him worse by making him a hypocrite, but it will never make him a truer man." See Jefferson, "Query XVII: Religion," p. 159. Later in the same essay Jefferson makes the very Millian argument that a diversity of opinion in religious matters is good for society and for each individual in it. See ibid., pp. 160 f.

Part VI

Feminist Justice

22   The Subjection of Women

JOHN STUART MILL

THE OBJECT OF THIS ESSAY is to explain as clearly as I am able, the grounds of an opinion which I have held from the very earliest period when I had formed any opinions at all on social or political matters, and which, instead of being weakened or modified, has been constantly growing stronger by the progress of reflection and the experience of life: That the principle which regulates the existing social relations between the two sexes—the legal subordination of one sex to the other—is wrong in itself, and now one of the chief hindrances to human improvements; and that it ought to be replaced by a principle of perfect equality, admitting no power or privilege on the one side, nor disability on the other.

The very words necessary to express the task I have undertaken, show how arduous it is. But it would be a mistake to suppose that the difficulty of the case must lie in the insufficiency or obscurity of the grounds of reason on which my conviction rests. The difficulty is that which exists in all cases in which there is a mass of feeling to be contended against. So long as an opinion is strongly rooted in the feelings, it gains rather than loses in stability by having a preponderating weight of argument against it. For if it were accepted as a result of argument, the refutation of the argument might shake the solidity of the conviction; but when it rests solely on feeling, the worse it fares in argumentative contest, the more persuaded its adherents are that their feeling must have some deeper grounds, which the arguments do not reach; and while the feeling remains, it is always throwing up fresh intrenchments of argument to repair any breach made in the old. And there are so many causes tending to make the feelings connected with this subject the most intense and most deeply rooted of all those which gather round and protect old institutions and customs, that we need not wonder to find them as yet less undermined and loosened than any of the rest by the progress of the great modern spiritual and social transition; nor suppose that the barbarisms to which men cling longest must be less barbarisms than those which they earlier shake off. . . .

In the first place, the opinion in favour of the present system, which entirely subordinates the weaker sex to the stronger, rests upon theory only; for there never has been trial made of any other; so that experience, in the sense in which it is vulgarly opposed to theory, cannot be pretended to have pronounced any verdict. And in the second place, the adoption of this system of inequality never was the result of deliberation, or forethought, or any social ideas, or any notion whatever of what conduced to the benefit of humanity or the good order of society. It arose simply from the fact that from the very earliest twilight of human society, every woman (owing to the value attached to her by men, combined with her inferiority in muscular strength) was found in a state of bondage to some man. Laws and systems of polity always begin by recognising the relations they find already existing between individuals. They con-

From The Subjection of Women, *Chap. 1. First published in 1869.*

vert what was a mere physical fact into a legal right, give it the sanction of society, and principally aim at the substitution of public and organized means of asserting and protecting these rights, instead of the irregular and lawless conflict of physical strength. Those who had already been compelled to obedience became in this manner legally bound to it. Slavery, from being a mere affair of force between the master and the slave, became regularized and a matter of compact among the masters, who, binding themselves to one another for common protection, guaranteed by their collective strength the private possessions of each, including his slaves. In early times, the great majority of the male sex were slaves, as well as the whole of the female. And many ages elapsed, some of them ages of high cultivation, before any thinker was bold enough to question the rightfulness and absolute social necessity, either of the one slavery or of the other. . . .

If people are mostly so little aware how completely, during the greater part of the duration of our species, the law of force was the avowed rule of general conduct—any other being only a special and exceptional consequence of peculiarities—and from how very recent a date it is that the affairs of society in general have been even pretended to be regulated according to any moral law, as little do people remember or consider how institutions and customs, which never had any ground but the law of force, last on into ages and states of general opinion which never would have permitted their first establishment. Less than forty years ago, Englishmen might still by law hold human beings in bondage as saleable property; within the present century they might kidnap them and carry them off, and work them literally to death. This absolutely extreme case of the law of force, condemned by those who can tolerate almost every other form of arbitrary power, and which, of all others, presents features the most revolting to the feelings of all who look at it from an impartial position, was the law of civilized and Christian England within the memory of persons now living: and in one half of Anglo-Saxon Amer-

ica three or four years ago, not only did slavery exist, but the slave trade, and the breeding of slaves expressly for it, was a general practice between slave states. Yet not only was there a greater strength of sentiment against it, but, in England at least a less amount either of feeling or of interest in favour of it, than of any other of the customary abuses of force: for its motive was the love of gain, unmixed and undisguised; and those who profited by it were a very small numerical fraction of the country, while the natural feeling of all who were not personally interested in it, was unmitigated abhorrence. So extreme an instance makes it almost superfluous to refer to any other; but consider the long duration of absolute monarchy. In England at present it is the almost universal conviction that military despotism is a case of the law of force, having no other origin or justification. Yet in all the great nations of Europe except England it either still exists, or has only just ceased to exist, and has even now a strong party favourable to it in all ranks of the people, especially among persons of station and consequence. Such is the power of an established system, even when far from universal, when not only in almost every period of history there have been great and well-known examples of the contrary system, but these have almost invariably been afforded by the most illustrious and most prosperous communities. In this case, too, the possessor of the undue power, the person directly interested in it, is only one person, while those who are subject to it and suffer from it are literally all the rest. The yoke is naturally and necessarily humiliating to all persons, except the one who is on the throne, together with, at most, the one who expects to succeed to it. How different are these cases from that of the power of men over women! I am not now prejudging the question of its justifiableness. I am showing how vastly more permanent it could not but be, even if not justifiable, than these other dominations which have nevertheless lasted down to our own time. Whatever gratification of pride there is in the possession of power, and whatever personal interest in its exercise, is in this case not confined to a limited class, but common to the whole male sex. Instead of being, to most of its supporters, a thing desirable chiefly in the abstract, or, like the political ends usually contended for by factions, of little private importance to any but the leaders, it comes home to the person and hearth of every male head of a family, and of every one who looks forward to being so. The clodhopper exercises, or is to exercise, his share of the power equally with the highest nobleman. And the case is that in which the desire of power is the strongest: for every one who desires power, desires it most over those who are nearest to him with whom his life is passed, with whom he has most concerns in common, and in whom any independence of his authority is oftenest likely to interfere with his individual preferences. If, in the other cases specified, power manifestly grounded only on force, and having so much less to support them, are so slowly and with so much difficulty got rid of, much more must it be so with this, even if it rests on no better foundation than those. We must consider, too, that the possessors of the power have facilities in this case, greater than in any other, to prevent any uprising against it. Every one of the subjects lives under the very eye, and almost, it may be said, in the hands, of some of the masters—in closer intimacy with him than with any of her fellow-subjects—with no means of combining against him, no power of even locally overmastering him, and, on the other hand, with the strongest motives for seeking his favour and avoiding to give him offence. In struggles for political emancipation, everybody knows how often its champions are bought off by bribes, or daunted by terrors. In the case of women, each individual of the subject-class is in a chronic state of bribery and intimidation combined. In setting up the standard of resistance, a large number of the leaders, and still more of the followers, must make an almost complete sacrifice of the pleasures or the alleviations of their own individual lot. If ever any system of privilege and enforced subjection had its yoke tightly riveted on the necks of those who are kept down by it, this has. . . .

All causes, social and natural, combine to make it unlikely that women should be collectively rebellious to the power of men. They are so far in a position different from all other subject classes, that their masters require something more from them than actual service. Men do not want solely the obedience of women, they want their sentiments. All men, except the most brutish, desire to have in the woman most nearly connected with them, not a forced slave but a willing one, not a slave merely, but a favourite. They have therefore put everything in practice to enslave their minds. The masters of all other slaves rely, for maintaining obedience, on fear; either fear of themselves, or religious fears. The masters of women wanted more than simple obedience, and they turned the whole force of education to effect their purpose. All women are bought up from the very earliest years in the belief that their ideal of character is the very opposite to that of men; not self-will, and government by self-control, but submission, and yielding to the control of others. All the moralities tell them that it is the duty of women, and all the current sentimentalities that it is their nature, to live for others; to make complete abnegation of themselves, and to have no life but in their affections. And by their affections are meant the only ones they are allowed to have—those to the men with whom they are connected, or to the children who constitute an additional and indefeasible tie between them and a man. When we put together three things—first, the natural attraction between opposite sexes; secondly, the wife's entire dependence on the husband, every privilege or pleasure she has being either his gift, or depending entirely on his will; and lastly, that the principal object of human pursuit, consideration, and all objects of social ambition, can in general be sought or obtained by her only through him, it would be a miracle if the object of being attractive to men had not become the polar star of feminine education and formation of character. And, this great means of influence over the minds of women having been acquired, an instinct of selfishness made men avail themselves of it to the utmost as a means of holding women in subjection, by representing to them meekness, submissiveness, and resignation of all individual will into the hands of a man, as an essential part of sexual attractiveness. Can it be doubted that any other yokes which mankind have succeeded in breaking, would have subsisted till now if the same means had existed, and had been as sedulously used, to bow down their minds to it? If it had been made the object of the life of every young plebeian to find personal favour in the eyes of some patrician, of every young serf with some seigneur; if domestication with him, and a share of his personal affections, had been held out as the prize which they all should look out for, the most gifted and aspiring being able to reckon on the most desirable prizes; and if, when this prize had been obtained, they had been shut out by a wall of brass from all interests not centering in him, all feelings and desires but those which he shared or inculcated; would not serfs and seigneurs, plebeians and patricians, have been as broadly distinguished at this day as men and women are? and would not all but a thinker here and there, have believed the distinction to be a fundamental and unalterable fact in human nature?

The preceding considerations are amply sufficient to show that custom, however universal it may be, affords in this case no presumption, and ought not to create any prejudice, in favour of the arrangements which place women in social and political subjection to men. But I may go farther, and maintain that the course of history, and the tendencies of progressive human society, afford not only no presumption in favour of this system of inequality of rights, but a strong one against it; and that, so far as the whole course of human improvement up to this time, the whole stream of modern tendencies, warrants any inference on the subject, it is, that this relic of the past is discordant with the future, and must necessarily disappear.

For, what is the peculiar character of the modern world—the difference which chiefly distinguishes modern institutions, modern social ideas, modern life itself, from those of times long past? It is, that human beings are no longer born to

their place in life, and chained down by an inexorable bond to the place they are born to, but are free to employ their faculties, and such favourable chances as offer, to achieve the lot which may appear to them most desirable. Human society of old was constituted on a very different principle. All were born to a fixed social position, were mostly kept in it by law, or interdicted from any means by which they could emerge from it. As some men are born white and others black, so some were born slaves and others freemen and citizens; some were born patricians, others plebeians; some were born feudal nobles, others commoners and *roturiers*. A slave or serf could never make himself free, nor, except by the will of his master, become so. In most European countries it was not till towards the close of the middle ages, and as a consequence of the growth of regal power, that commoners could be ennobled. Even among nobles, the eldest son was born the exclusive heir to the paternal possessions, and a long time elapsed before it was fully established that the father could disinherit him. Among the industrious classes, only those who were born members of a guild, or were admitted into it by its members, could lawfully practise their calling within its local limits; and nobody could practise any calling deemed important, in any but the legal manner—by processes authoritatively prescribed. Manufacturers have stood in the pillory for presuming to carry on their business by new and improved methods. In modern Europe, and most in those parts of it which have participated most largely in all other modern improvements, diametrically opposite doctrines now prevail. Law and government do not undertake to prescribe by whom any social or industrial operation shall or shall not be conducted, or what modes of conducting them shall be lawful. These things are left to the unfettered choice of individuals. Even the laws which required that workmen should serve an apprenticeship, have in this country been repealed: there being ample assurance that in all cases in which an apprenticeship is necessary, its necessity will suffice to enforce it. The old theory was, that the least possible should be left to the choice of the individual agent; that all he had to do should, as far as practicable, be laid down for him by superior wisdom. Left to himself he was sure to go wrong. The modern conviction, the fruit of a thousand years of experience is, that things in which the individual is the person directly interested, never go right but as they are left to his own discretion; and that any regulation of them by authority, except to protect the rights of others, is sure to be mischievous. This conclusion, slowly arrived at, and not adopted until almost every possible application of the contrary theory had been made with disastrous result, now (in the industrial department) prevails universally in the most advanced countries, almost universally in all that have pretensions to any sort of advancement. It is not that all processes are supposed to be equally good, or all persons to be equally qualified for everything; but that freedom of individual choice is now known to be the only thing which procures the adoption of the best processes, and throws each operation into the hands of those who are best qualified for it. Nobody thinks it necessary to make a law that only a strong-armed man shall be a blacksmith. Freedom and competition suffice to make blacksmiths strong-armed men, because the weak-armed can earn more by engaging in occupations for which they are more fit. In consonance with this doctrine, it is felt to be an overstepping of the proper bounds of authority to fit beforehand, on some general presumption, that certain persons are not fit to do certain things. It is now thoroughly known and admitted that if some such presumptions exist, no such presumption is infallible. Even if it be well grounded in a majority of cases, which it is very likely not to be, there will be a minority of exceptional cases in which it does not hold; and in those it is both an injustice to the individuals, and a detriment to society, to place barriers in the way of their using their faculties for their own benefit and for that of others. In the cases, on the other hand, in which the unfitness is real, the ordinary motives of human conduct will on the whole suffice to prevent the incompetent

person from making, or from persisting in, the attempt.

If this general principle of social and economical science is not true; if individuals, with such help as they can derive from the opinion of those who know them, are not better judges than the law and the government, of their own capacities and vocation; the world cannot too soon abandon this principle, and return to the old system of regulations and disabilities. But if the principle is true, we ought to act as if we believed it, and not to ordain that to be born a girl instead of a boy, and more than to be born black instead of white, or a commoner instead of a nobleman, shall decide the person's position through all life—shall interdict people from all the more elevated social positions, and from all, except a few, respectable occupations. Even were we to admit the utmost that is ever pretended as to the superior fitness of men for all the functions now reserved to them, the same argument applies which forbids a legal qualification for members of Parliament. If only once in a dozen years the conditions of eligibility exclude a fit person, there is a real loss, while the exclusion of thousands of unfit persons is no gain; for if the constitution of the electoral body disposes them to choose unfit persons, there are always plenty of such persons to choose from. In all things of any difficulty and importance, those who can do them well are fewer than the need, even with the most unrestricted latitude of choice; and any limitation of the field of selection deprives society of some chances of being served by the competent, without ever saving it from the incompetent.

At present, in the more improved countries, the disabilities of women are the only case, save one, in which laws and institutions take persons at their birth, and ordain that they shall never in all their lives be allowed to compete for certain things. . . .

The social subordination of women thus stands out an isolated fact in modern social institutions; a solitary breach of what has become their fundamental law; a single relic of an old world of thought and practice exploded in everything else, but retained in the one thing of most universal interest. . . .

The least that can be demanded is, that the question should not be considered as prejudged by existing fact and existing opinion, but open to discussion on its merits, as a question of justice and expediency; the decision on this, as on any of the other social arrangements of mankind, depending on what an enlightened estimate of tendencies and consequences may show to be most advantageous to humanity in general, without distinction of sex. And the discussion must be a real discussion descending to foundations, and not resting satisfied with vague and general assertions. It will not do, for instance, to assert in general terms, that the experience of mankind has pronounced in favour of the existing system. Experience cannot possibly have decided between two courses, so long as there has only been experience of one. If it be said that the doctrine of the equality of the sexes rests only on theory, it must be remembered that the contrary doctrine also has only theory to rest upon. All that is proved in its favour by direct experience, is that mankind have been able to exist under it, and to attain the degree of improvement and prosperity which we now see; but whether that prosperity has been attained sooner, or is now greater, than it would have been under the other system, experience does not say. On the other hand, experience does say, that every step in improvement has been so invariably accompanied by a step made in raising the social position of women, that historians and philosophers have been led to adopt their elevation or debasement as on the whole the surest test and most correct measure of the civilization of a people or an age. Through all the progressive period of human history, the condition of women has been approaching nearer to equality with men. This does not of itself prove that the assimilation must go on to complete equality; but it assuredly affords some presumption that such is the case.

Neither does it avail anything to say that the *nature* of the two sexes adapts them to their present functions and position, and renders these appropriate to them. Standing on the ground of common sense and the constitutions of the human mind, I deny that any one knows, or can know, the nature of the two sexes, as long as they have only been seen in their present relation to one another. If men had ever been found in society without women, or women without men, or if there had been a society of men and women in which the women were not under the control of the men, something might have been positively known about the mental and moral differences which may be inherent in the nature of each. What is now called the nature of women is an eminently artificial thing—the result of forced repression in some directions, unnatural stimulation in others. It may be asserted without scruple, that no other class of dependents have had their character so entirely distorted from its natural proportions by their relation with their masters; for, if conquered and slave races have been, in some respects, more forcibly repressed, whatever in them has not been crushed down by an iron heel has generally been let alone, and if left with any liberty of development, it has developed itself according to its own laws; but in the case of women, a hot-house and stove cultivation has always been carried on of some of the capabilities of their nature, for the benefit and pleasure of their masters. . . .

Hence, in regard to that most difficult question, what are the natural differences between the two sexes—a subject on which it is impossible in the present state of society to obtain complete and correct knowledge—while almost everybody dogmatizes upon it, almost all neglect and make light of the only means by which any partial insight can be obtained into it. This is, an analytic study of the most important department of psychology, the laws of the influence of circumstances on character. For, however great and apparently ineradicable the moral and intellectual differences between men and women might be, the evidence of their being natural differences could only be negative. Those only could be inferred to be natural which could not possibly be artificial—the residuum, after deducting every characteristic of either sex which can admit of being explained from education or external circumstances. The profoundest knowledge of the laws of the formation of character is indispensable to entitle any one to affirm even that there is any difference, much more what the difference is, between the two sexes considered as moral and rational beings; and since no one, as yet, has the knowledge, (for there is hardly any subject which, in proportion to its importance, has been so little studied), no one is thus far entitled to any positive opinion on the subject. Conjectures are all that can at present be made; conjectures more or less probable, according as more or less authorized by such knowledge as we yet have of the laws of psychology, as applied to the formation of character.

Even the preliminary knowledge, what the differences between the sexes now are, apart from all questions as to how they are made what they are, is still in the crudest and most incomplete state. . . .

One thing we may be certain of—that what is contrary to women's nature to do, they never will be made to do by simply giving their nature free play. The anxiety of mankind to interfere in behalf of nature, for fear lest nature should not succeed in effecting its purpose, is an altogether necessary solicitude. What women by nature cannot do, it is quite superfluous to forbid them from doing. What they can do, but not so well as the men who are their competitors, competition suffices to exclude them from, since nobody asks for protective duties and bounties in favour of women; it is only asked that the present bounties and protective duties in favour of men should be recalled. If women have a greater natural inclination for some things than for others, there is no need of laws or social inculcation to make the majority of them do the former in preference to the latter. Whatever women's services are most wanted for, the free play of competition will hold out the strongest inducements to them to undertake. And, as the words imply, they are most wanted for the things for which they are most fit; by the apportionment of which to them, the collective faculties of the two sexes can be applied on the whole with greatest sum of valuable result.

The general opinion of men is supposed to be, that the natural vocation of a woman is that of a wife and mother. I say, is supposed to be, because, judging from acts—from the whole of the present constitution of society—one might infer that their opinion was the direct contrary. They might be supposed to think that the alleged natural vocation of women was of all things the most repugnant to their nature; insomuch that if they are free to do anything else—if any other means of living, or occupation of their time and faculties, is open, which has any chance of appearing desirable to them—there will not be enough of them who will be willing to accept the condition said to be natural to them. If this is the real opinion of men in general, it would be well that it should be spoken out. I should like to hear somebody openly enunciating the doctrine (it is already implied in much that is written on the subject)—"It is necessary to society that women should marry and produce children. They will not do so unless they are compelled. Therefore it is necessary to compel them." The merits of the case would then be clearly defined. It would be exactly that of the slaveholders of South Carolina and Louisiana. "It is necessary that cotton and sugar should be grown. White men cannot produce them. Negroes will not, for any wages which we choose to give. *Ergo* they must be compelled." An illustration still closer to the point is that of impressment. Sailors must absolutely be had to defend the country. It often happens that they will not voluntarily enlist. Therefore there must be the power of forcing them. How often has this logic been used! and, but for one flaw in it, without doubt it would have been successful up to this day. But it is open to the retort—First pay the sailors the honest value of their labour. When you have made it as well worth their while to serve you, as to work for other employers, you will have no more difficulty than others have in obtaining their services. To this there is no logical answer except "I will not": and as people are now not only ashamed, but are not desirous, to rob the labourer of his hire, impressment is no longer advocated. Those who attempt to force women into marriage by closing all other doors against them, lay themselves open to a similar retort. If they mean what they say, their opinion must evidently be, that men do not render the married condition so desirable to women, as to induce them to accept it for its own recommendations. It is not a sign of one's thinking the boon one offers very attractive, when one allows only Hobson's choice, "that or none." And here, I believe, is the clue to the feelings of those men, who have a real antipathy to the equal freedom of women. I believe they are afraid, not lest women should be unwilling to marry, for I do not think that any one in reality has that apprehension; but lest they should insist that marriage should be on equal conditions; lest all women of spirit and capacity should prefer doing almost anything else, not in their own eyes degrading, rather than marry, when marrying is giving themselves a master, and a master too of all their earthly possessions. And truly, if this consequence were neces-

sarily incident to marriage, I think that the apprehension would be very well founded. I agree in thinking it probable that few women, capable of anything else, would, unless under an irresistible *entrainement,* rendering them for the time insensible to anything but itself, choose such a lot, when any other means were open to them of filling a conventionally honourable place in life: and if men are determined that the law of marriage shall be a law of despotism, they are quite right, in point of mere policy, in leaving to women only Hobson's choice. But, in that case, all that has been done in the modern world to relax the chain on the minds of women, has been a mistake. They never should have been allowed to receive a literary education. Women who read, much more women who write, are, in the existing constitution of things, a contradiction and a disturbing element: and it was wrong to bring women up with any acquirements but those of an odalisque, or of a domestic servant.

23   Justice and Gender

SUSAN OKIN

WE AS A SOCIETY PRIDE ourselves on our democratic values. We don't believe people should be constrained by innate differences from being able to achieve desired positions of influence to improve their well-being; equality of opportunity is our professed aim. The Preamble to our Constitution stresses the importance of justice, as well as the general welfare and the blessings of liberty. The Pledge of Allegiance asserts that our republic preserves "liberty and justice for all."

Yet substantial inequalities between the sexes still exist in our society. In economic terms, full-time working women (after some very recent improvement) earn on average 71 percent of the earnings of full-time working men. One-half of poor and three-fifths of chronically poor households with dependent children are maintained by a single female parent. The poverty rate for elderly women is nearly twice that for elderly men.[1] On the political front, two out of a hundred U.S. senators are women, one out of nine justices seems to be considered sufficient female representation on the Supreme Court, and the number of men chosen in each congressional election far exceeds the number of women elected in the entire history of the country. Underlying and intertwined with all these inequalities is the unequal distribution of the unpaid labor of the family.

An equal sharing between the sexes of family responsibilities, especially child care, is "the great revolution that has not happened."[2] Women, including mothers of young children, are, of course, working outside the household far more than their mothers did. And the small proportion of women who reach high-level positions in politics, business, and the professions command vastly disproportionate amount of space in the media, compared with the millions of women who work at low-paying, dead-end jobs, the millions who do part-time work with its lack of benefits, and the millions of others who stay home performing for no pay what is frequently not even acknowledged as work. Certainly, the fact that women are doing more paid work does not imply that they are more equal. It is often said that we are living in a post-feminist era. This claim, due in part to the distorted emphasis on women who have "made it," is false, no matter which of its meanings is intended. It is certainly not true that feminism has been vanquished, and equally untrue that it is no longer needed because its aims have been fulfilled. Until there is justice within the family, women will not be able to gain equality in politics, at work, or in any other sphere.

. . . The typical current practices of family life, structured to a large extent by gender, are not just. Both the expectation and the experience of the division of labor by sex make women vulnerable. As I shall show, a cycle of power relations and decisions pervades both family and workplace, each reinforcing the inequalities between the sexes that already exist within the other. Not only women, but children of both sexes, too, are often made vulnerable by gender-structured marriage.

One-quarter of children in the United States now live in families with only one parent—in almost 90 percent of cases, the mother. Contrary to common perceptions—in which the situation of never-married mothers looms largest—65 percent of single-parent families are a result of marital separation or divorce.[3] Recent research in a number of states has shown that, in the average case, the standard of living of divorced women and the children who live with them plummets after divorce, whereas the economic situation of divorced men tends to be better than when they were married.

A central source of injustice for women these days is that the law, most noticeably in the event of divorce, treats more or less as equals those whom custom, workplace discrimination, and the still conventional division of labor within the family have made very unequal. Central to this socially created inequality are two commonly made but inconsistent presumptions: that women are primarily responsible for the rearing of children; and that serious and committed members of the work force (regardless of class) do not have primary responsibility, or even shared responsibility, for the rearing of children. The old assumption of the workplace, still implicit, is that workers have wives at home. It is built not only into the structure and expectations of the workplace but into other crucial social institutions, such as schools, which make no attempt to take account, in their scheduled hours or vacations, of the fact that parents are likely to hold jobs.

Now, of course, many wage workers do not have wives at home. Often, they *are* wives and mothers, or single, separated, or divorced mothers of small children. But neither the family nor the workplace has taken much account of this fact. Employed wives still do by far the greatest proportion of unpaid family work, such as child care and housework. Women are far more likely to take time out of the workplace or to work part-time because of family responsibilities than are their husbands or male partners. And they are much more likely to move because of their husbands'

employment needs or opportunities than their own. All these tendencies, which are due to a number of factors, including the sex segregation and discrimination of the workplace itself, tend to be cyclical in their effects: wives advance more slowly than their husbands at work and thus gain less seniority, and the discrepancy between their wages increases over time. Then, because both the power structure of the family and what is regarded as consensual "rational" family decision-making reflect the fact that the husband usually earns more, it will become even less likely as time goes on that the unpaid work of the family will be shared between the spouses. Thus the cycle of inequality is perpetuated. Often hidden from view within a marriage, it is in the increasingly likely event of marital breakdown that the socially constructed inequality of married women is at its most visible.

This is what I mean when I say that gender-structured marriage *makes* women vulnerable. These are not matters of natural necessity, as some people would believe. Surely nothing in our natures dictates that men should not be equal participants in the rearing of their children. Nothing in the nature of work makes it impossible to adjust it to the fact that people are parents as well as workers. That these things have not happened is part of the historically, socially constructed differentiation between the sexes that feminists have come to call *gender*. We live in a society that has over the years regarded the innate characteristic of sex as one of the clearest legitimizers of different rights and restrictions, both formal and informal. While the legal sanctions that uphold male dominance have begun to be eroded in the past century, and more rapidly in the last twenty years, the heavy weight of tradition, combined with the effects of socialization, still works powerfully to reinforce sex roles that are commonly regarded as of unequal prestige and worth. The sexual division of labor has not only been a fundamental part of the marriage contract, but so deeply influences us in our formative years that feminists of both sexes who try to reject it can find themselves, struggling against it with varying degrees of ambivalence. Based on the linchpin, "gender"—by which I mean *the deeply entrenched institutionalization of sexual difference*—still permeates our society.

The Construction of Gender

Due to feminism and feminist theory, gender is coming to be recognized as a social factor of major importance. Indeed, the new meaning of the word reflects the fact that so much of what has traditionally been thought of a sexual difference is now considered by many to be largely socially produced.[4] Feminist scholars from many disciplines and with radically different points of view have contributed to the enterprise of making gender fully visible and comprehensible. At one end of the spectrum are those whose explanations of the subordination of women focus primarily on biological difference as causal in the construction of gender,[5] and at the other end are those who argue that biological difference may not even lie at the core of the social construction that is gender;[6] the views of the vast majority of feminists fall between these extremes. The rejection of biological determinism and the corresponding emphasis on gender as a social construction characterize most current feminist scholarship. Of particular relevance is work in psychology, where scholars have investigated the importance of female primary parenting in the formation of our gendered identities,[7] and in history and anthropology,[8] where emphasis has been placed on the historical and cultural variability of gender. Some feminists have been criticized for developing theories of gender that do not take sufficient account of differences *among* women, especially race, class, religion, and ethnicity.[9] While such critiques should always inform our research and improve our arguments, it would be a mistake to allow them to detract our attention from gender itself as a factor of significance. Many injustices are experienced by women *as women*, whatever the differences among them and whatever other injustices they also suffer from. The past and present gendered nature of the family, and the ideology that surround it, affects virtually all women, whether or not they live or ever lived in traditional families. Recognizing this is not to deny or de-emphasize the fact that gender may affect different subgroups of women to a different extent and in different ways.

The potential significance of feminist discoveries and conclusions about gender for issues of social justice cannot be overemphasized. They undermine centuries of argument that started with the notion that not only the distinct differentiation of women and men but the domination of women by men, being natural, was therefore inevitable and not even to be considered in discussions of justice. As I shall make clear in later chapters, despite the fact that such notions cannot stand up to rational scrutiny, they not only still survive but flourish in influential places.

During the same two decades in which feminists have been intensely thinking, researching, analyzing, disagreeing about, and rethinking the subject of gender, our political and legal institutions have been increasingly faced with issues concerning the injustices of gender and their effects. These issues are being decided within a fundamentally patriarchal system, founded in a tradition in which "individuals" were assumed to be male heads of households. Not surprisingly, the system has demonstrated a limited capacity for determining what is just, in many cases involving gender. Sex discrimination, sexual harassment, abortion, pregnancy in the workplace, parental leave, child care, and surrogate mothering have all become major and well-publicized issues of public policy, engaging both courts and legislatures. Issues of family justice, in particular—from child custody and terms of divorce to physical and sexual abuse of wives and children—have become increasingly visible and pressing, and are commanding increasing attention from the police and court systems. There is clearly a major "justice crisis" in contemporary society arising from issues of gender.

Theories of Justice and the Neglect of Gender

During these same two decades, there has been a great resurgence of theories of social justice. Political theory, which had been sparse for a period before the late 1960s except as an important branch of intellectual history, has become a flourishing field, with social justice as its central concern. Yet, remarkably, major contemporary theorists of justice have almost without exception ignored the situation I have just described. They have displayed little interest in or knowledge of the findings of feminism. They have largely bypassed the fact that the society to which their theories are supposed to pertain is heavily and deeply affected by gender, and faces difficult issues of justice stemming from its gendered past and present assumptions. Since theories of justice are centrally concerned with whether, how, and why persons should be treated differently from one another, this neglect seems inexplicable. These theories are *about* which initial or acquired characteristics or positions in society legitimize differential treatment of persons by social institutions, laws, and customs. They are *about* how and whether and to what extent beginnings should affect outcomes. The division of humanity into two sexes seems to provide an obvious subject for such inquires. But, as we shall see, this does not strike most contemporary theorists of justice, and their theories suffer in both coherence and relevance because of it. This book is about this remarkable case of neglect. It is also an attempt to rectify it, to point the way toward a more fully humanist theory of justice by confronting the question, "How just is gender?"

Why is that when we turn to contemporary theories of justice, we do not find illuminating and positive contributions to this question? How can theories of justice that are ostensibly about people in general neglect women, gender, and all the inequalities between the sexes? One reason is that most theorists *assume,* though they do not discuss, the traditional, gender-structured family. Another is that they often employ gender-neutral

language in a false, hollow way. Let us examine these two points.

THE HIDDEN GENDER-STRUCTURED FAMILY

In the past, political theorists often used to distinguish clearly between "private" domestic life and the "public" life of politics and the marketplace, claiming explicitly that the two spheres operated in accordance with different principles. They separated out the family from what they deemed the subject matter of politics, and they made closely related, explicit claims about the nature of women and the appropriateness of excluding them from civil and political life. Men, the subjects of the theories, were able to make the transition back and forth from domestic to public life with ease, largely because of the functions performed by women in the family.[10] When we turn to contemporary theories of justice, superficial appearances can easily lead to the impression that they are inclusive of women. In fact, they continue the same "separate spheres" tradition, by ignoring the family, its division of labor, and the related economic dependency and restricted opportunities of most women. The judgment that the family is "nonpolitical" is implicit in the fact that it is simply not discussed in most works of political theory today. In one way or another, as will become clear in the chapters that follow, almost all current theorists continue to assume that the "individual" who is the basic subject of their theories is the male head of a fairly traditional household. Thus the application of principles of justice to relations between the sexes, or within the household, is frequently, though tacitly ruled out from the start. In the most influential of all twentieth-century theories of justice, that of John Rawls, family life is not only assumed, but is assumed to be just—and yet the prevalent gendered division of labor within the family is neglected, along with the associated distribution of power, responsibility, and privilege. . . .

Moreover, this stance is typical of contemporary theories of justice. They persist, despite the wealth of feminist challenges to their assumptions, in their refusal even to discuss the family and its gender structure, much less to recognize the family as a political institution of primary importance. Recent theories that pay even less attention to issues of family justice than Rawls's include Bruce Ackerman's *Social Justice in the Liberal State,* Ronald Dworkin's *Taking Rights Seriously,* William Galston's *Justice and the Human Good,* Alasdair MacIntyre's *After Virtue* and *Whose Justice? Whose Rationality?,* Robert Nozick's *Anarchy, State, and Utopia,* and Robert Unger's *Knowledge and Politics* and *The Critical Legal Studies Movement.*[11] Philip Green's *Retrieving Democracy* is a welcome exception.[12] Michael Walzer's *Spheres of Justice,* too, is exceptional in this regard, but . . . the conclusion that can be inferred from his discussion of the family—that its gender structure is unjust—does not sit at all easily with his emphasis on the shared understandings of a culture as the foundation of justice.[13] For gender is one aspect of social life about which clearly, in the United States in the latter part of the twentieth century, there are no shared understandings.

What is the basis of my claim that the family, while neglected, is *assumed* by theorists of justice? One obvious indication is that they take mature, independent human beings as the subjects of their theories without any mention of how they got to be that way. We know, of course, that human beings develop and mature only as a result of a great deal of attention and hard work, by far the greater part of it done by women. But when theorists of justice talk about "work," they mean paid work performed in the marketplace. They must be assuming that women, in the gender-structured family, continue to do their unpaid work of nurturing and socializing the young and providing a haven of intimate relations—otherwise there would be no moral subjects for them to theorize about. But these activities apparently take place outside the scope of their theories. Typically, the family itself is not examined in the light of whatever standard of justice the theorist arrives at.[14]

The continued neglect of the family by theorists of justice flies in the face of a great deal of persuasive feminist argument. . . . Scholars have clearly revealed the interconnections between the gender structure inside and outside the family and the extent to which the personal is political. They have shown that the assignment of primary parenting to women is crucial, both in forming the gendered identities of men and women and in influencing their respective choices and opportunities in life. Yet, so far, the simultaneous assumption and neglect of the family has allowed the impact of these arguments to go unnoticed in major theories of justice.

FALSE GENDER NEUTRALITY

Many academics in recent years have become aware of the objectionable nature of using the supposedly generic male forms of nouns and pronouns. As feminist scholars have demonstrated, these words have most often *not* been used, throughout history and the history of philosophy in particular, with the intent to include women. *Man, mankind,* and *he* are going out of style as universal representations, though they have by no means disappeared. But the gender-neutral alternatives that most contemporary theorists employ are often even more misleading than the blatantly sexist use of male terms of reference. For they serve to disguise the real and continuing failure of theorists to confront the fact that the human race consists of persons of two sexes. They are by this means able to ignore the fact that there are *some* socially relevant physical differences between women and men, and the even more important fact that the sexes have had very different histories, very different assigned social roles and "nature," and very different degrees of access to power and opportunity in all human societies up to and including the present.

False gender neutrality is not a new phenomenon. Aristotle, for example, used *anthropos*—"human being"—in discussions of "the human good" that turn out not only to exclude women but to depend on their subordination. Kant even wrote of "all rational beings as such" in making arguments that he did not mean to apply to women. But it was more readily apparent that such arguments or conceptions of the good were not about all of us, but only about male heads of families. For their authors usually gave at some point an explanation, no matter how inadequate, of why what they were saying did not apply to women and of the different characteristics and virtues, rights, and responsibilities they thought women ought to have. Nevertheless, their theories have often been read as though they pertain (or can easily be applied) to all of us. Feminist interpretations of the last fifteen years or so have revealed the falsity of this "add women and stir" method of reading the history of political thought.[15]

The falseness of the gender-neutral language of contemporary political theorists is less readily apparent. Most, though not all, contemporary moral and political philosophers use "men and women," "he or she," "persons," or the increasingly ubiquitous "self." Sometimes they even get their computers to distribute masculine and feminine terms of reference randomly.[16] Since they do not explicitly exclude or differentiate women, as most theorists in the past did, we may be tempted to read their theories as inclusive of all of us. But we cannot. Their merely terminological responses to feminist challenges, in spite of giving a superficial impression of tolerance and inclusiveness, often strain credulity and sometimes result in nonsense. They do this in two ways: by ignoring the irreducible biological differences between the sexes, and/or by ignoring their different assigned social roles and consequent power differentials, and the ideologies that have supported them. Thus gender-neutral terms frequently obscure the fact that so much of the real experience of "persons," so long as they live in gender-structured societies, *does* in fact depend on what sex they are.

False gender neutrality is by no means confined to the realm of theory. Its harmful effects can be seen in public policies that have directly affected large numbers of women adversely. It was used, for example, in the Supreme Court's 1976 decision that the exclusion of pregnancy-related disabilities from employers' disability insurance plans was "not a gender-based discrimination at all." In a now infamous phrase of its majority opinion, the Court explained that such plans did not discriminate against women because the distinction drawn by such plans was between pregnant women and "non-pregnant *persons*."[17]

Examples of false gender neutrality in contemporary political theory will appear throughout this book; I will illustrate the concept here by citing just two examples. Ackermans' *Social Justice in the Liberal State* is a book containing scrupulously gender-neutral language. He breaks with this neutrality only, it seems, to *defy* existing sex roles; he refers to the "Commander," who plays the lead role in the theory, as "she." However, the argument of the book does not address the existing inequality or role differentiation between the sexes, though it has the potential for doing so.* The full impact of Ackerman's gender-neutral language without attention to gender is revealed in his section on abortion: a two-page discussion written, with the exception of a single "she," in the completely gender-neutral language of fetuses and their "parents."[18] The impression given is that there is no relevant respect in which the relationship of the two parents to the fetus differs. Now it is, of course, possible to imagine (and in the view of many feminists, would be desirable to achieve) a society in which differences in the relation of women and men to fetuses would be so slight as to reasonably play only a minor role in the discussion of abortion. But this would have to be a society without gender—one in which sexual difference carried no social significance, the sexes were equal in power and interdependence, and "mothering" and "fathering" a child meant the same thing, so that parenting and earning responsibilities were equally shared. We certainly do not live

---

*Ackerman's argument about how we arrive at social justice is in most essentials similar to Rawls's. . . . I think such methods can be useful in challenging gender and achieving a humanist theory of justice.

in such a society. Neither is there any discussion of one in Ackerman's theory, in which the division of labor between the sexes is not considered a matter of social (in)justice. In such a context, a "gender-neutral" discussion of abortion is almost as misleading as the Supreme Court's "gender-neutral" discussion of pregnancy.

A second illustration of false gender neutrality comes from Derek Phillips's *Toward a Just Social Order*. Largely because of the extent of his concern—rare among theorists of justice—with how we are to *achieve and maintain* a just social order, Phillips pays an usual amount of attention to the family. He writes about the family as the locus for the development of a sense of justice and self-esteem, of an appreciation of the meaning of reciprocity, of the ability to exercise unforced choice, and of an awareness of alternative ways of life.[19] The problem with this otherwise admirable discussion is that, apart from a couple of brief exceptions, the family itself is presented in gender-neutral terms that bear little resemblance to actual, gender-structured life.*[20] It is because of "parental affection," "parental nurturance," and "child rearing" that children in Phillips's families become the autonomous moral agents that his just society requires its citizens to be. The child's development of a sense of identity is very much dependent upon being raised by "parental figures who themselves have coherent and well-integrated personal identities," and we are told that such a coherent identity is "ideally one built around commitments to work and love." This all sounds very plausible. But it does not take into account the multiple inequalities of gender. In gender-structured societies—in which the child rearers are women, "parental nurturance" is largely mothering, and those who do what society re-

gards as "meaningful work" are assumed *not* to be primary parents—women in even the best of circumstances face considerable conflicts between love (a fulfilling family life) and "meaningful work." Women in less fortunate circumstances face even greater conflicts between love (even basic care of their children) and any kind of paid work at all.

It follows from Phillips's own premises that these conflicts are very likely to affect the strength and coherence in women of that sense of identity and self-esteem, coming from love and meaningful work, that he regards as essential for being an autonomous moral agent. In turn, if they are mothers, it is also likely to affect their daughters' and sons' developing senses of their identity. Gender is clearly a major obstacle to attainment of a social order remotely comparable to the just one Phillips aspires to—but his false gender-neutral language allows him to ignore this fact. Although he is clearly aware of how distant in some other respects this vision of a just social order is from contemporary societies,[21] his use of falsely gender-neutral language leaves him quite unaware of the distance between the type of family that might be able to socialize just citizens and typical families today.

The combined effect of the omission of the family and the falsely gender-neutral language in recent political thought is that most theorists are continuing to ignore the highly political issue of gender. The language they use makes little difference to what they actually do, which is to write about men and about only those women who manage, in spite of the gendered structures and practices of the society in which they live, to adopt patterns of life that have been developed to suit the needs of men. The fact that human beings are born as helpless infants—not as the purportedly autonomous actors who populate political theories—is obscured by the implicit assumption of gendered families, operating outside the range of the theories. To a large extent, contemporary theories of justice, like those of the past, are about men with wives at home.

---

*He points out the shortcomings of the "earlier ethic of sacrifice," especially for women. He also welcomes the recent lessening of women's dependence on their husbands, but at the same time blames it for tending to weaken family stability. The falseness of Phillips's gender neutrality in discussing parenting is clearly confirmed later in the book (chaps 8 and 9), where paid work is "men's" and it is "fathers" who bequeath wealth or poverty on their children.

Gender as a Issue of Justice

For three major reasons, this state of affairs is unacceptable. The first is the obvious point that women must be fully included in any satisfactory theory of justice. The second is that equality of opportunity, not only for women but for children of both sexes, is seriously undermined by the current gender injustices of our society. And the third reason is that, as has already been suggested, the family—currently the linchpin of the gender structure—must be just if we are to have a just society, since it is within the family that we first come to have that sense of ourselves and our relations with others that is at the root of moral development.

COUNTING WOMEN IN

When we turn to the great tradition of Western political thought with questions about the justice of the treatment of the sexes in mind, it is to little avail. Bold feminists like Mary Astell, Mary Wollstonecraft, William Thompson, Harriet Taylor, and George Bernard Shaw have occasionally challenged the tradition, often using its own premises and arguments to overturn its explicit or implicit justification of the inequality of women. But John Stuart Mill is a rare exception to the rule that those who hold central positions in the tradition almost never question the justice of the subordination of women.[22] This phenomenon is undoubtedly due in part to the fact that Aristotle, whose theory of justice has been so influential, relegated women to a sphere of "household justice"—populated by persons who are not fundamentally equal to the free men who participate in political justice, but inferiors whose natural function is to serve those who are more fully human. The liberal tradition, despite its supposed foundation of individual rights and human equality, is more Aristotelian in this respect than is generally acknowledged.[23] In one way or another, almost all liberal theorists have assumed that the "individual" who is the basic subject of the theories is the male head of a patriarchal household.[24] Thus they have not usually considered applying the principles of justice to women or to relations between the sexes.

When we turn to contemporary theories of justice, however, we expect to find more illuminating and positive contributions to the subject of gender and justice. As the mission of the family and the falseness of their gender-neutral language suggest, however, mainstream contemporary theories of justice do not address the subject any better than those of the past. Theories of justice that apply to only half of us simply won't do; the inclusiveness falsely implied by the current use of gender-neutral terms must become real. Theories of justice must apply to all of us, and to all of human life, instead of *assuming* silently that half of us take care of whole areas of life that are considered outside the scope of social justice. In a just society, the structure and practices of families must afford women the same opportunities as men to develop their capacities, to participate in political power, to influence social choices, and to be economically as well as physically secure.

Unfortunately, much feminist intellectual energy in the 1980s has gone into the claim that "justice" and "rights" are masculinist ways of thinking about morality that feminists should eschew or radically revise, advocating a morality of care.[25] The emphasis is misplaced, I think, for several reasons. First, what is by now a vast literature on the subject shows that the evidence for differences in women's and men's ways of thinking about moral issues is not (at least yet) very clear; neither is the evidence about the source of whatever differences there might be.[26] It may well turn out that any differences can be readily explained in terms of roles, including female primary parenting, that are socially determined and therefore alterable. There is certainly no evidence—nor could there be, in such a gender-structured society—for concluding that women are somehow naturally more inclined toward contextuality and away from universalism in their moral thinking, a false concept that unfortunately reinforces the old stereotypes that justify separate spheres. The capacity of reactionary forces to capitalize on the "different moralities" strain in feminism is particularly evident in Pope John Paul II's recent Apostolic Letter, "On the Dignity of Women," in which he refers to women's special capacity to care for others in arguing for confining them to motherhood or celibacy.[27]

Second, . . . I think the distinction between an ethic of justice and an ethic of care has been overdrawn. The best theorizing about justice, I argue, has integral to it the notions of care and empathy, of thinking of the interests and well-being of others who may be very different from ourselves. It is, therefore, misleading to draw a dichotomy as though they were two contrasting ethics. The best theorizing about justice is not some abstract "view from nowhere," but results from the carefully attentive consideration of *everyone's* point of view. This means, of course, that the best theorizing about justice is not good enough if it does not, or cannot readily be adapted to, include women and their points of view as fully as men and their points of view.

GENDER AND EQUALITY OF OPPORTUNITY

The family is a crucial determinant of our opportunities in life, of what we "become." It has frequently been acknowledged by those concerned with real equality of opportunity that the family presents a problem.[28] But though they have discerned a serious problem, these theorists have underestimated it because they have seen only half of it. They have seen that the disparity among families in terms of the physical and emotional environment, motivation, and material advantages they can give their children has a tremendous effect upon children's opportunities in life. We are not born as isolated, equal individuals in our society, but into family situations: some in the social middle, some poor and homeless, and some superaffluent; some to a single or soon-to-be-separated parent, some to parents whose marriage is fraught with conflict, some to parents who will stay together in love and happiness. Any claims that equal opportunity exists are therefore completely unfounded. Decades of neglect of the poor, especially of poor black and Hispanic households, accentuated by the policies of the Reagan years, have brought us farther from the principles of equal opportunity. To come close to them would require, for example, a high and uniform standard of public education and the provision of equal social services—including health care, employment training, job opportunities, drug rehabilitation, and decent housing—for all who need them. In addition to redistributive taxation, only massive reallocations of resources from the military to social services could make these things possible.

But even if all these disparities were somehow eliminated, we would still not attain equal opportunity for all. This is because what has not been recognized as an equal opportunity problem, except in feminist literature and circles, is the disparity *within* the family, the fact that its gender structure is itself a major obstacle to equality of opportunity. This is very important in itself, since one of the factors with most influence on our opportunities in life is the social significance attributed to our sex. The opportunities of girls and women are centrally affected by the structure and practices of family life, particularly by the fact that women are almost invariably primary parents. What nonfeminists who see in the family an obstacle to equal opportunity have *not* seen is that the extent to which a family is gender-structured can make the sex we belong to a relatively insignificant aspect of our identity and our life prospects or an all-pervading one. This is because so much of the social construction of gender takes place in the family, and particularly in the institution of female parenting.

Moreover, especially in recent years, with the increased rates of single motherhood, separation, and divorce, the inequalities between the sexes have *compounded* the first part of the problem. This disparity among families has grown largely because of the impoverishment of many women and children after separation or divorce. The division of labor in the typical family leaves most women far less capable than men of supporting themselves, and this disparity is accentuated by the fact that children of separated or divorced parents usually live with their mothers. The inadequacy—and frequent nonpayment—of child support has become recognized as a major social problem. Thus the inequalities of gender are now directly harming many children of both sexes as well as women themselves. Enhancing equal opportunity for women, important as it is in itself, is also a crucial way of improving the opportunities of many of the most disadvantaged children.

As there is a connection among the parts of this problem, so is there a connection among some of the solutions: much of what needs to be done to end the inequalities of gender, and to work in the direction of ending gender itself, will also help to equalize opportunity from one family to another. Subsidized, high-quality day care is obviously one such thing; another is the adaptation of the workplace to the needs of parents. . . .

THE FAMILY AS A SCHOOL OF JUSTICE

One of the things that theorists who have argued that families need not or cannot be just, or who have simply neglected them, have failed to explain is how, within a formative social environment that is *not* founded upon principles of justice, children can learn to develop that sense of justice they will require as citizens of a just society. Rather than being one among many co-equal institutions of a just society, a family is its essential foundation.

It may seem uncontroversial, even obvious, that families must be just because of the vast influence they have on the moral development of children. But this is clearly not the case. I shall argue that unless the first and most formative example of adult interaction usually experienced by children is one of justice and reciprocity, rather than one of domination and manipulation or of unequal altruism and one-sided self-sacrifice, and unless they themselves are treated with concern and respect, they are likely to be considerably hindered in becoming people who are guided by principles of justice. Moreover, I claim, the sharing of roles by men and women, rather than the division of roles between them, would have a further positive impact because the experience of *being* a physical and psychological nurturer—

whether of a child or of another adult—would increase that capacity to identify with and fully comprehend the viewpoints of others that is important to a sense of justice. In a society that minimized gender this would be more likely to be the experience of all of us.

Almost every person in our society starts life in a family of some sort or other. Fewer of these families now fit the usual, though by no means universal, standard of previous generations, that is, wage-working father, homemaking mother, and children. More families these days are headed by a single parent; lesbian and gay parenting is no longer so rare; many children have two wage-working parents, and receive at least some of their early care outside the home. While its forms are varied, the family in which a child is raised, especially in the earliest years, is clearly a crucial place for early moral development and for the formation of our basic attitudes to others. It is, potentially, a place where we can *learn to be just*. It is especially important for the development of a sense of justice that grows from sharing the experiences of others and becoming aware of the points of view of others who are different in some respects from ourselves, but with whom we clearly have some interests in common.

The importance of the family for the moral development of individuals was far more often recognized by political theorists of the past than it is by those of the present. Hegel, Rousseau, Tocqueville, Mill, and Dewey are obvious examples that come to mind. Rousseau, for example, shocked by Plato's proposal to abolish the family, says that it is

> as though there were no need for a natural base on which to form conventional ties; as though the love of one's nearest were not the principle of the love one owes the state; as though it were not by means of the small fatherland which is the family that the heart attaches itself to the large one.[29]

Defenders of both autocratic and democratic regimes have recognized the political importance of different family forms for the formation of citizens. On the one hand, the nineteenth-century monarchist Louis de Bonald argued against the divorce reforms of the French Revolution, which he claimed had weakened the patriarchal family, on the grounds that "in order to keep the state out of the hands of the people, it is necessary to keep the family out of the hands of women and children."[30] Taking this same line of thought in the opposite direction, the U.S. Supreme Court decided in 1879 in *Reynolds v. Nebraska* that familial patriarchy fostered despotism and was therefore intolerable. Denying Mormon men the freedom to practice polygamy, the Court asserted that it was an offense "subversive of good order" that "leads to the patriarchal principle, . . . [and] when applied to large communities, fetters the people in stationary despotism, while that principle cannot long exist in connection with monogamy."[31]

However, while de Bonald was consistent in his adherence to an hierarchical family structure as necessary for an undemocratic political system, the Supreme Court was by no means consistent in promoting an egalitarian family as an essential underpinning for political democracy. For in other decisions of the same period—such as *Bradwell v. Illinois,* the famous 1872 case that upheld the exclusion of women from the practice of law—the Court rejected women's claims to legal equality, in the name of a thoroughly patriarchal, though monogamous, family that was held to require the dependence of women and their exclusion from civil and political life.[32] While bigamy was considered patriarchal, and as such a threat to republican, democratic government, the refusal to allow a married woman to employ her talents and to make use of her qualifications to earn an independent living was not considered patriarchal. It was so far from being a threat to the civil order, in fact, that it was deemed necessary for it, and as such was ordained by both God and nature. Clearly in both *Reynolds* and *Bradwell,* "state authorities enforced family forms preferred by those in power and justified as necessary to stability and order."[33] The Court noticed the despotic potential of polygamy, but was blind to the despotic potential of patriarchal monogamy. This was perfectly acceptable to them as a training ground for citizens.

Most theorists of the past who stressed the importance of the family and its practices for the wider world of moral and political life by no means insisted on congruence between the structures or practices of the family and those of the outside world. Though concerned with moral development, they bifurcated public from private life to such an extent that they had no trouble reconciling inegalitarian, sometimes admittedly unjust, relations founded upon sentiment within the family with a more just, even egalitarian, social structure outside the family. Rousseau, Hegel, Tocqueville—all thought the family was centrally important for the development of morality in citizens, but all defended the hierarchy of the marital structure while spurning such a degree of hierarchy in institutions and practices outside the household. Preferring instead to rely on love, altruism, and generosity as the basis for family relations, none of these theorists argued for *just* family structures as necessary for socializing children into citizenship in a just society.

The position that justice within the family is irrelevant to the development of just citizens was not plausible even when only men were citizens. John Stuart Mill, in *The Subjection of Women,* takes an impassioned stand against it. He argues that the inequality of women within the family is deeply subversive of justice in general in the wider social world, because it subverts the moral potential of men. Mill's first answer to the question, "For whose good are all these changes in women's rights to be undertaken?" is: "the advantage of having the most universal and pervading of all human relations regulated by justice instead of injustice." Making marriage a relationship of equals, he argues, would transform this central part of daily life from "a school of despotism" into a "a school of moral cultivation."[34] He goes on to discuss, in the strongest of terms, the noxious effect of growing up in a family not regulated by justice. Consider, he says, "the self-worship, the unjust self-preference," nourished in a boy growing up in a household in which "by the mere fact of being born a male he is by right the superior of all and every one of an entire half of the human race."

Mill concludes that the example set by perpetuating a marital structure "contradictory to the first principles of social justice" must have such "a perverting influence" that it is hard even to imagine the good effects of changing it. All other attempts to educate people to respect and practice justice, Mill claims, will be superficial "as long as the citadel of the enemy is not attacked." Mill felt as much hope for what the family might be as he felt despair at what it was not. "The family, justly constituted, would be the real school of the virtues of freedom," primary among which was "justice, . . . grounded as before on equal, but now also on sympathetic association."[35] Mill both saw clearly and had the courage to address what so many other political philosophers either could not see, or saw and turned away from.

Despite the strength and fervor of his advocacy of women's rights, however, Mill's idea of a just family structure falls far short of that of many feminists even of his own time, including his wife, Harriet Taylor. In spite of the fact that Mill recognized both the empowering effect of earnings on one's position in the family and the limiting effect of domestic responsibility on women's opportunities, he balked at questioning the traditional division of labor between the sexes. For him, a woman's choice of marriage was parallel to a man's choice of a profession: unless and until she had fulfilled her obligations to her husband and children, she should not undertake anything else. But clearly, however equal the legal rights of husbands and wives, this position largely undermines Mill's own insistence upon the importance of marital equality for a just society. His acceptance of the traditional division of labor, without making any provision for wives who were thereby made economically dependent upon their husbands, largely undermines his insistence upon family justice as the necessary foundation for social justice.

Thus even those political theorists of the past who have perceived the family as an important school of moral development have rarely acknowledged the need for congruence between the family and the wider social order, which suggests that families themselves need to be just. Even

when they have, as with Mill, they have been unwilling to push hard on the traditional division of labor within the family in the name of justice or equality.

Contemporary theorists of justice, with few exceptions, have paid little or no attention to the question of moral development—of how we are to *become* just. Most of them seem to think, to adapt slightly Hobbes's notable phrase, that just men spring like mushrooms from the earth.[36] Not surprisingly, then, it is far less often acknowledged in recent than in past theories that the family is important for moral development, and especially for instilling a sense of justice. As I have already noted, many theorists pay no attention at all to either the family or gender. In the rare case that the issue of justice within the family is given any sustained attention, the family is not viewed as potential school of social justice.[37] In the rare case that a theorist pays any sustained attention to the development of a sense of justice or morality, little if any attention is likely to be paid to the family.[38] Even in the rare event that theorists pay considerable attention to the family *as* the first major locus of moral socialization, they do not refer to the fact that families are almost all still thoroughly gender-structured institutions.[39]

Among major contemporary theorists of justice, John Rawls alone treats the family seriously as the earliest school of moral development. He argues that a just, well-ordered society will be stable only if its members continue to develop a sense of justice. And he argues that families play a fundamental role in the stages by which this sense of justice is acquired. From the parents' love for their child, which comes to be reciprocated, comes the child's "sense of his own value and the desire to become the sort of person that they are."[40] The family, too, is the first of that series of "associations" in which we participate, from which we acquired the capacity, crucial for a sense of justice, to see things from the perspectives of others. . . . This capacity—the capacity for empathy—is essential for maintaining a sense of justice of the Rawlsian kind. For the perspective that is necessary for maintaining a sense of justice is not that of the egoistic or disembodied self, or of the dominant few who overdetermine "our" traditions or "shared understandings," or (to use Nagel's term) of "the view from nowhere," but rather the perspective of every person in the society for whom the principles of justice are being arrived at. . . . The problem with Rawls's rare and interesting discussion of moral development is that it rests on the unexplained *assumption* that family institutions are just. If gendered family institutions are *not* just, but are, rather, a relic of caste or feudal societies in which responsibilities, roles, and resources are distributed, not in accordance with the principles of justice he arrives at or with any other commonly respected values, but in accordance with innate differences that are imbued with enormous social significance, then Rawls's theory of moral development would seem to be built on uncertain ground. This problem is exacerbated by suggestions in some of Rawls's most recent work that families are "private institutions," to which it is not appropriate to apply standards of justice. But if families are to help form just individuals and citizens, surely they must be *just families.*

In a just society, the structure and practices of families must give women the same opportunities as men to develop their capacities, to participate in political power and influence social choices, and to be economically secure. But in addition to this, families must be just because of the vast influence that they have on the moral development of children. The family is the primary institution of formative moral development. And the structure and practices of the family must parallel those of the larger society if the sense of justice is to be fostered and maintained. While many theorists of justice, both past and present, appear to have denied the importance of at least one of these factors, my own view is that both are absolutely crucial. A society that is committed to equal respect for all of its members, and to justice in social distributions of benefits and responsibilities, can neither neglect the family nor accept family structures and practices that violate these norms, as do current gender-based structures and practices. It is essential that children who are to develop into adults with a strong sense of justice and commitment to just institutions spend their earliest and most formative years in an environment in which they are loved and nurtured, *and* in which principles of justice are abided by and respected. What is a child of either sex to learn about fairness in the average household with two full-time working parents, where the mother does, at the very least, twice as much family work as the father? What is a child to learn about the value of nurturing and domestic work in a home with a traditional division of labor in which the father either subtly or not so subtly uses the fact that he is the wage earner to "pull rank" on or to abuse his wife? What is a child to learn about responsibility for others in a family in which, after many years of arranging her life around the needs of her husband and children, a woman is faced with having to provide for herself and her children but is totally ill-equipped for the task by the life she agreed to lead, has led, and expected to go on leading?

NOTES

1. U.S. Department of Labor, *Employment and Earnings: July 1987* (Washington, D.C.; Government Printing Office, 1987); Ruth Sidel, *Women and Children Last: The Plight of Poor Women in Affluent America* (New York: Viking, 1986), pp. xvi, 158. See also David T. Ellwood, *Poor Support: Poverty in the American Family* (New York: Basic Books, 1988), pp. 84–85, on the chronicity of poverty in single-parent households.

2. Shirley Williams, in Williams and Elizabeth Holtzman, "Women in the Political World: Observations," *Daedalus* 116, no. 4 (Fall 1987): 30.

3. Twenty-three percent of single parents have never been married and 12 percent are widowed. (U.S. Bureau of the Census, Current Population Reports, *Household and Family Characteristics: March 1987* [Washington, D.C.: Government Printing Office, 1987], p. 79). In 1987, 6.8 percent of children under eighteen were living with a never-married parent. ("Study Shows Growing Gap Between Rich and Poor," *New York Times,* March 23, 1989, p. A24). The proportions for the total population are very different from those for black families, of whom in 1984 half of those with adult members under thirty-five years of age were maintained by single, female parents, three-quarters of whom were never married. (Frank Levy, *Dollars and Dreams: The*

Changing American Income Distribution [New York: Russel Sage, 1987], p. 156).

4. As Joan Scott has pointed out, *gender* was until recently used only as a grammatical term. See "Gender: A Useful Category of Historical Analysis," in Joan Wallach Scott, *Gender and the Politics of History* (New York: Columbia University Press, 1988), p. 28, citing Fowler's *Dictionary of Modern English Usage*.

5. Among Anglo-American feminists see, for example, Mary Daly, *Gyn/Ecology: The Metaethics of Radical Feminism* (Boston: Beacon Press, 1978); Susan Griffin, *Woman and Nature: The Roaring Inside Her* (New York: Harper & Row, 1978). For a good succinct discussion of radical feminist biological determinism, see Alison Jaggar, *Feminist Politics and Human Nature* (Totowa, N.J.: Rowman and Allanheld, 1983).

6. See, for example, Sylvia Yanagisako and Jane Collier, "The Mode of Reproduction in Anthropology," in *Theoretical Perspectives on Sexual Difference,* ed. Deborah Rhode (New Haven: Yale University Press, in press).

7. Nancy Chodorow, *The Reproduction of Mothering: Psychoanalysis and the Sociology of Gender* (Berkeley: University of California Press, 1978); Dorothy Dinnerstein, *The Mermaid and the Minotaur: Sexual Arrangements and Human Malaise* (New York: Harper & Row, 1976). For further discussion of this issue and further references to the literature, see chapter 6, note 58, and accompanying text.

8. Linda Nicholson, *Gender and History* (New York: Columbia University Press, 1986); Michelle Z. Rosaldo, "The Use and Abuse of Anthropology," *Signs* 5, no. 3 (1980); Joan Wallach Scott, *Gender and the Politics of History* (New York: Columbia University Press, 1986).

9. For such critiques, see Bell Hooks, *Ain't I a Woman: Black Women and Feminism* (Boston: South End Press, 1981), and *Feminist Theory: From Margin to Center* (Boston: South End Press, 1984); Elizabeth V. Spelman, *Inessential Woman: Problems of Exclusion in Feminist Thought* (Boston: Beacon Press, 1989).

10. There is now an abundant literature on the subject of women, their exclusion from nondomestic life, and the reasons given to justify it, in Western political theory. See, for example, Lorenne J. Clark and Lynda Lange, eds., *The Sexism of Social and Political Thought* (Toronto: University of Toronto Press, 1979); Jean Bethke Elshtain, *Public Man, Private Woman: Women in Social and Political Thought* (Princeton: Princeton University Press, 1981); Genevieve Lloyd, *The Man of Reason: "Male" and "Female" in Western Philosophy* (Minneapolis: University of Minnesota Press, 1984); Mary O'Brien, *The Politics of Reproduction* (London: Routledge & Kegan Paul, 1981); Susan Moller Okin, *Women in Western Political Thought* (Princeton: Princeton University Press, 1979); Carole Pateman, "Feminist Critiques of the Public/Private Dichotomy," in *Public and Private in Social Life,* ed. S. Benn and G. Gaus (London: Croom Helm, 1983); Carole Pateman and Elizabeth Gross, eds., *Feminist Challenges: Social and Political Theory* (Boston: Northeastern University Press, 1987); Carole Pateman, *The Sexual Contract* (Stanford: Stanford University Press, 1988); Carole Pateman and Mary L. Shanley, eds. *Feminist Critiques of Political Theory* (Oxford: Polity Press, in press).

11. Bruce Ackerman, *Social Justice in the Liberal State* (New Haven: Yale University Press, 1980); Ronald Dworkin, *Taking Rights Seriously* (Cambridge: Harvard University Press, 1977); William Galston, *Justice and the Human Good* (Chicago: University of Chicago Press, 1980); Alasdair MacIntyre, *After Virtue* (Notre Dame: University of Notre Dame Press, 1981), and *Whose Justice? Which Rationality?* (Notre Dame: University of Notre Dame Press, 1988); Robert Nozick, *Anarchy, State, and Utopia* New York: Basic Books, 1974); Roberto Unger, *Knowledge and Politics* (New York: The Free Press, 1975), and *The Critical Legal Studies Movement* (Cambridge: Harvard University Press, 1986).

12. Philip Green, in *Retrieving Democracy: In Search of Civic Equality* (Totowa, N.J.: Rowman and Allanheld, 1985), argues that the social equality that is prerequisite to real democracy is incompatible with the current division of labor between the sexes. See pp. 96–108.

13. Michael Walzer, *Spheres of Justice* (New York: Basic Books, 1983).

14. This is commented on and questioned by Francis Schrag, "Justice and the Family," *Inquiry* 19 (1976): 200, and Walzer, *Spheres of Justice,* chap. 9.

15. See note 10 of this chapter. The phrase is Dale Spender's.

16. See, for example, David Gauthier, *Morals by Agreement* (Oxford: Oxford University Press, 1986), passim and p. vi. Fortunately, Gauthier's computer was able to control its zeal for randomization enough to avoid referring to Plato and Rawls as "she" and Queen Gertrude and Mary Gibson as "he."

17. *General Electric v. Gilbert,* 429 U.S. 125 (1976), 135–36; second phrase quoted from *Geduldig v. Aiello,* 417 U.S. 484 (1974), 496–97, emphasis added.

18. Ackerman, *Social Justice,* pp. 127–28. He takes gender neutrality to the point of suggesting a hypothetical case in which "a couple simply *enjoy* abortions so much that they conceive embryos simply to kill them a few months later."

19. Derek L. Phillips, *Toward a Just Social Order* (Princeton: Princeton University Press, 1986), esp. pp. 187–96.

20. Ibid., pp. 224–26.

21. Ibid., esp. chap. 9.

22. I have analyzed some of the ways in which theorists in the tradition avoided considering the justice of gender in "Are Our Theories of Justice Gender-Neutral?" in *The Moral Foundations of Civil Rights*, ed. Robert Fullinwider and Claudia Mills (Totowa, N.J.: Rowman and Littlefield, 1986).

23. See Judith Hicks Stiehm, "The Unit of Political Analysis: Our Aristotelian Hangover," in *Discovering Reality: Feminist Perspectives on Epistemology, Metaphysics, Methodology, and Philosophy of Science*, ed. Sandra Harding and Merrill B. Hintikka (Dordrecht, Holland: Reidel, 1983).

24. See Carole Pateman and Theresa Brennan, "'Mere Auxiliaries to the Commonwealth': Women and the Origins of Liberalism," *Political Studies* 27, no. 2 (June 1979); also Susan Moller Okin, "Women and the Making of the Sentimental Family," *Philosophy and Public Affairs* 11, no. 1 (Winter 1982). This issue is treated at much greater length in Pateman, *The Sexual Contract.*

25. This claim, originating in the moral development literature, has significantly influenced recent feminist moral and political theory. Two central books are Carol Gilligan, *In a Different Voice* (Cambridge: Harvard University Press, 1982); and Nel Noddings, *Caring: A Feminine Approach to Ethics and Moral Education* (Berkeley: University of California Press, 1984). For the influence of Gilligan's work on feminist theory, see, for example, Seyla Benhabib, "The Generalized and the Concrete Other: The Kohlberg-Gilligan controversy and Feminist Theory," in *Feminism as Critique*, ed. Benhabib and Drucilla Cornell (Minneapolis: University of Minnesota Press, 1987); Lawrence Blum, "Gilligan and Kohlberg: Implications for Moral Theory," *Ethics* 98, no. 3 (1988); and Eva Kittay and Diana Meyers, eds., *Women and Moral Theory* (Totowa N.J.: Rowman and Allenheld, 1986). For a valuable alternative approach to the issues, and an excellent selective list of references to what has now become a vast literature, see Owen Flanagan and Kathryn Jackson, "Justice, Care and Gender: The Kohlberg-Gilligan Debate Revisited," *Ethics* 97, no. 3 (1987).

26. See, for example, John M. Broughton, "Women's Rationality and Men's Virtues: A Critique of Gender Dualism in Gilligan's Theory of Moral Development," *Social Research* 50, no. 3 (1983); Owen Flanagan, *Varieties of Moral Personality: Ethics and Psychological Realism* (Cambridge: Harvard University Press, forthcoming), ch. 8; Catherine G. Greeno and Eleanor E. Maccoby, "How Different Is the 'Different Voice'?" and Gilligan's reply, *Signs* 11, no. 2 (1986); Debra Nails "Social-Scientific Sexism: Gilligan's Mismeasure of Man," *Social Research* 50, no. 3 (1983); Joan Tronto, "'Women's Morality': Beyond Gender Difference to a Theory of Care," *Signs* 12, no. 2 (1987); Lawrence J. Walker, "Sex Differences in the Development of Moral Reasoning: A Critical Review," *Child Development* 55 (1984).

27. See extracts from the Apostolic Letter in *New York Times*, October 1, 1988, pp. A1 and 6. On the reinforcement of the old stereotypes in general, see Susan Moller Okin, "Thinking Like a Woman," in Rhode, ed., *Theoretical Perspectives.*

28. See esp. James Fishkin, *Justice, Equal Opportunity and the Family* (New Haven: Yale University Press, 1983); Phillips, *Just Social Order*, esp. pp. 346–49; Rawls, *Theory*, pp. 74, 300–301, 511–12.

29. Jean-Jacques Rousseau, *Emile: or On Education*, trans. Allan Bloom (New York: Basic Books, 1979), p. 363.

30. Louis de Bonald, in *Archives Parlementaires*, 2e série (Paris, 1869), vol. 15, p. 612; cited and translated by Roderick Phillips, "Women and Family Breakdown in Eighteenth-Century France: Rouen 1780–1800," *Social History* 2, (1976): 217.

31. *Reynolds v. Nebraska*, 98 U.S. 145 (1879), 164, 166.

32. *Bradwell v. Illinois*, 83 U.S. 130 (1872).

33. Martha Minow, "We, the Family: Constitutional Rights and American Families," *The American Journal of History* 74, no. 3 (1987); 969, discussing *Reynolds* and other nineteenth-century cases.

34. John Stuart Mill, *The Subjection of Women* (1869), in *Collected Works*, ed. J. M. Robson (Toronto: University of Toronto Press, 1984), vol. 21, pp. 324, 293–95. At the time Mill wrote, women had no political rights and coverture deprived married women of most legal rights, too. He challenges all this in his essay.

35. Mill, *Subjection of Women*, pp. 324–25, 294–95.

36. Hobbes writes of "men . . . as if but even now sprung out of the earth . . . like mushrooms." "Philosophical rudiments Concerning Government and Society," in *The English Works of Thomas Hobbes*, ed. Sir William Molesworth (London: John Bohn, 1966), vol. 2, p. 109.

37. For example, Walzer, *Spheres of Justice*, chap. 9, "Kinship and Love."

38. See Alan Gewirth, *Reason and Morality* (Chicago: University of Chicago Press, 1978). He discusses moral development from time to time, but places families within the broad category of "voluntary associations" and does not discuss gender roles within them.

39. This is the case with both Rawls's *A Theory of Justice* (Cambridge: Harvard University Press, 1971), . . . and Phillips's sociologically oriented *Toward a Just Social Order*, as discussed above.

40. Rawls, *Theory*, p. 465.

24   Feminist Justice and the Family

JAMES P. STERBA

CONTEMPORARY FEMINISTS almost by definition seek to put an end to male domination and to secure women's liberation. To achieve these goals, many feminists support the political ideal of a gender-free or androgynous society.[1] According to these feminists, all assignments of rights and duties are ultimately to accord with the ideal of a gender-free or androgynous society. Since a conception of justice is usually thought to provide the ultimate grounds for the assignment of rights and duties, I refer to this ideal of a gender-free or androgynous society as "feminist justice."

The Ideal of a Gender-Free or Androgynous Society

But how is this ideal of a gender-free or androgynous society to be interpreted? It is a society where basic rights and duties are not assigned on the basis of a person's biological sex. Being male or female is not the grounds for determining what basic rights and duties a person has in a gender-free society. But this is to characterize the feminist ideal only negatively. It tells us what we need to get rid of, not what we need to put in its place. A more positive characterization is provided by the ideal of androgyny. Putting the ideal of feminist justice more positively in terms of the ideal of androgyny also helps to bring out why men should be attracted to feminist justice.

In a well-known article, Joyce Trebilcot distinguishes two forms of androgyny.[2] The first postulates the same ideal for everyone. According to this form of androgyny, the ideal person "combines characteristics usually attributed to men with characteristics usually attributed to women." Thus, we should expect both nurturance and mastery, openness and objectivity, compassion and competitiveness from each and every person who has the capacities for these traits.

By contrast, the second form of androgyny does not advocate the same ideal for everyone but rather a variety of options from "pure" femininity to "pure" masculinity. As Trebilcot points out, this form of androgyny shares with the first the view that biological sex should not be the basis for determining the appropriateness of gender characterization. It differs in that it holds that "all alternatives with respect to gender should be equally available to and equally approved for everyone, regardless of sex."

It would be a mistake, however, to distinguish sharply between these two forms of androgyny. Properly understood, they are simply two different facets of a single ideal. For, as Mary Ann Warren has argued, the second form of androgyny is appropriate *only* "with respect to feminine and masculine traits which are largely matters of personal style and preference and which have little direct moral significance."[3] However, when we consider so-called feminine and masculine *virtues,* it is

Adapted from Perspectives on the Family *(1990) edited by Robert Moffat, Joseph Grcic, and Michael Bayles. Reprinted with revisions by permission.*

the first form of androgyny that is required, because then, other things being equal, the same virtues are appropriate for everyone.

We can even formulate the ideal of androgyny more abstractly so that it is no longer specified in terms of so-called feminine and masculine traits. We can specify the ideal as requiring no more than that the traits that are truly desirable in society be equally open to both women and men or, in the case of virtues, equally expected of both women and men, other things being equal.

There is a problem, of course, in determining which traits of character are virtues and which are largely matters of personal style and preference. To make this determination, Trebilcot has suggested that we seek to bring about the second form of androgyny, where people have the option of acquiring the full range of so-called feminine and masculine traits.[4] But surely when we already have good grounds for thinking that such traits as courage and compassion, fairness and openness are virtues, there is no reason to adopt a laissez-faire approach to moral education. Although, as Trebilcot rightly points out, proscribing certain options would involve a loss of freedom, nevertheless we should be able to determine, at least with respect to some character traits, when a gain in virtue is worth the loss of freedom. It may even be the case that the loss of freedom suffered by an individual now will be compensated for by a gain of freedom to that same individual in the future once the relevant virtues have been acquired.

So understood, the class of virtues will turn out to be those desirable traits which can be reasonably expected of both women and men. Admittedly, this is a restrictive use of the term "virtue." In normal usage, "virtue" is almost synonymous with "desirable trait."[5] But there is good reason to focus on those desirable traits that can be reasonably expected of both women and men, and for present purposes I will refer to this class of desirable traits as virtues.[6]

Unfortunately, many of the challenges to the ideal of androgyny fail to appreciate how the ideal can be interpreted to combine a required set of virtues with equal choice from among other desirable traits. For example, some challenges interpret the ideal as attempting to achieve "a proper balance of moderation" among opposing feminine and masculine traits and then question whether traits such as feminine gullibility or masculine brutality could ever be combined with opposing gender traits to achieve such a balance.[7] Other challenges interpret the ideal as permitting unrestricted choice of personal traits and then regard the possibility of Total Women and Hells Angels androgynes as a *reductio ad absurdum* of the idea.[8] But once it is recognized that the ideal of androgyny cannot only be interpreted to require of everyone a set of virtues (which need not be a mean between opposing extreme traits) but can also be interpreted to limit everyone's choice to desirable traits, then such challenges to the ideal clearly lose their force because they only work against objectionable interpretations of androgyny.

Actually, the main challenge raised by feminists to the ideal of androgyny is that the ideal is self-defeating in that it seeks to eliminate sexual stereotyping of human beings at the same time that it is formulated in terms of the very same stereotypical concepts it seeks to eliminate.[9] Or, as Warren puts it, "Is it not at least mildly paradoxical to urge people to cultivate both 'feminine' and 'masculine' virtues, while at the same time holding that virtues ought not to be sexually stereotyped?"

One response to this challenge contends that to build a better society we must begin where we are now, and where we are now people still speak of feminine and masculine character traits. Consequently, if we want to refer easily to such traits and to formulate an ideal with respect to how these traits should be distributed in society, it is plausible to refer to them in the way that people presently refer to them, that is, as feminine or masculine traits.

Another response, which attempts to avoid misunderstanding altogether, is to formulate the ideal in the more abstract way I suggested earlier, so that it no longer specifically refers to so-called feminine or masculine traits. So formulated, the ideal requires that the traits that are truly desirable in society be equally open to both women and men or, in the case of virtues, be equally expected of both women and men. So characterized, the ideal of androgyny represents neither a revolt against so-called feminine virtues and traits nor their exaltation over so-called masculine virtues and traits.[10] Accordingly, the ideal of androgyny does not view women's liberation as *simply* the freeing of women from the confines of traditional roles, which makes it possible for them to develop in ways heretofore reserved for men. Nor does the ideal view women's liberation as *simply* the reevaluation and glorification of so-called feminine activities such as housekeeping or mothering or so-called feminine modes of thinking as reflected in an ethic of caring. The first perspective ignores or devalues genuine virtues and desirable traits traditionally associated with women while the second ignores or devalues genuine virtues and desirable traits traditionally associated with men. In contrast, the ideal of androgyny seeks a broader-based ideal for both women and men that combines virtues and desirable traits traditionally associated with women with virtues and desirable traits traditionally associated with men. Nevertheless, the ideal of androgyny will clearly reject any so-called virtues or desirable traits traditionally associated with women or men that have been supportive of discrimination or oppression against women or men. In general, the ideal of androgyny substitutes a socialization based on natural ability, reasonable expectation, and choice for socialization based on sexual difference.

It also seems that those who claim that we cannot escape a gendered society are simply confused about what a gender-free society would be like;[11] for they seem to agree with those who favor a gender-free or androgynous society that the assignments of roles in society should be based on (natural) ability, rational expectation, and choice. But what they also maintain is that some of these assignments will be based on sex as well, because some of the natural abilities that people possess will be determined by their sex. But even assuming this is the case, it wouldn't show that society was gendered in the sense that its roles in society

are based on sex rather than on (natural) ability, rational expectation, and choice. And this is the only sense of gendered society to which defenders of feminist justice would be objecting.[12] So once the notion of a gender-free society is clarified, there should be widespread agreement that the assignments of roles in society should be based on (natural) ability, rational expectation, and choice. The ideal of androgyny simply specifies this notion of a gender-free society a bit further by requiring that the traits that are truly desirable in society be equally open to (equally qualified) women and men or, in the case of virtues, equally expected of (equally capable) women and men.

Of course, insofar as natural abilities are a function of sexual difference, there will be differences in the desirable traits and virtues that women and men acquire, even in a gender-free or androgynous society. And some contend that these differences will be substantial.[13] But given that we have been slow to implement the degree of equal opportunity required by the ideal of a gender-free or androgynous society, it is difficult to know what differences in desirable traits and virtues, if any, will emerge that are both sex-based and natural-ability-based. What we can be sure of is that given the variety and types of discrimination employed against women in existing societies, a gender-free or androgynous society will look quite different from the societies that we know.

Defenses of Androgyny

Now there are various contemporary defenses of the ideal of androgyny. Some feminists have attempted to derive the ideal from a Liberal Democratic Conception of Justice. Others have attempted to derive the ideal from a Socialist Conception of Justice. Let us briefly consider each of these defenses in turn.

In attempting to derive the ideal of androgyny from a Democratic Liberal Conception of Justice, feminists have tended to focus on the right to equal opportunity which is a central requirement of a Liberal Democratic Conception of Justice.[14] Of course, equal opportunity could be interpreted minimally as providing people only with the same legal rights of access to all advantaged positions in society for which they are qualified. But this is not the interpretation given the right by liberal democrats. In a Liberal Democratic Conception of Justice, equal opportunity is interpreted to require in addition the same prospects for success for all those who are relevantly similar, where the relevant similarity involves more than simply present qualifications. For example, Rawls claims that persons in his original position would favor a right to "fair equality of opportunity," which means that persons who have the same natural assets and the same willingness to use them would have the necessary resources to achieve similar life prospects.[15] The point feminists have been making is simply that failure to achieve the ideal of androgyny translates into a failure to guarantee equal opportunity to both women and men. The present evidence for this failure to provide equal opportunity is the discrimination that exists against women in education, employment and personal relations. Discrimination in education begins early in a child's formal educational experience as teachers and school books support different and less desirable roles for girls than for boys.[16] Discrimination in employment has been well documented.[17] Women continue to earn only a fraction of what men earn for the same or comparable jobs and although women make up almost half of the paid labor force in the U.S., 70% of them are concentrated in just 20 different job categories, only 5 more than in 1905.[18] Finally, discrimination in personal relations is the most entrenched of all forms of discrimination against women.[19] It primarily manifests itself in traditional family structures in which the woman is responsible for domestic work and childcare and the man's task is "to protect against the outside world and to show how to meet this world successfully."[20] In none of these areas, therefore, do women have the same prospects for success as compared with men with similar natural talents and similar desires to succeed.

Now the support for the ideal of androgyny provided by a Socialist Conception of Justice appears to be much more direct than that provided by a Liberal Democratic Conception of Justice.[21] This is because the Socialist Conception of Justice and the ideal of androgyny can be interpreted as requiring the very same equal right of self-development. What a Socialist Conception of Justice purports to add to this interpretation of the ideal of androgyny is an understanding of how the ideal is best to be realized in contemporary capitalist societies. For according to advocates of this defense of androgyny, the ideal is best achieved by socializing the means of production and satisfying people's nonbasic as well as their basic needs. Thus, the general idea behind this approach to realizing the ideal of androgyny is that a cure for capitalist exploitation will also be a cure for women's oppression.

Yet despite attempts to identify the feminist ideal of androgyny with a right to equal opportunity endorsed by a Liberal Democratic Conception of Justice or an equal right of self-development endorsed by a Socialist Conception of Justice, the ideal still transcends both of these rights by requiring not only that desirable traits be equally available to both women and men but also that the same virtues be reasonably expected of both women and men. Of course, part of the rationale for reasonably expecting the same virtues in both women and men is to support such rights. And if support for such rights is to be fairly allocated, the virtues needed to support such rights must be reasonably expected of both women and men. Nevertheless, to hold that the virtues required to support a right to equal opportunity or an equal right to self-development must be reasonably expected of both women and men is different from claiming, as the ideal of androgyny does, that human virtues, sans phrase, should be reasonably expected of both women and men. Thus, the ideal of androgyny clearly requires an inculcation of virtues beyond what is necessary to support a right to equal opportunity or an equal right to self-development. What additional virtues are required by the ideal obviously depends upon what other rights should be recognized. In this regard, the ideal of androgyny is somewhat open-ended.

Feminists who endorse the ideal would simply have to go along with the best arguments for additional rights and corresponding virtues. In particular, I would claim that they would have to support a right to welfare that is necessary for meeting the basic needs of all legitimate claimants given the strong case that can be made for such a right from liberal democrat, socialist, and even libertarian perspectives.[22]

Now, in order to provide all legitimate claimants with the resources necessary for meeting their basic needs, there obviously has to be a limit on the resources that will be available for each individual's self-development, and this limit will definitely have an effect upon the implementation of the ideal of androgyny. Of course, some feminists would want to pursue various possible technological transformations of human biology in order to implement their ideal. For example, they would like to make it possible for women to inseminate other women and for men to lactate and even to bring fertilized ova to term. But bringing about such possibilities would be very costly indeed.[23] Consequently, since the means selected for meeting basic needs must be provided to all legitimate claimants including distant peoples and future generations, it is unlikely that such costly means could ever be morally justified. Rather it seems preferable radically to equalize the opportunities that are conventionally provided to women and men and wait for such changes to ultimately have their effect on human biology as well. Of course, if any "technological fixes" for achieving androgyny should prove to be cost efficient as a means for meeting people's basic needs, then obviously there would be every reason to utilize them.

Unfortunately, the commitment of a Feminist Conception of Justice to a right of equal opportunity raises still another problem for the view. For some philosophers have contended that equal opportunity is ultimately an incoherent goal. As Lloyd Thomas has put the charge, "We have a problem for those who advocate competitive equality of opportunity: the prizes won in the competitions of the first generation will tend to defeat the requirements of equality of opportunity for the next."[24] The only way to avoid this result, Thomas claims, "is by not permitting persons to be dependent for their self-development on others at all," which obviously is a completely unacceptable solution.

But this is a problem, as Thomas points out, that exists for competitive opportunities. They are opportunities for which, even when each person does her best, there are considerably more losers than winners. With respect to such opportunities, the winners may well be able to place themselves and their children in an advantageous position with respect to subsequent competitions. But under a Liberal Democratic Conception of Justice, and presumably a Feminist Conception of Justice as well, most of the opportunities people have are not competitive opportunities at all, but rather noncompetitive opportunities to acquire the resources necessary for meeting their basic needs. These are opportunities with respect to which virtually everyone who does her best can be a winner. Of course, some people who do not do their best may fail to satisfy their basic needs, and this failure may have negative consequences for their children's prospects. But under a Liberal Democratic Conception of Justice, and presumably a Feminist Conception of Justice as well, every effort is required to ensure that each generation has the same opportunities to meet their basic needs, and as long as most of the opportunities that are available are of the noncompetitive sort, this goal should not be that difficult to achieve.

Now it might be objected that if all that will be accomplished under the proposed system of equal opportunity is, for the most part, the satisfaction of people's basic needs, then that would not bring about the revolutionary change in the relationship between women and men that feminists are demanding. For don't most women in technologically advanced societies already have their basic needs satisfied, despite the fact that they are not yet fully liberated?

In response, it should be emphasized that the concern of defenders of the ideal of androgyny is not just with women in technologically advanced societies. The ideal of androgyny is also applicable to women in Third World and developing societies, and in such societies it is clear that the basic needs of many women are not being met. Furthermore, it is just not the case that all the basic needs of most women in technologically advanced societies are being met. Most obviously, their basic needs for self-development are still not being met. This is because they are being denied an equal right to education, training, jobs and a variety of social roles for which they have the native capabilities. In effect, women in technologically advanced societies are still being treated as second-class persons, no matter how well-fed, well-clothed, well-housed they happen to be. This is why there must be a radical restructuring of social institutions even in technologically advanced societies if women's basic needs for self-development are to be met.

Androgyny and the Family

Now the primary locus for the radical restructuring required by the ideal of androgyny is the family. Here two fundamental changes are needed. First, all children irrespective of their sex must be given the same type of upbringing consistent with their native capabilities. Second, mothers and fathers must also have the same opportunities for education and employment consistent with their native capabilities.

Surprisingly, however, some liberal democrats have viewed the existence of the family as imposing an acceptable limit on the right to equal opportunity. Rawls, for example, claims the principle of fair opportunity can be only imperfectly carried out, at least as long as the institution of the family exists. The extent to which natural capacities develop and reach fruition is affected by all kinds of social conditions and class attitudes. Even the willingness to make an effort, to try, and so to be deserving in the ordinary sense is itself dependent upon happy family and social circumstances. It is impossible in practice to secure equal chances of achievement and culture for those similarly en-

dowed, and therefore we may want to adopt a principle which recognizes this fact and also mitigates the arbitrary effects of the natural lottery itself.[25]

Thus, according to Rawls, since different families will provide different opportunities for their children, the only way to fully achieve "fair equality of opportunity" would require us to go too far and abolish or radically modify traditional family structures.

Yet others have argued that the full attainment of equal opportunity requires that we go even further and equalize people's native as well as their social assets.[26] For only when everyone's natural and social assets have been equalized would everyone have exactly the same chance as everyone else to attain the desirable social positions in society. Of course, feminists have no difficulty recognizing that there are moral limits to the pursuit of equal opportunity. Accordingly, feminists could grant that other than the possibility of special cases, such as sharing a surplus organ like a second kidney, it would be too much to ask people to sacrifice their native assets to achieve equal opportunity.

Rawls, however, proposes to limit the pursuit of equal opportunity still further by accepting the inequalities generated by families in any given sector of society, provided that there is still equal opportunity between the sectors or that the existing inequality of opportunity can be justified in terms of its benefit to those in the least-advantaged position.[27] Nevertheless, what Rawls is concerned with here is simply the inequality of opportunity that exists between individuals owing to the fact that they come from different families. He fails to consider the inequality of opportunity that exists in traditional family structures, especially between adult members, in virtue of the different roles expected of women and men. When viewed from the original position, it seems clear that this latter inequality of opportunity is sufficient to require a radical modification of traditional family structures, even if the former inequality, for the reasons Rawls suggests, does not require any such modifications.

Yet at least in the United States this need radically to modify traditional family structures to guarantee equal opportunity confronts a serious problem. Given that a significant proportion of the available jobs are at least 9 to 5, families with pre-school children require day care facilities if their adult members are to pursue their careers. Unfortunately, for many families such facilities are simply unavailable. In New York City, for example, more than 144,000 children under the age of six are competing for 46,000 full-time slots in day care centers. In Seattle, there is licensed day care space for 8,800 of the 23,000 children who need it. In Miami, two children, 3 and 4 years old, were left unattended at home while their mother worked. They climbed into a clothes dryer while the timer was on, closed the door and burned to death.[28]

Moreover, even the available day care facilities are frequently inadequate either because their staffs are poorly trained or because the child/adult ratio in such facilities is too high. At best, such facilities provide little more than custodial care; at worst, they actually retard the development of those under their care. What this suggests is that at least under present conditions if pre-school children are to be adequately cared for, frequently, one of the adult members of the family will have to remain at home to provide that care. But since most jobs are at least 9 to 5, this will require that the adult members who stay at home temporarily give up pursuing a career. However, such sacrifice appears to conflict with the equal opportunity requirement of Feminist Justice.

Families might try to meet this equal opportunity requirement by having one parent give up pursuing a career for a certain period of time and the other give up pursuing a career for a subsequent (equal) period of time. But there are problems here too. Some careers are difficult to interrupt for any significant period of time, while others never adequately reward latecomers. In addition, given the high rate of divorce and the inadequacies of most legally mandated child support, those who first sacrifice their careers may find themselves later faced with the impossible

task of beginning or reviving their careers while continuing to be the primary caretaker of their children.[29] Furthermore, there is considerable evidence that children will benefit more from equal rearing from both parents.[30] So the option of having just one parent doing the child-rearing for any length of time is, other things being equal, not optimal.

It would seem, therefore, that to truly share child-rearing within the family what is needed is flexible (typically part-time) work schedules that also allow both parents to be together with their children for a significant period every day. Now some flexible job schedules have already been tried by various corporations.[31] But if equal opportunity is to be a reality in our society, the option of flexible job schedules must be guaranteed to all those with pre-school children. Of course, to require employers to guarantee flexible job schedules to all those with pre-school children would place a significant restriction upon the rights of employers, and it may appear to move the practical requirements of Feminist Justice closer to those of Socialist Justice. But if the case for flexible job schedules is grounded on a right to equal opportunity then at least defenders of Liberal Democratic Justice will have no reason to object. This is clearly one place where Feminist Justice with its focus on equal opportunity within the family tends to drive Liberal Democratic Justice and Socialist Justice closer together in their practical requirements.

Recently, however, Christina Hoff Sommers has criticized feminist philosophers for being "against the family."[32] Sommer's main objection is that feminist philosophers have criticized traditional family structures without adequately justifying what they would put in its place. In this paper, I have tried to avoid any criticism of this sort by first articulating a defensible version of the feminist ideal of androgyny which can draw upon support from both Liberal Democratic and Socialist Conceptions of Justice and then by showing what demands this ideal would impose upon family structures. Since Sommers and other critics of the feminist ideal of androgyny also support a strong requirement of equal opportunity, it is difficult to see how they can consistently do so while denying the radical implications of that requirement (and the ideal of androgyny that underlies it) for traditional family structures.[33]

NOTES

1. See, for example, Ann Ferguson, "Androgyny as an Ideal for Human Development," in *Feminism and Philosophy,* Mary Vetterling-Braggin *et al.,* eds. (Totowa: Rowman and Littlefield, 1977), pp. 45–69; Mary Ann Warren, "Is Androgyny the Answer to Sexual Stereotyping?" in *"Femininity," "Masculinity," and "Androgyny,"* Mary Vetterling-Braggin, ed. (Totowa: Rowman and Littlefield, 1982), pp. 170–186; A. G. Kaplan and J. Bean, Eds. *Beyond Sex-Role Stereotypes: Reading Toward a Psychology of Androgyny* (Totowa: Rowman and Littlefield, 1976); Andrea Dworkin, *Women Hating* (New York: Dutton, 1974), Part IV; Carol Gould, "Privacy Rights and Public Virtues: Women, the Family and Democracy," in Carol Gould, *Beyond Domination* (Totowa: Rowman and Littlefield, 1983), pp. 3–18; Carol Gould, "Women and Freedom," *The Journal of Social Philosophy* Vol. 15 (1984), 20–34; Linda Lindsey, *Gender Roles* (Englewood Cliffs, NJ: Prentice Hall, 1990); Marilyn Friedman, "Does Sommers like Women?" *Journal of Social Philosophy* Vol. 22 (1991), 75–90. For some feminists who oppose the ideal of androgyny, see Mary Daly *Gyn-Ecology: The Meta-Ethics of Radical Feminism* (Boston: Beacon Press, 1978); Kathryn Pauly Morgan, "Androgyny: A Conceptual Critique," *Social Theory and Practice,* Vol. 8 (1982); Jean Bethke Elshtain, "Against androgyny," *Telos,* Vol. 47 (1981), 5–21; Kari Weil, *Androgyny and the Denial of Difference* (Charlottesville: University of Virginia, 1992), especially Part III.

2. Joyce Trebilcot, "Two Forms of Androgynism" reprinted in *Feminism and Philosophy,* Mary Vetterling-Braggin, *et al.,* eds. (Totowa: Rowman and Littlefield, 1977), pp. 70–78.

3. Mary Ann Warren, "Is Androgyny the Answer to Sexual Stereotyping?" pp. 178–179.

4. Trebilcot, "Two Forms of Androgynism," pp. 74–77.

5. On this point, see Edmund Pincoffs, *Quandaries and Virtues* (Lawrence: University of Kansas, 1986), Chapter 5.

6. Of course, I cannot provide a full account of how these virtues are to be justifiably inculcated, although I will make some specific recommendations later in this chapter.

7. See, for example, Morgan, "Androgyny: A Conceptual Critique," pp. 256–257.

8. See, for example, Mary Daly, *Gyn-Ecology: The Meta-Ethics of Radical Feminism,* p. xi.

9. Margrit Eichler, *The Double Standard* (New York: St. Martin's Press, 1980), pp. 69–71; Elizabeth Lane Beardsley, "On Curing Conceptual Confusion" in *"Feminity," "Masculinity," and "Androgyny,"* Mary Vetterling-Braggin, *et al.,* eds. (Totowa: Littlefield and Adams, 1982), pp. 197–202; Mary Daly, "The Qualitative Leap Beyond Patriarchal Religion," *Quest* Vol. 1 (1975), 20–40; Janice Raymond, "The Illusion of Androgyny," *Quest* Vol. 2 (1975), 57–66.

10. For a valuable discussion and critique of these two viewpoints, see Iris Young, "Humanism, Gynocentrism and Feminist Politics," *Women's Studies International Forum* (1985) Vol. 8, pp. 173–183.

11. Elizabeth Wolgast, *Equality and the Rights of Women* (Ithaca: Cornell University Press, 1980).

12. Moreover, given that the basic rights that we have in society, such as a right to equal opportunity and a right to welfare, are equal for all citizens and are not based on our differing natural abilities, these rights are not even in this derivative sense based on one's sex.

13. Anne Moir and David Jessel, *Brain Sex* (New York: Dell Publishing Co., 1991).

14. See, for example, Virginia Held, *Rights and Goods* (New York: Free Press, 1984), especially chap. 11; and Gloria Steinem "What It Would Be Like if Women Win," *Time,* 31 August 1979, pp. 22–23; Mary Jeanne Larrabee, "Feminism and Parental Roles: Possibilities for Changes," *Journal of Social Philosophy* 14 (1983): 18. See also National Organization for Women (NOW) Bill of Rights, and United States Commission on Civil Rights, *Statement on the Equal Rights Amendment* (1978).

15. John Rawls, *A Theory of Justice* (Cambridge: Harvard University Press, 1971), p. 73.

16. See, for example, Elizabeth Allgeier and Naomi McCormick, eds. *Changing Boundaries* (Palo Alto, Calif.: Mayfield Publishing Co., 1983), Part I.

17. See, for example, *Toward Economic Justice for Women,* prepared by Women's Economic Agenda Working Group (Institute for Policy Studies, Washington, D.C., 1985); Jo Freeman, ed., *Women: A Feminist Perspective* (Palo Alto, Calif.: Mayfield Publishing Co. 1984), Part 4; *The Women's Movement: Agenda for the '80s,* an Editorial Research Report (Washington, D.C.: Congressional Quarterly Inc., 1981).

18. Alison M. Jagger and Paula Rothenberg, *Feminist Frameworks,* 2nd ed. (New York: McGraw-Hill, 1984), p. 216.

19. See, for example, Joyce Trebilcot, *Mothering* (Totowa, N.J.: Rowman & Allanheld, 1984); Irene Dia-

mond, *Families, Politics and Public Policy* (New York: Longman Inc., 1983).

20. Bruno Bettelheim, "Fathers Shouldn't Try to Be Mothers," *Parents Magazine,* October 1956, pp. 40 and 126–29.

21. See, for example, Ann Ferguson, "Androgyny as an Ideal for Human Development," in *Feminism and Philosophy,* ed. Vetterling-Braggin et al.; and Evelyn Reed, "Women: Caste, Class or Oppressed Sex?", in *Morality in Practice,* ed. James P. Sterba (Belmont, Calif.: Wadsworth Publishing Co., 1983), pp. 222–28.

22. See James P. Sterba, *How to Make People Just* (Totowa, N.J.: Rowman & Allanheld, 1988), especially chaps. 7–9.

23. See Barbara Katz Rothman, "How Science Is Redefining Parenthood." *Ms.,* August 1982, pp. 154–58.

24. D. A. Lloyd Thomas, "Competitive Equality of Opportunity," *Mind* (1977): 398.

25. Rawls, *Theory of Justice,* p. 74.

26. See Bernard Williams, "The Idea of Equality," in *Philosophy, Politics and Society,* 2nd series, ed. Peter Laslett and W. G. Runciman (Oxford: Oxford University Press, 1969), pp. 110–31. For a literary treatment, see Kurt Vonnegut, Jr., "Harrison Bergeron," in *Welcome to the Monkey House* (New York: Dell, 1968), pp. 7–13.

27. Rawls, *Theory of Justice,* pp. 300–01.

28. *New York Times,* 25 November 1987.

29. See Lenore Weitzman, *The Divorce Revolution: The Unexpected Social and Economic Consequences for Women and Children in America* (New York: Free Press, 1985).

30. Dorothy Dinnerstein, *The Mermaid and the Minotaur* (New York: 1977); Nancy Chodorow, *Mothering: Psychoanalysis and the Sociology of Gender* (Berkeley: 1978); Vivian Gornick, "Here's News: Fathers Matter as Much as Mothers," *Village Voice,* 13 October 1975.

31. *New York Times,* 27 November 1987.

32. Christina Hoff Sommers, "Philosophers Against the Family," in *Person to Person,* ed. Hugh LaFollette and George Graham (Philadelphia: Temple University Press, 1988).

33. In "The Equal Obligation of Mothers and Fathers," in *Having Children,* ed. Onora O'Neill and William Ruddick (New York: Oxford University Press, 1979), pp. 227–40, Virginia Held approaches the problem of what should be the relationship of parents to child-rearing by first assuming that both parents have an equal obligation to contribute to the rearing of their children and then seeking to determine what that equal obligation requires. She determines that parents have an obligation to exert an equal effort in contributing what their children need. As far as I can tell, Held's results about what parents owe their children complement my results about what parents ought to have coming to them in rearing their children, namely, day care facilities and/or flexible job schedules sufficient to maintain equal opportunity.

25 Philosophers against the Family

CHRISTINA SOMMERS

MUCH OF WHAT COMMONLY counts as personal morality is measured by how well we behave within family relationships. We live our moral lives as son or daughter to this mother and that father, as brother or sister to that sister or brother, as father or mother, grandfather, granddaughter to that boy or girl or that man or woman. These relationships and the moral duties defined by them were once popular topics of moral casuistry; but when we turn to the literature of recent moral philosophy, we find little discussion on what it means to be a good son or daughter, a good mother or father, a good husband or wife, a good brother or sister.

Modern ethical theory concentrates on more general topics. Perhaps the majority of us who do ethics accept some version of Kantianism or utilitarianism, and these mainstream doctrines are better designed for telling us about what we should do as persons in general than about our special duties as parents or children or siblings. We believe, perhaps, that these universal theories can fully account for the morality of special relations. In any case, modern ethics is singularly silent on the bread and butter issues of personal morality in daily life. But silence is only part of it. With the exception of marriage itself, the relationships in the family are biologically given. The contemporary philosopher is, on the whole, actively unsympathetic to the idea that we have *any* duties defined by relationships that we have not voluntarily entered into. We do not, after all, choose our parents or siblings, and even if we do choose to have children, this is not the same as choosing, say, our friends. Because the special relationships that constitute the family as a social arrangement are, in this sense, not voluntarily assumed, many moralists feel bound in principle to dismiss them altogether. The practical result is that philosophers are to be found among those who are contributing to an ongoing disintegration of the traditional family. In what follows I expose some of the philosophical roots of the current hostility to family morality. My own view that the ethical theses underlying this hostility are bad philosophy is made evident throughout the discussion.

The Moral Vantage

Social criticism is a heady pastime to which philosophers are professionally addicted. One approach is Aristotelian in method and temperament. It is antiradical, though it may be liberal, and it approaches the task of needed reform with a prima facie respect for the norms of established morality. It is conservationist and cautious in its recommendations for change. It is therefore not given to such proposals as abolishing the family or abolishing private property and, indeed, does not look kindly on such proposals from other philosophers. The antiradicals I am concerned about are not those who would be called Burkean. I call them liberal but this use of the term is somewhat perverse since, in my stimulative use, a liberal is a philosopher who advocates social reform but always in a conservative spirit. My liberals share with Aristotle the conviction that the traditional arrangements have great moral weight and that common opinion is a primary source of moral truth. A good modern example is Henry Sidgwick with his constant appeal to common sense. But philosophers like John Stuart Mill, William James, and Bertrand Russell can also be cited. On the other hand, since no radical can be called a liberal in my sense, many so-called liberals could be perversely excluded. Thus when John Rawls toys with the possibility of abolishing the family because kinship bias is a force inimical to equality of opportunity, he is no liberal.

The more exciting genre of social criticism is not liberal-Aristotelian but radical and Platonist in spirit. Its vantage is external or even supernal to the social institutions it has placed under moral scrutiny. Plato was as aware as anyone could be that what he called the cave was social reality. One reason for calling it a cave was to emphasize the need, as he saw it, for an external, objective perspective on established morality: Another point in so calling it was his conviction that common opinion was benighted, and that reform could not be accomplished except by a great deal of consciousness raising and enlightened social engineering. Plato's supernal vantage made it possible for him to look on social reality in somewhat the way the Army Corps of Engineers looks upon a river that needs to have its course changed and its waywardness tamed. In our own day much social criticism of a Marxist variety has taken this radical approach to social change. And of course much of contemporary feminist philosophy is radical. . . .

Feminism and the Family

I have said that the morality of the family has been relatively neglected. The glaring exception to this is, of course, the feminist movement. This movement is complex, but I am primarily confined to its moral philosophers, of whom the most influen-

tial is Simone de Beauvoir. For de Beauvoir, a social arrangement that does not allow all its participants the scope and liberty of a human subjectivity is to be condemned. De Beauvoir criticizes the family as an unacceptable arrangement since, for women, marriage and childbearing are essentially incompatible with their subjectivity and freedom:

> The tragedy of marriage is not that it fails to assure woman the promised happiness . . . but that it mutilates her: It dooms her to repetition and routine. . . . At twenty or thereabouts mistress of a home, bound permanently to a man, a child in her arms, she stands with her life virtually finished forever (1952, 534).

For de Beauvoir the tragedy goes deeper than marriage. The loss of subjectivity is unavoidable as long as human reproduction requires the woman's womb. De Beauvoir starkly describes the pregnant woman who ought to be a "free individual" as a "stockpile of colloids, an incubator of an egg." And as recently as 1977 she compared childbearing and nurturing to slavery.

It would be a mistake to say that de Beauvoir's criticism of the family is outside the mainstream of Anglo-American philosophy. Her criterion of moral adequacy may be formulated in continental existentialist terms, but its central contention is generally accepted: Who would deny that an arrangement that systematically thwarts the freedom and autonomy of the individual is *eo ipso* defective? What is perhaps a bit odd to Anglo-American ears is that de Beauvoir makes so little appeal to ideals of fairness and equality. For her, it is the loss of autonomy that is decisive.

De Beauvoir is more pessimistic than most feminists she has influenced about the prospects for technological and social solutions. But implicit in her critique is the ideal of a society in which sexual differences are minimal or nonexistent. This ideal is shared by many contemporary feminist philosophers: . . . Richard Wasserstrom (1980), Ann Ferguson (1977), and Alison Jaggar (1977; 1983; 1986) are representative.

Wasserstrom's approach to social criticism is Platonist in its use of a hypothetical good society.

The ideal society is nonsexist and "assimilationist": "In the assimilationist society in respect to sex, persons would not be socialized so as to see or understand themselves or others as essentially or significantly who they were or what their lives would be like because they were either male or female" (1980, 26). Social reality is scrutinized for its approximation to this ideal, and criticism is directed against all existing norms. Take the custom of having sexually segregated bathrooms: Whether this is right or wrong "depends on what the good society would look like in respect to sexual differentiation." The key question in evaluating any law or arrangement in which sex difference figures is: "What would the good or just society make of [it]?"

Thus the supernal light shines on the cave revealing its moral defects. *There,* in the ideal society; gender in the choice of lover or spouse would be of no more significance than eye color. *There* the family would consist of adults but not necessarily of different sexes and not necessarily in pairs. *There* we find equality ensured by a kind of affirmative action which compensates for disabilities. If women are somewhat weaker than men, or if they are subject to lunar disabilities, then this must be compensated for. (Wasserstrom compares women to persons with congenital defects for whom the good society makes special arrangements.) Male-dominated sports such as wrestling and football will . . . be eliminated, and marriage as we know it will not exist.

Other feminist philosophers are equally confident about the need for sweeping change. Ann Ferguson (1977) wants a "radical reorganization of child rearing." She recommends communal living and a deemphasis on biological parenting. In the ideal society "love relationships would be based on the meshing together of androgynous human beings." Carol Gould (1983) argues for androgyny and for abolishing legal marriage. She favors single parenting, co-parenting, and communal parenting. The only arrangement she emphatically opposes is the traditional one where the mother provides primary care for the children. Janice Raymond (1975) is an assimila-

tionist who objects to the ideal of androgyny, preferring instead to speak of a genderless ideal free of male or female stereotypes. Alison Jaggar's ideal is described in a science-fiction story depicting a society in which "neither sex bears children, but both sexes, through hormone treatments, suckle them . . . thus [the author] envisions a society where every baby has three social 'mothers,' who may be male or female, and at least two of whom agree to breast-feed it" (1983). To those of us who find this bizarre, Jaggar replies that this shows the depth of our prejudice in favor of the natural family.

Though they differ in detail, these feminists hold to a common social ideal that is broadly assimilationist in character and inimical to the traditional family. Sometimes it seems as if the radical feminist simply takes the classical Marxist eschatology of the *Communist Manifesto* and substitutes "gender" for "class." Indeed, the feminist and the old-fashioned Marxist do have much in common. Both see their caves as politically divided into two warring factions: one oppressing, the other oppressed. Both see the need of raising the consciousness of the oppressed group to its predicament and to the possibility of removing its shackles. Both look forward to the day of a classless or genderless society. And both are zealots, paying little attention to the tragic personal costs to be paid for the revolution they wish to bring about. The feminists tell us little about that side of things. To begin with, how can the benighted myriads in the cave who do not wish to mesh together with other androgynous beings be reeducated? And how are children to be brought up in the genderless society? Plato took great pains to explain his methods. Would the new methods be as thoroughgoing? Unless these questions can be given plausible answers, the supernal attack on the family must always be irresponsible. The appeal to the just society justifies nothing until it can be shown that the radical proposals do not have monstrous consequences. That has not been shown. Indeed, given the perennially dubious state of the social sciences, it is precisely what *cannot* be shown.

Any social arrangement that falls short of the assimilationist ideal is labeled sexist. It should be noted that this characteristically feminist use of the term differs significantly from the popular or literal sense. Literally, and popularly, sexism connotes unfair discrimination. But in its extended philosophical use it connotes discrimination, period. Wasserstrom and many feminists trade on the popular pejorative connotations of sexism when they invite us to be antisexist. Most liberals are antisexist in the popular sense. But to be antisexist in the technical, radical philosophical sense is not merely to be opposed to discrimination against women; it is to be *for* what Wasserstrom calls the assimilationist ideal. The philosopher antisexist opposes any social policy that is nonandrogynous, objecting, for example, to legislation that allows for maternity leave. As Alison Jaggar remarks: "We do not, after all, elevate 'prostate leave' into a special right of men" (1977). From being liberally opposed to sexism, one may in this way insensibly be led to a radical critique of the family whose ideal is assimilationist and androgynous. For it is very clear that the realization of the androgynous ideal is incompatible with the survival of the family as we know it.

The neological extension of labels such as "sexism," "slavery," and "prostitution" is a feature of radical discourse. The liberal too will sometimes call for radical solutions to social problems. Some institutions are essentially unjust. To reform slavery or totalitarian systems of government is to eliminate them. The radical trades on these extreme practices in characterizing other practices—for example, characterizing low wages as "slave" wages and the worker who is paid them as a "slave" laborer. Taking these descriptions seriously may put one on the way to treating a system of a free labor market as a "slave system," which, in simple justice, must be overthrown and replaced by an alternative system of production.

Comparing mothers and wives to slaves is a common radical criticism of the family: Presumably most slaves do not want to be slaves. In fact, the majority of wives and mothers want to be wives and mothers. Calling these women slaves is

therefore a pejorative extension of the term. To be slaves in the literal sense these women would have to be too dispirited and oppressed or too corrupt even to want freedom from slavery. Yet that is how some feminist philosophers look upon women who opt for the traditional family. It does seem fanciful and not a little condescending to see them so, but let us suppose that it is in fact a correct and profound description of the plight of married women and mothers. Would it now follow that the term "slave" literally applies to them? Not quite yet. Before we could call these women slaves, we should have to have made a further assumption. Even timorous slaves too fearful of taking any step to freedom are under no illusion that they are not slaves. Yet it is a fact that most women and mothers do not *think* of themselves as slaves, so we must assume that the majority of women have been systematically deluded into thinking they are free. And that assumption, too, is often explicitly made. Here the radical feminist will typically explain that, existentially, women, being treated by men as sex objects, are especially prone to bad faith and false consciousness. Marxist feminists will see them as part of an unawakened and oppressed economic class. Clearly we cannot call on a deluded woman to cast off her bonds before we have made her *aware* of her bondage. So the first task of freeing the slave woman is dispelling the thrall of a false and deceptive consciousness. One must raise her consciousness to the reality of her situation. (Some feminists acknowledge that it may in fact be too late for many of the women who have fallen too far into the delusions of marriage and motherhood. But the educative process can save many from falling into the marriage and baby trap.)

In this sort of rhetorical climate nothing is what it seems. Prostitution is another term that has been subjected to a radical enlargement. Alison Jaggar believes that a feminist interpretation of the term "prostitution" is badly needed and asks for a "philosophical theory of prostitution" (1986). Observing that the average woman dresses for men, marries a man for protection, and so on, she says: "For contemporary radical feminists, prostitution is the archetypal relationship of women to men" (1986, 115).

Of course, the housewife Jaggar has in mind might be offended at the suggestion that she herself is a prostitute, albeit less well paid and less aware of it than the professional street prostitute. To this the radical feminist reply is, to quote Jaggar:

> Individuals' intentions do not necessarily indicate the true nature of what is going on. Both man and woman might be outraged at the description of their candlelit dinner as prostitution, but the radical feminist argues this outrage is due simply to the participants' failure or refusal to perceive the social context in which the dinner occurs (1986, 117).

Apparently, this failure or refusal to perceive affects most women. Thus we may even suppose that the majority of women who have been treated by a man to a candlelit dinner prefer it to other dining alternatives they have experienced. To say that these preferences are misguided is a hard and condescending doctrine. It would appear that most feminist philosophers are not overly impressed with Mill's principle that there can be no appeal from a majority verdict of those who have experienced two alternatives.

The dismissive feminist attitude to the widespread preferences of women takes its human toll. Most women, for example, prefer to have children, and few of those who have them regret having them. It is no more than sensible, from a utilitarian standpoint, to take note of the widespread preference and to take it seriously in planning one's own life. But a significant number of women discount this general verdict as benighted, taking more seriously the idea that the reported joys of motherhood are exaggerated and fleeting, if not altogether illusory. These women tell themselves and others that having babies is a trap to be avoided. But for many women childlessness has become a trap of its own, somewhat lonelier than the more conventional traps of marriage and babies. Some come to find their childlessness re-

grettable; this sort of regret is common to those who flout Mill's reasonable maxim by putting the verdict of ideology over the verdict of human experience.

It is a serious defect of American feminism that it concentrates its zeal on impugning femininity and feminine culture at the expense of the grassroot fight against economic and social injustices to which women are subjected. As we have seen, the radical feminist attitude to the woman who enjoys her femininity is condescending or even contemptuous. Indeed, the contempt for femininity reminds one of misogynist biases in philosophers such as Kant, Rousseau, and Schopenhauer, who believed that femininity was charming but incompatible with full personhood and reasonableness. The feminists deny the charm, but they too accept the verdict that femininity is weakness. It goes without saying that an essential connection between femininity and powerlessness has not been established by *either* party.

By denigrating conventional feminine roles and holding to an assimilationist ideal in social policy, the feminist movement has lost its natural constituency. The actual concerns, beliefs, and aspirations of the majority of women are not taken seriously *except* as illustrations of bad faith, false consciousness, and successful brainwashing. What women actually want is discounted and reinterpreted as to what they have been led to *think* they want (a man, children). What most women *enjoy* (male gallantry; candlelit dinners, sexy clothes, makeup) is treated as an obscenity (prostitution).

As the British feminist Jennifer Radcliffe Richards says:

> Most women still dream about beauty, dress, weddings, dashing lovers, domesticity, and babies . . . but if feminists seem (as they do) to want to eliminate nearly all of these things—beauty, sex conventions, families, and all—for most people that simply means the removal of everything in life which is worth living for (1980, 341–342).

Radical feminism creates a false dichotomy between sexism and assimilation, as if there were nothing in between. This is to ignore completely the middle ground in which it could be recognized that a woman can be free of oppression and nevertheless feminine in the sense abhorred by many feminists. For women are simply not waiting to be freed from the particular chains the radical feminists are trying to sunder. The average woman enjoys her femininity. She wants a man, not a roommate. She wants fair economic opportunities, and she wants children and the time to care for them. These are the goals that women actually have, and they are not easily attainable. But they will never be furthered by an elitist radical movement that views the actual aspirations of women as the product of a false consciousness. There is room for a liberal feminism that would work for reforms that would give women equal opportunity in the workplace and in politics, but would leave untouched and unimpugned the basic institutions that women want and support: marriage and motherhood. Such a feminism is already in operation in some European countries. But it has been obstructed in the United States by the ideologues who now hold the seat of power in the feminist movement (Hewlett, 1986).

In characterizing and criticizing American feminism, I have not taken into account the latest revisions and qualifications of a lively and variegated movement. There is a kind of feminism-of-the-week that one cannot hope to keep abreast of, short of giving up all other concerns. The best one can do for the present purposes is attend to central theses and arguments that bear on the feminist treatment of the family. Nevertheless, even for this limited purpose, it would be wrong to omit discussion of an important turn taken by feminism in the past few years. I have in mind the recent literature on the idea that there is a specific female ethic that is more concrete, less rule-oriented, more empathetic and caring, and more attentive to the demands of a particular context. The kind of feminism that accepts the idea that women differ from men in approaching ethical dilemmas and social problems from a care perspective is not oriented to androgyny as an ideal. Rather it seeks to develop this special female ethic and give it greater practical scope.

The stress on context might lead one think these feminists are more sympathetic to the family as the social arrangement that shapes the moral development of women and is the context for many of the moral dilemmas that women actually face. However, one sees as yet no attention being paid to the fact that feminism itself is a force working against the preservation of the family. Psychologists like Carol Gilligan and philosophers like Lawrence Blum concentrate their attention on the moral quality of the caring relationships, but these relationships are themselves not viewed in their concrete embeddedness in any formal social arrangement.

It should also be said that some feminists are moving away from earlier hostility to motherhood (Trebilcot, 1984). Here, too, one sees the weakening of the assimilationist ideal in the acknowledgment of a primary gender role. However, childrearing is not primarily seen within the context of the family but as a special relationship between mother and daughter or—more awkwardly—between mother and son, a relationship that effectively excludes the male parent. And the often cultist celebration of motherhood remains largely hostile to traditional familial arrangements.

It is too early to say whether a new style of nonassimilationist feminism will lead to a mitigation of the assault on the family or even on femininity. In any case, the recognition of a female ethic of care and responsibility is hardly inconsistent with a social ethic that values the family as a vital, perhaps indispensable, institution. And the recognition that women have their own moral style may well be followed by a more accepting attitude to the kind of femininity that the more assimilationist feminists reject.

REFERENCES

De Beauvoir, Simone. 1952. *The Second Sex*. H. M. Parshley, trans. New York: Random House.

————. 1977. "Talking to De Beauvoir." In *Spare Rib*.

Ferguson, Ann. 1977. "Androgyny as an Ideal for Human Development." In M. Vetterling-Braggin, F. Elliston, and J. English, eds. *Feminism and Philosophy*, pp. 45–69. Totowa: N.J.: Rowman and Littlefield.

Gould, Carol. 1983. "Private Rights and Public Virtues: Woman, the Family and Democracy." In Carol Gould, ed. *Beyond Domination*, pp. 3–18. Totowa, N.J.: Rowman and Allanheld.

Hewlett, Sylvia Ann. 1986 *A Lesser Life: The Myth of Woman's Liberation in America*. New York: Morrow.

Jaggar, Alison. 1977. "On Sex Equality." In Jane English, ed. *Sex Equality*, Englewood Cliffs, N.J.: Prentice-Hall.

————. 1983. "Human Biology in Feminist Theory: Sexual Equality Reconsidered." In Gould, ed. *Beyond Domination*.

————. 1986. "Prostitution." In Marilyn Pearsell, ed. *Women and Values: Readings in Recent Feminist Philosophy*, pp. 108–121. Belmont, Calif.: Wadsworth.

Raymond, Janice. 1975. "The Illusion of Androgyny." *Quest: A Feminist Quarterly*. 2.

Richards, Jennifer Radcliffe. 1980. *The Skeptical Feminist*. Hardmondsworth: Penguin.

Trebilcot, Joyce, ed. 1984. *Mothering: Essays in Feminist Theory*. Totowa, N.J.: Rowman and Allanheld.

Wasserstrom, Richard. 1980. *Philosophy and Social Issues*. Notre Dame, Ind.: University of Notre Dame Press.

26   Sommers and the Family

MARILYN FRIEDMAN

1. IN A SERIES OF PAPERS which has recently appeared in several philosophical and general academic publications,[1] Christina Sommers mounts a campaign against feminist philosophers (1989a, 85; 1989b, B2) and "American feminism" in general (1989a, 90–91). Sommers blames feminists for contributing to the current divorce rate and the breakdown of the traditional family, and she repudiates feminist critiques of traditional forms of marriage, family, and femininity. In this paper, I explore Sommers's views in some detail. My aim is not primarily to defend her feminist targets, but to ferret out Sommers's own views of traditional marriage, family, and femininity, and to see whether or not they have any philosophical merit.

2. In her writings, Sommers generally defends what she claims that feminists have challenged. Whether or not she is actually discussing the same things is often open to question since she fails to define the key terms behind which she rallies. Sommers, for examples, endorses "the family," the "traditional family," and "the family as we know it" (1989a, 87–88). These are not equivalent expressions. The so-called traditional family—a nuclear family consisting of a legally married heterosexual couple and their children, in which the man is the sole breadwinner and "head" of the household, and the woman does the domestic work and childcare—comprised only 16% of all U.S. households in 1977, according to the U.S. Census Bureau.[2] Hence, the "traditional family" is no longer "*the family*" or "*the* family as

we know it" (italics mine) but is only one sort of family that we know.

Sommers also rallies behind "femininity," "feminine culture," "conventional feminine roles," and "a primary gender role" (1989a, 90, 92). These expressions, as well, call for clarification; they do not necessarily refer to the same practices. In recent years, many feminists have defended various aspects of what might also be called "feminine culture." Sommers notes a few of these authors and works (Carol Gilligan, for example), but finds one reason or another for repudiating each one that she cites.[3]

3. To see what Sommers is promoting under the banner of "feminine culture," we should look to Sommers's claims about what women value, want, and enjoy.[4] First, there are wants, values, and enjoyments pertaining to men.[5] Sommers claims that women want "a man," "marriage," and "to marry good providers."[6] She asserts that "most women" enjoy "male gallantry," that the "majority of women" enjoy being "treated by a man to a candlelit dinner," and that "many women . . . swoon at the sight of Rhett Butler carrying Scarlett O'Hara up the stairs to a fate undreamt of in feminist philosophy."[7]

Second, there are wants, values, and enjoyments having to do with children. Women, Sommers tells us, want children, motherhood, "*conventional* motherhood," "family," and "the time to care for children."[8] In a revealing turn of phrase, Sommers also asserts that women are

From "They Lived Happily Ever After: Sommers on Women and Marriage," Journal of Social Philosophy *Vol. XXI (1990). Reprinted by permission.*

"willing to pay the price" for family and motherhood (1989b, B2). Sommers does not say, however, what she thinks the price is.

Third, there are wants, values, and enjoyments having to do with femininity: Women are said to enjoy their "femininity," makeup, "sexy clothes," and, even more specifically, "clothes that render them 'sex objects.'"[9] On the topic of femininity, Sommers also quotes approvingly (1989a, 90–91) the words of Janet Radcliffe Richards who wrote that, "Most women still dream about beauty, dress, weddings, dashing lovers," and "domesticity," and that, for "most people," "beauty, sex conventions, families, and all" comprise "everything in life which is worth living for."[10]

4. A very few of the wants which Sommers attributes to women do not fit into my three-part classification scheme (men, children, femininity.) Sommers claims that women want "fair economic opportunities" (1989a, 91), and that they are "generally receptive to liberal feminist reforms that enhance their political and economic powers" (1989b, B2). Sommers ironically, does not recognize that the enhanced economic and political power of women makes them less needful of traditional marriage to a "good provider," and when they are married, makes them less afraid to resort to divorce to solve marital and family problems. The economic concerns of liberal feminism directly threaten one colossal support for the "traditional family," namely, the extreme economic vulnerability of the non-income-earning woman and her concomitant material dependence on a "good provider."

Under traditional arrangements, most women not only *wanted* marriage, they *needed* it. It was by far a woman's most socially legitimate option for economic survival. Take away the need, as liberal feminism seeks to do, and at least some of the want also disappears. One otherwise very traditional aunt of mine became a wealthy widow in her late fifties when my rich uncle died. She never remarried. Now a dynamic woman of 82 who travels widely and lives well, she confesses that no man has interested her enough to make it worthwhile to give up her freedom a second time. "I'm

lucky," she confides, "I don't need a meal-ticket." Even a nonfeminist can understand what she is getting at.

5. Before assessing Sommers's overall views, let us rescue Scarlett O'Hara. Sommers's remark that Scarlett O'Hara's rape by Rhett Butler is a fate undreamt of in feminist philosophy is . . . simply stunning. (Note that Sommers does not use the word *rape* here—one of many omissions in her writings.) Even a passing knowledge of feminist philosophy reveals that rape is hardly undreamt of in it.[11] Rape, of course, is not a dream; it is a nightmare. Any form of sexual aggression can involve coercion, intimidation, degradation, physical abuse, battering, and, in extreme cases, death.

The reality of rape is rendered invisible by the many novels and films, such as *Gone With the Wind,* which romanticize and mystify it. They portray the rapist as a handsome man whose domination is pleasurable in bed, and portray women as happy to have their own sexual choices and refusals crushed by such men. In a culture in which these sorts of portrayals are routine, it is no surprise that this scene arouses the sexual desire of some women. However, the name of Richard Speck,[12] to take one example, can remind us that real rape is not the pleasurable fantasy intimated in *Gone With the Wind.* To put the point graphically: Would "many women" still swoon over Butler's rape of O'Hara if they knew that he urinated on her? When you're the victim of rape, you don't have much choice over what goes on.

6. Let us move on to femininity. Sommers never spells out exactly what she means by femininity. For guidance on this topic, we could turn to literature in social psychology which identifies the important traits of femininity and which explores the social devaluation of the feminine (Eagly, 1987). However, it might be more revealing to turn to a different sort of "expert." By a lucky coincidence, I recently acquired a gem of a cultural artifact, a 1965 book entitled, *Always Ask a Man: Arlene Dahl's Key to Femininity,* written by a rather well-known actress and model of the 1960s, Arlene Dahl. I have learned a great deal from this femininity manifesto.

As you might guess from the title, one guiding theme of the book, and of the femininity it aims to promote, is utter deference to the opinions of men. Dahl instructs the female reader: "Look at Yourself Objectively (try to see yourself through a man's eyes)" (p. 2). In Dahl's view, the "truly feminine" woman works "instinctively" at pleasing men and making men feel important. "When [a man] speaks to her, she listens with rapt attention to every word" (p. 5). Dahl believes that every woman has the capacity to measure up to men's ideals of femininity. This is because "Every woman is an actress. (Admit it!) Her first role is that of a coquette. (If you have any doubts just watch a baby girl with her father)" (p. 6).

Dahl's book is laced with quotations from male celebrities who are treated as incontrovertible authorities on what women should be like. Yul Brynner, for example, wants women to be good listeners who are not particularly logical (p. 3). Richard Burton likes women who are "faintly giggly" (p. 3). Tony Perkins thinks that a "girl should act like a girl and not like the head of a corporation—even if she is" (p. 8). The most revealing observation comes from George Hamilton: "A woman is often like a strip of film—obliterated, insignificant—until a man puts a light behind her" (pp. 5–6).

Surprisingly, some of the traits advocated for women by these male celebrities are actually valuable traits; honesty, straightforwardness, maturity, ingenuity, understanding, dignity, generosity, and humor. These traits are not distinctively feminine, however, and that may be the reason why they quickly disappear from Dahl's discussion. The twin themes that resound throughout this femininity manual are that of cultivating one's physical attractiveness and slavishly deferring to men. Instead of a chapter on honesty, a chapter on dignity, and so on, the book features chapters on every aspect of bodily grooming and adornment, including a separate chapter on each of the four basic categories of Caucasian hair color: blonde, redhead, "brownette," and brunette.

The slavish deference to men is crucial, since the whole point of the enterprise is to get a man.

Thus, Dahl explains in the introduction that this book is written to counteract a tendency for women to dress to please other women, and it is also not for "women who want to be beautiful for beauty's sake. Such beauty serves no purpose, other than self-satisfaction, if that can be considered a purpose" (pp. x–xi).

The quintessential prohibition involved in femininity seems to be this: "NEVER upstage a man. Don't try to top his joke, even if you have to bite your tongue to keep from doing it. Never launch loudly into your own opinion on a subject—whether it's petunias or politics. Instead, draw out his ideas to which you can gracefully add your footnotes from time to time" (p. 12). Dahl is less sanguine than Sommers that the role of motherhood fits comfortably into a feminine life; she advises, ". . . don't get so involved with your role of MOTHER that you forget to play WIFE" (p. 9). Once married, your own interests should never override your husband's interests, job, and even hobbies, and, "There should be nothing that takes precedence in your day's schedule over making yourself attractive and appealing for the man in your life," not even your "children's activities" (p. 175)!

Voila, femininity. Such servility shows the dubiousness of Sommers's claim that "a woman can be free of oppression and nevertheless feminine in the sense abhorred by many feminists" (1989a, 91).

7. Let us turn now to Sommer's overall philosophical defense of traditional marriage, family, and femininity. Having asserted that most women value or want all of these traditions, Sommers charges feminist views with a serious defect: They either dismiss or disparage these popular feminine wants and values.[13] Sommers herself defers to these alleged views of most women as if they were as such authoritative: Because "most women" (as she alleges) want traditional marriage and family, therefore these practices must be better than any alternatives. It is important to note that Sommers does not argue that traditional marriage and so on, on balance, promote important moral values better than any feminist alternatives.[14] No

comprehensive moral comparisons appear in her writings. Her argument begins (and ends, as I will argue) with an appeal to popular opinion.

8. Is Sommers right about what "most women" think? She refers to no studies, no representative samples whatsoever to support her generalizations. Whole categories of women are patently excluded from her reference group and are invisible in her writings. This is a fitting moment to mention the "L" word—and I don't mean "liberal." Obviously, no lesbians, unless seriously closeted, are among Sommers's alleged majority of women who want "a man," conventional marriage, or a traditional family.

Even among nonlesbians, [many] women these days do not want a *traditional* marriage or a *traditional* family. Some heterosexual women simply do not want to marry or to have children at all, and many others want *nontraditional* marriages and *nontraditional* families. Surveys show that this attitude, and not the preference for tradition alleged by Sommers, is actually in the majority. In one 1983 study, 63 percent of women surveyed expressed preferences for nontraditional family arrangements (Sapiro, 1990, 355). Sommers's factual claims are, thus, debatable.

Even apart from questions of popularity, the wants, values, and enjoyments which Sommers attributes to "most women" are frankly suspicious as an ensemble. Candlelit dinners do not combine easily with babies. Dashing lovers (extramarital) can be disastrous for a marriage. This list of wants and values seems to show a failure to separate what is idealized and mythic from what is (to put it very advisedly) authentic and genuinely possible in the daily reality of marital and family relationships over the long haul. To hear Sommers tell it, women are blandly unconcerned about wife-battering, incest, marital rape, or the profound economic vulnerability of the traditional non-income-earning wife. This is hard to believe. What is more likely is that, for many women, ". . . they got married and lived happily ever after," is only a fairy tale—especially for those who have been married for a while. Even the most traditional of women, I am convinced, has some sense of the risks involved in traditional heterosexual relationships. As an old saying goes, "When two hearts beat as one, someone is dead."[15]

Sommers's list of women's wants and values is also woefully short. It suggests that this is *all* that "most women" want, that women's aspirations extend no farther than to being "feminine," getting a man—any man—and having babies. On the contrary, many women want meaningful and fulfilling work apart from childcare and domestic labor. Many women aspire to making a social contribution, or they have artistic impulses seeking expression, spiritual callings, deep friendships with other women, and abiding concerns for moral value and their own integrity.[16] One foundational motivation for feminism has always been the aim to overcome the *constraints* on women's genuinely wide-ranging aspirations posed by traditional marital and family arrangements.

9. What philosophical difference would it make if Sommers were right about women's wants and values in general? The popularity of an opinion is hardly an infallible measure of its empirical or moral credibility. Even popular opinions may be based on misinformation, unfounded rumor, and so on. Sommers ignores these possibilities and recommends that we defer to popular opinion on the basis of ". . . Mill's principle that there can be no appeal from a majority verdict of those who have experienced two alternatives" (1989a, 89–90). Sommers is evidently suggesting that feminist critiques of traditional family, marriage, and femininity should be judged by whether or not they conform to the "majority verdict of those who have experienced" the relevant alternatives. Now, carefully understood, this is actually not such a bad idea. However, rather than supporting Sommers's deference to popular opinion, this principle repudiates it.

First, there are more than just "two" feminist alternatives to any of the traditions in question. Consider, for example, the traditionally married, heterosexual couple comprised of dominant, breadwinning male and domestic, childrearing female. Feminists have recommended various alternative family arrangements, including egalitarian heterosexual marriage, communal living, lesbian relationships, and single parenting when economic circumstances are favorable.[17] To decide the value of traditional marriage and family, one would have to try all the relevant alternatives—or at least *some* of them. And on Mill's view, merely experiencing alternatives is not enough; one must also be capable of "appreciating and enjoying" them (Mill, 1979, 9). If Sommers is right, however, most women want and choose traditional family, traditional marriage, and traditional femininity, and thus, do not either experience or enjoy living according to any feminist alternatives. Women such as they are not what Mill calls "competent judges" of the value of those traditions since "they know only their own side of the question" (p. 10). And it is only from the verdict of *competent judges* that Mill believes that "there can be no appeal" (p. 11).

Second, of the "competent judges," in Mill's sense that is, of the women who *have* experienced and enjoyed feminist alternatives to traditional marriage and family, most (I would wager) *prefer the feminist alternatives.* I am referring, among others, to women in lesbian relationships, and women in genuinely egalitarian heterosexual relationships. If I am right about this, then by Mill's principle, we must reject "popular opinion" along with traditional marriage and the rest.

10. The truth of the matter is that in the end, Sommers does not rest her case on Mill's principle. Apparently without realizing that she changes her argument, she ends by appealing to something less vaunted than the majority verdict of those who have experienced and enjoyed *both* traditional family, etc., and various feminist alternatives. Her final court of appeal is simply to "what most people think," "common sense," and "tradition" itself (1989a, 95, 97). Sommers urges that "A moral philosophy that does not give proper weight to the customs and opinions of the community is presumptuous in its attitude and pernicious in its consequences" (1989a, 103). She speaks warmly of the Aristotelian conviction that "traditional arrangements have great moral weight and that common opinion is a primary source of moral truth" (1989a, 83). When it comes to tradition, Sommers would do well to consider Mill again. Mill often deferred to tradition, but it was not a deference from which he thought there was "no appeal," as he amply demonstrated in the important *indictment* of nineteenth century marital traditions on which he collaborated with Harriet Taylor (Mill & Taylor, 1970). (It would be interesting to know what "pernicious . . . consequences," to use Sommers' phrase, flowed from Mill's and Taylor's critique.)

Tradition is a fickle husband. He is constantly changing his mind. On the grounds of tradition, eighty years ago, Sommers would have opposed women's suffrage. One hundred and fifty years ago, she would have opposed women speaking in public (She would have had to do so in private!), opposed the rights of married women to property in their own names, opposed the abolition of slavery, and so on. She would have supported wife-battering since it was permitted by legal tradition—so long as the rod was no bigger around than the size of the husband's thumb.

Not only is tradition ever-changing, it is also plural, both within our own society and globally. Which tradition shall we follow when there is more than one from which to choose? Islam is the world's most widely practiced religion. Shall we non-Islamic women heed the most globally numerous of our sisters' voices and don the veil, retire from public life, and allow husbands to marry up to four wives? Within our own society, marital traditions also vary. Shall we follow the traditions of orthodox Jewish and orthodox Catholic women and avoid all contraceptives? My maternal grandmother did so; she had fourteen births. At nine months per gestation, she spent ten and a half years of her life being pregnant. Although she lingered to the age of eighty-seven, she seemed even older than her age for the final sixteen, worn-out years in which I knew her. Doubtless, that too was part of her tradition.

Why suppose that there is special merit to any of the alternative traditions that we happen to have at this historical moment in this particular geopolitical location? Why suppose that any of our current traditions are better or more deserving of loyalty and support than the traditions toward which we are evolving? And how will we ever evolve if we remain deadlocked in loyalty to all of the traditions we happen to have today?

11. Sommers allows that our traditions may need reform and even recommends "piecemeal social engineering" to deal with "imperfections" in the family (1989a, 97)—although it is noteworthy that she never specifies what these imperfections are, and, in a different passage, she inconsistently calls upon American feminism to leave marriage and motherhood simply "untouched and unimpugned" (1989a, 91).[18] Nevertheless, she insists that her arguments are directed only against those radical feminists who seek the abolition of the family and the "radical reform of preferences, values, aspirations, and prejudices" (1990, 151, 148).

A serious concern to reform imperfections in the family should lead someone to consider the views of nonradical feminist reformers who also criticize marital and family traditions. Many feminists would be content with piecemeal family reform—so long as it was genuine reform (Thorne & Yalom, 1982; Okin, 1987, 1989). Anyway, this issue is a red herring. A dispute over the pace of reform does not show that radical feminist critiques of family traditions are wrong in substance. Most important, by allowing that change is *needed* in family traditions, Sommers effectively concedes that we should not automatically defer to tradition. To admit that reform of tradition is morally permissible is to reject tradition *per se* as an incontestable moral authority. The controversy can only be decided by directly evaluating the conditions of life established by marital and family traditions— and their alternatives.

12. Sommers has one final twist to her argument which we should consider. She notes briefly—all too briefly—that traditions "have *prima facie* moral force" so long as they are not "essentially unjust" (1989a, 97). Sommers does not explain what she means by "essential injustice." Just how much injustice makes a traditional practice "essentially unjust?"

Despite its vagueness, this concession to injustice is critically important. It makes the merit of Sommers's own appeal to tradition contingent on the essential noninjustice of the particular traditions in question. Sommers, however, provides no argument to establish that traditional marriage practices and so forth are not essentially unjust. Nor does she respond substantively to those feminist arguments which claim to locate important injustices in these traditional practices. She rejects all feminist criticisms of the traditional family because they do not coincide with "popular opinion," "common sense," or tradition. Traditional marriage and family are not essentially unjust, in Sommers's view, simply because most people allegedly do not *think* they are.

We seem to have come full circle. Sommers rejects feminist critiques of traditional marriage and so on because they are inconsistent with popular opinion, common sense, and tradition. Tradition is to be relied on, in turn, so long as it is not essentially unjust. But Sommers rejects feminist arguments to show injustices in marital and family traditions simply on the grounds that those arguments are inconsistent with popular opinion, common sense, and tradition itself. Sommers's defense of traditional marriage and family is, in the final analysis, circular and amounts to nothing more than simple *deference to tradition*—indeed, to particular traditions which are no longer so pervasive or popular as Sommers thinks.

13. One final concern: Sommers blames feminists for contributing to the growing divorce rate and the "disintegration of the traditional family."[19] However, feminism could only contribute to the divorce rate if married women ended their marriages as a result of adopting feminist ideas. If Sommers is right, however, in thinking that "most women" reject nonliberal feminist values, then nonliberal feminists could not be having a significant impact on the divorce rate. Sommers cannot have it both ways. Either feminism *is* significantly contributing to the growing divorce rate, in which case it must be in virtue of the wide appeal of feminist ideas about marriage and family, or feminist ideas do *not* have wide appeal, in

which case they cannot be significantly contributing to the growing divorce rate.

14. To conclude: My overall assessment of Sommers's views on marriage, family, and femininity is grim.[20] Most important, Sommers rejects feminist views of marriage, family, and femininity ultimately on the basis of her own simple deference to (allegedly) popular opinion, common sense, and tradition. This deference is defensible only if feminist views about injustices in those traditions can be shown, on *independent* grounds, to be misguided—and Sommers never provides this independent argument.

NOTES.

1. Sommers, 1988, 1989a, 1989b, and 1990.
2. Cited in Thorne & Yalom, 1982, 5.
3. Sommers repudiates the feminist literature which explores the value of mothering (e.g., Trebilcot, 1984) on the grounds that it "remains largely hostile to traditional familial arrangements." She also claims that this literature focuses only on an abstracted mother-child relationship, especially the mother-daughter relationship—a focus that "effectively excludes the male parent" (1989a, 92). Aside from inaccurately summarizing a body of literature, this latter comment, ironically, ignores the fact that under "traditional familial arrangements," the male parent plays a *negligible role* in day-to-day primary childcare, especially in a child's early years.

The comment also ignores the work of Dorothy Dinnerstein (1977) and, especially, of Nancy Chodorow (1978), which precisely urges *shared parenting* and a prominent role for the male parent. This work has been extremely influential and widely cited among feminists. I suspect, however, that shared parenting is not the way in which Sommers wants to include the male parent, since this arrangement is not "traditional" and it challenges the idea of a "primary gender role" that Sommers appears to support (1989a, 92). Sommers, herself, thus fails to clarify the role of the male parent in her account.

4. Sommers complains that feminist philosophers have not been entrusted by ordinary women with a mission of speaking on behalf of those ordinary women (1989b, B3). Sommers, however, appears to think that she is thus entrusted, since she does not hesitate to make claims about what "most women . . . prefer," what "women actually want," and what "most women *enjoy*" (1989a, 90).

5. The following classification scheme is my own. The categories are not meant to be mutually exclusive.

6. Quotations are, respectively, from: 1989a, 90; 1989a, 91; and 1990, 150.

7. Quotations are, respectively, from: 1989a, 90; 1989a, 89; and 1989b, B3.

8. Quotations are, respectively, from: 1989a, 90; 1989a, 91; 1990, 150, italics mine; 1989b, B2; and 1989a, 91.

9. Quotations are, respectively, from: 1989a, 90; 1989a, 90; 1989a, 90; and 1990, 150.

10. Richards, 1980, 341–342. Quoted in Sommers, 1989a, 90–91.

11. Some important early papers are anthologized in: Vetterling-Braggin et al., 1977, Part VI. Another important, relatively early study is Brownmiller, 1976.

12. In 1966, Richard Speck stunned the city of Chicago and the nation by raping, killing, and, in some cases, mutilating the bodies of eight out of nine nursing students who shared a house together on Chicago's South Side. The nurse who survived did so by hiding under a bed until Speck left the house after having apparently lost count. That woman might well swoon over Scarlett O'Hara's rape, but it would not be a swoon of ecstasy.

13. 1989a, 88–91. Sommers writes: "It is a serious defect of American feminism that it concentrates its zeal on impugning femininity and feminine culture at the expense of the grass root fight against economic and social injustices to which women are subjected" (p. 90). American feminism has hardly neglected the fight against economic or social injustice against women. Apart from that, the *Philosopher's Index* back to 1970 contains no citations of writings by Sommers herself on "the economic and social injustices to which women are subjected." In the essays reviewed here, she does not even identify the injustices she has in mind.

14. Sommers does warn that "many women" who avoid motherhood find themselves lonely (1989a, 90), and she suggests that those who avoid or divorce themselves from the patriarchal family "often" suffer harm and "might" feel "betrayed by the ideology" which led them to this state (1989b, B3). These faintly threatening suggestions are left unexplained and unsupported.

15. I was reminded of this old saying by an article by Janyce Katz (1990, 88) in which Dagmar Celeste, then the "First Lady of Ohio," is quoted as mentioning it.

16. Raising children involves awesome moral responsibilities, as Sommers herself emphasizes when lamenting the increasing divorce rate. These profound moral responsibilities entail that we should not casually reinforce the cultural ideology which declares that the only hope of women's fulfillment in life depends on their *having* children. Sommers complains about divorce because of the harm it inflicts on children (1989a, 98–102), but she never cautions women to consider these

moral obligations before marrying or having children in the first place.

17. Cf. Hunter College Women's Studies Collective, 1983, Ch. 9.

18. My worry is that Sommers's occasional, reasonable call for piecemeal family reform disguises a hidden agenda that aims to deadlock us in certain family traditions as we know them now (or knew them three decades ago). This appearance might be dispelled if she were to identify the imperfections she recognizes in the family.

19. 1989a, 82–83, 99–102. Sommers admits that "no reliable study has yet been made comparing children of divorced parents to children from intact families who [sic] parents do not get on well together." She claims cavalierly that "any such study would be compromised by some arbitrary measures of parental incompatibility and one could probably place little reliance on them" (1989a, 101). However, she ignores her own claims of limited evidence on this issue and argues as if it were fact that children of divorced parents are invariably worse off than if their parents had remained married.

When Sommers discusses the problem of divorce, she tends to assimilate the philosophical culprits onto one model: They are all wrong for disregarding "special duties" to family members, especially to children. This latter accusation is simply irrelevant in regard to feminists; no serious feminist literature suggests that responsibilities toward children should be disregarded.

20. Overall, her presentations are marred by ambiguities, inconsistencies, dubious factual claims, misrepresentations of feminist literature, and faulty arguments.

REFERENCES

Brownmiller, Susan. 1976. *Against Our Will: Men, Women and Rape.* New York: Bantam.

Chodorow, Nancy: 1978. *The Reproduction of Mothering.* Berkeley: University of California Press.

Dahl, Arlene. 1965. *Always Ask a Man: Arlene Dahl's Key to Femininity.* Englewood Cliffs, N.J.: Prentice-Hall.

Dinnerstein, Dorothy: 1977. *The Mermaid and the Minotaur: Sexual Arrangements and Human Malaise.* New York: Harper & Row.

Eagly, Alice. 1987. *Sex Differences in Social Behavior.* Hillsdale, N.J.: Erlbaum.

Hunter College Women's Studies Collective. 1983. *Women's Realities, Women's Choices.* New York: Oxford University Press.

Katz, Janyce. 1990. "Celestial Reasoning: Ohio's First Lady Talks About Love and Feminism." *Ms: The World of Women, 1, 2* (September/October), p. 88.

Mill, John Stuart, 1979. *Utilitarianism.* George Sher, ed. Indianapolis: Hackett.

Mill, John Stuart and Harriet Taylor. 1970. *Essays on Sex Equality.* Alice S. Rossi, ed. Chicago: University of Chicago Press.

Okin, Susan Moller. 1987. "Justice and Gender." *Philosophy & Public Affairs, 16* (Winter), pp. 42–72.

————. 1989. *Justice, Gender, and the Family.* New York: Basic Books.

Richards, Janet Radcliffe, 1980. *The Sceptical Feminist.* Harmondsworth: Penguin.

Sapiro, Virginia, 1990. *Women in American Society.* Mountain View, Calif.: Mayfield Publishing Co.

Sommers, Christina. 1988. "Should the Academy Support Academic Feminism?" *Public Affairs Quarterly, 2, 3* (July), 97–120.

————. 1989a. "Philosophers Against the Family." In: George Graham and Hugh LaFollette, eds. *Person to Person.* Philadelphia: Temple University Press, 82–105.

————. 1989b. "Feminist Philosophers Are Oddly Unsympathetic to the Women They Claim to Represent." *Chronicle of Higher Education,* October 11, pp. B2–B3.

————. 1990. "The Feminist Revelation," *Social Philosophy and Policy Center, 8, 1* (Autumn), 141–158.

Thorne, Barrie, with Marilyn Yalom, eds. 1982. *Rethinking the Family.* New York: Longman.

Trebilcot, Joyce, ed. 1984. *Mothering: Essays In Feminist Theory.* Totowa, N.J.: Rowman and Allanheld.

Vetterling-Braggin, Mary, Frederick A. Elliston, and Jane English, eds. 1977. *Feminism and Philosophy.* Totowa, N.J.: Littlefield, Adams & Co.

Part VII

Postmodern Justice

27   The Postmodern Condition

JEAN-FRANÇOIS LYOTARD

THE OBJECT OF THIS STUDY is the condition of knowledge in the most highly developed societies. I have decided to use the word *postmodern* to describe that condition. The word is in current use on the American continent among sociologists and critics: it designates the state of our culture following the transformations which, since the end of the nineteenth century, have altered the game rules for science, literature, and the arts. The present study will place these transformations in the context of the crisis of narratives.

Science has always been in conflict with narratives. Judged by the yardstick of science, the majority of them prove to be fables. But to the extent that science does not restrict itself to stating useful regularities and seeks the truth, it is obliged to legitimate the rules of its own game. It then produces a discourse of legitimation with respect to its own status, a discourse called philosophy. I will use the term modern to designate any science that legitimates itself with reference to a metadiscourse of this kind making an explicit appeal to some grand narrative, such as the dialectics of Spirit, the hermeneutics of meaning, the emancipation of the rational or working subject, or the creation of wealth.[1] For example, the rule of consensus between the sender and addresse of a statement with truth-value is deemed acceptable if it is cast in terms of a possible unanimity between rational minds: this is the Enlightenment narrative, in which the hero of knowledge works toward a good ethico-political end—universal peace. As can be seen from this example, if a metanarrative implying a philosophy of history is used to legitimate knowledge, questions are raised concerning the validity of the institutions governing the social bond: these must be legitimated as well. Thus justice is consigned to the grand narrative in the same way as truth.

Simplifying to the extreme, I define *postmodern* as incredulity toward metanarratives. This incredulity is undoubtedly a product of progress in the sciences: but that progress in turn presupposes it. To the obsolescence of the metanarrative apparatus of legitimation corresponds, most notably the crisis of metaphysical philosophy and of the university institutions which in the past relied on it. The narrative function is losing its functors, its great hero, its great dangers, its great voyages, its great goal. It is being dispersed in clouds of narrative language elements—narrative, but also denotative, prescriptive, descriptive, and so on. Conveyed within each cloud are pragmatic valencies specific to its kind. Each of us lives at the intersection of many of these. However, we do not necessarily establish stable language combinations, and the properties of the ones we do establish are not necessarily communicable.

Jean-François Lyotard, The Postmodern Condition: A Report on Knowledge, *trans. Geoff Bennington and Brian Massumi (Minneapolis: University of Minnesota Press. 1984). Introduction and Sections 9 to 11, and 14, pp. xxiii–xxv. 31–47, 64–67. Originally published in France as* Le condition postmoderne: rapport sur le savoir, *copyright 1979 by Les Editions de Minuit. English translation and Forward copyright 1984 by the University of Minnesota. Reprinted by permission.*

Thus the society of the future falls less within the province of a Newtonian anthropology (such as structuralism or systems theory) than a pragmatics of language particles. There are many different language games—a heterogeneity of elements. They only give rise to institutions in patches—local determinism.

The decision makers, however, attempt to manage these clouds of sociality according to input/output matrices, following a logic which implies that their elements are commensurable and that the whole is determinable. They allocate our lives for the growth of power. In matters of social justice and of scientific truth alike, the legitimation of that power is based on its optimizing the system's performance—efficiency. The application of this criterion to all of our games necessarily entails a certain level of terror, whether soft or hard: be operational (that is, commensurable) or disappear.

The logic of maximum performance is no doubt inconsistent in many ways, particularly with respect to contradiction in the socio-economic field: it demands both less work (to lower production costs) and more (to lessen the social burden of the idle population). But our incredulity is now such that we no longer expect salvation to rise from these inconsistencies, as did Marx.

Still, the postmodern condition is as much a stranger to disenchantment as it is the blind positivity of delegitimation. Where, after the metanarratives, can legitimacy reside? The operativity criterion is technological; it has no relevance for judging what is true or just. Is legitimacy to be found in consensus obtained through discussion, as Jürgen Habermas thinks? Such consensus does violence to the heterogeneity of language games. And invention is always born of dissension. Postmodern knowledge is not simply a tool of the authorities; it refines our sensitivity to differences and reinforces our ability to tolerate the incommensurable. . . .

In contemporary society and culture—post-industrial society, postmodern culture [2]—the question of the legitimation of knowledge is for-mulated in different terms. The grand narrative has lost its credibility, regardless of what mode of unification it uses, regardless of whether it is a speculative narrative or a narrative of emancipation.

The decline of narrative can be seen as an effect of the blossoming of techniques and technologies since the Second World War, which has shifted emphasis from the ends of action to its means; it can also be seen as an effect of the redeployment of advanced liberal capitalism after its retreat under the protection of Keynesianism during the period 1930–60, a renewal that has eliminated the communist alternative and valorized the individual enjoyment of goods and services.

Anytime we go searching for causes in this way we are bound to be disappointed. Even if we adopted one or the other of these hypotheses, we would still have to detail the correlation between the tendencies mentioned and the decline of the unifying and legitimating power of the grand narratives of speculation and emancipation.

It is, of course, understandable that both capitalist renewal and prosperity and the disorienting upsurge of technology would have an impact on the status of knowledge. But in order to understand how contemporary science could have been susceptible to those effects long before they took place, we must first locate the seeds of "delegitimation" [3] and nihilism that were inherent in the grand narratives of the nineteenth century.

First of all, the speculative apparatus maintains an ambiguous relation to knowledge. It shows that knowledge is only worthy of that name to the extent that it reduplicates itself ("lifts itself up," *hebt sich auf:* is sublated) by citing its own statements in a second-level discourse (autonymy) that functions to legitimate them. This is as much as to say that, in its immediacy, denotative discourse bearing on a certain referent (a living organism, a chemical property, a physical phenomenon, etc.) does not really know what it thinks it knows. Positive science is not a form of knowledge. And speculation feeds on its suppression. The Hegelian speculative narrative thus harbors a certain skepticism toward positive learning, as Hegel himself admits. [4]

A science that has not legitimated itself is not a true science; if the discourse that was meant to legitimate it seems to belong to a prescientific form of knowledge, like a "vulgar" narrative, it is demoted to the lowest rank, that of an ideology or instrument of power. And this always happens if the rules of the science game that discourse denounces as empirical are applied to science itself.

Take for example the speculative statement: "A scientific statement is knowledge if and only if it can take its place in a universal process of engendering." The question is: Is this statement knowledge as it itself defines it? Only if it can take its place in a universal process of engendering. Which it can. All it has to do is to presuppose that such a process exists (the Life of spirit) and that it is itself an expression of that process. This presupposition, in fact, is indispensable to the speculative language game. Without it, the language of legitimation would not be legitimate; it would accompany science in a nosedive into nonsense, at least if we take idealism's word for it.

But this presupposition can also be understood in a totally different sense, one which takes us in the direction of postmodern culture: we could say, in keeping with the perspective we adopted earlier, that this presupposition defines the set of rules one must accept in order to play the speculative game.[5] Such an appraisal assumes first that we accept that the "positive" sciences represent the general mode of knowledge and second, that we understand this language to imply certain formal and axiomatic presuppositions that it must always make explicit. This is exactly what Nietzsche is doing, though with a different terminology, when he shows that "European nihilism" resulted from the truth requirement of science being turned back against itself.[6]

There thus arises an idea of perspective that is not far removed, at least in this respect, from the idea of language games. What we have here is a process of delegitimation fueled by the demand for legitimation itself. The "crisis" of scientific knowledge, signs of which have been accumulating since the end of the nineteenth century, is not born of a chance proliferation of sciences, itself an effect of progress in technology and the expansion of capitalism. It represents, rather, an internal erosion of the legitimacy principle of knowledge. There is erosion at work inside the speculative game, and by loosening the weave of the encyclopedic net in which each science was to find its place, it eventually sets them free.

The classical dividing lines between the various fields of science are thus called into question—disciplines disappear, overlappings occur at the borders between sciences, and from these new territories are born. The speculative hierarchy of learning gives way to an immanent and, as it were, "flat" network of areas of inquiry, the respective frontiers of which are in constant flux. The old "faculties" splinter into institutes and foundations of all kinds, and the universities lose their function of speculative legitimation. Stripped of the responsibility for research (which was stifled by the speculative narrative), they limit themselves to the transmission of what is judged to be established knowledge, and through didactics they guarantee the replication of teachers rather than the production of researchers. This is the state in which Nietzsche finds and condemns them.[7]

The potential for erosion intrinsic to the other legitimation procedure, the emancipation apparatus flowing from the *Aufklärung* [Enlightenment], is no less extensive than the one at work within speculative discourse. But it touches a different aspect. Its distinguishing characteristic is that it grounds the legitimation of science and truth in the autonomy of interlocutors involved in ethical, social, and political praxis. As we have seen, there are immediate problems with this form of legitimation: the difference between a denotative statement with cognitive value and a prescriptive statement with practical value is one of relevance therefore of competence. There is nothing to prove that if a statement describing a real situation is true, it follows that a prescriptive statement based upon it (the effect of which will necessarily be a modification of that reality) will be just.

Take, for example, a closed door. Between "The door is closed" and "Open the door" there is no relation of consequence as defined in propositional logic. The two statements belong to two autonomous sets of rules defining different kinds of relevance, and therefore of competence. Here, the effect of dividing reason into cognitive or theoretical reason on the one hand, and practical reason on the other, is to attack the legitimacy of the discourse of science. Not directly, but indirectly, by revealing that it is a language game with its own rules (of which the a priori conditions of knowledge in Kant provide a first glimpse) and that it has no special calling to supervise the game of praxis (nor the game of aesthetics, for that matter). The game of science is thus put on a par with the others.

If this "delegitimation" is pursued in the slightest and if its scope is widened (as Wittgenstein does in his own way, and thinkers such as Martin Buber and Emmanuel Lévinas in theirs)[8] the road is then open for an important current of postmodernity: science plays its own game; it is incapable of legitimating the other language games. The game of prescription, for example, escapes it. But above all, it is incapable of legitimating itself, as speculation assumed it could.

The social subject itself seems to dissolve in this dissemination of language games. The social bond is linguistic, but is not woven with a single thread. It is a fabric formed by the intersection of at least two (and in reality an indeterminate number) of language games, obeying different rules. Wittgenstein writes: "Our language can be seen as an ancient city: a maze of little streets and squares, of old and new houses, and of houses with additions from various periods; and this surrounded by a multitude of new boroughs with straight regular streets and uniform houses."[9] And to drive home that the principle of unitotality—or synthesis under the authority of a metadiscourse of knowledge—is inapplicable, he subjects the "town" of language to the old sorites paradox by asking" "how many houses or streets does it take before a town begins to be a town?"[10]

New languages are added to the old ones, forming suburbs of the old town: "the symbolism of chemistry and the notation of the infinitesimal calculus."[11] Thirty-five years later we can add to the list: machine languages, the matrices of game theory, new systems of musical notation, systems of notation for nondenotative forms of logic (temporal logics, deontic logics, modal logics), the language of the genetic code, graphs of phonological structures, and so on.

We may form a pessimistic impression of this splintering: nobody speaks all of those languages, they have no universal metalanguage, the project of the system-subject is a failure, the goal of emancipation has nothing to do with science, we are all stuck in the positivism of this or that discipline of learning, the learned scholars have turned into scientists, the diminished tasks of research have become compartmentalized and no one can master them all.[12] Speculative or humanistic philosophy is forced to relinquish its legitimation duties,[13] which explains why philosophy is facing a crisis wherever it persists in arrogating such functions and is reduced to the study of systems of logic or the history of ideas where it has been realistic enough to surrender them.[14]

Turn-of-the-century Vienna was weaned on this pessimism: not just artists such as Musil, Kraus, Hofmannsthal, Loos, Schönberg, and Broch, but also the philosophers Mach and Wittgenstein.[15] They carried awareness of and theoretical and artistic responsibility for delegitimation as far as it could be taken. We can say today that the mourning process has been completed. There is no need to start all over again. Wittgenstein's strength is that he did not opt for the positivism that was being developed by the Vienna Circle,[16] but outlined in his investigation of language games a kind of legitimation not based on performativity. That is what the postmodern world is all about. Most people have lost the nostalgia for the lost narrative. It in no way follows that they are reduced to barbarity. What saves them from it is their knowledge that legitimation can only spring from their own linguistic practice and communicational interaction. Science "smiling into its beard" at every other belief has taught them the harsh austerity of realism. . . .[17]

. . . Let us say at this point that the facts we have presented concerning the problem of the legitimation of knowledge today are sufficient for our purposes. We no longer have recourse to the grand narratives—we can resort neither to the dialectic of Spirit nor even to the emancipation of humanity as a validation for postmodern scientific discourse. But as we have just seen, the little narrative remains the quintessential form of imaginative invention, most particularly in science.[18] In addition, the principle of consensus as a criterion of validation seems to be inadequate. It has two formulations. In the first, consensus is an agreement between men, defined as knowing intellects and free wills, and is obtained through dialogue. This is the form elaborated by Habermas, but his conception is based on the validity of the narrative of emancipation. In the second, consensus is a component of the system, which manipulates it in order to maintain and improve its performance.[19] It is the object of administrative procedures, in Luhmann's sense. In this case, its only validity is as an instrument to be used toward achieving the real goal, which is what legitimates the system—power. . . .

From the beginning of this study, I have emphasized the differences (not only formal, but also pragmatic) between the various language games, especially between denotative, or knowledge, games and prescriptive, or action, games. The pragmatics of science is centered on denotative utterances, which are the foundation upon which it builds institutions of learning (institutes, centers, universities, etc.). But its postmodern development brings a decisive "fact" to the fore: even discussions of denotative statements need to have rules. Rules are not denotative but prescriptive utterances, which we are better off calling metaprescriptive utterances to avoid confusion (they prescribe what the moves of language games must be in order to be admissible). The function of the differential or imaginative or paralogical activity of the current pragmatics of science is to point out these metaprescriptives (science's "presuppositions")[20] to petition the players to accept different

ones. The only legitimation that can make this kind of request admissible is that it will generate ideas, in other words, new statements.

Social pragmatics does not have the "simplicity" of scientific pragmatics. It is a monster formed by the interweaving of various networks of heteromorphous classes of utterances (denotative, prescriptive, performative, technical, evaluative, etc.). There is no reason to think that it would be possible to determine metaprescriptives common to all of these language games or that a revisable consensus like the one in force at a given moment in the scientific community could embrace the totality of metaprescriptions regulating the totality of statements circulating in the social collectivity. As a matter of fact, the contemporary decline of narratives of legitimation—be they traditional or "modern" (the emancipation of humanity, the realization of the Idea)—is tied to the abandonment of this belief. It is its absence for which the ideology of the "system," with its pretensions to totality, tries to compensate and which it expresses in the cynicism of its criterion of performance.

For this reason, it seems neither possible, nor even prudent, to follow Habermas in orienting our treatment of the problem of legitimation in the direction of a search for universal consensus[21] through what he calls *Diskurs*, in other words, a dialogue of argumentation.[22]

This would be to make two assumptions. The first is that it is possible for all speakers to come to agreement on which rules or metaprescriptions are universally valid for language games, when it is clear that language games are heteromorphous, subject to heterogeneous sets of pragmatic rules.

The second assumption is that the goal of dialogue is consensus. But as I have shown in the analysis of the pragmatics of science, consensus is only a particular state of discussion, not its end.

This double observation (the heterogeneity of the rules and the search for dissent) destroys a belief that still underlies Habermas's research, namely, that humanity as a collective (universal) subject seeks its common emancipation through the regularization of the "moves" permitted in all language games and that the legitimacy of any statement resides in contributing to that emancipation.[23]

It is easy to see what function this recourse plays in Habermas's argument against Luhmann. *Diskurs* is his ultimate weapon against the theory of the stable system. The cause is good, but the argument is not.[24] Consensus has become an outmoded and suspect value. But justice as a value is neither outmoded nor suspect. We must thus arrive at an idea and practice of justice that is not linked to that of consensus.

A recognition of the heteromorphous nature of language games is a first step in that direction. This obviously implies a renunciation of terror, which assumes that they are isomorphic and tries to make them so. The second step is the principle that any consensus on the rules defining a game and the "moves" playable within it *must* be local, in other words, agreed on by its present players and subject to eventual cancellation. The orientation then favors a multiplicity of finite meta-arguments, by which I mean argumentation that concerns metaprescriptives and is limited in space and time.

This orientation corresponds to the course that the evolution of social interaction is currently taking; the temporary contract is in practice supplanting permanent institutions in the professional, emotional, sexual, cultural, family, and international domains, as well as in political affairs. This evolution is of course ambiguous: the temporary contract is favored by the system due to its greater flexibility, lower cost, and the creative turmoil of its accompanying motivations—all of these factors contribute to increased operativity. In any case, there is no question here of proposing a "pure" alternative to the system: we all now know, that an attempt at an alternative of that kind would end up resembling the system it was meant to replace. We should be happy that the tendency toward the temporary contract is ambiguous: it is not totally subordinated to the goal of the system, yet the system tolerates it. This

bears witness to the existence of another goal within the system: knowledge of language games as such and the decision to assume responsibility for their rules and effects.

We are finally in a position to understand how the computerization of society affects this problematic. It could become the "dream" instrument for controlling and regulating the market system, extended to include knowledge itself and governed exclusively by the performativity principle. In that case, it would inevitably involve, the use of terror. But it could also aid groups discussing metaprescriptives by supplying them with the information they usually lack for making knowledgeable decisions. The line to follow for computerization to take the second of these two paths is, in principle, quite simple: give the public free access to the memory and data banks.[25] Language games would then be games of perfect information at any given moment. But they would also be non-zero-sum games, and by virtue of that fact discussion would never risk fixating in a position of minimax equilibrium because it had exhausted its stakes. For the stakes would be knowledge (or information, if you will) and the reserve of knowledge—language's reserve of possible utterances—is inexhaustible. This sketches the outline of a politics that would respect both the desire for justice and the desire for the unknown.

NOTES

1. These grand narratives are what Lyotard calls "metanarratives," philosophical stories which legitimate all other discourse.

2. Certain scientific aspects of postmodernism are inventoried by Ihab Hassan in "Culture, Indeterminacy, and Immanence: Margins of the (Postmodern) Age," *Humanitites in Society,* 1 (1978): 51–85.

3. Claus Mueller uses the expression "a process of delegitimation" in *The Politics of Communication* (New York: Oxford University Press, 1973), p. 164.

4. "Road of doubt . . . road of despair . . . skepticism," writes Hegel in the preface to the *Phenomenology of Spirit* to describe the effect of the speculative drive on natural knowledge.

5. For fear of encumbering this account, I have postponed until a later study the exposition of this group of rules.

6. Nietzsche, "Der europäische Nihilismus" (MS. N VII 3): "der Nihilism, ein normaler Zustand" (MS. W II 1): "Kritik der Nihilism" (MS. W VII 3): "Zum Plane" (MS. W II 1), in *Nietzshes Werke kritische Gesamtausgabe*, vol. 7, pts. 1 and 2 (1887–89) (Berlin: De Gruyter, 1970). These texts have been the object of a commentary by K. Ryjik, *Nietzsche, le manuscrit de Lenzer Heide* (typescript, Départent de philosophie, Université de Paris VIII [Vincennes]).

7. "On the future of our educational institutions," in *Complete Works,* vol. 3.

8. Martin Buber, *Ich und Du* (Berlin: Schocken Verlag, 1922) [Eng. trans. Ronald G. Smith, *I and Thou* (New York: Charles Scribner's Sons, 1937)], and *Dialogisches Leben* (Zürich: Müller, 1947); Emmanuel Lévinas, *Totalité et Infinité* (Lay Haye: Nijhoff, 1961) [Eng. trans. Alphonso Lingis, *Totality and Infinity: An Essay on Exteriority* (Pittsburgh: Duquesne University Press, 1969)], and "Martin Buber und die Erkenntnish theorie" (1958), in *Philosophen des 20. Jahrhunderts* (Stuttgart: Kohlhammer, 1963).

9. *Philosophical Investigations,* sec. 18, p. 8 [by Ludwig Wittgenstein, trans. G. E. M. Anscombe (New York: Macmillan, 1958)].

10. Ibid.

11. Ibid.

12. See for example, "La taylorisation de la recherche," in *(Auto) critique de la science,* pp. 291–3. And especially D. J. de Solla Price. *Little Science, Big Science* (New York: Columbia University Press, 1963), who emphasizes the split between a small number of highly productive researchers (evaluated in terms of publication) and a large mass of researchers with low productivity. The number of the latter grows as the square of the former, so that the number of high productivity researchers only really increases every twenty years. Price concludes that science considered as a social entity is "undemocratic" (p. 59) and that "the eminent scientist" is a hundred years ahead of "the minimal one" (p. 56).

13. See J. T. Desanti, "Sur le rapport traditional des sciences et de la philosophie," in *La Philosophie silencieuse, ou critique des philosophies de la science* (Paris: Seuil, 1975).

14. The reclassification of academic philosophy as one of the human sciences in this respect has a significance far beyond simply professional concerns. I do not think that philosophy as legitimation is condemned to disappear, but it is possible that it will not be able to carry out this work, or at least advance it, without revising its ties to the university institution. See on this matter the preamble to the *Projet d'un institut polytechnique de philosophie* (typescript, Départment de philosophie, Université de Paris VIII, 1979).

15. See Allan Janik and Stephan Toulmin, *Wittgenstein's Vienna* (New York: Simon & Schuster, 1973), and J. Piel (ed.) "Vienne début d'un siècle," *Critique,* 330–40 (1975).

16. See Jürgen Habermas, "Dogmatismus, Vernunft unt Entscheidung—Zu Theorie und Praxis in der verwissenschaftlichen Zivilisation" (1963), in *Theorie und Praxis [Theory and Practice,* abr. edn of 4th German edn. trans. John Viertel (Boston: Beacon Press, 1971)].

17. "Science Smiling into its Beard" is the title of chap. 72, vol. 1 of Musil's *The Man Without Qualities.* Cited and discussed by J. Bouveresse, "La Problématique du sujet".

18. It has not been possible within the limits of this study to analyze the form assumed by the return of narrative in discourses of legitimation. Examples are: the study of open systems, local determinism, antimethod—in general, everything that I group under the name *paralogy.*

19. Nora and Minc, for example, attribute Japan's success in the field of computers to an "intensity of social consensus" that they judge to be specific to Japanese society (*L'Informatisation de la Société,* p. 4). They write in their conclusion, "The dynamics of extended social computerization leads to a fragile society: such a society is constructed with a view to facilitating consensus, but already presupposes its existence, and comes to a standstill if that consensus cannot be realized" (p. 125). Y. Stourdzé, "Les Etats-Unis", emphasizes the fact that the current tendency to deregulate, destabilize, and weaken administration is encouraged by society's loss of confidence in the State's performance capability.

20. This is at least one way of understanding this term, which comes from Ducrot's problematic, *Dire.*

21. *Legitimationsprobleme,* passim, especially pp. 21–2: "Language functions in the manner of a transformer . . . changing cognitions into propositions needs and feelings into normative expectations (commands, values). This transformation produces the far-reaching distinction between the subjectivity of intention and willing, of pleasure and unpleasure on the one hand, and expressions and norms with a *pretension to universality* on the other. Universality signifies the objectivity of knowledge and the legitimacy of prevailing norms: both assume the community constitutive of lived social experience." We see that by formulating the problematic in this way, the question of legitimacy is fixated on one type of reply, universality. This on the one hand presupposes that the legitimation of the subject of knowledge is identical to that of the subject of action (in opposition to Kant's critique, which dissociates conceptual universality, appropriate to the former, and ideal universality, or "supersensible nature," which forms the

horizon of the latter, on the other hand), and maintains that consensus (*Gemeinschaft*) is the only possible horizon for the life of humanity.

22. Ibid., p. 20. The subordination of the metaprescriptives of prescription (i.e. the normalization of laws) to *Diskurs* [Discourse] is explicit, for example, on p. 144: "The normative pretension to validity is itself cognitive in the sense that it always assumes it could be accepted in a rational discussion."

23. Garbis Kortian, *Métacritique* (Paris: Editions de Minuit, 1979) [Eng. trans. John Raffan, *Metacritique: The Philosophical Argument of Jürgen Habermas* (Cambridge: Cambridge University Press, 1980)], pt. 5, examines this enlightenment aspect of Habermas's thought. See by the same author, "Le Discours philosophique et son objet," *Critique*, 384 (1979): 407–19.

24. See J. Poulain ("Vers une pragmatique nucléaire"), and for a more general discussion of the pragmatics of Searle and Gehlen, see J. Poulain, "Pragmatique de la parole et pragmatique de la vie," *Phi zéro* 7, no. 1 (Université de Montréal, September 1978): 5–50.

25. See Tricot et al., *Informatique et libertés,* government report (La Documentation française, 1975); L. Joinet, "Les 'pièges liberaticides' de l'informatique," *Le Monde dipolomatique,* 300 (March 1979): these traps (pièges) are "the application of the technique of 'social profiles' to the management of the mass of the population; the logic of security produced by the automatization of society." See too the documents and analysis in *Interférences,* 1 and 2 (Winter 1974–Spring 1975), the theme of which is the establishment of popular networks of multimedia communication. Topics treated include: amateur radios (especially their role in Quebec during the FLQ affair of October 1970 and that of the "Front commun" in May 1972); community radios in the United States and Canada; the impact of computers on editorial work in the press; pirate radios (before their development in Italy); administrative files, the IBM monopoly, computer sabotage. The municipality of Yverdon (Canton of Vaud), having voted to buy a computer (operational in 1981), enacted a certain number of rules: exclusive authority of the municipal council to decide which data are collected, to whom and under what conditions they are communicated; access for all citizens to all data (on payment); the right of every citizen to see the entries on his file (about 50), to correct them and address a complaint about them to the municipal council and if need be to the Council of State; the right of all citizens to know (on request) which data concerning them is communicated and to whom (*La Semaine media* 18, 1 March 1979, 9).

28 Postmodern Argumentation and Post-Postmodern Liberalism

JEFFREY REIMAN

The Paradox of Postmodernism

MODERNISM IS, ROUGHLY SPEAKING, the Enlightenment belief in a single unified rational perspective, founded on some indubitable evidence given in human experience—either innate concepts à la Descartes and the rationalists or sensations à la Locke and the empiricists—and elaborated according to reliable logical rules. This view was first attacked for its "foundationalism." Philosophers such as Nietzsche, Dewey, Heidegger, and the later Wittgenstein denied that there is any indubitable given upon which truth can be founded. There is no experience, no testimony of the senses or of reason, that blazons forth the undeniable truth. Rather, the "given" is, so to speak, constructed—which is to say, not given to us, but made by us. Some experience or other evidence is interpreted as this or that with this or that epistemological status, on the basis of beliefs that one already has about, say, space or mathematics or sense perception or the nature of what is ultimately real. Postmodernism is an intensification of this attack, with a distinctive political spin.

The intensification takes the following form. If there is no given, interpretation is "fundamental" (not, of course, in the sense of a new foundational given, rather quite the reverse, in the sense of something beneath or behind which we cannot get, something that stands eternally between us and any foundational given). Interpretation is fundamental in the sense that it is the furthest down we can ever get.[1] If interpretation is as far as we can ever get, then every experience is part of a tapestry (textile, text) of beliefs against which it gets its interpretation. And the beliefs themselves are only what they are for us as a result of interpretation of their meaning in light of other beliefs, and other interpretations, and so on.

Accordingly, there can never be just one interpretation of anything. This is sometimes exaggerated into the claim that there are unlimited valid interpretations of everything, a claim that would make it impossible to write a single sentence, since one would have no reason for choosing one string of words rather than another to express one's thoughts! The more modest claim is enough, however, to ground the distinctive postmodern strategy of *deconstruction*. Any supposedly canonical interpretation can be shown to have been purchased by the arbitrary exclusion of other possible ones. There can only be a canonical interpretation if some meaning in a text has been taken as if it were an unquestioned given from which the canonical interpretation then follows. The deconstructer finds the meaning that has been taken as if simply given and shows that it is in fact only one interpretation among other possible ones in view of the "textily" way in which it is woven together with other beliefs. Then, taking a different mean-

From Critical Moral Liberalism *by Jeffrey Reiman (1997), pp. 53–56, 67–69. Reprinted by permission of the publisher, Rowman & Littlefield.*

ing than the supposedly given one as her starting point, the deconstructer shows that other interpretation of the whole text can be spun. Such alternative interpretations must still meet the normal standards for successful interpretation, namely, plausibility, fit with the text, and so on. This is not the "anything goes" that is sometimes associated with deconstructive technique. Rather, the canonical interpretation is deconstructed by means of showing its illicit appeal to sheer given meanings, and the way in which it has been promoted by excluding other possible plausible interpretations.

Related to this technique is the political dimension of postmodernism. Much as any canonical interpretation is necessarily based on excluding alternative possible interpretations, any universal vision is based on excluding what doesn't fit by defining it as "other," "lesser," "lower," "bad," "crazy," "primitive," and so forth. Consequently, Enlightenment universalism based on, say, the shared rationality of human beings reflects (in various versions of the critique) the definition of rationality by exclusion of deviants, or women, or third-world people. Or, at the very least, the establishment of the universal standard becomes a tool or weapon by means of which some can be defined as second rate because they are held not to share the prevailing trait, or not to embody it completely, or the like. Thus, for example, Zygmunt Bauman, in his *Postmodern Ethics,* describes the moral universalism of the modern era "as but a thinly disguised declaration of intent to embark on *Gleichschaltung,* on an arduous campaign to smother the differences."[2] With this, deconstruction becomes a political weapon in defense of the people who have been oppressed because their natures or ways have been excluded from the universal standard—as the means to define that very standard.

Here enters the paradox: The critique of universal standards because they exclude certain individuals or groups of individuals is a critique of those standards for not being universal enough! Consequently, rather than abandoning or oppos-

ing universalism, the critique is itself based on an implicit universal valuation, albeit one that aims to be more inclusive than the ones critiqued.

In short, what postmodernism needs, what virtually every postmodern writer writes as if he or she had, but in fact does not have, is a universal standard for valuing human beings that is compatible with the postmodern critique of universals. I will argue that such a universal can be found and can be defined while keeping to postmodernism's own critical requirements of argumentation.

The Requirements of Postmodern Argumentation

If postmodernism understands itself as (*a*) a form of antifoundationalism and (*b*) a protest against the exclusion of certain human individuals and/or groups from the universal measure of full moral standing, then certain things follow about the way arguments must be made if they are to be acceptable to postmodernists. First of all, arguments must be explicitly based on assumptions actually held by those to whom they are addressed (rather than appealing to foundational givens). Second, arguments must be addressed to all human beings. Putting the two together, arguments must start from assumptions that are shared by all human beings. Arguments must be *universal* in their aim and *ad hominem* in their logical structure.

Actually, the second condition is already suggested by antifoundationalism. If there is no indubitable given, if all starting points are, so to speak, created by interpretation in light of other beliefs, then there is no Archimedean point from which all of a person's beliefs can be shown true or false. Consequently, all arguments must proceed from beliefs that people already hold, which is to say, they must be ad hominem.

Two examples from different contemporary philosophical directions will show the prevalence of ad hominem argumentation in present-day thought. Consider, for example, Rawls's political liberalism, which starts openly by appeal to beliefs held by participants in liberal democratic cultures, assumes explicitly that even within this framework there will be irreconcilable disagreements among reasonable people on fundamental metaphysical and moral beliefs, and proceeds to argue for its very modest liberalism from the hopefully actual overlapping consensus among those fundamental views that presumably permit allegiance to liberal ideals.[3] Consider, for a quite different example, the approach of Habermas's "discourse ethics," which starts from the presuppositions of rational argument aimed at justifying moral norms. Since the implicit aim of such argument is rational persuasion, and since rational persuasion is uncoerced assent in the face of open argumentation and full information, those who engage in justification can be taken as implicitly committed to seeking uncoerced and fully informed assent to their proposals.[4] Accordingly, one can justify only moral norms to which all can freely and informedly consent—the result being not very far from contractarianism of the Rawlsian sort.

There can be postmodern universals if there are ad hominem arguments that can appeal to assumptions necessarily made by all human beings. However, the demand that arguments must appeal to assumptions that all human beings can be taken to share surely seems impossible in the condition of postmodernism, with its objections to universalism and its emphasis on irreducible differences. But the situation is more hopeful than it appears at first, for postmodernists do assume that human beings are rational insofar as postmodernists speak of and to human beings as users of language, interpreters of texts, bearers of culture, and so on—all of which require rational operations. I shall argue that the assumption that human beings are rational leads to other beliefs, which form the basis for a universal moral principle. . . .

Habermas maintains that anyone who engages in rational justification to others implicitly accepts rational argument's commitment to uncoerced and informed assent from its audience. On these grounds, Habermas contends that the arguer is committed to treating the other according to norms to which the other can uncoercedly and informedly assent.[5] The problem, however, is that, even if the arguer presupposes commitment to persuasion by uncoerced consent, *nothing requires him to shape his actions by the conditions of interpersonal argument.* Put otherwise, even if there are morally laden commitments built into justification to others, these commitments do not require people (*a*) to engage in justification in the first place or (*b*) to conform their actions to their justifications if they do so engage. Requirements (*a*) and (*b*) are separate substantive moral requirements, not provided for by the conditions of justification themselves. Thus Habermas's theory can have no moral claim on anyone who does not believe that he must justify his actions to others before acting or that he must act only in ways that he can justify to others.

The needed substantive moral requirements are provided by . . . the notion that wholehearted recognition of people as rational authority-claiming subjects requires that we allow them to form their own judgments and that we refrain from treating them according to judgments they do not themselves make—except where necessary to assure that no one is so treated. Here, then, we derive the obligation to conform to the conditions of argument, regarding both beliefs and actions, from recognition of, and respect for, the nature of human beings as rational subjects.

In *Political Liberalism,*[6] Rawls defends a version of liberalism that is political both in its subject and in its justification. Its subject is the basic structure of society (the main political, economic, and social institutions), thus leaving large areas of "private" or "civil" life subject to citizens' personally held ideals. As for justification, Rawls's liberalism is put forth as a "freestanding view."[7] By this Rawls means that it is not based on a comprehensive philosophical, religious, or moral doctrine that aims to determine all or most of what is valuable in life. Thus it is unlike Mill's liberalism, which was founded on the comprehensive doctrine of utilitarianism, and unlike Kant's, which was founded on his comprehensive doctrine of pure reason. To establish his liberalism as a free-standing view, Rawls hopes to avoid taking a position on any metaphysical issues by starting instead from an idea he finds embedded in our democratic culture: the idea "of society as a fair system of social cooperation between free and equal persons."[8] This way, Rawls's political liberalism is meant to appeal to the holders of a wide range of irreconcilable though reasonable comprehensive doctrines—religious, philosophical, and moral—as long as they can find within their particular doctrines some reasons to join an "overlapping consensus" on the ideas distinctive to liberal democratic culture. As he has recently summarized it in replying to Habermas,

> The central idea is that political liberalism moves within the category of the political and leaves philosophy as it is. It leaves untouched all kinds of doctrines religious, metaphysical, and moral, with their long traditions of development and interpretation. Political philosophy proceeds apart from all such doctrines, and presents itself in its own terms as freestanding. Hence, it cannot argue its case by invoking any comprehensive doctrines, or by criticizing or rejecting them, so long of course as those doctrines are reasonable, politically speaking. When attributed to persons, the two basic elements of the conception of the reasonable are, first, a willingness to propose fair terms of social cooperation that others as free and equal also might endorse, and to act on these terms, provided others do, even contrary to one's own interest; and, second, a recognition of the burdens of judgment [grounds for expecting that reasonable people will differ irreconcilably in their comprehensive doctrines] and accepting their consequences for one's attitude (including toleration) toward other comprehensive doctrines.[9]

As for the notion of "citizens as reasonable," it is drawn "from the public political culture of a democratic society."[10]

The problem here is that if the concept of the reasonable only holds for those who share a democratic culture, then those who do not share that culture—though they live within its midst as say, Ku Klux Klanners or other extremists—cannot be said to be unreasonable, only different. Then, the upholders of democratic liberal politics cannot say that the dissenters are wrong, only different. And that means that the relation between the democratic liberal state and the dissenters, particularly when the state uses force to repress the dissenters' "principled" violence, is strictly a power relation rather than a moral one. The dissenters cannot be said to have failed in an obligation owed to the democratic liberal citizens, since the claim for that obligation goes no further than the shared beliefs of those citizens.

Put more generally, a liberal political theory that aims to be "political not metaphysical"[11] cannot generate a moral obligation for those who do not share its liberal political culture. Indeed, even those who do share that political culture only *believe* they are obligated. They are *truly* obligated only if liberal political values are truly worthy of allegiance independent of any comprehensive doctrine and/or if the comprehensive doctrines that teach them that liberal values are worthy are true. However, as a political doctrine, Rawls's theory eschews appeal to, or even judgment about, its own truth (Rawls will only call it reasonable)[12] or the truth of the comprehensive doctrines held by citizens. Thus, political liberalism cannot generate a moral obligation to its own liberal values. It must rest content with the hope that the citizens will fill this in for themselves.

The needed moral obligation is provided by . . . the notion that it is most appropriate to the nature of rational beings to treat them only according to the judgments they are prepared to make. Then, it is wrong not to be reasonable in just the way that Rawls and democratic culture have defined it. And there is a moral obligation to be reasonable that goes beyond subscribing to reasonable comprehensive doctrines supportive of reasonable liberal political values. It is an obligation on all rational beings, including the extremists in, but not of, "the public political culture of a democratic society." Of course, this would make Rawls's theory, not just political, but ever so slightly metaphysical.[13]

NOTES

This chapter is a revised version of an article originally published in the *Canadian Journal of Philosophy,* supplementary volume 21: *On the Relevance of Metaethics: New Essays on Metaethics,* ed. J. Couture and K. Nielsen (1996): 251–72. I am indebted to Joseph Flay, emeritus professor of philosophy at Pennsylvania State University, and Jonathan Loesberg, professor of literature at American University, for numerous helpful comments, many of which I have incorporated into this chapter.

1. In *Speech and Phenomena,* Jacques Derrida gives an argument for nongivenness of meaning and thus for the fundamentality of interpretation from within phenomenology itself. He does so by playing Husserl's *Phenomenology of Internal Time-Consciousness* (trans. James Churchill [Bloomington, Ind.: Indiana University Press, 1964; originally published 1928]) off against Husserl's own theory of the intuitive givenness of linguistic meaning. The latter requires there to be an instantaneous grasp of the meaning of a term, while the former shows that there is nothing in consciousness that is instantaneous. Everything in consciousness is elapsing in time, and that implies that the appearance of an instantaneous grasp of meaning is really the product of a gathering up of flowing elements of experience into some meaningful totality, which is to say, interpretation. Nor should the term "elements" here be taken as implying yet other instantaneous givens, since that too is denied by the elapsing nature of consciousness. As far down as we go, all we get are interpretations. See Jacques Derrida, *Speech and Phenomena, and Other Essays on Husserl's Theory of Signs* (Evanston, Ill.: Northwestern University Press, 1973).

2. Zygmunt Bauman, *Postmodern Ethics* (Oxford: Blackwell, 1993), p. 13.

3. John Rawls, *Political Liberalism* (New York: Columbia University Press, 1993).

4. See Jürgen Habermas, "Discourse Ethics," in his *Moral Consciousness and Communicative Action* (Cambridge, Mass.: Massachusetts Institute of Technology Press, 1990), pp. 43–115.

5. See Habermas, "Discourse Ethics."

6. See Rawls, *Political Liberalism.*

7. Ibid., pp. 12–13, inter alia.

8. Ibid., p. 9, inter alia.

9. John Rawls, "Reply to Habermas," *Journal of Philosophy* 92, no. 3 (March 1995): 134 (I have omitted Rawls's references).

10. Ibid., 135.

11. Rawls, *Political Liberalism,* p. 10; see also Rawls, "Justice as Fairness: Political Not Metaphysical," *Philosophy and Public Affairs* 14 (Summer 1985): 223–51.

12. "[P]olitical liberalism, rather than referring to its political conception of justice as true, refers to it as reasonable instead." Rawls, *Political Liberalism,* p. xx.

13. Actually, I think that this would vastly improve Rawls's theory and that it is in any event necessary at other points in the theory as well. Consider the fact that the abortion controversy needs a solution within the nonmetaphysical framework of political liberalism. Rawls is quite sure this is possible, as he points out in a lengthy footnote:

As an illustration, consider the troubled question of abortion. Suppose . . . that we consider the question in terms of three important political values: the due respect for human life, the ordered reproduction of political society over time, including the family in some form, and finally the equality of women as equal citizens. (There are, of course, other important political values besides these.) Now I believe *any reasonable balance of these three political values will give a woman a duly qualified right to decide whether or not to end her pregnancy during the first trimester.* The reason for this is that at this early stage of pregnancy the political value of the equality of women is overriding, and this right is required to give it substance and force. (Rawls, *Political Liberalism,* p. 243, n. 32 [emphasis mine])

But note right away that Rawls's conclusion about abortion only follows on the assumption that a first-trimester fetus is not among those equal persons who are to be protected by the laws of a liberal state (otherwise, the political value of women's equality would not be overriding). This is clearly a metaphysical, not merely a political, claim.

29 An Encounter between Feminism and Postmodernism

NANCY FRASER AND LINDA J. NICHOLSON

FEMINISM AND POSTMODERNISM have emerged as two of the most important political-cultural currents of the last decade. So far, however, they have kept an uneasy distance from one another. Indeed, so great has been their mutual wariness that there have been remarkably few extended discussions of the relations between them.[1]

Initial reticences aside, there are good reasons for exploring the relations between feminism and postmodernism. Both have offered deep and far-reaching criticisms of the institution of philosophy. Both have elaborated critical perspectives on the relation of philosophy to the larger culture. And, most central to the concerns of this essay, both have sought to develop new paradigms of social criticism which do not rely on traditional philosophical underpinnings. Other differences notwithstanding, one could say that during the last decade feminists and postmodernists have worked independently on a common nexus of problems: They have tried to rethink the relation between philosophy and social criticism so as to develop paradigms of criticism without philosophy.

The two tendencies have proceeded from opposite directions. On the one hand, postmodernists have focused primarily on the philosophy side of the problem. They have begun by elaborating antifoundational metaphilosophical perspectives and from there have drawn conclusions about the shape and character of social criticism. For feminists, on the other hand, the question of philosophy has always been subordinate to an interest in social criticism. Consequently, they have begun by developing critical political perspectives and from there have drawn conclusions about the status of philosophy. As a result of this difference in emphasis and direction, the two tendencies have ended up with complementary strengths and weaknesses. Postmodernists offer sophisticated and persuasive criticisms of foundationalism and essentialism, but their conceptions of social criticism tend to be anemic. Feminists offer robust conceptions of social criticism, but they tend at times to lapse into foundationalism and essentialism.

Thus, each of the two perspectives suggests some important criticisms of the other. A postmodernist reflection on feminist theory reveals disabling vestiges of essentialism while a feminist reflection on postmodernism reveals androcentrism and political naivete.

This essay has previously appeared in Communication, Vol. 10, Nos. 3 and 4, 1988, pp. 345–366; Theory, Culture and Society, Vol. 5, Nos. 2 and 3, June 1988, pp. 373–394; Universal Abandon? The Politics of Postmodernism, ed. Andrew Ross (Minneapolis: University of Minnesota Press, 1988) pp. 83–104; The Institution of Philosophy; A Discipline in Crisis? ed. Avner Cohen and Marcelo Dascal (Peru, Illinois: Open Court Press, 1989). We are grateful for the helpful suggestions of many people, especially Jonathan Arac, Ann Ferguson, Marilyn Frye, Nancy Hartsock. Alison Jaggar, Berel Lang, Thomas McCarthy, Karsten Struhl, Iris Young, Thomas Wartenburg, and the members of SOFPHIA. We are also grateful for word-processing help from Marina Rosiene. Reprinted by permission.

It follows that an encounter between feminism and postmodernism will initially be a trading of criticism. But there is no reason to suppose that this is where matters must end. In fact, each of these tendencies has much to learn from the other; each is in possession of valuable resources which can help remedy the deficiencies of the other. Thus, the ultimate stake of an encounter between feminism and postmodernism is the prospect of a perspective which integrates their respective strengths while eliminating their respective weaknesses. It is the prospect of a postmodernist feminism.

In what follows, we aim to contribute to the development of such a perspective by staging the initial, critical phase of the encounter. In the first section, we examine the ways in which one exemplary postmodernist, Jean-François Lyotard, has sought to derive new paradigms of social criticism from a critique of the institution of philosophy. We argue that the conception of social criticism so derived is too restricted to permit an adequate critical grasp of gender dominance and subordination. We identify some internal tensions in Lyotard's arguments, and we suggest some alternative formulations which could allow for more robust forms of criticism without sacrificing the commitment to antifoundationalism. In the second section, we examine some representative genres of feminist social criticism. We argue that in many cases feminist critics continue tacitly to rely on the sorts of philosophical underpinnings which their own commitments, like those of the postmodernists, ought in principle to rule out. We identify some points at which such underpinnings could be abandoned without any sacrifice of social-critical force. Finally, in a brief conclusion, we consider the prospects for a postmodernist feminism. We discuss some requirements which constrain the development of such a perspective, and we identify some pertinent conceptual resources and critical strategies.

Postmodernism

Postmodernists seek, *inter alia,* to develop conceptions of social criticism which do not rely on traditional philosophical underpinnings. The typical starting point for their efforts is a reflection on the condition of philosophy today. Writers like Richard Rorty and Jean-François Lyotard begin by arguing that Philosophy with a capital *P* is no longer a viable or credible enterprise. They go on to claim that philosophy and, by extension, theory in general, can no longer function to *ground* politics and social criticism. With the demise of foundationalism comes the demise of the view that casts philosophy in the role of *founding* discourse vis-à-vis social criticism. That "modern" conception must give way to a new "postmodern" one in which criticism floats free of any universalist theoretical ground. No longer anchored philosophically, the very shape or character of social criticism changes; it becomes more pragmatic, *ad hoc,* contextual, and local. With this change comes a corresponding change in the social role and political function of intellectuals.

Thus, in the postmodern reflection of the relationship between philosophy and social criticism, the term 'philosophy' undergoes an explicit devaluation; it is cut down to size, if not eliminated altogether. Yet, even as this devaluation is argued explicitly, the term 'philosophy' retains an implicit structural privilege. It is the changed condition of philosophy which determines the changed character of social criticism and of engaged intellectual practice. In the new postmodern equation, then, philosophy is the independent variable while social criticism and political practice are dependent variables. The view of theory which emerges is not determined by considering the needs of contemporary criticism and engagement. It is determined, rather, by considering the contemporary status of philosophy. This way of proceeding has important consequences, not all of which are positive. Among the results is a certain underestimation and premature foreclosing of possibilities for social criticism and engaged intellectual practice.

This limitation of postmodern thought will be apparent when we consider its results in the light of the needs of contemporary feminist theory and practice.

Let us consider as an example the postmodernism of Jean-François Lyotard, since it is genuinely exemplary of the larger tendency. Lyotard is one of the few social thinkers widely considered postmodern who actually uses the term; indeed, it was he himself who introduced it into current discussions of philosophy, politics, society, and social theory. His book *The Postmodern Condition* has become the *locus classicus* for contemporary debates, and it reflects in an especially acute form the characteristic concerns and tensions of the movement.[2]

For Lyotard, postmodernism designates a general condition of contemporary Western civilization. The postmodern condition is one in which "grand narratives of legitimation" are no longer credible. By grand narratives he means overarching philosophies of history like the Enlightenment story of the gradual but steady progress of reason and freedom, Hegel's dialectic of Spirit coming to know itself, and most importantly, Marx's drama of the forward march of human productive capacities via class conflict culminating in proletarian revolution. For Lyotard, these metanarratives instantiate a specifically modern approach to the problem of legitimation. Each situates first-order discursive practices of inquiry and politics within a broader totalizing metadiscourse which legitimates them. The metadiscourse narrates a story about the whole of human history which purports to guarantee that the pragmatics of the modern sciences and of modern political processes—the norms and rules which govern these practices, determining what counts as a warranted move within them—are themselves legitimate. The story guarantees that some sciences and some politics have the *right* pragmatics, and so, are the *right* practices.

We should not be misled by Lyotard's focus on narrative philosophies of history. In his conception of legitimating metanarrative, the stress properly belongs on the *meta* and not on the *narrative*. For what most interests him about the Enlightenment, Hegelian, and Marxist stories is what they share with other nonnarrative forms of philosophy. Like ahistorical epistemologies and moral theories, they aim to show that specific first-order discursive practices are well formed and capable of yielding true and just results. *True* and *just* here mean something more than results reached by adhering scrupulously to the constitutive rules of some given scientific and political games. They mean, rather, results which correspond to Truth and Justice as they really are in themselves independently of contingent, historical social practices. Thus, in Lyotard's view, a metanarrative is *meta* in a very strong sense. It purports to be a privileged discourse capable of situating, characterizing, and evaluating all other discourses but not itself to be infected by the historicity and contingency which render first-order discourses potentially distorted and in need of legitimation.

In *The Postmodern Condition,* Lyotard argues that metanarratives, whether philosophies of history or nonnarrative foundational philosophies, are merely modern and dépassé. We can no longer believe, he claims, in the availability of a privileged metadiscourse capable of capturing once and for all the truth of every first-order discourse. The claim to *meta* status does not stand up. A so-called metadiscourse is in fact simply one more discourse among others. It follows for Lyotard that legitimation, both epistemic and political, can no longer reside in philosophical metanarratives. Where, then, he asks, does legitimation reside in the postmodern era?

Much of *The Postmodern Condition* is devoted to sketching an answer to that question. The answer, in brief, is that in the postmodern era legitimation becomes plural, local, and immanent. In this era, there will necessarily be many discourses of legitimation dispersed among the plurality of first-order discursive practices. For example, scientists no longer look to prescriptive philosophies of science to warrant their procedures of inquiry.

Rather, they themselves problematize, modify, and warrant the constitutive norms of their own practice even as they engage in it. Instead of hovering above, legitimation descends to the level of practice and becomes immanent in it. There are no special tribunals set apart from the sites where inquiry is practiced. Rather, practitioners assume responsibility for legitimizing their own practice.

Lyotard intimates that something similar is or should be happening with respect to political legitimation. We cannot have and do not need a single, overarching theory of justice. What is required, rather, is a "justice of multiplicities."[3] What Lyotard means by this is not wholly clear. On one level, he can be read as offering a normative vision in which the good society consists in a decentralized plurality of democratic, self-managing groups and institutions whose members problematize the norms of their practice and take responsibility for modifying them as situations require. But paradoxically, on another level, he can be read as ruling out the sort of larger-scale, normative political theorizing which, from a modern perspective at least, would be required to legitimate such a vision. In any case, his justice of multiplicities conception precludes one familiar, and arguably essential, genre of political theory: identification and critique of macrostructures of inequality and injustice which cut across the boundaries separating relatively discrete practices and institutions. There is no place in Lyotard's universe for critique of pervasive axes of stratification, for critique of broad-based relations of dominance and subordination along lines like gender, race, and class.

Lyotard's suspicion of the large extends to historical narrative and social theory as well. Here, his chief target is Marxism, the one metanarrative in France with enough lingering credibility to be worth arguing against. The problem with Marxism, in his view, is twofold. On the one hand, the Marxian story is too big, since it spans virtually the whole of human history. On the other hand, the Marxian story is too theoretical, since it relies on a *theory* of social practice and social relations which claims to *explain* historical change. At one level,

Lyotard simply rejects the specifics of this theory. He claims that the Marxian conception of practice as production occludes the diversity and plurality of human practices; and that the Marxian conception of capitalist society as a totality traversed by one major division and contradiction occludes the diversity and plurality of contemporary societal differences and oppositions. But Lyotard does not conclude that such deficiencies can and should be remedied by a better social theory. Rather, he rejects the project of social theory *tout court*.

Once again, Lyotard's position is ambiguous, since his rejection of social theory depends on a theoretical perspective of sorts of its own. He offers a postmodern conception of sociality and social identity, a conception of what he calls "the social bond." What holds a society together, he claims, is not a common consciousness or institutional substructure. Rather, the social bond is a weave of crisscrossing threads of discursive practices, no single one of which runs continuously throughout the whole. Individuals are the nodes or posts where such practices intersect, and so, they participate in many practices simultaneously. It follows that social identities are complex and heterogeneous. They cannot be mapped onto one another nor onto the social totality. Indeed, strictly speaking, there is no social totality and *a fortiori* no possibility of a totalizing social theory.

Thus, Lyotard insists that the field of the social is heterogeneous and nontotalizable. As a result, he rules out the sort of critical social theory which employs general categories like gender, race, and class. From his perspective, such categories are too reductive of the complexity of social identities to be useful. There is apparently nothing to be gained, in his view, by situating an account of the fluidity and diversity of discursive practices in the context of a critical analysis of large-scale institutions and social structures.

Thus, Lyotard's postmodern conception of criticism without philosophy rules out several recognizable genres of social criticism. From the premise that criticism cannot be grounded by a foundationalist philosophical metanarrative, he infers the illegitimacy of large historical stories, normative theories of justice, and social-theoretical accounts of macrostructures which institutionalize inequality. What, then, *does* postmodern social criticism look like?

Lyotard tries to fashion some new genres of social criticism from the discursive resources that remain. Chief among these is smallish, localized narrative. He seeks to vindicate such narrative against both modern totalizing metanarrative and the scientism that is hostile to all narrative. One genre of postmodern social criticism, then, consists in relatively discrete, local stories about the emergence, transformation, and disappearance of various discursive practices treated in isolation from one another. Such stories might resemble those told by Michel Foucault, although without the attempts to discern larger synchronic patterns and connections that Foucault sometimes made.[4] Like Michael Walzer, Lyotard evidently assumes that practitioners would narrate such stories when seeking to persuade one another to modify the pragmatics or constitutive norms of their practice.[5]

This genre of social criticism is not the whole postmodern story, however. For it casts critique as strictly local, *ad hoc,* and ameliorative, thus supposing a political diagnosis according to which there are not large-scale, systemic problems which resist local, *ad hoc,* ameliorative initiatives. Yet, Lyotard recognizes that postmodern society does contain at least one unfavorable structural tendency which requires a more coordinated response. This is the tendency to universalize instrumental reason, to subject *all* discursive practices indiscriminately to the single criterion of efficiency, or "performativity." In Lyotard's view, this threatens the autonomy and integrity of science and politics, since these practices are not properly subordinated to performative standards. It would pervert and distort them, thereby destroying the diversity of discursive forms.

Thus, even as he argues explicitly against it, Lyotard posits the need for a genre of social criticism which transcends local mininarrative. Despite his strictures against large, totalizing stories, he narrates a fairly tall tale about a large-scale social

trend. Moreover, the logic of this story, and of the genre of criticism to which it belongs, calls for judgments which are not strictly practice-immanent. Lyotard's story presupposes the legitimacy and integrity of the scientific and political practices allegedly threatened by performativity. It supposes that one can distinguish changes or developments which are *internal* to these practices from externally induced distortions. But this drives Lyotard to make normative judgments about the value and character of the threatened practices. These judgments are not strictly immanent in the practices judged. Rather, they are metapractical.

Thus, Lyotard's view of postmodern social criticism is neither entirely self-consistent nor entirely persuasive. He goes too quickly from the premise that Philosophy cannot ground social criticism to the conclusion that criticism itself must be local, *ad hoc,* and nontheoretical. As a result, he throws out the baby of large historical narrative with the bathwater of philosophical metanarrative and the baby of social-theoretical analysis of large-scale inequalities with the bathwater of reductive Marxian class theory. Moreover, these allegedly illegitimate babies do not in fact remain excluded. They return like the repressed within the very genres of postmodern social criticism with which Lyotard intends to replace them.

We began this discussion by noting that postmodernists orient their reflections on the character of postmodern social criticism by the falling star of foundationalist philosophy. They posit that, with philosophy no longer able credibly to ground social criticism, criticism itself must be local, *ad hoc,* and untheoretical. Thus, from the critique of foundationalism, they infer the illegitimacy of several genres of social criticism. For Lyotard, the illegitimate genres include large-scale historical narrative and social-theoretical analyses of pervasive relations of dominance and subordination.[6]

Suppose, however, one were to choose another starting point for reflecting on postfoundational social criticism. Suppose one began, not with the condition of Philosophy, but with the nature of the social object one wished to criticize. Suppose, further, that one defined that object as the subordination of women to and by men. Then, we submit, it would be apparent that many of the genres rejected by postmodernists are necessary for social criticism. For a phenomenon as pervasive and multifaceted as male dominance simply cannot be adequately grasped with the meager critical resources to which they would limit us. On the contrary, effective criticism of this phenomenon requires an array of different methods and genres. It requires at minimum large narratives about changes in social organization and ideology, empirical and social-theoretical analyses of macrostructures and institutions, interactionist analyses of the micropolitics of everyday life, criticalhermeneutical and institutional analyses of cultural production, historically and culturally specific sociologies of gender, and so on. The list could go on.

Clearly, not all of these approaches are local and untheoretical. But all are nonetheless essential to feminist social criticism. Moreover, all can in principle be conceived in ways that do not take us back to foundationalism, even though, as we argue in the next section, many feminists have not wholly succeeded in avoiding that trap.

Feminism

Feminists, like postmodernists, have sought to develop new paradigms of social criticism which do not rely on traditional philosophical underpinnings. They have criticized modern foundationalist epistemologies and moral and political theories, exposing the contingent, partial, and historically situated character of what has passed in the mainstream for necessary, universal, and ahistorical truths. They have called into question the dominant philosophical project of seeking objectivity in the guise of a "God's eye view" which transcends any situation or perspective.[7]

However, if postmodernists have been drawn to such views by a concern with the status of philosophy, feminists have been led to them by the demands of political practice. This practical interest has saved feminist theory from many of the mistakes of postmodernism: Women whose theorizing was to serve the struggle against sexism were not about to abandon powerful political tools merely as a result of intramural debates in professional philosophy.

Yet, even as the imperatives of political practice have saved feminist theory from one set of difficulties, they have tended at times to incline it toward another. Practical imperatives have led some feminists to adopt modes of theorizing which resemble the sorts of philosophical metanarrative rightly criticized by postmodernists. To be sure, the feminist theories we have in mind here are not pure metanarratives; they are not ahistorical normative theories about the transcultural nature of rationality or justice. Rather, they are very large social theories—theories of history, society, culture, and psychology—which claim, for example, to identify causes and constitutive features of sexism that operate cross-culturally. Thus, these social theories purport to be empirical rather than philosophical. But, as we hope to show, they are actually quasi-metanarratives. They tacitly presuppose some commonly held but unwarranted and essentialist assumptions about the nature of human beings and the conditions for social life. In addition, they assume methods and concepts which are uninflected by temporality or historicity and which therefore function *de facto* as permanent, neutral matrices for inquiry. Such theories then, share some of the essentialist and ahistorical features of metanarratives: They are insufficiently attentive to historical and cultural diversity, and they falsely universalize features of the theorist's own era, society, culture, class, sexual orientation and ethnic, or racial group.

On the other hand, the practical exigencies inclining feminists to produce quasi-metanarratives have by no means held undisputed sway. Rather, they have had to coexist, often uneasily, with counterexigencies which have worked to opposite effect, for example, political pressures to acknowledge differences among women. In general, then, the recent history of feminist social theory reflects a tug of war between forces which have encouraged and forces which have discouraged metanarrative-like modes of theorizing. We can illustrate this dynamic by looking at a few important turning points in this history.

When in the 1960s, women in the New Left began to extend prior talk about women's rights into the more encompassing discussion of women's liberation, they encountered the fear and hostility of their male comrades and the use of Marxist political theory as a support for these reactions. Many men of the New Left argued that gender issues were secondary because they were subsumable under more basic modes of oppression, namely, class and race.

In response to this practical-political problem, radical feminists such as Shulamith Firestone resorted to an ingenious tactical maneuver: Firestone invoked biological differences between women and men to explain sexism. This enabled her to turn the tables on her Marxist comrades by claiming that gender conflict was the most basic form of human conflict and the source of all other forms, including class conflict.[8] Firestone drew on the pervasive tendency within modern culture to locate the roots of gender differences in biology. Her coup was to use biologism to establish the primacy of the struggle against male domination rather than to justify acquiescence to it.

The trick, of course, is problematic from a postmodernist perspective in that appeals to biology to explain social phenomena are essentialist and monocausal. They are essentialist insofar as they project onto all women and men qualities which develop under historically specific social conditions. They are monocausal insofar as they look to one set of characteristics, such as women's physiology or men's hormones, to explain women's oppression in all cultures. These problems are only compounded when appeals to biology are used in conjunction with the dubious claim that women's oppression is the cause of all other forms of oppression.

Moreover, as Marxists and feminist anthropologists began insisting in the early 1970s, appeals to biology do not allow us to understand the enormous diversity of forms which both gender and sexism assume in different cultures. In fact, it was not long before most feminist social theorists came to appreciate that accounting for the diversity of the forms of sexism was as important as accounting for its depth and autonomy. Gayle Rubin aptly described this dual requirement as the need to formulate theory which could account for the oppression of women in its "endless variety and monotonous similarity."[9] How were feminists to develop a social theory adequate to both demands?

One approach which seemed promising was suggested by Michelle Zimbalist Rosaldo and other contributors in the influential 1974 anthropology collection, *Woman, Culture, and Society*. They argued that common to all known societies was some type of separation between a domestic sphere and a public sphere, the former associated with women and the latter with men. Because in most societies to date, women have spent a good part of their lives bearing and raising children, their lives have been more bound to the domestic sphere. Men, on the other hand, have had both the time and mobility to engage in those out of the home activities which generate political structures. Thus, as Rosaldo argued, while in many societies women possess some or even a great deal of power, women's power is always viewed as illegitimate, disruptive, and without authority.[10]

This approach seemed to allow for both diversity and ubiquity in the manifestations of sexism. A very general identification of women with the domestic and of men with the extra-domestic could accommodate a great deal of cultural variation both in social structures and in gender roles. At the same time, it could make comprehensible the apparent ubiquity of the assumption of women's inferiority above and beyond such variation. This hypothesis was also compatible with the idea that the extent of women's oppression differed in different societies. It could explain such differences by correlating the extent of gender inequality in a society with the extent and rigidity of the separation between its domestic and public spheres. In short, the domestic/public theorists seemed to have generated an explanation capable of satisfying a variety of conflicting demands.

However, this explanation turned out to be problematic in ways reminiscent of Firestone's account. Although the theory focused on differences between men's and women's spheres of activity rather than on differences between men's and women's biology, it was essentialist and monocausal nonetheless. It posited the existence of a domestic sphere in all societies and thereby assumed that women's activities were basically similar in content and significance across cultures. (An analogous assumption about men's activities lay behind the postulation of a universal public sphere.) In effect, the theory falsely generalized to all societies an historically specific conjunction of properties: women's responsibility for early child rearing, women's tendency to spend more time in the geographical space of the home, women's lesser participation in the affairs of the community, a cultural ascription of triviality to domestic work, and a cultural ascription of inferiority to women. The theory thus failed to appreciate that, while each individual property may be true of many societies, the conjunction is not true of most.[11]

One source of difficulty in these early feminist social theories was the presumption of an overly grandiose and totalizing conception of theory. Theory was understood as the search for the one key factor which would explain sexism cross-culturally and illuminate all of social life. In this sense, to theorize was by definition to produce a quasi-metanarrative.

Since the late 1970s, feminist social theorists have largely ceased speaking of biological determinants or a cross-cultural domestic/public separation. Many, moreover, have given up the assumption of monocausality. Nevertheless, some feminist social theorists have continued implicitly to suppose a quasi-metanarrative conception of theory. They have continued to theorize in terms of a putatively unitary, primary, culturally universal type of activity associated with women, generally an activity conceived as domestic and located in the family.

One influential example is the analysis of mothering developed by Nancy Chodorow. Setting herself to explain the internal, psychological dynamics which have led many women willingly to reproduce social divisions associated with female inferiority, Chodorow posited a cross-cultural activity, mothering, as the relevant object of investigation. Her question thus became: How is mothering as a female-associated activity reproduced over time? How does mothering produce a new generation of women with the psychological inclination to mother and a new generation of men not so inclined? The answer she offered was in terms of gender identity: Female mothering produces women whose deep sense of self is relational and men whose deep sense of self is not.[12]

Chodorow's theory has struck many feminists as a persuasive account of some apparently observable psychic differences between men and women. Yet, the theory has clear metanarrative overtones. It posits the existence of a single activity, mothering, which while differing in specifics in different societies, nevertheless constitutes enough of a natural kind to warrant one label. It stipulates that this basically unitary activity gives rise to two distinct sorts of deep selves, one relatively common across cultures to women, the other relatively common across cultures to men. It claims that the difference thus generated between feminine and masculine gender identity causes a variety of supposedly cross-cultural social phenomena, including the continuation of female mothering, male contempt for women, and problems in heterosexual relationships.

From a postmodern perspective, all of these assumptions are problematic because they are essentialist. But the second one, concerning gender identity, warrants special scrutiny, given its political implications. Consider that Chodorow's use of the notion of gender identity presupposes three major premises. One is the psychoanalytic premise that everyone has a deep sense of self which is constituted in early childhood through one's interactions with one's primary parent and which remains relatively constant thereafter. Another is the premise that this deep self differs significantly for men and for women but is roughly similar among women, on the one hand, and among men, on the other hand, both across cultures and within cultures across lines of class, race, and ethnicity. The third premise is that this deep self colors everything one does; there are no actions, however trivial, which do not bear traces of one's masculine or feminine gender identity.

One can appreciate the political exigencies which made this conjunction of premises attractive. It gave scholarly substance to the idea of the pervasiveness of sexism. If masculinity and femininity constitute our basic and ever present sense of self, then it is not surprising that the manifestations of sexism are systemic. Moreover, many feminists had already sensed that the concept of sex-role socialization, an idea Chodorow explicitly criticized, ignored the depth and intractability of male dominance. By implying that measures such as changing images in school textbooks or allowing boys to play with dolls would be sufficient to bring about equality between the sexes, this concept seemed to trivialize and coopt the message of feminism. Finally, Chodorow's depth-psychological approach gave a scholarly sanction to the idea of sisterhood. It seemed to legitimate the claim that the ties which bind women are deep and substantively based.

Needless to say, we have no wish to quarrel with the claim of the depth and pervasiveness of sexism nor with the idea of sisterhood. But we do wish to challenge Chodorow's way of legitimating them. The idea of a cross-cultural, deep sense of self, specified differently for women and men, becomes problematic when given any specific content. Chodorow states that women everywhere differ from men in their greater concern with "relational interaction." But what does she mean by this term? Certainly not any and every kind of human interaction, since men have often been more concerned than women with some kinds of interactions, for example, those which have to do with the aggrandizement of power and wealth. Of course, it is true that many women in modern Western societies have been expected to exhibit strong concern with those types of interactions associated with intimacy, friendship, and love, interactions which dominate one meaning of the late

twentieth-century concept of relationship. But surely this meaning presupposes a notion of private life specific to modern Western societies of the last two centuries. Is it possible that Chodorow's theory rests on an equivocation on the term *relationship*?[13]

Equally troubling are the aporias this theory generates for political practice. While gender identity gives substance to the idea of sisterhood, it does so at the cost of repressing differences among sisters. Although the theory allows for some differences among women of different classes, races, sexual orientations, and ethnic groups, it construes these as subsidiary to more basic similarities. But it is precisely as a consequence of the request to understand such differences as secondary that many women have denied an allegiance to feminism.

We have dwelt at length on Chodorow because of the great influence her work has enjoyed. But she is not the only recent feminist social theorist who has constructed a quasi-metanarrative around a putatively cross-cultural female-associated activity. On the contrary, theorists like Ann Ferguson and Nancy Folbre, Nancy Hartsock, and Catharine MacKinnon have built similar theories around notions of sex-affective production, reproduction, and sexuality, respectively.[14] Each claims to have identified a basic kind of human practice found in all societies which has cross-cultural explanatory power. In each case, the practice in question is associated with a biological or quasi-biological need and is construed as functionally necessary to the reproduction of society. It is not the sort of thing, then, whose historical origins need be investigated.

The difficulty here is that categories like sexuality, mothering, reproduction, and sex-affective production group together phenomena which are not necessarily conjoined in all societies while separating off from one another phenomena which are not necessarily separated. As a matter of fact, it is doubtful whether these categories have any determinate cross-cultural content. Thus, for a theorist to use such categories to construct a universalistic social theory is to risk projecting the socially dominant conjunctions and dispersions of her own society onto others, thereby distorting important features of both. Social theorists would do better first to construct genealogies of the *categories* of sexuality, reproduction, and mothering before assuming their universal significance.

Since around 1980, many feminist scholars have come to abandon the project of grand social theory. They have stopped looking for *the* causes of sexism and have turned to more concrete inquiry with more limited aims. One reason for this shift is the growing legitimacy of feminist scholarship. The institutionalization of women's studies in the United States has meant a dramatic increase in the size of the community of feminist inquirers, a much greater division of scholarly labor, and a large and growing fund of concrete information. As a result, feminist scholars have come to regard their enterprise more collectively, more like a puzzle whose various pieces are being filled in by many different people than like a construction to be completed by a single grand theoretical stroke. In short, feminist scholarship has attained its maturity.

Even in this phase, however, traces of youthful quasi-metanarratives remain. Some theorists who have ceased looking for *the* causes of sexism still rely on essentialist categories such as gender identity. This is especially true of those scholars who have sought to develop gynocentric alternatives to mainstream androcentric perspectives but who have not fully abandoned the universalist pretensions of the latter.

Consider, as an example, the work of Carol Gilligan. Unlike most of the theorists we have considered so far, Gilligan has not sought to explain the origins or nature of cross-cultural sexism. Rather, she set herself the more limited task of exposing and redressing androcentric bias in the model of moral development of psychologist Lawrence Kohlberg. Thus, she argued that it is illegitimate to evaluate the moral development of women and girls by reference to a standard drawn exclusively from the experience of men and boys. She proposed to examine women's moral discourse on its own terms in order to uncover its immanent standards of adequacy.[15]

Gilligan's work has been rightly regarded as important and innovative. It challenged mainstream psychology's persistent occlusion of women's lives and experiences and its insistent but false claims to universality. Yet insofar as Gilligan's challenge involved the construction of an alternative feminine model of moral development, her position was ambiguous. On the one hand, by providing a counterexample to Kohlberg's model, she cast doubt on the possibility of any single, universalist development schema. On the other hand, by constructing a female countermodel, she invited the same charge of false generalization she had herself raised against Kohlberg, although now from other perspectives such as class, sexual orientation, race, and ethnicity. Gilligan's disclaimers notwithstanding,[16] to the extent that she described women's moral development in terms of *a* different voice; to the extent that she did not specify which women, under which specific historical circumstances have spoken with the voice in question; and to the extent that she grounded her analysis in the explicitly cross-cultural framework of Nancy Chodorow, her model remained essentialist. It perpetuated in a newer, more localized fashion traces of previous more grandiose quasi-metanarratives.

Thus, vestiges of essentialism have continued to plague feminist scholarship, even despite the decline of grand theorizing. In many cases, including Gilligan's, this represents the continuing subterranean influence of those very mainstream modes of thought and inquiry with which feminists have wished to break.

On the other hand, the practice of feminist politics in the 1980s has generated a new set of pressures which have worked against metanarratives. In recent years, poor and working-class women, women of color, and lesbians have finally won a wider hearing for their objections to feminist theories which fail to illuminate their lives and address their problems. They have exposed the earlier quasi-metanarratives, with their assumptions of universal female dependence and confinement to the domestic sphere, as false extrapolations from the experience of the white, middle-class, heterosexual women who dominated the beginnings of the second wave. For example, writers like Bell Hooks, Gloria Joseph, Audre Lord, Maria Lugones, and Elizabeth Spelman have unmasked the implicit reference to white Anglo women in many classic feminist texts. Likewise, Adrienne Rich and Marilyn Frye have exposed the heterosexist bias of much mainstream feminist theory.[17] Thus, as the class, sexual, racial, and ethnic awareness of the movement has altered, so has the preferred conception of theory. It has become clear that quasi-metanarratives hamper rather than promote sisterhood, since they elide differences among women and among the forms of sexism to which different women are differentially subject. Likewise, it is increasingly apparent that such theories hinder alliances with other progressive movements, since they tend to occlude axes of domination other than gender. In sum, there is growing interest among feminists in modes of theorizing which are attentive to differences and to cultural and historical specificity.

In general, then, feminist scholarship of the 1980s evinces some conflicting tendencies. On the one hand, there is decreasing interest in grand social theories as scholarship has become more localized, issue-oriented, and explicitly fallibilistic. On the other hand, essentialist vestiges persist in the continued use of ahistorical categories like gender identity without reflection as to how, when, and why such categories originated and were modified over time. This tension is symptomatically expressed in the current fascination, on the part of U.S. feminists, with French psychoanalytic feminisms: The latter propositionally decry essentialism even as they performatively enact it.[18] More generally, feminist scholarship has remained insufficiently attentive to the *theoretical* prerequisites of dealing with diversity, despite widespread commitment to accepting it politically.

By criticizing lingering essentialism in contemporary feminist theory, we hope to encourage such theory to become more consistently postmodern. This is not, however, to recommend merely any form of postmodernism. On the contrary, as we have shown, the version developed by Jean-François Lyotard offers a weak and inadequate conception of social criticism without phi-

losophy. It rules out genres of criticism, such as large historical narrative and historically situated social theory, which feminists rightly regard as indispensable. But it does not follow from Lyotard's shortcomings that criticism without philosophy is in principle incompatible with criticism with social force. Rather, as we argue next, a robust postmodern-feminist paradigm of social criticism without philosophy is possible.

Toward a Postmodern Feminism

How can we combine a postmodernist incredulity toward metanarratives with the social-critical power of feminism? How can we conceive a version of criticism without philosophy which is robust enough to handle the tough job of analyzing sexism in all its endless variety and monotonous similarity?

A first step is to recognize, *contra* Lyotard, that postmodern critique need forswear neither large historical narratives nor analyses of societal macrostructures. This point is important for feminists, since sexism has a long history and is deeply and pervasively embedded in contemporary societies. Thus, postmodern feminists need not abandon the large theoretical tools needed to address large political problems. There is nothing self-contradictory in the idea of a postmodern theory.

However, if postmodern-feminist critique must remain theoretical, not just any kind of theory will do. Rather, theory here would be explicitly historical, attuned to the cultural specificity of different societies and periods and to that of different groups within societies and periods. Thus, the categories of postmodern-feminist theory would be inflected by temporality, with historically specific institutional categories like the modern, restricted, male-headed, nuclear family taking precedence over ahistorical, functionalist categories like reproduction and mothering. Where categories of the latter sort were not eschewed altogether, they would be genealogized, that is, framed by a historical narrative and rendered temporally and culturally specific.

Moreover, postmodern-feminist theory would be nonuniversalist. When its focus became cross-cultural or transepochal, its mode of attention would be comparativist rather than universalizing, attuned to changes and contrasts instead of to covering laws. Finally, postmodern-feminist theory would dispense with the idea of a subject of history. It would replace unitary notions of woman and feminine gender identity with plural and complexly constructed conceptions of social identity, treating gender as one relevant strand among others, attending also to class, race, ethnicity, age, and sexual orientation.

In general, postmodern-feminist theory would be pragmatic and fallibilistic. It would tailor its methods and categories to the specific task at hand, using multiple categories when appropriate and forswearing the metaphysical comfort of a single feminist method or feminist epistemology. In short, this theory would look more like a tapestry composed of threads of many different hues than one woven in a single color.

The most important advantage of this sort of theory would be its usefulness for contemporary feminist political practice. Such practice is increasingly a matter of alliances rather than one of unity around a universally shared interest or identity. It recognizes that the diversity of women's needs and experiences means that no single solution, on issues like child care, social security, and housing, can be adequate for all. Thus, the underlying premise of this practice is that, while some women share some common interests and face some common enemies, such commonalities are by no means universal; rather, they are interlaced with differences, even with conflicts. This, then, is a practice made up of a patchwork of overlapping alliances, not one circumscribable by an essential definition. One might best speak of it in the plural as the practice of feminisms. In a sense, this practice is in advance of much contemporary feminist theory. It is already implicitly postmodern. It would find its most appropriate and useful theoretical expression in a postmodern-feminist form of critical inquiry. Such inquiry would be the theoretical counterpart of a broader, richer, more complex, and multilayered feminist solidarity, the sort of solidarity which is essential for overcoming the oppression of women in its "endless variety and monotonous similarity."

NOTES

1. Exceptions are Jane Flax, "Gender as a Social Problem: In and For Feminist Theory," *American Studies/Amerika Studien,* June 1986, (an earlier version of the paper in this book); Sandra Harding, *The Science Question in Feminism* (Ithaca, NY: Cornell University Press, 1986) and "The Instability of the Analytical Categories of Feminist Theory," *Signs: Journal of Women in Culture and Society,* Vol. 11, No. 4, 1986, pp. 645–664; Donna Haraway, "A Manifesto for Cyborgs: Science, Technology, and Socialist Feminism in the 1980s," *Socialist Review,* No. 80, 1983, pp. 65–107; Alice A. Jardine, *Gynesis: Configurations of Women and Modernity* (Ithaca, NY: Cornell University Press, 1985); Jean-François Lyotard, "Some of the Things at Stake in Women's Struggles," trans. Deborah J. Clarke, Winifred Woodhull, and John Mowitt, *Sub-Stance,* No. 20, 1978; Craig Owens, "The Discourse of Others: Feminists and Postmodernism," *The Anti-Aesthetic: Essays on Postmodern Culture,* ed. Hal Foster (Port Townsend, WA: Bay Press, 1983).

2. Jean-François Lyotard, *The Postmodern Condition: A Report on Knowledge,* trans. G. Bennington and B. Massumi (Minneapolis: University of Minnesota Press, 1984).

3. Ibid. Cf. Jean-François Lyotard and Jean-Loup Thebaud, *Just Gaming* (Minneapolis: University of Minnesota Press, 1987); also Jean-François Lyotard, "The Differend," *Diacritics,* Fall 1984, trans. Georges Van Den Abbeele, pp. 4–14.

4. See, for example Michel Foucault, *Discipline and Punish: The Birth of the Prison,* trans. Alan Sheridan (New York: Vintage Books, 1979).

5. Michael Walzer, *Spheres of Justice: A Defense of Pluralism and Equality* (New York: Basic Books, 1983).

6. It should be noted that, for Lyotard, the choice of philosophy as a starting point is itself determined by a metapolitical commitment, namely, to antitotalitarianism. He assumes erroneously, in our view, that totalizing social and political theory necessarily eventuates in totalitarian societies. Thus, the "practical intent" that subtends Lyotard's privileging of philosophy (and which is in turn attenuated by the latter) is anti-Marxism. Whether it should also be characterized as neoliberalism is a question too complicated to be explored here.

7. See, for example, the essays in *Discovering Reality: Feminist Perspectives on Epistemology, Metaphysics, Methodology, and Philosophy of Science,* ed. Sandra Hard-

ing and Merrill B. Hintikka (Dordrecht, Holland: D. Reidel, 1983).

8. Shulamith Firestone, *The Dialectic of Sex* (New York: Bantam, 1970).

9. Gayle Rubin, "The Traffic in Women," *Toward an Anthropology of Women,* ed. Rayna R. Reiter, (New York: Monthly Review Press, 1975), p. 160.

10. Michelle Zimbalist Rosaldo, "Woman, Culture, and Society: A Theoretical Overview," *Woman, Culture, and Society,* ed. Michelle Zimbalist Rosaldo and Louise Lamphere (Stanford: Stanford University Press, 1974), pp. 17–42.

11. These and related problems were soon apparent to many of the domestic/public theorists themselves. See Rosaldo's self-criticism, "The Use and Abuse of Anthropology: Reflections on Feminism and Cross-cultural Understanding," *Signs: Journal of Women in Culture and Society,* Vol. 5, No. 3, 1980, pp. 389–417. A more recent discussion, which points out the circularity of the theory, appears in Sylvia J. Yanagisako and Jane F. Collier, "Toward a Unified Analysis of Gender and Kinship," *Gender and Kinship: Essays Toward a Unified Analysis,* ed. Jane Fishburne Collier and Sylvia Junko Yanagisako, (Stanford: Stanford University Press, 1987).

12. Nancy Chodorow, *The Reproduction of Mothering: Psychoanalysis and the Sociology of Gender* (Berkeley: University of California Press, 1978).

13. A similar ambiguity attends Chodorow's discussion of the family. In response to critics who object that her psychoanalytic emphasis ignores social structures, Chodorow has rightly insisted that the family is itself a social structure, one frequently slighted in social explanations. Yet, she generally does not discuss families as historically specific social institutions whose specific relations with other institutions can be analyzed. Rather, she tends to invoke the family in a very abstract and general sense defined only as the locus of female mothering.

14. Ann Ferguson and Nancy Folbre, "The Unhappy Marriage of Patriarchy and Capitalism" *Women and Revolution,* ed. Lydia Sargent (Boston: South End Press, 1981), pp. 313–338; Nancy Hartsock, *Money, Sex, and Power: Toward a Feminist Historical Materialism* (New York: Longman, 1983); Catharine A. MacKinnon, "Feminism, Marxism, Method, and the State: An Agenda for Theory," *Signs: Journal of Women in Culture and Society,* Vol. 7, No. 3, Spring 1982, pp. 515–544.

15. Carol Gilligan, *In a Different Voice: Psychological Theory and Women's Development* (Cambridge, MA: Harvard University Press, 1983).

16. Cf. Ibid., p. 2.

17. Marilyn Frye, *The Politics of Reality: Essays in Feminist Theory* (Trumansburg, NY: The Crossing Press, 1983); Bell Hooks, *Feminist Theory from Margin to Center* (Boston: South End Press, 1984); Gloria Joseph, "The Incompatible Menage à Trois: Marxism, Feminism and Racism," *Women and Revolution,* ed. Lydia Sargent (Boston: South End Press, 1981), pp. 91–107; Audre Lord, "An Open Letter to Mary Daly," *This Bridge Called My Back: Writings by Radical Women of Color,* ed. Cherríe Moraga and Gloria Anzaldúa (Watertown, MA: Persephone Press, 1981), pp. 94–97; Maria C. Lugones and Elizabeth V. Spelman, "Have We Got a Theory for You! Feminist Theory, Cultural Imperialism and the Demand for the Woman's Voice," *Hypatia, Women's Studies International Forum,* Vol. 6, No. 6, 1983, pp. 578–581; Adrienne Rich, "Compulsory Heterosexuality and Lesbian Existence," *Signs: Journal of Women in Culture and Society,* Vol. 5, No. 4, Summer 1980, pp. 631–660; Elizabeth Spelman, "Theories of Race and Gender: The Erasure of Black Women," *Quest,* Vol. 5, No. 4, 1980/81, pp. 36–62.

18. See, for example, Hélène Cixous, "The Laugh of the Medusa," trans. Keith Cohen and Paula Cohen, *New French Feminisms,* ed. Elaine Marks and Isabelle de Courtivron (New York: Schocken Books, 1981), pp. 245–261; Hélène Cixous and Catherine Clément, *The Newly Born Woman,* trans. Betsy Wing (Minneapolis: University of Minnesota Press, 1986); Luce Irigaray, *Speculum of the Other Woman* (Ithaca, NY: Cornell University Press, 1985) and *This Sex Which Is Not One* (Ithaca, NY: Cornell University Press, 1985); Julia Kristeva, *Desire in Language: A Semiotic Approach to Literature and Art,* ed. Leon S. Roudiez (New York: Columbia University Press, 1980) and "Women's Time," trans. Alice Jardine and Harry Blake, *Signs: Journal of Women in Culture and Society* Vol. 7, No. 1, Autumn 1981, pp. 13–35. See also the critical discussions by Ann Rosalind Jones, "Writing the Body: Toward an Understanding of l'Ecriture Féminine," *The New Feminist Criticism: Essays on Women, Literature and Theory,* ed. Elaine Showalter (New York: Pantheon Books, 1985), and Toril Moi, *Sexual/Textual Politics: Feminist Literary Theory* (London: Methuen, 1985).

Part VIII

Environmental Justice

30   Chimpanzee Justice

FRANS DE WAAL

THE INFLUENCE OF THE RECENT PAST is always overestimated. When we are asked to name the greatest human inventions we tend to think of the telephone, the electric light bulb and the silicon chip rather than the wheel, the plough and the taming of fire. Similarly the origins of modern society are sought in the advent of agriculture, trade and industry, whereas in fact our social history is a thousand times older than these phenomena. It has been suggested that food sharing was a strong stimulus in furthering the evolution of our tendency to reciprocal relations. Would it not be more logical to assume that social reciprocity existed earlier, and that tangible exchanges such as food sharing stem from this phenomenon?

Be this as it may, there are indications of reciprocity in the non-material behaviour of chimpanzees. This is seen, for instance, in their coalitions (A supports B, and vice versa), non-intervention alliances (A remains neutral if B does the same), sexual bargaining (A tolerates B mating after B has groomed A) and reconciliation blackmail (A refuses to have contact with B unless B 'greets' A). It is interesting that reciprocity occurs in both the negative and the positive sense. Nikkie's habit of individually punishing females who a short time before joined forces against him has already been described. In this way he repaid a negative action with another negative action. We regularly see this mechanism in operation before the group separates for the night. This is the time when differences are squared, no matter when these differ-

ences may have arisen. For example, one morning a conflict breaks out between Mama and Oor. Oor rushes to Nikkie and with wild gestures and exaggeratedly loud screams persuades him to attack her powerful opponent. Nikkie attacks Mama and Oor wins. That evening, however, a good six hours later, we hear the sound of a scuffle in the sleeping quarters. The keeper later tells me that Mama has attacked Oor in no uncertain manner. Needless to say Nikkie was nowhere in the vicinity. . . .

The principle of exchange makes it possible actively to teach someone something: good behaviour is rewarded, bad behaviour is punished. A development in the relationship between Mama and Nikkie demonstrates just how complex such influencing processes can be. Their relationship is ambivalent. There are numerous indications that the two of them are very fond of each other. For example, when Mama returned to the group after an absence of over a month, she spent hours grooming Nikkie, and not Gorilla, Jimmie, Yeroen or any of the other individuals with whom she normally spends her time. And of all the children in the colony Moniek, Mama's daughter, is obviously Nikkie's favourite. But for a while it was the hostile side of their relationship which got the upper hand. This was at the beginning of Nikkie's leadership. Yeroen used to mobilize adult females against the young leader and Mama was his major ally. At the end of such incidents, when Nikkie

From Chimpanzee Politics *(Jonathan Cape: London, 1982), pp. 205–7. Reprinted by permission.*

had been reconciled with Yeroen, he would go over to Mama to punish her for the part she had played. This could take a very long time, because Mama usually punished Nikkie in return by rejecting his subsequent attempts at reconciliation. For instance, Nikkie slaps Mama, but a little later he comes back and sits down by her 'shyly' plucking at some wisps of grass. Mama pretends she has not seen him, gets up and walks off. Nikkie waits a while, then starts all over again, with his hair on end. This was clearly a phase of negative reciprocity.

As Yeroen's resistance to Nikkie decreased, Mama became more favourably inclined towards Nikkie. She still supported Yeroen, but when Nikkie made his peace with her later she no longer took any 'affective revenge' and their conflict remained brief. Later still—a process taking years—Mama reconciled her differences with Nikkie before his conflict with Yeroen had ended. One moment the two older apes were chasing after Nikkie, the next moment Mama affectionately embraced him. The conflict then continued between the two males, but Mama declined to take any further part.

In time the situation became even stranger. Nikkie began kissing Mama before or even during his display against Yeroen. This developed gradually from their reconciliations, until it took place without any preceding conflict. It could be seen as a mark of Mama's neutrality. Nikkie and Mama were showing positive reciprocity.

I have done a statistical study of the bilateral nature of coalitions by comparing how each individual intervenes in the conflicts of the others. In periods of stability such interventions are symmetrical, both in a positive sense (two individuals support each other) and in a negative sense (two individuals support each other's opponents). If we are to get a full picture of reciprocity, however, we will have to analyse more kinds of behaviour. Interventions need not necessarily be offset by other interventions. The receipt of regular support may be answered by greater tolerance towards the supporter, or by grooming. Perhaps we will eventually be able to conduct such an analysis in Arnhem. For the time being I should like to sum up as follows: chimpanzee group life is like a market in power, sex, affection, support, intolerance and hostility. The two basic rules are 'one good turn deserves another' and 'an eye for an eye, a tooth for a tooth'.

The rules are not always obeyed and flagrant disobedience may be punished. This happened once after Puist had supported Luit in chasing Nikkie. When Nikkie later displayed at Puist she turned to Luit and held out her hand to him in search of support. Luit, however, did nothing to protect her against Nikkie's attack. Immediately Puist turned on Luit, barking furiously, chased him across the enclosure and even hit him. If her fury was in fact the result of Luit's failure to help her after she had helped him, this would suggest that reciprocity among chimpanzees is governed by the same sense of moral rightness and justice as it is among humans.

31   All Animals are Equal

PETER SINGER

. . . "ANIMAL LIBERATION" MAY SOUND more like a parody of other liberation movements than a serious objective. The idea of "The Rights of Animals" actually was once used to parody the case for women's rights. When Mary Wollstonecraft, a forerunner of today's feminists, published her *Vindication of the Rights of Women* in 1792, her views were widely regarded as absurd, and before long an anonymous publication appeared entitled *A Vindication of the Rights of Brutes*. The author of this satirical work (now known to have been Thomas Taylor, a distinguished Cambridge philosopher) tried to refute Mary Wollstonecraft's arguments by showing that they could be carried one stage further. If the argument for equality was sound when applied to women, why should it not be applied to dogs, cats, and horses? The reasoning seemed to hold for these "brutes" too; yet to hold that brutes had rights was manifestly absurd; therefore the reasoning by which this conclusion had been reached must be unsound, and if unsound when applied to brutes, it must also be unsound when applied to women, since the very same arguments had been used in each case.

In order to explain the basis of the case for the equality of animals, it will be helpful to start with an examination of the case for the equality of women. Let us assume that we wish to defend the case for women's rights against the attack by Thomas Taylor. How should we reply?

One way in which we might reply is by saying that the case for equality between men and women cannot validly be extended to nonhuman animals. Women have a right to vote, for instance, because they are just as capable of making rational decisions about the future as men are; dogs, on the other hand, are incapable of understanding the significance of voting, so they cannot have the right to vote. There are many other obvious ways in which men and women resemble each other closely, while humans and animals differ greatly. So, it might be said, men and women are similar beings and should have similar rights, while humans and nonhumans are different and should not have equal rights.

The reasoning behind this reply to Taylor's analogy is correct up to a point, but it does not go far enough. There *are* important differences between humans and other animals, and these differences must give rise to *some* differences in the rights that each have. Recognizing this obvious fact, however, is no barrier to the case for extending the basic principle of equality to nonhuman animals. The differences that exist between men and women are equally undeniable, and the supporters of Women's Liberation are aware that these differences may give rise to different rights. Many feminists hold that women have the right to an abortion on request. It does not follow that since these same feminists are campaigning for equality between men and women they must sup-

From Animal Liberation *(New York: New York Review, 1975), pp. 1–22. Reprinted by permission of* Peter Singer.

port the right of men to have abortions too. Since a man cannot have an abortion, it is meaningless to talk of his right to have one. Since a dog can't vote, it is meaningless to talk of its right to vote. There is no reason why either Women's Liberation or Animal Liberation should get involved in such nonsense. The extension of the basic principle of equality from one group to another does not imply that we must treat both groups in exactly the same way, or grant exactly the same rights to both groups. Whether we should do so will depend on the nature of the members of the two groups. The basic principle of equality does not require equal or identical *treatment;* it requires equal *consideration.* Equal consideration for different beings may lead to different treatment and different rights.

So there is a different way of replying to Taylor's attempt to parody the case for women's rights, a way that does not deny the obvious differences between humans and nonhumans but goes more deeply into the question of equality and concludes by finding nothing absurd in the idea that the basic principle of equality applies to so-called "brutes." At this point such a conclusion may appear odd; but if we examine more deeply the basis [for] our opposition to discrimination on grounds of race or sex ultimately, we will see that we would be on shaky ground if we were to demand equality for Blacks, women, and other groups of oppressed humans while denying equal consideration to nonhumans. To make this clear we need to see first exactly why racism and sexism are wrong.

When we say that all human beings, whatever their race, creed, or sex, are equal, what is it that we are asserting? Those who wish to defend hierarchical, inegalitarian societies have often pointed out that by whatever test we choose it simply is not true that all humans are equal. Like it or not we must face the fact that humans come in different shapes and sizes; they come with different moral capacities, different intellectual abilities, different amounts of benevolent feeling and sensitivity to the needs of others, different abilities to

communicate effectively, and different capacities to experience pleasure and pain. In short, if the demand for equality were based on the actual equality of all human beings, we would have to stop demanding equality.

Still, one might cling to the view that the demand for equality among human beings is based on the actual equality of the different races and sexes. Although, it may be said, humans differ as individuals there are no differences between the races and sexes *as such.* From the mere fact that a person is Black or a woman we cannot infer anything about that person's intellectual or moral capacities. This, it may be said, is why racism and sexism are wrong. The white racist claims that whites are superior to Blacks, but this is false—although there are differences among individuals, some Blacks are superior to some whites in all of the capacities and abilities that could conceivably be relevant. The opponent of sexism would say the same: A person's sex is no guide to his or her abilities, and this is why it is unjustifiable to discriminate on the basis of sex.

The existence of individual variations that cut across the lines of race or sex, however, provides us with no defense at all against a more sophisticated opponent of equality, one who proposes that, say, the interests of all those with IQ scores below 100 be given less consideration than the interests of those with ratings over 100. Perhaps those scoring below the mark would, in this society, be made the slaves of those scoring higher. Would a hierarchical society of this sort really be so much better than one based on race or sex? I think not. But if we tie the moral principle of equality to the factual equality of the different races or sexes, taken as a whole, our opposition to racism and sexism does not provide us with any basis for objecting to this kind of inegalitarianism.

There is a second important reason why we ought not to base our opposition to racism and sexism on any kind of actual equality, even the limited kind that asserts that variations in capacities and abilities are spread evenly between the different races and sexes: We can have no absolute guarantee that these capacities and abilities really are distributed evenly, without regard to race or sex, among human beings. So far as actual abilities are concerned there do seem to be certain measurable differences between both races and sexes. These differences do not, of course, appear in each case, but only when averages are taken. More important still, we do not yet know how much of these differences is really due to the different genetic endowments of the different races and sexes, and how much is due to poor schools, poor housing, and other factors that are the result of past and continuing discrimination. Perhaps all of the important differences will eventually prove to be environmental rather than genetic. Anyone opposed to racism and sexism will certainly hope that this will be so, for it will make the task of ending discrimination a lot easier; nevertheless it would be dangerous to rest the case against racism and sexism on the belief that all significant differences are environmental in origin. The opponent of, say, racism who takes this line will be unable to avoid conceding that *if* differences in ability do after all prove to have some genetic connection with race, racism would in some way be defensible.

Fortunately there is no need to pin the case for equality to one particular outcome of a scientific investigation. The appropriate response to those who claim to have found evidence of genetically based differences in ability between the races or sexes is not to stick to the belief that the genetic explanation must be wrong, whatever evidence to the contrary may turn up: Instead we should make it quite clear that the claim to equality does not depend on intelligence, moral capacity, physical strength, or similar matters of fact. Equality is a moral idea, not an assertion of fact. There is no logically compelling reason for assuming that a factual difference in ability between two people justifies any difference in the amount of consideration we give to their needs and interests. *The principle of the equality of human beings is not a description of an alleged actual equality among humans: It is a prescription of how we should treat humans.*

Jeremy Bentham, the founder of the reforming utilitarian school of moral philosophy, incorporated the essential basis of moral equality into his system of ethics by means of the formula: "Each to count for one and none for more than one." In other words, the interests of every being affected by an action are to be taken into account and given the same weight as the like interests of any other being. A later utilitarian, Henry Sidgwick, put the point in this way: "The good of any one individual is of no more importance, from the point of view (if I may say so) of the Universe, than the good of any other." More recently leading figures in contemporary moral philosophy have shown a great deal of agreement in specifying as a fundamental presupposition of their moral theories some similar requirement which operates so as to give everyone's interests equal consideration—although these writers generally cannot agree on how this requirement is best formulated.[1]

It is an implication of this principle of equality that our concern for others and our readiness to consider their interests ought not depend on what they are like or on what abilities they may possess. Precisely what this concern or consideration requires us to do may vary according to the characteristics of those affected by what we do: Concern for the well-being of a child growing up in America would require that we teach him to read; concern for the well-being of a pig may require no more than that we leave him alone with other pigs in a place where there is adequate food and room to run freely. But the basic element—the taking into account of the interests of the being, whatever those interests may be—must, according to the principle of equality, be extended to all beings, Black or white, masculine or feminine, human or nonhuman.

Thomas Jefferson, who was responsible for writing the principle of the equality of men into the American Declaration of Independence, saw this point. It led him to oppose slavery even though he was unable to free himself fully from his slaveholding background. He wrote in a letter to the author of a book that emphasized the notable intellectual achievements of Negroes in order to refute the then common view that they had limited intellectual capacities:

> Be assured that no person living wishes more sincerely than I do, to see a complete refutation of the doubts I have myself entertained and expressed on the grade of understanding allotted to them by nature, and to find that they are on a par with ourselves . . . but whatever be their degree of talent it is no measure of their rights. Because Sir Isaac Newton was superior to others in understanding, he was not therefore lord of the property or person of others.[2]

Similarly when in the 1850s the call for women's rights was raised in the United States a remarkable Black feminist named Sojourner Truth made the same point in more robust terms at a feminist convention:

> . . . they talk about this thing in the head; what do they call it? ["Intellect," whispered someone near by.] That's it. What's that got to do with women's rights or Negroes' rights? If my cup won't hold but a pint and yours holds a quart, wouldn't you be mean not to let me have my little half-measure full?[3]

It is on this basis that the case against racism and the case against sexism must both ultimately rest; and it is in accordance with this principle that the attitude that we may call "speciesism," by analogy with racism, must also be condemned. Speciesism—the word is not an attractive one, but I can think of no better term—is a prejudice or attitude of bias toward the interests of members of one's own species and against those of members of other species. It should be obvious that the fundamental objections to racism and sexism made by Thomas Jefferson and Sojourner Truth apply equally to speciesism. If possessing a higher degree of intelligence does not entitle one human to use another for his own ends, how can it entitle humans to exploit nonhumans for the same purpose?[4]

Many philosophers and other writers have proposed the principle of equal consideration of interests, in some form or other, as a basic moral principle; but not many of them have recognized that this principle applies to members of other species as well as to our own. Jeremy Bentham was one of the few who did realize this. In a forward-looking passage written at a time when Black slaves had been freed by the French but in the British dominions were still being treated in the way we now treat animals, Bentham wrote:

> The day *may* come when the rest of the animal creation may acquire those rights which never could have been withholden from them but by the hand of tyranny. The French have already discovered that the blackness of the skin is no reason why a human being should be abandoned without redress to the caprice of a tormentor. It may one day come to be recognized that the number of the legs, the villosity of the skin, or the termination of the *os sacrum* are reasons equally insufficient for abandoning a sensitive being to the same fate. What else is it that should trace the insuperable line? Is it the faculty of reason, or perhaps the faculty of discourse? But a full-grown horse or dog is beyond comparison a more rational, as well as a more conversable animal, than an infant of a day or a week or even a month, old. But suppose they were otherwise, what would it avail? The question is not, Can they *reason*? nor Can they *talk*? but, *Can they suffer*?[5]

In this passage Bentham points to the capacity for suffering as the vital characteristic that gives a being the right to equal consideration. The capacity for suffering—or more strictly, for suffering and/or enjoyment or happiness—is not just another characteristic like the capacity for language or higher mathematics. Bentham is not saying that those who try to mark "the insuperable line" that determines whether the interests of a being should be considered happen to have chosen the wrong characteristic. By saying that we must consider the interests of all beings with the capacity for suffering or enjoyment Bentham does not arbitrarily exclude from consideration any interests at all—as those who draw the line with reference to the possession of reason or language do. The capacity for suffering and enjoyment is *a prerequisite for having interests at all,* a condition that must be satisfied before we can speak of interests in a meaningful way. It would be nonsense to say that it was not in the interests of a stone to be kicked along the road by a schoolboy. A stone does not have interests because it cannot suffer. Nothing that we can do to it could possibly make any difference to its welfare. A mouse, on the other hand, does have an interest in not being kicked along the road, because it will suffer if it is.

If a being suffers there can be no moral justification for refusing to take that suffering into consideration. No matter what the nature of the being, the principle of equality requires that its suffering be counted equally with the like suffering—in so far as rough comparisons can be made—of any other being. If a being is not capable of suffering, or of experiencing enjoyment or happiness, there is nothing to be taken into account. So the limit of sentience (using the term as a convenient if not strictly accurate shorthand for the capacity to suffer and/or experience enjoyment) is the only defensible boundary of concern for the interests of others. To mark this boundary by some other characteristic like intelligence or rationality would be to mark it in an arbitrary manner. Why not choose some other characteristic, like skin color?

The racist violates the principle of equality by giving greater weight to the interests of members of his own race when there is a clash between their interests and the interests of those of another race. The sexist violates the principle of equality by favoring the interests of his own sex. Similarly the speciesist allows the interests of his own species to override the greater interests of members of other species. The pattern is identical in each case.

Most human beings are speciesists. . . . Ordinary human beings—not a few exceptionally cruel or heartless humans, but the overwhelming majority of humans—take an active part in, acquiesce in, and allow their taxes to pay for practices that require the sacrifice of the most important interests of members of other species in order to promote the most trivial interests of our own species.

There is, however, one general defense of these practices . . . that needs to be disposed of. . . . It is a defense which, if true, would allow us to do anything at all to nonhumans for the slightest reason, or for no reason at all, without incurring any justifiable reproach. This defense claims that we are never guilty of neglecting the interests of other animals for one breathtakingly simple reason: They have no interests. Nonhuman animals have no interests, according to this view, because they are not capable of suffering. By this is not meant merely that they are not capable of suffering in all the ways that humans are—for instance, that a calf is not capable of suffering from the knowledge that it will be killed in six months time. That modest claim is, no doubt, true; but it does not clear humans of the charge of speciesism, since it allows that animals may suffer in other ways—for instance, by being given electric shocks, or being kept in small, cramped cages. The defense I am about to discuss is the much more sweeping, although correspondingly less plausible, claim that animals are incapable of suffering in any way at all; that they are . . . unconscious automata, possessing neither thoughts nor feelings nor a mental life of any kind.

Although . . . the view that animals are automata was proposed by the seventeenth-century French philosopher René Descartes, to most people, then and now, it is obvious that if, for example, we stick a sharp knife into the stomach of an unanesthetized dog, the dog will feel pain. That this is so is assumed by the laws in most civilized countries which prohibit wanton cruelty to animals. Readers whose common sense tells them that animals do suffer may prefer to skip the next few paragraphs . . . since they do nothing but refute a position which they do not hold. Implausible as it is, though, for the sake of completeness this skeptical position must be discussed.

Do animals other than humans feel pain? How do we know? Well, how do we know if anyone, human or nonhuman, feels pain? We know that we ourselves can feel pain. We know this from the direct experiences of pain that we have when, for instance, somebody presses a lighted cigarette against the back of our hand. But how do we know that anyone else feels pain? We cannot directly experience anyone else's pain, whether that "anyone" is our best friend or a stray dog. Pain is a state of consciousness, a "mental event," and as such it can never be observed. Behavior like writhing, screaming, or drawing one's hand away from the lighted cigarette is not pain itself; nor are the recordings a neurologist might make of activity within the brain observations of pain itself. Pain is something that we feel, and we can only infer that others are feeling it from various external indications.

In theory, we *could* always be mistaken when we assume that other human beings feel pain. It is conceivable that our best friend is really a very cleverly constructed robot, controlled by a brilliant scientist so as to give all the signs of feeling pain, but really no more sensitive than any other machine. We can never know, with absolute certainty, that this is not the case. But while this might present a puzzle for philosophers, none of us has the slightest real doubt that our best friends feel pain just as we do. This is an inference, but a perfectly reasonable one, based on observations of their behavior in situations in which we would feel pain, and on the fact that we have every reason to assume that our friends are beings like us, with nervous systems like ours that can be assumed to function as ours do, and to produce similar feelings in similar circumstances.

If it is justifiable to assume that other humans feel pain as we do, is there any reason why a similar inference should be unjustifiable in the case of other animals?

Nearly all the external signs that lead us to infer pain in other humans can be seen in other species, especially [those] most closely related to us—other species of mammals, and birds. Behavioral signs—writhing, facial contortions, moaning, yelping, or other forms of calling, attempts to avoid the source of pain, appearance of fear at the prospect of its repetition, and so on—are present. In addition, we know that these animals have nervous systems very like ours, which respond physiologically as ours do when the animal is in

circumstances in which we would feel pain: an initial rise of blood pressure, dilated pupils, perspiration, an increased pulse rate, and, if the stimulus continues, a fall in blood pressure. Although humans have a more developed cerebral cortex than other animals, this part of the brain is concerned with thinking functions rather than with basic impulses, emotions, and feelings. These impulses, emotions, and feelings are located in the diencephalon, which is well developed in many other species of animals, especially mammals and birds.[6]

We also know that the nervous systems of other animals were not artificially constructed to mimic the pain behavior of humans, as a robot might be artificially constructed. The nervous systems of animals evolved as our own did, and in fact the evolutionary history of humans and other animals, especially mammals, did not diverge until the central features of our nervous systems were already in existence. A capacity to feel pain obviously enhances a species' prospects of survival, since it causes members of the species to avoid sources of injury. It is surely unreasonable to suppose that nervous systems which are virtually identical physiologically, have a common origin and a common evolutionary function, and result in similar forms of behavior in similar circumstances should actually operate in an entirely different manner on the level of subjective feelings.

It has long been accepted as sound policy in science to search for the simplest possible explanation of whatever it is we are trying to explain. Occasionally it has been claimed that it is for this reason "unscientific" to explain the behavior of animals by theories that refer to the animal's conscious feelings, desires, and so on—the idea being that if the behavior in question can be explained without invoking consciousness or feelings, that will be the simpler theory. Yet we can now see that such explanations, when placed in the overall context of the behavior of both human and nonhuman animals, are far more complex than their rivals. We know from our own experience that explanations of our own behavior that did not refer to consciousness and the feeling of pain would be incomplete; it is simpler to assume that the similar behavior of animals with similar nervous systems is to be explained in the same way than to try to invent some other explanation for the behavior of nonhuman animals as well as an explanation for the divergence between humans and nonhumans in this respect.

The overwhelming majority of scientists who have addressed themselves to this question agree. Lord Brain, one of the most eminent neurologists of our time, has said:

> I personally can see no reason for conceding mind to my fellow men and denying it to animals. . . . I at least cannot doubt that the interests and activities of animals are correlated with awareness and feeling in the same way as my own, and which may be, for aught I know, just as vivid.[7]

While the author of a recent book on pain writes:

> Every particle of factual evidence supports the contention that the higher mammalian vertebrates experience pain sensations at least as acute as our own. To say that they feel less because they are lower animals is an absurdity; it can easily be shown that many of their senses are far more acute than ours—visual acuity in certain birds, hearing in most wild animals, and touch in others; these animals depend more than we do today on the sharpest possible awareness of a hostile environment. Apart from the complexity of the cerebral cortex (which does not directly perceive pain) their nervous systems are almost identical to ours and their reactions to pain remarkably similar, though lacking (so far as we know) the philosophical and moral overtones. The emotional element is all too evident, mainly in the form of fear and anger.[8]

In Britain, three separate expert government committees on matters relating to animals have accepted the conclusion that animals feel pain. After noting the obvious behavioral evidence for this view, the Committee on Cruelty to Wild Animals said:

> . . . we believe that the physiological, and more particularly the anatomical, evidence fully justifies and reinforces the commonsense belief that animals feel pain.

And after discussing the evolutionary value of pain they concluded that pain is "of clear-cut biological usefulness" and this is "a third type of evidence that animals feel pain." They then went on to consider forms of suffering other than mere physical pain, and added that they were "satisfied that animals do suffer from acute fear and terror." In 1965, British government [reports] on experiments on animals, and on the welfare of animals under intensive farming methods, agreed with this view, concluding that animals are capable of suffering both from straightforward physical injuries and from fear, anxiety, stress, and so on.[9]

That might well be thought enough to settle the matter; but there is one more objection that needs to be considered. There is, after all, one behavioral sign that humans have when in pain which non-humans do not have. This is a developed language. Other animals may communicate with each other, but not, it seems, in the complicated way we do. Some philosophers, including Descartes, have thought it important that while humans can tell each other about their experience of pain in great detail, other animals cannot. (Interestingly, this once neat dividing line between humans and other species has now been threatened by the discovery that chimpanzees can be taught a language.)[10] But as Bentham pointed out long ago, the ability to use language is not relevant to the question of how a being ought to be treated—unless that ability can be linked to the capacity to suffer, so that the absence of a language casts doubt on the existence of this capacity.

This link may be attempted in two ways. First, there is a hazy line of philosophical thought, stemming perhaps from some doctrines associated with influential philosopher Ludwig Wittgenstein, that maintains we cannot meaningfully attribute states of consciousness to beings without language. This position seems to me very implausible. Language may be necessary for abstract thought, at some level anyway; but states like pain are more primitive, and have nothing to do with language.

The second and more easily understood way of linking language and the existence of pain is to say that the best evidence that we can have that another creature is in pain is when he tells us that he is. This is a distinct line of argument, for it is not being denied that a non-language-user conceivably *could* suffer, but only that we could ever have sufficient reason to *believe* that he is suffering. Still, this line of argument fails too. As Jane Goodall has pointed out in her study of chimpanzees, *In the Shadow of Man,* when it comes to the expressions of feelings and emotions language is less important than in other areas. We tend to fall back on nonlinguistic modes of communication such as a cheering pat on the back, an exuberant embrace, a clasp of the hands, and so on. The basic signals we use to convey pain, fear, anger, love, joy, surprise, sexual arousal, and many other emotional states are not specific to our own species.[11]

Charles Darwin made an extensive study of this subject, and the book he wrote about it, *The Expression of the Emotions in Man and Animals,* notes countless nonlinguistic modes of expression. The statement "I am in pain" may be one piece of evidence for the conclusion that the speaker is in pain, but it is not the only possible evidence, and since people sometimes tell lies, not even the best possible evidence.

Even if there were stronger grounds for refusing to attribute pain to those who do not have a language, the consequences of this refusal might lead us to reject the conclusion. Human infants and young children are unable to use language. Are we to deny that a year-old child can suffer? If not, language cannot be crucial. Of course, most parents understand the responses of their children better than they understand the responses of other animals; but this is just a fact about the relatively greater knowledge that we have of our own species, and the greater contact we have with infants, as compared to animals. Those who have studied the behavior of other animals, and those who have pet animals, soon learn to understand their responses as well as we understand those of an infant, and sometimes better. Jane Goodall's account of the chimpanzees she watched is one [example], but the same can be said of those who have observed species less closely related to our own. Two among many possible examples are Konrad Lorenz's observations of geese and jackdaws, and N. Tinbergen's extensive studies of herring gulls.[12] Just as we can understand infant human behavior in the light of adult human behavior, so we can understand the behavior of other species in the light of our own behavior—and sometimes we can understand our own behavior better in the light of the behavior of other species.

So to conclude: There are no good reasons, scientific or philosophical, for denying that animals feel pain. If we do not doubt that other humans feel pain we should not doubt that other animals do so too.

Animals can feel pain. As we saw earlier, there can be no moral justification for regarding the pain (or pleasure) that animals feel as less important than the same amount of pain (or pleasure) felt by humans. But what exactly does this mean, in practical terms? To prevent misunderstanding I shall spell out what I mean a little more fully.

If I give a horse a hard slap across its rump with my open hand, the horse may start, but it presumably feels little pain. Its skin is thick enough to protect it against a mere slap. If I slap a baby in the same way, however, the baby will cry and presumably does feel pain, for its skin is more sensitive. So it is worse to slap a baby than a horse, if both slaps are administered with equal force. But there must be some kind of blow . . . perhaps a blow with a heavy stick . . . that would cause the horse as much pain as we cause a baby by slapping it with our hand. That is what I mean by "the same amount of pain" and if we consider it wrong to inflict that much pain on a baby for no good reason then we must, unless we are speciesists, consider it equally wrong to inflict the same amount of pain on a horse for no good reason.

There are other differences between humans and animals that cause other complications. Normal adult human beings have mental capacities which will, in certain circumstances, lead them to suffer more than animals would in the same circumstances. If, for instance, we decided to perform extremely painful or lethal scientific experiments on normal adult humans, kidnapped at random from public parks for this purpose, every adult who entered a park would become fearful that he would be kidnapped. The resultant terror would be a form of suffering additional to the pain of the experiment. The same experiments performed on nonhuman animals would cause less suffering since the animals would not have the anticipatory dread of being kidnapped and experimented upon. This does not mean, of course, that it would be right to perform the experiment on animals, but only that there is a reason, which is *not* speciesist, for preferring to use animals rather than normal adult humans, if the experiment is to be done at all. Note, however, that this same argument gives us a reason for preferring to use human infants—orphans perhaps—or retarded humans for experiments, rather than adults, since infants and retarded humans would also have no idea of what was going to happen to them. So far as this argument is concerned nonhuman animals and infants and retarded humans are in the same category; and if we use this argument to justify experiments on nonhuman animals we have to ask ourselves whether we are also prepared to allow experiments on human infants and retarded adults; and if we make a distinction between animals and these humans, on what basis can we do it, other than a barefaced—and morally indefensible—preference for members of our own species?

There are many areas in which the superior mental powers of normal adult humans make a difference: anticipation, more detailed memory, greater knowledge of what is happening, and so on. Yet these differences do not all point to greater suffering on the part of the normal human being. Sometimes an animal may suffer more because of his more limited understanding. If, for instance, we are taking prisoners in wartime we can explain to them that while they must submit to capture, search, and confinement they will not otherwise be harmed and will be set free at the conclusion of hostilities. If we capture a wild animal, however, we cannot explain that we are not threatening its life. A wild animal cannot distinguish an attempt to overpower and confine from an attempt to kill; the one causes as much terror as the other.

It may be objected that comparisons of the sufferings of different species are impossible to make, and that for this reason when the interests of animals and humans clash the principle of equality gives no guidance. It is probably true that comparisons of suffering between members of different species cannot be made precisely, but precision is not essential. Even if we were to prevent the infliction of suffering on animals only when it is quite certain that the interests of humans will not be affected to anything like the extent that animals are affected, we would be forced to make radical changes in our treatment of animals that would involve our diet, the farming methods we use, experimental procedures in many fields of science, our approach to wildlife and to hunting, trapping, and the wearing of furs, and areas of entertainment like circuses, rodeos, and zoos. As a result, a vast amount of suffering would be avoided.

So far I have said a lot about the infliction of suffering on animals, but nothing about killing them. This omission has been deliberate. The application of the principle of equality to the infliction of suffering is, in theory at least, fairly straightforward. Pain and suffering are bad and should be prevented or minimized, irrespective of the race, sex, or species of the being that suffers. How bad a pain is depends on how intense it is and how long it lasts, but pains of the same intensity and duration are equally bad, whether felt by humans or animals.

The wrongness of killing a being is more complicated. I have kept, and shall continue to keep, the question of killing in the background because in the present state of human tyranny over other species the more simple, straightforward principle of equal consideration of pain or pleasure is a sufficient basis for identifying and protesting all the major abuses of animals that humans practice. Nevertheless, it is necessary to say something about killing.

Just as most humans are speciesists in their readiness to cause pain to animals when they would not cause a similar pain to humans for the same reason, so most humans are speciesists in their readiness to kill other animals when they would not kill humans. We need to proceed more cautiously here, however, because people hold widely differing views about when it is legitimate to kill humans, as the continuing debates over abortion and euthanasia attest. Nor have moral philosophers been able to agree on exactly what it is that makes it wrong to kill humans, and under what circumstances killing a human being may be justifiable.

Let us consider first the view that it is always wrong to take an innocent human life. We may call this the "sanctity of life" view. People who take this view oppose abortion and euthanasia. They do not usually, however, oppose the killing of nonhumans—so perhaps it would be more accurate to describe this view as the "sanctity of *human* life" view.

The belief that human life, and only human life, is sacrosanct is a form of speciesism. To see this, consider the following example.

Assume that, as sometimes happens, an infant has been born with massive and irreparable brain damage. The damage is so severe that the infant can never be any more than a "human vegetable," unable to talk, recognize other people, act independently of others, or develop a sense of self-awareness. The parents of the infant, realizing that they cannot hope for any improvement in their child's condition and being in any case unwilling to spend, or ask the state to spend, the thousands of dollars that would be needed annually for proper care of the infant, ask the doctor to kill the infant painlessly.

Should the doctor do what the parents ask? Legally, he should not, and in this respect the law reflects the sanctity of life view. The life of every human being is sacred. Yet people who would say this about the infant do not object to the killing of nonhuman animals. How can they justify their different judgments? Adult chimpanzees, dogs, pigs, and many other species far surpass the brain-damaged infant in their ability to relate to others, act independently, be self-aware, and any other capacity that could reasonably be said to give value

to life. With the most intensive care possible, there are retarded infants who can never achieve the intelligence level of a dog. Nor can we appeal to the concern of the infant's parents, since they themselves, in this imaginary example (and in some actual cases), do not want the infant kept alive.

The only thing that distinguishes the infant from the animal, in the eyes of those who claim it has a "right to life," is that it is, biologically, a member of the species *Homo sapiens,* whereas chimpanzees, dogs, and pigs are not. But to use *this* difference as the basis for granting a right to life to the infant and not to the other animals is, of course, pure speciesism.[13] It is exactly the kind of arbitrary difference that the most crude and overt kind of racist uses in attempting to justify racial discrimination.

This does not mean that to avoid speciesism we must hold that it is as wrong to kill a dog as it is to kill a normal human being. The only position that is irredeemably speciesist is the one that tries to make the boundary of the right to life run exactly parallel to the boundary of our own species. Those who hold the sanctity of life view do this because while distinguishing sharply between humans and other animals they allow no distinctions to be made within our own species, objecting to the killing of the severely retarded and the hopelessly senile as strongly as they object to the killing of normal adults.

To avoid speciesism we must allow that beings which are similar in all relevant respects have a similar right to life—and mere membership in our own biological species cannot be a morally relevant criterion for this right. Within these limits we could still hold that, for instance, it is worse to kill a normal adult human, with a capacity for self-awareness, and the ability to plan for the future and have meaningful relations with others, than it is to kill a mouse, which presumably does not share all of these characteristics; or we might appeal to the close family and other personal ties which humans have but mice do not have to the same degree; or we might think that it is the consequences for other humans, who will be put in fear of their own lives, that make the crucial difference; or we might think it is some combination of these factors, or other factors altogether.

Whatever criteria we choose, however, we will have to admit that they do not follow precisely the boundary of our own species. We may legitimately hold that there are some features of certain beings which make their lives more valuable than those of other beings; but there will surely be some nonhuman animals whose lives, by any standards, are more valuable than the lives of some humans. A chimpanzee, dog, or pig, for instance, will have a higher degree of self-awareness and a greater capacity for meaningful relations with others than a severely retarded infant or someone in a state of advanced senility. So if we base the right to life on these characteristics we must grant these animals a right to life as good as, or better than, such retarded or senile humans.

Now this argument cuts both ways. It could be taken as showing that chimpanzees, dogs, and pigs, along with some other species, have a right to life and we commit a grave moral offense whenever we kill them, even when they are old and suffering and our intention is to put them out of their misery. Alternatively one could take the argument as showing that the severely retarded and hopelessly senile have no right to life and may be killed for quite trivial reasons, as we now kill animals.

Since the focus of this [reading] is on ethical questions concerning animals and not on the morality of euthanasia I shall not attempt to settle this issue finally. I think it is reasonably clear, though, that while both of the positions just described avoid speciesism, neither is entirely satisfactory. What we need is some middle position which would avoid speciesism but would not make the lives of the retarded and senile as cheap as the lives of pigs and dogs now are, nor make the lives of pigs and dogs so sacrosanct that we think it wrong to put them out of hopeless misery. What we must do is bring nonhuman animals within our sphere of moral concern and cease to treat their lives as expendable for whatever trivial purposes we may have. At the same time, once we realize that the fact that a being is a member of our own species is not in itself enough to make it always wrong to kill that being, we may come to reconsider our policy of preserving human lives at all costs, even when there is no prospect of a meaningful life or of existence without terrible pain.

I conclude, then, that a rejection of speciesism does not imply that all lives are of equal worth. While self-awareness, intelligence, the capacity for meaningful relations with others, and so on are not relevant to the question of inflicting pain—since pain is pain, whatever other capacities, beyond the capacity to feel pain, the being may have—these capacities may be relevant to the question of taking life. It is not arbitrary to hold that the life of a self-aware being, capable of abstract thought, of planning for the future, of complex acts of communication, and so on, is more valuable than the life of a being without these capacities. To see the difference between the issues of inflicting pain and taking life, consider how we would choose within our own species. If we had to choose to save the life of a normal human or a mentally defective human, we would probably choose to save the life of the normal human; but if we had to choose between preventing pain in the normal human or the mental defective—imagine that both have received painful but superficial injuries, and we only have enough painkiller for one of them—it is not nearly so clear how we ought to choose. The same is true when we consider other species. The evil of pain is, in itself, unaffected by the other characteristics of the being that feels the pain; the value of life is affected by these other characteristics.

Normally this will mean that if we have to choose between the life of a human being and the life of another animal we should choose to save the life of the human; but there may be special cases in which the reverse holds true, because the human being in question does not have the capacities of a normal human being. So this view is not speciesist, although it may appear to be at first glance. The preference, in normal cases, for saving a human life over the life of an animal when a choice *has* to be made is a preference based on the characteristics that normal humans have, and not on the mere fact that they are members of our own species. This is why when we consider members of our own species who lack the characteristics of normal humans we can no longer say their lives are always to be preferred to those of other animals. . . . In general, though, the question of when it is wrong to kill (painlessly) an animal is one to which we need give no precise answer. As long as we remember that we should give the same respect to the lives of animals as we give to the lives of those humans at a similar mental level, we shall not go far wrong.

NOTES

1. For Bentham's moral philosophy, see his *Introduction to the Principles of Morals and Legislation,* and for Sidgwick's see *The Methods of Ethics* (the passage quoted is from the seventh edition, p. 382). As examples of leading contemporary moral philosophers who incorporate a requirement of equal consideration of interests, see R. M. Hare, *Freedom and Reason* (New York: Oxford University Press, 1963) and John Rawls, *A Theory of Justice* (Cambridge: Harvard University Press, Belknap Press, 1972). For a brief account of the essential agreement on this issue between these and other positions, see R. M. Hare, "Rules of War and Moral Reasoning," *Philosophy and Public Affairs,* vol. 1, no. 2 (1972).

2. Letter to Henri Gregoire, February 25, 1809.

3. Reminiscences by Francis D. Gage, from Susan B. Anthony, *The History of Woman Suffrage,* vol. 1; the passage is to be found in the extract in Leslie Tanner, ed., *Voices from Women's Liberation* (New York: Signet, 1970).

4. I owe the term "speciesism" to Richard Ryder.

5. *Introduction to the Principles of Morals and Legislation,* chapter 17.

6. Lord Brian, "Presidential Address," in C. A. Keele and R. Smith, eds., *The Assessment of Pain in Men and Animals* (London: Universities Federation for Animal Welfare, 1962).

7. Ibid., p. 11.

8. Richard Serjeant, *The Spectrum of Pain* (London: Hart-Davis, 1969), p. 72.

9. See the reports of the Committee on Cruelty to Wild Animals (Command Paper 8268, 1951), paragraphs 36–42; the Departmental Committee on Experiments on Animals (Command Paper 2641, 1965), paragraphs 179–182; and the Technical Committee to Enquire into the Welfare of Animals Kept under Intensive Livestock Husbandry Systems (Command Paper 2836, 1965), paragraphs 26–28 (London: Her Majesty's Stationery Office).

10. One chimpanzee, Washoe, has been taught the sign language used by deaf people, and acquired a vocabulary of 350 signs. Another, Lana, communicates in structured sentences by pushing buttons on a special machine. For a brief account of Washoe's abilities, see Jane van Lawick-Goodall, *In the Shadow of Man* (Boston: Houghton Mifflin, 1971), pp. 252–254; and for Lana, see *Newsweek,* 7 January 1974, and *New York Times,* 4 December 1974.

11. *In the Shadow of Man,* p. 225; Michael Peters makes a similar point in "Nature and Culture," in Stanley and Roslind Godlovitch and John Harris, eds., *Animals, Men and Morals* (New York: Taplinger Publishing Co., 1972).

12. Konrad Lorenz, *King Solomon's Ring* (New York: T. Y. Crowell, 1952); N. Tinbergen, *The Herring Gull's World,* rev. ed. (New York: Basic Books, 1974).

32   The Ethics of Respect for Nature

PAUL W. TAYLOR

Human-Centered and Life-Centered Systems of Environmental Ethics

In this paper I show how the taking of a certain ultimate moral attitude toward nature, which I call "respect for nature," has a central place in the foundations of a life-centered system of environmental ethics. I hold that a set of moral norms (both standards of character and rules of conduct) governing human treatment of the natural world is a rationally grounded set if and only if, first, commitment to those norms is a practical entailment of adopting the attitude of respect for nature as an ultimate moral attitude, and second, the adopting of that attitude on the part of all rational agents can itself be justified. When the basic characteristics of the attitude of respect for nature are made clear, it will be seen that a life-centered system of environmental ethics need not be holistic or organicist in its conception of the kinds of entities that are deemed the appropriate objects of moral concern and consideration. Nor does such a system require that the concepts of ecological homeostasis, equilibrium, and integrity provide us with normative principles from which could be derived (with the addition of factual knowledge) our obligations with regard to natural ecosystems. The "balance of nature" is not itself a moral norm, however important may be the role it plays in our general outlook on the natural world that underlies the attitude of respect for nature. I argue that finally it is the good (well-being, welfare) of individual organisms, considered as entities having inherent worth, that determines our moral relations with the Earth's wild communities of life.

In designating the theory . . . as life-centered, I intend to contrast it with all anthropocentric views. According to the latter, human actions that affect the natural environment and its nonhuman inhabitants are right (or wrong) by either of two criteria: They have consequences that are favorable (or unfavorable) to human well-being, or they are consistent (or inconsistent) with the system of norms that protect and implement human rights. From this human-centered standpoint it is to humans and only to humans that all duties are ultimately owed. We may have responsibilities *with regard to* the natural ecosystems and biotic communities of our planet, but these responsibilities are in every case based on the contingent fact that our treatment of those ecosystems and communities of life can further the realization of human values and/or human rights. We have no obligation to promote or protect the good of nonhuman living things, independently of this contingent fact.

A life-centered system of environmental ethics is opposed to human-centered ones precisely on this point. From the perspective of a life-centered theory, we have prima facie moral obligations that are owed to wild plants and animals themselves as members of the Earth's biotic community. We are morally bound (other things being equal) to protect or promote their good for *their* sake. Our du-

From "The Ethics of Respect for Nature," Environmental Ethics (1986), pp. 197–218. Reprinted by permission of the publisher. Notes renumbered.

ties to respect the integrity of natural ecosystems, to preserve endangered species, and to avoid environmental pollution stem from the fact that these are ways in which we can help make it possible for wild species populations to achieve and maintain a healthy existence in a natural state. Such obligations are due those living things out of recognition of their inherent worth. They are entirely additional to and independent of the obligations we owe to our fellow humans. Although many of the actions that fulfill one set of obligations also fulfill the other, two different grounds of obligation are involved. Their well-being, as well as human well-being, is something to be realized *as an end in itself.*

If we were to accept a life-centered theory of environmental ethics, a profound reordering of our moral universe would take place. We would begin to look at the whole of the Earth's biosphere in a new light. Our duties with respect to the "world" of nature would be seen as making prima facie claims on us to be balanced against our duties with respect to the "world" of human civilization. We could no longer simply take the human point of view and consider the effects of our actions exclusively from the perspective of our own good.

The Good of a Being and the Concept of Inherent Worth

What would justify acceptance of a life-centered system of ethical principles? In order to answer this it is first necessary to make clear the fundamental moral attitude that underlies and makes intelligible the commitment to live by such a system. It is then necessary to examine the considerations that would justify any rational agent's adopting that moral attitude.

Two concepts are essential to the taking of a moral attitude of the sort in question. A being which does not "have" these concepts, that is, which is unable to grasp their meaning and conditions of applicability, cannot be said to have the attitude as part of its moral outlook. These concepts

are, first, that of the good (well-being, welfare) of a living thing, and second, the idea of an entity possessing inherent worth. I examine each concept in turn.

(1) Every organism, species population, and community of life has a good of its own which moral agents can intentionally further or damage by their actions. To say that an entity has a good of its own is simply to say that, without reference to any *other* entity, it can be benefited or harmed. One can act in its overall interest or contrary to its overall interest, and environmental conditions can be good for it (advantageous to it) or bad for it (disadvantageous to it). What is good for an entity is what "does it good" in the sense of enhancing or preserving its life and well-being. What is bad for an entity is something that is detrimental to its life and well-being.[1]

We can think of the good of an individual nonhuman organism as consisting in the full development of its biological powers. Its good is realized to the extent that it is strong and healthy. It possesses whatever capacities it needs to successfully cope with its environment and so preserve its existence throughout the various stages of the normal life cycle of its species. The good of a population or community of such individuals consists in the population or community maintaining itself from generation to generation as a coherent system of genetically and ecologically related organisms whose average good is at an optimum level for the given environment. (Here *average good* means that the degree of realization of the good of *individual organisms* in the population or community is, on average, greater than would be the case under any other ecologically functioning order of interrelations among those species populations in the given ecosystem.)

The idea of a being having a good of its own . . . does not entail that the being must have interests or take an interest in what affects its life for better or for worse. We can act in a being's interest or contrary to its interest without its being interested in what we are doing to it in the sense of wanting or not wanting us to do it. It may, indeed, be wholly unaware that favorable and unfavorable events are taking place in its life. [Trees], for example, have no knowledge or desires or feelings. Yet it is undoubtedly the case that trees can be harmed or benefited by our actions. We can crush their roots by running a bulldozer too close to them. We can see to it that they get adequate nourishment and moisture by fertilizing and watering the soil around them. Thus we can help or hinder them in the realization of their good. It is the good of trees themselves that is thereby affected. We can similarly act so as to further the good of an entire tree population of a certain species (say, all the redwood trees in a California valley) or the good of a whole community of plant life in a given wilderness area, just as we can do harm to such a population or community.

When construed in this way, the concept of a being's good is not coextensive with sentience or the capacity for feeling pain. William Frankena has argued for a general theory of environmental ethics in which the ground of a creature's being worthy of moral consideration is its sentience. I have offered some criticisms of this view elsewhere, but the full refutation of such a position . . . finally depends on the positive reasons for accepting a life-centered theory of the kind I am defending in this essay.[2]

It should be noted further that I am leaving open the question of whether machines—in particular, those which are not only goal-directed, but also self-regulating—can properly be said to have a good of their own.[3] Since I am concerned only with human treatment of wild organisms, species populations, and communities of life as they occur in our planet's natural ecosystems, it is to those entities alone that the concept "having a good of its own" will here be applied. I am not denying that other living things, whose genetic origin and environmental conditions have been produced, controlled, and manipulated by humans for human ends, do have a good of their own in the same sense as do wild plants and animals. It is not my purpose in this essay, however, to set out or defend the principles that should

guide our conduct with regard to their good. It is only insofar as their production and use by humans have good or ill effects upon natural ecosystems and their wild inhabitants that the ethics of respect for nature comes into play.

(2) The second concept essential to the moral attitude of respect for nature is the idea of inherent worth. We take that attitude toward wild living things (individuals, species populations, or whole biotic communities) when and only when we regard them as entities possessing inherent worth. Indeed, it is only because they are conceived in this way that moral agents can think of themselves as having validly binding duties, obligations, and responsibilities that are *owed* to them as their *due*. I am not at this juncture arguing why they *should* be so regarded; I consider it at length below. But so regarding them is a presupposition of our taking the attitude of respect toward them and accordingly understanding ourselves as bearing certain moral relations to them. This can be shown as follows:

What does it mean to regard an entity that has a good of its own as possessing inherent worth? Two general principles are involved: the principle of moral consideration and the principle of intrinsic value.

According to the principle of moral consideration, wild living things are deserving of the concern and consideration of all moral agents simply in virtue of their being members of the Earth's community of life. From the moral point of view their good must be taken into account whenever it is affected for better or worse by the conduct of rational agents. This holds no matter what species the creature belongs to. The good of each is to be accorded some value and so acknowledged as having some weight in the deliberations of all rational agents. Of course, it may be necessary for such agents to act in ways contrary to the good of this or that particular organism or group of organisms in order to further the good of others, including the good of humans. But the principle of moral consideration prescribes that, with respect to each being an entity having its own good, every individual is deserving of consideration.

The principle of intrinsic value states that, regardless of what kind of entity it is in other respects, if it is a member of the Earth's community of life, the realization of its good is something *intrinsically* valuable. This means that its good is prima facie worthy of being preserved or promoted as an end in itself and for the sake of the entity whose good it is. Insofar as we regard any organism, species population, or life community as an entity with inherent worth, we believe that it must never be treated as if it were a mere object or thing whose entire value lies in being instrumental to the good of some other entity. The well-being of each is judged to have value in and of itself.

Combining these two principles, we can now define what it means for a living thing or group of living things to possess inherent worth. To say that it possesses inherent worth is to say that its good is deserving of the concern and consideration of all moral agents, and that the realization of its good has intrinsic value, to be pursued as an end in itself and for the sake of the entity whose good it is.

The duties owed to wild organisms, species populations, and communities of life in the Earth's natural ecosystems are grounded on their inherent worth. When rational, autonomous agents regard such entities as possessing inherent worth, they place intrinsic value on the realization of their good and so hold themselves responsible for performing actions that will have this effect and for refraining from actions having the contrary effect.

The Attitude of Respect for Nature

Why should moral agents regard wild living things in the natural world as possessing inherent worth? To answer this question we must first take into account the fact that, when rational, autonomous agents subscribe to the principles of moral consideration and intrinsic value and so conceive of wild living things as having that kind of worth, such agents are *adopting a certain ultimate moral attitude toward the natural world*. This is the attitude I call "respect for nature." It parallels the attitude of respect for persons in human ethics. When we adopt the attitude of respect for persons as the proper (fitting, appropriate) attitude to take toward all persons as persons, we consider the fulfillment of the basic interests of each individual to have intrinsic value. We thereby make a moral commitment to live a certain kind of life in relation to other persons. We place ourselves under the direction of a system of standards and rules that we consider validly binding on all moral agents as such.[4]

Similarly, when we adopt the attitude of respect for nature as an ultimate moral attitude we make a commitment to live by certain normative principles. These principles constitute the rules of conduct and standards of character that are to govern our treatment of the natural world. This is, first, an *ultimate* commitment because it is not derived from any higher norm. The attitude of respect for nature is not grounded on some other, more general, or more fundamental attitude. It sets the total framework for our responsibilities toward the natural world. It can be justified, as I show below, but its justification cannot consist in referring to a more general attitude or a more basic normative principle.

Second, the commitment is a *moral* one because it is understood to be a disinterested matter of principle. It is this feature that distinguishes the attitude of respect for nature from the set of feelings and dispositions that comprise the love of nature. The latter stems from one's personal interest in and response to the natural world. Like the affectionate feelings we have toward certain individual human beings, one's love of nature is nothing more than the particular way one feels about the natural environment and its wild inhabitants. And just as our love for an individual person differs from our respect for all persons as such (whether we happen to love them or not), so love of nature differs from respect for nature. Respect for nature is an attitude we believe all moral agents ought to have simply as moral agents, regardless of whether or not they also love nature. Indeed, we have not truly taken the attitude of respect for nature ourselves unless we believe this. To put it in a Kantian way, to adopt the attitude of respect for nature is to take a stance that one wills it to be a universal law for all rational beings. It is to hold that stance categorically, as being validly applicable to every moral agent without exception, irrespective of whatever personal feelings toward nature such an agent might have or might lack.

Although the attitude of respect for nature is, in this sense, a disinterested and universalizable attitude, anyone who does adopt it has certain steady, more or less permanent dispositions. These dispositions, which are themselves to be considered disinterested and universalizable, comprise three interlocking sets: dispositions to seek certain ends, dispositions to carry on one's practical reasoning and deliberation in a certain way, and dispositions to have certain feelings. We may accordingly analyze the attitude of respect for nature into the following components. (a) The disposition to aim at, and to take steps to bring about, as final and disinterested ends, the promoting and protecting of the good of organisms, species populations, and life communities in natural ecosystems. (These ends are "final" in not being pursued as means to further ends. They are "disinterested" in being independent of the self-interest of the agent.) (b) The disposition to consider actions that tend to realize those ends to be prima facie obligatory *because* they have that tendency. (c) The disposition to experience positive and negative feelings toward states of affairs in the world *because* they are favorable or unfavorable to the good of organisms, species populations, and life communities in natural ecosystems.

The logical connection between the attitude of respect for nature and the duties of a life-centered system of environmental ethics can now be made clear. Insofar as one sincerely takes that attitude and so has the three sets of dispositions, one will at the same time be disposed to comply with certain rules of duty (such as nonmaleficence and noninterference) and with standards of character (such as fairness and benevolence) that determine the obligations and virtues of moral agents with regard to the Earth's wild living things. We can say that the actions one performs and the character

traits one develops in fulfilling these moral requirements are the way one *expresses* or *embodies* the attitude in one's conduct and character. In his famous essay, "Justice as Fairness," John Rawls describes the rules of the duties of human morality (such as fidelity, gratitude, honesty, and justice) as "forms of conduct in which recognition of others as persons is manifested."[5] I hold that the rules of duty governing our treatment of the natural world and its inhabitants are forms of conduct in which the attitude of respect for nature is manifested.

The Justifiability of the Attitude of Respect for Nature

I return to the question posed earlier, which has not yet been answered: Why *should* moral agents regard wild living things as possessing inherent worth? I now argue that the only way we can answer this question is by showing how adopting the attitude of respect for nature is justified for all moral agents. Let us suppose that we were able to establish that there are good reasons for adopting the attitude, reasons which are intersubjectively valid for every rational agent. If there are such reasons, they would justify anyone's having the three sets of dispositions mentioned above as constituting what it means to have the attitude. Since these include the disposition to promote or protect the good of wild living things as a disinterested and ultimate end, as well as the disposition to perform actions for the reason that they tend to realize that end, we see that such dispositions commit a person to the principles of moral consideration and intrinsic value. To be disposed to further, as an end in itself, the good of any entity in nature just because it is that kind of entity, is to be disposed to give consideration to *every* such entity and to place intrinsic value on the realization of its good. Insofar as we subscribe to these two principles we regard living things as possessing inherent worth. Subscribing to the principles is what it *means* to so regard them. To justify the attitude of respect for nature, then, is to justify commitment to these principles and thereby to justify regarding wild creatures as possessing inherent worth.

We must keep in mind that inherent worth is not some mysterious sort of objective property belonging to living things that can be discovered by empirical observation or scientific investigation. To ascribe inherent worth to an entity is not to describe it by citing some feature discernible by sense perception or inferable by inductive reasoning. Nor is there a logically necessary connection between the concept of a being having a good of its own and the concept of inherent worth. We do not contradict ourselves by asserting that an entity that has a good of its own lacks inherent worth. In order to show that such an entity "has" inherent worth we must give good reasons for ascribing that kind of value to it (placing that kind of value upon it, conceiving of it to be valuable in that way). Although it is humans (persons, valuers) who must do the valuing, for the ethics of respect for nature, the value so ascribed is not a human value. That is to say, it is not a value derived from considerations regarding human well-being or human rights. It is a value that is ascribed to nonhuman animals and plants themselves, independently of their relationship to what humans judge to be conducive to their own good.

Whatever reasons, then, justify our taking the attitude of respect for nature as defined above are also reasons that show why we *should* regard the living things of the natural world as possessing inherent worth. We saw earlier that, since the attitude is an ultimate one, it cannot be derived from a more fundamental attitude nor shown to be a special case of a more general one. On what sort of grounds, then, can it be established?

The attitude we take toward living things in the natural world depends on the way we look at them, on what kind of beings we conceive them to be, and on how we understand the relations we bear to them. Underlying and supporting our attitude is a certain *belief system* that constitutes a particular world-view or outlook on nature and the place of human life in it. To give good reasons for adopting the attitude of respect for nature, then, we must first articulate the belief system which underlies and supports that attitude. If it appears that the belief system is internally coherent and well ordered, and if, as far as we can now tell, it is consistent with all known scientific truths relevant to our knowledge of the object of the attitude (which in this case includes the whole set of the Earth's natural ecosystems and their communities of life), then there remains the task of indicating why scientifically informed and rational thinkers with a developed capacity of reality awareness can find it acceptable as a way of conceiving of the natural world and our place in it. To the extent we can do this we provide at least a reasonable argument for accepting the belief system and the ultimate moral attitude it supports.

I do not hold that such a belief system can be *proven* to be true, either inductively or deductively. As we shall see, not all of its components can be stated in the form of empirically verifiable propositions. Nor is its internal order governed by purely logical relationships. But the system as a whole, I contend, constitutes a coherent, unified, and rationally acceptable "picture" or "map" of a total world. By examining each of its main components and seeing how they fit together, we obtain a scientifically informed and well-ordered conception of nature and the place of humans in it.

This belief system underlying the attitude of respect for nature I call (for want of a better name) "the biocentric outlook on nature." Since it is not wholly analyzable into empirically confirmable assertions, it should not be thought of as simply a compendium of the biological sciences concerning our planet's ecosystems. It might best be described as a philosophical world-view, to distinguish it from a scientific theory or explanatory system. However, one of its major tenets is the great lesson we have learned from the science of ecology: the interdependence of all living things in an organically unified order whose balance and stability are necessary conditions for the realization of the good of its constituent biotic communities.

Before turning to an account of the main components of the biocentric outlook, it is convenient here to set forth the overall structure of my theory of environmental ethics as it has now emerged. The ethics of respect for nature is made up of three basic elements: a belief system, an ultimate moral attitude, and a set of rules of duty and standards of character. These elements are connected with each other in the following manner. The belief system provides a certain outlook on nature which supports and makes intelligible an autonomous agent's adopting, as an ultimate moral attitude, the attitude of respect for nature. It supports and makes intelligible the attitude in the sense that, when an autonomous agent understands its moral relations to the natural world in terms of this outlook, it recognizes the attitude of respect to be the only *suitable* or *fitting* attitude to take toward all wild forms of life in the Earth's biosphere. Living things are now viewed as *the appropriate objects of the attitude of respect* and are accordingly regarded as entities possessing inherent worth. One then places intrinsic value on the promotion and protection of their good. As a consequence of this, one makes a moral commitment to abide by a set of rules of duty and to fulfill (as far as one can by one's own efforts) certain standards of good character. Given one's adoption of the attitude of respect, one makes that moral commitment because one considers those rules and standards to be validly binding on all moral agents. They are seen as embodying forms of conduct and character structures in which the attitude of respect for nature is manifested.

This three-part complex which internally orders the ethics of respect for nature is symmetrical with a theory of human ethics grounded on respect for persons. Such a theory includes, first, a conception of oneself and others as persons, that is, as centers of autonomous choice. Second, there is the attitude of respect for persons as persons. When this is adopted as an ultimate moral attitude it involves the disposition to treat every person as having inherent worth or "human dignity." Every human being, just in virtue of her or his humanity, is understood to be worthy of moral consideration, and intrinsic value is placed on the autonomy and well-being of each. This is what Kant

meant by conceiving of persons as ends in themselves. Third, there is an ethical system of duties which are acknowledged to be owed by everyone to everyone. These duties are forms of conduct in which public recognition is given to each individual's inherent worth as a person.

This structural framework for a theory of human ethics is meant to leave open the issue of consequentialism (utilitarianism) versus nonconsequentialism (deontology). That issue concerns the particular kind of system of rules defining the duties of moral agents toward persons. Similarly, I am leaving open [here] the question of what particular kind of system of rules defines our duties with respect to the natural world.

The Biocentric Outlook on Nature

The biocentric outlook on nature has four main components. (1) Humans are thought of as members of the Earth's community of life, holding that membership on the same terms as apply to all the nonhuman members. (2) The Earth's natural ecosystems as a totality are seen as a complex web of interconnected elements, with the sound biological functioning of each being dependent on the sound biological functioning of the others. (This is the component referred to above as the great lesson that the science of ecology has taught us.) (3) Each individual organism is conceived of as a teleological center of life, pursuing its own good in its own way. (4) Whether we are concerned with standards of merit or with the concept of inherent worth, the claim that humans by their very nature are superior to other species is a groundless claim and, in the light of elements (1), (2), and (3) above, must be rejected as nothing more than an irrational bias in our own favor. . . .

The Denial of Human Superiority

This fourth component of the biocentric outlook on nature is the single most important idea in establishing the justifiability of the attitude of respect for nature. Its central role is due to the special relationship it bears to the first three components of the outlook. This relationship will be brought out after the concept of human superiority is examined and analyzed.[6]

In what sense are humans alleged to be superior to other animals? We are different from them in having certain capacities that they lack. But why should these capacities be a mark of superiority? From what point of view are they judged to be signs of superiority and what sense of superiority is meant? After all, various nonhuman species have capacities that humans lack. There is the speed of a cheetah, the vision of an eagle, the agility of a monkey. Why should not these be taken as signs of *their* superiority over humans?

One answer . . . is that these capacities are not as *valuable* as the human capacities that are claimed to make us superior. Such uniquely human characteristics as rational thought, aesthetic creativity, autonomy and self-determination, and moral freedom, it might be held, have a higher value than the capacities found in other species. Yet we must ask: valuable to whom, and on what grounds?

The human characteristics mentioned are all valuable to humans. They are essential to the preservation and enrichment of our civilization and culture. Clearly it is from the human standpoint that they are being judged to be desirable and good. It is not difficult here to recognize a begging of the question. Humans are claiming human superiority from a strictly human point of view, that is, from a point of view in which the good of humans is taken as the standard of judgment. All we need to do is to look at the capacities of nonhuman animals (or plants, for that matter) from the standpoint of *their* good to find a contrary judgment of superiority. The speed of the cheetah, for example, is a sign of its superiority to humans when considered from the standpoint of the good of its species. If it were as slow a runner as a human, it would not be able to survive. And so for all the other abilities of nonhumans which further their good but which are lacking in humans. In each case the claim to human superiority would be rejected from a nonhuman standpoint.

When superiority assertions are interpreted in this way, they are based on judgments of *merit*. To judge the merits of a person or an organism one must apply grading or ranking standards to it. (As I show below, this distinguishes judgments of merit from judgments of inherent worth.) Empirical investigation then determines whether it has the "good-making properties" (merits) in virtue of which it fulfills the standards being applied. In the case of humans, merits may be either moral or nonmoral. We can judge one person to be better than (superior to) another from the moral point of view by applying certain standards to their character and conduct. Similarly, we can appeal to nonmoral criteria in judging someone to be an excellent piano player, a fair cook, a poor tennis player, and so on. Different social purposes and roles are implicit in the making of such judgments, providing the frame of reference for the choice of standards by which the nonmoral merits of people are determined. Ultimately such purposes and roles stem from a society's way of life as a whole. Now a society's way of life may be thought of as the cultural form given to the realization of human values. Whether moral or nonmoral standards are being applied, then, all judgments of people's merits finally depend on human values. All are made from an exclusively human standpoint.

The question that naturally arises at this juncture is: Why should standards that are based on human values be assumed to be the only valid criteria of merit and hence the only true signs of superiority? This question is especially pressing when humans are being judged superior in merit to nonhumans. [A] human being may be a better mathematician than a monkey, but the monkey may be a better tree climber than a human being. If we humans value mathematics more than tree climbing, that is because our conception of civilized life makes the development of mathematical ability more desirable than the ability to climb trees. But is it not unreasonable to judge nonhumans by the values of human civilization, rather than by values connected with what it is for a member of *that* species to live a good life? If all living things have a good of their own, it makes sense to judge the merits of nonhumans by standards derived from *their* good. To use only standards based on human values is already to commit oneself to holding that humans are superior to nonhumans, which is the point in question.

A further logical flaw arises in connection with the widely held conviction that humans are *morally* superior beings because they possess, while others lack, the capacities of a moral agent (free will, accountability, deliberation, judgment, practical reason). This view rests on a conceptual confusion. As far as moral standards are concerned, only beings that have the capacities of a moral agent can properly be judged to be *either* moral (morally good) or immoral (morally deficient). Moral standards are simply not applicable to beings that lack such capacities. Animals and plants cannot therefore be said to be morally inferior in merit to humans. Since the only beings that can have moral merits *or be deficient in such merits* are moral agents, it is conceptually incoherent to judge humans as superior to nonhumans on the ground that humans have moral capacities while nonhumans don't.

Up to this point I have been interpreting the claim that humans are superior to other living things as a grading or ranking judgment regarding their comparative merits. There is, however, another way of understanding the idea of human superiority. According to this interpretation, humans are superior to nonhumans not as regards their merits but as regards their inherent worth. Thus the claim of human superiority is to be understood as asserting that all humans, simply in virtue of their humanity, have *a greater inherent worth* than other living things.

The inherent worth of an entity does not depend on its merits.[7] To consider something as possessing inherent worth, we have seen, is to place intrinsic value on the realization of its good. This is done regardless of whatever particular merits it might have or might lack, as judged by a set of grading or ranking standards. In human affairs, we are all familiar with the principle that one's worth as a person does not vary with one's merits or lack of merits. The same can hold true of animals and plants. To regard such entities as possessing inher-

ent worth entails disregarding their merits and deficiencies, whether they are being judged from a human standpoint or from the standpoint of their own species.

The idea of one entity having more merit than another, and so being superior to it in merit, makes perfectly good sense. Merit is a grading or ranking concept, and judgments of comparative merit are based on the different degrees to which things satisfy a given standard. But what can it mean to talk about one thing being superior to another in inherent worth? In order to get at what is being asserted in such a claim it is helpful first to look at the social origin of the concept of degrees of inherent worth.

The idea that humans can possess different degrees of inherent worth originated in societies having rigid class structures. Before the rise of modern democracies with their egalitarian outlook, one's membership in a hereditary class determined one's social status. People in the upper classes were looked up to, while those in the lower classes were looked down upon. In such a society one's social superiors and social inferiors were clearly defined and easily recognized.

Two aspects of these class-structured societies are especially relevant to the idea of degrees of inherent worth. First, those born into the upper classes were deemed more worthy of respect than those born into the lower orders. Second, the superior worth of upper class people had nothing to do with their merits nor did the inferior worth of those in the lower classes rest on their lack of merits. One's superiority or inferiority entirely derived from a social position one was born into. The modern concept of a meritocracy simply did not apply. One could not advance into a higher class by any sort of moral or nonmoral achievement. Similarly, an aristocrat held his title and all the privileges that went with it just because he was the eldest son of a titled nobleman. Unlike the bestowing of knighthood in contemporary Great Britain, one did not earn membership in the nobility by meritorious conduct.

We who live in modern democracies no longer believe in such hereditary social distinctions. Indeed, we would wholeheartedly condemn them on moral grounds as fundamentally unjust. We have come to think of class systems as a paradigm of social injustice, it being a central principle of the democratic way of life that among humans there are no superiors and no inferiors. Thus we have rejected the whole conceptual framework in which people are judged to have different degrees of inherent worth. That idea is incompatible with our notion of human equality based on the doctrine that all humans, simply in virtue of their humanity, have the same inherent worth. (The belief in universal human rights is one form that this egalitarianism takes.)

The vast majority of people in modern democracies, however, do not maintain an egalitarian outlook when it comes to comparing human beings with other living things. Most people consider our own species to be superior to all other species and this superiority is understood to be a matter of inherent worth, not merit. There may exist thoroughly vicious and depraved humans who lack all merit. Yet because they are human they are thought to belong to a higher class of entities than any plant or animal. That one is born into the species *Homo sapiens* entitles one to have lordship over those who are one's inferiors, namely, those born into other species. The parallel with hereditary social classes is very close. Implicit in this view is a hierarchical conception of nature according to which an organism has a position of superiority or inferiority in the Earth's community of life simply on the basis of its genetic background. The "lower" orders of life are looked down upon and it is considered perfectly proper that they serve the interests of those belonging to the highest order, namely humans. The intrinsic value we place on the well-being of our fellow humans reflects our recognition of their rightful position as our equals. No such intrinsic value is to be placed on the good of other animals, unless we choose to do so out of fondness or affection for them. But their well-being imposes no moral requirement on us. In this respect there is an absolute difference in moral status between ourselves and them.

This is the structure of concepts and beliefs that people are committed to insofar as they regard humans to be superior in inherent worth to all other species. I now wish to argue that this structure of concepts and beliefs is completely groundless. If we accept the first three components of the biocentric outlook and from that perspective look at the major philosophical traditions which have supported that structure, we find it to be at bottom nothing more than the expression of an irrational bias in our own favor. The philosophical traditions themselves rest on very questionable assumptions or else simply beg the question. I briefly consider three of the main traditions to substantiate the point. These are classical Greek humanism, Cartesian dualism, and the Judeo-Christian concept of the Great Chain of Being.

The inherent superiority of humans over other species was implicit in the Greek definition of man as a rational animal. Our animal nature was identified with "brute" desires that need the order and restraint of reason to rule them (just as reason is the special virtue of those who rule in the ideal state). Rationality was then seen to be the key to our superiority over animals. It enables us to live on a higher plane and endows us with a nobility and worth that other creatures lack. This familiar way of comparing humans with other species is deeply ingrained in our Western philosophical outlook. The point to consider here is that this view does not actually provide an argument *for* human superiority but rather makes explicit the framework of thought that is implicitly used by those who think of humans as inherently superior to nonhumans. The Greeks who held that humans, in virtue of their rational capacities, have a kind of worth greater than any nonrational being, never looked at rationality as but one capacity of living things among many others. But when we consider rationality from the standpoint of the first three elements of the ecological outlook, we see that its value lies in its importance for *human* life. Other creatures achieve their species-specific good without the need of rationality, although they often make use of capacities that humans lack. So the humanistic outlook of classical Greek thought does not give us a neutral (non-question-begging) ground on which to construct a scale of degrees of inherent worth possessed by different species of living things.

The second tradition, centering on the Cartesian dualism of soul and body, also fails to justify the claim to human superiority. That superiority is supposed to derive from the fact that we have souls while animals do not. Animals are mere automata and lack the divine element that makes us spiritual beings. I will not go into the now familiar criticisms of this two-substance view. I only add the point that, even if humans are composed of an immaterial, unextended soul and a material, extended body, this in itself is not a reason to deem them of greater worth than entities that are only bodies. Why is a soul substance a thing that adds value to its possessor? Unless theological reasoning is offered here (which many, including, myself, would find unacceptable on epistemological grounds), no logical connection is evident. An immaterial something that thinks is better than a material something that doesn't think only if thinking itself has value, either intrinsically or instrumentally. Now it is intrinsically valuable to humans alone, who value it as an end in itself, and it is instrumentally valuable to those who benefit from it, namely humans.

For animals that neither enjoy thinking for its own sake nor need it for living the kind of life for which they are best adapted, it has no value. Even if "thinking" is broadened to include all forms of consciousness, there are still many living things that can do without it and yet live what is, for their species, a good life. The anthropocentricity underlying the claim to human superiority runs throughout Cartesian dualism.

A third major source of the idea of human superiority is the Judeo-Christian concept of the Great Chain of Being. Humans are superior to animals and plants because their Creator has given them a higher place on the chain. It begins with God at the top, and then moves to the angels, who are lower than God but higher than humans, then to humans, positioned between the angels and the beasts (partaking of the nature of both), and then on down to the lower levels occupied by nonhuman animals, plants, and finally inanimate objects. Humans, being "made in God's image," are inherently superior to animals and plants by virtue of their being closer (in their essential nature) to God.

The metaphysical and epistemological difficulties with this conception of a hierarchy of entities are, in my mind, insuperable. Without entering into this matter here, I point out that if we are unwilling to accept the metaphysics of traditional Judaism and Christianity, we are again left without good reasons for holding to the claim of inherent human superiority.

The foregoing considerations (and others like them) leave us with but one ground for the assertion that a human being, regardless of merit, is a higher kind of entity than any other living thing. This is the mere fact of the genetic makeup of the species *Homo sapiens*. But this is surely irrational and arbitrary. Why should the arrangement of genes of a certain type be a mark of superior value, especially when this fact about an organism is taken by itself, unrelated to any other aspect of its life? We might just as well refer to any other genetic makeup as a ground of superior value. Clearly we are confronted here with a wholly arbitrary claim that can only be explained as an irrational bias in our own favor.

That the claim is nothing more than a deep-seated prejudice is brought home to us when we look at our relation to other species in the light of the first three elements of the biocentric outlook. Those elements taken conjointly give us a certain overall view of the natural world and of the place of humans in it. When we take this view we come to understand other living things, their environmental conditions, and their ecological relationships in such a way as to awake in us a deep sense of our kinship with them as fellow members of the Earth's community of life. Humans and nonhumans alike are viewed together as integral parts of one unified whole in which all living things are functionally interrelated. Finally, when our awareness focuses on the individual lives of plants and animals, each is seen to share with us the characteristic of being a teleological center of life striving to realize its own good in its own unique way.

As this entire belief system becomes part of the conceptual framework by which we understand

and perceive the world, we come to see ourselves as bearing a certain moral relation to nonhuman forms of life. Our ethical role in nature takes on a new significance. We begin to look at other species as we look at ourselves, seeing them as beings which have a good they are striving to realize just as we have a good we are striving to realize. We accordingly develop the disposition to view the world from the standpoint of their good as well as from the standpoint of our own good. Now if the groundlessness of the claim that humans are inherently superior to other species were brought clearly before our minds, we would not remain intellectually neutral toward that claim but would reject it as fundamentally at variance with our total world outlook. In the absence of any good reasons for holding it, the assertion of human superiority would then appear simply as the expression of an irrational and self-serving prejudice that favors one particular species over several million others.

Rejecting the notion of human superiority entails its positive counterpart: the doctrine of species impartiality. One who accepts that doctrine regards all living things as possessing inherent worth—the *same* inherent worth, since no one species has been shown to be either "higher" or "lower" than any other. Now we saw earlier that, insofar as one thinks of a living thing as possessing inherent worth, one considers it to be the appropriate object of the attitude of respect and believes that attitude to be the only fitting or suitable one for all moral agents to take toward it.

Here, then, is the key to understanding how the attitude of respect is rooted in the biocentric outlook on nature. The basic connection is made through the denial of human superiority. Once we reject the claim that humans are superior either in merit or in worth to other living things, we are ready to adopt the attitude of respect. The denial of human superiority is itself the result of taking the perspective on nature built into the first three elements of the biocentric outlook.

Now the first three elements of the biocentric outlook, it seems clear, would be found acceptable to any rational and scientifically informed thinker who is fully "open" to the reality of the lives of non-human organisms. Without denying our distinctively human characteristics, such a thinker can acknowledge the fundamental respects in which we are members of the Earth's community of life and in which the biological conditions necessary for the realization of our human values are inextricably linked with the whole system of nature. In addition, the conception of individual living things as teleological centers of life simply articulates how a scientifically informed thinker comes to understand them as the result of increasingly careful and detailed observations. Thus, the biocentric outlook recommends itself as an acceptable system of concepts and beliefs to anyone who is clear-minded, unbiased, and factually enlightened, and who has a developed capacity of reality awareness with regard to the lives of individual organisms. This is as good a reason for making the moral commitment involved in adopting the attitude of respect for nature as any theory of environmental ethics could possibly have.

Moral Rights and the Matter of Competing Claims

I have not asserted anywhere in the foregoing account that animals or plants have moral rights. This omission was deliberate. I do not think that the reference class of the concept, bearer of moral rights, should be extended to include nonhuman living things. My reasons for taking this position, however, go beyond the scope of this paper. I believe I have been able to accomplish many of the same ends which those who ascribe rights to animals or plants wish to accomplish. There is no reason, moreover, why plants and animals, including whole species populations and life communities, cannot be accorded *legal* rights under my theory. To grant them legal protection could be interpreted as giving them legal entitlement to be protected, and this would be a means by which a society that subscribed to the ethics of respect for nature could give public recognition to their inherent worth.

There remains the problem of competing claims, even when wild plants and animals are not thought of as bearers of moral rights. If we accept the biocentric outlook and accordingly adopt the attitude of respect for nature as our ultimate moral attitude, how do we resolve conflicts that arise from our respect for persons in the domain of human ethics and our respect for nature in the domain of environmental ethics? This is a question that cannot adequately be dealt with here. My main purpose in this paper has been to try to establish a base point from which we can start working toward a solution to the problem. I have shown why we cannot just begin with an initial presumption in favor of the interests of our own species. It is after all within our power as moral beings to place limits on human population and technology with the deliberate intention of sharing the Earth's bounty with other species. That such sharing is an ideal difficult to realize even in an approximate way does not take away its claim to our deepest moral commitment.

NOTES

1. The conceptual links between an entity *having* a good, something being good *for* it, and events doing good *to* it are examined by G. H. Von Wright in *The Varieties of Goodness* (New York: Humanities Press, 1963), chaps. 3 and 5.

2. See W. K. Frankena, "Ethics and the Environment," in K. E. Goodpaster and K. M. Sayre, eds., *Ethics and Problems of the 21st Century* (Notre Dame: University of Notre Dame Press, 1979), pp. 3–20. I critically examine Frankena's views in "Frankena on Environmental Ethics," *Monist* (1981): 237–243.

3. In the light of considerations set forth in Daniel Dennett's *Brainstorms: Philosophical Essays on Mind and Psychology* (Montgomery, Vt.: Bradford Books, 1978), it is advisable to leave this question unsettled at this time. When machines are developed that function in the way our brains do, we may well come to deem them proper subjects of moral consideration.

4. I have analyzed the nature of this commitment of human ethics in "On Taking the Moral Point of View," *Midwest Studies in Philosophy,* vol. 3, *Studies in Ethical Theory* (1978), pp. 35–61.

5. John Rawls, "Justice as Fairness," *Philosophical Review* 67 (1958): 183.

6. My criticisms of the dogma of human superiority gain independent support from a carefully reasoned essay by R. and V. Routley showing the many logical weaknesses in arguments for human-centered theories of environmental ethics. R. and V. Routley, "Against the Inevitability of Human Chauvinism," in K. E. Goodpaster and K. M. Sayre, eds., *Ethics and Problems of the 21st Century* (Notre Dame: University of Notre Dame Press, 1979), pp. 36–59.

7. For this way of distinguishing between merit and inherent worth, I am indebted to Gregory Vlastos, "Justice and Equality," in R. Brandt, ed., *Social Justice* (Englewood Cliffs, N.J.: Prentice-Hall, 1962), pp. 31–72.

33 Morality as a Compromise Between Anthropocentrism and Nonanthropocentrism*

JAMES P. STERBA

IN DEFENSE OF AN ENVIRONMENTAL ethics it would be helpful to show that an environmental ethics is grounded in rationality. This requires not simply showing that an environmental ethics is rationally permissible, because that would imply that a rejection of an environmental ethics is rationally permissible as well. Rather, what needs to be shown is that an environmental ethics is rationally required, thus excluding its rejection as rationally permissible. No doubt most contemporary philosophers would like to have an argument showing that an environmental ethics is rationally required, but given the history of past failures to provide a convincing argument of this sort, most of them have simply given up hope of defending an environmental ethics in this way. In this paper, I propose to provide just such a defense of an environmental ethics.

I The Moral Status of All Living Beings

Clearly what we are looking for from ethics is a really good argument that nonhuman living beings should count morally. A really good argument, by definition, must be a non-question-begging argument. So what we are looking for is a non-question-begging argument that nonhuman living beings should count morally. Is there such an argument?

Consider. We clearly have the capacity of entertaining and acting upon both anthropocentric reasons that take only the interests of humans into account and nonanthropocentric reasons that take only the interests of nonhuman living beings into account.[1] Given that capacity, the question we are seeking to answer is what sort of reasons it would be rational for us to accept.

Now right off, we might think that we have non-question-begging grounds for only taking the interests of humans into account, namely, the possession by human beings of the distinctive traits of rationality and moral agency. But while human beings clearly do have such distinctive traits, the members of nonhuman species also have distinctive traits that humans lack, like the homing ability of pigeons, the speed of the cheetah, and the ruminative ability of sheep and cattle. Nor will it do to claim that the distinctive traits that humans possess are more valuable than the distinctive traits that members of other species possess because there is no non-question-begging standpoint from which to justify that claim. From a human standpoint, rationality and moral agency are more valuable than any of the distinctive traits found in nonhuman species, because, as humans, we would not be better off if we were to trade in those traits for the distinctive traits found in nonhuman species. Yet the same holds true of nonhuman species. Generally, pigeons, cheetahs, sheep and cattle would not be better off if they were to trade in their distinctive traits for the distinctive traits of other species.[2]

Of course, the members of some species might be better off if they could retain the distinctive traits of their species while acquiring one or another of the distinctive traits possessed by some

331

other species. For example, we humans might be better off if we could retain our distinctive traits while acquiring the ruminative ability of sheep and cattle.[3] But many of the distinctive traits of species cannot be even imaginatively added to the members of other species without substantially altering the original species. For example, in order for the cheetah to acquire the distinctive traits possessed by humans, presumably it would have to be so transformed that its paws became something like hands to accommodate its humanlike mental capabilities, thereby losing its distinctive speed, and ceasing to be a cheetah. So possessing distinctively human traits would not be good for the cheetah.[4] And with the possible exception of our nearest evolutionary relatives, the same holds true for the members of other species: they would not be better off having distinctively human traits. Only in fairy tales and in the world of Disney can the members of nonhuman species enjoy a full array of distinctively human traits.[5] So there would appear to be no non-question-begging perspective from which to judge that distinctively human traits are more valuable than the distinctive traits possessed by other species, and so no non-question-begging justification for only taking anthropocentric reasons into account. Judged from a non-question-begging perspective, we would seemingly have to grant the prima facie relevance of both anthropocentric and nonanthropocentric reasons to rational choice and then try to determine which reasons we would be rationally required to act upon, all things considered.

In this regard, there are two kinds of cases that must be considered. First, there are cases in which there is a conflict between the relevant anthropocentric and nonanthropocentric reasons. Second, there are cases in which there is no such conflict.

It seems obvious that where there is no conflict and both reasons are conclusive reasons of their kind, both reasons should be acted upon. In such

contexts, we should do what is favored both by anthropocentrism and by nonanthropocentrism.

Now when we turn to rationally assess the relevant reasons in conflict cases, three solutions are possible. First, we could say that anthropocentric reasons always have priority over conflicting nonanthropocentric reasons. Second, we could say, just the opposite, that nonanthropocentric reasons always have priority over conflicting anthropocentric reasons. Third, we could say that some kind of compromise is rationally required. In this compromise, sometimes anthropocentric reasons would have priority over nonanthropocentric reasons, and sometimes nonanthropocentric reasons would have priority over anthropocentric reasons.

Once the conflict is described in this manner, the third solution can be seen to be the one that is rationally required. This is because the first and second solutions give exclusive priority to one class of relevant reasons over the other, and only a question-begging justification can be given for such an exclusive priority. Only by employing the third solution, and sometimes giving priority to anthropocentric reasons, and sometimes giving priority to nonanthropocentric reasons, can we avoid a question-begging resolution.

Notice also that this standard of rationality will not support just any compromise between the relevant anthropocentric and nonanthropocentric reasons. The compromise must be a nonarbitrary one, for otherwise it would beg the question with respect to the opposing anthropocentric and nonanthropocentric views. Such a compromise would have to respect the rankings of anthropocentric and nonanthropocentric reasons imposed by the anthropocentric and nonanthropocentric views, respectively. Since for each individual there is a separate ranking of that individual's relevant anthropocentric and nonanthropocentric reasons, we can represent these rankings from the most important reasons to the least important reasons as follows:

Individual A		Individual B	
Anthropocentric Reasons	Nonanthropocentric Reasons	Anthropocentric Reasons	Nonanthropocentric Reasons
1	1	1	1
2	2	2	2
3	3	3	3
.	.	.	.
N	N	N	N

Accordingly, any nonarbitrary compromise among such reasons in seeking not to beg the question against anthropocentrism or nonanthropocentrism will have to give priority to those reasons that rank highest in each category. Failure to give priority to the highest-ranking anthropocentric or nonanthropocentric reasons would, other things being equal, be contrary to reason.

It might be objected that this defense of Morality as Compromise could be undercut if we simply give up any attempt to show that any one view is rationally preferable to the others. But we cannot rationally do this. For we are people who can act anthropocentrically and can act nonanthropocentrically, and we are trying to discover which way of acting is rationally justified. To rationally resolve this question, we must be committed to finding out which view is more rationally defensible than the others. So as far as I can tell, there is no escaping the conclusion that Morality as Compromise is more rationally defensible than either anthropocentrism and nonanthropocentrism, which means that we have a non-question-begging argument that all living beings should count morally.

II Conflict Resolution Principles

But how is this compromise to be specified? Surely, even if we hold that all living beings should count morally, we can justify a preference for humans on grounds of preservation. Accordingly, we have

A Principle of Human Preservation: Actions that are necessary for meeting one's basic needs or the basic needs of other human beings are permissible even when they require aggressing against the basic needs of individual animals and plants or even of whole species or ecosystems.[6]

Now needs, in general, if not satisfied, lead to lacks or deficiencies with respect to various standards. The basic needs of humans, if not satisfied, lead to lacks or deficiencies with respect to a standard of a decent life. The basic needs of animals and plants, if not satisfied, lead to lacks or deficiencies with respect to a standard of a healthy life. The basic needs of species and ecosystems, if not satisfied, lead to lacks or deficiencies with respect to a standard of a healthy living system. The means necessary for meeting the basic needs of humans can vary widely from society to society. By contrast, the means necessary for meeting the basic needs of particular species of animals and plants tend to be invariant.[7] Of course, while only some needs can be clearly classified as basic, and others clearly classified as nonbasic, there still are other needs that are more or less difficult to classify. Yet the fact that not every need can be clearly classified as either basic or nonbasic, as is true of a whole range of dichotomous concepts like moral/immoral, legal/illegal, living/nonliving, human/nonhuman, should not immobilize us from acting at least with respect to clear cases.[8]

In human ethics, there is no principle that is strictly analogous to this Principle of Human Preservation.[9] There is a principle of self-preservation in human ethics that permits actions that are necessary for meeting one's own basic needs or the basic needs of other people, even if this requires *failing to meet* (through an act of omission) the basic needs of still other people. For example, we can use our resources to feed ourselves and our families, even if this necessitates failing to meet the basic needs of people in underdeveloped countries. But, in general, we don't have a principle that allows us to *aggress against* (through an act of commission) the basic needs of some people in order to meet our own basic needs or the basic needs of other people to whom we are committed or happen to care about. One place where we do permit aggressing against the basic needs of other people in order to meet our own basic needs or the basic needs of people to whom we are committed or happen to care about is our acceptance of the outcome of life and death struggles in lifeboat cases, where no one has an antecedent right to the available resources. For example, if you had to fight off others in order to secure the last place in a lifeboat for yourself or for a member of your family, we might say that you justifiably aggressed against the basic needs of those whom you fought to meet your own basic needs or the basic needs of the members of your family.[10]

Now the Principle of Human Preservation does not permit aggressing against the basic needs of humans even if it is the only way to meet our own basic needs or the basic needs of other human beings.[11] Rather this principle is directed at a different range of cases with respect to which we can meet our own basic needs and the basic needs of other humans simply by aggressing against the basic needs of nonhuman living beings. With respect to those cases, the Principle of Human Preservation permits actions that are necessary for meeting one's own basic needs or the basic needs of other human beings, even when they require aggressing against the basic needs of individual animals and plants or even of whole species or ecosystems.

Of course, we could envision an even more permissive principle of human preservation, one that would permit us to aggress against the basic needs of both humans and nonhumans to meet our own basic needs or the basic needs of other human beings. But while adopting such a principle, by permitting cannibalism, would clearly reduce the degree of predation of humans on other species, and so would be of some benefit to other species, it would clearly be counterproductive with respect to meeting basic human needs. This is because implicit nonaggression pacts based on a reasonable expectation of a comparable degree of altruistic forbearance from fellow humans have been enormously beneficial and probably were necessary for the survival of the human species. So it is difficult to see how humans could be justifiably required to forgo such benefits.

Moreover, beyond the prudential value of such implicit nonaggression pacts against fellow humans, there is no morally defensible way to exclude some humans from their protection. This is because any exclusion would fail to satisfy one of the most basic principles of morality, the "ought" implies "can" principle, given that it would impose a sacrifice on at least some humans that would be unreasonable to accept.[12]

But what about the interests of nonhuman living beings? Doesn't the Principle of Human Preservation impose a sacrifice on nonhumans that it would be unreasonable for any would-be guardian of their interests to accept. Surely, we would expect the animals and plants to fight us however they can to prevent being used in this fashion. Why then would it not be reasonable for would-be guardians of the interests of nonhuman living beings to also try to prevent their being used in this fashion? But this would mean that it would be morally permissible for would-be guardians of the interest of nonhumans to prevent other humans from meeting their own basic needs, or the basic needs of other humans, when this requires aggressing against the basic needs of nonhumans. Understood as "strong permissibility," it would imply that other humans would be *prohib-*

ited from interfering with such preventive actions, even if it meant that their own basic needs would not be met as a result. But surely, this would be an unreasonable imposition for humans to impose on other humans—one that would not accord with the "ought" implies "can" principle.

But suppose we understood the permissibility involved to be that of weak permissiblity according to which virtually everything is permissible and virtually nothing is morally required or prohibited. Then the Principle of Human Preservation would imply that it was permissible, in this weak sense, for humans to aggress against the basic needs of nonhumans when this was necessary for meeting their own basic needs, and at the same time imply that it was permissible, in this same weak sense, for would-be guardians of the interests of nonhumans to prevent humans from meeting their basic needs by aggressing against the basic needs of nonhumans. Since under this interpretation of moral permissibility, virtually nothing is morally required or prohibited, what gets done will tend to depend on the relative power of the contending parties. The purpose of morality, however, is to provide resolutions in just such severe conflict-of-interest situations. Moreover, since a moral resolution must satisfy the "ought" implies "can" principle, it cannot impose moral requirements on humans that would be unreasonable for them to accept. This would seem to imply that the permissibility in the Principle of Human Preservation must be that of strong permissibility. This means that would-be guardians of the interests of nonhumans would be prohibited from interfering with humans who are taking the necessary action to meet their basic needs, even when this requires them to aggress against the basic needs of nonhumans.

But are there no exceptions to the Principle of Human Preservation? Consider, for example, the following real-life case.[13] Thousands of Nepalis have cleared forests, cultivated crops, and raised cattle and buffalo on land surrounding the Royal Chitwan National Park in Nepal, but they have also made incursions into the park to meet their own basic needs. In so doing, they have threatened the rhino, the Bengal tiger, and other endangered species in the park. Assume that the basic needs of no other humans are at stake.[14] For this case, then, would the would-be guardians of these nonhuman endangered species be justified in preventing the Nepalis from meeting their basic needs in order to preserve these endangered species? It seems to me that before the basic needs of disadvantaged Nepalis could be sacrificed, the would-be guardians of these endangered species first would be required to use whatever surplus was available to them and to other humans to meet the basic needs of the Nepalis whom they propose to restrict.[15] Yet clearly it would be very difficult to have first used up all the surplus available to the whole human population for meeting basic human needs. Under present conditions, this requirement has certainly not been met. So for all present purposes, the moral permissibility in the Principle of Human Preservation remains that of strong permissibility, which means that other humans are prohibited from interfering with the aggression against nonhumans that is permitted by the principle.[16]

Nevertheless, preference for humans can go beyond bounds, and the bounds that are required are captured by the following:

A Principle of Disproportionality: Actions that meet nonbasic or luxury needs of humans are prohibited when they aggress against the basic needs of individual animals and plants or even of whole species or ecosystems.

This principle is strictly analogous to the principle in human ethics that similarly prohibits meeting some people's nonbasic or luxury needs by aggressing against the basic needs of other people. Without a doubt, the adoption of such a principle with respect to nonhumans would significantly change the way we live our lives. Such a principle is required, however, if there is to be any substance to the claim that the members of all species count morally. We can no more consistently claim that the members of all species count morally and yet aggress against the basic needs of some animals or plants whenever this serves our own nonbasic or luxury needs than we can consistently claim that all humans count morally and then aggress against the basic needs of other human beings whenever this serves our nonbasic or luxury needs. Consequently, if saying that species count morally is to mean anything, it must be the case that the basic needs of the members of nonhuman species are protected against aggressive actions that only serve to meet the nonbasic needs of humans, as required by the Principle of Disproportionality.[17] Another way to put the central claim here is to hold that counting morally rules out domination, where domination means aggressing against the basic needs of some for the sake of satisfying the nonbasic needs of others.

To see why these limits on preference for the members of the human species are what is required for recognizing that species and their members count morally, we need to understand the nondomination of species by analogy with the nondomination of humans. We need to see that just as we claim that humans should not be dominated but treat them differently, so too we can claim that species should not be dominated but also treat them differently. In human ethics, there are various interpretations given to human nondomination that allow for different treatment of humans. In ethical egoism, everyone is *equally at liberty* to pursue his or her own interests, but this allows us to always prefer ourselves to others, who are understood to be like opponents in a competitive game. In libertarianism, everyone has an *equal right to liberty*, but although this imposes some limits on the pursuit of self-interest, it is said to allow us to refrain from helping others in severe need. In welfare liberalism, everyone has an *equal right to welfare and opportunity*, but this need not commit us to providing everyone with exactly the same resources. In socialism, everyone has an *equal right to self-development*, and although this may commit us to providing everyone with the same resources, it still sanctions some degree of self-preference. So just as there are these various ways to interpret the nondomination of humans that still allow us to treat humans differently, there are various ways that we can interpret the nondomination of species that allow us to treat species differently.

Now one might interpret the nondomination of species in a very strong sense, analogous to the interpretation of nondomination found in socialism. But the kind of nondomination of species that I have defended here is more akin to the nondomination found in welfare liberalism or in libertarianism than it is to the nondomination found in socialism. In brief, this form of nondomination requires that we not aggress against the basic needs of the members of other species for the sake of the nonbasic needs of the members of our own species (the Principle of Disproportionality), but it permits us to aggress against the basic needs of the members of other species for the sake of the basic needs of the members of our own species (the Principle of Human Preservation). In this way, I have argued that we can endorse the nondomination of species, while avoiding imposing an unreasonable sacrifice on the members of our own species.

In addition, what helps to avoid imposing an unreasonable sacrifice on the members of our own species is that we can also justify a preference for humans on grounds of defense. Thus, we have

A Principle of Human Defense: Actions that defend oneself and other human beings against harmful aggression are permissible even when they necessitate killing or harming individual animals or plants, or even destroying whole species or ecosystems.

This Principle of Human Defense allows us to defend ourselves and other human beings from harmful aggression first against our persons and the persons of other humans beings that we are committed to or happen to care about and second against our justifiably held property and the justifiably held property of other humans beings that we are committed to or happen to care about.[18]

Here there are two sorts of cases. First, there are cases where humans are defending their own basic needs against harmful aggression from nonhumans. In cases of this sort, not only would the human defenders be perfectly justified in defending themselves against aggression but also no would-be guardians of nonhuman interests would be justified in opposing that defense.

Second, there are cases where humans are defending their nonbasic needs against harmful aggression from nonhumans which, let's assume, are trying to meet their basic needs. In cases of this sort, would it be justified for would-be human guardians of the interests of nonhuman living beings to assist them in their aggression against humans? In analogous cases in human ethics, we can see how just this type of aggression can be justified when the poor, who have exhausted all the other means that are legitimately available to them, take from the surplus possessions of the rich just what they require to meet their basic needs. Expressed in terms of an ideal of negative liberty endorsed by libertarians, the justification for this aggression is the priority of the liberty of the poor not to be interfered with when taking from the surplus possessions of the rich what they require to meet their basic needs over the liberty of the rich not to be interfered with when using their surplus for luxury purposes.[19] Expressed in terms of an ideal of fairness endorsed by welfare liberals, the justification for this aggression is the right to welfare that the needy have against those with a surplus. And expressed in terms of an ideal of equality endorsed by socialists, the justification for this aggression is the right that everyone has to equal self-development. Under each of these justifications, would-be guardians of the poor (e.g., real or idealized Robin Hoods) would certainly be justified in assisting the poor in their aggression against the rich. Would then would-be guardians of nonhuman living beings (e.g., real or idealized Earth Firsters) be similarly justified in assisting plants and animals in their aggression against the nonbasic needs of humans to meet the basic needs of nonhumans?

There are two reasons why this is unlikely to be the case. First, as the above justifications from human ethics suggest, achieving either libertarian, welfare liberal or socialist justice for humans will require a considerable redistribution of resources in order to meet the basic needs of humans in both existing and future generations.[20] So if justice is done in this regard, it will significantly constrain the availability of resources for legitimately meeting nonbasic human needs, and thereby limit the possibilities where humans could be justifiably defending their nonbasic needs against aggression from nonhumans. Second, the Principle of Disproportionality further constrains those possibilities where humans could be justifiably defending their nonbasic needs against aggression from nonhumans. This is because the principle prohibits humans from aggressing against the basic needs of nonhumans in order to meet their own nonbasic needs, and thereby significantly constrains the ways that humans could legitimately acquire resources that are used simply for meeting nonbasic human needs. For these two reasons, therefore, the possibilities for legitimately exercising the Principle of Human Defense in defense of nonbasic needs would be drastically limited, thus providing few occasions where would-be guardians of the interests of nonhumans could have any role with regard to its exercise. Of course, some nonbasic human needs can still be legitimately met indirectly through meeting basic human needs. But any attempt by would-be guardians of the interests of nonhumans to help nonhumans aggress against the nonbasic needs of other humans in such contexts would most likely result in aggressing against the basic needs of those humans as well, and thus would not be justified. Of course, in the nonideal societies in which we live, many humans still have access to a surplus for meeting nonbasic needs. But in these circumstances, other humans would surely have a claim to a significant part of that surplus, and much of what remains would have been illegitimately acquired in violation of the Principle of Disproportionality. In any case, the Principle of Defense would not apply because it presupposes for its application that the means for meeting the nonbasic needs of humans have been legitimately acquired.

Lastly, we need one more principle to deal with violations of the above three principles. Accordingly, we have

> A *Principle of Rectification:* Compensation and reparation are required when the other principles have been violated.

Obviously, this principle is somewhat vague, but for those who are willing to abide by the other three principles, it should be possible to remedy that vagueness in practice. Here too would-be guardians of the interests of nonhumans could have a useful role figuring out what is appropriate compensation or reparation for violations of the Principle of Disproportionality, and, even more importantly, designing ways to get that compensation or reparation enacted.

Taken altogether, these four principles, I claim, constitute a defensible set of principles for resolving conflicts between human and nonhuman living beings.

III Individualism and Holism

It might be objected, however, that I have not yet taken into account the conflict between holists and individualists. According to holists, the good of a species, or the good of an ecosystem, or the good of the whole biotic community can trump the good of individual living things.[21] According to individualists, the good of each individual living thing must be respected.[22]

Now one might think that holists would require that we abandon my Principle of Human Preservation. Yet consider. Assuming that people's basic needs are at stake, how could it be morally objectionable for them to try to meet those needs, even if this were to harm nonhuman individuals, or species, or whole ecosystems, or even, to some degree, the whole biotic community? Of course, we can *ask* people in such conflict cases not to meet their basic needs in order to prevent harm to nonhuman individuals or species, ecosystems or

the whole biotic community. But if people's basic needs are at stake, it will be a very unusual case where we can reasonably demand that they make such a sacrifice.

Consider the following often discussed example.[23] A fat person who is leading a party of spelunkers gets himself stuck in the mouth of a cave in which flood waters are rising. The trapped party of spelunkers just happens to have a stick of dynamite with which they can blast the fat person out of the mouth of the cave; either they use the dynamite or they all drown, the fat person with them. Now it is usually assumed in this case that it is morally permissible to dynamite the fat person out of the mouth of the cave. After all, if that is not done, the whole party of spelunkers will die, the fat person with them. So the sacrifice imposed on the fat person in this case would not be that great. But what if the fat person's head is outside rather than inside the cave as it must have been in the previous interpretation of the case. Under those circumstances, the fat person would not die when the other spelunkers drown. Presumably after slimming down a bit, he would eventually just squeeze his way out of the mouth of the cave. In this case, could the party of spelunkers trapped in the cave still legitimately use the stick of dynamite they have to save themselves rather than the fat person?

Suppose there were ten, twenty, one hundred, or whatever number you want of spelunkers trapped in the cave. At some point, won't the number be sufficiently large that it would be morally acceptable for those in the cave to use the stick of dynamite to save themselves rather than the fat person, even if this meant that the fat person would be morally required to sacrifice his life? The answer has to be yes, but surely it has to be a very unusual case when we can reasonably demand that people thus sacrifice their lives or basic needs.

We could demand, of course, that people do all that they reasonably can to keep such conflicts from arising in the first place, for, just as in human ethics, many severe conflicts of interest can be avoided simply by doing what is morally required early on. Nevertheless, when lives or basic needs are at stake, the individualist perspective seems generally incontrovertible. We cannot normally require people to be saints.

At the same time, when people's basic needs are not at stake, we would be justified in acting on holistic grounds to prevent serious harm to nonhuman individuals, or species, or ecosystems, or the whole biotic community. Obviously, it will be difficult to know when our interventions will have this effect, but when we can be reasonably sure that they will, such interventions (e.g. culling elk herds in wolf-free ranges or preserving the habitat of endangered species) would be morally permissible, and would even be morally required, when the Principle of Rectification applies. This shows that it is possible to agree with individualists when the basic needs of human beings are at stake, and to agree with holists when they are not.[24]

Yet this combination of individualism and holism appears to conflict with recognizing that all species count morally by imposing greater sacrifices on the members of nonhuman species than it imposes on the members of the human species. Fortunately, appearances are deceiving here. Although the proposed resolution only justifies imposing holism when people's basic needs are not at stake, it does not justify imposing individualism at all. Rather it would simply permit individualism when people's basic needs *are* at stake. Of course, we could impose holism under all conditions. But given that this would, in effect, involve going to war against people who are simply striving to meet their own basic needs in the only way they can, as permitted by the Principle of Human Preservation, intervention in such cases would generally not be justified. It would involve taking away the means of survival from people, even when these means are not required for one's own survival.

Nevertheless, this combination of individualism and holism may leave animal liberationists wondering about the further implications of this resolution for the treatment of animals. Obviously, a good deal of work has already been done on this topic. Initially, philosophers thought that humanism could be extended to include animal liberation and eventually environmental concern.[25] Then Baird Callicott argued that animal liberation and environmental concern were as opposed to each other as they were to humanism.[26] The resulting conflict Callicott called "a triangular affair." Agreeing with Callicott, Mark Sagoff contended that any attempt to link together animal liberation and environmental concern would lead to "a bad marriage and a quick divorce."[27] Yet more recently, such philosophers as Mary Ann Warren, have tended to play down the opposition between animal liberation and environmental concern, and even Callicott now thinks he can bring the two back together again.[28] There are good reasons for thinking that such a reconciliation is possible.

Right off, it would be good for the environment if people generally, especially people in the developed world, adopted a more vegetarian diet of the sort that animal liberationists are recommending. This is because a good portion of livestock production today consumes grains that could be more effectively used for direct human consumption. For example, 90% of the protein, 99% of the carbohydrate, and 100% of the fiber value of grain is wasted by cycling it through livestock, and currently 64% of the U.S. grain crop is fed to livestock.[29] So by adopting a more vegetarian diet, people generally, and especially people in the developed world, could significantly reduce the amount of farmland that has to be kept in production to feed the human population. This, in turn, could have beneficial effects on the whole biotic community by eliminating the amount of soil erosion and environmental pollutants that result from raising livestock. For example, it has been estimated that 85% of U.S. topsoil lost from cropland, pasture, range land and forest land is directly associated with raising livestock.[30] So, in addition to preventing animal suffering, there are these additional reasons to favor a more vegetarian diet.

But even though a more vegetarian diet seems in order, it is not clear that the interests of farm animals would be well served if all of us became complete vegetarians. Sagoff assumes that in a completely vegetarian human world people would continue to feed farm animals as before.[31] But it is not clear that we would have any obligation to do so. Moreover, in a completely vegetarian human world, we would probably need about half of the grain we now feed livestock to meet people's nutritional needs, particularly in underdeveloped countries. There simply would not be enough grain to go around. And then there would be the need to conserve cropland for future generations. So in a completely vegetarian human world, it seems likely that the population of farm animals would be decimated, relegating many of the farm animals that remain to zoos. But raising farm animals can be seen to be mutually beneficial for humans and the farm animals involved. Surely, it would benefit farm animals to be brought into existence, maintained under healthy conditions, and hence not in the numbers sustainable only with factory farms, but then killed relatively painlessly and eaten, rather than that they not be brought into existence or maintained at all.[32] So a completely vegetarian human world would not be in the interest of farm animals.[33] Of course, no one would be morally required to bring farm animals into existence and maintain them in this manner. Morally, it would suffice just to maintain representative members of the various subspecies in zoos. Nevertheless, many will find it difficult to pass up an arrangement that is morally permissible and mutually beneficial for both humans and farm animals.

Nor, it seems, would it be in the interest of wild species who no longer have their natural predators not to be at least therapeudically hunted by humans.[34] Of course, where possible, it may be preferable to reintroduce natural predators. But this may not always be possible because of the unavoidable proximity of farm animals and human populations, and then if action is not taken to control the populations of wild species, disaster could result for the species and their environments. For example, ungulates (hooved mammals such as white-tailed and mule deer, elk and bison) as well as elephants in the absence of predators regularly tend to exceed the carrying capacity of their environments.[35] So it may be in the interest of these

wild species and their environments that humans intervene periodically to maintain a balance. Of course, there will be many natural environments where it is in the interest of the environment and the wild animals that inhabit it to be simply left alone. But here too animal liberation and environmental concern would not be in conflict. For these reasons, animal liberationists would have little reason to object to the proposed combination of individualism and holism within Morality as Compromise.

IV The "Is/Ought" Problem Again

Nevertheless, it might still be objected that if Morality as Compromise is going to maintain that all living beings count morally, it must be presupposing a derivation from "is" to "ought," or from "facts" to "values," or more explicitly from "X is a living being" to "X counts morally," "in such a way that we can always ask why these "facts" and not others are the grounds for the derivation.[36] Of course, animal liberationists, who hold that only sentient beings or experiencing subjects of life count morally, and most people, who appear to be anthropocentrists and hold that only humans or, more generally, rational beings count morally, face the same problem. But is there any way out of this problem? Haven't I claimed that ethics, or more specifically, Morality as Compromise, can do better than this?

Clearly, according to Morality as Compromise, our basic ethical concern is to determine what prerogatives and constraints hold for in our relationship with other living beings. The prerogatives specify the ways that we can justifiably harm nonhuman living beings (the Principles of Human Defense and Human Preservation) while the constraints specify the ways that we cannot justifiably harm them (the Principle of Disproportionality). Now it is important to notice that the constraints specifying ways that we should not harm other living beings are simply requirements that, under certain conditions, we should leave other living beings alone, that is, not interfere with them. They are not requirements that we do anything for them. To generally require that we do something beneficial for nonhuman living beings (except when restitution is required) would be to require much more of us. It would entail positive obligations to benefit nonhuman living beings not just negative obligations not to harm them by interfering with them. In general, this would be to demand too much from us, in effect, requiring us to be saints, and, as we have noted before, morality is not usually in the business of requiring us to be saints. Accordingly, the general obligation of noninterference that we have with respect to nonhuman living beings is fixed not so much by the nature of those other living beings as by what constraints or requirements can be reasonably imposed on ourselves.[37] Thus, we can see that those who benefit from the obligations that can be reasonably imposed on ourselves must have a certain independence to their lives; they must be able to get along on their own, without the help of others. In other words, they must have a good of their own.[38]

Accordingly, I have specified the class of those nonhumans to which we can have moral obligations not primarily in terms of the factual characteristics of those to whom we have those obligations, but rather in terms of what constraints or requirements can reasonably be imposed on us in this regard.[39] This is not a derivation of values from facts or of "ought" from "is" where we can always ask why these facts and not some others support the derivation. But rather it is a derivation of values from values or of "ought" from "ought" where the necessity of the derivation can be displayed.

We can more clearly display this derivation by the following argument:

1 All human beings ought to abide by the requirements of morality.
2 The requirements of morality are reasonable to impose on human beings.
3 The Principles of Human Defense, Human Preservation, Disproportionality and Rectification, in contrast with the alternatives, are reasonable to impose on human beings.

4 The Principles of Human Defense, Human Preservation, Disproportionality, and Rectification are requirements of morality.
5 All human beings ought to abide by the Principles of Human Defense, Human Preservation, Disproportionality, and Rectification.

Since the basic premises of this argument (1) and (2) are widely accepted as a fundamental characterization of morality, I think that the conclusions (3) and (4) can be seen to clearly follow.[40] Of course, a fuller statement of this argument would require an elaboration of all the considerations that I have advanced in this paper.[41] Nevertheless, I think that I have said enough to indicate how Morality as Compromise with its conflict resolution principles avoids an unjustifiable leap from facts to values. Moreover, by showing how Morality as Compromise is grounded in a standard of non-question-beggingness, I think I have also shown how it provides a foundation for environmental policy that we cannot rationally reject.

NOTES

1. Nonanthropocentric reasons are not usually thought to be reasons that take only the interests of nonhuman living beings into account, but rather reasons that take the interests of all (human and nonhuman) living beings into account. However, nonanthropocentric reasons, as I define them, are truly distinct from anthrocentric reasons in just the way that altruistic reasons are distinct from self-interested reasons, and it is important that when trying to decide what we ought rationally to do that we start with classifications of reasons that are truly distinct. For more on why this is the case, see my *Justice for Here and Now* (Cambridge, 1998), p. 25 and note #42

2. See Paul Taylor, *Respect for Nature* (Princeton: Princeton University Press, 1987) pp.129–135 and R. and V. Routley, "Against the Inevitability of Human Chauvinism," in *Ethics and Problems of the 21st Century* edited by K. E. Goodpaster and K. M. Sayre (Notre Dame: University of Notre Dame, 1979).

3. Assuming God exists, humans might also be better off if they could retain their distinctive traits while acquiring one or another of God's qualities, but consideration of this possibility would take us too far afield. Nonhuman animals might also be better off if they

could retain their distinctive traits and acquire one or another of the distinctive traits possessed by other non-human animals.

4. This assumes that there is an environmental niche that cheetahs can fill.

5. Since some things that are good for some (like rationality) are not good for others, there are no universal standard of excellences that apply to all living beings, even though there are some basic goods that all living beings need (like water).

6. For the purposes of this essay, I will follow the convention of excluding humans from the denotation of "animals."

7. For further discussion of basic needs, see my *How To Make People Just* (Totowa: Rowman & Littlefield, p. 45ff.

8. Moreover, this kind of fuzziness in the application of the distinction between basic and nonbasic needs is characteristic of the application of virtually all our classificatory concepts, and so is not an objection to its usefulness.

9. It should be pointed out that the Principle of Human Preservation must be implemented in a way that causes the least harm possible, which means that, other things being equal, basic needs should be meet by aggressing against nonsentient rather than against sentient living beings so as to avoid the pain and suffering that would otherwise be inflicted on sentient beings.

10. It is important to recognize here that we also have a strong obligation to prevent lifeboat cases from arising in the first place.

11. The principle just does not speak to the issue, although I do discuss in the text what is permissible and impermissible in this regard.

12. For my most recent discussion of the "ought" implies "can" principle, *see Justice for Here and Now* (Cambridge, Cambridge University Press, 1998) Chapter 3.

13. See Holmes Rolston III, "Enforcing Environmental Ethics: Civil Law and Natural Value," in James P. Sterba, *Social and Political Philosophy: Contempoary Perspectives* (London: Routledge, 2001) where Rolston uses this example to object to my Principle of Human Preservation and I respond.

14. This did not hold in the real-life case that Rolston actually presented. See my response in *Social and Political Philosophy: Contemporary Perspectives*.

15. If this requirement were ever met, then, we would be in something like that of a lifeboat situation among humans where both parties with their allies would be morally free to do what they can to meet their basic needs. In that situation, the moral permissibility in the Principle of Human Preservation would be that of weak permissibility where virtually nothing is morally required or prohibited.

16. Of course, we may be required to meet our basic needs and the basic needs of other humans by aggressing against the basic needs of the members of some nonhuman species rather than others, for example, in order to protect, in this way, certain endangered species. But clearly this requirement would not undermine the present and prevailing moral acceptability of the Principle of Human Preservation understood as involving strong permissibility.

17. It should be pointed out that although the Principle of Disproportionality prohibits aggressing against basic needs of nonhumans to serve nonbasic needs of humans, the Principle of Human Defense permits defense of nonbasic needs of humans against aggression of nonhumans. So while we cannot legitimately aggress against nonhumans to meet our nonbasic needs, we can legitimately defend our nonbasic needs against the aggression of nonhumans seeking to meet their basic needs, although this will tend to rarely happen for the reasons given in the text.

18. For an account of what constitutes justifiably held property within human ethics, see *Justice for Here and Now*, especially Chapter 3.

19. For a detailed discussion of this argument, see my article "From Liberty to Welfare," *Ethics* (1994), pp. 64–98, and Chapter 3 *of Justice for Here and Now.*

20. For further argument for this conclusion, *see Justice for Here and Now*, Chapter 3 and *How To Make People Just,* Chapters 2–10

21. Aldo Leopold's view is usually interpreted as holistic in this sense. Leopold wrote "A thing is right when it tends to preserve the integrity, stability and beauty of the biotic community. It is wrong when it tends otherwise." See his *A Sand County Almanac* (Oxford, 1949).

22. For a defender of this view, see Paul Taylor, *Respect for Nature.*

23. See Philippa Foot, "The Problem of Abortion and the Doctrine of Double Effect," *Oxford Review* Vol. 5 [1967], pp. 5–15.

24. Of course, actions justified on wholist grounds, may sometimes preclude the satisfaction of nonbasic human needs (e.g., by restricting urban sprawl), but they will only rarely involve aggressing against nonbasis human needs for the reasons given earlier, except when compensation and reparation is required.

25. Peter Singer's *Animal Liberation* (New York: Avon Books, 1975) inspired this view.

26. Baird Callicott, "Animal Liberation: A Triangular Affair," *Environmental Ethics* (1980) 311–328.

27. Mark Sagoff, "Animal Liberation and Environmental Ethics: Bad Marriage, Quick Divorce," *Osgood Hall Law Journal* (1984) 297–307.

28. Mary Ann Warren, "The Rights of the Nonhuman World," in *Environmental Philosophy,* edited by

Robert Elliot and Arran Gare (University Park: Penn State University Press, 1983) 109–134 and Baird Callicott, *In Defense of the Land Ethic* (Albany: Suny, 1989) Chapter 3.

29. *Realities for the 90's,* (Santa Cruz, 1991) p. 4

30. *Ibid,* p. 5

31. Mark Sagoff, *op. cit.* pp. 301–5.

32. There is an analogous story to tell here about "domesticated" plants, but hopefully there is no analogous story about "extra humans" who could be raised for food. Given the knowledge these "extra humans" would have of their fate, a similar use of humans would not be mutually beneficial, would most likely make their lives not worth living. But even assuming that this were not the case, with the consequence that this particular justification for domestication would be ruled out because of its implications for a similar use of humans, it still would be the case that domestication is justified in a sustainable agriculture to provide fertilizer for crops to meet basic human needs.

33. To say that the proposed arrangement is in the interest of farms animals implies that the farm animals who would come into existence by means of that arrangement would benefit overall, not that there are some pre-existent farm animals who will benefit from the arrangement. However, the arrangement can be in the interest of some existing animals as well.

34. For a valuable discussion of this issue, see Gary Varner, *In Nature's Interests?* New York: Oxford University Press 1998), pp. 100–18.

35. There are other species such as mourning doves, cottontail rabbits, gray squirrels, bobwhite and blue quail which each year produce more young than their habitat can support through the winter, but they usually do not degrade their environment. With respect to such species, it might be argued that hunting is morally permissible. Nevertheless, unless such hunting is either therapeudic or required to meet basic human needs, it is difficult to see how it could be permissible.

36. I am not objecting here to all attempts to derive, or better ground "values" on "facts" but just to the arbitrariness that seems to characterize the one under consideration. For a discussion of what good derivations or groundings of values would look like, see Kurt Baier, *The Rational and the Moral Order* (Chicago: Open Court, 1995) Chapter 1.

37. Although the living beings must be capable of being benefited and harmed, unlike cars, refrigerators, etc., in a nonderivative way. See my article, "A Biocentrist Fights Back," *Environmental Ethics* (1998), pp.361–376.

38. One notable exception to the requirement of independence are some species and subspecies of domesticated animals who have been made into beings who are dependent for their survival on humans. I contend that because of their historic interaction with these domesticated animals, humans have acquired a positive obligation to care for these animals provided certain mutually beneficial arrangements can be maintained.

39. Even the requirement that those who can be benefited or harmed in a nonderivative way must have a certain independence to their lives or a good of their own is, on my account, *derived* from what we can reasonably expect of moral agents.

40. For further discussion of this fundamental characterization of morality (1) and (2), see *Justice for Here and Now,* Chapter 3.

34 The Power and the Promise of Ecological Feminism

KAREN J. WARREN

Ecological feminism (ecofeminism) has begun to receive a fair amount of attention lately as an alternative feminism and environmental ethic. Since Francoise d'Eaubonne introduced the term *ecofeminisme* in 1974 to bring attention to women's potential for bringing about an ecological revolution, the term has been used in a variety of ways. As I use the term here, ecological feminism is the position that there are important connections—historical, experiential, symbolic, and theoretical—between the domination of women and the domination of nature, an understanding of which is crucial to both feminism and environmental ethics. I argue that the promise and power of ecological feminism is that *it provides a distinctive framework both for reconceiving feminism and for developing an environmental ethic which takes seriously connections between the domination of women and the domination of nature.* I do so by discussing the nature of a feminist ethic and the ways in which ecofeminism provides a feminist and environmental ethic. I conclude that any feminist theory *and* any environmental ethic which fails to take seriously the twin and interconnected dominations of women and nature is at best incomplete and at worst simply inadequate.

Feminism, Ecological Feminism, and Conceptual Frameworks

Whatever else it is, feminism is at least the movement to end sexist oppression. It involves the elimination of any and all factors that contribute to the continued and systematic domination or subordination of women. While feminists disagree about the nature of and solutions to the subordination of women, all feminists agree that sexist oppression exists, is wrong, and must be abolished.

A "feminist issue" is any issue that contributes in some way to understanding the oppression of women. Equal rights, comparable pay for comparable work, and food production are feminist issues whenever an understanding of them contributes to an understanding of the continued exploitation or subjugation of women. Carrying water and searching for firewood are feminist issues wherever and whenever women's primary responsibility for these tasks contributes to their lack of full participation in decision making, income producing, or high status positions engaged in by men. What counts as a feminist issue, then, depends largely on context, particularly the historical and material conditions of women's lives.

Reprinted from Environmental Ethics *(1990) by permission of the author.*

Environmental degradation and exploitation are feminist issues because an understanding of them contributes to an understanding of the oppression of women. In India, for example, both deforestation and reforestation through the introduction of a monoculture species tree (e.g., eucalyptus) intended for commercial production are feminist issues because the loss of indigenous forests and multiple species of trees has drastically affected rural Indian women's ability to maintain a subsistence household. Indigenous forests provide a variety of trees for food, fuel, fodder, household utensils, dyes, medicines, and income-generating uses, while monoculture species forests do not. Although I do not argue for this claim here, a look at the global impact of environmental degradation on women's lives suggests important respects in which environmental degradation is a feminist issue.

Feminist philosophers claim that some of the most important feminist issues are *conceptual* ones: These issues concern how one conceptualizes such mainstay philosophical notions as reason and rationality, ethics, and what it is to be human. Ecofeminists extend this feminist philosophical concern to nature. They argue that, ultimately, some of the most important connections between the domination of women and the domination of nature are conceptual. To see this, consider the nature of conceptual frameworks.

A *conceptual framework* is a set of *basic* beliefs, values, attitudes, and assumptions which shape and reflect how one views oneself and one's world. It is a socially constructed lens through which we perceive ourselves and others. It is affected by such factors as gender, race, class, age, affectional orientation, nationality, and religious background.

Some conceptual frameworks are oppressive. An *oppressive conceptual framework* is one that explains, justifies, and maintains relationships of domination and subordination. When an oppressive conceptual framework is *patriarchal*, it explains, justifies, and maintains the subordination of women by men.

I have argued elsewhere that there are three significant features of oppressive conceptual frameworks: (1) value-hierarchical thinking, i.e., "up-down" thinking which places higher value, status, or prestige on what is "up" rather than on what is "down"; (2) value dualisms, i.e., disjunctive pairs in which the disjuncts are seen as oppositional (rather than as complementary) and exclusive (rather than as inclusive), and which place higher value (status, prestige) on one disjunct rather than the other (e.g., dualisms which give higher value or status to that which has historically been identified as "mind," "reason," and "male" than to that which has historically been identified as "body," "emotion," and "female"); and (3) logic of domination, i.e., a structure of argumentation which leads to a justification of subordination.

The third feature of oppressive conceptual frameworks is the most significant. A logic of domination is not *just* a logical structure. It also involves a substantive value system, since an ethical premise is needed to permit or sanction the "just" subordination of that which is subordinate. This justification typically is given on grounds of some alleged characteristic (e.g., rationality) which the dominant (e.g., men) have and the subordinate (e.g., women) lack.

Contrary to what many feminists and ecofeminists have said or suggested, there may be nothing *inherently* problematic about "hierarchical thinking" or even "value-hierarchical thinking" in contexts other than contexts of oppression. Hierarchical thinking is important in daily living for classifying data, comparing information, and organizing material. Taxonomies (e.g., plant taxonomies) and biological nomenclature seem to require *some* form of "hierarchical thinking." Even "value-hierarchical thinking" may be quite acceptable in certain contexts. (The same may be said of "value dualisms" in nonoppressive contexts.) For example, suppose it is true that what is unique about humans is our conscious capacity to radically reshape our social environments (or "societies"), as Murray Bookchin suggests. Then one could truthfully say that humans are better equipped to radically reshape their environments than are rocks or plants—a "value-hierarchical" way of speaking.

The problem is not simply that value-hierarchical thinking and value dualisms are used, but *the way* in which each has been used *in oppressive conceptual frameworks* to establish inferiority and to justify subordination.[1] It is the logic of domination, *coupled* with value-hierarchical thinking and value dualisms, which "justifies" subordination. What is explanatorily basic, then, about the nature of oppressive conceptual frameworks is the logic of domination.

For ecofeminism, that a logic of domination is explanatorily basic is important for at least three reasons. First, without a logic of domination, a description of similarities and differences would be just that: a description of similarities and differences. Consider the claim, "Humans are different from plants and rocks in that humans can (and plants and rocks cannot) consciously and radically reshape the communities in which they live; humans are similar to plants and rocks in that they are both members of an ecological community." Even if humans are "better" than plants and rocks with respect to the conscious ability of humans to radically transform communities, one does not *thereby* get any *morally* relevant distinction between humans and nonhumans, or an argument for the domination of plants and rocks by humans. To get *those* conclusions one needs to add at least two powerful assumptions, viz., (A2) and (A4) in argument A below:

A1 Humans do, and plants and rocks do not, have the capacity to consciously and radically change the community in which they live.

A2 Whatever has the capacity to consciously and radically change the community in which it lives is morally superior to whatever lacks this capacity.

A3 Thus, humans are morally superior to plants and rocks.

A4 For any X and Y, if X is morally superior to Y, then X is morally justified in subordinating Y.

A5 Thus, humans are morally justified in subordinating plants and rocks.

Without the two assumptions that *humans are morally superior* to (at least some) nonhumans, (A2), and that *superiority justifies subordination*, (A4), all one has is some difference between humans and some nonhumans. This is true *even if* that difference is given in terms of superiority. Thus, it is the logic of domination, (A4), which is the bottom line in ecofeminist discussions of oppression.

Second, ecofeminists argue that, at least in Western societies, the oppressive conceptual framework which sanctions the twin dominations of women and nature is a patriarchal one characterized by all three features of an oppressive conceptual framework. Many ecofeminists claim that, historically, within at least the dominant Western culture, a patriarchal conceptual framework has sanctioned the following argument B:

B1 Women are identified with nature and the realm of the physical; men are identified with the "human" and the realm of the mental.

B2 Whatever is identified with nature and the realm of the physical is inferior to ("below") whatever is identified with the "human" and the realm of the mental; or, conversely, the latter is superior to ("above") the former.

B3 Thus, women are inferior to ("below") men; or, conversely, men are superior to ("above") women.

B4 For any X and Y, if X is superior to Y, then X is justified in subordinating Y.

B5 Thus, men are justified in subordinating women.

If sound, argument B establishes *patriarchy*, i.e., the conclusion given at (B5) that the systematic domination of women by men is justified. But according to ecofeminists, (B5) is justified by just those three features of an oppressive conceptual framework identified earlier: value-hierarchical thinking, the assumption at (B2); value dualisms, the assumed dualism of the mental and the physical at (B1) and the assumed inferiority of the physical vis-á-vis the mental at (B2); and a logic of domination, the assumption at (B4), the same as the previous premise (A4). Hence, according to ecofeminists, insofar as an oppressive patriarchal conceptual framework has functioned historically (within at least dominant Western culture) to sanction the twin dominations of women and nature (argument B), both argument B and the patriarchal conceptual framework, from whence it comes, ought to be rejected.

Of course, the preceding does not identify which premises of B are false. What is the status of premises (B1) and (B2)? Most, if not all, feminists claim that (B1), and many ecofeminists claim that (B2), have been assumed or asserted within the dominant Western philosophical and intellectual tradition.[2] As such, these feminists assert, as a matter of historical fact, that the dominant Western philosophical tradition has assumed the truth of (B1) and (B2). Ecofeminists, however, either deny (B2) or do not affirm (B2). Furthermore, because some ecofeminists are anxious to deny any historical identification of women with nature, some ecofeminists deny (B1) when (B1) is used to support anything other than a strictly historical claim about what has been asserted or assumed to be true within patriarchal culture—e.g., when (B1) is used to assert that women properly are identified with the realm of nature and the physical.[3] Thus, from an ecofeminist perspective, (B1) and (B2) are properly viewed as problematic though historically sanctioned claims: They are problematic precisely because of the way they have functioned historically in a patriarchal conceptual framework and culture to sanction the dominations of women and nature.

What *all* ecofeminists agree about, then, is the way in which the *logic of domination* has func-tioned historically within patriarchy to sustain and justify the twin dominations of women and nature.[4] Since *all* feminists (and not just ecofeminists) oppose patriarchy, the conclusion given at (B5), all feminists (including ecofeminists) must oppose at least the logic of domination, premise (B4), on which argument B rests—whatever the truth-value status of (B1) and (B2) *outside* of a patriarchal context.

That *all* feminists must oppose the logic of domination shows the breadth and depth of the ecofeminist critique of B: It is a critique not only of the three assumptions on which this argument for the domination of women and nature rests, viz., the assumptions at (B1), (B2), and (B4); it is also a critique of patriarchal conceptual frameworks generally, i.e., of those oppressive conceptual frameworks which put men "up" and women "down," allege some way in which women are morally inferior to men, and use that alleged difference to justify the subordination of women by men. Therefore, ecofeminism is necessary to *any* feminist critique of patriarchy, and, hence, necessary to feminism (a point I discuss again later).

Third, ecofeminism clarifies why the logic of domination, and any conceptual framework which gives rise to it, must be abolished in order both to make possible a meaningful notion of difference which does not breed domination and to prevent feminism from becoming a "support" movement based primarily on shared experiences. In contemporary society, there is no one "woman's voice," no *woman* (or *human*) *simpliciter*: Every woman (or human) is a woman (or human) of some race, class, age, affectional orientation, marital status, regional or national background, and so forth. Because there are no "monolithic experiences" that all women share, feminism must be a "solidarity movement" based on shared beliefs and interests rather than a "unity in sameness" movement based on shared experiences and shared victimization. In the words of Maria Lugones, "Unity—not to be confused with solidarity—is understood as conceptually tied to domination."

Ecofeminists insist that the sort of logic of domination used to justify the domination of humans by gender, racial or ethnic, or class status is also used to justify the domination of nature. Because eliminating a logic of domination is part of a feminist critique—whether a critique of patriarchy, white supremacist culture, or imperialism—ecofeminists insist that *naturism* is properly viewed as an integral part of any feminist solidarity movement to end sexist oppression and the logic of domination which conceptually grounds it.

Ecofeminism Reconceives Feminism

The discussion so far has focused on some of the oppressive conceptual features of patriarchy. As I use the phrase, the "logic of traditional feminism" refers to the location of the conceptual roots of sexist oppression, at least in Western societies, in an oppressive patriarchal conceptual framework characterized by a logic of domination. Insofar as other systems of oppression (e.g., racism, classism, ageism, heterosexism) are also conceptually maintained by a logic of domination, appeal to the logic of traditional feminism ultimately locates the basic conceptual interconnections among *all* systems of oppression in the logic of domination. It thereby explains at a *conceptual* level why the eradication of sexist oppression requires the eradication of the other forms of oppression. It is by clarifying this conceptual connection between systems of oppression that a movement to end sexist oppression—traditionally the special turf of feminist theory and practice—leads to a reconceiving of feminism as *a movement to end all forms of oppression*.

Suppose one agrees that the logic of traditional feminism requires the expansion of feminism to include other social systems of domination (e.g., racism and classism). What warrants the inclusion of nature in these "social systems of domination"? Why must the logic of traditional feminism include the abolition of "naturism" (i.e., the domination or oppression of nonhuman nature) among the "isms" feminism must confront? The conceptual justification for expanding feminism to include ecofeminism is twofold. One basis has already been suggested: By showing that the conceptual connections between the dual dominations of women and nature are located in an oppressive and, at least in Western societies, patriarchal conceptual framework characterized by a logic of domination, ecofeminism explains how and why feminism, conceived as a movement to end sexist oppression, must be expanded and reconceived as also a movement to end naturism. This is made explicit by the following argument C:

C1 Feminism is a movement to end sexism.
C2 But sexism is conceptually linked with naturism (through an oppressive conceptual framework characterized by a logic of domination).
C3 Thus, feminism is (also) a movement to end naturism.

Because, ultimately, these connections between sexism and naturism are conceptual—embedded in an oppressive conceptual framework—the logic of traditional feminism lends to the embracement of ecological feminism.

The other justification for reconceiving feminism to include ecofeminism has to do with the concepts of gender and nature. Just as conceptions of gender are socially constructed, so are conceptions of nature. Of course, the claim that women and nature are social constructions does not require anyone to deny that there are actual humans and actual trees, rivers, and plants. It simply implies that *how* women and nature are conceived is a matter of historical and social reality. These conceptions vary cross-culturally and by historical time period. As a result, any discussion of the "oppression or domination of nature" involves reference to historically specific forms of social domination of nonhuman nature by humans, just as discussion of the "domination of women" refers to historically specific forms of social domination of women by men. Although I do not argue for it here, an ecofeminist defense of the historical connections between the dominations of women and of nature, claims (B1) and (B2) in argument B, involves showing that within patriarchy the feminization of nature and the naturalization of women have been crucial to the historically successful subordinations of both.

If ecofeminism promises to reconceive traditional feminism in ways which include naturism as a legitimate feminist issue, does ecofeminism also promise to reconceive environmental ethics in ways which are feminist? I think so. This is the subject of the remainder of the paper.

Climbing from Ecofeminism to Environmental Ethics

Many feminists and some environmental ethicists have begun to explore the use of first-person narrative as a way of raising philosophically germane issues in ethics often lost or underplayed in mainstream philosophical ethics. Why is this so? What is it about narrative which makes it a significant resource for theory and practice in feminism and environmental ethics? Even if appeal to first-person narrative is a helpful literary device for describing ineffable experience or a legitimate social science methodology for documenting personal and social history, how is first-person narrative a valuable vehicle of argumentation for ethical decision making and theory building? One fruitful way to begin answering these questions is to ask them of a particular first-person narrative.

Consider the following first-person narrative about rock climbing:

> For my very first rock climbing experience, I chose a somewhat private spot, away from other climbers and onlookers. After studying "the chimney," I focused all my energy on making it to the top. I climbed with intense determination, using whatever strength and skills I had to accomplish this challenging feat. By midway I was exhausted and anxious. I couldn't see what to do next—where to put my hands or feet. Growing increasingly more weary as I clung somewhat desperately to the rock, I made a move. It didn't work. I fell. There I was, dangling midair above the rocky ground below, frightened but terribly relieved that the belay rope had held me. I knew I was safe. I took a look up at the climb that re-

mained. I was determined to make it to the top. With renewed confidence and concentration, I finished the climb to the top.

> On my second day of climbing, I rappelled down about 200 feet from the top of the Palisades at Lake Superior to just a few feet above the water level. I could see no one—not my belayer, not the other climbers, no one. I unhooked slowly from the rappel rope and took a deep cleansing breath. I looked all around me—really looked—and listened. I heard a cacophony of voices—birds, trickles of water on the rock before me, waves lapping against the rocks below. I closed my eyes and began to feel the rock with my hands—the cracks and crannies, the raised lichen and mosses, the almost imperceptible nubs that might provide a resting place for my fingers and toes when I began to climb. At that moment I was bathed in serenity. I began to talk to the rock in an almost inaudible, child-like way, as if the rock were my friend. I felt an overwhelming sense of gratitude for what it offered me—a chance to know myself and the rock differently, to appreciate unforeseen miracles like the tiny flowers growing in the even tinier cracks in the rock's surface, and to come to know a sense of *being in relationship* with the natural environment. It felt as if the rock and I were silent conversational partners in a longstanding friendship. I realized then that I had come to care about this cliff which was so different from me, so unmovable and invincible, independent and seemingly indifferent to my presence. I wanted to be with the rock as I climbed. Gone was the determination to conquer the rock, to forcefully impose my will on it; I wanted simply to work respectfully with the rock as I climbed. And as I climbed, that is what I felt. I felt myself *caring* for this rock and feeling thankful that climbing provided the opportunity for me to know it and myself in this new way.

There are at least four reasons why use of such a first-person narrative is important to feminism and environmental ethics. First, such a narrative gives voice to a felt sensitivity often lacking in traditional analytical ethical discourse, viz., a sensitivity to conceiving of oneself as fundamentally "in relationship with" others, including the non-human environment. It is a modality which *takes relationships themselves seriously*. It thereby stands in contrast to a strictly reductionist modality that takes relationships seriously only or primarily because of the nature of the *relators* or parties to those relationships (e.g., relators conceived as moral agents, right holders, interest carriers, or sentient beings). In the rock-climbing narrative above, it is the climber's relationship with the rock she climbs which takes on special significance—which is itself a locus of value—in addition to whatever moral status or moral considerability she or the rock or any other parties to the relationship may also have.[5]

Second, such a first-person narrative gives expression to a variety of ethical attitudes and behaviors often overlooked or underplayed in mainstream Western ethics, e.g., the difference in attitudes and behaviors toward a rock when one is "making it to the top" and when one thinks of oneself as "friends with" or "caring about" the rock one climbs.[6] These different attitudes and behaviors suggest an ethically germane contrast between two different types of relationship humans or climbers may have toward a rock: an imposed conqueror-type relationship, and an emergent caring-type relationship. This contrast grows out of, and is faithful to, felt, lived experience.

The difference between conquering and caring attitudes and behaviors in relation to the natural environment provides a third reason why the use of first-person narrative is important to feminism and environmental ethics: It provides a way of conceiving of ethics and ethical meaning as *emerging out of* particular situations moral agents find themselves in, rather than as being *imposed on* those situations (e.g., as a derivation or instantiation of some predetermined abstract principle or rule). This emergent feature of narrative centralizes the importance of *voice*. When a multiplicity of cross-cultural *voices* are centralized, narrative is able to give expression to a range of attitudes, values, beliefs, and behaviors which may be overlooked or silenced by imposed ethical meaning and theory. As a reflection of and on felt, lived experiences, the use of narrative in ethics provides a stance from which ethical discourse can be held accountable to the historical, material, and social realities in which moral subjects find themselves.

Lastly, and for our purposes perhaps most importantly, the use of narrative has argumentative significance. Jim Cheney calls attention to this feature of narrative when he claims, "To contextualize ethical deliberation is, in some sense, to provide a narrative or story, from which the solution to the ethical dilemma emerges as the fitting conclusion." Narrative has argumentative force by suggesting *what counts* as an appropriate conclusion to an ethical situation. One ethical conclusion suggested by the climbing narrative is that what counts as a proper ethical attitude toward mountains and rocks is an attitude of respect and care (whatever that turns out to be or involve), not one of domination and conquest.

In an essay entitled "In and Out of Harm's Way: Arrogance and Love," feminist philosopher Marilyn Frye distinguishes between "arrogant" and "loving" perception as one way of getting at this difference in the ethical attitudes of care and conquest. Frye writes:

> The loving eye is a contrary of the arrogant eye.
>
> The loving eye knows the independence of the other. It is the eye of a seer who knows that nature is indifferent. It is the eye of one who knows that to know the seen, one must consult something other than one's own will and interests and fears and imagination. One must look at the thing. One must look and listen and check and question.
>
> The loving eye is one that pays a certain sort of attention. This attention can require a discipline but not a self-denial. The discipline is one of self-knowledge, knowledge of the scope and boundary of the self. . . . In particular, it is a matter of being able to tell one's own interests from those of others and of knowing where one's self leaves off and another begins. . . .
>
> The loving eye does not make the object of perception into something edible, does not try to assimilate it, does not reduce it to the size of the seer's desire, fear, and imagination, and hence does not have to simplify. It knows the complexity of the other as something which will forever present new things to be known. The science of the loving eye would favor The Complexity Theory of Truth [in contrast to The Simplicity Theory of Truth] and presuppose The Endless Interestingness of the Universe.

According to Frye, the loving eye is not an invasive, coercive eye which annexes others to itself, but one which "knows the complexity of the other as something which will forever present new things to be known."

When one climbs a rock as a conqueror, one climbs with an arrogant eye. When one climbs with a loving eye, one constantly "must look and listen and check and question." One recognizes the rock as something very different, something perhaps totally indifferent to one's own presence, and finds in that difference joyous occasion for celebration. One knows "the boundary of the self," where the self—the "I," the climber—leaves off and the rock begins. There is no fusion of two into one, but a complement of two entities *acknowledged* as separate, different, independent, yet *in relationship;* they are in relationship *if only* because the loving eye is perceiving it, responding to it, noticing it, attending to it.

An ecofeminist perspective about both women and nature involves this shift in attitude from "arrogant perception" to "loving perception" of the nonhuman world. Arrogant perception of nonhumans by humans presupposes and maintains *sameness* in such a way that it expands the moral community to those beings who are thought to resemble (be like, similar to, or the same as) humans in some morally significant way. Any environmental movement or ethic based on arrogant perception builds a moral hierarchy of beings and assumes some common denominator of moral considerability in virtue of which like beings deserve similar treatment or moral consideration and unlike beings do not. Such environmental ethics are or generate a "unity in sameness." In contrast, "loving perception" presupposes and maintains *difference*—a distinction between the self and the other, between human and at least some nonhumans—in such a way that perception of the other as other is an expression of love for one who/which is recognized at the outset as independent, dissimilar, different. As Maria Lugones says, in loving perception, "Love is seen not as fusion and erasure of difference but as incompatible with them." "Unity in sameness" alone is an *erasure of difference*.

"Loving perception" of the nonhuman natural world is an attempt to understand what it means *for humans* to care about the nonhuman world, a world *acknowledged* as being independent, different, perhaps even indifferent to humans. Humans are different from rocks in important ways, even if they are also both members of some ecological community. A moral community based on loving perception of oneself *in relationship with* a rock, or with the natural environment as a whole, is one which acknowledges and respects difference, whatever "sameness" also exists. The limits of loving perception are determined only by the limits of one's (e.g., a person's, a community's) ability to respond lovingly (or with appropriate care, trust, or friendship)—whether it is to other humans or to the nonhuman world and elements of it.

If what I have said so far is correct, then there are very different ways to climb a mountain, and *how* one climbs it and *how* one narrates the experience of climbing it matter ethically. If one climbs with "arrogant perception," with an attitude of "conquer and control," one keeps intact the very sorts of thinking that characterize a logic of domination and an oppressive conceptual framework. Since the oppressive conceptual framework which sanctions the domination of nature is a patriarchal one, one also thereby keeps intact, even if unwittingly, a patriarchal conceptual framework. Because the dismantling of patriarchal conceptual frameworks is a feminist issue, *how* one climbs a mountain and *how* one narrates—or tells the story—about the experience of climbing also are *feminist issues*. In this way, ecofeminism makes visible why, at a conceptual level, environmental ethics is a feminist issue.

Conclusion

I have argued in this paper that ecofeminism provides a framework for a distinctively feminist and environmental ethic. Ecofeminism grows out of the felt and theorized about connections between the domination of women and the domination of nature. As a contextualist ethic, ecofeminism refocuses environmental ethics on what nature might mean, morally speaking, *for* humans, and on how the relational attitudes of humans to others—humans as well as nonhumans—sculpt both what it is to be human and the nature and ground of human responsibilities to the nonhuman environment. Part of what this refocusing does is to take seriously the voices of women and other oppressed persons in the construction of that ethic.

A Sioux elder once told me a story about his son. He sent his seven-year-old son to live with the child's grandparents on a Sioux reservation so that he could "learn the Indian ways." Part of what the grandparents taught him was how to hunt the four-leggeds of the forest. As I heard the story, the boy was taught, "to shoot your four-legged brother in his hind area, slowing it down but not killing it. Then, take the four-legged's head in your hands, and look into his eyes. The eyes are where all the suffering is. Look into your brother's eyes and feel his pain. Then, take your knife and cut the four-legged under his chin, here, on his neck, so that he dies quickly. And as you do, ask your brother, the four-legged, for forgiveness for what you do. Offer also a prayer of thanks to your four-legged kin for offering his body to you just now, when you need food to eat and clothing to wear. And promise the four-legged that you will put yourself back into the earth when you die, to become nourishment for the earth, and for the sister flowers, and for the brother deer. It is appropriate that you should offer this blessing for the four-legged and, in due time, reciprocate in turn with your body in this way, as the four-legged gives life to you for your survival." As I reflect on that story, I am struck by the power of the environmental ethic that grows out of and takes seriously narrative, context, and such values and relational attitudes as care, loving perception, and appropriate reciprocity, and doing what is appropriate in a given situation—however that notion of appropriateness eventually gets filled out. I am also struck by what one is able to see, once one begins to explore some of the historical and conceptual connections between the dominations of women and of nature. A *re-conceiving* and *re-visioning* of both feminism and environmental ethics, is, I think, the power and promise of ecofeminism.

NOTES

1. It may be that in contemporary Western society, which is so thoroughly structured by categories of gender, race, class, age, and affectional orientation, that there simply is no meaningful notion of "value-hierarchical thinking" which does not function in an oppressive context. For the purposes of this paper, I leave that question open.

2. Many feminists who argue for the historical point that claims (B1) and (B2) have been asserted or assumed to be true within the dominant Western philosophical tradition do so by discussion of that tradition's conceptions of reason, rationality, and science. For a sampling of the sorts of claims made within that context, see "Reason, Rationality, and Gender," ed. Nancy Tuana and Karen J. Warren, a special issue of the American Philosophical Association's *Newsletter on Feminism and Philosophy* 88, no. 2 (March 1989): 17–71. Ecofeminists who claim that (B2) has been assumed to be true within the dominant Western philosophical tradition include: Gray, *Green Paradise Lost:* Griffin, *Woman and Nature: The Roaring Inside Her;* Merchant, *The Death of Nature;* Ruether, *New Woman/New Earth.* For a discussion of some of these ecofeminist historical accounts, see Plumwood, "Eco-feminism." While I agree that the historical connections between the domination of women and the domination of nature is a crucial one, I do not argue for that claim here.

3. Ecofeminists who deny (B1) when (B1) is offered as anything other than a true, descriptive, historical claim about patriarchal culture often do so on grounds that an objectionable sort of biological determinism, or at least harmful female sex-gender stereotypes, underlie (B1). For a discussion of this "split" among those ecofeminists ("nature feminists") who assert and those ecofeminists ("social feminists") who deny (B1) as anything other than a true historical claim about how women are described in patriarchal culture, see Griscom, "On Healing the Nature/History Split."

4. I make no attempt here to defend the historically sanctioned truth of these promises.

5. Suppose . . . that a necessary condition for the existence of a moral relationship is that at least one party to the relationship is a moral being (leaving open for our purposes what counts as a "moral being"). If this is so, then the Mona Lisa cannot properly be said to have or stand in a moral relationship with the wall on which she hangs, and a wolf cannot have or properly be said to have or stand in a moral relationship with a moose. Such a necessary-condition account leaves open the question whether *both* parties to the relationship must be moral beings. The point here is simply that however one resolves *that* question, recognition of the relationships themselves as a locus of value is a recognition of a source of value that is different from and not reducible to the values of the "moral beings" in those relationships.

6. It is interesting to note that the image of being friends with the Earth is one which cytogeneticist Barbara McClintock uses when she describes the importance of having "a feeling for the organism," "listening to the material [in this case the corn plant]," in one's work as a scientist. See Evelyn Fox Keller, "Women, Science, and Popular Mythology," in *Machina Ex Dea: Feminist Perspectives on Technology,* ed. Joan Rothschild (New York: Pergamon Press, 1983), and Evelyn Fox Keller, *A Feeling For the Organism: The Life and Work of Barbara McClintock* (San Francisco: W. H. Freeman, 1983).

Suggestions for Further Reading

Anthologies

Garner, Richard T., and Andrew Oldenquist, *Society and the Individual: Readings in Political and Social Philosophy.* Belmont, CA: Wadsworth, 1990.
Solomon, Robert, and Mark Murphy, *What is Justice?* 2nd edition. New York: Oxford University Press, 1999.
Sterba, James P., *Social and Political Philosophy: Classical Western Texts in Feminist and Multicultural Perspectives.* 3rd edition. Belmont: Wadsworth. 2002.
Sterba, James P. *Social and Political Philosophy:* Contemporary Perspectives. London: Routledge, 2001.

Basic Concepts

Plato, *The Republic.* Trans. Francis Cornford. New York: Oxford University Press, 1945.
Sterba, James P., *Contemporary Social and Political Philosophy.* Belmont: Wadsworth, 1995.

Libertarian Justice

Hospers, John, *Libertarianism.* Los Angeles: Nash, 1971.
Machan, Tibor, *Individuals and Their Rights.* LaSalle, IL: Open Court, 1989.
——, and Rasmussen, Douglas, *Liberty for the 21st Century.* Lanham, MD: Rowman and Littlefield, 1995.
Narveson, Jan, *Respecting Persons in Theory and Practice.* London: Rowman & Littlefield, 2002.
Nozick, Robert, *Anarchy, State and Utopia.* New York: Basic Books, 1974.
Rasmussen, Douglas, and Douglas Den Uyl, *Liberty and Nature.* LaSalle, IL: Open Court, 1990.

Socialist Justice

Buchanan, A., *Marx and Justice: The Radical Critique of Liberalism.* Totowa, NJ: Rowman and Allanheld, 1982.
Cauthen, Kenneth, *The Passion for Equality.* Totowa, NJ: Rowman and Littlefield, 1987.
Engels, Friedrich, "Socialism: Utopian and Scientific," in Arthur Mendel, Ed., *Essential Works of Marxism,* pp. 45–82. New York: Bantam Books, 1961.
Fisk, Milton, *Ethics and Society: A Marxist Interpretation of Value.* New York: New York University Press, 1980.
Harrington, Michael, *Socialism Past and Future.* New York: Arcade, 1989.
Peffer, R. G., *Marxism, Morality, and Social Justice.* Princeton, NJ: Princeton University Press, 1990.

Liberal Democratic Justice: The Contractarian Perspective

Barry, Brian, *Justice as Impartiality.* Oxford: Oxford University Press, 1995.
Kekes, John, *Against Liberalism.* Ithaca: Cornell University Press, 1997.

Rawls, John, *A Theory of Justice*. Cambridge, MA: Harvard University Press, 1971.
——, *Political Liberalism*. New York: Columbia University Press, 1993.
Raz, J. *The Morality of Freedom*. Oxford: Oxford University Press, 1986.
Sterba, James P., *Justice for Here and Now*. New York: Cambridge University Press, 1998.

Liberal Democratic Justice: The Utilitarian Perspective

Glover, Jonathan, *Utilitarianism and its Critics*. New York: Macmillan, 1990.
Goodin, Robert, *Utilitarianism as a Public Philosophy*. New York: Cambridge University Press, 1995.
Sidgwick, Henry, *The Methods of Ethics*. New York: Dover, 1966.
Singer, Peter, *Practical Ethics*. 2nd edition. Cambridge, England: Cambridge University Press, 1993.
Smart, J. J. C., and Bernard Williams, *Utilitarianism For and Against*. Cambridge, England: Cambridge University Press, 1973.

Liberal Democratic Justice: The Discourse Ethics Perspective

Baynes, Kenneth, *Normative Grounds of Social Criticism*. New York: SUNY Press, 1992.
Benhabib, Seyla, *Situating the Self*. New York: Routledge, 1992.
——, and Dallmayr, Fred, *The Communicative Ethics Controversy*. Cambridge: MIT, 1990.
Fraser, N., "What's Critical about Critical Theory?, The Case of Habermas and Gender," in *Feminism as Critique: On the Politics of Gender,* edited by S. Benhabib and D. Cornell. Minneapolis, MN: University of Minnesota Press, 1987.
Habermas, Jürgen, *Between Facts and Norms*. Cambridge: MIT, 1996.
White, Stephen, *The Cambridge Companion to Habermas*. Cambridge: Cambridge University Press, 1995.

Communitarian Justice

Daly, Markate, *Communitarianism*. Belmont: Wadsworth, 1994.
Hegel, G. W. F., *Philosophy of Right*. Trans. T. M. Knox. New York: Oxford University Press, 1962. (Originally published 1921.)
Horton, John, and Mendus, Susan, Eds., *After MacIntyre*. Notre Dame, IN: University of Notre Dame Press, 1994.
Kymlika, W., *Liberalism, Community and Culture*. Oxford: Oxford University Press, 1989.
MacIntyre, Alasdair, *After Virtue*. Notre Dame, IN: University of Notre Dame Press, 1981.
Sandel, Michael, *Democracy's Discontent*. Cambridge: Harvard University Press, 1996.

Feminist Justice

Held, Virginia, *Justice and Care,* Boulder, CO: Westview Press, 1995.
Kourany, Janet, James Sterba, and Rosemarie Tong, *Feminist Philosophies*. 2nd edition. Upper Saddle River, NJ: Prentice Hall, 1998.
Sommers, Christina, *Who Stole Feminism?* New York: Simon and Schuster, 1994.
Tong, Rosemarie, *Feminist Thought*. 2nd edition. Boulder, CO: Westview Press, 1998.
Wollstonecraft, Mary, *A Vindication of the Rights of Women*. New York: Norton, 1967. (Originally published 1792.)
Young, Iris, *Justice and the Politics of Difference*. Princeton: Princeton University Press, 1990.

Postmodern Justice

Best, Steven, and Douglas Kellner, *Postmodern Theory*. New York: The Guilford Press, 1991.

Cahoone, Lawrence, *From Modernism to Postmodernism*. Cambridge: Blackwell, 1996.

Foucault, Michel, *The Archaeology of Knowledge*. New York: Pantheon, 1972.

Lyotard, Jean-François, *The Postmodern Condition*. Minneapolis: University of Minnesota Press, 1984.

Nicholson, Linda, *Feminism/Postmodernism*. New York: Routledge, 1990.

Rabinow, Paul, Ed., *Foucault Reader*. New York: Pantheon Books, 1984.

Environmental Justice

Carruthers, Peter. *The Animals Issue*. Cambridge: Cambridge University Press, 1992.

Gore, Al. *Earth in the Balance*. New York: Houghton Mifflin, 1992.

Hargrove, Eugene. *The Foundations of Environmental Ethics*. Englewood Cliffs, N.J.: Prentice-Hall, 1988.

Plumwood, Val. *Feminism and the Mastery of Nature*. London: Routledge, 1993.

Rachels, James. *Created from Animals*. Oxford: Oxford University Press, 1990.

Regan, T. *The Case for Animal Rights*. Berkeley: University of California Press, 1984.

Singer, P. *Animal Liberation* (rev. ed.). New York: New York Review, 1990.

Stone, C. *Earth and Other Ethics*. New York: Harper & Row, 1987.

Ohio Reading Aicle

9th Grade   1978

Get Those Rebounds!

Get
Those
Rebounds!

by
LES ETTER

Illustrated by James Calvin

HASTINGS HOUSE, PUBLISHERS
New York

Library of Congress Cataloging in Publication Data
Etter, Les.   Get those rebounds.

    SUMMARY: Although he loves basketball, sixteen-year-
old Rick is convinced he'll never attain the star status
of his older brother.

    [1. Basketball-Fiction.   2. Family life—Fiction]
I. Title.
PZ7.E858Ge   [Fic]   77-17217
ISBN 0-8038-2685-0

Published simultaneously in Canada by
Saunders of Toronto, Ltd., Don Mills, Ontario
Printed in the United States of America

Get Those Rebounds!

· CHAPTER ONE ·

RICK HANLEY stared at the mirror in the Rock Hill High School dressing room. His swollen cheekbone, cut and bleeding, stood out against his dark skin. His ribs ached, and when he clenched his right fist, the knuckles stung.

The blast of Coach Kenney's whistle still rang in his ears. So did the coach's words: "Get off the floor, Hanley! I'll have no fighting on this squad! Get showered and dressed, but don't leave. I want to see you after practice!"

Rick had stalked off the court in silence. He didn't even wait to see if Joe Smallwood made the free throw. Hadn't Kenney seen Joe swing his elbow under the basket? How did the coach think he got that lump on his cheek?

Smallwood always got away with murder. Joe still

played an alleyball game—shoving, holding, elbowing and tripping. But let Rick Hanley try to defend himself—that was different.

He undressed in the empty dressing room. The heck with Coack Kenney, he thought. He'd get his shower, dress, and take off. No use hanging around for another chewing out.

Rick looked into the mirror once more as he brushed his hair. Something in the reflection reminded him of his brother Bill. A wave of guilt swept through him. What would Bill think if he knew about this?

Rick grew bitter as he studied his own ungainly body in the glass, with its spindly arms and legs. Any resemblance between that body and Bill's was strictly accidental. You couldn't look at it no other way,—just no other way.

Bill Hanley was a legend at Rock Hill High. He had led the Rockets to two state championships his last two seasons. Then he had gone on to college to become a two-time All-American. When he graduated, the Los Angeles Lakers were waiting for him with a fat contract. Last year the mayor of Rock City had proclaimed a "Bill Hanley Day" and the whole city had turned out. That was when Rick was trying desperately to make the Rock Hill freshmen team— and failing.

Bill had been his idol ever since he could remember. Bill had taught him how to play basketball. No kid ever had a better big brother.

But as he grew older, Rick began to notice differences between them. He could not learn to do the things Bill did so naturally. The harder he tried, the worse he looked. Then all at once he was a teen-ager, and a 6-foot one who still had room to "shoot up" as his parents called it. He felt lanky and awkward, and his muscles never obeyed his will.

He still remembered the day a couple of men had stopped to watch him shooting baskets on the playground. He missed an easy shot and leaped for the rebound, missed, and sprawled in the dust.

Both men had laughed. "That kid is Bill Hanley's brother?" asked one. "You've got to be kidding!"

Rick froze. That was the first time he had seen the vast difference between Bill and himself. The hurt inside him grew as things got worse instead of better.

Sometimes, some wise guy would grin at him and ask, "Say, aren't you Bill Hanley's brother? Kid, you'd better get some meat on your bones if you're going to be anything like the star."

Rick couldn't help getting angry and embarrassed, but he never came up with any quick, witty answers the way other guys did. By the time he thought up a real crusher, the wise guy was long gone.

But he loved basketball, and he would not quit. During summers he got into pickup games, although he soon learned that nobody wanted him on their side. He was too light to muscle under the basket, and he was a lousy outside shot. These games were

rough—alleyball games they called them—where anything went. The guy who fouled the most was the
hero.

He was surprised when he tried out for the Rock
Hill freshman squad—and made it. When he first
heard them reel off the list of names, he thought he
had heard wrong. But he checked over the coach's
shoulder, and sure enough, his name was there.

The coach looked up at him and smiled. "You're
Rick Hanley, aren't you?"

Rick nodded, trying to think of something to say.

"Bill's brother," the coach went on, half to himself. "We'll be glad to have a Hanley on the team
again."

"Thanks coach," he said, swallowing the lump in
his throat, the one that always came at any mention of
Bill. "I hope I'll live up to the name."

Someone laughed. He turned around to face a
boy he'd never seen before. "Your name is all you've
got, Hanley. I saw you try out today. You looked like
a lame giraffe."

That was the beginning of his feud with Joe
Smallwood. Joe was a wiry kid, with all the moves of
the natural athlete. Whenever Rick made the slightest
mistake, Joe was ready with some comment that made
the whole team laugh. By the end of the season Rick
knew he'd had enough of Joe Smallwood.

This year he'd made the Jayvee squad by the skin
of his teeth. But he still had his problems. In an early

practice, as the Jayvees went through a simple shooting drill with Jim Saylor, the assistant coach, he'd
blown a layup. There was no one near him but somehow he got his feet crossed and he fell with a crash.
Even the coach grinned as he got up, red-faced and
angry.

Joe Smallwood had been behind him, waiting his
turn to shoot. "Hey, Rick!" he had cried. "What's
that—your stork shot? You learn that from Bill?"

All of Rick's pent-up fury exploded in a round-
house swing to Joe's jaw. The surprised player tum-
bled backward to the floor. As Smallwood struggled to
his feet, Rick swung again. He missed, and Jim Saylor
seized his arms.

"Get over to the bench and cool off!" Saylor
snapped. "Try that again and you're off the squad!"

As he sat on the bench, Rick admitted that Smallwood's gibe had not even been worth answering, and
his own reaction had been even dumber. Later he
told Saylor he was sorry.

"I didn't mean to blow up. It was my fault."

"All right," Saylor said wearily. "Shake hands with
Joe and go get your shower."

Shake hands with Joe! That was about the last
thing he wanted to do, thought Rick as he trudged
across the court. But he went up to Joe and muttered,
"Saylor said to shake hands and forget about it."

Smallwood started to sneer, but he saw the assistant coach watching him from across the gym. He

stuck out his hand and let Rick touch it. Neither boy smiled.

As he headed for the shower, still scowling, Rick's friend Rudy Thompson caught up to him. "Don't worry about it Rick," Rudy advised. "Joe's just a smart punk."

Rick shrugged and kept on walking. "I don't know. Sometimes I think Joe's right. Who else but me could have bungled that lay-up like that?"

"My dad's seen you play. He says you're just growing too fast right now. When you stop growing your head and body will get to know each other and you'll be okay."

"Where did he get that idea?"

"He's a doctor. He knows."

Rick had to smile at the blond, curly-haired guard. "Thanks, Rudy. But by then I'll be an old man. What about right now?"

That had been a year ago. Right now meant today, even the next few minutes, for Rick Hanley. Now he must face Coach Kenney and probably the end of his basketball career at Rock Hill High.

When the squad streamed in, panting and noisy, Rudy Thompson stopped beside Rick again. "Coach wants you upstairs right away," Rudy said. "He asked me to tell you. Good luck buddy. I'll wait around."

Suddenly Rick was angry again. Why make a big deal out of this? He didn't want any preaching from the coach. Just get it over. "Don't bother, Rudy," he said shortly. "I don't need anybody to hold my hand."

"Don't be like that," Rudy said as he slapped a towel across his back and went to shower. "You know how Coach is. Take it easy and he'll probably let you off. Pop off, and you've had it."

"I've already had it," Rick shrugged, heading for the stairs.

Coach Kenney's tiny office was on a balcony over-looking the gym floor. As Rick climbed the steps some of his anger faded, but he dreaded the scene ahead. He halted abruptly when he saw the office door partly open and heard voices inside.

"I don't want to give up on the boy, Jim," he heard Kenney say. "But we can't have this fighting and hard feeling. That can infect the whole squad."

The coach sighed. "This kid's not like Bill—he's moody and he's got a temper. Bill was steady as a rock. I will say this for Rick—he tries hard. Maybe if we suspend him for a few days he'll simmer down."

Saylor's retort echoed through the empty hall. "Why bother—we've got enough problems. It's not just his temper—the kid simply hasn't got it. Bill's got all the talent in the family. The sooner this kid learns that, the better."

"I can't drop him from the squad. After all, I owe Bill that much."

Rick stood frozen in his tracks, sick at what he

heard. He tried to turn silently and go back downstairs. But a board creaked loudly under his feet. The two men in the office stopped talking instantly.

Coach Kenney looked around the door. 'Oh, Rick," he said, "Come in. We're waiting for you."

Rick took a half-step toward the stairway. Then he stopped. He might be Bill's no-good kid brother, but he was still Rick Hanley, and no coward.

Both men watched him as he entered the office. "Sit down, Rick," Kenney said. "We've got to get something straightened out."

"That's not necessary, Coach," Rick blurted. "I know what you're going to say. I couldn't help hearing you just now. I don't want to be a drag around here. I'll clean out my locker tomorrow."

That was all he could manage to say before he walked out of the office. Before either coach could speak, Rick dashed down the stairs.

Behind him he heard Kenney shout. "Wait, Rick! Come back here for a minute—"

The outside door banged shut against the coach's words. Rick ran through the darkness, across the football field, past the stands and into the street. He didn't stop until he was sobbing for breath. Then he turned toward home.

·CHAPTER TWO·

"You're late," Rick's mother greeted him with a smile. She was a slender pleasant-faced woman with skin a shade darker than her son's. "But I saved your dinner for you. The rest of us got hungry and ate." That meant herself, his father, and Francine, his thirteen-year-old sister.

"No thanks, Mom," Rick muttered, "I'm not hungry."

His mother's eyes widened. "You—not hungry!" she exclaimed. "Are you sick, honey? You *do* look done in." She looked at him more closely. "Don't tell me that Mr. Kenney is working you kids that hard!"

Rick swallowed the lump in his throat. The family had to know sometime; it might as well be now. "I—

I—well, I quit the squad—I'm all through," he said, adding quickly "I was going to get cut off soon, anyway."

His mother's soft brown eyes searched his face. "What's really happened, Rick? More trouble?"

"Yeah, I guess so, Mom. I tangled with Smallwood again."

"Oh, Rick—not Joe again! When will you learn to keep your temper? You can't go around hitting everyone who gets in your way!"

"I didn't mean to, mom, but Smallwood—he really bugs me. He's always bad-mouthing me. When he gave me an elbow under the basket—well, I popped him."

Rick heard the rustle of a newspaper in the living room, then the sound of his father's heavy footsteps coming toward the kitchen. His dad was a big man, tall and wide-shouldered like Bill, who resembled him closely.

"What's this I hear? Something about quitting the squad? How come? I thought you were doing better this year."

"Coach Kenney doesn't think so," replied Rick. He felt uneasy under his father's steady gaze. "He was going to cut me anyway, so I quit."

"Kenney drop you—Bill's brother?" His father sounded doubtful. "That's hard to believe. Why, nobody ever heard of Kenney until Bill came along! Rock Hill hasn't even got past the first round of the

State tournament since he graduated. Besides, I know you're not that bad—not Bill's—"

Rick's lips tightened. Here we go again, he thought—Bill's brother! Couldn't anyone understand that he might want to be something on his own? All his life it had been Bill who brought home the prizes, the trophies, the troops of hungry boys after basketball practices on cold autumn afternoons. And now, even after Bill had been gone over a year, Rick still felt like "the star's" younger brother.

"Oh, hush!" cried Mrs. Hanley to her husband. "That's no way to talk! Let Rick tell you what really happened."

Rick's father waited silently.

Reluctantly Rick repeated what he'd told his mother. He saw his father's eyes harden behind his glasses. Then his face relaxed as he listened.

"What's so bad about that?" he asked his wife. "Kids are always getting into scraps. That's a sign they're healthy—got spirit." He looked at Rick. "Of course, you can't go around slugging people, Rick— your mother's right, there. That's part of sports, to learn to control yourself. Kenney understands that, too. Why not go back and see him? Tell him you're sorry. I'll bet he'll take you back in a minute."

Rick felt the anger inside him rise as he looked down at the floor. "Not me, Dad," he said flatly. "I already told him I quit. Besides, I'm low man on the Jayvees now. I'd never have a chance."

His father stared at him. "You mean you're just dropping out? That's not the way Bill would handle it."

"I'm not Bill, Dad!" Rick burst out. "Bill's a great athlete! He's a superstar! He's got everything all the tools—always had it. I'm just his kid brother. That doesn't make me great. I want to make it on my own, whatever I am. I want to be *Rick* Hanley!"

"So what're you going to do—take up prize-fighting?" his father retorted. "Even in boxing, the first thing you've got to learn is to keep your temper."

"Now Joe," protested Mrs. Hanley. "We're getting nowhere with everybody shouting at each other."

His father shrugged. "I guess you're right, Mary," he said. "I'm sorry." He turned to Rick. "I'll leave the decision to you. Maybe one star athlete in the family is enough. It's hard to understand, though—you've always been so crazy about basketball. I hope you don't miss it. If you do, maybe I can find something for you to do at the plant in your free time. You could pick up a few extra bucks, you know.

"Rick can spend the extra time on his studies," Mrs. Hanley suggested. "Besides, playing basketball every day is too much for a boy growing as fast as he is. He's not even sixteen, and he's over six feet tall."

"Six feet!" cried Rick. "Six feet, two and a half, Mom!"

"All right—and what do you weigh—one hundred and thirty pounds?"

Rick's lips tightened again. "More than that!" he protested. "At least one-thirty-seven."

"Let's see," said his father thoughtfully. "When Bill was your age he weighed the same as I did at sixteen—one hundred and seventy-two."

"Oh, let's not have any more of that—sounds like we're raising beef for the market." Mrs. Hanley looked at Rick in alarm. "My goodness! We've been talking so much, you haven't eaten a bite—and all this talk about gaining weight!"

Suddenly Rick was very hungry. His mother bustled about the kitchen and in a moment set a plate of chicken and rice before him.

"Put that away," she said. "There's good solid muscle in that."

After he had finished dinner, he felt better. His mother began to clear the dishes. He got up to go.

"Rick—"

He stopped in the doorway.

"Rick, maybe all these years you thought you had to play basketball just because Bill did."

"That's not true, Mom, I love basketball!" he blurted out and then bit his lip. He could already hear her next question—then why did you quit?

Just then the phone rang. Relieved, Rick started toward his room as his mother picked up the receiver. But then he heard her exclaim,

"Bill! Well isn't this a surprise! How are you? Just a second, let me get Dad on the other phone."

He stopped in the hallway. Now he'd have to tell Bill about his decision to quit the team. What could he say? Bill had spent hours coaching him last time he was home, promising Rick if he practiced he'd be able to make the Jayvees. And he'd been right. What would he think when he found out it was all for nothing, that his younger brother wasn't going to play basketball anymore?

Rick heard his Dad picking up the phone in the living room, and he leaned against the wall with a sinking feeling. Now Bill would get the story before he even had a chance to explain!

But Mr. Hanley didn't say a word about the day's events. Maybe he's hoping Coach Kenney will ask me back, thought Rick. I bet Dad doesn't want to admit that I won't be a basketball star.

"Rick!" his mother called. "Bill's on the phone and wants to talk to you!"

Rick went reluctantly into the kitchen and took the receiver from her.

"Hi, Bill."

"Hey, how's it going!" his brother's deep cheerful voice greeted him. "I thought I'd just surprise you folks and give you a call. How's the Jayvee squad?"

Rick swallowed the lump in his throat. He closed his eyes and answered in a low voice, "Pretty good, I guess."

"No news? Practices rough?"

"Oh no . . . not more than usual."

"Well, it's good to hear your voice again. Tell Coach Kenney I said hi, and that things are as hectic as ever."

"Sure. I will next time I talk to him," Rick answered, thinking that there wouldn't be a next time. "Well, I gotta go, Bill. Here's mom again."

He handed the phone to his mother without looking at her. After she had said goodbye, Rick murmured,

"I'll write him a letter or something. I just didn't feel like telling him right then."

His mother smiled and said gently, "Changes are always hard to get used to. But I'm sure it will all work out for the best."

·CHAPTER THREE·

THE NEXT FEW days dragged by for Rick. He dreaded the afternoons most of all, especially when Rudy and the other guys left the study hall for practice.

Once he even started to join them without thinking. He sat down so quickly that his knee banged his desk and everyone looked around. He saw Joe Smallwood grinning at him. It would be that creep, he thought.

When the desire to at least watch practice became almost too strong for him a week later, he hiked the eight blocks to McKerson Furniture, the factory where his dad was production foreman.

"So you want to get your mind off basketball?" his father asked, smiling. "Come with me. We can use some help in the shipping department."

It did not take Rick long, however, to become

bored with the routine work. The ache and resentment returned. Rudy Thompson was no help either.
Rudy either dropped by his house or called him on
the phone to tell him about practice. And when he
picked up the local newspaper, there was always
something about the Lakers. The Rock Hill sports editor still played up Bill's name.

Rick became even more restless when the Jayvee
team approached its first game with a smaller school
in a nearby town. Rudy had told him that Smallwood
was slated to start at center. Rick was glad the Jayvee
opener would be away from home.

That evening he saw a column of City Recreation
League basketball scores on the local sport page. The
City League results seldom registered with Rick. But
now he began to read the few brief paragraphs that
highlighted the more important games.

Suddenly his interest perked up. He spotted the
name of Ted Newcombe, a guy in his science class.
Ted was the best student in the class, a wiry, dark-
haired kid with glasses. Rick had not known he played
basketball, but the newspaper account said Newcombe led the scoring in the junior division of the
League for boys under 18. What would it be like to
play in that league? He rubbed the palms of his hands
on the arms of his chair. They itched to hold a basketball again.

Next day after class, he spoke to Newcombe.
"Congratulations," he said. "I didn't know you played

basketball until I saw your name in the paper last night."

Newcombe smiled with pleasure. "Gee thanks, Rick," he said. "I didn't know anybody ever looked at our scores except the players and maybe their families."

"Do you think there's a chance for me to get into the league?"

The other boy eyed him doubtfully. "You're not putting me on are you? Aren't you playing with the Jayvee squad?"

"Past tense. I *used* to play," replied Rick. "I—I sort of got cut—some things happened. I'd sure like to play basketball some place."

Ted Newcombe gripped his arm. "Man, I hope you're serious! Do we need a tall center! Our guy is the shortest one in the league, and we get hurt badly off the boards. We've got only one tall guy, and he's our best outside shot, but he's not as big as you. Our speed has helped us so far, and we've got the best coach in the league."

"Who is he?" asked Rick. "Some former high school coach?"

"No sir. Don't tell me you've never heard of Jerry Caswell?"

Rick looked at Ted in amazement. Jerry Caswell was an All-America from a small black college in Kentucky. "Is that the Jerry Caswell who led the NCAA in scoring when he played for Mountain Central? The guy who almost took them to the national champion-ship?"

"That's our coach," cried Newcombe proudly. "He's also the new pastor at the Second Baptist Church!"

"How come he's not playing with the pros?" Rick asked suddenly. "A big star like him?"

"We asked him that, too," said Ted seriously. "He said he felt he could do more good as a minister. He's a real dedicated man. Wait until you meet him. He's great!"

Rick frowned suddenly. "But I don't belong to the Baptist Church. Neither do my folks."

"I don't either," Ted said. "This is a city league team. As long as you're under eighteen, and not play-ing with any other outfit, you're eligible. Of course, you've got to keep in training and live up to the rules."

"That sounds fine," he remarked. "What do I do next?"

"We practice at the church gym tomorrow night at seven," Ted said. "Come around about twenty min-utes early, and I'll introduce you to Jerry."

"I'll be there," Rick answered eagerly.

He felt better than he had in a long time. When he got home, he dropped his books on the lawn and went to shoot a few baskets in the driveway. Jerry Caswell, thought Rick. A new coach—a whole new team—and no Joe Smallwood. Now he had a real chance.

Rick hurried inside. "I'm home, Mom!" he called. He went into his room and saw a letter lying on his dresser.

It was from Bill! As always, he tore the envelope open and read avidly all the inside stories on the national teams.

"I'm glad you wrote me about quitting Rock Hill's team," Rick read. "But I bet it won't keep you away from basketball long."

Rick put the letter down, smiling. Sometimes he could almost feel lucky to have an older brother like Bill, someone who felt the same way he did about basketball. If only it didn't mean living up to Bill's reputation. Well, wait until his brother heard the news!

His parents were delighted when he told them at dinner. "Jerry Caswell—the All-American?" His father beamed at him.

"I'm so glad, Rick," his mother added. "It looks like maybe you needed basketball after all."

"What do you mean, needed basketball?" his father snorted. "He's a Hanley, isn't he? Basketball needs him!"

·CHAPTER FOUR·

AFTER AN EARLY dinner the next day, Rick packed his basketball gear and hurried to the church gym. He arrived so early that no one was there, not even Newcombe. A light drizzle began to fall, and a chill wind whipped around the corner.

Rick tried the door but it was locked. As he rattled it in disgust, a deep voice sounded behind him. "Looking for someone, son? Can I help you?"

Rick turned to see a tall, well-built black man smiling at him. He wore a sweatshirt beneath an open windbreaker, gray slacks and basketball shoes.

"I'm waiting for Ted Newcombe," Rick replied. "I'm to meet him here to see if I can try out for the team."

"Well, I'm glad to hear that. We can use all the help we can get, and you've got something we're missing—height. I'm the coach, Reverend Caswell—Jerry to my friends. And you are—?"

"Rick Hanley." He accepted the huge hand the minister thrust forward.

"Hanley, eh?" said Reverend Caswell. "Let's get out of the rain where we can talk until the others come." He unlocked the door and switched on the lights. The gym was small but well-kept.

The minister repeated Rick's name. "Hanley," he said. "Any relation to Bill Hanley?" he asked. "I understand he came from around here. I never played against him in college, but I saw him play a couple of times. He was one of the best, and still is."

"I'm just his kid brother," replied Rick. "That's it, period." He tried to sound light and witty but the words seemed flat and bitter.

Reverend Caswell nodded. "Oh?" he said. There was a questioning look in his eyes.

"I didn't mean it to sound that way," Rick said hastily. "What I mean is—Bill's the basketball player in the family. I'm crazy about the game—but it looks like that's all I am—just crazy." Then he added, "I sort of lost out in the Jayvee squad at school, but I'd like to play somewhere."

Jerry Caswell was quiet as he studied Rick.

Rick felt he hadn't been quite honest. He took a deep breath. "I got into some fights in scrimmage," he blurted. "But I was going to be cut anyway." There it was. He stared back at Caswell defiantly.

"I'm glad you told me," replied the minister. "But it's what you do from now on that matters, right?"

The door banged open. Ted Newcombe and two other boys hurried in out of the rain. "Sorry we're late, Coach," Ted apologized. "I had to pick up these two guys, and it's slippery driving." He turned to Rick. "Guess you've already met Jerry. You tell him you want to join us?"

Caswell smiled. "He told me. What do you fellows think?"

"Okay!" cried the others together.

The shorter of Ted's two companions shook his head. "Just my luck," he said. "You must be all of six-two. There goes my center job—unless you can lend me a few inches. He grinned and thrust out his hand. "I'm Stan Maxwell," he said.

Rick liked Maxwell instantly. As Newcombe had told him, Stan was short for a center, but he was husky. His face was freckled, he had a thatch of reddish brown hair and a wide smile.

"Glad to know you," replied Rick. "But about those inches—no way. Height is all I've got."

Russ Williams, the other boy, was black, almost as tall and scrawny as Rick. His arms and legs were long and thin, too. There was something familiar about him.

"Haven't I seen you somewhere before?" Rick asked. "Maybe at Rock Hill High?"

"Could be," replied Williams. He was a good-looking kid with a grave smile. "I was on the freshman team there a few days last year. I had to drop out of school when my father died.

"I've got a job now at McKerson's. Between Mom and me, we get by."

"McKerson's!" exclaimed Rick. My dad works there, too. He's a foreman."

"I know," replied Russ Williams, smiling. "He hired me. A real nice man."

Ted Newcombe spoke up quickly. "Come on, guys, let's move it. The rest of the gang is coming."

Rick was impressed with Caswell as the coach put the squad through some warm-up drills. Caswell made his points quickly and clearly as he gave directions.

It was soon clear to Rick that aside from Newcombe, Russ Williams was the best player on the squad. Russ was long-geared like himself, but he had a certain cat-like quickness and he could shoot. With more weight and strength, he was certain to become a fine player.

Stan Maxwell surprised Rick as the scrimmage began. The shorter boy outleaped him on the tipoff. Then he stole a pair of rebounds under the basket. Maxwell might lack height, but he never stopped trying.

Buster Hinton, a pint-sized black kid, and Pete DeLong, a slow but rugged player, held the guard positions. Hinton was a good dribbler and the fastest man down the floor. DeLong wore a head band to keep the blond hair out of his eyes. After a few minutes Caswell halted the workout. "Hanley," he said, "you've got to make better use of your reach. When you're near the basket, keep your hands up all the time. "Reach—reach—stretch as high as you can for the ball! Get those hands on it! And watch for someone to pass to!"

Rick began to tire from the stiff pace as scrimmage was resumed. Caswell coached a running type of game. Rick had never played so long in one stretch before. His feet felt heavy and he panted for breath.

Suddenly Williams whipped the ball to him beneath the basket. It slapped into his hands for a perfect layup. Rick forgot his weary body as he leaped high. Two points!

"That's the way, Rick!" the coach shouted. Rick was still elated when the scrimmage ended, tired as he was. He started toward the dressing room as Caswell blew his whistle. "We'll wind up with the usual wind sprints," he ordered. "Get set!"

Wind sprints! Rick wondered if he could run another step. Man—this coach was a real slave-driver! When the session finally ended Rick dragged himself to his locker and collapsed on the bench in front of it.

Caswell walked over and smiled down at him. "No use asking if you're tired," he said warmly. "But remember, this is a game of legs. The fellows you play against will be tired, too. Maybe even more than you are. That's why you've got to push yourself a little harder each day. You're going to play a lot for us, Hanley—I want you to have the stamina to do it."

Tired as he was, Rick managed a smile. He felt a glow he'd never known at Rock Hill High. Jerry Caswell had faith in him. He would do something about it.

·CHAPTER FIVE·

RICK PLAYED his first game for the Warriors against the Forreston Rangers in the Rock Hill Civic Center. Last year the Rangers had beaten them twice, but this was a new season.

Although he had not played with the Warriors before, Rick felt the closeness and determination among his new teammates. A year ago they had finished near the bottom of the junior division standings. The players had been discouraged and hopeless.

But Jerry Caswell had changed all that. Ted Newcombe voiced the Warriors' new feeling. "We're going to win this Forreston game to show Jerry what we can do. If we can take them, we've got a chance against anybody in this league."

Rick sensed the tension as soon as he entered the dressing room before the game. There was a world of difference between the way he felt now and the way he had felt when he first talked to Newcombe about joining the squad. Then he had just wanted a chance to play basketball again. There would be no pressure. Tonight all he could think of was how well he must play.

Caswell spoke to Rick briefly. "We'll start Maxwell at center because he's more experienced," the coach said. "But you're going to play a lot tonight. Just remember one thing—you've got the height to get those rebounds. So get 'em! The Rangers are bigger and they're good shots. But they can't score without the ball!"

Rick watched Maxwell lose the opening tip-off to his taller rival as the game began. A pair of accurate passes led to the Rangers' first basket. A moment later Pete DeLong's pass was intercepted, and the Warriors trailed, 4–0.

The Rangers lead shot up to eight points as the Warriors remained scoreless. The taller Forreston boys owned the backboards.

Caswell tapped Rick's shoulder. "Stan's having trouble clearing the boards," he said. "Let's see what you can do."

Rick struggled out of his sweat shirt. In his hurry to reach the court, he stumbled awkwardly. The coach called to him. "Take it easy, Hanley! Report to the scorer's table first!"

His ears burned when he heard several fans hoot

as he bent over the scorer's table to report his entry into the lineup. "Easy does it, son," one of the men at the table said. "They won't start without you."

Russ Williams came over to meet him. "Watch your man," he whispered. "He'll try the same pick and roll he used on Maxwell. "You're as tall as he is— stay with him and watch his baseline fake."

Rick nodded. He had watched the Rangers center from the bench. But trying to stop him near the basket was something else, he soon discovered.

Back on defense he saw the Rangers sweep toward him behind a two man screen. The ball came in high to the center. The Ranger pivot man made a sweeping hook shot that missed, and leaped up for the rebound.

Rick's hand caught his opponent's shoulder as they went up for the ball. The whistle sounded, and the Ranger sank one free throw. The Warriors trailed, 9–0.

Buster Hinton took the inbounds pass and dribbled swiftly up the court. Rick hurried toward the basket as Buster's hasty shot bounced off the backboard, straight into his hands. He held the ball high and pitched to Newcombe. Ted dribbled once, then fired a jumper through the net to put the Warriors on the scoreboard, 9–2.

The Rangers speeded up to force the Warriors back on defense. Rick remembered Williams' warning about the Ranger center's fake, and managed to block the shot before he stumbled off balance.

Williams scooped up the bounding ball and flipped it to Hinton far down the court. Buster was open for an easy shot to give the Warriors another two points. Then Newcombe raised them to six with his first basket of the game. But the Rangers spurted and still led 17–11 as the first quarter ended.

The redheaded Ranger center leaned hard on Rick at both ends of the court. He was strong, quick and rough. But the referee saw him hack Rick's arm, and Rick scored his first point as a Warrior on the free throw attempt. A minute later he tapped in a rebound for his first basket.

Midway in the second period Rick began to tire. The constant racing up and down the floor and the pushing and shoving around the basket made him pant for breath. Both of his knees were skinned in a fall. Another fall knocked the wind out of him.

Rick was happy when Maxwell came in to relieve him. That was the longest stretch he had ever played, even in the Rock Hill Jayvee practice sessions. His legs ached and the sweat stung his eyes as he sank down on the bench. He knew he had played well and it was a good feeling. But the Warriors still trailed at halftime, 25–22.

Rick did not see action again until late in the third period. Both teams were tired and shooting wildly. Maxwell had picked up three personal fouls as he struggled against the Ranger post man.

As Rick took his place beneath the basket, Hinton faked a pass to him, and then hooked in a shot behind the Ranger guarding him. Newcombe tied it up with a free throw at 33 all.

In the final period, the score was still even at 45–45, with two minutes left in the game. When Rick blew a layup and lost the rebound out of bounds, the Rangers moved ahead, 47–45. Williams sank a free throw to cut the Rangers' lead to a single point.

The red light on the clock showed 50 seconds left. The Rangers held the ball and began to play keep away with it. They wanted to play the clock and keep the Warriors from ever attempting the go-ahead shot.

Buster Hinton hounded a Ranger forward and slapped the ball away. He managed to control it and dribble down the court. From his spot beneath the basket, Rick waved at him frantically. But Buster threw to Newcombe in a corner.

Two Rangers thrust their hands in front of Ted's face to block his shot. But Newcombe wheeled and fired to Rick in the open underneath.

The winning points were on Rick's fingertips. But he shot too quickly. The ball caromed off the back of the rim.

An alert Ranger gobbled it up and fired it far up the floor. A waiting teammate took it and dribbled in for an easy basket. When the final whistle blew the Rangers still led, 49–46.

Rick shook his head dazedly. How could he have missed an easy shot like that? He started slowly off the court, his head hanging. Someone whacked him across the shoulders. "Man—what kind of luck was that?" asked Russ Williams. "Don't let that get you down!"

"I just plain blew it, that's all," replied Rick feebly.

Jerry Caswell met him at the sideline. "Too bad Rick," he said. "You played a good game but you must learn to relax on a shot like that. Never hurry an easy one. I ought to know—I've missed plenty of them myself. All right, boys—get your showers. Then we'll start thinking about the next game."

·CHAPTER SIX·

WHEN RICK AWOKE Saturday morning, he could hear his mother making breakfast. He flexed his long legs beneath the covers and sighed contentedly. The soreness was gone. Then he winced as he turned over; someone had dug a sharp elbow into his ribs. But the twinge was not enough to wipe out the good feeling he had about the game.

He recalled Russ Williams' encouragement and his pat on the back. And Jerry Caswell's quiet words. Hinton, Ted Newcombe and Pete DeLong—a good bunch of guys! He was going to enjoy this season.

As he lay there, he thought about Russ. What kind of life did Williams have aside from basketball? All he knew about Russ was that he'd dropped out of school to help support his family.

His mother's voice broke up his thoughts. "Everybody up!" she cried cheerfully. "Pancakes!"

As they finished eating, his sister Francie announced with all the importance of her thirteen years that she was going shopping. "Can I have my allowance now?" she asked.

"After you've helped with the dishes and cleaned your room," said Mrs. Hanley.

While the usual argument went on, Rick turned to his father. "Do you remember a kid at the plant named Russ Williams?" he asked. "A tall skinny kid about my size?"

"Sure—I hired him a few months ago, after his father passed away. I hear he's a great worker, and smart enough to get a raise soon. Too bad he had to quit school."

"Guess what; Russ is on our basketball team."

"No kidding. Is he good?"

"He's *really* good, Dad."

Mr. Hanley nudged his son. "Not as good as a Hanley, is he?"

"Probably better," Rick retorted, but he kept his smile. "What about the rest of the family? The only thing Russ told me is that his mother works too."

"Well, I always liked his dad. He worked for us for a long time. And I believe there are six children in all. His older brother, Frank, and four younger sisters."

"He has a brother?"

"In name if nothing else. Frank is different—a

wild sort of kid. He tried working for us, but he didn't last long. Always late, always taking time off. When he didn't show up for almost a week we had to let him go. That was the last I saw of him."

Mr. Hanley sighed. "It's too bad. When he lost his job his mother came to me but I couldn't do a thing. Later I heard he was mixed up in some kind of trouble. He should be helping to support the family so Russ can finish school."

Mr. Hanley got up from the table. "I've got some things to do this morning, but I'll be back in time to watch the football game on TV."

"Speaking of TV," said Mrs. Hanley, "Bill's on the tube Sunday afternoon. The Lakers play the Knicks in the Garden."

"What do you know!" exclaimed her husband. "We mustn't miss that!"

Rick decided to take a long hike after breakfast to loosen up his legs. It was a perfect day for walking, a crisp, sunny December morning. He thought again about Russ Williams. Some people got awful bad breaks. He wondered what Frank Williams was really like.

Gradually he stepped up his stride. Before he realized it, he had turned left on the broad, tree-lined avenue that led past the Baptist Church. Rick was about to pass the building when he saw two bikes parked beside the gym in the rear. He halted as he heard the muffled thump of a basketball inside.

Who could be working out there this time of the

day? His curiosity brought him along the flag-stone walk to the door. He opened it quietly. To his surprise he saw Russ in an old sweat shirt and jeans, shooting baskets one after another. Jerry Caswell watched him from the sidelines.

Caswell saw Rick in the doorway. "Come in and join the party," he called across the gym. "We're working on Russ's jump shot. Get your shoes and loosen up with a few baskets."

"Okay," said Rick eagerly. "I'll be right back."

Caswell glanced at his watch. "You know, I think I'll join you fellows. I've got a half hour or so to spare."

In a few minutes all three were popping the ball at the basket. Caswell was heavier than he had been in college, but he was still loose and agile. Rick marveled at the way he swished the ball through the net from all angles. The pros had lost a great player when Jerry Caswell became a minister.

"Get that jumper off quicker, Russ," the coach told Williams. "Get up higher. It's too easy to block your shots if you don't. And try a head fake—like this—just before you make your move."

Later they played a one-on-one game, in which the player with the ball tried to drive around a lone defender to score.

"Watch Earl Monroe of the Knicks on TV, or Dr. J— fellows like that, if you want to see how it's done," said Caswell.

When Rick took his place against Caswell, the minister dribbled in from midcourt. He faked to the left, then fired a jump shot off his right hand. He hardly seemed to look at the basket but the ball didn't even ripple the net on its way through.

"Work up a good feint to make the defensive man hesitate. He'll try to outguess you—but it's that split-second that counts."

As they took a breather, Caswell motioned Rick over to his side. "Your stride is too long when you dribble. You can't change direction quickly enough if you stretch out like that. Shorten your steps and dribble closer to the floor. You'll have better balance and you can protect the ball better."

Forty minutes passed before Caswell looked at the time. "I've got to leave," he said. "You fellows stick around if you want to. Just be sure everything is locked when you go."

By noon the two boys finally had enough. "How come you came down here this morning?" Rick asked Williams as they dressed.

"Last week I asked the coach if I could practice here by myself if I swept out the gym and mopped the dressing room. I've got to clean the place now."

"I'll help you," Rick said. Then he had another idea. "How'd you like to come over to my house tomorrow afternoon and watch the Lakers and Knicks on TV? My brother's playing."

Russ's eyes lit. "Sure—We've got an old TV at

home, but try and use it! The girls have a half dozen programs they battle over."

Outside the gym as they left, Russ took an old bike from the rack. "This baby isn't much but it gets me back and forth to work. Good for my legs, too. I'm no hunk of muscle like Caswell."

Rick eyed his own body. "I wouldn't complain. Look at me."

Williams looked him over and said shyly, "You know—you're not as clumsy as you looked when I first saw you play. You were really loose today."

"You just made my week!" exclaimed Rick. "See you Sunday."

They enjoyed the Laker-Knicks game. The whole family was gathered around the TV set, and Mrs. Hanley passed cookies around. To top it off, the Lakers beat the Knicks in an overtime thriller by three points. And Bill Hanley scored 23 for Los Angeles.

"So that's your brother," Russ murmured when it was over. His face clouded over. "Guess I'd better take off now," he said abruptly. After thanking Mrs. Hanley, he left the house.

Rick watched from the window as his new friend pedaled down the street. He wondered at the sudden change in Russ's manner. Was he thinking of his own brother?

·CHAPTER SEVEN·

AS THE WEEKS passed, Rick Hanley realized he was living in two worlds. One was his daily life at home and school. The other centered around the Warriors.

The world at school meant seeing Joe Smallwood every day. But things weren't as bad as he'd anticipated. In fact, except for a mumbled "Hi" or a nod, Joe had been ignoring him.

"I guess now that I'm off Jayvees," Rick told Rudy one morning as they walked to school, "Joe's forgotten about me."

Rudy shifted his backpack onto his left shoulder. "I think Joe's forgotten about everyone lately. All *I've* seen him doing is shooting baskets."

"Really?"

"Lunch hours, after school, even after practice. It's amazing."

"Is he getting any better?" Rick tried to keep his voice even, but the old jealousy flared up in him.

"You're not kidding. Coach Kenney's been talking about him." Rudy stopped and lowered his voice a register. "That boy," he bellowed, "is gonna be our next star."

"Kenney really said that?"

Rudy nodded emphatically. They went on talking about the team, but Rick found his mind wandering. He was thinking about the next Warrior practice, and Jerry's latest pointers. Sometimes he wondered if he could keep them all straight. "Use your reach, Hanley, your reach," was what Coach Caswell said most often.

Later that day, Rick talked to Ted Newcombe after science class.

"Practice this evening," Ted greeted him.

"Right," Rick grinned. Ted had become the only link between Rick's divided interests. Ted understood what it meant to play for Jerry Caswell.

"I'm reading a book about Wilt Chamberlain," Ted held out a paperback. "I'm almost done with it. It's really great."

As they walked down the hall, they passed Coach Kenney. Flustered, Rick lowered his head hastily and started to pass him.

"Rick," Kenney exclaimed. "How are you?"

Rick looked up, his cheeks burning, but the coach was smiling at him.

"Fine, I guess, Coach."

"I saw Bill against the Knicks on TV," he said. "Twenty-three points!"

"Yeah," replied Rick somewhat lamely, "We watched him at home. He played real well."

"What about you? How's school going?"

Rick looked over at Ted. Suddenly Ted spoke up, "He's joined our junior city league, Coach, with the Warriors."

"The Warriors?" Kenney seemed to approve. "You two boys with the Warriors? That's Jerry—I mean Reverend Caswell's team, isn't it? Good going!"

Rick was surprised. "You know about him?"

Kenney laughed. "Who doesn't know about Jerry Caswell?" Then he added more quietly, "You couldn't find a better man to play for. Jerry can teach you a lot."

Rick stared at the stocky coach. Maybe Kenney wasn't such a bad guy after all, he thought. He glanced over at Ted. Ted Newcombe was definitely one of the *best* guys around.

Friday night rolled around again. This time the Warriors faced the Rockets, one of the weaker teams in the league. Rick scored four baskets and split playing time with Maxwell. They won easily.

Ted Newcombe's 18 points made him the Warriors' high point man and increased his lead as the top scorer in the junior division. He wondered why Ted wasn't playing for Rock Hill High. He certainly could make the varsity.

As they dressed afterward, Rick asked him. "How

come you didn't go out for the varsity, Ted? You'd be starting for sure."

Ted crammed his gear into his bag. "Thanks, Rick, but it's like this. I'm not big enough to ever make a college team. Besides, I'm trying for a scholarship at M.I.T. I'm no genius, so I have to study hard—it takes up all my spare time. Playing in this league doesn't cut in on the books. I need that scholarship if I'm going to become an aerospace engineer."

Rick felt uncomfortable. He envied Ted and wondered about himself. Secretly, he wanted to become a pro star like his brother some day. But it sounded crazy to admit it when he couldn't even stay on the Jayvee squad. If he couldn't be a pro, he'd have to find something else. It was worth thinking about . . .

The Warriors won their next two games. They moved ahead until they found themselves tied for second place in the eight-team league. But Caswell warned them it was too early to get excited. "We haven't really hit the top teams yet. The Panthers and the Barton Eagles are both tough. Our big job is still ahead."

Rick felt he was improving steadily. He was playing more than Maxwell now as he learned to anticipate his teammates' moves and use his height and reach better.

He knew Jerry Caswell was watching his closely. For the first time in his life, Rick shook off the image of his older brother Bill. He was alone on the court now, the tallest kid on the team, and it was his job to help the Warriors win the league championship.

He felt free. The coach advised him, and he listened without a hint of the old tension. "Don't hop about under the basket," Jerry suggested. "Try to take a position about five or six feet in front of the backboard and be ready to move to either side in the direction of the ball. Practice your pivot shot every chance you get, and remember to put the ball up there softly."

Russ Williams, too, was improving. Russ's jumper wasn't as good as Newcombe's but it was getting better, and he led the team in free throw percentage.

When the Warriors defeated the Hawks, Rick's name appeared in the local newspaper story for the first time. It was only a sentence in a one paragraph report, but it was a big thrill.

The sentence read: "Rick Hanley's rebounding, four baskets and three free throws, brought 11 points to the winner's total." After dinner that night he tried to sound casual as he called the family's attention to the story. His father seized the paper from him and read it aloud.

"Well, how about that?" he cried delightedly. "Looks like the Hanleys have another basketball star in the family!"

Rick protested modestly as he tried to keep from smiling too much at his father's praise. He felt very good.

But his kid sister, Francie, whose sports interests

were limited, brought him back to earth. She sniffed loudly. "Oh, I thought it was a Rock Hill High game," she said disdainfully. "Who're the Warriors? I never even *heard* of them!"

As Rick seized another section of the paper and rolled it up, Francie dashed into the other room screaming, "Mama—Rick's after me—make him stop!"

·CHAPTER EIGHT·

THE GAME WITH the Panthers was the most important of the early season for the Warriors. The Panthers were defending champs of the junior division. They had won the title easily the past two seasons. Although the Rangers had upset them earlier, they were still picked to make it three championships in a row. It would be the Warriors' toughest game to date. If they could win it, they might have a chance at the title themselves.

Suddenly a new problem arose. A week-long auto show in the Rock Hill Civic Center made it necessary to shift the game to another floor. The only place available on that Friday night was Haskell Center—the Panthers' home court.

Haskell Center was run by the city recreation department "to offer sports and crafts to underpriv-

ileged youth." Located in an old, rundown district of
the city, the Panthers' three-story home stood out like
a jewel among the rickety stores, old wooden houses,
the sagging porches and overgrown lawns. It was a
dangerous neighborhood. Even the police rolled up
their squad car windows when they drove by.

Russ Williams, who had grown up there, said
simply, "It's a good place to be *from,* Rick—not to
move to."

The Williams family had obviously agreed with
Russ and left that section of the city. Russ seemed uneasy about returning.

"The Panthers are still top team in the league," he
explained to Rick. "They won't like an old teammate
coming back to try and push them out of first place."

Rick realized how worried Russ was when he lost
the handle on the ball three times in a row in their
final scrimmage before the game. Even Coach Caswell, who seldom raised his voice, snapped, "Get with
it, Williams! This is no time to go to sleep!"

As they left the gym, Rick brought it up again.

"You still upset, Russ?"

"I get a funny feeling about Haskell," Russ admitted. "I know what basketball means there. It's everything to them. If we win they might see that we regret
it."

"Oh, come on, Russ. You're imagining things.
The officials won't stand for any rough stuff."

"What about the crowd? Besides—" He hesi-

tated. "Something else is bugging me too," he finally said. "My brother Frank still hangs out down there."

"What does he do?"

"I don't know," Russ frowned. "Last time we saw him he said he had a job. If he did, I don't know where the money went. Five months ago he borrowed about $500 from us and never payed it back."

"Five months? Have you seen him since?"

"He only comes by two or three times a year. Just when Mom's starting to give up on him he brings her some flowers or something, sweet talks her and ends up with the bucks.

"It sounds like you're more worried about your brother than the game."

"Maybe," Russ sighed. "If I see him I'll have to ask about the money and I hate that. It's like I'm some kind of bill collector or something. Not his brother. We used to get along real good, Frank and me. He always looked out for me in the neighborhood and, I don't know, Frank's got a lot of style. He's exciting to be around. You never know what he's going to do next. But this money thing has come between us. It's got me all mixed up."

Russ slammed his fist into his palm.

"Take it easy, Russ," Rick soothed his friend. "Let's just worry about basketball."

As the night of the game approached, the tension spread through the squad. Normally, city junior league games received little attention in the press. Class A high schools like Rock Hill, or the nearby colleges, received the coverage.

But this was different. The Panthers' unusual record captured the interest of fans far beyond the Haskell area. A lot of good players had come out of the Center in the past. The name of Jerry Caswell, the minister-coach, was an added attraction.

Then a reporter learned that Bill Hanley's brother played for the Warriors. The family was delighted at the boxed-in paragraph that appeared on the sports page. But Rick was not. It set the butterflies in his stomach fluttering even faster.

He realized the power of publicity when he came to school the next day. Students who had barely nodded to him before stopped to chat. Some kidded him good naturedly and others wished him good luck. A few wanted to know why he wasn't on the Rock Hill team.

While he was talking to a couple of them, Joe Smallwood came down the hall. "Hey—how's the headline hero?" he jeered. "How come you got cut off the poor old Jayvee squad, if you're so good, man? Anybody can play in that rinky-dink league you're in."

Rick's fists tightened angrily. He wanted to wipe that grin off Joe's face once more. He stepped forward and raised his right arm.

But this time Smallwood was ready. Joe blocked

the blow aimed at his jaw and landed a swing of his own. It glanced off Rick's forehead as he charged in.

Someone yelled, "Fight! fight!"

"Cream him, Hanley!" cried another student.

The scuffle ended as abruptly as it began. A husky upperclassman seized Rick's arms. Another shoved Smallwood away. "Beat it, both of you!" one of them said sharply. "or you'll both be in trouble!"

Rick was slightly dazed and filled with chagrin. Why had he let Smallwood bug him again? The news would be all over the school before his next class ended.

He dropped into a seat beside Newcombe in the classroom, feeling the spot on his forehead where Joe's blow skidded off.

"I saw what happened, Rick," said Newcombe. "Forget about Joe—he's always trying to ride someone. Must get his kicks that way. Besides, he's not setting the Jayvees on fire."

When he came home from school, Francie met him at the front door. Her eyes were sparkling. "I know a secret! I know a secret!" she announced in a loud whisper.

Rick stared at her. He knew that look on her face. If she told Mother what happened at school, he'd be in trouble again.

Francie tossed her head teasingly. "I'll bet I know something you don't think I know!" she taunted.

"Listen, brat—" he began. Then he decided to

use strategy instead. "Oh, you mean that scuffle at school with Smallwood?" He laughed. "Nothing at all, Little Sister. Just a bit of friendly by-play."

He looked at her coolly. "I suppose you've already told Mom."

"I did not!" Francie cried. "What kind of a fink do you think I am?"

Rick didn't answer. Instead he waited to see what would come out of her next.

Francie eyed him shrewdly. "Real cute, aren't you?" she said. "You aren't going to tell her either. You know what she'd say!" She changed her tone. "I won't say anything either—only—well—"

"What's the deal this time?" Rick asked patiently. "How much?"

"I need two dollars."

"Two dollars! What happened to your allowance?"

"You call that an allowance? I already spent it."

He winked at her. "Maybe Mom ought to hear about that, too."

Francie withered under his steady gaze. "You wouldn't dare," she said weakly. "Okay then—maybe I can squeeze by on a dollar."

Rick handed her one of the two dollars in his billfold. She snatched it from his hand and dashed to her room. "You're a real darling!" she howled gleefully. "I only needed fifty cents!" She slammed the door behind her with another shriek.

"Brat!" he shouted after her, grinning in spite of himself. But the grin quickly faded. Why did he fly off the handle over a creep like Smallwood?

Rick decided to work on his lay-ups for a while. With each shot at the basket that "had launched Bill Hanley," he reminded himself that the Warriors were going to be playing the toughest team in the division. And he'd be pitted against one of the best centers around. Even Coach Kenney praised the Panthers and George Carson.

"No *matter* what Joe Smallwood thinks, this is the most important game I've played yet. And I've got to be ready for it."

·CHAPTER NINE·

RICK HANLEY glanced up at the sign above the entrance to the weathered gray stone building. Dirt-encrusted letters carved there read: HASKELL YOUTH CENTER. Below them someone had scrawled boldly in chalk: *Home of the Champion Panthers!*

As they passed through the lobby, the Warriors saw a row of photographs of famous players along one wall. These were athletes who got their start at the Center before they became college and pro stars.

Before they descended to their basement locker room, Caswell let them to the court on the main floor. People were already coming in, a full hour before game time. From the balcony came a chorus of boos as the fans saw the visiting team. It was plain that Haskell crowds did not favor outsiders.

Rick grinned at Russ Williams. "They don't like us much, do they?" he asked.

"Things haven't changed a bit since I lived around here," replied Russ. "Even the boos sound familiar."

Both boys laughed, and felt better.

They went downstairs and dressed in their blue and gold uniforms. Caswell cautioned them briefly before they went up to the court. "Don't let the fans bother you," he said. "Just keep your minds on the game. The Panthers have a fine record, but games are won or lost on the floor—not in the record books."

When the Warriors came out on the court they saw the Panthers already warming up. They were a big team, smooth and fast-moving.

As the squads were introduced, the crowd noise became deafening. The boos drowned out the cheers as the Warriors, particularly Russ Williams, were introduced.

"My old buddies and friendly neighbors," Russ muttered, wetting his lips. "How they love me!"

Rick faced George Carson at the center circle. Carson was slightly taller and perhaps twenty pounds heavier than he was.

Carson jumped too soon at the whistle and Rick managed to tip the ball to Williams. Russ passed to Hinton, but Buster was called for traveling as he started his dribble, and the home team took over.

"Defense! defense!" called out Newcombe. But it

was too late. A lightning flip by Carson to Al Langford, the swift Panther forward, set up the first score of the game.

Hinton took the inbounds pass and dribbled to the front court. Williams, deep in the corner, reached for the ball but a Panther tipped it away. Russ got his hands on it again for a jump ball. He controlled the tap back to Newcombe. Ted's arching shot tied the score at a basket apiece.

The Panthers quickly broke the tie and were off to a 9–2 lead before Hinton sank a layup over Carson's hands. The home team worked their fast break well and led 14–6 at the end of the first period.

The second quarter began at an even faster pace. It looked as if the Warriors would be blasted off the court. The Panther lead increased 19–6.

The Warriors took time out and gathered around Caswell on the sideline. The coach spoke sharply. "We can't score without the ball," he said. "Hanley, you've got to get us those rebounds. And Russ—you get in there and help him. Don't let these guys intimidate you!"

It was good advice. When play was resumed, Rick slapped the ball away from Carson, and Newcombe snatched it off the floor. Immediately, the tempo of the game slowed.

Russ Williams sank an open shot from outside the foul line. Two baskets by Newcombe and a pair of free throws, cut the Panther lead to five points, 19–14.

The Panthers rallied again, but the Warriors kept creeping closer with their careful shooting. Just before the half ended, however, a bad pass gave the Panthers a breakaway, and they led 25–20 at the intermission.

"We've got them worried," Caswell said during the rest period. "Let's keep them running. It's bound to tire them. Just keep working for that open shot! We'll catch them."

But the Panthers put on a blitz as the third period opened. They led 29 to 20 before the dogged Warriors began to cut into the lead again. The Panthers led only 33–29 as the quarter ended. There was muttering among the home court fans, while the handful of Warrior rooters cheered madly.

"Keep the ball away from them," cautioned Caswell. "They'll try to rush you off your feet again. Keep working for the open shot and watch out for fouling. We can't afford any mistakes now."

Caswell's prediction proved right. The Panthers charged out furiously for the final quarter. But the stubborn Warriors still held them to a four point lead halfway through the period.

Play became rougher as the Panthers tried to force the pace. They were a proud team, and they were not used to being checked so closely. More fouls were called against them. Three successive free tosses brought the Warriors within a single point of their rivals. Then the Panthers got a turn at the foul line to make it 40–38.

Carson snatched a Panther pass and went high to shoot. Rick tried to match his leap and caught a jolting elbow in the ribs that made him gasp. The whistle sounded. Rick grunted with satisfaction as he turned to march the length of the court for his free throw.

Then he stared at the official in amazement. The foul was on him! "Wh—what—what?" cried Rick.

"You fouled him in the act of shooting!" the referee snapped. "Basket counts! One free throw!"

"He almost caved in my ribs with his elbow! Where were you?" Rick was angry through and through. "He's been shoving me all night!"

The referee stared at him coldly. "One more word from you, young man, and you're out of the game!"

Rick was still speechless as Maxwell relieved him. Coach Caswell was waiting on the sideline. As he started to protest, the coach cut him short. "You've got three personals now," Caswell snapped. "Don't make it any worse."

"But Carson fouled *me!*" sputtered Rick. "He shoved me aside when we jumped. That ref is really blind!"

"Enough of that, Rick! Even if he made a mistake, we can't change his decision. Now sit down and relax."

Rick sat down still seething. Carson sank the free throw for a three-point play. Now the Warriors trailed 43–38 as the clock ticked away.

George Carson brought the Warriors even more trouble as he caged a layup over Maxwell's groping hands. The Panthers began to move away and Caswell called Rick over to him.

"Can you control yourself if you go back in?" he asked.

"Yes sir!"

Rick managed to block a couple of Carson's shots, intercept a pass and score one basket before the game ended. But the final gun found the Panthers the winner, 50 to 44.

Someone seized his hand as he started off the floor. He looked up to see George Carson smiling at him. "Good game, Rick," he said. "You guys gave us fits. See you next time! Good luck!"

Rick still felt bitter. "Yeah? That referee—" He checked himself in time. "You guys played a great game, too," he said.

As Carson was swept away by the mass of Panther rooters, Rick began to work his way through the crowd. Suddenly he became aware of something else. Ahead of him he saw several boys blocking Russ Williams' path. A couple of them closed in behind him.

Russ tried to walk past the group but they did not move. Rick hurried forward just as one of them sneered, "Who you think you're shovin', Williams. We all know you, boy!"

"Excuse me," Russ said quietly. "Let me through."

A large, tough-looking youth placed a hand on Russ's chest. "Excuse me!" he mimicked. "Real polite—ain't he?"

Rick squeezed forward beside his friend. His heart was pounding, and his throat was dry as he stared at the group.

"Oh my—" said the burly youth. "The man's got a friend!"

"Come on, Russ," said Rick. "Let's go through."

"You wanna try it?" snarled another of the gang.

Suddenly there was the sound of scuffling behind them, and a quick cry of pain. Rick glanced over his shoulder to see a husky young man seize one of their tormentors and hurl him to the floor. He sent another spinning with a hard slap. Then he stepped up to the bully in front of the two Warriors.

"Buzz off," he snapped, "before I lose my temper!" He raised two big fists and stepped forward. "Beat it!" he said. "That means all of you!"

The group melted back into the crowd as Rick stared at the brawny newcomer. He had the same handsome features as Russ, but he was shorter, with a thick neck and heavy shoulders. He wore an expensive-looking leather jacket.

He smiled at Russ. "See how things are around here? But everything's cool. They don't mess around with Frank—they got respect." He looked at Rick. "Who's your friend, Russ? Aren't you going to introduce me?"

"Rick, this is my brother, Frank. You've already heard about him. Frank, this is Rick Hanley."

"The Hanley kid?"

Rick was still a bit stunned. Everything had happened so fast. So this was Russ' big brother. He tried to remember how he had imagined him.

"I'm sure glad to meet you, Frank," Rick stammered, still trying to make sense of things.

"Hear that, Russ, baby? At least *he's* glad to meet me." Frank grinned, smoothing the front of his leather jacket. "They're tough around here—my, my!—but they sure cool down fast! Hey, Russell— ain't you got a good word for me—just once?"

Russ smiled hesitantly. "Believe me, Frank, I'm glad you were around." He glanced at his brother's clothes. "You must be doing okay, Frank."

Frank Williams chuckled. "Yeah, I get around."

"Well," Russ hedged, "do you have a little extra? Mom could sure use some of that bread you owe her."

"In due time, Brother, in due time," replied Frank easily. "Right now, though, I've got an idea that might interest you. Go on, get dressed. I'll wait around."

"What kind of idea?" asked Russ uneasily. "How about paying us back? That's what I'm really interested in."

Frank Williams eyes narrowed. "You always did have a one-track mind. Listen—I can get you out of that sweat-shop you're in. No more shovin' boxes. A couple of minutes of your time is all I ask."

Rick saw Russ hesitate. "Okay, then. I'll be right out. But a minute's all I got. I'm going back with the team."

Frank Williams chuckled. "Take your time—but hurry. I'll be right here." He peeled the silver foil from a cigar. He lit it slowly, humming to himself.

·CHAPTER TEN·

RICK HANLEY faced a problem of his own when he reported for the Warriors next practice.

Coach Caswell had said nothing after the Panther game about his argument with the referee. The coach seemed to be more concerned about getting the team into the station wagon for the return trip to the church gym. All through the weekend Rick had worried about what Caswell would have to say.

As he opened his locker to dress for the workout, he saw Caswell coming toward him. For an instant he wished he could slip quietly from the room but there was no way.

Caswell's brown eyes were serious as he stood before Rick. "Now that you've had some time to think about it, Rick I wish you'd tell me exactly what happened between you and the referee in the game."

This was no time for an alibi, Rick knew. He took a deep breath. "I'm sorry I blew up," he said. "I got tired of being shoved around, I guess. That's the roughest team we've played. When the referee called that foul, it cost us three points—maybe even the game. I still figure there's no way he could have been right—no way."

"I see," replied the coach. "Rick—officials are human just like us. Sometimes they make mistakes, but they try to be fair."

Caswell paused for a moment. Then he said, "Some of them may give the man with the ball the benefit of a doubt; others may lean toward the defense. The best thing to do is play your own game and let them do their job. Nothing is solved if you get thrown out of a game."

"But I didn't get thrown out!" protested Rick.

"Let's face it. You'll never come closer."

The coach studied him for a moment. "Maybe a story I once heard about Wilt Chamberlain can get my point across," he said. "A man who used to see Wilt play when he was about your age told it to me.

"Wilt had the same problem you have—he grew too rapidly for a time. He played for Overbrook High School in Philadelphia when my friend knew him. The 'brook produced some great college and pro players in those days. There was always a game going on. Most of the players were older, stronger boys, even men, and they played rough around the basket. Wilt was awkward, and, at that time, he lacked the strength to match them. He took a hard beating.

"But Wilt was smart, as he was proven since. When he caught an elbow or a fist, or when he was mauled, he didn't retaliate. Instead, the next time the other player came in toward the basket, he'd get his shot blocked, or the ball stolen from him."

Caswell smiled at Rick. "Now that's what I call constructive protest," he said. "Soon the other fellows were so busy trying to play basketball they had no time to cheat. Think it over. Let the other fellow's mistakes work for you. Forget the officials."

Rick nodded thoughtfully as Caswell walked away. He felt both relieved and grateful. He had expected a bawling out. Instead, he'd gotten some good advice. Reverend Jerry Caswell was a real solid man.

He glanced around to see Ted Newcombe laughing and talking with Hinton and Pete DeLong as they dressed. He watched them for a moment. He was glad he was playing with the Warriors.

Russ Williams hurried in. "Sorry I'm late," he said briefly. "I got tied up."

"How'd you make out with your brother the other night?" Rick asked.

"Don't waste your breath on him," replied Russ tightly. He didn't say anything more.

When they gathered on the court Coach Caswell announced a change in the team's strategy. After he had talked about the Panther game briefly, he said,

"Rick, I want you to concentrate on your pivot shot. We've got to get more scoring from you. We've got to take better advantage of your height. If you can score more from out around the circle, they won't be able to crowd you so much inside."

He turned to Williams. "You've got to help more on both boards," he said. "Make better use of your height and those quick hands of yours. You're protecting yourself under the boards better, but you've got to get up higher on close-in shots. They say a tap-in isn't a true shot, but it still scores two points every time."

His plans called for Hinton and Newcombe to handle the outside shooting. Pete DeLong, the poorest shooter on the team, but a steady floor player, would hang back to protect against break-aways by the other team.

Caswell drilled Rick hard on hook and pivot shots. He showed him how to fake toward the basket and set up shots for Newcombe with high passes just outside the foul circle. He did not let him forget rebounds and layups. When Rick missed a close shot, Caswell's whistle blasted instantly.

"Rick, we can't afford to miss shots like that. Those easy ones are the easiest to blow," he said. "They count two points, the same as a flashy jumper from fifteen feet away. Keep your touch soft and pick your spot on the backboard."

They faced the Junior Celtics, a team that also had lost only two games, on Friday night. The Celtics were good but nothing like the Panthers. After an even first quarter, the Warriors opened up a small halftime lead of 20–16.

Newcombe and Rick broke the contest wide open in the third period. Ted scored twice in the first minute. Then Rick's new pivot shot began to click. They kept up the pace between them through the last quarter. The Warriors won, 47–36.

Rick was surprised the next day when he saw the results in the *Rock Hill News*. Instead of the usual brief paragraph for a Warriors' game, this account was stretched to three, and it headed the city league basketball column. It read:

> After being dumped by the league-leading Panthers last week, the Warriors bounced back solidly to down the Junior Celtics, 47–36.
>
> As a result, the Warriors are one of the top teams in the league today. They loom as the chief threat to the Panthers in the championship race.
>
> Ted Newcombe was the game's high scorer for both teams with 22 points. Rick Hanley, at center, was the real surprise of the game as he racked up 17 points, his best showing to date. His 10 rebounds also helped the Warriors' cause.

There was only one thing wrong with the Warriors' victory in Rick's eyes as he studied the box score. Next to the name of Russ Williams, only two points were listed—just two free throws.

He frowned as he remembered that Russ had

missed a couple of his favorite jump shots, and at least one easy layup under the basket. The box score told only the bare facts of Russ's performance. What had happened to him?

Then he shrugged off the thought. Every player has a bad game. Even his brother Bill, during his best college season, had a slump in which he couldn't "buy as basket," as he had put it. It was a mental block, Bill had said. He'd even had a few dry scoring spells with the Lakers. Fatigue or nerves could throw a player's timing off enough to make the ball rim the basket.

Rick wondered if Russ Williams was still worried about his brother. He decided to wait and see.

·CHAPTER ELEVEN·

THE WARRIORS won their next two games, and then began the final round of their schedule by playing the Rangers once more. Although the Rangers had upset the Panthers, and the Warriors, too, they had lost their next three games.

Rich had not forgotten that his turnover beneath the basket had cost the Warriors the first Ranger contest. He was determined to make up for his misplay this time, and he did. He scored 14 points in the Warriors' easy victory.

Their next opponent was the strong Barton Eagles team. After losing their first two starts, the Eagles had gone unbeaten. They and the Warriors were ranked as the only teams with a chance against the Panthers.

"Barton isn't as big and fast as the Panthers,"

Caswell told the squad. "But they can shoot, and their man-to-man defense is tough to score on. We'll have to be really sharp to win."

As the Warriors practiced for the game with the Eagles, Russ Williams seemed alert and enthusiastic again. Rick thought it was safe to ask about Frank. But when he did, his friend's face clouded.

"Frank said he'd found a great job. Said he'd get in touch again," Russ shrugged. "But we haven't heard a word from him. I guess he'll turn up one of these days."

Rick let the matter drop. Both he and Russ needed to keep their minds on the game ahead.

The Warriors started fast against the Eagles. The crowd was in an uproar as they ran on the Barton defense and began to pile up the score. Coach Caswell sent his team out to use a fast-break offense and the Eagles became confused. Before they pulled themselves together the Barton team was down by eight.

Then they shifted to the same tactics the Warriors had used in previous games. They moved the ball deliberately and took only open shots. Their new style worked so well that the score was tied at 14 in the second quarter. But Newcombe and Hinton broke away enough to give the Warriors a halftime lead.

The stubborn Eagles refused to become discouraged, however, and they chipped away at the Warriors' lead until they tied and finally passed them. The

Warriors tired as they continued to rely on the fast break.

Caswell ordered them to switch to their old style of working for open shots and the game slowed down.

Rick was having trouble with the Barton center. His rival was no great jumper but he clung to Rick like a shadow. He stripped the ball from Rick several times, and his waving hands spoiled one shot after another.

Rick didn't score his first clean two-pointer until the third period. His rival had held him to a single tip-in during the first half. Russ Williams had broken loose for three baskets and a free throw during the same time.

Suddenly Rick whirled and hit a 12-footer from the pivot. The timely basket placed the Warriors within one point of the Eagles, 28–27. Outside shots by Newcombe and Hinton put the Warriors ahead 31–28 as the third period ended.

Early in the final quarter Rick scored twice, the second time on a high pass from Williams. The Eagles sent two men to guard him.

Barton started to fight desperately for the ball. They pressed the Warriors the length of the court. Hinton dribbled to eat up the clock, looking for the open man.

Suddenly Newcombe shouted. "Watch it, Buster—behind you!" It was too late. An Eagle forward slapped the ball away from Buster and passed far down the floor. A teammate had a step and a half on Pete DeLong and scored easily. The quick basket started a rally cutting the Warriors lead to 37–35.

Then Newcombe, who seldom fouled, hacked an opponent and with the converted free throw the gap narrowed to a single point. It was a whole new ball game at 37–36. Caswell called time-out with only three minutes left to play.

"Keep moving and work for an open shot," Caswell urged. "If you're fouled, make sure you sink the free throw. Whatever you do, don't let them steal the ball again!"

But the Warriors' strategy backfired. The Eagles intercepted a pass to put them ahead 38–37. Hinton tied it up with a free throw, and Newcombe picked up two points on a pass from Russ Williams. The Warriors had the lead again 40 to 38.

The Eagles came back with a rush. They went down the court too fast and Williams snaked out a long arm to seize a wildly flung ball.

Russ stood holding the ball high above his head with both hands, searching for an open man. Rick barely had time to hurry down the court before he heard Hinton's shout.

He turned to take the ball over his shoulder, and took a giant stride toward the basket, leaping high. The ball bounced off the backboard like a feather and fell straight, barely rippling the net.

Rick's effort carried him beneath the boards and

across the end line. He landed awkwardly on his right foot and thudded to the floor.

He doubled up as he felt a sharp pain knife through his ankle. He tried to get up but fell back clutching his foot.

The referee blew his whistle. Then he motioned to the Warriors' bench. Caswell and Newcombe raised Rick gently to his feet.

"Can you stand on it?" asked the coach. Pain flooded through his lower leg as he tried. They helped him to the bench and Caswell probed the ankle carefully. It was already swelling.

"We'll have to get you to the dressing room and put ice packs on it," said Caswell. "There's a doctor friend of mine sitting behind us. We'll have him look at it."

A moment later the Warrior fans leaped up as the clock ran out. Rick's basket cinched the game, 42–38.

The doctor made a more thorough examination of the ankle in the dressing room. "It's not broken," he said. "But you'll have to stay off of it for a while. Ever use crutches before, Rick?"

"Crutches!" Rick gasped. "Is it that bad?"

The physician chuckled. "Don't get upset," he said. "We'll check it again when the swelling goes down. I'm sure you'll be walking by the end of the week. But we'll have to wait and see."

"You mean I'll be out a week, or even longer?"

asked Rick. "But I can't do that—we play the Panthers in three weeks!"

The doctor smiled at him. "Sometimes these ankles heal faster than we expect. But all you can do is hope."

·CHAPTER TWELVE ·

RICK REPLACED his crutches with a cane on Tuesday. By Friday he was able to walk with the ankle tightly bandaged. He sat on the bench as the Warriors defeated the Comets, the last-place team in the league. It was little more than a workout for them but Caswell was not satisfied.

"We have only two games left, with an open date in between," he said, "and we've got to be a lot sharper than we were tonight before we're ready for the Panthers."

The thought of the open date did not make Rick too unhappy. His ankle would have more time to mend, and he would be back at full strength by the Panther game.

He was able to shoot a few baskets as the Warriors held their first practice, but when he felt some

twinges in his ankle, he stopped. The coach promised to let him dress for Friday night's game. Possibly he might even get to play a few minutes.

Then Caswell made a surprising announcement.

"I've arranged for a practice game to fill our open date," he said. "Coach Kenney at high High school has agreed to a game with their Jayvee squad in the school gym a week from Thursday afternoon."

Rick was startled by the coach's words. His first thought was that this would bring him face-to-face with Joe Smallwood. Smallwood was now the regular center for the Jayvees. It might be only a practice session for the others, Rick thought grimly, but it would be real enough for him. It would be a test, a personal challenge, a chance to see if he could handle Joe.

A sudden doubt crossed his mind. How about his ankle? There could be no alibis in this game. All that mattered now was being ready.

After practice he asked Caswell if he could work out daily in the church gym to strengthen his ankle. He carefully avoided any mention of the Jayvee game.

The coach agreed on one condition. "Okay, but if it starts to bother you," said Caswell, "I want you to lay off and tell me right away. Your ankle is much more important than the Panther game."

Rick began his extra workouts eagerly. A quick spasm of pain brought him up sharply during the first one. He walked slowly around the court until it went away. The warning made him practice more carefully.

The news of the coming Jayvee-Warriors game caused scarcely a ripple among the students at Rock Hill High. Their interest was centered around the varsity which was engaged in a battle for a place in the district playoffs. The Jayvees, too, had a good record. Joe Smallwood was their most promising candidate for next year's varsity squad.

Smallwood had not changed, Rick learned the next day as he entered the school library. Joe glanced up from a book he was reading, and spoke with his usual mocking grin. "Hi, Rick. How're things in the Little League these days?"

Rick's anger rose but he kept his voice steady. "Guess you'll have a chance to find out for yourself next week," he replied. "That is, if you're still on the Jayvee squad."

Joe's eyes narrowed. "I'll be around, buddy. Don't you worry about that."

"That's nice," replied Rick. "I hope I can give you some competition." Joe's snort of derision followed him as he left the room.

Rick sat on the bench as the Warriors easily defeated the Hawks. He was not disappointed, for earlier that day the doctor had checked his ankle and told him he'd be ready to play against the Jayvees.

There had been an added thrill after the Hawks' game when they learned that the Barton Eagles had upset the Panthers that same night. That meant they were now tied with the defending division champions. The Warriors and Panthers would play for the junior title.

But the Jayvee game still came first in Rick's mind. That and meeting with Joe Smallwood.

Rick returned to scrimmage to share the center duties with Maxwell. After the drill Caswell asked about his ankle, and Rick replied quickly, "It's okay. Didn't feel a thing."

"Good—maybe we'll start you against the Jayvees. You need more work in scrimmage. "Get plenty of rest tomorrow night. Remember, we play the Jayvees on Thursday."

Rick suppressed a grin. As if he could forget!

Russ Williams bent down to finish lacing his shoes as he sat beside Rick in the Rock Hill High dressing room. "You know," he said, "last year I used to wonder what it would be like to be in here getting ready for a varsity game. Guess this is as close as I'll get."

Coach Caswell sent them out to warm up. The Jayvees were already on the floor. Joe Smallwood sank a fancy hook shot and Rick saw him drop another cleanly through the hoop. Joe always looked good in warm-up drills. How would he do with hands waving in front of his face, or with someone leaping up to block his shots?

Rick glanced around and saw Jim Saylor watching

him. His lips tightened as he remembered what had happened in Kenney's office three months ago. *"Why waste your time on him?"* Saylor had said. So let's see who's right today, Rick thought bitterly. Let's get on with it.

Across the court he saw Caswell talking to Ed Kenney. The Rock Hill coach was holding the whistle. He was going to referee.

The teams moved to their positions. Joe Smallwood stood before him, a tight grin on his face. Kenney told him to shake hands, then stepped back to toss the ball high.

Rick forgot about his ankle as he put everything he had into his jump. He felt a thrill as his fingers reached the leather first and guided it back to Newcombe.

The Warriors moved swiftly to the forecourt. Smallwood outran him and blocked Newcombe's shot. Russ Williams picked the ball up on the first bounce and fired toward the pivot spot. Rick seized it eagerly, turned and leaped. The shot was good.

The Jayvees put the ball in play against a partial pressing defense and advanced toward the Warriors basket. Rick tried to move in front of Smallwood, but Joe nudged him lightly and leaped to one side. Rick followed him and was screened out of the play as a Jayvee forward dribbled in for a short jumper. The shot was no good, but Joe seized it as it caromed off the backboard and passed back to a waiting teammate.

Ten seconds later the ball arched high above him to drop through the basket. There was no chance to block it with Joe in his way.

The score see-sawed back and forth through the first quarter. Hinton and Newcombe did most of the Warriors' scoring. They did their shooting from outside since Smallwood kept Rick bottled up. Every time the ball came toward the post position, Joe was right with him. All Rick could manage was two or three rebounds.

As the second period began, Caswell sent in Stan Maxwell. Rick was panicky as he went to the bench. He knew he had improved since he'd joined the Warriors, but so had Joe Smallwood. Joe was better than he had thought.

Beside him, Caswell said, "You're tight, Rick. What's the matter—your ankle bothering you?"

He shook his head, and Caswell smiled. "Watch what's going on under the basket while you have a chance," he said.

Rick studied Smallwood and saw something he hadn't noticed before. Joe kept faking Maxwell off balance to get open for a shot. On defense he clung to Stan like a shadow. He wondered if he, too, had looked that bad against Joe Smallwood.

"All right," said Caswell finally. "Get back in. And play your own game."

The first time he tried to block Joe's pass attempt, he accidentally struck his arm. Joe quickly sank the free throw, and a moment later scored on a jumper.

Rick became confused. Nobody had outplayed him that badly. He was glad when the Jayvees took time out. He took a deep breath and leaned forward, his hands on his knees, and tried to think about what he'd seen from the bench.

The whistle blew and the Warriors came down the floor. As Rick positioned himself in front of the backboard, he felt Smallwood at his elbow. Suddenly he jumped forward and stepped to one side, waving his hands. Newcombe's bullet pass reached him and in the same motion he jumped, turned and shot. Joe stared at him in chagrin as the ball arched through the net.

When he repeated the play on another toss from Newcombe, Ted shouted, "Now you're cooking, Rick—keep it up!"

But the next time the Warrior forwards came down, Joe stretched out to block the pass. It was Rick's turn to stand helplessly as the Jayvees took the ball down the floor.

During the half-time rest, it occurred to Rick that Joe hadn't been giving out with his usual corny line of chatter. Maybe they were both too busy playing basketball. He flexed his ankle as it began to ache slightly. Nothing to worry about, he decided.

In the third period Joe showed that he had not completely changed his habits. When he blocked

Rick's shot, he failed to control the ball and it was deflected to Russ. The tall Warrior forward promptly scored.

"Lucky dog!" snapped Joe.

Rick grinned at him but did not reply. Toward the end of the quarter, Rick stopped suddenly, leaped back and shot from the edge of the foul circle.

As the ball dropped through the basket to the floor, Smallwood looked at him in surprise. "I hate to say it, but that was a good shot. I sure goofed that time."

It was Rick's turn to look surprised. But he did not reply as he felt a quick shock of pain. He had put all his weight on the ankle when he'd landed on the fadeaway jumper. He took another step but it got no worse. He couldn't leave the game now.

A moment later Smallwood drove by him to spin a lay-up off the backboard. "Not bad, eh?" he asked with a grin.

"Very good," muttered Rick but his mind was not on the shot, but on his ankle. It had begun to throb under the tight bandage.

He saw Caswell watching him from the sideline. The coach signaled for a time-out. Maxwell was already peeling off his warm-up shirt.

"It's not that bad, Coach," protested Rick as he came to the bench. "Maybe the bandage is too tight."

Caswell shook his head. "Sit down," he said. "We'll have a look at it."

Rick did not get out on the court again that day. The Jayvees won by five points and Joe Smallwood had scored fourteen in the game. His own total was nine, he reflected sadly. All because of an ankle!

As he got up to leave the bench, he saw Smallwood coming toward him. He braced himself for another wisecrack. Joe looked at him for a moment. "I didn't realize your ankle was that bad," he said. "You did all right for a cripple," he added with a grin.

As Joe turned to walk away, he said, "Good luck against the Panthers."

Rick stared after him. How, he wondered, do you figure a guy like that?

CHAPTER THIRTEEN·

RICK LOOKED UP at the clock on the gym wall. Practice was due to begin in two minutes, and the Warriors were warming up—all except Russ Williams.

Coach Caswell asked, "Any idea where Williams is, Rick? He's never been late before. This is an important practice. I hate to start without him."

"Maybe he had to work late, or he could be sick. Want me to call his house and find out?"

"Why don't you do that? If he's on his way, we'll wait a few minutes."

Russ's mother seemed surprised when she answered the phone.

"Why, Russell's at basketball practice at the church," she said. "Is there any message?"

"This is Rick Hanley, Mrs. Williams. I'm calling

from the gym. He isn't here yet. How long ago did he leave?"

"Well, he called from the plant an hour ago—said Frank was going to pick him up. They're both supposed to come home after practice. What could have happened?"

Rick hastened to reassure her. "Oh, he'll probably be along any minute. We were about to start practice and Coach Caswell wondered if he was sick or something."

"Reverend Caswell asked about him?" Mrs. Williams sounded anxious. "Where in the world could those two boys have gone?"

Rick was suddenly alert. If Russ had gone somewhere with Frank, it might mean trouble. Rick tried to keep the concern out of his voice as he said, "I'll ask him to call you the minute he comes in."

"I'd really appreciate that." said Mrs. Williams. "Thank you."

When Coach Caswell looked at him, he shook his head. "His mother said he left the plant about an hour ago," Rick said. "His brother was supposed to drop him off at practice. Maybe they were held up some place. Russ will probably show any minute."

"Well, we can't wait any longer. Let's go."

It was not a good workout. Rick couldn't make himself concentrate. When practice ended, Caswell beckoned to Rick. "I don't want to alarm his mother, but I'm concerned about Russ. It's not like him to miss practice without even giving us a call."

"If what his mother said was right, both Russ and his brother should be at home now, or very shortly."

"After you get dressed, call him again. I'll feel better when I know he's all right."

Rick dialed the Williams' number. He half expected Russ to answer. Instead, he heard Mrs. Williams voice. "No—I haven't heard a word from them! It's just not like Russell to not even call me—not like him at all. Do you think they've had an accident? What'll I do?"

Caswell motioned Rick aside and took the phone. "This is Reverend Caswell, Mrs. Williams. We hope we didn't upset you but we're concerned about Russ, too. I'm sure there's a good reasons for whatever has happened. If you'd like, I can do some checking for you and call you back."

Mrs. Williams agreed, almost tearfully, and Caswell called the police department and the hospitals. There was no report on the two brothers.

Caswell called Mrs. Williams again and left his home phone number. "Have Russ call me when he comes in," he said. "I want to be sure he's all right."

As he hung up he turned to Rick. "We might as well go home," he said. "If you hear anything, call me."

Rick found he was very tired as he began walking home. The workout and the worry about Russ had

worn him down. His ankle began to throb. He saw
the lights of a Spring Street bus coming up behind
him. That would take him only a couple of blocks from
home.

Something else flashed through his mind. Russ
had mentioned a pizza place farther out on Spring
Street where he sometimes stopped after work. He
smiled as he thought of the corny name—Crazy Joe's
Pizza Palace—a neighborhood hangout.

Crazy Joe's was easy to find. If the sign in front
were not enough, the music that bellowed from a
loudspeaker would have guided a deaf person there. It
was filled with noisy people.

"You know a guy named Russ Williams?" he
yelled in the ear of a passing waiter. "Has he been in
tonight? I'm supposed to meet him."

"Russ Williams? Sure, man, sure. Follow your
nose around the corner to the back room. Him and his
brother got the second booth on the right."

What a stroke of luck, Rick thought, as he hurried into the back room. Russ was seated facing him as
he approached the booth. "Rick!" he gasped. "Hi,
man—what brings you way out here!"

"You!" snapped Rick. "When you didn't show up
for practice, I called your home. Your mother's all
upset and Caswell's worried, what gives?"

Russ jumped up. "I called the church gym. First
there was no answer and then it was busy."

"Well, what did you expect? The phone's no-

where near the gym. It's in the office. The only reason
it was busy was because Jerry and I were calling your
mother, the hospital and the police!"

"The police?" a low voice interrupted. Rick
looked down to see Frank's long, leather-clad body
stretched out in the seat, fingers tapping a pack of cigarettes. "Just because Russ missed a practice!"

Russ snapped, "It wouldn't have happened if you
showed up on time." He turned to Rick. "Frank was
an hour late. We were supposed to talk."

Rick eyed his friend suspiciously. Russ stared
back, his lips frozen into a tight line. Rick shrugged
and decided to let it go.

Frank's eyes glittered as he pulled out a cigarette
and appraised the two boys coolly. "What did you tell
the police?" he addressed Rick.

"We thought there might be an accident. They
said they'd keep a lookout for you guys."

"I'll drive you both home." Frank stood up, dig-
ging into his back pocket and pulling out a few dollar
bills. "My car's outside."

"I can walk," Rick replied. But Frank Williams
wouldn't hear of it. Reluctantly, Rick followed the
brothers to the lot.

Frank stopped before a shiny late model sports
car. "How do you like this little beauty?" he asked
with a grin. "Hop in—relax on a real set of wheels."

Rick stared uneasily at the expensive little machine. How could Frank Williams own a car like this?

Russ read his mind. "Quit snowing him, Frank. You said you borrowed it."

"The trouble with you, Russell baby, is that you got no imagination. Can't a man have his little joke?"

"Little is right!"

They pulled out smoothly into the street. Frank drove fast, but well, hitting the traffic lights just right, and talking easily as they sped through town.

Suddenly he made a right turn, then swung left at the next corner to follow a parallel street. "Too much traffic back there," he explained briefly.

Both boys stared at him, surprised. A moment later he snapped, "Hang on—fuzz!" The car leaped forward with a roar of skid around the next corner.

"Wait a minute, Frank!" shouted Russ. "Is this car hot?"

"No, but I am. I forgot to renew my driver's license, and got a mess of tickets hanging over me. They'll hit me with the book!"

A siren sounded behind them, and a flashing red light swung around the corner. Frank stepped on the gas pedal.

"Pull over!" cried Russ frantically. "We got enough trouble now!"

But Frank Williams did not see the wet spot at the intersection as he tried another sharp turn. They skidded halfway across the street, narrowly missing an oncoming car.

Frank twisted the wheel savagely, but the little

machine had no traction. He let go of the wheel as the car spun around and they crashed broadside against the curb. There was the hissing sound of air escaping from a tire as they sat helplessly part way across the sidewalk.

Frank tried to gun the engine but it quit with a harsh cough. For the first time he looked scared. He leaped to the street.

"Scatter!" he yelled. A police car whirled to a halt in front of them and two officers sprang out. Frank started running but slipped and fell headlong to the walk. A policeman jerked him to his feet.

Rick found himself with his hands against the side of the car, his feet spread wide. The Williams brothers stood next to him. Another police car pulled up behind them.

"These two don't know a thing!" protested Frank. "One of them's my brother. I was just driving them home."

"In a stolen car?" asked one of the officers coldly.

"Stolen—nothing!" Frank cried. "I just borrowed it!"

"Come off it! It was reported stolen two hours ago!"

"Advise him of his rights," one policeman stated. "You two get in the squad car."

The policemen led Russ and Rick, who were speechless, over to the car.

"What do you kids know about this?" one said roughly. "Did you help your friend out?"

"We didn't know anything," Rick answered, his voice cracking.

"We'll see about that at the station."

Frank got in a minute later, and the other policeman slid into the front seat. At police headquarters a sergeant questioned them. He looked at Rick and at Russ Williams curiously and asked their ages. "Minors, huh? You can call your folks and be released in their custody. We'll have to set up an appointment with the juvenile division for you later. Better get on the phone if you don't want to spend the night in jail."

"Jail? My folks?" exclaimed Rick in dismay. "But I—I—can't do that!"

Russ spoke up quickly. "Couldn't we call Caswell? Maybe he could explain it to them first."

The officer leaned forward. "Jerry Caswell? You know him?"

"We're on his basketball team—the Warriors."

The sergeant talked in low tones with the other two officers, then nodded. "Okay, one of you call Reverend Caswell." He stared at Frank Williams. "Not you. We got some questions for you. You're no juvenile."

Caswell listened carefully as Rick tried to explain what had happened. "Anyone hurt?" he asked. "You didn't run into anyone, did you?"

"Just the car, it got banged up some," replied Rick.

"Lucky. I'll be right down."

After a brief discussion with the sergeant, who seemed to know Jerry Caswell quite well, the boys were released in his custody. He promised to talk to their parents.

Rick's folks were shocked when Caswell drove them home. But they soon accepted his explanation. Mrs. Williams, however, was greatly upset, particularly about Frank. Again Caswell seemed to know just what to say.

"Maybe it's for the best," he told her. "Things had to come to a head sometime. It might have been much worse. You try to get a good night's sleep and I'll see what I can do."

Next day Caswell told both boys they would have to be present with their parents for a conference with a juvenile court officer Friday afternoon. "And we play the Panthers at seven o'clock," Rick said.

"That can't be helped. It shouldn't take long—it's just routine," explained Caswell. "But both of you may have to be present Monday at Frank's hearing. I don't think he knew the car was stolen. I'll try and get him on probation." Caswell sighed. "It won't be easy. Well, I'll see you at the game tonight. Good luck at the hearing—and don't worry, it's nothing!"

Caswell was right. The conference was informal.

The boys and their parents left the court office, Rick and Russ trailing behind at a distance.

"What did you have to talk to Frank about, anyway?" Rick asked curiously.

Russ heaved a sigh. "He said a friend of his had this high-paying job for me. I could do it part-time and still make enough to go back to school."

"Sounds great. What was it?"

"Delivering packages. Nothing to it, as long as I didn't talk about it to anybody—or ask any questions, like about what was in the packages."

Rick swallowed. "Sounds like a good job to forget."

Russ nodded. "Yeah. I tried to get Frank to tell me what it was all about, but he said he's smart enough not to ask questions."

"Do you think he stole the car?"

"Who knows? I wouldn't put it past him. He must have known the car was hot. Even so, Frank wouldn't lose the chance to drive a car like that. His car is an old dump and my brother's big on images."

Suddenly Rick saw Frank Williams standing about twenty feet away, watching them.

"Speaking of the devil," he said in a low voice. "There's your brother."

"Frank?" Russ looked over as Frank began striding confidently toward them. "What are you doing here?"

"I'm free till Monday," Frank shrugged as he approached them. He stopped, pulled a cigarette out and lit it. "Thought I'd come around and set you guys straight."

"About what?"

"Just this—if I rip something off, I don't get caught. I borrowed that car and the guys I borrowed it from are the thieves. I had no idea it was hot."

Russ spat on the ground. "Why didn't you? Because you're too smart to ask questions?"

Frank's eyes narrowed and he looked quickly at Rick. "Believe me, if I wanted to make something up, I could do a lot better."

Suddenly Russ's anger spilled out. "All you care about is looking good, looking cool. You got yourself busted and us too, but that doesn't mean a thing as long as everybody still thinks you're a big man. I'll tell you, Frank, you better do some thinking yourself. You've got a lot of style, but it takes more than that to make it as a hustler."

As the two boys walked away, Frank called after them, "How'd I ever get a brother like you?" But Rick looked back and saw him standing uncertainly, fiddling with his watch band and frowning.

Russ heaved a long sigh. "I've never told him off. I can't believe he just took it like that." He shook his head. "I sure wish we weren't playing tonight."

"I know what you mean," Rick smiled. "Listen, if

you don't think about your brother, I won't think about mine."

"Yours?" Russ shot a look at Rick to see if he was serious. "Your brother is the best there is!"

"Sure," Rick said, "but sometimes it's hard trying to measure up to the best there is."

Russ stopped. "I never even thought of that," he admitted. He said wryly, "So what can we do?"

"I think I'm going to forget it all and try to get some shut-eye before 7:00. Ready or not, we've got a game to play."

·CHAPTER FOURTEEN·

ACROSS THE COURT the Panthers huddled tightly around their coach. The officials stood chatting at the scorers' table. Rick Hanley bent down to tighten his shoe laces, and as he straightened up a firm hand clapped his shoulder.

"You're sure the ankle is okay, Rick? asked Caswell.

"I'm sure," Rick replied.

Caswell stepped out on the floor and the Warriors gathered around him. "You all know what to do," he said. They nodded quickly and clasped their hands together. "All right! Go get 'em!" snapped the coach.

The crowd began to shout as they scattered to their posts and shook hands with their opponents. Both teams tensed as the referee walked to the center circle.

Suddenly the official tossed the ball high. The championship game was on!

The action began with a bang. George Carson easily outjumped Rick and tapped the ball back to Al Langford. As Al fired it to Carson again, Russ Williams stole it from behind. Hinton took a pass and dribbled up the floor. As he slanted toward a corner, he threw to Rick underneath. Rick grabbed the ball and went up to plant it in the basket before Carson could reach him.

The Panthers came back with a rush and Langford dodged around Russ to sink a shot that tied the score at 2-all. When the defending champs took the ball on a turnover, they came racing through the Warriors' defense again. But Langford took too many steps.

Pete DeLong threw the ball inbounds and the Warriors fanned out watching for an opening. But the alert defenders held them in check.

The crowd began to shout for action. Russ Williams raced toward the basket throwing his hands high. The defense shifted to meet the threat and Hinton dribbled in from the other side to score. Again the Panthers came back to tie it up.

Fifteen seconds later the Warriors seized another turnover. Hinton whipped the ball to Williams who relayed it to Rick. When Carson beat him to the basket, Rick passed back to Ted Newcombe, and Ted promptly sank a fifteen footer.

Both teams maintained the hot scoring pace through the first quarter with the Panthers leading 16–14 at the intermission.

George Carson increased the lead with a free throw and a lay-up as the second quarter opened. The Warriors pushed the ball quickly down the floor, but Newcombe missed. Russ and Rick tried to follow up, but both missed rebound shots. A moment later the Panthers scored after a long pass down the floor.

The Warriors struck a cold shooting streak as they missed half a dozen attempts in a row. Their opponents meanwhile scored another basket to boost their lead, 23–14.

Newcombe tried to drive through the zone, and when he found his way blocked, he whipped a backward pass to Russ. Williams attempted to attack the zone from the side but again there was no opening.

As a defender came toward him, he threw hastily in to Rick in the post. Rick had to leap out beyond the foul circle to take the throw. Finding himself unexpectedly open, he turned and fired in one sweeping motion. The ball dropped through the basket with a swish.

Rick leaped high, waving his arms. The Warriors' shooting slump was broken! "Come on guys—let's get some more buckets! We can do it!"

Hinton sprinted through to count with a hook shot a few seconds later. But the rally ended abruptly as the Panthers switched to a man-to-man defense.

Rick did not get another basket in the first half. Carson's hands waved constantly before his face, and he had to hurry the shots he did get. Only accurate outside shooting by Newcombe and Russ in the final minutes of the period, reduced the scoring gap to five, 29–24 at halftime.

Caswell offered criticism and advice while they rested. "Rick, remember how you scored on that turn-around jumper from outside?" he asked. "Why not try that again? Carson didn't go out with you, just stayed planted under the basket." He spoke to the others. "Let's try it as a play. Rick can raise his hand when he sees he's clear in front. Then pass in to him just outside the circle. If he breaks out fast enough, he should have an open shot."

They did not try the play immediately. Russ Williams intercepted the opening tip-off for the second half and fired the ball to Hinton who dribbled in for a driving hook shot off the boards. A moment later Williams slipped away from another bucket that brought the Warriors within one point of their rivals, 29–28.

As the Panther defense stiffened, Rick kept his eyes on Newcombe, dribbling down the side of the floor. Suddenly Ted whipped a pass to Williams. When he saw Williams take the throw, Rick's arm shot up, and he took three long strides forward.

Russ's pass came to him waist high. He gripped the ball easily as he turned and leaped toward the basket. He saw Carson lean back and watch the leather sail above his head and drop through the hoop. The Warriors now led 30–29.

Seconds later Newcombe scooped up a loose ball and passed to Hinton. Rick screened Carson away from Buster whose shot made it 32–29. The Panthers called time out.

When the champions got the ball again, they hit a hot streak and regained the lead on three quick baskets.

Once more Newcombe moved the ball into position for a pass to Williams. Rick's sweeping turn-around shot got back two points but the Panthers still led by one.

Hinton was fouled and he made the free throw that knotted the game at 35-all.

Suddenly both teams found the shooting range at the same time. They traded basket for basket until the last ten seconds of the third period when Langford gave the Panthers a two-point lead, 48–46.

Both teams came out with a rush for the final quarter but the rest period had dulled their shooting touch. A minute passed before Newcombe's jumper scored for the Warriors. Seconds later Carson out-leaped Rick to score a lay-up. The Panthers still led by two points, 50–48.

There was a Panther time-out and while the Warriors, too, huddled around their coach, Newcombe said, "Why not try that pivot play of yours again, Rick? Maybe if we can score on it, Carson won't stick so close to the backboard."

"Good idea," agreed Caswell. "Try it, Rick. We've got to loosen up that defense."

The Warriors took the ball inbounds and play was resumed. Newcombe moved into the forecourt. He shot a quick glance at Rick and saw him sprint out past the foul circle.

Rick took the pass perfectly and turned, his arm sweeping high. But the ball seemed to slide off his fingers and as it left his hand, he knew it wasn't good. He dashed in for the rebound.

The leather slapped off the backboard as he and Carson leaped for it. Both got their hands on it, tugging hard. Rick was knocked off his feet and Carson fell heavily across his legs.

The referee whistled for a jump ball. As Rick got to his feet, shaken and panting, he felt a stab of pain in his right ankle. He walked around for a moment and the pain subsided to a dull ache. He signaled to Caswell, who was standing with his hand on Maxwell's shoulder, that he was all right. Ten seconds later Langford increased his team's lead, 52–48.

As the period wore on the Panthers reached the 60-point mark, but the Warriors stayed with them to make it 60–58.

Rick was tired now. The fall under the basket had taken more out of him than he realized. He longed for a chance to catch his breath on the bench, but the game was too close. Caswell did not want to give Carson any further advantage beneath the basket against the shorter Maxwell.

The clock moved to the two-minute mark. Rick's chest was burning and his right leg throbbed. Play centered around midcourt for the moment. Then Hinton seized a loose ball and Rick pumped his legs toward the basket.

He heard Newcombe's shout and turned to find himself alone. Ted's pass was long and high and Rick had to leap for it. As he came down, a flash of pain in his ankle made him miss his stride. He took another step and fired. The ball struck the backboard and shot down through the rim.

The referee's whistle cut through Rick's feeling of elation like a knife. "No basket—too many steps!" cried the official.

Russ Williams dashed over to slap him on the back. "Come on, Rick!" he shouted. "Let's get it back. We've got time!"

As they tried to catch up with the racing Panthers, Hinton gave them a break. Buster dashed between two opponents to intercept a bounce-pass and flip it to Newcombe.

Before the Panthers could change direction, Ted dribbled the length of the court and laid it in to the the score at 60–60.

The quick, easy basket against them unsettled the

Panthers. Instead of taking time out, they charged back furiously and Langford's jump shot bounded back into Russ Williams' hands. Two passes and Newcombe was heading down the right sideline.

Rick backed into the pivot spot, his eyes on Ted, waiting for the pass-in. It came, a little underthrown, and he had to take an extra step to get it. As he turned toward the basket, his ankle gave way and he stumbled forward as he shot. The ball bounded off the backboard to the sidelines.

A Panther player seized it, glanced at the clock and hurled the ball far down the court as the buzzer ended the regular play.

The game would go into overtime.

Rick was sick at heart. He'd muffed two big chances to win. Then he saw the others gathering around Caswell. There would be a one-minute intermission and then a three-minute extra period.

"Hurry it up, Rick!" shouted Caswell.

"I'm sorry, guys," Rick panted as he limped into the huddle.

"Never mind that!" snapped Caswell. "We're going to win! We'll play for the open shot. Keep moving!" He looked at Rick.

"I'm putting Maxwell in to give you a rest."

The coach glanced toward the Panthers huddle. "They'll be pressing us all over the court. Russ, you cover Langford! We've got to get that ball!"

A moment later Rick watched the two teams

move tensely into position for the tipoff. Carson guided it easily toward Langford, but Russ grabbed at it for a jump ball. He sent it spinning over to Maxwell. The Warriors began to move the leather around the front court.

Buster Hinton dribbled to an open spot but two Panthers quickly converged on him. The cat-and-mouse passing game began again. Suddenly Russ faked a pass to Hinton, turned and spun it toward Stan Maxwell.

Maxwell hesitated, looked around for an open man, and somehow the ball slipped away from him. Before Stan could recover his wits, the Panthers were racing down the floor. Their first shot missed, and so did a rebound by Carson. Then Langford went above Maxwell, and the Panthers led by two points.

The Warriors took the inbounds pass down the floor, only to miss a lay-up and the rebound.

Rick sprang to his feet but Caswell paid no attention as Hinton was fouled and sank the free throw, and the Panthers led by only a single point now, 62–61. But the period was half over.

Rick trotted a half-dozen steps down the sideline and back toward the bench. Each stride cost him a twinge of pain but it grew no worse. He stopped beside Caswell.

"I can run on it, Coach," he said. "Let me go in."

"But you can't jump," replied Caswell quietly. "That's what we need now."

"I know I can make that pivot shot," he pleaded. "Let me try it, just once."

Caswell looked at him for a moment. Then he said, "All right, try it. Tell Newcombe."

As the whistle sounded and Rick trotted back in, the Warriors looked surprised. While Maxwell was leaving the floor Rick leaned close to Ted Newcombe. "Coach said to try that pivot shot. They won't be looking for it."

Newcombe nodded. "The first time we get our hands on the ball."

It took nearly thirty seconds to get the ball again, but Russ deflected a pass that Hinton caught on the run. Rick was already in position, but Ted and Williams were playing catch in the front court as the clock kept ticking.

Suddenly Hinton dashed along the left sideline, stretched out his arms for a pass. But Williams turned and threw to Ted Newcombe as Rick leaned forward.

Ted came in fast. He passed the ball just as a Panther leaped at him. It came in hard and low. Rick caught it a step past the circle. He twisted around and suddenly pain shot through his ankle and up his leg. He saw a Panther running toward him, and, for an instant, the entire year seemed to flash before him—his humiliation on the Jayvees, Joe Smallwood's taunts, the new world that had opened up to him since he started playing with the Warriors.

His leg throbbed again as the guard moved in and Rick twisted away. Steeling himself against the pain, he lept up into a sweeping turn and aimed for the basket.

There was loud roar from the Warrior's bench and then the sound of clapping hands, stamping feet and whistles from the crowd. The ball spun gently against the backboard and dropped through the net to the floor.

Everything seemed suspended in a montage of bright faces, baskets and the high, arched walls of the gymnasium.

Rick took another step and stopped as his team crowded around him. He felt dizzy and needed to be helped off court. But what made him dizzier was the feeling of astonishment running through him.

There was no time for congratulations as the referee whistled frantically and gave the ball to the Panthers in the end zone. There were still ten seconds left, and the Warriors led, 63–62. He could hear the crowd starting its count-down.

And then it was over.

When Rick untangled himself from his happy teammates, he saw George Carson waiting for him with an outstretched hand.

"You did all right," Carson said with a reluctant smile. "I guess you're the champs after all."

Suddenly a pair of powerful arms locked around

Rick from behind. He was swung off the floor and spun around in the air. Then he was staring into the face of his brother Bill.

"Great game, Rick!" cried Bill Hanley. "Congratulations! You did it—ankle and all!"

"But how did you know—" Rick started, and then stopped as he saw Mom and Dad and Francie hurrying up. Mr. Hanley enveloped Rick in a tremendous bear hug. Rick laughed and struggled free.

"Where'd you come from?" he gasped. "You mean you saw the whole game?"

"You bet!" exclaimed his brother. "Mom let me in on the news a week ago. We have a game in New York on Sunday and I got an okay to take an earlier plane. I couldn't miss your first championship, could I?"

"I guess not," Rick grinned. "I still can't believe we did it!"

"I can," Bill said, "That was a great play at the end, Rick."

Proudly Rick introduced Bill to Reverend Caswell, and to Russ and the rest of his teammates.

"So this is our star's brother," Caswell said, winking at Rick. "I'm glad to meet you, Bill."

"It's an honor to meet *you*," Bill replied.

Rick was smiling. Caswell had called *him* the star! Then he realized that he'd introduced Bill to everyone, without any sense of becoming less in their eyes, of fading into the background.

There was a knock on the dressing-room door and Coach Kenney came in. Bill greeted him with a shout. After a moment Kenney turned to Rick. "I didn't really expect to find Bill here. I wanted to talk to you— you and Russ Williams. Coach Caswell says you two will make a fine addition to the Rock Hill squad next year. How about it?"

Rick stared at him and so did Russ.

Russ said soberly. "But I'm not in high school, Mr. Kenney. No way I can do it."

"Oh yes you can," spoke up Caswell. "Frank already has a job. That's one of the conditions of his— well, his probation—he'll be responsible to me."

"But I thought the hearing wasn't until Monday," said Russ. "How can you say that?"

"The judge already has agreed to that, and so has Frank."

Russ was speechless.

"With you two fellows and Joe Smallwood, Rock Hill has something to look forward to next season," said Kenney. "With you at center, Rick, and Williams and Smallwood at forward—"

"Smallwood at forward?" asked Rick, his face clouding. "He won't like that."

"Oh no?" replied Kenney. "Joe says he always wanted to play forward."

"Well, how do you like that?" muttered Rick dazedly.

He felt stunned. It seemed just yesterday that

he'd almost been booted off the Jayvee squad. And now Kenney was standing there, offering him center position for the Varsity.

Rick turned to Jerry Caswell, who was smiling broadly. But the sight of the coach only confused him, only made him indecisive. It was Jerry who was behind the success, who'd worked them so hard, who'd believed they could win, who'd actually trusted Rick to play center.

He'd felt elated on the court tonight, but it wasn't only because he'd done things right for once. It was that term he'd heard of so often, but never once felt on the Jayvee squad—"team spirit." Rick glanced at Coach Kenney, who was beginning to look puzzled, and back at Caswell. Then he turned to Russ.

Russ' face must have been an exact mirror of his own. Eagerness, incredulity and doubt were mingled there. The boys stared at each other uncertainly, while the two coaches waited.

Russ doesn't want to leave the Warriors either, thought Rick. But how can we turn Kenney down?

"Well," Russ began, eyeing Rick. "I'm not sure."

"What do you mean, Russ? Is there something I haven't thought of?" Coach Kenney inquired.

"No, no, Coach, it's not that. I appreciate your offer and I know yours is one of the best teams around, but—" He paused, and finished quickly. "I think I'd like to stay with the Warriors next year."

The Coach seemed surprised, but he smiled and said only, "Why?"

"I've gotten kind of used to the team, and to Jerry. And I think we could become first rate if we work hard. I'm not speaking for Rick—"

Rick had never been so relieved in his life. The minute Russ stopped, he spoke up. "I'll stay with the Warriors, too."

"Well," Coach Kenney exclaimed, turning to Jerry Caswell. 'I've got to hand it to you, Jerry! It looks like you've got two great kids on your team."

Rick looked from Kenney to Caswell. Jerry's smile was warmer than Rick had ever seen it, and his eyes were sparkling. He put his arms around the two boys.

"Until they go pro!" he said.

DATE DUE